A TRINITARIAN ANTHROPOLOGY

A TRINITARIAN ANTHROPOLOGY

*Adrienne von Speyr & Hans Urs von Balthasar
in Dialogue with Thomas Aquinas*

MICHELE M. SCHUMACHER

The Catholic University of America Press
Washington, D.C.

Copyright © 2014
The Catholic University of America Press
All rights reserved
The paper used in this publication meets the minimum
requirements of American National Standards for Information
Science—Permanence of Paper for Printed Library Materials,
ANSI Z39.48-1984.

Library of Congress Cataloging-in-Publication Data
Schumacher, Michele M.
A Trinitarian anthropology : Adrienne Von Speyr and
Hans Urs Von Balthasar in dialogue with Thomas Aquinas /
Michele M. Schumacher.
pages cm
Includes bibliographical references and index.
ISBN 978-0-8132-2697-2 (cloth)
1. Speyr, Adrienne von. 2. Balthasar, Hans Urs von, 1905–1988.
3. Thomas, Aquinas, Saint, 1225?–1274. 4. Trinity—History of
doctrines. 5. Catholic Church—Doctrines.—I. Title.
BX4705.S7 S38 2014
233.092′2—dc23
2014020724

*For Bernard
with all my love always*

CONTENTS

Acknowledgments xi

Abbreviations xiii

Introduction
1

1. Analogies of the Trinity: St. Thomas Aquinas, Hans Urs von Balthasar, and Adrienne von Speyr
25

The Historical Context of the "Tension" between the Theology of Balthasar and that of St. Thomas	27
The Analogy of Being and the Psychological Model of the Trinity: St. Thomas Aquinas	32
A Trinitarian Analogy of Freedom: Hans Urs von Balthasar	41
An Analogy of Surrender: Adrienne von Speyr	57
A Trinitiarian "Resolution" of Human "Tensions" or Polarities	63

2. The Difference-in-Unity of Faith's Object and Act: A Speyrian Methodology of Gift Encountering Gift
67

Discerning the Unity of Adrienne's Mission and Theology of Mission under Balthasar's Regard	68
A "Theodramatic" Hermeneutic: The Theologian's Openness to the Divine "Ever-More"	76
Faith: A Participation in the Revelatory Disposition of Christ	81
Adrienne, the Mystic: Balthasar's Model "Theologian"	86
The Fruits of Adrienne's Faith as a Gift for the Church	94

3. The Nature-Grace Difference-in-Unity: The Expansion of Human Liberty to the "Measure" of the Divine (Theological Persons)
99

Introduction: The Question of Human Fulfillment	99
St. Thomas on Human Fulfillment: Human Participation in Divine Knowledge and Love	103
A Balthasarian Understanding of Human Fulfillment: Human Surrender within Divine Surrender	112
A Speyrian Understanding of the Image of God: Nature and Grace	123
Human Perfection in Divine Communion as Viewed by Adrienne von Speyr	126
The Mystery of Grace and Merit from the Perspective of the Mutual Immanence of Christ and the Christian	130
Breaking Boundaries from Within: The Expansion of Human Nature by Christ in the Christian	138
The Expansion of the Christian's Assent to the "Proportion" of God's Surrender	142
Mary-Church or Person as Response: An Anticipation of Balthasar's "Theological Person"	149
Conclusion: Breaking the Boundary between Nature and Grace	156

4. The Body-Spirit Difference-in-Unity: A Speyrian Theology of the Body
160

Introduction to a Speyrian Theology of the Body	160
The Body-Spirit "Tension" in Balthasar's Work	165
The Heart of Adrienne's Theology of the Body: The Incarnation as a Revelation of Trinitarian Love	172
Adrienne's Incarnational Perspective: A Corporal-Spiritual Unity	176
Sacraments as the Archetypal Form of Human Life: The Example of Christian Marriage	179
The Eucharist of the Father and the Son: Our Inclusion in Trinitarian Love	182
The Eucharist of Believers: A Corporal-Spiritual Participation in Christ's Mission	185
Mary-Church, the Body of Christ	192

5. The Individual-Community Difference-in-Unity: The Trinitarian Face of Redemption and the Ecclesial Existence of the Christian
196

An Introduction to the Individual-Community Difference-in-Unity in the Works of Adrienne von Speyr and Hans Urs von Balthasar	196
The Trinitarian Difference-in-Unity Revealed in "Alienation": Balthasar's Redemption by Substitution	200
The Love Command at the Service of Divine Communion: Toward a More Adequate Theology of Redemption	214
The Redemptive Gift of Surrender	228
Abiding in Love: Communicating Love Received	233
Conclusion: Redemption as a Mystery of Reciprocal Surrender	238
Postscript: An Alternative Interpretation of Christological "Abandonment"	240

6. The Man-Woman Difference-in-Unity: A "Trinitarian" Theology of the Sexes
246

Introduction: Sexual Differentiation Viewed from the Perspective of Christ's Assumption of Human Nature	246
Balthasar's Regard from Above in His Treatment of the Difference-in-Union of the Sexes	250
The Complementarity of the Sexes within the Sublime Order of Redemption as Viewed by Adrienne von Speyr	262
The Natural "Tension" between the Sexes and Their Reciprocity in View of Grace	265
"Masculine" and "Feminine" Forms of Surrender	271
The Transition between the "Feminine" and "Masculine" Qualities of Love in Christ	283
"Masculine" and "Feminine" Missions	291
Conclusion: Sexual Differentiation and Divine Differentiation	301

7. A Critical Appraisal of the Trinitarian Anthropology of Adrienne von Speyr as Appropriated by Hans Urs von Balthasar
308

The Trinitarian Dynamic Called into Question: Analogical and Metaphorical Descriptions of the Godhead	310
Confusion of the Divine and Human Natures in Christ?	320

A Distortion of the Catholic Balance between Philosophy and
Theology? 336
A "Loss" in the Godhead? 341
The Center of the Whole: Descent or Surrender? 344
The Grounding of the Analogy between Creator and Creature: The
"Distance" Implied in Surrender 351

General Conclusion: Difference-in-Unity: An Invitation to Dialogue in the Spirit of Catholicism
357

Analogical and Katalogical Reasoning: Balthasar and St. Thomas 357
An Analogy of Reciprocal Surrender: Divine "Enrichment" or
Human Fulfillment? 366
A Challenge for Balthasarian Scholars: Situating His Appropriation
of Adrienne's Doctrine within the Tradition 371
The Question of Interpreting Adrienne von Speyr's Presumably
Mystical Experiences 383

Bibliography   399

Index of Names   441

Subject Index   443

ACKNOWLEDGMENTS

All charisms of Christians are inextricably interwoven; everyone owes himself not only to God but to the whole Church; everyone is borne by invisible prayers and sacrifices, has been nourished by countless gifts of love, is continually strengthened and preserved by the affection of others.[1]

If this truism, beautifully expressed by Hans Urs von Balthasar, was already evident to me long before engaging in the research for this book, how much more vivid is this truth today, as I bring the volume to its conclusion! So many people and institutions have contributed to its birth that I hardly dare to claim it as my own.

From the very inception of this work—which began with a grant from the National Swiss Scientific Foundation, for which I am extremely grateful—until its completion, the Speyrian-Balthasarian specialist Father Jacques Servais, SJ, faithfully accompanied me at every turn. He has been a constant source of helpful encouragement and critical insight. Even before launching on this adventure, Antoine Birot generously shared with me his enthusiastic knowledge of the united work of Adrienne von Speyr and Hans Urs von Balthasar. May this completed work stand as proof that his enthusiasm was indeed contagious. A more recent, but highly faithful contributor by way of his provocative questions, helpful criticisms, excellent suggestions for reading, ever pertinent remarks, and never failing support is Father Bernhard Blankenhorn, OP. It is largely due to my ongoing discussions with him, within the context of our friendship, that my initial project on the correspondence between Balthasar and Adrienne von Speyr became a dialogue with Thomism.

My reader will quickly discern how much my reading of St. Thomas is also influenced by the theology of Fr. Gilles Emery, OP, to whom I owe an obvious debt, as well as to Fr. Jean-Pierre Torrell, OP. Less obvious, perhaps, but highly significant is the helpful encouragement and support of Fr. Michael Sherwin, OP, also of the University of Fribourg,

---

1. Hans Urs von Balthasar, *My Work: In Retrospect*, trans. Brian McNeil et al. (San Francisco: Ignatius Press, 1993), 88.

who helped me obtain the degree of habilitation for an earlier version of this work. I am also very grateful for his faithful reading of my manuscript and for his helpful suggestions and references. Likewise, I am very grateful to Michael Waldstein, whose careful reading of an earlier version of this manuscript gave rise to pertinent challenges that have helped to shape this volume into its present form. The role of midwife was, however, played out by Father Edward Oakes, SJ, who is largely responsible for the present state of the volume with its emphasis upon analogical and metaphorical language. I am particularly grateful for his meticulous editing work and his often very challenging remarks.

In my attempt to find a publisher for this volume, I am especially grateful to the helpful suggestions, encouragement, and intercession of Matthew Levering, Father Thomas Joseph White, OP, and Reinhard Hütter. A special word of thanks is also due to the acquisitions editor at the Catholic University of America Press, Jim Kruggel, who has been very helpful and encouraging at every juncture of the process of getting my manuscript approved, and to my copy editor, Paul Higgins, for his careful work, kindness, and enduring patience.

No less significant than the help of those who actively assisted in the challenges of writing and publishing is the aid of those who accompanied me in silence. So many people prayed for me that I can hardly list them by name, but three stand out as particularly exemplary of the gift of self in the form of surrender that is constantly referred to throughout these pages: Sr. Bernarda Kötting, OSB; Sr. Allison Braus, OCD; and Sr. Gloria Therese Laven, OCD. My thanks also to Alison Grey for her constant encouragement and support and for her careful reading of chapter six.[2]

Of course, my overwhelming appreciation must be expressed to my wonderful family: to my children—Myriam, Sophia, Teresa, and Nicolas—who literally grew up with this book and patiently endured the challenges of an occupied mother; to my wonderful mother-in-law, Emma Schumacher, who often cared for the children during those occupied hours, including the year that found me busy behind the computer with a broken leg; and to my loving husband, Bernard, who not only accompanied me at every turn of the venture but often pushed me into the playing field, as it were. This book is rightfully dedicated to him.

2. I greatly regret that I was unable to incorporate into my research here the notable work of Étienne Vetö, *Penser les mystères du Christ après Thomas d'Aquin et Balthasar* (Paris: Cerf, 2012) and that of Pascal Ide, *Une théologie du don: le don dans la 'Trilogie' de Hans Urs von Balthasar* (Leuven: Peeters, 2013).

ABBREVIATIONS

Comp	*Compendium theologiae* (St. Thomas Aquinas)
De Pot	*De Potentia* (*Quaestiones Disputatae*) (St. Thomas Aquinas)
DZ	*Compendium of Creeds, Definitions, and Declarations on Matters of Faith and Morals* (Denzinger, ed.)
De Ver	*De Veritate* (*Quaestiones Disputatae*) (St. Thomas Aquinas)
PL	*Patrologia Latina* (Migne, ed.)
PG	*Patrologia Graeca* (Migne, ed.)
SC	*Sources chrétiennes* (Paris: Cerf)
SCG	*Summa Contra Gentiles* (St. Thomas Aquinas)
Sent	*Scriptum super libros Sententiarum* (St. Thomas Aquinas)
ST	*Summa Theologiae* (St. Thomas Aquinas)
Super Col	*Super Epistolam B. Pauli ad Colossenses lectura* (St. Thomas Aquinas)
Super ad I Cor	*Super I Epistolam B. Pauli ad Corinthios lectura* (St. Thomas Aquinas)
Super ad II Cor	*Super II Epistolam B. Pauli ad Corinthios lectura* (St. Thomas Aquinas)
Super Eph	*Super Epistolam B. Pauli ad Ephesios lectura* (St. Thomas Aquinas)
Super Gal	*Super Epistolam B. Pauli ad Galatas lectura* (St. Thomas Aquinas)
Super Ioan	*Super Evangelium S. Ioannis lectura* (St. Thomas Aquinas)
Super Phil	*Super Epistolam B. Pauli ad Philipenses lectura* (St. Thomas Aquinas)
Super Rom	*Super Epistolam B. Pauli ad Romanus lectura* (St. Thomas Aquinas)

A TRINITARIAN ANTHROPOLOGY

Introduction

The Trinitarian foundation of anthropology is a theme that has abundantly marked theological discussion since the Second Vatican Council. An anthropological account of the Trinity, on the other hand, is obviously less apparent; for it is man who is the image of God, and not God who is the image of man. In virtue, however, of that important event whereby God became man, man himself has become—as the Swiss theologian Hans Urs von Balthasar (1905–88) insists throughout his vast opus—the language of God. Theology has become inseparable from anthropology and anthropology from theology. Indeed, "the whole of what God has to say to the world is said," Balthasar firmly believes, "in *a single* man."[1]

From this perspective, the work of the theologian consists in unfolding the whole Christian faith from the fullness of Christ, in whom "the whole fullness of deity dwells bodily" (Col 2:9), or, in reverse, of converging, or integrating, the various dogmas or truths of the faith within the one truth of Christ, in union with his Church, on the one hand, and in union with the Father and the Holy Spirit, on the other hand. It is thus not surprising that Balthasar should maintain—with specific reference to St. Thomas Aquinas—that "great men communicate with one another not in their forms, but in the depth of the reality made known to them through these forms."[2]

This conviction was in fact so overriding for Balthasar that he explicitly refused to believe "in pluralism," that is, in the legitimacy of a diversity of religious, or even secular, beliefs. Instead, as he explained in an interview toward the end of his life, he believed "in catholicity," by which he meant to emphasize the universal dimension of the one truth of Christ. After all, "we, at least we Christians, are always looking at the same thing even if our view

---

1. Balthasar and Michael Albus, "Spirit and Fire: An Interview with Hans Urs von Balthasar," *Communio* 32, no. 3 (2005): 593. See also Balthasar, *My Work*, 105.

2. Balthasar, *Explorations in Theology* I: *The Word Made Flesh*, trans. A. V. Littledale and Alexander Dru (San Francisco: Ignatius Press, 1989), 220. Cf. Adrienne von Speyr, *Light and Images: Elements of Contemplation*, trans. David Schindler, Jr. (San Francisco: Ignatius Press, 2004), 30.

is always only partial."[3] Such is also the conviction that has been the guiding thread of this volume: a conviction that is now expressed as a hope that it might launch an authentic dialogue between disciples of Hans Urs von Balthasar and those of the Church's common doctor, St. Thomas Aquinas, whose teaching has been endorsed by various popes throughout the centuries as a model of truth and avoidance of error, and whom Balthasar himself calls upon in his own work "as guarantor that we have not departed from the great tradition."[4]

Assuredly such a dialogue is challenging given the present state of affairs which admits of undeniable tensions between these two theological "schools" (for lack of a better word). These tensions are perhaps due to misunderstandings, but might more positively, I will argue, they point to the mystery of difference-in-unity and unity-in-difference, which Balthasar, not unlike St. Thomas, presents as typifying the richness of Catholicism and ultimately of the Holy Trinity. In these pages I will thus point to the unifying mystery which lies simultaneously beyond and within the differences of the theologies of St. Thomas and Balthasar: a mystery which is necessarily articulated in analogical and metaphorical terms, whence the particular focus in this volume upon theological anthropology as pointing to Trinitarian theology.

It was not, however, so much in the analogical discourse of St. Thomas that Balthasar found the inspiration for his own theological perspective, I will maintain, but that of the Swiss mystic and physician Adrienne von Speyr (1902–67) with whom he shared—such was clearly his belief—a common theological mission.[5] To be sure, it is among the most important goals of this volume to point to the profound unity of the theological perspectives of Balthasar and Adrienne von Speyr. For the moment, however, it suffices

---

3. Balthasar and Albus, "Spirit and Fire," 580. See also Balthasar, *In the Fullness of Faith: On the Centrality of the Distinctively Catholic*, trans. Graham Harrison (San Francisco: Ignatius Press, 1988), 27. Strikingly similar is the insight of Emmanuel Perrier, who observes that "as a whole, the program of contemporary theology opposes formalism from every angle: whether soteriological (St. Anselm), Christological (K. Rahner), historical (W. Pannenberg) or narrative (E. Schillebeeckx, J. Moingt). It is never Christ who is reached [*atteint*], but rather a concept by which one 'thinks Christ': gift, story, consciousness, solidarity" ("L'enjeu christologique de la satisfaction (I)," *Revue thomiste* 103, no. 1 [2003]: 123).

4. Hans Urs von Balthasar, *Theo-Logic. Theological Logical Theory* I: *Truth of the World*, trans. Adrian J. Walker (San Francisco: Ignatius Press, 2000), 11. On papal endorsement of the teaching of St. Thomas, see, for example, Leo XIII, *Aeterni Patris*, encyclical letter on The Restoration of Christian Philosophy, August 4, 1879 (DZ-3135-3146); Canons 589 and 1366 §2 of the Code of Canon Law issued by authority of Pope Benedict XV in 1917; and Pope John Paul II, *Fides et Ratio* (September 14, 1998) (Washington, D.C.: United States Catholic Conference, 1998), no. 43.

5. See, for example, Hans Urs von Balthasar, *Our Task: A Report and a Plan*, trans. John Saward (San Francisco: Ignatius Press / Communio Books, 1994), 13 and 72–73; Balthasar, *My Work*, 19–20 and 89; and Balthasar and Angelo Scola, *Test Everything, Hold Fast to What Is Good: An Interview with Hans Urs von Balthasar by Angelo Scola*, trans. Maria Shrady (San Francisco: Ignatius Press, 1989), 88–90.

to mention that in my attempt to launch a dialogue between disciples of St. Thomas and those of Balthasar, I have contextualized the latter's theology within what he describes as the inseparability of his work from that of Dr. von Speyr, who is referred to throughout this work simply as "Adrienne."[6] In so doing, I hope to provide for Balthasar's theology what he sought to do for Adrienne's: "to gather it up and embed it in a space, such as the theology [...] of the Middle Ages," so as to permit the emergence of my reader's own conviction that Balthasar's "original proposition," as borrowed from Adrienne, "in no way contradicted it [medieval, especially Thomistic, theology]," but rather complements it in a special way.[7]

Admittedly, this woman is hardly an obvious candidate for opening new discussion in theology or for advancing the dialogue that this volume seeks to foster. Not only does she remain very much in Balthasar's shadow, but despite a new and growing interest in her work—presumably because of her place in this "shadow"—she still remains a relatively untapped source in any field of theological investigation. Indeed, as might be gathered from the rather limited nature of the secondary literature, she is rarely regarded as providing insights for contemporary theological discussion, even within the context of Balthasar's "own" theology. In 1975, eight years after her death, the theologian of Lucerne and editor of her very large opus of over sixty volumes of mystically and biblically-inspired theology, most of which she dictated to him in increments of twenty to thirty minutes, mourned the fact that despite the printing of thirty-seven of these books, thirty-four of which were available in bookstores at the time, "no one" had taken "serious notice of her writings."[8] Today, some forty years later—a moment coinciding with the mounting international renown of Balthasar—nearly all of her books are available in the original German, and many have been translated into English (which will be cited throughout whenever available), French, Italian, and Dutch, with some titles available in Spanish, Czechoslovakian, Portuguese, Polish, and Russian. Nonetheless, despite two international colloquia dedicated to her ecclesial mission and her spiritual theology,[9] an ever growing body

---

6. This decision to address Dr. von Speyr as simply "Adrienne" is in conscious union with Balthasar's own preference for the familiar first-name approach, which he—in his role as editor—adopts throughout his many introductions to and commentaries on her works, as well as in his presentations of her work and person—as, for example, in *First Glance at Adrienne von Speyr*, trans. Antje Lawry and Sergia Englund (San Francisco: Ignatius Press, 1981). Following Balthasar's example, other commentators and biographers tend to do the same.

7. Balthasar and Scola, *Test Everything*, 88.

8. Balthasar, *First Glance*, 12; see also 98 and 100.

9. See Balthasar, Georges Chantraine and Angelo Scola, eds., *Adrienne von Speyr und ihre kirchliche Sendung*, Akten des römischen Symposiums (27–29 September 1985) (Einsiedeln: Johannes Verlag,

of secondary literature,[10] two anthologies,[11] and five doctoral dissertations dedicated to specifically Speyrian themes,[12] her mystical theology still—and almost inevitably—presents itself as painfully unsystematic to systematically-minded theologians, for whom it is perhaps too quickly dismissed as "mere" spirituality.[13]

It is thus among my primary purposes in this volume to demonstrate that her presumably mystical insights have a profound theological value (albeit by way of image, analogy, and metaphor), particularly insofar as they are deeply rooted within the word of God.[14] Such—it must be admitted—was the conviction of Balthasar, and it would be "an injustice to history as well as to the extraordinary intelligence of Fr. Von Balthasar," as Antonio Sicari sees it, to consider his appropriation of her spiritual insights as arbitrary or, worse, as leading to the impoverishment of his more dogmatic theology.[15] Such is also,

---

1986) [*La mission ecclésiale d'Adrienne von Speyr* (Paris and Namur: Éditions Lethielleux and Culture et Vérité, 1986)] and Hans Urs von Balthasar Stiftung, ed., *Adrienne von Speyr und ihre spirituelle Theologie : die Referate am Symposium zu ihrem 100 Geburtstag (12–13 September 2002) im Freiburg im Breisgau* (Einsiedeln: Johannes Verlag, 2002).

10. Although I cannot claim to be exhaustive, the bibliography included at the end of this book is a good display of this secondary literature, although most of it (admittedly) treats Balthasar's theology and thus only indirectly (at best) that of Adrienne.

11. See Barbara Albrecht's two-volume anthology of Adrienne: *Eine Theologie des Katholischen: Einführung in das Werk Adriennes von Speyr*, vol. 1: *Durchblick in Texten* (Einsiedeln: Johannes Verlag, 1972); vol. 2: *Darstellung* (1973), as well as that of Balthasar: *Kostet und seht* (Einsiedeln: Johannes Verlag, 1988).

12. Johannes Schiettecatte, *Disponiblité aimante. L'attitude d'amour johannique chez Adrienne von Speyr à la lumière de l'exégèse contemporaine*, Pontifical Theology Faculty "Teresianum," 1998; Justin Matro, *Christian Suffering in the Spiritual Writings of Adrienne von Speyr*, Pontifical Gregorian University, 1999; William Schmitt, *The Sacrament of Confession as a "Sequela Christi" in the Writings of A. von Speyr*, Pontifical Lateran University, Pontifical John Paul II Institute of Studies on Marriage and Family, 1999; Blaise R. Berg, *Christian Marriage according to Adrienne von Speyr*, Pontifical Lateran University, Pontifical John Paul II Institute of Studies on Marriage and Family, 2003; and Matthew Lewis Sutton, *The Gate of Heaven Opens to the Trinity: The Trinitarian Mysticism of Adrienne von Speyr*, submitted to the faculty of the Graduate school, Marquette University, 2007. The latter has since been published under the same title: *Heaven Opens: The Trinitarian Mysticism of Adrienne von Speyr* (Minneapolis, Minn.: Fortress Press, 2014).

13. This attitude, it might be added, is particularly offensive to Balthasar, who insisted upon the unity of dogma and spirituality, of theology and holiness. This will be treated at greater length in chapter two of the present volume. See also Balthasar, *Explorations in Theology* I, 181–209 and 211–26.

14. As it lies beyond my expertise to judge the validity of Balthasar's claim to the mystical origin of Adrienne's insights—a claim grounded in his experience of relating to her in his two-fold role of spiritual director-confessor and editor of her works—I have simply taken this for granted. I will nonetheless argue for the significant theological value of her doctrine—a fact which might argue in favor of this claim—as exposited in chapters 2–6 and in my attempt (in chapter seven) to respond to many important criticisms of Balthasar's doctrine attributable to Adrienne's influence. For more detail concerning Balthasar's conviction of the mystical nature of her doctrine and his estimation of its profound theological value, see chapter two of the present work. On the challenging question of judging the mystical nature of her work, see my general conclusion. On the biblical nature of her mysticism, see Balthasar, *First Glance*, 87–90 and 100.

15. Antonio Sicari, "Hans Urs von Balthasar: Theology and Holiness" in David L. Schindler, (ed.),

presumably, the conviction of the well-reputed commentator and translator of Balthasar, Edward T. Oakes, who sets as the goal of one of his important works the healing of the latter's isolation "from the wider guild of professional theologians" due "no doubt" to Balthasar's encounter with Adrienne "more than [to] any other event in Balthasar's life."[16]

While Balthasar's "isolation" during his lifetime might, in fact, have been due largely to what readers such as Oakes regard—and understandably so—as "disconcerting"[17] passages borrowed from Adrienne's works, it would be hard to deny Balthasar's increasing popularity in the years that followed the publication of Oakes's book in 1994. Fergus Kerr noted in 2007, for example, the "overwhelmingly positive tenor" of the "ever-expanding secondary literature" dedicated to the thought of the Swiss theologian, to whom Kerr himself accords a less than glowing report, but whom he nonetheless accredits as being "widely regarded as the greatest Catholic theologian of the century" and "by far the most discussed Catholic theologian at present."[18] In that same year, however, Alyssa Lyra Pitstick virtually accused Balthasar in her much-discussed book of nothing less than heresy.[19] To be sure, no one has been more vigorous, forceful, and sustained in responding to Pitstick's concerns than has Oakes.[20] Because, however, Pitstick—not unlike other critics of Balthasar—implicitly points to his appropriation of Adrienne's doctrine, we can hardly do otherwise than admit to Oakes's insightful remark: "the

---

Hans Urs von Balthasar: His Life and Work (San Francisco: Communio Books / Ignatius Press, 1991), 126. As a case in point, Kevin Mongrain holds that "von Speyr's influence on his theology was deforming rather than constructive, derived rather than original" (Kevin Mongrain, *The Systematic Thought of Hans Urs von Balthasar: An Irenaean Retrieval* [New York: Herder & Herder, 2002], 11–12).

16. Edward T. Oakes, *Pattern of Redemption: The Theology of Hans Urs von Balthasar* (New York & London: Continuum, 1994), 3. See also ibid., 5. Cf. Nicholas Healy, *The Eschatology of Hans Urs von Balthasar* (Oxford: Oxford University Press, 2005), 5.

17. See Oakes, *Pattern of Redemption*, 302; and Fergus Kerr, "Adrienne von Speyr and Hans Urs von Balthasar," *New Blackfriars* 79, no. 923 (1998): 26–32. See also Balthasar's own judgement on this matter in Balthasar, *Our Task*, 15.

18. Fergus Kerr, *Twentieth-Century Theologians: From Neoscholasticism to Nuptial Mysticism* (Oxford: Blackwell, 2007), 121 and 144. For an up-to-date list of the secondary literature on Hans Urs von Balthasar, see http://homepage.bluewin.ch/huvbslit.

19. Alyssa Lyra Pitstick, *Light in Darkness: Hans Urs von Balthasar and the Catholic Doctrine of Christ's Descent into Hell* (Grand Rapids, Mich.: Eerdmans, 2007). See also Pitstick, "Development of Doctrine, or Denial? Balthasar's Holy Saturday and Newman's *Essay*," *International Journal of Systematic Theology*, 11, no. 2 (2009): 129–45; and R. R. Reno, "Was Balthasar A Heretic?" *First Things*, October 15, 2008; http://www.firstthings.com/web-exclusives/2008/10/was-balthasar-a-heretic.

20. See, for example, the series of articles by Alyssa Lyra Pitstick and Edward T. Oakes: "Balthasar, Hell and Heresy: An Exchange," *First Things* (December 2006): 25–29; "More on Balthasar, Hell, and Heresy," *First Things* (January 2007): 16–18; "The Internal Logic of Holy Saturday in the Theology of Hans Urs von Balthasar," *International Journal of Systematic Theology* 9, no. 2 (2007): 184–99; and "*Descensus* and Development: A Response to Recent Rejoinders," *International Journal of Systematic Theology* 13, no. 1 (2011): 3–24.

greatest hindrance" in assessing Balthasar's work "comes from its symbiotic relation to the parallel (and equally lengthy) work" of Adrienne. The American Jesuit concludes that any evaluation of Balthasar "will involve a parallel evaluation of her."[21]

This parallel evaluation is no easy task. Because Adrienne's profound insights are scattered in an unsystematic manner throughout her very large corpus of more than 15,000 pages of mystical prose, uniting her thoughts on any particular theme is a rather daunting challenge, even given the two anthologies of her work (regrettably still not translated into English). This may explain why so few disciples of Balthasar—with several notable exceptions[22]—explicitly address Adrienne's theology, despite his insistence upon the unity of their theological missions and despite his attesting to the importance of her theological perspective for understanding his own.[23] Another essential aim of my work is, therefore, that of rendering readers of Balthasar more conscious of his indebtedness to Adrienne, more pointedly to assess her influence upon his vast opus, and to better appreciate the unity of their theological perspectives. Jacques Servais, for example, argues for "the strictly unified work of Hans Urs von Balthasar and Adrienne von Speyr,"[24] and Joseph Ratzinger recognizes Balthasar as "inconceivable without Adrienne von Speyr."[25] As for Balthasar himself, he maintains that "her work and mine

---

21. Oakes, *Pattern of Redemption*, 300; cf. Oakes and David Moss, "Introduction" to their co-edited volume, *The Cambridge Companion to Hans Urs von Balthasar* (Cambridge: Cambridge University Press, 2004, 2006), 4–5. Similarly, although Manfred Lochbrunner considers it "impossible" to separate Balthasar from Speyr, he humbly admits to limiting his investigation to Balthasar's "enormous mountain of books," at the foot of which lies the tremendous "sea" of Adrienne's works. See his *Analogia Caritatis. Darstellung und Deutung der Theologie Hans Urs von Balthasars* (Freiburg: Herder, 1981), 320–21.

22. See, for example, Robert Nandkisore, *Hoffnung auf Erlösung. Die Eschatologie im Werk Hans Urs von Balthasars* (Rome: Editrice Pontificia Università Gregoriana, 1997); Antoine Birot, *La dramtique trinitaire de l'amour: Pour une introduction à la théologie trinitaire de Hans Urs von Balthasar et Adrienne von Speyr* (Paris: Parole et Silence, 2009); Marcello Paradiso, *Il blu e il giallo. Hans Urs von Balthasar e Adrienne von Speyr: un'avventura spirituale* (Cantalupa, Italy: Effatà Editrice, 2009); Paolo Martinelli, *La morte di Cristo come rivelazione dell'amore trinitario nella teologia di Hans Urs von Balthasar* (Milano: Jaca Book, 1995); Jacques Servais, "The *Ressourcement* of Contemporary Spirituality under the Guidance of Adrienne von Speyr and Hans Urs von Balthasar," trans. David Louis Schindler, Jr., *Communio* 23, no. 2 (1996): 300–321, and "Per una valutazione dell'influsso di Adrienne von Speyr su Hans Urs von Balthasar," *Rivista Teologica di Lugano* 6, no. 1 (2001): 67–89. Many of the authors contributing to the 1985 Roman colloquium, *La mission ecclésiale d'Adrienne von Speyr / Adrienne von Speyr und ihre kirchliche Sendung*, are well-respected disciples of Balthasar, including Angelo Scola, Georges Chantraine, Marc Ouellet, and Joseph Fessio. Other authors point to Adrienne's influence upon Balthasar, but rather than citing her directly, they tend to read her indirectly, namely through Balthasar's explicit integration of her work into his own.

23. "Perhaps my writings will be really understood only when serious attention is given to Adrienne von Speyr" (Balthasar and Albus, "Spirit and Fire," 574).

24. Jacques Servais, "The *Ressourcement* of Contemporary Spirituality," 300. Similar are the judgments of Lochbrunner, *Analogia Caritatis*, 321; and Paradiso, *Il blue e il giallo*, 179–85.

25. Joseph Ratzinger, "Das Problem der christlichen Prophetie, Neils Christian Hvidt im Gespräch

are neither psychologically nor philologically to be separated; two halves of a single whole, which has as its center a unique foundation."[26] It is thus that he authored *Our Task* with "one chief aim" in mind: "to prevent any attempt being made after my death to separate my work from that of Adrienne von Speyr."[27]

This goal of mine is thus opposed to that of Kevin Mongrain, for example, who hopes to "give scholars the tools for refuting von Balthasar's misleading claims about her [Adrienne's] role in shaping his theology."[28] Although Mongrain drops the debate that he thus proposes (that of arguing for or against Adrienne's influence upon Balthasar),[29] one might argue—even in granting Mongrain's thesis that Balthasar understood his theology as "an Irenaean retrieval"—that the Swiss theologian saw this retrieval, along with all the theological tools at his disposal, as a means of better articulating Adrienne's insights and of situating them within the realm of the tradition as presented, for example, in the theology of Irenaeus of Lyons (to hold to Mongrain's thesis), or still more significantly (I maintain throughout this work) by Thomas Aquinas. This is explicit, for example, when Balthasar writes of de Lubac's theology—which Mongrain presents as providing "the general source of the internal logic in von Balthasar's theology"[30]—that it enabled him to better understand and communicate Adrienne's dictated works "in the exactness of their insights and the almost immeasurable variety of their theological opinions."[31] As for Irenaeus, "the anti-Gnostic theologian of the enfleshing

---

mit Joseph Kardinal Ratzinger," in *Internationale katholische Zeitschrift: Communio* 28 (March-April 1999): 183.

26. Balthasar, *My Work*, 89; see also 19–20; and Balthasar, *Our Task*, 72–73.
27. Balthasar, *Our Task*, 13.
28. Mongrain, *The Systematic Thought of Hans Urs von Balthasar*, 12.
29. Mongrain's own argumentation concerning Adrienne's influence, or lack thereof, is closed with the above statement. No mention is made of her from this point forward. She does not enter into his bibliography, and one has the impression that he is, in fact, ignorant of the content of her teaching.
30. Kevin Mongrain, *The Systematic Thought of Hans Urs von Balthasar*, 16. By this, Mongrain means that de Lubac's theology "determines his conceptual priorities, regulative themes, and privileged theological, philosophical, and literary sources" (ibid.). See also Gilbert Narcisse, "The Supernatural in Contemporary Theology," in Serge-Thomas Bonino (ed.), *Surnaturel: A Controversy at the Heart of Twentieth-Century Thomistic Thought* (Naples, Fla.: Sapientia Press, 2009), 302; John Milbank, *The Suspended Middle: Henri de Lubac and the Debate Concerning the Supernatural* (Grand Rapids, Mich.: Eerdmans, 2005), 5 and 12–13; and Guy Mansini, "The Abiding Significance of de Lubac's *Surnaturel*," *The Thomist* 73, no. 4 (2009): 596; and Henri de Lubac, *Mémoire sur l'occasion de mes écrits* (Namur, Belgium: Culture et Verité, 1989), 478.
31. Balthasar, *Our Task*, 39. See also ibid., 44. Reference is also made within the context of this passage to the influence of Erich Przywara, Gustav Siewerth, and Ferdinand Ulrich. See also my general conclusion to this volume for a more largely developed argument of how Balthasar understood all of his own theological, philosophical and literary training as preparing and sustaining him in the mission of handing on Adrienne's insights to the Church.

of the Word," he is acknowledged by Balthasar as enabling him to point the way past the Christian mystical theology influenced by Neo-Platonism, for "bodiliness was to play a key role in Adrienne's theory of mysticism."[32] Fergus Kerr, on the other hand, argues that "von Balthasar comes close to saying [in his introduction to *Herrlichkeit*] that the whole idea of contemplating the divine glory comes from [Karl Barth's] *Church Dogmatics*."[33] Meanwhile, Balthasar actually does say that if he had not striven to bring his "way of looking at Christian revelation into conformity" with that of Adrienne, "the basic perspective of *Herrlichkeit* would never have existed."[34]

In my defense of what Balthasar esteemed the inseparability of his work and that of Adrienne, I will not only (nor primarily) draw out the explicit connections between his insights and hers, but I will also (and perhaps more importantly) allow Adrienne to "speak" in her "own"—presumably mystical—voice: a voice which certain critics argue, ironically enough, was reduced to silence by the very one (namely Balthasar) who put all of her dictations into writing, founded a publishing house to get them into print, and spent the last twenty years of his life trying to get her mission recognized by the Church.[35] This goal I set out to achieve by way of a general exposition and roughly "systematic"[36] presentation of Adrienne's theological an-

---

32. Ibid. On Irenaeus as read by Balthasar, see *The Scandal of the Incarnation: Irenaeus Against the Heresies*, selected and introduced by Hans Urs von Balthasar, trans. John Saward (San Francisco: Ignatius Press, 1990).

33. Kerr, "Adrienne von Speyr and Hans Urs von Balthasar," 28.

34. Balthasar, *First Glance at Adrienne von Speyr*, 13. See also Balthasar, *My Work*, 89, where he simultaneously addresses his thanks to both Adrienne and Barth in nonetheless very different terms.

35. These details are provided by Peter Henrici, "Hans Urs von Balthasar: A Sketch of Von Balthasar's Life," in Schindler, *Hans Urs von Balthasar: His Life and His Work*, 27–28; and Balthasar, *My Work*, 89. On the "silencing" of Adrienne by Balthasar, see, for example, Tina Beattie, "A Man and Three Women—Hans, Adrienne, Mary and Luce," *New Blackfriars* 79, no. 927 (1998): 97–105. On the silencing of women in general by Balthasar, see Rachel Muers, "The Mute Cannot Keep Silent: Barth, von Balthasar, and Irigaray, on the Construction of Women's Silence" in Susan Frank Parsons (ed.), *Challenging Women's Orthodoxies in the Context of Faith* (Sydney: Ashgate, 2000), 109–20; Lucy Gardner and David Moss, "Something Like Time; Something Like the Sexes: An Essay in Reception," in Moss, Gardner, Benjamin Quash, and Graham Ward (eds.), *Balthasar at the End of Modernity* (Edinburgh: T. & T. Clark, 1999), 69–137, esp. 88–89; and Michelle Gonzalez, "Hans Urs von Balthasar and Contemporary Feminist Theology," *Theological Studies* 65, no. 3 (2004): 566–95, who points to "the prominence of women in Balthasar's theology" and "his push to lift the voices of women" (580), all in arguing that "the manner in which women's voices are constructed" by him "limit[s] their intellectual contribution" (585). In short, women are "characterized as mystics and not theologians" (583).

36. This does not mean that I will purposefully counter Adrienne and Balthasar's explicit disdain for any attempt to systematize the divine mystery. See the following passages in Balthasar's works: *First Glance at Adrienne von Speyr*, 50; *The Grain of Wheat: Aphorisms*, trans. Erasmo Leiva-Merikakis (San Francisco: Ignatius Press, 1995), 21–22; *My Work*, 105; *Explorations in Theology* IV: *Spirit and Institution*, trans. Edward T. Oakes (San Francisco: Ignatius Press, 1995), 333; and *Theo-Drama: Theological Dramatic Theory* IV: *The Action*, trans. Graham Harrison (San Francisco: Ignatius Press, 1994), 319. Rather,

thropology—which, as shall soon be apparent, is absolutely inseparable from her Trintiarian theology—scattered throughout her very extensive corpus in a largely unsystematic manner. This exposition is set in parallel with a development of the same subject in the still more lengthy work of Balthasar,[37] who sets the tone for the volume by providing the thematic basis from which Adrienne's doctrine is exposited. This fundament, more specifically, is the mystery of difference-in-unity, which Balthasar presents in terms—popular to contemporary theological and philosophical discourse (as shall be made evident later in this introduction)—of certain anthropological "tensions" (*Spannungen*): those of the body and soul; the individual and the community; man and woman; and finally of nature and grace, or person and mission. In each case, the tension in question points to the same mystery: the union-in-difference or the difference-in-union of the Holy Trinity as revealed by Christ in his attitude of archetypal surrender (*Hingabe*).

Balthasar does not, however, simply mark this volume by inspiring the subjects that it addresses, for his own theological perspective opens each of the four thematically-based chapters (three, four, five, and six) by way of introduction. In the ensuing exposition of Adrienne's anthropology—wherein the Trinitiarian connection becomes evident—references to her works are cross-referenced to his, attesting to the truth of Balthasar's claim: "the greater part of so much of what I have written is a translation of what is present in more immediate, less technical fashion in the powerful work of Adrienne von Speyr."[38]

This already daunting task of presenting the theological (especially Trinitarian) anthropology of Adrienne von Speyr in systematic terms supplied by a profound reading of Balthasar's "own" theological anthropology serves still another important goal highlighted above, namely that of responding to Balthasar's critics, most of whom represent the Thomistic tradition. It is within this context that I seek—throughout all of these chapters but most especially in the first chapter and in my general conclusion—to situate the common theological work of Balthasar and Adrienne within the whole of the Catholic theological tradition as represented by Aquinas. Noteworthy is the fact that these criticisms, which are taken up in a succinct manner in chapter seven (notwithstanding our critical exposition of certain aspects of Balthasar's theology throughout), are almost inevitably directed to insights

---

my intention is to gather together her insights on any one theme, in view of further enlightening or enhancing our perception of the mystery of the triune God.

37. See *Hans Urs von Balthasar. Bibliographie 1925–2005*, eds. Cornelia Capol and Claudia Müller (Einsiedeln: Johannes Verlag, 2005).

38. Balthasar, *My Work*, 105; see also 89.

attributable to Adrienne. She, in turn, is seldom criticized: proof, perhaps, that she is rarely taken seriously by theologians.[39]

As shall become increasingly apparent, Adrienne's theology is inseparable from her anthropology, which is to say that she approaches the mystery of the Trinity and of our graced participation therein through various images borrowed largely from human life and experiences, especially those touching upon the experiences of difference-in-unity and unity-in-difference, whence her constant reference to the anthropological "tensions" cited above. These serve, more specifically, to clarify the mystery of the communion in one divine nature of the three divine persons, which Adrienne presents as archetypal for the many differences that make true unity, and thus true love, possible.[40] In this way, there is a constant movement in her theological reflection from God to man (from archetype to image) and from man to God (from image to archetype); from her theology to her anthropology and from her anthropology to her theology.

The primary focus in this volume upon her theological anthropology should thus in no way be thought of as limiting the mystery contained therein to that of the human person, for the latter becomes the lens through which the mystery of the divine life is analogically approached, just as the divine mystery will constantly be cited as indicating the heights (or depths)[41] to which the human being is called. In this way, Adrienne's anthropology is not unlike that of St. Thomas in the *Summa Theologiae*, who does not leave the doctrine of God (the subject of the *Prima Pars*) behind in his treatment of the human person (in the *Prima Secundae* and the *Secunda Secundae*). Precisely as God's image, the human person is, in the theology of St. Thomas as read by Colman E. O'Neil, "the place where God reveals himself, where he can be known, where he can be loved."[42]

---

39. Other than passing remarks of those who, for example, find her theology "disconcerting," the one exception, of which I am aware, comes from a philologist (rather than a theologian) who, not surprisingly, concentrates upon Adrienne's "ambiguities of language" as potentially misleading. See Anne Barbeau Gardiner, "Correcting the Deposit of Faith? The Dubious Adrienne von Speyr," *New Oxford Review* 69, no. 8 (September 2002): 36. This, of course, is of no little importance for theological argumentation. See, in that regard, my general conclusion to this volume, as well as Servais's "A Response from Jacques Servais," *New Oxford Review* 69, no. 8 (September 2002): 36–42; and "Anne Barbeau Gardiner Answers Jacques Servais," *New Oxford Review* 69, no. 8 (September 2002): 42–45.

40. See, for example, by Speyr: *Apokalypse: Betrachtungen über die geheime Offenbarung* (Einsiedeln: Johannes Verlag, 1950, 1999³), 64; *Theologie der Geschlechter*, vol. 12 of *Die Nachlasswerke* (Einsiedeln: Johannes Verlag, 1969), 79; and *John II: Discourses of Controversy. Meditations on John 6–12*, trans. Brian McNeil (San Francisco: Ignatius Press, 1993), 166.

41. As we shall see, the central movement here is that of surrender, which is perhaps more habitually understood as a descent than an ascent, although Adrienne will argue that there is no authentic transcendence in its absence.

42. C. E. O'Neil, "L'homme ouvert à Dieu (Capax Dei)" in N. A. Luyten, *L'anthropologie de saint*

As for the unity of Adrienne's own theology and anthropology, this is achieved, not surprisingly, by the mediating figure of the God-man, Jesus Christ, whom Balthasar presents—in perfect union with Adrienne's insights—as the "concrete analogy of being,"[43] the "measure"[44] between God and man, the "hypostatic union between archetype and image,"[45] and "the original idea" of all creation in whom everything was created and finds meaning.[46] He thus reveals God and man simultaneously and likewise mediates between them.[47]

This united role of prophet and priest is realized by Christ, as Adrienne and Balthasar see it, by virtue of his attitude of archetypal surrender; for by it—as we shall see throughout this work, but most especially in chapter five—he simultaneously receives the Father's gift of life and being and mediates it to humankind by way of a generous outpouring in the form of grace. Because Adrienne recognizes this attitude as characterizing Christ not only in his human nature, but also in his divine nature, she likewise recognizes it as contained within the very gift of grace that is thus outpoured: in, that is to say, the form of the most characteristic of the Christian virtues, faith and

---

Thomas (Fribourg: Éditions universitaires, 1974), 72. See also Servais Pinckaers, *The Sources of Christian Ethics*, trans. Mary Thomas Noble (Washington, D.C.: The Catholic University of America Press, 1995), 221; and Marie-Dominique Chenu, *Introduction à l'étude de Saint Thomas d'Aquin* (Montréal / Paris: Institute d'études médievales / Vrin, 1950), 266–73. Similarly, Balthasar maintains that "to parcel up theology into isolated tracts is by definition to destroy it" (*Theo-Logic* I, 8).

43. See Hans Urs von Balthasar, *A Theology of History* (San Francisco: Ignatius Press, 1994), 69; *Theo-Drama: Theological Dramatic Theory* III: *The Dramatis Personae: Persons in Christ*, trans. Graham Harrison (San Francisco: Ignatius Press, 1992), 222 and 230; and *Theo-Drama: Theological Dramatic Theory* II: *The Dramatis Personae: Man in God*, trans. Graham Harrison (San Francisco: Ignatius Press, 1990), 267.

44. Hans Urs von Balthasar, *The Glory of the Lord: A Theological Aesthetics* I: *Seeing the Form*, trans. Erasmo Leiva-Merikakis, eds. Joseph Fessio and John Riches (San Francisco: Ignatius Press, 1982, 1989), 472. See also ibid., 432–33 and 474; *Theo-Logic: Theological Logical Theory* II: *Truth of God*, trans. Adrian J. Walker (San Francisco: Ignatius Press, 2004), 316; *Theo-Drama* II, 407; and Ellero Babini, "Jesus Christ: Form and Norm of Man according to Hans Urs von Balthasar" in Schindler, *Hans Urs von Balthasar: His Life and Work*, 221–30.

45. Balthasar, *Glory of the Lord* I, 432.

46. Hans Urs von Balthasar, *The Christian State of Life*, trans. Mary Frances McCarthy (San Francisco: Ignatius Press, 1986), 184. See also Victoria S. Harrison, *Homo Orans*: Von Balthasar's Christocentric Philosophical Anthropology," *Heythrop Journal* 40, no. 3 (1999): 280–300, esp. 287–90. Such is close to the Thomistic presentation of God creating through the conception of his intellect, that is to say, his Word. See Gilles Emery, *The Trinitarian Theology of St. Thomas Aquinas* (Oxford: Oxford University Press, 2007), 338; and Emery, "The Ecclesial Fruit of the Eucharist in St. Thomas Aquinas," trans. Therese C. Scarpelli, in *Trinity, Church, and the Human Person* (Ave Maria, Fla.: Sapientia Press, 2007), 129. See also Balthasar's account of the three states of life—original, fallen, and final (repaired and glorified)—from this perspective, in his *The Christian State of Life* (not to be confused with Adrienne's book by the same title); *Theo-Drama* II, 12–13; and *A Theology of History*, 42–43.

47. "Between the divine and created natures there is an essential abyss. It cannot be circumvented. The fact that the person of Jesus Christ bridges this abyss without harm to his unity should render us speechless in the presence of the mystery of his person" (Balthasar, *Theo-Drama* II, 220).

charity. By means of his or her own surrender to Christ, the Christian thus simultaneously receives the virtue of charity (cf. Jn 17:26) and the revelation of the Christian faith in the form of the Son's love for the Father (cf. 14:31) and the Father's love for the Son (cf. 17:23, 26).

It follows that the dynamic of this theological anthropology is not so much that of the human being advancing toward God, who is presented as the term of his or her transcendence or search for happiness, as it is that of God descending toward the human being to take him or her up into his own Trinitarian life.[48] Herein there can be no doubt of the absolute priority of divine *agape*, "which clothes itself in the language of the body." On the other hand, it is precisely this priority, which grants to human freedom the possibility of being "lifted above itself and elevated into the eternal, in order there, as creaturely *eros*, to be the tent and dwelling-place of the divine love!"[49] This, then, is not simply "a one-sided movement"[50] of the divine person of Christ to the human person, for the later becomes increasingly capable—in virtue, it must be admitted, of the primacy of grace—of grasping God and of committing him- or herself to God "in obedience and love."[51] Our incorporation into the Trinitarian communion thus "requires"[52] of us the kenotic movement of loving obedience, which we experience as a participation in Christ's unlimited obedience to the Father.[53]

---

48. See Speyr, *John III: The Farewell Discourses. Meditations on John 13–17*, trans. E. A. Nelson (San Francisco: Ignatius Press, 1987), 310; and Speyr, *Der Mensch vor Gott* (Einsiedeln: Johannes Verlag, 1966), 11. Cf. Balthasar, *A Theology of History*, 37 and 118; *Love Alone Is Credible*, trans. David C. Schindler (San Francisco: Ignatius Press, 2004), 86–87; *The Glory of the Lord: A Theological Aesthetics* V: *The Realm of Metaphysics in the Modern Age*, trans. Oliver Davies et al., eds. Rian McNeil and John Riches (San Francisco: Ignatius Press, 1991), 22; and "Current Trends in Catholic Theology and the Responsibility of the Christian," *Communio* 5, no. 1 (1978): 82–83. Such is also the perspective of Benedict XVI in his first encyclical, *Deus caritas est* (San Francisco: Ignatius Press, 2006).

49. Hans Urs von Balthasar, *The Glory of the Lord: A Theological Aesthetics* VII: *Theology. The New Covenant*, trans. Brian McNeil, ed. John Riches (San Francisco: Ignatius Press, 1989), 470. On the absolute priority of God's action, see also Balthasar, *Epilogue*, trans. Edward T. Oakes (San Francisco: Ignatius Press, 2004), 86.

50. Speyr, *The Boundless God*, trans. Helena M. Tomko (San Francisco: Ignatius Press, 2004), 37.

51. Speyr, *The Letter to the Ephesians*, ed. Hans Urs von Balthasar, trans. Adrian Walker (San Francisco: Ignatius Press, 1996), 19. Hence, "neither direction can be designated as the definitive one: from earth to heaven or from heaven to earth. It is an eternal circuit between God and man, heaven and earth, spiritual world and material world" (Speyr, *Handmaid of the Lord*, trans. E. A. Nelson [San Francisco: Ignatius Press, 1985], 146).

52. Cf. Speyr, *Die katholischen Briefe* II: *Die Johannesbriefe* (Einsiedeln: Johannes Verlag, 1961), 179.

53. See Speyr, *John I: The Word Becomes Flesh. Meditations on John 1–5*, trans. Lucia Wiedenhöver and Alexander Dru (San Francisco: Ignatius Press, 1994), 63; Speyr, *Das Buch vom Gehorsam*, ed. Hans Urs von Balthasar (Einsiedeln: Johannes Verlag, 1966), 20; Speyr, *Korinther I*, ed. Hans Urs von Balthasar (Einsiedeln: Johannes Verlag, 1956), 506; and Balthasar, *Explorations in Theology* IV, 141–53. On the unlimited character of Christ's obedience, see Speyr, *Bereitschaft: Dimensionen christlichen Gehorsams*, ed. Hans Urs von Balthasar, (Einsiedeln: Johannes Verlag, 1975), 3–4; and *Bereitschaft*, 70. Cf. Pope John Paul II, *Veritatis Splendor* (Washington, D.C.: United States Catholic Conference, 2003), nos. 19 and 21;

On the other hand, our graced participation in the divine nature is presented by Balthasar, in perfect union with Adrienne's rich insights, as a *"proportionalitas"*: a proportional relation between two relations, namely the relation of difference between the Creator and the creature, on the one hand, and the relation of difference—and herein lies Adrienne's influence—between the divine persons, on the other.[54] As such—in what constitutes an important distinction between his use of the concept (proportionality) and that of Karl Barth[55]—it implies our "stretching to God's measure"[56] or our sharing in the rhythm of Christ's ever greater surrender to the Father and to the world for love of the Father (cf. Jn 14:31), wherein lies the specifically religious character of Balthasar's own analogy between the Creator and the creature.[57] Similarly, Adrienne recognizes all of creation, but most especially human creation, as "bearing the sign of the Son," of striving toward him, of being held together by him, and of "freely surrendering" itself "inwardly, in an obedience that comes from the Son's obedience."[58]

Thomas Aquinas, *Summa theologiae*, vols. 13–20 in *Works of St. Thomas Aquinas*, trans. Laurence Shapcote, eds. John Mortensen and Enrique Alarcón (Lander, Wyo.: The Aquinas Institute for the Study of Sacred Doctrine, 2012), III, q. 20, a. 2; hereafter "*ST*." The Latin text for this edition is based on the Leonine Edition, transcribed by Roberto Busa and revised by Enrique Alarcón. See also Balthasar's general introduction to the posthumous works of Speyr, in his *Book of All Saints, Part One*, trans. D. C. Schindler (San Francisco: Ignatius Press, 2008), 5–6, for an explication of the importance of this theme in Adrienne's work.

54. See Balthasar, *Theo-Logic* II, 316; cf. Speyr, *The Boundless God*, 18–19. See also Gardner and Moss, "Something Like Time; Something Like the Sexes," 124.

55. Although Barth takes recourse to the term, he rejects the analogy of proper proportionality for the same reason that he rejects the analogy of intrinsic attribution. "According to him [Barth] the analogous form belongs 'originally, primarily, independently and properly' to God alone and 'only subsequently, secondarily, dependently' to us. Hence he admits only of an extrinsic or metaphorical analogy of proportionality" (Joseph Palakeel, *The Use of Analogy in Theological Discourse: An Investigation in Ecumenical Perspective* [Rome: Editrice Pontificia Università Gregoriana, 1995], 56–57). See also Georges de Schrijver (*Le merveilleux accord de l'homme et de Dieu. Étude de l'analogie de l'être chez Hans Urs von Balthasar* [Leuven: Leuven University Press, 1983], 160–63 and 288–96) who explains that Barth's *analogia fidei* entails the rejection of any human role in salvation—including the role of Christ's own humanity—other than that of allowing oneself to be overpowered (*envahir*) by the divine action. It follows that the religious attitude of the human person is, for Barth, that of total receptivity. See also Archie Spencer, "Causality, the *Analogia Entis*, and Karl Barth," *Nova et Vetera* (English Edition) 6, no. 2 (2008): 329–76; and Hans Urs von Balthasar, *The Theology of Karl Barth: Exposition and Interpretation*, trans. Edward T. Oakes (San Francisco: Ignatius Press, 1992).

56. Adrienne von Speyr, *Das Wort und die Mystik* II: *Objektive Mystik* (Einsiedeln: Johannes Verlag, 1970), 59; cf. Balthasar, *Theo-Drama* V, 101.

57. See Schrijver, *Le merveilleux accord*, 258. Schrijver recognizes "the central preoccupation which dominates all of his [Balthasar's] thought" as "situated on the existential level where the analogy of proportionality, emerging from the metaphysical plan, develops in a mysticism of obedience (correspondence, *Entsprechung*), which is at the same time the means used by God to reveal himself" (ibid., 57). See also Balthasar, *Theo-Drama* III, 123.

58. Speyr, *Korinther* I, 506; cited by Balthasar in *Theo-Drama: Theological Dramatic Theory* V: *The Last Act*, trans. Graham Harrison (San Francisco: Ignatius Press, 1998), 520; cf. ibid., 484. See also Speyr, *The Letter to the Colossians*, trans. Michael J. Miller (San Francisco: Ignatius Press, 1998), 37; *Das Buch von Gehorsam*, 20; and *Korinther* I, 185.

In virtue of this primary importance awarded to the notion of surrender as mediating—via the figure of Christ—between Adrienne's theology and her anthropology, we might recognize her work as anticipating the anthropology that arose out of what Michael Waldstein appropriately calls "the Trinitarian nucleus of the Council."[59] Adrienne's work might, more specifically, be viewed as anticipating, as Fergus Kerr has rightly noted,[60] that key insight of the Second Vatican Council, which was of supreme significance for the magisterial teaching of Pope John Paul II and which provided the central intuition at the heart of his theological anthropology and of those inspired by him. Particularly drawn to the Council's presentation of Christ as revealing man to himself within the mystery of the Father and his love,[61] Pope John Paul II recognized "the whole of Christian anthropology"[62] as summed up in the Council's presentation of the specifically human vocation to love in terms of "a certain likeness [*aliquam similitudinem*]" revealed in the Lord's priestly prayer (Jn 17:21–22) "between the union of the divine persons and the union of the sons [and daughters] of God in truth and in charity." From this Johannine insight, the Council concluded—and Pope John Paul II continually returned to this insight in his pontifical teaching—that the human person, "the only creature on earth willed by God for its own sake," cannot find him- or herself "except through a sincere gift of himself [or herself]."[63] From this key insight was, in fact, born the famous theology of the body of Pope John Paul II,[64] as well as

---

59. See his introduction to Pope John Paul II, *Man and Woman He Created Them: A Theology of the Body*, trans. Michael Waldstein (Boston: Pauline Books & Media, 2006), 87. A good example of this development may be found in the 2004 document of the International Theological Commission entitled *Communion and Stewardship: Human Persons Created in the Image of God*, in *International Theological Commission: Texts and Documents*, Volume II: 1986–2007 (San Francisco: Ignatius Press, 2009), 319–51.

60. Anticipating Pope John Paul II's nuptial theology—including, most especially, the role of sexual difference in the presentation of the human creature as the 'image of God'—is, Kerr observes, the theology of Hans Urs von Balthasar "in obedience to the visions of the mystic Adrienne Kaegi-von Speyr" (*Twentieth-Century Catholic Theologians*, 201).

61. "Christ, the final Adam, by the revelation of the mystery of the Father and his love, fully reveals man to man himself and makes his supreme calling clear" (Second Vatican Council, Pastoral Constitution on the Church in the Modern World, *Gaudium et Spes*, no. 22; in Heinrich Denzinger, *Compendium of Creeds, Definitions, and Declarations on Matters of Faith and Morals*, 43rd edition, ed. Robert Fastiggi and Anne Englund Nash [San Francisco: Ignatius Press, 2012], 4322 [hereafter "*DZ*"]). See also *Vatican Council II. The Conciliar and Post Conciliar Documents*, ed. Austin Flannery (Collegeville, Minn.: The Liturgical Press, 1975, 1979⁴).

62. Pope John Paul II, *Dominum et Vivificantem* (Boston: Pauline Books and Media, 1986), no. 59. Cf. also his *Mulieris Dignitatem* (Boston: Pauline Books and Media, 1988), no. 7.

63. *Gaudium et Spes*, no. 24 (*DZ* 4324). On the extensive reference to this passage in the teaching of Pope John Paul II, see Pascal Ide, "Une théologie du don. Les occurrences de *Gaudium et spes*, nr. 24, §3 chez Jean-Paul II," *Anthropotes* 17, no. 1 (2001): 149–78; and 17, no. 2 (2001): 313–44.

64. See Pope John Paul II, *Man and Woman He Created Them*. Fergus Kerr does well to point out that the last major doctrinal text to be issued by the Congregation of the Doctrine of the Faith under Ratzinger as prefect, namely the *Letter to the Bishops of the Catholic Church on the Collaboration of Men*

the "new feminism"[65] inspired by this same pope, and what Fergus Kerr refers to as the "nuptial mysticism"[66] characterizing the perspectives of the most reputed Catholic theologians of the twentieth century.

While this anticipation is certainly not without interest to many readers of this volume, my primary intention is not so much to situate the united theological perspective of Adrienne and Balthasar within the context of present theological trends or developments of doctrine as—it bears repeating—to argue for its congruity with respect to the rich theological tradition of the Church's "common doctor," St. Thomas Aquinas. It is to this end that Aquinas's psychological presentation of the Trinity will be presented in the first chapter of this volume. This presentation will serve, more specifically, to demonstrate the continuity and the novelty of Balthasar's "own" analogical presentation of the Trinity in terms of human freedom, as borrowed from Adrienne's insights into the reciprocal surrender of the divine persons. In so doing, he reasons that we must consider the likeness and difference between the Creator and the creature not only from an *analogical* perspective, which proceeds upward from creation to Creator, but also and especially from a *katalogical* perspective: a perspective proceeding downward from the re-

---

and Women in the Church and the World (May 31, 2004), which sought to respond to the challenge of feminism, originated in Pope John Paul II's theology of the body, although—Kerr adds—it is "anticipated to some degree in the work of Henri de Lubac and Hans Urs von Balthasar" (Kerr, *Twentieth-Century Theologians*, 193). See chaps. 5 and 6 of this volume for a thorough exposé of Adrienne's insights into this theme and Antoine Birot, "Le fondement christologique et trinitaire de la difference sexuelle chez Adrienne von Speyr" in *Revue Catholique Internationale: Communio* 31, nos. 5–6 (2006): 123–35.

65. See Pope John Paul II, *Evangelium Vitae* (Boston: Pauline Books and Media, 1995), no. 99; and Michele M. Schumacher (ed.), *Women in Christ: Toward a New Feminism* (Grand Rapids, Mich.: Eerdmans, 2004), including the extensive bibliography.

66. See Kerr, *Twentieth-Century Theologians*. On Kerr's disapproval of the concept, see his "Discipleship of Equals or Nuptial Mystery?," *New Blackfriars* 75, no. 884 (1994): 344–54, esp. 349, where reference is made to Balthasar. Similar is the critique of Karen Kilby, *Balthasar: A (Very) Critical Introduction* (Grand Rapids, Mich.: Eerdmans, 2012), 123–46. This nuptial theme is particularly evident in works inspired by the anthropology of Pope John Paul II. See, for example, Angelo Scola, *The Nuptial Mystery*, trans. Michelle K. Borras (Grand Rapids, Mich.: Eerdmanns, 2005); "The Nuptial Mystery: A Perspective for Systematic Theology?"; *Communio* 30, no. 2 (Summer 2003): 208–33. See also Marc Ouellet, *Divine Likeness: Toward a Trinitarian Anthropology of the Family*, trans. Philip Milligan and Linda M. Cicone (Grand Rapids, Mich.: Eerdmanns, 2006); Mary Shivanandan, *Crossing the Threshold of Love: A New Vision of Marriage in the Light of John Paul II's Anthropology* (Edinburgh: T. & T. Clark, 1999); David L. Schindler, "The Significance of World and Culture for Moral Theology: *Veritatis Splendor* and the 'Nuptial-Sacramental' Nature of the Body," *Communio* 31 (Spring 2004): 111–42; and David Crawford, "Christian Community and the States of Life: A Reflection on the Anthropological Significance of Virginity and Marriage," *Communio* 29 (2002): 337–65. As for the theme in Balthasar's work, see for example his *Explorations in Theology* II: *Spouse of the Word*, trans. A. V. Littledale, Alexander Dru, Brian McNeil, John Saward, and Edward T. Oakes (San Francisco: Ignatius Press, 1991), 157–66; *A Short Primer for Unsettled Laymen*, trans. Michael Waldstein (San Francisco: Ignatius Press, 1985), 92; *Theo-Drama* V, 462; *Theo-Logic* II, 62; *Elucidations*, trans. John Riches (San Francisco: Ignatius Press, 1998), 67; and (with Scola), *Test Everything*, 81.

vealed archetype to the image. In accord with this perspective and in unity with the profound insights of Adrienne von Speyr, Balthasar presents the divine processions as archetypal for all that we recognize in the world as love by self-surrender. He thus faults—ironically enough, when one considers the critiques that have been launched against his own theology, as we shall see in chapter seven—the Thomistic ordering of the processions, in accord with the principle that something can be loved only when it is known, for importing a human restriction into the divine Trinity. Instead, he suggests that we should—in accord with the facts of revelation—present the Father's generation of the Son as an act of primal "surrender" attributable to love, rather than knowledge.

For this same reason—that we should begin our theological reasoning with the facts of revelation—he also argues that our analogical descriptions of God must address not only the divine unity of being (essence or nature) but also the plurality of persons (which, he insists, presupposes differences or distinctions in the Godhead). This accounts for his constant attempt to account for the "difference-in-unity" or "unity-in-difference"[67] of divine life in terms of various anthropological "tensions," borrowed from Erich Przywara,[68] but transposed—I will argue—in accord with the mystical insights of Adrienne von Speyr and most especially the central importance that she accords to the notion of surrender as describing the dynamism at the heart of the Trinity. This is particularly apparent in our presentation of Adrienne's own "analogy of surrender."

As shown in the first chapter, because Adrienne's anthropology serves to demonstrate how God's being in Trinitarian form is reflected in creaturely being, a bi-directional analysis is constantly at work in her anthropology, no less than that of Balthasar.[69] Hence the revelation of the inner life of the Trinity by Christ will be presented as illuminating the various human "tensions" (body-spirit; man-woman; individual-community; nature-grace) which Balthasar investigates in his "own" theological anthropology; these human tensions, in turn, will serve to illuminate the mystery of the difference-in-unity and unity-in-difference of the Trinity. Because, Balthasar reasons, God has created the world "out of free love, out of free self-expression, freely glorifying himself," the world "necessarily contain[s] within itself traces and images of the intradivine difference."[70] On the other hand, the united perspective of Adrienne and Balthasar is such that every likeness between the Creator and his creation is presented within the context of a greater unlikeness: the infinite freedom of

---

67. Cf. Balthasar, *Theo-Drama* III, 187.
68. See Balthasar, *Theo-Drama* II, 355n26.
69. See Balthasar, *Theo-Logic* I, 15.
70. Balthasar, *Epilogue*, 86.

God "shows himself, *in* (but not of necessity *through*) the existence of what is not God, to be 'He-who-is-always-greater': we can never catch up with him."[71]

With all due respect to this "greater dissimilitude"[72] between Creator and creature, Adrienne's anthropology—which is united (such is my conviction) to that of Balthasar as a "single whole"[73]—remains inseparable from her theology, which in turn is inseparable from her anthropology, thanks to the mediation of her Christology and the important concept of surrender. Focal importance is, in fact, awarded within each of the thematic chapters to this concept, as that whereby the unity of each tension is realized and continues to "reside."

The second chapter, for example, addresses the "tension" (difference-in-unity) between action and contemplation, and thus also the tension between theology and prayer, wherein also lies the question of methodology. All of these tensions, it is argued, achieve unity through the specific Christological "attitude" or disposition of obedient letting-go or letting-happen in virtue of which is realized the mission of the theologian. Christ thus exemplifies the attitude of the theologian, and still more generally of every Christian, in his receptive surrender of love to the Father, wherein he is said to be the "archetype of faith." Because, moreover, Christ mirrors both the divine "attitude" of generous surrender (cf. Phil 2:6–7) and the human attitude of obedience (2:8), he is presented as simultaneously mediating faith's object, or content (*Glaubenslehre*), and faith's act or disposition: the theological virtue (*Glaubenshaltung*). The Christian's own surrender is thus simultaneously an imitation of and a participation in the divine surrender, mediated by Christ. He (Christ), in turn, is presented as revealing the Father precisely by allowing the Father to "be" and act *in him*.

Such also, Adrienne and Balthasar argue, is the mission of the theologian: to give form and figure, by way of obedient surrender, to the "ever-greater" God. Within this context, Adrienne will be presented as exhibiting, from the perspective of Balthasar's regard, the unity of theology and sanctity that he esteems to be essential to the credibility of the Christian message. The emphasis here, however, is not upon Adrienne's interior state, but rather—as typifies the teaching of both Balthasar and Adrienne—what is believed to be her God-given mission. This chapter will be of particular interest to those seeking to better understand Balthasar's own methodology and to those who question the validity of his appropriation of Adrienne's presumably mystical theology.

The third chapter addresses this tension between faith's object and faith's

---

71. Balthasar, *Theo-Drama* II, 119.   72. Cf. *DZ* 806.
73. Balthasar, *My Work*, 89.

act, between the gift of revelation and the Christian's response to the gift in the form of self-gift, or obedient surrender; whence also the presentation of the tension between divine freedom and human freedom, including the tension between freedom and obedience. Such is also the mystery of nature and grace: the mutual indwelling of Christ and the Christian. Hence, as Balthasar puts it, "The end toward which the whole world is orientated is that unity of divine and human freedom in Jesus Christ, which God alone can effect, for in Christ man finds his own self and is taken up whole and entire into God."[74] In contrast to the essentially teleological model of human fulfillment found in Thomistic teaching, this Balthasarian-Speyrian perspective highlights the Ignatian call to mission, which can, Balthasar insists, in no way be discerned from the viewpoint of human nature. Instead human fulfillment requires the surrender of human freedom to divine freedom: *Soli Deo Gloria*.

This focus on the glory of God serves as the context for our examination of Balthasar's apparently original idea—arising out of Speyrian insights—of a "theological" person: one whose freedom is expanded by his or her willing participation in the universal mission and obedience (surrender) of Christ, as exemplified by Mary. This means, as we shall see, that every grace implies a mission. It also means that the Christian's incorporation into the divine life is realized by the very means that most profoundly characterize it: the loving surrender revealed by Christ, who simultaneously manifests the universal significance of human nature. As Balthasar explains in the context of Adrienne's insights, "the Christian lives from the strength of Christ's grace; his living faith is essentially 'infused virtue'; his mission, whether it succeed or miscarry, is answered for by Christ's word of commission."[75]

In the fourth chapter, this fundamental "tension" between person and mission will be examined as building upon and contributing to the "tension" between the human body and the human spirit: a tension which, not unlike the others, is unified within the basic disposition of Christian obedience, characterized by the fundamental attitude of surrender or willing "letting happen." This, more specifically, is an obedience arising out of the obedience of Christ: the lens from which his threefold body (*corpus natum, corpus eucharisticum, corpus mysticum*) is viewed by Adrienne, with reference, once again, to the example of Mary. The final word here, as elsewhere, is however given to the exemplarity of Trinitarian love, which is shown to be the first and final reason for the Incarnation.

---

74. Hans Urs von Balthasar, *Engagement with God. The Drama of Christian Discipleship*, trans. John Halliburton (San Francisco: Ignatius Press, 2008), 75.

75. Balthasar, *My Work*, 71.

From this perspective (that of the divine Incarnation), Christ's body is presented as an instrument of obedience: that whereby he realizes the world's salvation out of love for the Father, who in turn has eternally loved us in his eternal love for the Son (cf. Jn 17:23; 3:16). Such also is the mystery of human beings, who "upon receiving their essential [corporal-spiritual] form from the Creator, find it designed so as to give them their definitive place within the encompassing analogy of the *Verbum-Caro*."[76] This encompassing analogy is, more specifically, the mystery whereby "the Logos himself reads things together in himself [*ana-legein*] and inserts them into the likeness of his 'similitude' […] upward to himself, since he is both the ground and the end of all created things."[77] This ascent of creation to share in the likeness of his glory is nonetheless achieved by the surrender of love which can be described in no other way than by the descent of obedient love in the Incarnation and death of the eternal Word.

The mystery of this descent (that is to say, surrender) is examined more thoroughly in the fifth chapter, which treats the "tension" (or difference-in-unity) of the individual and the community as it arises out of the more fundamental "tension" (treated primarily in chapter three) between the individual and his or her "personalizing" mission and still more fundamentally out of the "tension" (that is to say, again, the difference-in-unity) between the incarnate Son's love for the Father and his love for those to whom the Father has sent him. In virtue, more specifically, of the Son's obedient and receptive surrender to the Father, he (the Son) is simultaneously disposed to receive the Father's gift of divine love and being and to bestow these gifts upon those to whom he is sent.

It is within this context that one confronts the problematic theme of redemption by substitution, as presented by Balthasar in light of Adrienne's mystical experiences. It is observed, more specifically, that the primacy of love that is so central to Balthasar's analogical presentation of the Trinity risks being overshadowed, in his doctrine of redemption, by his portrayal of the Father's wrath directed against the sin-bearing Son. After critically expositing Balthasar's doctrine on this challenging topic, I will propose what I judge a more fitting interpretation of both Adrienne's experiences and her doctrine in light of the Christian, that is to say Trinitarian, faith. I argue, more specifically—in terms borrowed directly from Adrienne—that Christ's generous gift of himself to the world in his passion, death and Eucharist simultaneously reveals and communicates the mystery of the Father's own generous gift of

---

76. Balthasar, *Theo-Logic* II, 315.
77. Ibid., 314.

the whole divine life and being to him (the Son): "As the Father has loved me so I have loved you" (Jn 15:9). It is this revelation, I will argue, which brings about the conversion from sin consisting in the surrender of finite (human) freedom to divine freedom.

Because, it is argued in this same (fifth) chapter, Christ's disciples are given, in virtue of his passion and death, to receive the gift of the Father's love—precisely by being given to imitate and participate in the Christ's own receptive surrender to the Father—they are likewise perfectly suited to communicate this divine gift beyond themselves: "Abide in my love. If you keep my commandments, you will abide in my love, just as I have kept my Father's commandments and abide in his love. [...] This is my commandment, that you love one another as I have loved you" (Jn 15:10, 12). As such—as imitating and participating in Christ's surrender—the Christian is said to be a *homo ecclesiasticus*: a notion apparently arising out of Balthasar's reading of the Fathers which is nonetheless strongly emphasized in Adrienne's doctrine.[78] Those who have become "one spirit in Christ" by the action of the Holy Spirit are, Balthasar explains in union with Adrienne, drawn into the "inner-trinitiarian process" so as to gain "a supernatural influence and attain something like a mutual osmosis or circumincession, first of all in faith and good works (in the 'exchange of merits') and ultimately in the 'vision' of the perfected *communio* of eternal life."[79]

In the sixth chapter, the "tension" (difference-in-unity) of the sexes is examined within the context of the same notion of surrender: a surrender, which Adrienne quite audaciously proposed for her time (1947) as profoundly mutual. After exposing Balthasar's treatment of sexual differentiation in light of certain criticisms, which will be refuted (that of biological reductionism, for example), our attention turns to Adrienne's presentation of the same. Not surprising to the reader who will have discovered the specifically Speyrian regard of the anthropological tensions of unity-in-difference "from on high"—from, that is to say, the perspective of redemption and the archetypical quality of divine (Trinitarian) love—this treatment of the sexes is viewed as illuminated by and as simultaneously illuminating what she contemplates as the mystery of the unity of the Trinity by means of reciprocal personal surrender: a willing gift of one person to the other by way of a generous outpouring or a responsive reception of the other's gift. Hence, for ex-

---

78. It is perhaps worth noting that Adrienne did not read the Fathers—not even at secondhand. Her only knowledge of them would have come from Balthasar's teaching, from a general Catholic culture, or, as Balthasar suggests, from her encounter with them in prayer. See Balthasar, *Our Task*, 40–41.

79. Balthasar, *Explorations in Theology* IV, 203.

ample, "the formation of Eve from the one living body of Adam" is presented by Balthasar in union with Adrienne as "a direct physical image of the origin from the Father's substance of the eternal Son who shares his nature." More significant still in pointing to the mystery of difference-in-unity within the Trinity, Balthasar understands the mystery of Eve's creation from Adam's rib as pointing to the fact that God "not only created them to be one in the duality of sex; he also created their duality out of their own oneness."[80]

From this perspective of granting primacy to divine love, the mediating figure of Christ again assumes central significance. In this chapter, he is presented as exemplifying both the paternal and filial aspects of surrender (and thus also of love), on the one hand, and both the feminine and the masculine qualities of love (by surrender), on the other. As such, he is also the origin of both "masculine" and "feminine" missions, without in any way usurping the particular mission of Mary. Indeed, she is presented as the first cell of the Church, who, in turn, is the unique bride of Christ and the new Eve. Hence, as Balthasar sees it, "The union of Christ and the Church is 'the primordial mystery,' and marriage is only the copy of this; the gift of self made by the Lord in the cult mystery is the 'nuptial gift,' indeed the 'joining in matrimony itself.'"[81] It follows that sexual difference is endowed with a fundamentally spiritual value from the very beginning.

> Man's natural sexuality is bestowed on him in view of the union of natural and supernatural fecundity in him. In no way does the sexual dominate only the physical sphere while the spiritual sphere, which is deemed to be the true seat of his 'likeness to God,' remains untouched by it. For the division of the sexes touches man's spirit so totally, from its deepest roots to its highest pinnacle, that the physical difference appears insignificant in comparison with this distinction that affects the whole person.[82]

The seventh chapter is reserved to a critical appraisal of Adrienne's Trinitarian anthropology as appropriated by Balthasar. While I do address various criticisms of Balthasar's doctrine throughout the volume, such as his method of drawing upon the lives of the saints and the doctrine of the mystics—especially that of Adrienne—as a critical source for his theology in chapter two, his alleged endorsement of an ethics of constraint and of voluntarism in chapter three, his questionable theology of redemption by substitution in chapter five, and his purported macho presentation of sexual differentia-

---

80. Balthasar, *The Christian State of Life*, 227.
81. Hans Urs von Balthasar, *Explorations in Theology* III: *Creator Spirit*, trans. Brian McNeil (San Francisco: Ignatius Press, 1993), 199.
82. Balthasar, *The Christian State of Life*, 226–27.

tion in chapter six, a systematic response is offered in this (seventh) chapter to those criticisms launched against his Trinitarian and Christological doctrines, such as those touching upon the divine immutability, the two natures of Christ, and his presentation of divine *kenosis*. The questionable nature of Balthasar's doctrine on each of these subjects inevitably arises once again out of his appropriation of Adrienne's presentation of the Trinity in terms proper to the human person and human relations. Herein is entertained the question of whether the mystical (often metaphorical) language and images are not misleading at best. I particularly recommend this chapter to those who wonder if Adrienne might not have led Balthasar "astray"[83] with this "too" human image of the Trinity: a Trinity which appears, as it were, in the image of man.

The question of the place of metaphor and analogy in theological language is examined still more thoroughly in my general conclusion, within the context of addressing the interpretation of Adrienne's experiences and doctrine: a question which is already treated to a lesser extent in previous chapters (especially chapters one and five), but which is more systematically treated here along with the question of the relationship between Adrienne and Balthasar in the context of what they regarded as a common mission. Herein is also launched the challenge to those who would continue the work that I have begun here to seriously entertain criticisms such as those addressed throughout this volume. Indeed, these might, it is hoped, incite disciples of Balthasar and Adrienne to situate their metaphorical and analogical images and mystical doctrines within the broad realm of Catholic tradition, including most especially, but not exclusively, that of Thomism. My own decision to focus upon this particular (Thomistic) tradition is due not only to various papal endorsements, but also to the precision of its metaphysical language, which many critics point to as lacking in the common doctrine of Adrienne and Balthasar. Ours is the task, more specifically, I will maintain, of rendering their insights not only intelligible, but also and more importantly, clear of misunderstanding, especially misunderstanding that would lead astray "an unwary or poorly instructed reader," as Anne Barbeau Gardiner fittingly remarks with regard to certain aspects of Adrienne's teaching.[84]

To this end of situating the doctrine of Balthasar and Adrienne within the context of Catholic theological tradition, I will propose a dialogue between disciples of Thomas and those of Balthasar based upon the theme—so

---

83. See, for example, Kerr, "Adrienne von Speyr and Hans Urs von Balthasar," 28; and Mongrain, *The Systematic Thought of Hans Urs von Balthasar*, 11–12.
84. See Gardiner, "Correcting the Deposit of Faith," 36.

central to both of their perspectives—of the integration of human freedom into divine communion. Before so doing, I will examine the very meaning of freedom itself, as it is understood by these two theologians, and I will then address the idea of transcendental participation within their analogical expression of the Creator-creature relation. Within that context, I will argue that disciples of Balthasar should be careful not to pass too quickly from the (theologically valid) notion of receptivity within the Godhead to the (theologically invalid) idea that God is receptive of his creatures.

At the same time, this concluding chapter launches the challenge to the critics of Balthasar (and thus indirectly of Adrienne) to be willing—in light most especially of the attempts made in chapter seven to respond to their arguments—to not simply dismiss this rich doctrine as unorthodox in virtue of its metaphorical language and imprecision. Indeed, it is my most profound hope—and with this I emphasize the final and most significant goal of this volume—that this critical exposé of their doctrine of the human person in the light of the Trinitarian God (as revealed in the terrestrial existence of the divine person of Christ) might convince the suspicious reader of the significant value of this teaching.

In each of these chapters the underlying "tension"—that is to say, the unity-in-difference or the difference-in-unity—between Adrienne's "Trinitarian" anthropology and that of Balthasar is also treated in such a way as to enable the reader to more objectively account for what Balthasar perceives as the profound unity of their works, even to the extent that it is quite impossible "to try to disentangle what is hers from what is mine."[85] It is to this end that each of the chapters is framed from a "properly" Balthasarian perspective: not so as to beg the question from the outset, but rather to facilitate the reader in the task of drawing out the connections and correspondences between their works—whence also the numerous cross-references—so as, in turn, to facilitate the reader's own judgment in this regard.

While it is incumbent upon me to provide a certain structure to this exposition—as expressed in my choice of thematically based chapters—it will quickly become evident to the reader that no matter where one begins within the context of the various tensions treated in this work, one is always led back to the whole of Trinitarian communion, which in turn is continuously "realized" in the reciprocal self-gift of the divine persons by way of their mutual surrender. For this same reason—that everything leads to this Trinitarian whole—there emerges in each succeeding chapter not so much a repetition

---

85. Balthasar, *Our Task*, 72–73.

of the same themes, as a view of the same mystery from still another angle. This in turn presupposes a certain complementarity of the themes exposited, such that each might serve to deepen and strengthen the insights exposited in the others, as various hues and shapes serve to bring out more vividly the other colors and forms within the same picture in service of a harmonic composition encouraging the beauty of the whole.[86]

This whole, on the other hand, serves to clarify each part, which means that the reader should never lose sight of an essential Speyrian insight: namely, that *the human person "can only understand himself and live rightly if he understands himself and lives through the Trinity."*[87] Indeed, "everything in creation is a mirror of the living God, and the mysteries of the created world of which we can never reach a simple understanding reflect the greater mysteries of the trinitarian life."[88] It is into this Trinitarian unity—that whereby each of the divine persons is "transparent" to the others in an eternal communion of mutual surrender—that each of us and all of humanity is called to enter by way of a surrender likened unto theirs[89]: likened, that is to say, in a manner that respects the "greater dissimilitude" than similitude between Creator and creature. This also means that the Christian perfection to which we are all called is not so much a process of gradual or systematic ascent as it is a participation in the kenotic descent of Christ through a participation in his obedience.[90] In precisely this way is realized the *admirabile commercium*, the wonderful exchange, of our salvation. "As far as man is concerned this means ... [that] he can no longer take his own standards from anything within the cosmos but only from the God who stands 'over against' him. He is face to face with his Creator, which implies that he can no longer use God in any way as a measuring rod for himself, for man: he himself must submit to being measured and judged by God."[91]

---

86. As Balthasar put it so well, "there is simply no way to do theology except by repeatedly circling around what is, in fact, always the same totality looked at from different angles." (*Theo-Logic* I, 8). See also *First Glance at Adrienne von Speyr*, 61.

87. Speyr, *John* I, 29; emphasis added. Cf. Balthasar, *Theo-Drama* V, 506.

88. Speyr, *John* I, 28.

89. See Speyr, *John* III, 364; *Korinther* I, 532; and Balthasar, *Theo-Drama* II, 259.

90. See, for example, Speyr, *Korinther* I, 506; *The Letter to the Colossians*, 37; *Das Buch von Gehorsam*, 19–20; and Matro, *Christian Suffering in the Spiritual Writings of Adrienne von Speyr*.

91. Balthasar, *Theo-Drama* II, 396; see also 428; *Theo-Logic* I, 244; *The Glory of the Lord* I, 473–74; and Speyr, *The Victory of Love: A Meditation on Romans 8*, trans. Lucia Wiedenhöver (San Francisco: Ignatius Press, 1990), 13.

ONE

Analogies of the Trinity

*St. Thomas Aquinas, Hans Urs von Balthasar,
and Adrienne von Speyr*

In what might be considered as a key challenge facing anyone attempting to construct a dialogue between theologians of the Thomistic tradition and those inspired by Balthasar, Pope Benedict XVI offered these thoughts in October 2010:

Aristotelian philosophy, as we well know, tells us that between God and man there is only a non-reciprocal relationship. Man refers to God, but God, the Eternal, is in Himself, He does not change: He cannot have this relationship today and another relationship tomorrow. He is within Himself, He does not have *ad extra* relations. It is a very logical term, but it is also a word that makes us despair: so God himself has no relationship with me. With the Incarnation, with the event of the *Theotókos,* this radically changed, because God drew us into Himself and God in Himself is the relationship and allows us to participate in His interior relationship. Thus we are in His being Father, Son and Holy Spirit, we are within His being in relationship, we are in relationship with Him and He truly created a relationship with us. At that moment, God wished to be born from woman and to remain Himself always: this is the great event.[1]

To be sure, as Balthasar acknowledges, "The possibility of distinguishing between God—who 'is all' (Sir 43:27) and thus needs nothing—and a world of finite beings who need God remains the fundamental mystery" grounding "everything that comes after, while not being deducible from anything." It follows that this mystery "can only be illuminated by the infinite freedom

---

1. Pope Benedict XVI, "Meditation of His Holiness Benedict XVI during the First General Congregation, Special Assembly for the Middle East of the Synod of Bishops, Synod Hall, Monday, 11 October 2010"; http://www.vatican.va/holy_father/benedict_xvi/speeches/2010/october/documents/hf_ben-xvi_spe_20101011_meditazione_en.html. I am particularly grateful to Stephen Merkelbach for this reference.

of God, who shows himself *in* (but not necessarily *through*) the existence of what is not God, to be 'He-who-is always-greater': we can never catch up with him."[2]

Within this context of the absolutely perfect God and a world completely dependent upon him, one might recall the apparently provocative question—shocking to Thomist ears—which concludes the final volume of Hans Urs von Balthasar's *Theo-Drama*. This, more specifically, is not the anthropological question concerning man's final fate vis-à-vis his Creator, but rather the strictly theological question of the Creator's own "fate," as it were. "What," Balthasar asks, "does God lose in losing man [to eternal damnation]? Of course, there are problems in formulating the question in this way," Balthasar admits; "but to do so obviously presupposes that God actually *can* lose something, and accordingly that he 'gains' something if his will 'for all men to be saved' (1 Tim 2:4) is achieved."[3]

What is in fact gained, Balthasar concludes after citing some twenty-five pages of excerpts from the very extensive work of Adrienne von Speyr, is not a new relationship with mankind but rather a new manifestation of his glory, which Balthasar, following Speyr, interprets in a Trinitarian sense: the glory consisting of an "additional gift, given to the Son by the Father, but equally a gift made by the Son to the Father, and by the Spirit to both."[4] Or, to put it in still other anthropomorphic terms borrowed from Adrienne, such is a sort of "divine 'conversation'" which from all eternity "envisages the possibility of involving a non-divine world in the Trinity's love."[5]

This involvement of the world in the divine conversation of love is, Balthasar suggests, what St. Paul means when he writes of the end times that God will be "all in all" (1 Cor 15:28).[6] In contrast is the simple and straightforward Thomistic understanding of this same Scriptural passage. "God may be everything in everyone," Aquinas explains, "because then it will be clear that whatever good we have is from God."[7]

In an attempt to point to the likenesses and differences between the analogical discourse in the theology of St. Thomas, on the one hand, and that of Hans Urs von Balthasar and Adrienne von Speyr, on the other, this chap-

---

2. Balthasar, *Theo-Drama* II, 119.
3. Balthasar, *Theo-Drama* V, 506–7; emphasis added.
4. Ibid., 521. 5. Ibid., 509.
6. See ibid., 507.
7. Thomas Aquinas, *Super ad I Cor I*, 15, lect. 3, no. 950 (= *Super I Epistolam B. Pauli ad Corinthios lectura*, in *Commentary on the Letters of Saint Paul to the Corinthians*, vol. 38 of Latin/English Edition of the *Works of St. Thomas Aquinas*, trans. Fabien R. Larcher, Elisabeth Mortensen and Daniel Keating, eds. John Mortensen and Enrique Alarcón [Lander, Wyo.: The Aquinas Institute for the Study of Sacred Doctrine, 2012]).

ter will begin by presenting the historical context of the "tensions" between these theologies before presenting Aquinas's analogy of being and his psychological model of the Trinity. This presentation of the analogical doctrine of the angelic doctor will then serve as the context for my presentation of Balthasar's own analogy of freedom which—although it assuredly draws from this valued tradition—nonetheless differs from it in what I would consider a complementary manner. This analogy of freedom is, more specifically, one which focuses—such is Balthasar's intention—not only nor primarily upon the divine *being*, or essence, but also and especially upon the personal *relations*. As such, it seeks (as does the Thomistic analogy) to account for both likeness and differences within the Trinity. What is perhaps most unique about Balthasar's approach, however, is his constant and overriding purpose of serving, within his analogy, the biblical revelation that "God is love" (1 Jn 4:16).

This analogy of personal freedom for describing the Godhead is further clarified in our treatment of the analogy of personal surrender, as it is used by Adrienne to point simultaneously to the tensions (differences-in-unity) of human life and to the differences-in-unity of the Trinity, which she presents as the archetype of all differences that make love possible. From this perspective, as we will see, all that is recognized in the world as polar, is shown by Adrienne to be first and finally—that is to say, *archetypically*—Trinitarian.

The Historical Context of the "Tension" between the Theology of Balthasar and that of St. Thomas

Before expositing the different analogies of the Trinity by St. Thomas, on the one hand, and by Balthasar and Adrienne, on the other, I wish to admit from the outset that my attempt to argue for a certain congruity between these perspectives is not immediately evident. Indeed, it was not even evident for Balthasar. While he praises St. Thomas for regarding "all metaphysics [...] as orientated towards 'theology,'" he nonetheless considers the angelic doctor as "more of a philosopher than a theologian."[8] By this remark, he means that "the general, suprahistorical essence (*quidditas*) of things" takes precedence in Thomas's work over "the historical and actualist dimensions."[9]

---

8. Hans Urs von Balthasar, *The Glory of the Lord: A Theological Aesthetics* IV: *The Realm of Metaphysics in Antiquity*, trans. Brian McNeil, Andrew Louth, John Saward, Rowan Williams, and Oliver Davies, ed. John Riches (Edinburgh / San Francisco: T. & T. Clark / Ignatius Press, 1989), 396; and *The Glory of the Lord: A Theological Aesthetics* III: *Studies in Theological Styles: Lay Styles*, trans. Andrew Louth, John Saward, Martin Simon, and Rowan Williams, ed. John Riches (Edinburgh / San Francisco: T. & T. Clark / Ignatius Press, 1986), 9.

9. Balthasar, *The Theology of Karl Barth*, 264.

> In accordance with the Aristotelian way of thinking, Thomism emphasizes thinking from below up: it moves from the world of concrete experience and sensation, through abstraction, to universal concepts and a demonstration of the principles contained in them. Here again we have a methodology that is predominantly philosophical, whose use in theology is quite limited. For theology deals primarily with God, the *concretisimum*, from whom nothing can be abstracted. And insofar as theology deals with the revelation of this one, only and unique God in the world, its object is historical [that is to say, incarnational].[10]

With these words written in 1951, Balthasar echoes those of Jean Daniélou in his 1946 "manifesto"[11] of the *nouvelle théologie* in its attack against neo-scholasticism and its presumed neglect of history: "Putting reality more in essences than in subjects, it [neo-scholastic theology] is ignorant of the dramatic world of persons, of concrete universals transcending every essence and distinguishing itself only by existence, and thus no longer by the intelligible and intellection, but rather by value and love or hatred."[12] Such, indeed, was the Thomism of Balthasar's student years: a Thomism which rejected experience, change, development, and pluralism, while simultaneously neglecting scriptural themes, the history of doctrine, personal faith, and liturgy.[13] This negligence was, moreover, highly significant given the historical changes that had put the human person at the center of the universe in such a way as to call into question the very significance of metaphysics:

> The traditional term "metaphysical" signified the act of transcending physics, which for the Greeks signified the totality of the cosmos, of which man was a part. For us, physics is something else: the science of the material world. For us, the cosmos perfects itself in man, who at the same time sums up the world and surpasses it. Thus our philosophy will be essentially a meta-anthropology, presupposing not only the cosmological sciences but also the anthropological sciences, and surpassing them toward the question of being and essence of man.[14]

It is thus not surprising that Aquinas, whom Balthasar approvingly acknowledges as bringing all of worldly knowledge to bear upon theology, be-

---

10. Ibid., 263–64. See also *The Glory of the Lord* I, 147; and "On the Tasks of Catholic Philosophy in Our Time," *Communio* 20, no. 1 (1993): 147–87.

11. Such is the designation of Aidan Nichols. See his "Thomism and the *nouvelle théologie*," *The Thomist* 64 (2000): 1–2.

12. Jean Daniélou, "Les orientations présentes de la pensée religieuse," *Études* 249 (1946): 14.

13. See Thomas F. O'Meara, *Thomas Aquinas Theologian* (Notre Dame, Ind.: University of Notre Dame Press, 1997), 167–73; Jean-Pierre Torrell, *La Somme de Saint Thomas* (Paris: Cerf, 1998), 150; and Karl Rahner, "The Present Situation of Catholic Theology" in *Theological Investigations* XXI (London: Darton, Longman & Todd, 1988), 70–77, esp. 71–72. Fergus Kerr qualifies this "Thomism" as, in fact, "Suárezianism"; see his *Twentieth-Century Theologians*, 124. Cf. Balthasar, *The Glory of the Lord* V, 21–29.

14. Balthasar, *My Work*, 114. The concept "meta-anthropology" he attributes to Peter Henrici. See Balthasar and Scola, *Test Everything*, 25. See also Balthasar, *A Theological Anthropology* (New York: Sheed and Ward, 1967), 81–83; and *Explorations in Theology* I, 253–54.

came too often (and falsely!) identified, as Thomas O'Meara explains, "with a past ontology, a dead language, and a fear of one's own age."[15] In contrast, Balthasar presents his own method in words which further expose his solidarity with the *ressourcement* movement of the *nouvelle théologie:*[16] "I have attempted to see Christianity or the figure of Christ as a form, and together with Christ also his Church. One can walk around a form and see it from various sides. One always sees something different and yet still the same thing."[17] That "same thing," he was convinced, was also the *whole* thing, for the "whole" of God's revelation is expressed for Balthasar, as we saw in the general introduction to this volume, "in *a single* man, *a single* Church."[18] It follows, then, that respect for the tradition "does not excuse one from the obligation of beginning everything from the beginning each time, not with Augustine or Thomas or Newman, but with Christ."[19]

In opposition to both the correlation method of Rahner, which seeks—by way of a so-called dialogue between the structure of human experience and the content of faith—to discover within the human experience of God the

---

15. O'Meara, *Thomas Aquinas Theologian*, 173. On the other hand, Balthasar does admit that Thomas was "no Thomist" (*Explorations in Theology* I, 220); see also "The Fathers, the Scholastics and Ourselves," *Communio* 24, no. 2 (1997): 345–96; and "On the Task of Catholic Philosophy in Our Time," trans. Brian McNeil, *Communio* 20, no. 1 (1993): 176. As for Balthasar's estimation of Thomas, he writes: "The entire breadth of human thought [...] is scarcely broad enough to serve the theological wisdom of a Thomas Aquinas as material for his presentation" (Balthasar, "On the Task of Catholic Philosophy," 158). See also ibid., 176; *Engagement with God*, 67; and *The Grain of Wheat*, 22.

16. The *nouvelle théologie* proposed to respond to the challenges posed by modernity and contemporary culture with the riches of the past in its engagement with contemporary thought; whence the term *ressourcement*: the return to the sources, namely the Bible, the Fathers of the Church, and the liturgy. For more detail, see (in addition to the references cited above) Jürgen Mettepenningen, *Nouvelle Théologie—New Theology: Inheritor of Modernism, Precursor of Vatican II* (New York: T. & T. Clark, 2010); Hans Boersma, *Nouvelle Théologie & Sacramental Ontology: A Return to Mystery* (Oxford: Oxford University Press, 2009); John Auricchio, *The Future of Theology* (New York: Alba House, 1970), esp. 257–315; Massimo Faggioli, *Vatican II: The Battle for Meaning* (New York: Paulist Press, 2012), 68–75; and John A. Gallagher, *Time Past, Time Future: An Historical Study of Catholic Moral Theology* (New York: Paulist Press, 1990), 141–51. For Balthasar's account of his involvement, see his *My Work*, 48–50. Interestingly enough, he also addresses his commitment to *aggiornomento* on 51.

17. Balthasar and Albus, "Spirit and Fire," 579–80. In the context of this citation, Balthasar explicitly makes reference to his indebtedness to Goethe's manner of seeing a "'form' in its interconnected wholeness" (Balthasar, *Our Task*, 37); see also *Epilogue*, 59; and Edward T. Oakes, *Pattern of Redemption*, 84–85 and 94. Louis Dupré presents Goethe's vision as embracing a Platonic ideal of beauty. "Yet he steadfastly denied any separation between the universal idea and the particular image. The image represents the entire universal type. 'The particular is always subject to the universal; the universal must always suit the particular.' Rendering the universal concrete, raising the particular to universal significance, seeing the eternal in the transient—that is for Goethe the goal of artistic genius" (Louis Dupré, *The Enlightenment and the Intellectual Foundations of Modern Culture* [New Haven, Conn.: Yale University Press, 2004], 111).

18. Balthasar and Albus, "Spirit and Fire," 593.

19. Hans Urs von Balthasar, *Razing the Bastions: On the Church in this Age*, trans. Brian McNeil (San Francisco: Ignatius Press, 1993), 34. Balthasar thus mourns the loss of mysticism in theology; see *The Glory of the Lord* V, 26.

explicit grounds for faith in him,[20] and the Thomistic method of employing the experience of causality as the conceptual link between our experience of God and our experience of the world,[21] Balthasar argues that the Word of God "will not consist in anything that man could have figured out about the world, about himself, and about God, on his own—whether a priori or a posteriori."[22] In precisely this way, the Swiss theologian launches the challenge to consider the similitude within "greater dissimilitude" between Creator and creature (*"tanta similitudo [. . .] maior sit dissimilitudo"*)[23] not only from an analogical perspective, which proceeds upward (*ana-*) from the creature to the Creator in accord with the doctrine of creation as viewed from the perspective of causality, but also, and even primarily, from a *katalogical* one: a

---

20. On Rahner's method, see J. Augustine DiNoia, "Karl Rahner" in David F. Ford (ed.), *The Modern Theologians* I (Oxford: Basil Blackwell, 1989), 183–204, esp. 190; Francis Schüssler Fiorenza, *Foundational Theology: Jesus and the Church* (New York: Crossroad, 1985), 278–79; Stephen Fields, "Balthasar and Rahner on the Spiritual Senses," *Theological Studies* 57 (1996): 224–41, esp. 233; and Fergus Kerr, *Immortal Longings: Versions of Transcending Humanity* (Notre Dame, Ind.: University of Notre Dame Press, 1997), 178. For a presentation of the method of correlation, see David F. Ford, "Introduction to Modern Christian Theology," in Ford (ed.), *The Modern Theologians*, 3. The debate between Balthasar and Rahner is evident in Balthasar's *Love Alone Is Credible*; *The Moment of Christian Witness*, trans. Richard Beckley (San Francisco: Ignatius Press, 1994); *The God Question and Modern Man*, trans. Hilda Graef (New York: Seabury Press, 1967); and to some extent, *Engagement with God*. See also *My Work*, 51–60; "Spirit and Fire"; *Theo-Drama* IV, 273–84; and "Current Trends in Catholic Theology."

21. This is so because causality is, as Coleman Eugene O'Neil explains, "the necessary context [*encadrement*] of all intellectual expressions of Christian experience, even at its most sublime heights (mysticism and the beatific vision). During the present life, in fact, God is known only through his effects in the natural order or in the order of grace" (O'Neil, "L'homme ouvert à Dieu [Capax Dei]," 60–61). Hence, St. Thomas reasons that "in all creatures there is found the trace of the Trinity, inasmuch as in every creature are found some things which are necessarily reduced to the divine Persons as to their cause" (*ST* I, q. 45, a. 7). Cf. *The Catechism of the Catholic Church* (New York: Doubleday, 1995), no. 41. See also Reinhard Hütter, "Attending to the Wisdom of God—from Effect to Cause, from Creation to God: A *Relecture* of the Analogy of Being according to Thomas Aquinas," in Thomas Joseph White (ed.), *The Analogy of Being: Invention of the Antichrist or the Wisdom of God?* (Grand Rapids, Mich.: Eerdmans, 2011), 209–45; and Thomas Joseph White, *Wisdom in the Face of Modernity: A Study in Thomistic Natural Theology* (Naples, Fla.: Sapientia Press, 2009).

22. Balthasar, *Love Alone Is Credible*, 50. See also *The Glory of the Lord* I, 222. It is more directly against Rahner that Balthasar will argue: "Christianity disappears the moment it allows itself to be dissolved into a transcendental precondition of human self-understanding in thinking or living, knowledge or deed" (ibid., 51). See also Balthasar's *Mysterium Paschale, The Mystery of Easter*, trans. Aidan Nichols (Edinburgh: T. & T. Clark, 1990), 140.

23. *DZ* 806. This is the formula adopted by the Fourth Lateran Council to describe the analogical relation between the Creator and his creature. Cf. Balthasar, *Theo-Drama* III, 221, especially n51; and *Explorations in Theology* III, 40–41. Balthasar's understanding of the analogy between Creator and creature in these terms is clearly indebted to Erich Przywara who, in turn, recognizes in Balthasar's work the "deeper form of analogy," or "the mystery of the cross that overcomes the 'no matter how great a similarity' by means of 'even greater dissimilarity,' so that the greatness of God can be participated in" (Erich Przywara, *Analogia Entis* [Einsiedeln: Johannes Verlag, 1962²], 250). See also James V. Zeitz, "Przywara and von Balthasar on Analogy," *The Thomist* 52 (1988): 473–98; and Peter Casarella, "Hans Urs von Balthasar, Erich Przywara's *Analogia Entis*, and the Problem of a Catholic *Denkform*" in Thomas Joseph White (ed.), *The Analogy of Being: Invention of the Antichrist or the Wisdom of God?* (Grand Rapids, Mich.: Eerdmans, 2011), 192–206.

perspective which proceeds downward (*kata-*) from the revealed archetype to the created image.[24]

Balthasar argues more specifically—in accord with Adrienne's perspective as is (in part) the intention of this volume to demonstrate—that because the divine processions give rise to both creation and the Son's earthly mission,[25] "the infinite distance" between God and his creation is founded in the "prototypical distance between God [the Father] and God [the Son]"[26] as revealed in the Son's "Eucharistic movement back and forth from the Father."[27] It is in drawing on Adrienne's insights, I will argue, that Balthasar thus recognizes "differences within creation (differences which are included in and also include the difference of creation from God)" as "analogous to (other) differences in God," as Lucy Gardner and David Moss accurately put it. "That is, both the differences of not-God from God and the differences of not-God from not-God participate in Trinitarian differencing."[28] It follows, for Balthasar—in close union with Adrienne—that precisely in virtue of the divine Incarnation "divine and creaturely difference" really does enter "into a certain relation of comparability."[29]

The "greater dissimilitude" than similitude between God and his creation is obvious to all world religions, Balthasar reasons. What is unique to Christianity is that this gulf is bridged by the difference—or otherness—that is revealed within God himself: "If," Balthasar reasons, "within God's identi-

---

24. See Krenski, *Passio Caritatis. Trinitarische Passiologie im Werk Hans Urs von Balthasar* (Einsiedeln: Johannes Verlag, 1990), 122–26; and W. Trietler, "True Foundations of Authentic Theology," in D. Schindler, ed., *Hans Urs von Balthasar: His Life and Work,* 170–78.

25. "According to God's gracious plan for the world, the *processio*, which includes the *creatio*, is to be fulfilled in the Son's *missio*" (Balthasar, *Theo-Drama* V, 81). See also *The Christian State of Life*, 189; *Theo-Drama* IV, 326; *A Theology of History*, 31; and Speyr, *Mary in the Redemption*, trans. Helena M. Tomko (San Francisco: Ignatius Press, 2003), 50–51. From still another perspective—that of the *reditus*—Balthasar argues that "the Son's *mission* has been taken up into his *processio*, rendering it timeless" (*Theo-Drama* III, 513). Hence, "the created world is, as it were, drawn into the begetting" (*Theo-Drama* V, 81; here, Balthasar makes reference to Speyr, *Die Schöpfung* [Einsiedeln: Johannes Verlag, 1972], 11).

26. Balthasar, *Theo-Drama* II, 266. Cf. Sepyr, *Theologie der Geschlecther*, 115–16 and 143. See also Balthasar, *Theo-Drama* III, 22, 261–62, and 530; *Explorations in Theology* IV, 333; and *Does Jesus Know Us? Do We Know Him?* trans. Graham Harrison (San Francisco: Ignatius Press, 1983), 52. It should be noted that the notion of "distance" is a metaphorical expression for "distinction" or "difference" with respect to the divine persons. See, for example, Speyr, *The World of Prayer*, trans. Graham Harrison (San Francisco: Ignatius Press, 1985), 66, where it is admitted that "no spatial separation is possible or necessary" in God.

27. Balthasar, *Theo-Drama* II, 268. Cf. Speyr, *John* II, 167; *Das Wort und die Mystik* II, 98–101; and *Korinther* I, 377. See also Balthasar, *The Threefold Garland: The World's Salvation in Mary's Prayer*, trans. Erasmo Leiva-Merikakis (San Francisco: Ignatius Press, 1982), 24; and Nicholas Healy and David L. Schindler, "For the Life of the World: Hans Urs von Balthasar on the Church as Eucharist," in *The Cambridge Companion to Hans Urs von Balthasar*, eds. Edward Oakes and David Moss (Cambridge: Cambridge University Press, 2004), 51–63.

28. Gardner and Moss, "Something Like Time; Something Like the Sexes," 124.

29. Balthasar, *Theo-Logic* II, 181.

ty, there is an Other [...], then both the otherness of creation, which is modeled on the archetypal otherness within God, and its sheer existence, which it owes to the intradivine liberality, are brought into a positive relationship to God."[30] When, however, this "positive relationship" of creation to God gives way to God's relation to creation, the tension between Balthasar's perspective and that of St. Thomas becomes particularly apparent, as we shall now see.

The Analogy of Being and the Psychological Model of the Trinity: St. Thomas Aquinas

To begin our investigation of both the Thomistic analogy of being and Aquinas's psychological model of the Trinity in view of illuminating the likenesses and differences between Aquinas's perspective and that of Balthasar, we do well to return to their contrasting vision of eschatological fulfillment. For Balthasar, we are reminded, the Pauline image of God as "all in all" (1 Cor 15:28) is interpreted to mean that all of creation will partake of the love of the divine persons for one another. For Thomas, on the other hand, this means that all created goodness will be manifest as having its goodness from God. Such is, for St. Thomas, the expression of the divine will; for God "wills both Himself to be, and other things to be; but Himself as the end, and other things as ordained to that end; inasmuch as it befits the divine goodness that other things should be partakers therein."[31] Or, to put it in other words, in willing his own goodness, God simultaneously wills things "apart from Himself."[32] It follows that "no perfection can accrue to Him from them."[33] Meanwhile, "each and every creature exists for the perfection of the entire universe," which in turn "with all its parts is ordained toward God as its end, inasmuch as it imitates, as it were, and shows forth the Divine goodness, to the glory of God."[34]

With these words, the angelic doctor points to what might be considered one of the chief characteristics of his analogical discourse, whereby the mystery of the Creator is addressed in terms of his creation. Here, more specifically, is employed not only the typically Aristotelian reasoning according to which a cause might be said to be present in the effect, and therefore also the Creator in his creation, but also the more typically Neo-Platonic reasoning whereby creatures are considered as participating in the perfections of the Creator: "[T]he last end is the first beginning of being, in Whom every per-

---

30. Ibid. See also ibid., 82; *Epilogue*, 35, 37, and 181; *Theo-Logic* I, 267; *My Work*, 118; *Theo-Drama* II, 288; and *Explorations in Theology* IV, 341.
31. Thomas Aquinas, *ST* I, q. 19, a. 2.
32. Ibid., ad. 2.
33. Ibid., ad. 3.
34. Ibid., q. 65, a. 2.

fection of being is."³⁵ Such, in other words, is a likeness, which is not to be found in form, but in "proportion": according as being is unequivocally ascribed to both the Creator and his creation. Because the agent (God) is "not contained in any 'genus,'" the effect (creation) does not, Thomas reasons, "participate in the likeness of the agent's form," as is the case of beings who belong to the same species, for example, "but only according to some sort of analogy; as existence is common to all. In this way all created things, so far as they are beings, are like God as the first and universal principle of all being."³⁶

Hence, as Balthasar fittingly presents the teaching of St. Thomas:

The analogy of Being between God and the creature allows neither the comparison on the basis of a neutral middle term (the 'concept of Being,' which does not exist) nor the comparison on the basis of a formal proportion (such as that between 'being' [*Sein*] and 'essence' [*Wesen*] that remains constant in both, nor such a derivation of the one (the creature) from the other (God) that the creature would come to stand in this attribution at a distance from the Creator that it could measure and determine, for that would mean that God's distance from the creature would also be somehow surveyable by the creature: the *maior dissimilitude* (DS [*DZ*] 806) always cuts through every possibility of comparison.³⁷

The difference between substantial being (God) and participated being (in creatures) thus accounts for the likeness and the distinction between the Creator and his creation and simultaneously points to the dynamism within all created beings whereby they are joined to God as source and end.³⁸ "God draws all things to Himself," Thomas reasons, "in so far as He is the source of being, since all things, in as much as they are, tend to be like God, who is Being itself."³⁹ Or, to put it otherwise: "every beginning of perfection is or-

---

35. Thomas Aquinas, *ST* I-II, q. 2, a. 5, ad. 3.
36. Thomas Aquinas, *ST* I, q. 4, a. 3; cf. q. 104, a. 1.
37. Balthasar, *Explorations in Theology* III, 40–41; translation slightly altered. See also Balthasar, *Epilogue*, 82 and 91–92; and *Theo-Logic* I, 17. Such is also Balthasar's own understanding of the analogy of being, which, as Lucy Gardner and David Moss explain, "is not based upon two terms (God and world, or Being and being) having become co-terminus in their sharing of a prior, common, third term which can be known apart from these two ('to be'). It is, rather, the participation of the second with the first, the asymmetric relation of two without 'a' third" ("Something Like Time; Something Like the Sexes," 118–19). Or, to put it in properly Thomistic terms: God is related to creatures "as transcending every *genus*, and as the principle of all *genera*" (*ST* I, q. 4, a. 3, ad. 2).
38. As Anna Williams rightly argues, "The notion of participation functions not only to assure the authenticity of the creature's share in divine life but just as much to ensure the distinction between creature and Creator articulated through the difference in possession by essence versus participation." (A. N. Williams, *The Ground of Union: Deification in Aquinas and Palamas* [Oxford: Oxford University Press, 1999], 95). Such is also implied by the doctrine of the divine simplicity, which Serge-Thomas Bonino qualifies as "a notion more fundamental than the [divine] immutability" of God in Thomas's *ST*. See Bonino, "La simplicité de Dieu" in *Instituto San Tommaso, Studi 1996*, ed. Dietrich Lorenz (Rome: Pontificia Università San Tommaso d'Aquino in Roma Angelicum: 1997), 118.
39. Thomas Aquinas, *ST* II-II, q. 34, a. 1, ad. 3.

dained to complete perfection, which is achieved through the last end."⁴⁰ The angelic doctor thus invites us to consider "a twofold order between creatures and God: the first is by reason of creatures being caused by God and depending on Him as on the principle of their being; and thus on account of the infinitude of His power God touches each thing immediately, by causing and preserving it [...]. But the second order is by reason of things being directed to God as to their end."⁴¹ And all of this, we might add, is accomplished by the missions of the Son and the Holy Spirit, who enable the created person to be united to God by knowledge (wisdom) and love (charity).

Herein is evident the famous *exitus-reditus* schema of St. Thomas's *Summa theologiae* such that the descending movement of creation's procession from God joins the ascending movement of its return to God, as to its final cause, in a dynamic of assimilation by way of Christ's mediating action.⁴² Hence, as Balthasar reads St. Thomas, all cosmic order is "at once immanent and transcendent: since all things have their principle in God and are related to him, they can also be ordered to one another by means of the relations that underlie them."⁴³

Such is also the origin of a fundamental insight at the heart of Balthasar's fifteen-volume trilogy—*The Glory of the Lord*, *Theo-Drama*, and *Theo-Logic*—which he acknowledges as attributable to the angelic doctor: "The 'to-be-real' that is given to every being thus hides a duality in itself that might at first seem contradictory: (1) it is grounded in itself (which a mere being cannot do on its own, or otherwise it would be God); and (2) it proceeds out of itself by virtue of a dynamic given to it in order to real-ize [sic] itself (its innerness) in the very act of expressing."⁴⁴

To be sure, the creature's procession out of itself ought not to be understood in strictly unequivocal terms, which is to say, that the same concept is

---

40. Thomas Aquinas, *ST* I-II, q. 1, a. 6.
41. Thomas Aquinas, *ST* III, q. 6, a. 1; ad. 1.
42. See, for example, the classic work of Marie-Dominique Chenu, *Introduction à l'étude de Saint Thomas d'Aquin*, 255–73.
43. Balthasar, *The Glory of the Lord* IV, 408–9. Balthasar recognizes Thomas as "the greatest artist of order and organization in the history of thought" (*The Glory of the Lord* II, 266). Cf. Marie-Joseph Nicolas, "L'idée de nature dans la pensée de saint Thomas d'Aquin," in *Revue thomiste* 74, no. 4 (1974): 533–90. On the unity of the Platonic and Aristotelian perspectives in St. Thomas, see the general conclusion to this volume and Fran O'Rourke, *Pseudo-Dionysius and the Metaphysics of Aquinas* (Leiden: Brill, 1992), 248–49.
44. Balthasar, *Epilogue*, 51. This "epiphanic character [...] permeates everything that exists" (ibid., 83). See also ibid., 109; and *Theo-Logic* II, 184. Cf. Thomas Aquinas, *ST* I, q. 19, a. 2; *SCG* III, c. 21 (= *Summa contra Gentiles*, Leonine edition, volumes 13–15 [Rome: Editori di San Tommaso, 1918, 1926, 1930], trans. Anton C. Pegis, James F. Anderson, Vernon J. Bourke, and Charles J. O'Neil [Notre Dame, Ind.: University of Notre Dame Press, 1997]); and O'Rourke, *Pseudo-Dionysius and the Metaphysics of Aquinas*, 247–50.

used by Balthasar to describe a phenomenon which is differentiated according to, on the one hand, a three-tiered hierarchy of being, and, on the other hand, a threefold category of transcendence that characterizes his trilogy (beauty, goodness, and truth): "(1) mere appearance is already appropriate for what is lifeless, while (2) self-giving receives a definite character on the level of life and consciousness (plants and animals 'give themselves' as nourishment in a way that is almost exemplary), and (3) actual self-saying remains reserved for the human word."[45]

Ultimately, then, Balthasar recognizes within this mysterious tension between immanence and transcendence in created being (between the creature's standing in itself as a substantial being and its proceeding out of itself in relation to other beings)[46] the important Aristotelian-Thomistic distinction between essence and operation as implicit to the concept of human freedom, whence the reciprocity of being and action: "Only the action itself will reveal who each individual is; and it will not reveal, through successive unveilings, primarily who the individual *always was,* but rather who he *is to become* through the action, through his encounter with others and through the decisions he makes."[47]

This, in fact, is the direction in which Balthasar recognizes the analogy of being as having pointed all along: to what Angelo Scola suggests is "an analogy of freedom."[48] "The basic presupposition for all understanding of existing things [*des Seienden*] and of Being [*des Sein*], is," Balthasar explains, "the relationship between uncreated and created freedom; it is the creature's freedom that causes him to be termed the 'image and likeness of God'—and this likewise is the concrete thrust of the '*analogia entis.*'"[49]

Such, arguably, is not far from the perspective of the angelic doctor in his *Summa theologiae* wherein it is reasoned: "While in all creatures there is some kind of likeness to God, in the rational creature alone we find a likeness of image." This image quality of the rational creature points more specifically, Thomas maintains, to an imitation of God "not only in being and life, but

---

45. Balthasar, *Epilogue,* 83. As for St. Thomas, he addresses this same distinction in terms of the degrees of being, whence the various desires for perfection: "some desire [perfection] as to being only, some as to living being, some as to being which is living, intelligent and happy" (*ST* I-II, q. 2, a. 5, ad. 3).
46. See Balthasar, *Epilogue,* 51.
47. Balthasar, *Theo-Drama* II, 11. Hence, "There is a reciprocal relationship between the 'was' and the 'will be.' '*Agere sequitur esse*' ['to act' follows 'to be'] also requires '*esse sequitur agere*' ['to be' follows 'to act']" (ibid.).
48. See Angelo Scola, *The Nuptial Mystery* (Grand Rapids, Mich.: Eerdmanns, 2005), 235–36; cf. Balthasar, *The God Question and Modern Man,* 114.
49. Balthasar, *Theo-Drama* II, 123. See also his *The Glory of the Lord: A Theological Aesthetics* VI: *Theology. The Old Covenant,* trans. Brian McNeil and Erasmo Leiva-Merikakism, ed. John Riches (San Francisco: Ignatius Press, 1991), 87.

also in intelligence";[50] for "we should understand what is said of God, not according to the mode of the lowest creatures, namely bodies," he reasons, "but from the similitude of the highest creatures, the intellectual substances."[51] These, he further explains, are those who are endowed "with free-will and self-movement,"[52] whence the presentation of the processions in God according to the analogy whereby "the intelligible word [...] proceeds from the speaker, yet remains in him"[53] and love proceeds from the lover with its object remaining within him.[54]

Here, in short, is an analogy borrowed from human psychology to explain the unity of nature and the difference of persons within the Trinity. This same analogy is then inverted by St. Thomas to explain, on the basis of our understanding of the Trinity, the deification of human persons: the mystery whereby we "become partakers of the divine nature" (2 Pet 1:4). "Because the Holy Ghost is Love, the soul is assimilated to the Holy Ghost by the gift of charity," Thomas reasons; and the Son, who is Word, is sent "according to the intellectual illumination, which breaks forth into the affection of love," that is to say, as "wisdom."[55] Or, to resume in the words of Gilles Emery:

> The divine person who is sent communicates a participation in his eternal property: the Son communicates a likeness or a resemblance to the proper mode by which he refers to the Father; the Holy Spirit communicates a likeness to the proper mode by which he proceeds. This likeness is the impression that the Son and the Holy Spirit dispose in the soul of the saints, such that the union to God is accomplished by an assimilation to the personal relation that both the Son and Holy Spirit have to the Father. Since the Holy Spirit proceeds personally as love, he leads us to join the Father by the love that he communicates to us when he is poured into our hearts. And just as the Son personally proceeds as the Word of the Father, he enables us to join the Father by the wisdom that he communicates to us when he is sent. [...] The Father who sends is thus manifest and present in the mission of the Son and [that] of the Holy Spirit.[56]

This assimilation of the human being to the divine persons presupposes, of course, the spiritual nature of the human person, for while other creatures "can be moved by a divine person," only a rational creature is capable—in virtue of grace—of actually partaking "of the divine Word and of the Love proceeding, so as freely to know God truly and to love God rightly."[57] The theological vir-

---

50. Thomas Aquinas, *ST* I, q. 93, a. 6.
51. Ibid., q. 27, a. 1.
52. Thomas Aquinas, *ST* I-II, Prologue.
53. Thomas Aquinas, *ST* I, q. 27, a. 1.
54. Cf. ibid., a. 3; and q. 37, a. 1.
55. Thomas Aquinas, *ST* I, q. 43, a. 5, ad. 2.
56. Gilles Emery, "Missions invisibiles et missions visibles: Le Christ et son Esprit," *Revue thomiste* 106, nos. 1–2 (2006): 54–55.
57. Thomas Aquinas, *ST* I, q. 38, a. 1; cf. q. 8, a. 3.

tues of faith, hope, and charity, which conform us to God, simultaneously direct us to him "in the same way" that our natural inclinations direct us toward perfection: "in respect to the reason or intellect" and "through the rectitude of the will which tends naturally to good as defined by reason."[58]

It is thus not surprising that the angelic doctor should recognize natural reason as "minister[ing] to faith as the natural bent of the will ministers to charity," whence the famous Thomist axiom: "grace does not destroy nature, but perfects it."[59] In other words, our deification whereby we are assimilated to God by partaking of his own nature, supposes that human nature is already *per se* an image of the Trinitarian God: "as the uncreated Trinity is distinguished by the procession of the Word from the Speaker, and of Love from both of these," so also within ourselves "we find a procession of the word in the intellect, and a procession of the love in the will."[60] Grace does not, therefore, create new faculties in human nature but rather extends the "range of possibility"[61] of those faculties already possessed by human nature, whence the progressive development of the image of God in the human person from nature to grace and finally to glory.[62]

In short, the dynamic relation of intellect and will determines the structure of Aquinas's doctrine of the Trinity, as well as that of his theological anthropology, as Anna Williams acutely observes.[63] Or, as Gilles Emery explains:

[The] theological anthropology [of St. Thomas] is directly rooted in Trinitarian theology, insofar as it rests on the doctrine of the Word and of Love. The same observation can be made about the study of the virtues, especially of the theological virtues, and of the gifts of the Holy Spirit, thus illuminating the fundamental structure of St. Thomas's moral theology. The doctrine of the Word and Love thus provides us with a unified understanding of the Trinity in itself, of Trinitarian action, of the divine missions, and of theological anthropology.[64]

From the perspective of this tightly woven synthesis of theology and anthropology in Thomas's doctrine, it is not surprising that Anna Williams should hold that his treatment of the knowledge of God[65] and of religious language[66] are not "investigations of these issues for their own sake or because of any methodological importance, but as a search for the grounds of relation between humanity and the God who is utterly Other."[67] Far from im-

---

58. Thomas Aquinas, *ST* I-II, q. 62, a. 3.
59. Thomas Aqinas, *ST* I, q. 1, a. 8, ad. 2.
60. Ibid., q. 93, a. 6.
61. Cf. Williams, *The Ground of Union*, 37.
62. Cf. Thomas Aquinas, *ST* I, q. 93, a. 4.
63. Williams, *The Ground of Union*, 36.
64. Gilles Emery, "*Theologia and Dispensatio:* The Centrality of the Divine Missions in St. Thomas's Trinitarian Theology," *The Thomist* 74, no. 4 (2010): 554–55. Cf. Williams, *The Ground of Union*, 36.
65. Cf. Thomas Aquinas, *ST* I, q. 12.
66. Cf. ibid., q. 13.
67. Williams, *The Ground of Union*, 41. Similarly, Williams recognizes: "In the very way he frames

plying the breaching of the Creator-creature distinction, however, Thomas's solution insists upon "the strong and startling claim of Christian scripture: 'We become partakers in divine nature.'"[68] To be more precise, it is the basic Thomistic distinction between "possession by essence versus participation"[69] that accounts for the unity and distinction between God, who "alone is good essentially"[70] and "contain[s] within Himself the whole perfection of being,"[71] and the deified human being, who can add nothing to God's goodness[72] when, in virtue of his perfection, he shares in God's own nature: in, that is to say, God's own knowledge and love of Himself.[73] This means that while all perfections flow from God to creatures, they do not do so "as from a univocal agent."[74] Hence, the being and goodness which belong to God and his creation "do not tie them inextricably to one another; creatures indeed depend wholly on God, but the act of creating [...] does not irrevocably implicate God in creation, nor bring about any change in divine nature."[75]

This fact that God is not a univocal agent also accounts, on the other hand, for an intimacy between the creature and the Creator that is far greater than that which could be conceived if they were in some sort of mutual relation. "[F]rom the beginning of creation," Thomas explains in his commentary on the Gospel of St. John, "he was always in the world, causing and preserving all things; because if God for even a moment were to withhold his power from the things he established, all would return to nothing and cease to be." And this, he continues, is what Origen meant when he drew a comparison between the spoken word and the idea conceived by the human mind, on the one hand, and the creation of the world by the Word of God, on the other.

---

the question of knowledge of God, he [Thomas] has created a foundation congenial to his doctrine, for by knowledge he means both God's knowledge of himself and our knowledge of God. The scope of the question thus encompasses divine nature, human nature, the distinction between them and the possibility of the intellectual union of the two" (ibid., 44).

68. Ibid., 47.

69. Ibid., 95; cf. Thomas Aquinas, *ST* I, q. 4, a. 3, ad. 3. "To predicate something of something *per essentiam* or *per participationem* is," Jan Aertsen explains, "to say that in the first case a simplicity and in the second a composition is expressed" (*Nature and Creature: Thomas Aquinas's Way of Thought* [Leiden: Brill, 1988], 136).

70. Thomas Aquinas, *ST* I, q. 6, a. 3; cf. q. 13, a. 6.

71. Ibid., q. 4, a. 2.

72. Cf. ibid., a. 2, obj. 1; ad. 1.

73. The "distinctive feature of Thomistic epistemology, the characteristic that renders it particularly suited to the development of a doctrine of theosis," is recognized by Anna Williams as "its understanding of knowledge as a form of participation" (*Ground of Union*, 45).

74. Thomas Aquinas, *ST* I, q. 6, a. 2.

75. Williams, *Ground of Union*, 51.

For as our vocal sound is the effect of the work conceived in our mind, so the creature is the effect of the Word conceived in the divine mind. "For he spoke, and they were created" (Ps 148:5). Hence, just as we notice that as soon as our inner word vanishes, the sensible vocal sound also ceases, so, if the power of the divine Word were withdrawn from things, all of them would immediately cease to be at that moment. And this is because he is "sustaining all things by his powerful word" (Heb 1:3).[76]

When, therefore, St. Thomas teaches that God has "no real relation to creatures"[77] for the simple reason that He is "outside the whole order of creation"[78] and thus absolutely immutable,[79] this doctrine ought not to be understood as implying some kind of defect in his knowledge or love of creatures: as is insinuated in Pope Benedict's statement that this doctrine—namely, that God does not have a real relation to creatures—leads to "despair." On the contrary, St. Thomas points to the perfection of divine knowledge and love in such a way that they might be considered—as are all the divine attributes—"identical with very essence of God."[80] God does not, in other words, know and love us beyond, or *in addition to*, himself. Rather, he knows and loves us *within* himself: his "relation to the creature is implied both in the Word [the Son] and in the proceeding Love [the Holy Spirit], as it were in a secondary way, inasmuch as the divine truth and goodness are a principle of understanding and loving all creatures."[81] We are not far from the Balthasarian affirmation that "the world can receive its possibility and reality nowhere else but in the eternal Son."[82] Nor from Balthasar's logic when he writes that "God alone [...] remains forever above the world, and for that very reason abides in the heart of the world."[83]

As if to make this evident to us who, in virtue of our real relation of absolute dependency upon God, tend to conceptualize a reciprocal relation of God to us (what St. Thomas calls a "logical" relation[84]), the angelic doctor

---

76. Thomas Aquinas, *Super Ioan* 1, lect. 5, no. 135 (= *Super Evangelium S. Ioannis lectura*, in *Commentary on the Gospel of John*, trans. Fabian R. Larcher, ed. Aquinas Institute. Biblical Commentaries, volumes 35–36 of the Latin/English Edition of the *Works of St. Thomas Aquinas* [Lander, Wyo.: The Aquinas Institute for the Study of Sacred Doctrine, 2013]); the Latin text is based on the 1972 Marietti edition.

77. Thomas Aquinas, *ST* I, q. 13, a. 7; cf. q. 28, a. 2, ad. 3; and q. 45, a. 3, ad. 1.

78. Ibid., q. 13, a. 7.

79. Cf. ibid., q. 9, a. 1; Jas 1:7; Mal 3:6; Num 23:19.

80. Gilles Emery, "*Theologia and Dispensatio*," 525; Cf. *The Trinitarian Theology of St. Thomas Aquinas*, trans. Francesca Aran Murphy (Oxford: Oxford University Press, 2007, 2010²), 86–88; "The Immutability of the God of Love and the Problem of Language Concerning the 'Suffering of God,'" in James F. Keating and Thomas J. White (eds.), *Divine Impassibility and the Mystery of Human Suffering* (Grand Rapids, Mich.: Eerdmans, 2009), 70–72; and "Contemporary Questions about God," *Nova et Vetera* (English edition) 8, no. 4 (2010): 799–811.

81. Thomas Aquinas, *ST* I, q. 37, a. 2, ad. 3.   82. Balthasar, *Theo-Drama* II, 261.

83. Balthasar, *Love Alone Is Credible*, 146.

84. Such is a relation which is "real" in the mind of the knowing subject but for the thing perceived

explains that all creatures "necessarily [...] pre-existed in the Word of God even before they are in their own proper nature[s]," just as the plans of a house exist within the mind of the architect before its actual construction.[85] Similarly, "The Father loves not only the Son, but also Himself and us, by the Holy Ghost. [...] [For] as the Father speaks Himself and every creature by His begotten Word, inasmuch as the Word *begotten* adequately represents the Father and every creature; so He loves Himself and every creature by the Holy Ghost, inasmuch as the Holy Ghost proceeds as the love of the primal goodness whereby the Father loves Himself and every creature."[86] Hence, the missions of the Son and the Holy Spirit are founded in the eternal processions that they include: "the procession of the Son and that of the Holy Spirit are the 'reason' for the production of creatures,[87] that is, for the 'natural gifts in which we subsist' (*exitus*: creation). And, at another level, the same processions are the reason for the gifts 'that unite us to the ultimate end, namely, sanctifying grace and glory' (*reditus*: the divine missions)."[88]

Because, moreover, the divine missions in time are a form of the eternal processions, the resultant relation between the divine and human natures in the person of the Son is "really in the creature [i.e. the human nature], by whose change the relation is brought into being; whereas it is not really in God, but only in our way of thinking, since it does not arise from any change in God, except only in our way of thinking."[89] In other words, "the divine person sent neither begins to exist where he did not previously exist, nor ceases to exist where He was."[90] There is thus "no separation between the eternal mystery of the Word and his saving action in the flesh," Gilles Emery explains. "On the contrary, the mystery itself is disclosed and given within the *dispensation*. The mission bears within itself the eternal procession of the

---

or known (God in the case at hand), there is no real relation to the knower, but merely a logical one; cf. *ST* I, q. 13, a. 7; q. 45, a. 3, ad. 1. For example, Gilles Emery draws a comparison to an art collection being admired by visitors of a gallery: "the fact of 'being admired' is not positively inscribed within the paintings themselves" nor does it add anything to the paintings. As far as the artwork is ontologically concerned, "the fact of being admired is a 'logical' relation. But when the visitor admires the artwork, it is very much an objective event in the person vis-à-vis the work of art, that is, a gaze, a knowledge, an emotion, a pleasure which positively qualifies the admirer: so far as the visitor is concerned, the relation to the artwork is very much 'real'" (*Trinitarian Theology of St. Thomas Aquinas*, 87–88).

85. Thomas Aquinas, *SCG* IV, c. 13; cf. Jn 1:3–4.
86. Thomas Aquinas, *ST* I, q. 37, a. 2, ad. 3.
87. Cf. ibid., q. 45, a. 6.
88. Emery, "*Theologia* and *Dispensatio*," 552–53. Elsewhere Emery describes the missions as temporal processions: "The temporal procession is an embassy of the eternal, bringing a part of its home country into our history. There are not two different processions, one eternal and one temporal" (*Trinitarian Theology of St. Thomas Aquinas*, 368).
89. Thomas Aquinas, *ST* III, q. 2, a. 7.
90. Thomas Aquinas, *ST* I, q. 43, a. 1, ad. 2; cf. a. 2, ad. 2.

Word, together with the effect of the saving action that the incarnate Word performed in the flesh."[91]

As differing from the circular movement of the intellect and will in human persons which tend to what is exterior to them—"the external good moving the intellect and the intellect moving the will, and the will by appetite and love tending to the external good"—in the case of God, "the circle ends in him. For God, by understanding himself, conceives his word which is the type of all things understood by him, inasmuch as he understands all things by understanding himself, and from this word he proceeds to love of all things and of himself."[92]

A Trinitarian Analogy of Freedom: Hans Urs von Balthasar

While St. Thomas thus acknowledges human freedom as capable of analogically describing the life of the triune God *despite* its exteriorization (its *ek-stasis* out of its self in virtue of which it is related to all beings),[93] Balthasar maintains—as if to follow up on an essential insight of Adrienne von Speyr, as shall be increasingly apparent—that it is *precisely* this exteriorization, this "movement [of finite freedom] toward self-realization within infinite freedom," which enables human freedom to be an appropriate image of the triune God.[94] Similarly, it is in the "social interchange," whereby finite freedoms "reciprocally enrich each other in 'self-lessness,'" that Balthasar intuits—again with reference to Adrienne von Speyr—an important insight into the "self-disclosure" of infinite freedom,[95] in whom "everything self-referential [*Fürsich*] has already been transcended in reference to a thou [*Fürdich*]."[96]

This mystery of the simultaneity of the immanence and transcendence of the human spirit is presented by Balthasar in terms of what he observes

---

91. Emery, "*Theologia* and *Dispensatio*," 546.

92. Thomas Aquinas, *De Pot* 9, 9 (= *De potentia* in *Quaestiones disputatae*, volume 2, ed. Pio Bazzi [Turin and Rome: Marietti, 1965]; *On the Power of God*, trans. English Dominican Fathers [Eugene, Ore.: Wipf & Stock Publishers, 2004]).

93. This is the origin of the objection to the question "Whether God loves all things?" (*ST* I, q. 20, a. 2): "It seems that God does not love all things. For according to Dionysius (*Div. Nom.* iv. 1), love places the lover outside himself, and causes him to pass, as it were, into the object of his love. But it is not admissible to say that God is placed outside of Himself, and passes into other things" (obj. 1). We are reminded that, according to St. Thomas, the Son begotten by the Father "is not outside the Father, but in Him" (*SCG* IV, ch. 11). See also *ST* I, q. 27, a. 1.

94. Balthasar, *Theo-Drama* II, 237.

95. Ibid., 228; see also *Mysterium Paschale*, 28. Cf. Speyr, *John* II, 188; and *Das Wort und die Mystik* II, 52.

96. Balthasar, *Epilogue*, 93.

to be two poles[97] of human freedom—that of self-possession, or autonomous motion (*autexousion*), and that of consent—which are merely the specific form, within the spiritual creature, of the universal tension (*Spannung*) characterizing all being between immanence and transcendence: the tension between the "to-be-in-itself" (*in-sich-sein*) and the "to-be-with" (*Mitsein*).[98] While all created being might thus be characterized by a so-called "polar" structure providing insight into the mystery of Trinitarian being,[99] pride of place is given by Balthasar to conscious being, which is capable of consciously acknowledging its being (and thus its autonomy) as a gift and, in a second moment, of consciously (and thus freely) engaging in the procession out of itself (to make of itself a gift). In precisely this way, the spiritual creature is capable of giving to both poles of its freedom the meaning of love. To be more exact, it is capable of experiencing itself as, first of all, "an *object* of love" that has been "granted entrance into a sheltering and encompassing world"[100] and secondly (and consequently), as a *subject* of love. Or to put it in other words, it is enabled, in virtue of this primary experience of gratuitous love, of willfully surrendering itself. The awareness of having been invited into existence out of love thus empowers the conscious being to recognize "letting-be and letting-stream, handing on further—as the inner fulfillment of the finite entity [and thus of itself]."[101]

From this perspective it becomes clear, as Nicholas J. Healy also insists, that Balthasar in no way seeks to replace ontological categories with personal ones.[102] Far from falling into the modernist trap of reducing interiority to subjectivity (*Geist*), Balthasar invites us, at least implicitly, to embrace a notion of being that includes what the Latin tradition referred to as *spiritus*: a concept ascribing interiority and immateriality—form, finality, and what Kenneth Schmitz presents as "participation in the cosmic web of existence"—to even sub-rational beings.[103] The Swiss theologian thus charac-

---

97. See Balthasar, *Theo-Drama* II, 205–60; and *The Glory of the Lord* I, 21.
98. Balthasar, *Epilogue*, 51; translation slightly altered. See also *Theo-Logic* I, 171.
99. See Balthasar, *Epilogue*, 85.
100. *The Glory of the Lord* V, 616; emphasis added. "It *is*, in so far as it is allowed to take part as an object of love" (ibid.).
101. Ibid., 627.
102. See Healy, *The Eschatology of Hans Urs von Balthasar*, 63. Healy maintains that for Balthasar, "analogy, in its first and deepest meaning, is neither a logical principle nor a linguistic tool governing speech about God, but is the ontological relationship that obtains between God and creation" (ibid., 21).
103. Kenneth Schmitz, "The First Principle of Personal Becoming," in his *The Texture of Being: Essays in First Philosophy*, ed. Paul O'Herron (Washington, D.C.: The Catholic University of America Press, 2007), 192. In traditional metaphysics of both the Greek and Latin tendencies, it is possible to speak of "an 'intelligent' organizing and creative force" by which even a subrational organism is ordained with a "constant regularity toward a precise determinate end, that is, the ultimate development of its

terizes *all* beings—and not just conscious ones—as having this immanent character (they are grounded in themselves), in virtue of which they are given to realize themselves in a dynamic that he figuratively presents as a procession "out"[104] of themselves. They are, in other words, "epiphanic," or "self-showing."[105]

As for consciousness, it is recognized by Balthasar as a specific characteristic of being in its "full measure."[106] This means that he roots consciousness within being; whence his account of the capacity of the spiritual creature to simultaneously grasp itself (its being) and being as such.

> But in recognizing itself as be-ing [sic], it [the spiritual creature] simultaneously grasps what being as such and as a whole is, so that in reflection it is given the measure not only of its own being but, in principle, of all being. [...] This coincidence is being's identity with itself in consciousness, in which the subject constitutes itself as such. Consequently, it gives the subject access both to the inner dimension of itself and, in principle, to the outer dimension of being. The two disclosures are exactly simultaneous and totally identical. [...] The coincidence of the two disclosures—that of the self and that of the world—guarantees the true objectivity both of the knowledge of the self and of the knowledge of the world.[107]

Hence, precisely as a spiritual being, "I am given to myself as the being that is both aware of itself and at the same time of others in the comprehensive light of Being as reality."[108]

Precisely as given to themselves, spiritual creatures—unlike sub-rational creatures who are naturally unveiled to one another—"must supplement natural unveiling with free self-surrender." As such, they are said by Balthasar to express themselves "not only to one another, but also in one another."[109] As such they are also receptive in a sense signifying "an unqualified perfection of being," namely that of "accessibility to another's being, openness to something other than the inner dimension of one's own subjectivity, the possession of windows looking out on all being and truth"; in short, "the power to welcome and, so to say, host another's being in one's own home."[110]

---

nature" (Bernard Schumacher, *A Philosophy of Hope: Josef Pieper and the Contemporary Debate on Hope*, trans. David C. Schindler [New York: Fordham University Press, 2003], 30).

104. Balthasar, *Epilogue*, 51.   105. Ibid., 59.
106. "The full measure of being entails self-consciousness" (*Theo-Logic* I, 44).
107. *Theo-Logic* I, 44. Similarly: "Insofar as consciousness understands itself as be-ing, it has in principle understood being as such [...]. Being and consciousness coincide so immediately that any distinction between them would be totally futile" (ibid., 166).
108. *Epilogue*, 53.
109. Balthasar, *Theo-Logic* I, 172; see also *Theo-Drama* II, 288; and *Presence and Thought: An Essay on the Religious Philosophy of Gregory of Nyssa*, trans. Mark Sebanc (San Francisco: Ignatius Press / Communio Books, 1995), 94.
110. Balthasar, *Theo-Logic* I, 44–45. Edith Stein speaks in similar terms in her phenomenological

It is, moreover, this act of willful surrender that makes of the spiritual creature a particularly appropriate one, Balthasar argues—with images borrowed from Adrienne von Speyr, as we shall see—for giving analogical expression to the mystery of the triune God:

> Here through the greater dissimilarity of the finite and the infinite existent, the positive aspect of the *analogia entis* appears, which makes of the finite the shadow, trace, likeness and image of the Infinite. And not in such a way that the finite 'first' constitutes itself as a 'closed' entity or subject (through the seizing and hoarding of the parcel of actuality which it is able to take into oneself from the stream of finite Being) in order 'then' (and perhaps for the rounding-out of its own perfection) to pass the surplus on. But rather in such a way that the finite, since it is subject, already constitutes itself as such through the letting-be of Being by virtue of an *ekstasis* out of its own closed self, and therefore through dispossession and poverty becomes capable of salvaging in recognition and affirmation the infinite poverty of the fullness of Being, and within it, that of the God who does not hold on to Himself.[111]

Despite certain interpretations to the contrary, Balthasar would not thereby suggest that God, as substantial being, can be thought of as "generously" pouring himself out by way of emanation into what subsequently amounts to creation. Nor would he otherwise subject divine freedom to the whims of human fancy.[112] Rather, the Swiss theologian stresses in this passage—as almost everywhere throughout this vast opus, as if to echo the same insight in Adrienne's equally vast work—that the God who, in the mystery of the Incarnation, does not "hold unto himself" (cf. Phil 2:7) is the very one who from all eternity surrenders himself, as it were, within the divine processions.

God is not an unmoved Absolute that endows the finite with its essence and to whom the finite must create a fitting space so that God can be in the finite what he

---

analysis of the difference between an animal and a human being: "I look in the eyes of an animal and from there, something looks at me. I look into his interior, into his soul, which perceives [*spürt*] my regard and my presence. But it is a mute and imprisoned soul: imprisoned in itself, unable to go back beyond itself and to grasp itself, unable to go out of itself to come to me. I look into the eyes of a man and his regard [*sein Blick*] answers me. He lets me penetrate in his interior or he repulses me. He is the master of his soul and can open or close its door. He can step out of himself and enter into the thing. When two men regard one another, an 'I' stands before another 'I.' There can be an encounter before their doors or an encounter in the interior. If there is an encounter in the interior, then the other 'I' is a 'you'" (Edith Stein, *Der Aufbau der menschlichen Person. Vorlesung zur philosophischen Anthropologie* [Wein: Herder, 2004], 78). We are also not far from the Thomistic presentation of a spiritual nature. See Marie-Joseph Nicolas, "L'idée de nature dans la pensée de saint Thomas d'Aquin," 551.

111. Balthasar, *The Glory of the Lord* V, 627. See also *Theo-Drama* II, 286–87; and *Love Alone Is Credible*, 144–45.

112. Balthasar, in fact, calls upon the analogy of being precisely in order to distinguish the Creator-creature relation from "a pantheism or theopanism which dissolves God into the world or the world into God (and hence, dissolving the interplay of divine and created freedoms, abolishing theo-drama)" (Balthasar, *Theo-Drama* II, 118–19).

already is in reality [...]. Much more is God always already the One who has lovingly surrendered himself in freedom and who thus seeks a free and loving space [*Raumgeben*] for his willed self-outpouring Love. [He does this] so as to be with [*bei*] himself in created freedom, to thus "inhabit" [*bewohnen*] (Jn 14:23) this created freedom with his own infinite freedom, to newly "beget" and "give birth" to created freedom (Jn 1:13; 3:5; 1 Jn 3:9) out of the womb of the infinite loving surrender (of the Father to the Son in the Holy Spirit).[113]

Herein it is evident that God does not need the world.[114] Nor does he pour himself forth by nature.[115] Because, rather, he chooses to create the world "out of free love, out of free self-expression, freely glorifying himself," the divine mysteries can never be deduced "from the perspective of a necessary analogy between worldly being and its origin."[116] On the other hand, Balthasar reasons—in a manner altogether akin to the reasoning of St. Thomas[117]—that "the freedom in which he determines that the world shall exist is, according to its nature, none other than the freedom by which he wills eternally to be what he is." Hence, the world is necessarily and "exclusively" grounded in God's freedom.[118]

By this fact of the world being grounded in God's freedom, Balthasar specifies that both its possibility and its reality are to be found in the eternal Son, "who eternally owes his divine being to the Father's generosity." And, because the Son is "the Father's eternal Word, the world in its totality is created by the Word (Jn 1:3), not only instrumentally but in the sense that the Word is the world's pattern and hence its goal." Of course, to be "in the Son" means to be "in the totality of the Godhead," Balthasar is careful to add; but we cannot even begin to fathom the world's location in "the entire ocean of being," who is God (John Damascene), without reference to the divine hypostases.[119] In fact, the "creature's metaphysical and theological locus is," as Balthasar sees it, "the diastasis of the divine 'Persons' in the unity of the divine nature."[120] Or, to put it in more metaphorical terms: "The infinite distance between the world and God is grounded in the other, prototypical distance between God and God."[121]

At this point in his reasoning, Balthasar does little more than follow

---

113. Balthasar, *Explorations in Theology* IV, 340; translation slightly altered. See also *Theo-Drama* V, 81.
114. This is still more explicit in Balthasar, *Theo-Drama* V, 507; and *Theo-Drama* II, 261.
115. See Balthasar, *Theo-Drama* V, 507.
116. Balthasar, *Epilogue*, 86; see also *Theo-Logic* II, 84.
117. Cf. Thomas Aquinas, *ST* I, q. 32, a. 1; ad. 3; q. 20, a. 2; q. 19, a. 2; *SCG* II, c. 28; etc.
118. Balthasar, *Theo-Drama* II, 261; see also "Creation and the Trinity," *Communio* 15, no. 4 (1988): 285–93, esp. 291.
119. Balthasar, *Theo-Drama* II, 262.   120. Ibid., 288.
121. Ibid., 266.

Thomistic doctrine, as I have exposited it above, with an exception being made for his metaphorical image of "distance." The novelty in his teaching—wherein we shall observe a definite similarity to the doctrine of Adrienne von Speyr, as shall be evident—arises in his metaphorical account of "the realms of freedom within the Godhead,"[122] which "come about both through the self-giving of the hypostases and by each hypostasis in turn 'letting' the other two 'be.'"[123] Hence, "the 'nothing-out-of-which' the world came into being can only be sought in infinite freedom itself: that is, in the realms of creatable being opened up by divine omnipotence and, at a deeper level, by the Trinitarian 'letting-be' of the hypostatic acts."[124]

As complementary to an analogy of being, Balthasar is thus proposing that we might describe the unity of the three divine persons within the unity of one divine nature in God in terms—it bears repeating—of an analogy of freedom which draws upon the created order in terms supplied by divine revelation:

"This day I have begotten you," says the Father to the Son. This day I have created you, says eternal freedom to finite freedom. The fact that no human "I" can awaken to itself unless it is called "thou" by some other "I" is only the prelude, within the parameters of the world, to what is meant here. For in and through the human "I" there is manifested an Absolute "I," who has from eternity generated an equally Absolute "Thou" and, in the Holy Spirit, is One God with him.[125]

Balthasar recommends, more specifically, that we might conceive of the eternal generation of the Son by the Father as a "giving and receiving of self" in virtue of which is manifest the "limitless self-affirmation and freedom" of God who is "never 'just there' in the Positivist sense." Rather, in the "reciprocal ecstasy" of the divine Persons the "limitless plenitude" of the divine essence is unfolded "as absolute love" and thus also as "absolute truth."[126] Balthasar's proposal for an adequate representation of the Godhead is thus based upon his firm conviction—wherein we might recognize a contrast to the analogy of St. Thomas—that the "immemorial priority of the self-surrender or self-expropriation thanks to which the Father *is* Father cannot be ascribed to knowledge but only to groundless love."[127]

---

122. Ibid., 262. "Naturally we can only speak of these [the realms of freedom within the Godhead] in metaphors" (ibid.).

123. Ibid. Cf. Aquinas, *ST* I, q. 42, a. 1, ad. 3: "[A]lthough movement is not in God, there is something that receives."

124. Balthasar, *Theo-Drama* II, 266; see also *Theo-Logic. Theological Logical Theory* III: *The Spirit of Truth*, trans. Graham Harrison (San Francisco: Ignatius Press, 2005), 236.

125. Balthasar, *Theo-Drama* II, 286.

126. Balthasar, *Theo-Logic* II, 180. Cf. Thomas Aquinas, *Super Ioan* 14, lect. 8, no. 1971.

127. Ibid., 177. In using the expression "groundless love," Balthasar specifies that is it not prior to

To be sure, Aquinas does, Matthew Levering points out, conceive of the Son's generation "as the Father's self-gift or self-communication": not so that we might conclude to the existence of three "selves" in God in the modern sense of the word (such that "self" is understood as a center of consciousness), of course, but in the sense that he "gives all that he is (the divine essence) in begetting."[128] Aquinas furthermore connects this generative communication or gift with the Father's love: not, however, as a power of generation, but as the fruit of generation. "The Father's love is a sign of what he has done for the Son in giving him everything that he, the Father, possesses," Levering explains. "It is love that manifests a giver who has generated his perfect likeness."[129] Hence, we might speak of a "unity of nature" (cf. Jn 10:30) and "a unity of love in the Father and Son, which is a unity of spirit." This love, moreover, "proceeds from them, for the Father and Son love themselves by the Holy Spirit."[130] Similarly, within the context of his exposition of the one God in the *Summa theologiae*, the angelic doctor presents love as "an entailment rather than an axiom," for it is, as Anna Williams accurately observes, "simplicity's inexorable consequent."[131] This is not to deny, Williams continues with reference to St. Thomas, that we might address love as a unitive force "even in God," but in so doing, there is implied no composition in the Godhead; "for the good that He wills for Himself, is no other than Himself, Who is good by His essence."[132]

Aquinas nonetheless argues that it would be heretical to maintain that the Father generates the Son out of love, since he presumes that this would *de facto* imply generation by an act of will: "If the Father gave a nature to the Son by his will, the will of the Father would be the principle of the generation of the Son; and then it would follow that the Father generated the Son by will, and not by nature; and this is the Arian heresy."[133] Hence, although he does

---

being but is rather "the supreme act of being" (ibid., 177n9). This means applying "the attribute 'love' to God's essence as an infinite surrender of himself to himself" (*Explorations in Theology* IV, 359). See also *Theo-Logic* III, 158; *The Glory of the Lord* VII, 248–49; and *Explorations in Theology* I, 169; cf. Adrienne Speyr, *Das Wort und die Mystik* I: *Subjektive Mystik*, vol. 6 of *Die Nachlasswerke* (Einsiedeln: Johannes Verlag, 1970), 87.

128. Matthew Levering, *Scripture and Metaphysics: Aquinas and the Renewal of Trinitarian Theology* (Oxford: Blackwell Publishing, 2004, 2006), 138 and 138n122. Cf. Balthasar, *Theo-Logic* III, 158, and *Theo-Logic* II, 130. On the limitations of the concept of "self" as a center of consciousness and the resultant reduction of the notion of personhood, see Bernard N. Schumacher, "La personne comme conscience de soi performante au cœur du débat bioéthique. Analyse critique de la position de John Locke," *Laval Théologique et Philosophique* 64, no. 3 (2008): 709–43.

129. Levering, *Scripture and Metaphysics*, 138. Cf. Thomas Aquinas, *Super Ioan* 5, lect. 3, no. 753; ibid., 17, lect. 5, no. 2251.

130. Super Ioan, 17, lect. 3, no. 2214.   131. Williams, *The Ground of Union*, 52.

132. Thomas Aquinas, *ST* I, q. 20, a. 1, ad. 3. See also q. 5, a. 1, ad. 1; and I-II, q. 30, a. 2, ad. 1.

133. Thomas Aquinas, *Super Ioan* 3, lect. 6, no. 545; see also ibid., 1, lect. 1, no. 41; 5, lect. 3, no. 753; *ST* I, q. 32, a. 1, ad. 3; and q. 41, a. 2.

conceive of the generation of the Son as a personal act of the Father, Aquinas attributes the power of generation (*potentia generandi*) to the divine essence: "Acts are personal," as John Boyle summarizes the teaching of St. Thomas, "but the power is essential, that is, according to a person's nature."[134]

This conviction actually represents a certain development in Aquinas's thought. While he initially attributed the power of generation equally to the divine essence and the person of the Father (in his *Liber sententiarum*, for example), he ends up (in the *Summa theologiae*) "firmly in the essentialist camp," Boyle explains, "but with qualifications."[135] Aquinas reasons, more specifically, that because the power of generation is attributed to nature in the created order, our analogical discourse of God should follow along the same lines. Because the meaning of fatherhood on the natural level is that of giving life to another of the same nature, its "supreme realization" lies "in the gift of the fullness of the divine nature to the Son, in the unity of the divinity."[136] "With increasing precision in articulating the natural analog comes increasing simplicity in articulating the divine analog."[137]

Balthasar, in contrast, points to the exceptional quality of the divine analogue over and above the natural analogue, that is, to the ever-greater dissimilarity between creature and Creator despite the real similarity. His emphasis is thus not only upon the analogical perspective, which might be thought to typify the theology of St. Thomas, but also and especially upon a *katalogical* (which is also transposed as "catalogical") one: a perspective, it bears repeating, proceeding downward (*kata-*) from the revealed archetype to the created image. As such, he presents the divine processions as archetypical for all that we might recognize in this world as authentic love by self-surrender.

Within this context, the theologian of Lucerne points out, for example, that it is uniquely when the act of divine surrender "simultaneously calls forth one who receives himself in this surrender and thus also necessarily responds as one-who-has-received,"[138] that it is possible to ascribe to this act the meaning of love. "Where God is defined as love, he must be in essence perfect self-giving, which," Balthasar maintains, "can only elicit from the Beloved, in return, an equally perfect movement of thanksgiving, service and self-giving."[139]

---

134. John F. Boyle, "St. Thomas and the Analogy of *Potentia Generandi*," *The Thomist* 64 (2000): 581-592, at 581. Cf. Thomas Aquinas, *SCG* IV, ch. 13.
135. Ibid., 583.
136. Gilles Emery, *The Trinity: An Introduction to Catholic Doctrine on the Triune God*, trans. Matthew Levering (Washington, D.C.: The Catholic University of America Press, 2011), 116.
137. Boyle, "St. Thomas and the Analogy of *Potentia Generandi*," 591.
138. Balthasar, *Explorations in Theology* IV, 35; translation slightly altered.
139. Balthasar, *Theo-Drama* V, 82.

If we were to define God, we "would have to put it in the form: unity as being-for-one another."[140]

While St. Thomas argues that "God's love is a logical consequence of his simplicity,"[141] Balthasar argues that God's love is a logical consequence of his Trinity of persons: "Without the difference between the hypostases, God cannot be the God whom revelation knows him to be: the God of love."[142] "God is one, good, true and beautiful because he is essentially Love, and Love supposes the one, the other and their unity."[143] "To think in any other way would be," he reasons, "Arianism."[144] Interestingly enough, St. Thomas reasons in much the same way in his *De Potentia*:

> True and perfect charity requires the trinity of persons in God. For the love whereby a person loves himself is selfish love and is not true charity. But God cannot love supremely another who is not supremely lovable; and none is supremely lovable that is not supremely good. Hence it is evident that true charity cannot be supreme in God if there be but one Person in him. Nor can it be perfect if there be but two Persons: since perfect charity demands that the lover wish that what he loves himself be equally loved by another. For it is a sign of great imperfection to be unwilling to share one's love, whereas to be willing to share it is a sign of great perfection: "The more one is pleased to receive a thing the greater our longing in seeking for it," as Richard says […]. In God therefore, since there is perfection of goodness, happiness and glory, there must be a trinity of persons.[145]

Of course, knowledge and love are not really distinct in God, and it is impossible to love in the absence of knowledge. This much Balthasar grants to St. Thomas.[146] Could we not however, he asks, acknowledge within the "all-embracing" love of God, which includes all of his other properties (knowledge, omnipotence, etc.), "something like a foundation for the distinction of the two processions"?[147] The Swiss theologian cannot help but inquire, more specifically, whether the Thomistic ordering of the processions according to the principle that something can be loved only when it is known[148] is not simply "an importation from the created order into the divine world?"[149] In God there is after all, Balthasar argues in terms supplied by Adrienne von Speyr, "no dominance of knowledge over love, no possibility of increasing insight to a point where it no longer corresponds to love."[150]

---

140. Balthasar, *Elucidations*, 29.
141. Williams, *The Ground of Union*, 52.
142. Balthasar, *Theo-Logic* II, 82.
143. Balthasar, *My Work*, 118; see also *Epilogue*, 181.
144. Balthasar, *Epilogue*, 93.
145. Thomas Aquinas, *De Pot* 9, 9.
146. See Balthasar, *Theo-Logic* II, 164. Cf. Thomas Aquinas, *ST* I, q. 27, a. 3, ad. 3; *De Pot* 9, 9, obj. 3, ad. 3
147. *Theo-Logic* II, 163.
148. Cf. Thomas Aquinas, *ST* I, q. 27, a. 3, ad. 3.
149. *Theo-Logic* II, 162.
150. Speyr, *World of Prayer*, 55. Meanwhile, Mark McIntosh notes—as if to defend Aquinas—that

Beyond the question, then, of whether the Father generated the Son "'by necessity' (yet by what constraint, if not that of love?) or 'freely' (though certainly not arbitrarily!),"[151] the Swiss theologian asks whether we might not imagine the Son, whom the Father is said to give to the world out of love (Jn 3:16), as being likewise generated "out of love" rather than by a cognitive act. "If the self-giving of the Father to the Son and of both to the Holy Spirit reflects neither an arbitrary choice nor a necessary constraint but God's inmost being,"[152] then it seems clear to Balthasar that "this most intimate nature—however the processions may be distinguished from one another—can in the end only be love."[153]

To view the divine mystery in this way enables us, Balthasar further maintains, to avoid, on the one hand, the Hegelian conception of a Father who generates the Son in order to perfectly know himself and, on the other hand, the Arian conception of a Father who generates the Son because he already knows himself perfectly.[154] More positively still, attributing the Father's act of generating the Son to love rather than knowledge has the advantage of better corresponding to the facts of revelation, Balthasar argues. The incarnate Son does not reveal the Father simply nor primarily "*per modum intellectus*." Rather, by means of his love for the Father and "for the men whom the Father loves," the Son reveals the Father's love.[155]

If, then, the Father's surrender of the Son and the Spirit for the salvation of the world and the Son's own surrender of himself and the Spirit are, as Scripture tells us, motivated by "pure love," ought we not, Balthasar reasons, to understand God's own essence in these terms? "How," he asks, "could this fundamental claim about the economy of salvation have no foundation in any property of the essence of the triune God,"[156] who is identified with every one of his qualities? Or to put it more positively: because we can discern within the events of the New Testament "an entirely free initiative" on God's part and the simultaneous "unveiling of his essence,"[157] we ought also to conceive of the "all-grounding deed of the Father's love"—that deed

---

at the highest level of the human person's union with God, knowing and loving are perfectly united in his theology. This unity, McIntosh further explains, is "not based on an analysis of the human subject but of the divine subject [...]. In the human subject, knowing and loving are distinct, and as directed towards other creatures they are often in conflict with each other; as directed towards God they are not just complementary but essential to their mutual fulfillment, indeed in the relationship with God they are united in each other" (*Mystical Theology* [Oxford: Basil Blackwell, 1998], 71).

151. Balthasar, *Theo-Logic* II, 162. Balthasar notes that "even the generation of the Son, which is termed 'natural,' does not occur involuntarily; even the procession of the Spirit has a 'natural' side" (ibid., 163).

152. Cf. *DZ* 71 and 526.
153. Balthasar, *Theo-Logic* II, 136; see also 164.
154. Ibid., 177; see also *Theo-Logic* III, 158.
155. Balthasar, *Theo-Logic* III, 162.
156. Balthasar, *Theo-Logic* II, 136.
157. Balthasar, *Explorations in Theology* IV, 35.

"whereby he gives all that is his to the Son (Jn 16:15)"—as "simply the first, indispensable act of the divine superabundance." It is, in other words, that act without which all the salvific acts of the New Testament—the Incarnation, Cross, Resurrection, Ascension, and sending of the Spirit—"could not be performed."[158] "It corresponds to his absolute being and essence to reveal himself in his unfathomable and absolutely uncompelled freedom as inexhaustible love."[159]

To explain what he means by the primal love of the Father accounting for the generation of the Son, Balthasar turns to a key intuition of Adrienne von Speyr, which was probably guiding his reasoning all along. "The Father's first, primal purpose," she explains in a passage, which is cited at a vital point in Balthasar's argumentation,[160] "is beyond necessity and freedom."

Once the Son is begotten, however, he adopts the Father's will by freely desiring to be what the Father's purpose has determined. And now, from the vantage point of this free will, it is as if even the Father's begetting and the Son's being begotten acquire characteristics of freedom, as if in their freedom Father and Son recapitulate their natural relationship, in order freely to be what they are by necessity. [...] But in God necessity is not a blind necessity of nature, preliminary to his qualities of mind and personhood. It is a divine necessity which expresses his spiritual nature. It has no parallel among us creatures; we can only describe it as lying beyond all creaturely freedom and necessity.[161]

Drawing directly from this insight, which is so central to Adrienne's Trinitarian-shaped anthropology, as we shall see, Balthasar argues for a "'recapitulation' of the nature-based processions in a divine freedom that goes to their very origin."[162] As such, he recommends that the Trinitarian mystery be regarded in such a way that "the divine essence would not only be coextensive with the event of the eternal processions," but would "also be concomitantly determined by the unrepeatably unique participation of Father, Son and Spirit in this event and so would never exist except as fatherly, sonly, or spirit-ually [sic]."[163] When we address the Father as "begetting" the Son, Balthasar thus recommends that we envisage him as "sharing his full divine freedom" with the Son, "and sharing it ultimately, irrevocable and forever."[164] Without in-

---

158. Balthasar, *Theo-Logic* II, 163–64.   159. Balthasar, *Love Alone Is Credible*, 145.
160. See, for example, *Theo-Logic* III, 163 and 236–37.
161. Speyr, *World of Prayer*, 58. Similarly, Adrienne intuits that the Father's act of begetting "is an act of surrender to the Son to which the Son replies with his surrender," and because there is no temporal succession within the Trinity, "the Father already receives the Son's surrender in begetting him" (ibid., 213).
162. Balthasar, *Theo-Logic* III, 163. Or, to put it in other words, we must exclude "every ontic priority of mere necessity over divine freedom, but [...] also [...] every arbitrary exercise of will" (ibid.).
163. Balthasar, *Theo-Logic* II, 136–37.   164. Balthasar, *Theo-Drama* V, 83.

fringing upon the order of the processions (*taxis*), "we can and must think of the Persons who proceed, the Son and the Spirit, as 'letting themselves be brought forth.'"[165] The Swiss theologian thus conceives of the generation of the Son by the Father as rooted, "on the one hand, in the ability to 'let be' and, on the other hand, in the ability to allow oneself to be brought to birth, to separate oneself, really and in fact, from what is one's own."[166] "Where absolute love is concerned, conceiving and letting be are just as essential as giving."[167]

This absolute self-giving [of the Father] can only be a "begetting" (within the divine identity). And its result can only be a total acceptance of, and a total responding gift to, the origin. Thus the "love" of giving back in return can never be less than that of the begetting. From this we conclude that the interpenetration of love elicits the identity of love equally powerfully in all three Persons, which [the identity of love] is both the fruit as well as the "conclusive" manifestation of the absoluteness of divine love (once more, with all this taking place within the divine identity). "God is love" and nothing else; in this love lies every possible form of self-expression, of truth, and of wisdom.[168]

In other words, "This love is not the absolute Good beyond being, but is the depth and height, the length and breadth of being itself."[169] It is thus not surprising that Balthasar should ask "whether this love might not be the hidden ground underlying the transcendentals and their circumincessive relation?"[170]

Without denying the "identical divinity of each hypostasis," Balthasar thus points to the "inappropriateness of making the one divine essence as such the agent of the processions of, and relations among, the Divine Persons."[171] So too in the doctrine of St. Thomas: "The personal distinction in God is never posed as an emanation from the essence: Neither in the doctrine of processions, nor in the knowledge of the person of the Father, nor in the study of the distinct persons," Gilles Emery observes. Hence, there is no attempt, nor any possibility within the work of the angelic doctor "of conceiving the person [sic] in God the Trinity as a divine Being personalized in a non-relational or pre-relational manner."[172] What "must" then "be entirely ruled out of the

---

165. Balthasar, *Theo-Logic* II, 136.   166. Balthasar, *Theo-Drama* V, 85.
167. Ibid., 86.
168. Balthasar, *Epilogue*, 93; see also *Theo-Drama* V, 82 and 122. In a similar manner Adrienne presents the divine love as "both 'transitive,' focusing on the other, and 'intransitive,' since God's entire being 'is love'" (Speyr, *Das Wort und die Mystik* I, 108; see also 113).
169. Balthasar, *Love Alone Is Credible*, 145.
170. Balthasar, *Theo-Logic* I, 9. This, in turn, would imply that "the 'good' now dominates as the central moment: self-showing and self-expressing culminate in absolute self-giving" (Balthasar, *Epilogue*, 93).
171. Balthasar, *Theo-Logic* II, 135.
172. Gilles Emery, "Essentialism or Personalism in the Treatise on God in St. Thomas Aquinas?" in his *Trinity in Aquinas*, 207–8.

discussion—if, that is, we wish to enter into the immanent Trinity through the portal of the missions of the Son and the Spirit—is," Balthasar explains, "a 'fruitfulness' of the divine essence as such, of a divine essence that supposedly releases the Trinitarian process from itself."[173] Nor might the divine essence be understood as a "blank, homogeneous block of identity."[174] "The Father generates the Son as God, that is, out of his substance."[175] If, however, we were to abstract from the persons, this substance "could not be designated as a 'who' (as the 'one God' for example)."[176]

Balthasar thus suggests that we look upon the divine essence as "a giving (in the Father), a receiving (in the Son), a gift given to the Spirit by Father and Son together, and a cause of thanksgiving by Son and Spirit."[177] This does not mean—as is further evident in the context[178]—that Balthasar confuses the divine essence, which is single and unique in all three divine persons, and the relations which distinguish the divine persons from one another.[179] His purpose in presenting the divine essence in terms of giving and receiving is, rather, to point out that "the divine nature is defined through and through by the modes of divine being (*tropos tès hyparxeos*)" so as to be "always both what is possessed and what is given away."[180] "This essence is no fourth element, something common to the three Persons. Rather, it is their eternal life itself in its processions."[181] To think otherwise, Balthasar argues, would be to call into question the biblically-founded doctrine—common to both the eastern and western theological traditions—that "God is love" (cf. 1 Jn 4:16).[182]

Again, it is important to insist that Balthasar is not proposing—contrary to certain assertions[183]—that we replace ontological categories with personal

---

173. Ibid., 130–31; cf. Thomas Aquinas, *I Sent* 23, q. 1, a. 3.
174. Balthasar, *Theo-Logic* II, 130.
175. Balthasar, *Theo-Drama* V, 76.
176. Balthasar, *Theo-Logic* II, 130; cf. Thomas Aquinas, *De Pot* 10, 3.
177. Balthasar, *Theo-Drama* V, 76.
178. Balthasar's purpose in this context is to distinguish finite beings who "are precisely *not* identical with their real (posited) being" and the divine hypostases who are each "identical with the divine essence" (Balthasar, *Theo-Drama* V, 76).
179. See Balthasar, *Theo-Logic* II, 132–34.
180. Balthasar, *Theo-Drama* II, 258; see also *Theo-Logic* III, 158.
181. Balthasar, *Epilogue*, 92–93. See also ibid., 85; and *Explorations in Theology* I, 169. God not only "exists in himself as an eternal essence (or Being)," Balthasar explains, but also—and herein we might discern Adrienne's influence—as "an equally eternal (that is, not temporal) 'happening.'" So essential, indeed, is this "fact" to Christian theology that it must not be forgotten, Balthasar maintains, even "for an instant" (Balthasar, *Theo-Drama* V, 67).
182. Cf. *The Catechism of the Catholic Church*, no. 221.
183. Gilbert Narcisse, for example, recognizes "an ontological jump" in Balthasar's movement from the analogy of being (wherein God is fully act of being) to its deepening in an analogy of persons. It is as if, Narcisse suggests, "everything occurs between person and being," which in turn requires that we pass "from one ontological degree to another: namely one permitting an analogy between created persons

ones in theological discourse. Rather, he reasons that because "God is essentially spirit, self-giving, receiving, and loving (that is, far beyond what Greek 'substance' philosophy understands as 'Being')," our description of God and of the creature's relation to him "should be located beyond the opposition between physic-ontic and purely personal concepts."[184] His is a "freedom that so pervades his whole Being that there cannot be a remainder of Being outside this freedom, nor could some corner of his Being manage to withdraw from this freedom."[185] Similarly, there is "no possibility of separating the life of the three Persons from God's essence."[186] Hence also in our analogical expression of the mystery of God, we should not simply refer to the creature's relation to God as its origin and end; for the creature's relation to God "extends just as expressly to the hypostases" and most especially (or "primarily") to the Son, who is the archetype of all creation and the perfect image of the Father.[187]

If then—Balthasar reasons—we wish to have an adequate analogy of the one God in three persons, we must have access to both essentialist and personalist concepts, and this—Balthasar maintains—implies that we must have access not only to the notion of likeness, but also to difference.[188] This means, more specifically, that the divine mystery should be analogically addressed not only in terms of the creature's unity of being (*ens*),[189] in virtue of which it might be likened unto him who identifies with Being (*Esse est*)—terms focusing upon the divine simplicity—but also in terms of creaturely differences: terms emphasizing the plurality of the divine persons.[190] Uniting the two—essence (unity) and persons (plurality)—in a fruitful tension is the key notion of surrender.

---

and the divine persons, and this in a quasi dialectical opposition with the analogy of being" ("Participer à la vie trinitaire," *Revue thomiste* 96 [1996]: 120; see also 124). Similarly, Joseph Palakeel recognizes in Balthasar's work "a relation concept of the Trinity where the reality of being is not substance but is self-surrendering love" (*The Use of Analogy in Theological Discourse: An Investigation in Ecumenical Perspective* [Rome: Editrice Pontificia Università Gregoriana, 1995], 106). In contrast to this assertion, see Balthasar, *Theo-Logic* II, 177n9 and 134–35n10. As for Margaret Turek, she recognizes in Balthasar's work a "shift in interpretative frameworks: from a substance-based ontology [...] to an intersubjective ontology given exposition according to the 'logic of love' and the '*analogia caritatis*' which together comprise the primary context of Balthasar's speech about God" (Margaret M. Turek, *Towards a Theology of God the Father: Hans Urs von Balthasar's Theodramatic Approach* [New York: Peter Lang, 2001], 112).

184. Balthasar, *Theo-Logic* III, 235.
185. Balthasar, *Epilogue*, 85.
186. Ibid., 92.
187. Balthasar, *Theo-Logic* II, 181.
188. See, for example, Balthasar, *Theo-Drama* III, 340, where the argument is made for these two categories in our description of the image of God.
189. In fact, Balthasar notes that this unity itself remains polar, as is evident in his question: where are we to "locate the unity of creaturely being: In the universal (which, however, must always contain the particular in order to be common to all) or in the particular (which in turn cannot be particular without the universal)?" (*Theo-Logic* II, 183).
190. Cf. Thomas Aquinas, *ST* I, q. 93, a. 5.

It is this concept which will play a vital role in each of the polar tensions marking Balthasar's anthropology. Such, for example, is the tension of difference between body and spirit, as we shall see in the fourth chapter of this volume. Such also, and more clearly, are the differences between creatures (such as the difference between man and woman, as we shall see in chapter six) or between the universal and the particular, which Balthasar treats in terms of the tension between the individual and the community within the context of his theology of substitution, as we shall see in chapter five. However, these are ultimately and primarily the differences between the creature and Creator, as finds expression in Balthasar's theology of mission and grace, as we shall see in chapter three. Indeed, the Swiss theologian recognizes that the very difference between divine and human freedom, in virtue of which the human being might be recognized as standing "over against" God, is "itself an image of the divine life within the Trinity (in the opposition of hypostases)."[191] In short, the various differences that remain in "tension," or unity, within the human creature, without being dissolved within him or her, serve to clarify the mystery of the three divine persons within the one divine nature. This insight has, of course, strong implications for Balthasar's Christology, which thereby assumes a central role in the Creator-creature analogy:

> If we wish to reprise the concepts of analogy handed down in the Scholastic tradition and adapt them to the foregoing, we must begin with a primary *attributio* [attribution] of all things to the Logos, who, being the ground and end of the creation, himself exemplifies prototypically the right *proportio* [proportion] between God and the creature and, through the Spirit, communicates it to creation. Yet this proportion transcends every human concept. Consequently, despite all appropriation (*attributio*) to Christ and all graced "participation in the divine nature," it remains a *proportionalitas*, a "proportional relation between proportional relations," that is, between the relation of difference between God and creature and the relation of difference between Father, Son, and Spirit.[192]

Although any faith statement must, Balthasar maintains, be interpreted from top-down (*kata*)—from God as the author of revelation to the human person, who is its recipient—we should begin our theological investigations with a Christology from below, recognizing in the man Jesus "the correspondence, the expression, the image (*ana*) of the one who can be glimpsed, not on the earthly plane, but 'above' (*ano*)," namely, the Father.[193] This role of

---

191. Balthasar, *Theo-Drama* III, 340.
192. Balthasar, *Theo-Logic* II, 316; cf. Speyr, *The Boundless God*, 18–19.
193. Ibid., 312–13; see also *Theo-Drama* IV, 324; *Theo-Drama* V, 122; and *Theo-Drama* III, 508. See also Paolo Martinelle, *La morte de Cristo come rivelazione dell'amore trinitario nella teologia di Hans Urs von Balthasar.*

mirroring the Father (as his perfect image) is not, however, unique to the Son as human, for "the exposition [of the Father that] he performs in the flesh naturally points back to his hypostatic property within God."[194] It is precisely in this sense that the Swiss theologian presents Christ as "the concrete analogy of being."[195]

By this term is meant more than that Christ embraces within himself, in virtue of the hypostatic union, both poles of the analogy between the Creator and the creature, although this idea is certainly not lacking in his teaching.[196] Balthasar is concerned, more specifically, that the teaching of Chalcedon—the union of the two (divine and human) natures in the one (divine) person of Christ—may not be sufficiently attentive to the fact that this divine person can only exist within a Trinitarian relation.[197] For this same reason, Christ does not—as would, Balthasar argues, be a consequence of monophysitism—represent his own divine nature; rather he "translates," or expresses in a revelatory manner, his eternal filial relation in temporal and creaturely terms, namely those of obedience.[198] As the eternal Son, who can exist only by possessing the fullness of the divinity in the mode of receptivity, on the one hand, and as the archetype of all creation, on the other,[199] he—the incarnate

---

194. Balthasar, *Theo-Logic* II, 160.

195. Balthasar, *A Theology of History*, 69; *Theo-Drama* II, 267; and *Theo-Drama* III, 222; *Epilogue*, 65; *Explorations in Theology* II, 78–79; and *Cosmic Liturgy: The Universe According to Maximus the Confessor*, trans. Brain E. Daley (San Francisco: Igantius Press and Communio Books, 2003), 239. Cf. Speyr, *Mary in the Redemption*, 34 and 116–17; and *The Mystery of Death*, trans. Graham Harrison (San Francisco: Ignatius Press, 1988), 74. See also Schrijver, *Le merveilleux accord*; Healy, *The Eschatology of Hans Urs von Balthasar*, 91–158; and Joseph Palakeel, *The Use of Analogy in Theological Discourse*, 67–123.

196. See, for example, Balthasar, *Theo-Drama* II, 268 and 407; *The Glory of the Lord* I, 472; *Epilogue*, 89; and *Theo-Drama* III, 506.

197. Hans Urs von Balthasar, "On the Concept of Person," trans. Peter Verhalen, *Communio* 13, no. 1 (1986), 22. Inspired undoubtedly by Adrienne, as shall be increasingly evident, the Swiss theologian argues that the Trinitarian union is the presupposition for the hypostatic union of Christ and thus also for the unity of the Creator and the creature, grace and nature, heaven and earth. See Balthasar, *Theo-Drama* V, 120; *The Glory of the Lord* I, 479; cf. *Theo-Drama* III, 187 and 225; and *A Theology of History*, 62. We nonetheless do well to respond to Balthasar's critique of the Council of Chalcedon with the wise insight of Emmanuel Perrier: "It was not the council Fathers who imposed the terms of the debate, but the doctrinal context. [...] It is one thing not to address a question, because it is not posed, another thing to deliberately ignore it or to block access to it" ("L'enjeu christologique de la satisfaction (I)," 130).

198. Christ's obedience is, more specifically (Balthasar explains) the "kenotic translation" of his eternal love for the Father, an idea which is likewise found in Adrienne's work, as consistent—Balthasar maintains—with the tradition. On that subject, see Balthasar, *First Glance at Adrienne von Speyr*, 59. See also Speyr, *Erde und Himmel* III: *Die späten Jahre*, vol. 10 of *Die Nachlasswerke* (Einsiedeln: Johannes Verlag, 1976), 193; *Das Wort und die Mystik* II, 82—and Balthasar, *Theo-Drama* III, 506; *Theo-Drama* V, 120; and *Epilogue*, 89–90. The question of Christological obedience is treated more thoroughly in light of Balthasar's critics in chapter seven.

199. It is worth noting that it is precisely on this point that the humanity of Christ plays a particularly important role in the drama of our salvation for Balthasar in contrast to the position of Karl Barth, for whom the redemptive value of Christ's humanity is precarious at best. See Schrijver, *Le merveilleux accord*, 160–63 and 288–96.

one—achieves the "identity between reception of one's being and adoring assent to the Father, between being and the act in which the whole of one's being is lovingly received."[200]

It is in this key notion of surrender—which not only assures the unity of Balthasar's Christology, his Trinitarian theology and his anthropology, but also bridges the three disciplines and unites them in what he esteems an inseparable whole—that I recognize the particular influence of Adrienne von Speyr, or at least the profound unity of his theological perspective with hers.

An Analogy of Surrender: Adrienne von Speyr

Given Balthasar's explicit recognition not only of "the fundamental consonance"[201] between his own theological perspective and that of Adrienne, but also his desire to bring his own thinking into conformity with hers[202] and even his estimation (it bears repeating) of the inseparability of his opus from hers, it should not come as a surprise to his reader that what is apparently most "novel" among his insights[203] might be traced back to the mystically and biblically inspired theology of his spiritual daughter. This theology, which was almost entirely dictated to him and which represents, as he attests, "about a third of the books written with my own hand," he credits as having "laid the basis"[204] for most of his publications since 1940. He—almost unquestionably one of the most influential theologians of our time—thus admits a remarkable statement regarding his indebtedness to this very intelligent but nonetheless theologically uneducated woman: "On the whole I received far more from her, theologically, than she from me, though, of course, the exact proportion can never be calculated."[205]

Adrienne's influence is apparent not so much in Balthasar's effort to concentrate, without dissolving,[206] the various "polarities" (Przywara) of human existence within the person of Christ;[207] nor in the dynamic aspect of his

---

200. Balthasar, *Theology of History*, 32.   201. See Balthasar, *Theo-Drama* V, 13.
202. See Balthasar, *First Glance at Adrienne von Speyr*, 13; and Johann Roten, "The Two Halves of the Moon: Marian Anthropological Dimensions in the Common Mission of Adrienne von Speyr and Hans Urs von Balthasar," *Communio* 16, no. 3 (Fall 1989): 419–45.
203. In the present case, this refers to his analogical description of the Trinity in terms of human persons and human relations.
204. Balthasar, *My Work*, 89.
205. Balthasar, *First Glance at Adrienne von Speyr*, 13. See also (with Scola), *Test Everything*, 88; and (with Albus), "Spirit and Fire," 574.
206. Balthasar argues that these tensions are actually "confirmed in the God-man" (*Theo-Drama* II, 405); see also ibid., 407; and *Epilogue*, 91–92.
207. In this we might recognize, for example, the influence of Karl Barth. See Balthasar, *The Theology of Karl Barth*, 55. Similarly, Balthasar recognizes in Przywara's thought "the ultimately christological interpretation of the analogy of being" (Balthasar, *The Theology of Karl Barth*, 328). See also Aidan

anthropology, founded in a dynamic of being itself[208] and continued in the individual's turning (in an act of conversion) from the old man (Adam) to the new (Christ);[209] but rather, or most especially (for her influence is not lacking in any of the above mentioned areas), in the explicitly *Trinitarian interpretation of the Creator-creature analogy*,[210] including the methodological consequences that follow therefrom. If, in fact, Balthasar's "distinctive contribution" to the Catholic concept of *analogia entis* consists, as Joseph Palakeel recognizes, in "the Trinitarian foundation, the Christological interpretation and the anthropological situating of analogy,"[211] the Swiss theologian owes "the final articulation" of his unique perspective, Palakeel also remarks,[212] to Adrienne's mystical insight into the paschal mystery and most especially—it bears repeating—to her categories of absolute availability or surrender and self-gift, as founded in the inner life of the Trinity.

In a manner altogether like that of Balthasar, and in what is presumably an insight preceding his, Adrienne presents the Son as being "nothing more" and as wishing to be nothing more "than the pure act of proceeding from the Father."[213] Hence his "Eucharistic movement"[214] to and from the Father is a revelation of the eternal "correspondence between the Father's self-giving, expressed in generation, and the Son's thanksgiving and readiness [...] the identity of the gift-as-given and the gift-as-received in thanksgiving."[215] This in turn accounts for his being the perfect image and revelation of the Father,[216] whose act of begetting is "an act of surrender to the Son, to which the Son replies with his surrender."[217]

Nichols, *No Bloodless Myth: A Guide through Balthasar's Dramatis* (Washington, D.C.: The Catholic University of America Press, 2000), 84.

208. For Pryzwara, the very essence of the analogy of being is, as Georges de Schrijver reads him, "unity in becoming" (Schrijver, *Le merveilleux accord*, 263). See also Zeitz, "Przywara and von Balthasar on Analogy," 484, 496, 498; and Balthasar, *Epilogue*, 49, 55, 59, and 109.

209. See Balthasar, *Theo-Drama* III, 33–34; *Theo-Drama* V, 33; and *The God Question and Modern Man*, 89–90. Cf. Speyr, *Korinther* I, 536.

210. Although Balthasar's exposition (see *Theo-Drama* V, 68) of "three attempts at a Trinitarian interpretation of the world's being" (those of Clemens Kaliba, Wilhelm Moock, and Klaus Hemerle) includes no explicit mention of Adrienne's theology, the conclusions that he draws therefrom (see ibid., 75–81) read as a defence of her insights, as is evident in the very extensive citations and references to her works there. In fact, Adrienne's "presence" is apparent throughout the entire volume, as Balthasar attests in an introductory note. See ibid., 13.

211. Palakeel, *The Use of Analogy in Theological Discourse*, 123.

212. See ibid., 119. 213. Speyr, *John* III, 372–73.

214. Balthasar, *Theo-Drama* II, 268.

215. Balthasar, *Theo-Drama* IV, 326. See also ibid., 324; "Christian Prayer," trans. André Emery, *Communio* 5, no. 1 (1978): 21; *Theo-Drama* II, 259; and *Theo-Drama* V, 85, with bountiful references to Adrienne's work.

216. See Speyr, *The Countenance of the Father*, trans. David Kipp (San Francisco: Ignatius Press, 1997), 10 and 11; and *John* III, 341.

217. Speyr, *World of Prayer*, 213.

In precisely this correspondence between gift and reception, Adrienne recognizes a certain "tension" of love within the Trinity,[218] arising not only from the differences, or distinction of the divine persons ("the heterogeny"), but also from the likeness or sameness of their one nature ("the homogeny").[219] It follows, she reasons, that unity and distance "are not opposites" in the Godhead.[220] In fact, "true unity never means the equalization of all, the levelling of differences," Adrienne explains in regard to the Trinity. Rather it "always contains in itself the greatest tension found in life. It is full of movement precisely because it is the point of stillness from which all movement proceeds, the ultimate origin of all life and therefore too its final goal."[221] Hence, although Adrienne holds that there is no becoming or development in God, she nonetheless recognizes within the Trinitarian communion of persons the archetype for the differences—she also uses the terms "tension" and "opposition," in addition to "surrender" and "receptivity"—that make love possible.[222]

To be sure, every distance between the divine persons is "exceeded" by the love which constantly bridges their "being-other [*das Anderssein*]."[223] "Between the initial bestowal of the Father's love and the answering love of the Son, there are no gradations, there is no diminution."[224] These processions also account for the "tension" (the difference-in-unity, or communion) among the divine persons that never slackens: it is unthinkable that their distinctiveness might be absolved in the uniqueness of the divine nature. Hence, "no tedium arises." Rather, there is a "perfect, self-surpassing correspondence": the discovering and fulfilling of each divine person "in his equal."[225] "If one un-

---

218. See ibid., 48. This tension is presented by Adrienne, more specifically, as the "food of their love," since it gives rise to the "boundless possibilities of mutual surrender [*Hingabe*] and receptivity [*Hinnahme*]" among the divine persons (Speyr, *Theologie der Geschlechter*, 143).

219. See Speyr, *World of Prayer*, 34. In a similar manner, Balthasar maintains that the intimacy of the divine persons requires that their personal distinctions be maintained. See Balthasar, *Theo-Drama* II, 257; *Theo-Drama* V, 85 and 486; and *Epilogue*, 93.

220. Speyr, *John* I, 48. In the Trinity, Adrienne explains, everything is "differentiated and decided to the highest degree. But [...] God differentiates in order continually to reunite; but he unites in order continually to make new decisions" (ibid., 72). In this uniting of difference, the Spirit assumes an important role. Proceeding from both, he "reunite[s] them in love across the distance between them. It is as if the Spirit is witness that the distance between them can never be separation because he constantly bridges the permanent, perpetual distance with the love of him who proceeds. Thus in triune being, distance and union are motive forces which can only increase and which are rooted so deeply in the life of God that they keep it forever new and fruitful" (*World of Prayer*, 48).

221. Speyr, *John* III, 366.

222. See, for example, Speyr, *Apokalypse*, 64; *Theologie der Geschlechter*, 79; and *John* II, 166.

223. Speyr, *Theologie der Geschlechter*, 80; see also *World of Prayer*, 48.

224. Speyr, *The Letter to the Ephesians*, 33. This love, she specifies, is "consubstantial" (ibid.). Similarly, Adrienne presents this triune love as "a continual weaving and flux of concessions and fulfillments" (*World of Prayer*, 65).

225. Ibid., 34–35. This also means that the Father can only be measured "against himself, the Son, and the Spirit" (*The Countenance of the Father*, 10).

derstands the Father as the one who begets, the Son as the one begotten and the Spirit as the one who issues from them both, then one also understands that each Person must be wholly and exclusively what he is if this exchange in God's one essence is to be possible. Each Person is wholly himself for the sake of the other two."[226] Unlike an exchange between human beings which is always limited—"no one can impart his memory or spirit to the other"—the exchange between the divine persons is presented by Adrienne as total and complete. Every gift in God "is the thing itself, not a representation of it."[227]

The inner-Trinitarian life is thus presented by Adrienne in terms of the infinite possibilities of surrender as gift and surrender as reception among the divine persons,[228] and the divine love as that "whereby each divine person, in his exchange of love with the others, surrenders himself unlimitedly, surpassingly." Indeed, it is the "unlimited and surpassing [*übertreffend*]"[229] surrender of each of the divine persons to the others—this dynamic exchange of love[230] accounting for what Adrienne refers to as "a real happening"[231] without becoming[232] in the Godhead—that makes it possible to recognize that "every I in God is in every You."[233]

This dynamic vision of the Trinity has, to be sure, profound implications for Adrienne's theological method, which Balthasar describes as character-

---

226. Adrienne von Speyr, *Confession*, trans. Douglas W. Stott (San Francisco: Ignatius Press, 1985), 22. "The Son, by proceeding from the Father, and the Spirit, by proceeding from Father and Son, both cause the Father to be Father. [...] All the Persons define each other reciprocally" (*Das Wort und die Mystik* II, 104). On the other hand, "Each shares himself with the other in such a way that he is not thereby compelled to be any less himself. This is part of God's firmness of decision" (Speyr, *John* I, 73).

227. Speyr, *World of Prayer*, 28; cf. Balthasar, *Theo-Drama* V, 74 (with reference to Klaus Hemmerle). "God not only possesses everything but also mediates everything he is and has: God gives God" (Speyr, *Mary in the Redemption*, 41).

228. See Speyr, *Theologie der Geschlechter*, 143.

229. Speyr, *Das Wort und die Mystik* II, 523; cf. *World of Prayer*, 59. See also Balthasar, *Theo-Drama* V, 87; and *Elucidations*, 92.

230. Cf. *The Catechism of the Catholic Church*, no. 221.

231. Speyr, *The Countenance of the Father*, 8.

232. This is explicit in Speyr, *Apokalypse*, 64; and *Korinther* I, 413. Similarly, Balthasar argues: "We must resolve to see these two apparently contradictory concepts as a unity: eternal or absolute Being—and 'happening' [...]. All earthly becoming is a reflection of the eternal 'happening' in God, which, we repeat, is per se identical with the eternal Being or essence" (Balthasar, *Theo-Drama* V, 67); hence his presentation of the perfection of divine life as "eternal movement" (ibid., 77). See also Gerard O'Hanlon, *The Immutability of God in the Theology of Hans Urs von Balthasar*; Thomas G. Dalzell, "The Enrichment of God in Balthasar's Trinitarian Eschatology," *Irish Theological Quarterly* 66 (2001): 3–18; Dalzell, *The Dramatic Encounter of Divine and Human Freedom in the Theology of Hans Urs von Balthasar* (Bern: Peter Lang, 1997), esp. 186; Antonio López, "Eternal Happening: God as an Event of Love," *Communio* 32 (2005): 214–45; cf. Marie-Joseph Nicolas, "L'idée de nature dans la pensée de saint Thomas d'Aquin," 554–55.

233. Speyr, *Das Wort und die Mystik* II, 523. "Each is so much everything to the other, that the Father's essence belongs to the Son; the Son's essence to the Spirit, and so on" (ibid., 524). Cf. Speyr, *Die Schöpfung*, 54.

ized by a realism "that goes into specific details," while remaining "dominated by a vision of the higher order."[234] This means not only that the order of creation is incorporated into the Christological and ecclesial order of redemption, but also that the latter has precedence over the former. It is with this precedence in mind that one should regard Adrienne's many anthropomorphisms: her common manner of approaching the divine by means of the human, or more correctly, of speaking of the divine in human terms.

To be more specific, as shall become increasingly evident, Adrienne often addresses the Trinity in terms analogical to human relations. This approach—so significant to her theology of the body, as we shall see in chapter four, but also to her theology of the sexes, which will be exposited in chapter six, and to her theology of ecclesial communion, examined in chapter five—should be understood within her general intention of recognizing the human (and even nature itself) as pointing to the divine, as originating in and as oriented toward the divine: as existing "in Him [in whom] we live and move and have our being" (cf. Acts 17:28). Through Christ, the whole multitude of creation is, Adrienne explains, "incorporated in the revelation of Trinitarian life."[235] "It is not about 'God in all things,' but about 'all things towards God, towards Christ; all things as signposts.'"[236] Indeed, Adrienne recognizes all of creation, but most especially human creation, as "bearing the sign of the Son," of striving toward him, of being held together by him, and of "freely surrendering" itself "inwardly, in an obedience that comes from the Son's obedience."[237] Creation, therefore, is not considered by Adrienne as merely "natural." "Behind it lies the free, powerful will of God to reveal himself."[238] In the (supernatural) intention of God to reveal himself, on the other hand, lies the origin of the natural order: the creature is willed by God as the receiver and bearer of his self-revelation.[239] The very fact that God can and

---

234. Balthasar, *Our Task*, 67.

235. Speyr, *Korinther* I, 376; see also *John* III, 366. See Balthasar, *First Glance at Adrienne von Speyr*, 61; and *Explorations in Theology* I, 175–77. In a similar manner, Balthasar argues that in virtue of God's profound abasement in the Incarnation, "everything" in the created world has been rendered useful for God's revelation, not excepting that which formerly appeared most remote from him: "the cross, opprobrium, anguish, death." Indeed, we have been made capable "of really finding God in all things" (Balthasar, *Explorations in Theology* I, 176); see also *The Glory of the Lord* I, 35–36; and Jacques Servais, "Finding God in all Things," *Communio* 30, no. 2 (2003): 260–81.

236. Speyr, *Der Mensch vor Gott*, 59. See also Balthasar, "Das literarische Werk Adriennes von Speyr," in *Adrienne von Speyr und ihre spirituelle Theologie. Symposium zu ihrem 100. Geburtstag*, ed. Hans Urs von Balthasar Stiftung, Georges Chantraine, and Angelo Scola (Einsiedeln: Johannes Verlag, 2002), 130–31.

237. Speyr, *Korinther* I, 506 (cited by Balthasar in *Theo-Drama* V, 520). See also Speyr, *The Letter to the Colossians*, 37; *Das Buch von Gehorsam*, 20; and *Korinther* I, 185.

238. Speyr, *Das Wort und die Mystik* II, 31.

239. See ibid., 34.

wills to reveal himself to the world implies "a living unity between God and the world": a unity, Adrienne adds, which is grounded within the Trinitarian unity.[240] It is therefore impossible in any given revelation of God to clearly distinguish nature from super-nature.[241]

While one might consequently fear a sort of profanation of the sacred—an objection that we will treat below—Adrienne herself mourns the absence of what had been the sanctifying of the profane. She observes, more specifically, that modern man and woman have lost the sense of wonder arising from the recognition of the created order as revelatory of the uncreated. Accustomed, instead, to seeing things with a sort of habitual reference to the past—as if to admit that there is nothing new under the sun (cf. Eccl 1:9)—we have lost the sense of creation itself: the orientation of all things in the future, in hope: *in the Son to the Father*.[242] Indeed, Adrienne thus challenges us to regard all of human life as "access to the life of God in heaven."[243]

From this perspective, and in response to the objection above—namely, that her perspective might be viewed as a sort of profanation of the sacred—Adrienne argues that God allows us to keep our human concepts—however inadequate—as a means of "initiating us into his inner-divine world of love, showing us ways to his Trinitarian nature and guiding us into the 'greater-than' of his being," precisely because these might be "transformed" by his grace. This means, more specifically, the Swiss mystic argues, that our experiences of God are a valid access to the mystery of his nature and to an interpretation of his being. To renounce these "would be to shut ourselves in our earthly world and reject the most precious gifts which give access to God."[244]

In this way, Adrienne might be thought to share with Balthasar the conviction that we ought "to see in the natural realm a breadth, abundance, and multiplicity that will prepare us to appreciate fully the work of grace, which uses this whole plenitude to exhibit itself and, in so doing, permeates it, forms it, elevates it, and gives it its ultimate efficacy." As such, she—together with him—might also be viewed as providing a bridge beyond the alleged tension between analogical and katalogical perspectives, just as St. Thomas is observed by Balthasar as getting "underneath the alleged incompatibility

---

240. Speyr, *John* I, 27.
241. See Speyr, *Das Wort und die Mystik* II, 31–32. For a concrete example, see Balthasar, *Our Task*, 89, and for the question of the relation between nature and grace, see chapter three of this volume.
242. See Speyr, *Der Mensch vor Gott*, 59.
243. Speyr, *Korinther* I, 377. Our "being here" is, Adrienne argues, the beginning of our "being with God" (ibid., 378).
244. Speyr, *World of Prayer*, 35. Cf. Balthasar, *Explorations in Theology* I, 176–77; *The Glory of the Lord* I, 35–36; and *Theo-Drama* V, 78–79.

between Platonism (or Augustinianism) and Aristotelianism."[245] It is, in other words, in profound union with both Adrienne and St. Thomas, as is the purpose of this volume to demonstrate, that Balthasar invites us to "recenter our intellectual effort on thinking through the analogy between the divine archetype and the world image from both sides."[246]

A Trinitiarian "Resolution" of Human "Tensions" or Polarities

From this Trinitarian perspective of anthropology, life takes on a still richer meaning than that of being created by the Father; it also means, for the Christian, being "newly created through the Son."[247] It is not as if the Father simply leads fallen man and woman back to the point from which they departed. Rather, he "unites him [and her] more profoundly with himself in his Son": the first Adam is included in the second Adam's return to the Father.[248] Because, more specifically, the Son's eternal return to the Father is already implied in his eternal generation by the Father—which, as we have seen, includes the act of creation—our own return to the Father through the Son is also implied in the creative act.[249]

It is thus not surprising that Adrienne also recognizes a profound unity between the work of creation and that of redemption, as symbolized by the presence of the Cross in her mystical vision of creation. The darkness that descends upon earth at the moment of Christ's death is likened by the Swiss mystic to the original darkness preceding creation: a heavenly sign of the dawning of a—the first—new day: "the intersection of that which is to be separated, but also of that which is already separated."[250] It is likewise the Cross, Adrienne discerns, which determines the divisions between day and night, earth and land, and which also rules over the division, within man himself, between body and soul.[251] Similarly, it is the Cross (and thus also the Eucharist, as shall

---

245. Balthasar, *Theo-Logic* I, 14.   246. Ibid., 15; see also *Theo-Logic* III, 234–35.

247. Adrienne von Speyr, *Dienst der Freude: Betrachtungen über den Philipperbrief* (Einsiedeln: Johannes Verlag, 1951), 35.

248. Speyr, *Das Wort und die Mystik* II, 261. See also Speyr, *The Mystery of Death*, 67; and *Korinther* I, 467. Cf. Balthasar, *Theo-Drama* II, 373–74.

249. See Balthasar, *Theo-Drama* V, 83. It is important to add that this return implies the creature's free adherence to God, his willingness to be "in Christ," as shall become increasingly evident.

250. See Speyr, *Apokalypse*, 385.

251. See ibid. and *Die Schöpfung*, 12–13 and 31–37. Similar is the vision of St. Irenaeus of Lyons, who recognizes the Son of God as encompassing "the breadth and length, the height and depth, of the whole world, for by God's Word all things are guided and ordered. Now God's Son was also crucified in the four dimensions, since He imprinted the form of the Cross on the universe. In becoming visible, He had to reveal the participation of the universe in His Cross" (*Demonstratio* 32, in Irenaeus, *The Scandal*

be increasingly evident) which, in the works of Adrienne—and herein resides an important thesis of this work—rules over what Balthasar presents as the various "tensions" (or better: the mystery of difference-in-unity) characterizing the human person in a fundamental manner. There is a "tension" not only between the body and soul, but also between man and woman, individual and community, nature and grace, and ultimately between the human person and God.[252] Because—it bears repeating—this word (tension, *Spannung*) is used by Adrienne to address the mystery of the difference-in-unity or unity-in-difference (communion) of the divine persons, it should not be understood as implying resistance or conflict, but rather unity, communion and love.[253] Because, moreover, the Cross—and with it the Eucharist[254]—meet in the heart of God (that is to say, in the Trinity), all of these "tensions" meet most fundamentally, without ever being resolved, in the "tension" of love (or again: the difference-in-unity and unity-in-difference) in the triune life of God.[255] Indeed, the whole mystery of the Lord's terrestrial life stands, within Adrienne's theology, as testimony of the Son's love for the Father and his (the Father's) creation as well as a testimony of the Father's love for the Son and creation: "testimony of a love within the Deity that in circulating has drawn into itself that creation which was created because the Son *is*."[256]

This means, finally, that all that appears within the mystery of human existence as *polar* is in the final and most fundamental sense *Trinitarian*, thanks most especially to the mediating presence of the "third" in God: the Holy Spirit who, in the words of Balthasar, is "the objective witness" to the "difference-in-unity or unity-in difference" of the Father and Son.[257] For this

---

of the Incarnation, 15 [= *Démonstrations de la prédication apostolique*, trans. L. M. Froideveaux, Sources chrétiennes 62 (Paris: Cerf, 1959, 1971, 1995)].

252. See, for example, Adrienne's image of the horizontal relation between man and woman as "firmly" united to the vertical line of the Eucharist which, in turn, she presents as the "common basis for everything," namely the fleshly relationship between Christ and mankind "represented in the Church-Bride" (*Erde und Himmel* II: *Die Zeit der großen Diktate*, vol. 9 of *Die Nachlasswerke* [Einsiedeln: Johannes Verlag, 1975], 248). This theme will be treated more completely in chapter four. See also Adrienne's *Das Wort und die Mystik* II, 525–26; and Balthasar, *Our Task*, 225.

253. See, for example, Speyr, *John* II, 166 and 292. As is typical of Adrienne's thought, "unity prevails over difference, the one mission over the differences of the persons and their life circumstances, holiness over the individual saints" (*Korinther* I, 322).

254. See Speyr, *Das Wort und die Mystik* II, 524–25; and *Gebetserfahrung* (Einsiedeln: Johannes Verlag, 1965, 1978²), 13.

255. See, for example, Speyr, *Theologie der Geschlechter*, 143; *Das Wort und die Mystik* II, 98. Cf. Balthasar, *Theo-Drama* III, 333; and Balthasar's presentation of Adrienne's theological perspective in his introduction to her *The Letter to the Ephesians*, 10. See chapter four for a more thorough development of this thesis.

256. Speyr, *The Letter to the Colossians*, 30; see also *The Letter to the Ephesians*, 29; and *Korinther* I, 378.

257. Balthasar, *Theo-Drama* III, 187.

reason, Balthasar argues that it is "impossible to approach the Holy Spirit except from two sides, as the (subjective) epitome of the reciprocal love of Father and Son—whereby he appears as the bond (*nexus*) between them—and as the (objective) fruit that is produced by this love and attests it."[258] As the "essence of love," he "maintains the infinite difference between them, seals it and, since he is the one Spirit of both [the Father and the Son], bridges it."[259]

[The Spirit] makes the One out of the Other (that is, he brings back the creation, which as regards God is the Other, into the divine law of life, and subordinates to it this otherness), and at the same time makes the Other out of the One (that is, from the hypostatic union of Christ he brings forth the double subject Christ-Church). Thus the return of the creature into God becomes simultaneously the outgoing of the divine life which, entering into the creature, draws it into the eternal opposition of the persons in love and through love.[260]

Indeed, as Balthasar puts it, the "whole becomes comprehensible only with the coming of the Holy Spirit into the heart."[261]

While it is the Son who realizes our salvation, Adrienne thus recognizes between his saving word and its effect (*Wirkung*) in us, "a sort of margin (*Spanne*) in believers which is filled by the Spirit."[262] It is thus not surprising that Adrienne should acknowledge "a Trinitarian solution" to "every human problem concerning the battle against evil and the redemption of the world."[263] It is not only the tensions due to sin—which Adrienne prefers in fact to address in terms of "limit"[264] rather than "tension," reserving the latter term for that which serves unity or love—that benefit from a Trinitarian solution in Adrienne's anthropology. After all, her theological method typifies what Balthasar means by *katalogy*, namely a method which regards "the tensions traversing the world" as "resolved only when a comprehensive vision or a reconciliation is given by God."[265] What is unique to Adrienne's own katalogical perspective, as shared with Balthasar, is that this comprehensive vision from on high is one of difference-in-unity or unity-in-difference,

---

258. Balthasar, *Theo-Logic* III, 160. Cf. Speyr, *World of Prayer*, 48; and *John* I, 26.
259. Balthasar, *Theo-Drama* IV, 324; see also *Theo-Logic* II, 156; and (with Scola) *Test Everything*, 87.
260. Balthasar, *Explorations in Theology* II, 191; cf. (with Scola) *Test Everything*, 64–65. Comparable is Adrienne's presentation of Mary, who bridges the "distance and difference between heaven and earth" insofar as she is received into heaven by her Son, whom she had received on earth. See Speyr, *Handmaid of the Lord*, 146.
261. Balthasar and Scola, *Test Everything*, 87.
262. Speyr, *Das Wort und die Mystik* II, 528. Cf. Balthasar, *The Threefold Garland*, 30.
263. Ibid., 98. Cf. Balthasar, *Theo-Drama* III, 333.
264. See, for example, Speyr, *Das Wort und die Mystik* I, 42; *Victory of Love*, 14; *John* IV, 157; and *Markus: Betrachtungspunkte für eine Gemeinschaft* (Einsiedeln: Johannes Verlag, 1971), 446.
265. Balthasar, *Theo-Logic* II, 188.

whence the question posed by Balthasar: "how God's absolute being, which […] can occur only in Trinitarian form, is reflected in the world's being."[266]

Adrienne's anthropology—in perfect union with that of Balthasar—will read as a response to this question, which constitutes the guiding thread throughout the next five chapters of this volume in preparation for our more direct conversation with St. Thomas and his disciples in chapter seven and the general conclusion.

266. Ibid., 173.

TWO

The Difference-in-Unity of Faith's Object and Act

A Speyrian Methodology of Gift Encountering Gift

Before addressing the various anthropological tensions that Balthasar and Adrienne present as images, analogies, or metaphors of the difference-in-unity of the Trinity, we would do well to focalize upon the mediating figure of Christ, whom Balthasar and Adrienne present as the revelation of the whole triune life in virtue of his archetypical surrender of obedience to the Father. Precisely by way of this surrender, Christ is said more specifically to reveal the Father who, in turn, is characterized essentially by the paternal "surrender" of the whole divine Being in the generation of the Son. As for the Son, he is said by Balthasar and Adrienne to contribute to his own generation by way of his filial "surrender" in the form of receptivity. Hence the acts of surrender that characterize Christ throughout his terrestrial existence in the form of human obedience—acts enabling, as it were, the eternal Father to be seen, heard, and loved in him (the incarnate Son)—are revelatory of both the Son's eternal (receptive) "surrender" to the Father and of the Father's own eternal (generative) surrender to the Son. In the incarnate Son—who, out of love, makes "space" for the Father—is thus seen the Father. The Son's revelatory disposition of obedience allows the believer to see the Father in him (the Son).

These acts of obedient surrender do not only reveal the divine persons, however, for they are also said by Balthasar and Adrienne to fundamentally characterize the Christian believer, who thus, by obedient surrender, allows God to be God within him- or herself. This, more specifically, is the disposition of faith, which is thus presented by Balthasar and Adrienne as archetypically present in Christ before it is said to belong to the Christian.[1] Hence, the incarnate Son of God reveals the meaning of faith as the act of being caught up within the dynamic life of the Trinity: a life characterized by surrender.

While the dramatic existence of the Christian who partakes of the universal mission of Christ will be examined more thoroughly in chapter three, in this (second) chapter we will consider the specifically dramatic existence of the theologian, who—in virtue of his or her faith—is recognized by Balthasar and Adrienne as participating in Christ's own revelatory disposition. To this end, we will begin by pointing to Balthasar's presentation—in the midst of various criticisms—of what he recognized as the profound unity of holiness and charisma in the figure of Adrienne von Speyr. Balthasar regards this unity as essential to the vocation of the theologian, who must allow him- or herself to be readily disposed (by way of surrender) to accomplish the ever-greater demands of the always-greater God. Such is also, we will see in this chapter, the profound unity, within the one saving "act"[2] of God's self-revelation, of the two dimensions of faith: the one word (faith) simultaneously designates that which is received and the means whereby it is received.[3] It is precisely the unity of these two dimensions of faith in the person and mission of Adrienne, as observed by Balthasar, that allows him to present her, in imitation of Christ, as a model "theologian." More significantly still, her experience of faith is recognized by Balthasar as an ecclesial gift: a gift to the Church for the enrichment of her own (ecclesial) faith and that of the Christian in the Church.

Discerning the Unity of Adrienne's Mission and Theology of Mission under Balthasar's Regard

"Charisms," writes Balthasar in reference to Adrienne von Speyr, "are not distributed at random but are dispensed by God to supply what is needful

---

1. See Henri Donneaud, "Hans Urs von Balthasar contre saint Thomas d'Aquin sur la foi du Christ," *Revue thomiste* 97, no. 2 (1997): 335–54.

2. God's revelation, Balthasar teaches, is "not primarily a doctrine but the occurrence of a deed" (*Convergences: To the Source of Christian Mystery*, trans. E. A. Nelson [San Francisco: Ignatius Press, 1983], 39).

3. By that which is received, I mean more specifically "that which is contained in the word of God [...] which the Church proposes for belief as divinely revealed" (*The Catechism of the Catholic Church*, no. 182). By the means whereby it is received, I mean "a personal adherence of the whole man to God who reveals himself" (ibid., no. 176). On the unity of these two dimensions of faith within the context of Church tradition, see, for example, ibid., no. 175; Second Vatican Council, Dogmatic Constitution on Divine Revelation, *Dei Verbum* (November Divine 18, 1965) in *DZ* 4201–35; and The Pontifical Biblical Commission, "The Interpretation of the Bible in the Church" in *Origins: CNS Documentary Service* 23 (January 6, 1994): 497–524.

and lacking in his Church at each historical moment. If they are from God they usually do not flow with the latest fashionable trend but much more likely contain an antidote and remedy for the perils of the time."[4] Certainly there was no shortage of needs in the Church of the twentieth century, nor of perils in the contemporary world. For the author of these words, however, what summed up everything then (in 1968), as in every historical period, was the pressing need for sanctity. Balthasar was convinced, more specifically, that the one who is charged to teach the truth of Christ must first become a living Gospel.[5] His (or hers) must be an existential theology: a theology which is first of all received and lived before it is transmitted; a theology which is founded in the experience of the living God, who gives himself to the human subject as an "object" to be known and loved, while nevertheless remaining the subject of truth *par excellence*.

In the work of Adrienne von Speyr, Balthasar recognized that this pressing need for spiritual depth in the midst of the world and in the heart of the Church had, without confrontation and reactionary guile, been addressed—thanks to his own humble stenographic efforts—with healing medicine: "Into confused and perplexing situations, she brings directions and solutions of penetrating, often painful clarity," Balthasar believed. "But they are directions which all flow from the source-waters of biblical revelation."[6]

To be sure, many a commentator of Balthasar has recognized a similar unity between his own theological and faith perspectives, but Antonio Sicari attributes this unity to Balthasar's participation—as Adrienne's confessor and spiritual director—in her mystical experiences and thus also and more profoundly in her ecclesial mission.[7] "A theologian who demands a necessary bond between holiness and theology (and this in the very person of the

---

4. Balthasar, *First Glance at Adrienne von Speyr*, 95–96.
5. See Balthasar, *Explorations in Theology* I, 182; and *Theo-Drama* III, 126.
6. Balthasar, *First Glance at Adrienne von Speyr*, 245; see also 96, 100. Similarly, in his contribution to the colloquium on the ecclesial mission of Adrienne von Speyr (held on September 27–29, 1985), he refers to "her ecclesial mission in the framework of divine Providence for our epoch" ("Le charisme d'Adrienne" in Balthasar, Georges Chantraine, and Angelo Scola [eds.], *La mission ecclésiale d'Adrienne von Speyr*, 187). Oddly, one does not find the same remark in the original German version: "Adriennes Charisma" in *Adrienne von Speyr und ihre kirchliche Sendung*, 173–78.
7. See Antonio Sicari, "Hans Urs von Balthasar: Theology and Holiness," in David L. Schindler, *Hans Urs von Balthasar: His Life and His Work*, 121–32, esp. 126. See also, for example, Marc Ouellet, "The Message of Balthasar's Theology to Modern Theology," *Communio* 23 (1996): 270–99; Jacques Servais, "The *Ressourcement* of Spirituality of Contemporary Spirituality under the Guidance of Adrienne von Speyr and Hans Urs von Balthasar," *Communio* 23, no. 2 (1996): 300–321; Angelo Scola, *Hans Urs von Balthasar: A Theological Style* (Grand Rapids, Mich.: Eerdmans, 1995): 9–16; Johann Roten, "Hans Urs von Balthasar's Anthropology in Light of his Marian Thinking," *Communio* 20 (1993): 306–33; and Adrian J. Walker, "Love Alone: Hans Urs von Balthasar as a Master of Theological Renewal," *Communio* 32 (Fall 2005): 517–40.

theologian himself) is," Sicari argues, "placed in a strange position—*he exposes himself*. And he, together with his own theology becomes, so to speak, subject to judgment and even to blackmail: 'Where then is your holiness? Where is your 'spirituality'?"[8]

The only way around the temptation of renouncing one's stand for this unity is, Sicari proposes, to have recourse—precisely as a member of the ecclesial community—to the Church's own holiness by way of the mystery of the communion of saints. Such, more specifically, Sicari proposes, is the experience mediated by "the contagion [...] between different ecclesial subjects [...] unified by the Spirit."[9] Not surprisingly, then, Sicari recognizes Balthasar as one whose ecclesial mission was guided by the same Spirit whom Balthasar himself held responsible for the unity of Adrienne's person and teaching, on the one hand, and of her mission and personal path of holiness, on the other. He (Sicari) thus points to the important quality that Cardinal Ratzinger also emphasized in his homily at Balthasar's funeral liturgy, namely, the "obedience of thought, which allows itself to be led away even from the highest peaks of mysticism by the true God."[10]

Ironically, however, it is precisely this willingness "to be led away" not so much "from" as *by* "the highest peaks of mysticism"—as he believed to be entrusted to the Church of our time in the charisma and mission of Adrienne von Speyr[11]—that Balthasar is faulted by certain of his critics. Unlike Ratzinger who credits Adrienne with providing "the charismatic, prophetic impulse" that made of Balthasar's work "a truly living theology,"[12] they question more specifically if she did not instead mislead him away from both his

---

8. Sicari, "Hans Urs von Balthasar: Theology and Holiness," 124.

9. Ibid. Beyond Balthasar's enormous work of editing and publishing Adrienne's dictations, Sicari points to his numerous translations, which Balthasar considers "an integral and not a secondary part of his own theological work. We can even say more: von Balthasar considers his whole enormous output secondary with respect to the living work of weaving ecclesial ties and forming people in holiness" (ibid., 126). Cf. Balthasar, *My Work*, 87. See also Speyr, *Light and Images*, 30.

10. Joseph Ratzinger, "Homily at the Funeral Liturgy of Hans Urs von Balthasar" (Lucerne, July 1, 1988), reprinted in Schindler, *Hans Urs von Balthasar: His Life and Work*, 292.

11. In Balthasar's presentation of Adrienne in *First Glance at Adrienne von Speyr*, for example, one readily discerns, as Claudia Lee points out, his conviction that "within the contemporary Church, ecclesial mysticism has found no truer expression than in the life of Adrienne von Speyr" (Claudia Lee, "The Role of Mysticism within the Church as Conceived by Hans Urs von Balthasar," *Communio* 16 [1989]: 118). On Balthasar's perception of mysticism, see also his "Understanding Christian Mysticism" in *Explorations in Theology* IV, 309–35; Christophe Potworowski, "Christian Experience in Hans Urs von Balthasar," *Communio* 20 (1993): 107–17; and *Revista Teologica di Lugano* 6, no. 1 (2001)—the entire volume—wherein are published the acts of the 14th colloquium of theology in Lugano: "Esperienza mistica e teologia. Ricerca epistemologica sulle proposte di Hans Urs von Balthasar" (May 25–26, 2000).

12. Joseph Cardinal Ratzinger, "Das Problem der christlichen Prophetie. Neils Christian Hvidt im Gespräch mit Joseph Kardinal Ratzinger," *Internationale katholische Zeitschrift "Communio"* 28 (March–April 1999): 183.

Jesuit vocation and the metaphysical precision of a more scholastic theology that might have spared him of certain "gnostic" tendencies and even errors in, for example, his presentation of the Godhead and the union of the two natures in Christ.[13] Such questions are hardly subdued when one reads of his unwavering conviction regarding the authenticity of her mystical mission and of his willing submission to her advice and insights: "As her [Adrienne's] confessor and spiritual director, I observed her interior life most closely, yet in twenty-seven years I never had the least doubt about the authentic mission that was hers, nor about the unpretentious integrity with which she lived it and communicated it to me. I not only made some of the most difficult decisions of my life—including my leaving the Jesuit Order—following her advice, but I also strove to bring my way of looking at Christian revelation into conformity with hers."[14]

For those, moreover, who question the prophetic or mystical nature of Adrienne's teaching, their concerns about her influence upon Balthasar are likely to be accented by his further conviction that God had entrusted him with a mission that he was to share with Adrienne—a so-called "double mission"[15]—wherein obedience "was fundamental to everything": so fundamental that he willingly subjected himself to what he believed was prophetically revealed to Adrienne regarding his own part within the common mission.[16]

From this perspective, Balthasar's claim that theology might—indeed *should*—draw upon the experience of the saints and mystics as an illumination of the Christian mysteries runs the risk of being read as a form of self-justification or a personal vindication of his theological debt to Adrienne.[17]

---

13. On the accusation of "gnostic" tendencies see, for example, Karl Rahner, *Im Gespräch* I, eds. Paul Imhof and Herbert Biallowons (Munich: Kösel Verlag, 1982), 245–46; and Richard Schenk, "Ist die Rede vom leidenden Gott theologisch zu vermeiden? Reflexionen über den Streit von K. Rahner und H. U. von Balthasar" in Peter Koslowski and Friedrich Hermanni (eds.), *Der leidende Gott. Eine philosophische und theologische Kritik* (Munich: Wilhelm Fink Verlag, 2001), 225–39. In anticipation of Rahner's criticism, see Balthasar, *Theo-Drama* V, 13. On the accusation of other errors see, for example, Gilbert Narcisse, "Participer à la vie trinitaire," *Revue thomiste* 96 (1996): 107–28, esp. 127–28; and Kerr, "Adrienne von Speyr and Hans Urs von Balthasar." For a more thorough treatment of the various images and themes borrowed from Adrienne's mystical theology in Balthasar's work, which are often the object of extensive criticism, see chapter seven of the present volume.

14. Balthasar, *First Glance at Adrienne von Speyr*, 13. See also the letter he addressed to his brothers in the Society of Jesus in March 1950, explaining his decision to renounce making his profession in the Society in order to carry out the foundation of the Community of St. John, in appendix VIII of Henri de Lubac, *At the Service of the Church: Henri de Lubac Reflects on the Circumstances that Occasioned His Writings*, trans. Anne Elizabeth Englund (San Francisco: Ignatius Press/Communio Books, 1993), 370–75. See also Peter Henrici's account of this event in *Hans Urs von Balthasar: Aspekte seiner Sendung* (Einsiedeln: Johannes Verlag, 2008), 25–31.

15. Balthasar, *Our Task*, 16.   16. See ibid., 19.

17. On Balthasar's turning to the saints and mystics as a theological source, see Mark McIntosh, *A Christology from Within: Spirituality and the Incarnation in Hans Urs von Balthasar* (Notre Dame, Ind.:

Some readers of Balthasar will undoubtedly exercise, therefore, a reserve of prudence—especially given Balthasar's estimation of Adrienne's own sanctity—when evaluating what David Moss recognizes as the "central task" of the theologian as viewed by Balthasar, namely, "the exegesis of the saints' objective mission," or the discerning of "the very *form and content* [*Gestalt*] of revelation as it appears in this particle of saintly existence."[18] Indeed, it is not surprising that some would suspiciously regard not only the relationship between the mystic (Adrienne) and her confessor-director-editor (Balthasar), but also the theology (hers, his, both), which apparently originated within the context of this relationship.[19] They suspect this theology, more specifically, of being motivated by a certain psychological symbiosis and thus also of being marked by the very subjectivism that Balthasar regards as opposed to the true spirit of Catholicism.

This accusation also stands in apparent contradiction with Balthasar's statement—as if to echo Adrienne—that it is "the mission, not the psychology of the saints, [that] must always have the last word."[20] It follows that the exegesis of the saint's (or the mystic's) life by the theologian—and, of course, we are interested in Balthasar's so-called exegesis of Adrienne's life—in no way involves an interpretation of "the intensity of their moral or ascetical achievement,"[21] nor, it would seem, of the extraordinary phenomena surrounding their lives. Rather, the emphasis is upon the discernment, within the confines of a properly human existence, of the God-given mission as it is more or less perfectly appropriated by the individual.[22] Indeed, the saints are esteemed by

---

University of Notre Dame Press, 2000), 26; Larry Chapp, "Revelation," in Oakes and Moss, *The Cambridge Companion to Hans Urs von Balthasar*, 11–23, esp. 23; David Moss, "The Saints" in ibid., 79–92, esp. 81–82; and Balthasar, "Theology and Sanctity" in *Explorations in Theology* I, 189–209. On the personal vindication of his reliance on Adrienne's presumably mystical experiences, see the extensive reflection of Karen Kilby, *Balthasar: A (Very) Critical Introduction*, 153–61, esp. 157.

18. David Moss, "The Saints," in Oakes and Moss, *Cambridge Companion to Hans Urs von Balthasar*, 81. Hence, for example, the questions: "what is from God? what is personality-determined? historically superseded? perennially valid?" (ibid.).

19. For a thorough presentation of the various positions taken by theologians with regard to Adrienne's influence upon Balthasar, see Jacques Servais, "Per una valutazione dell'influsso di Adrienne von Speyr su Hans Urs von Balthasar," *Rivista Teologica di Lugano* 6 (2001): 67–89. Perhaps the most extreme of these positions (which is not mentioned by Servais) is that of Tina Beattie, *New Catholic Feminism: Theology and Theory* (London: Routledge, 2006), esp. 145–83. See my response to her criticisms in chapter six, where I treat "Masculine and Feminine Missions." As for Servais, he argues for Adrienne's "decisive influence" upon Balthasar ("Per une valutazione," 85), not however in a psychological or subjective sense, but in virtue of what he esteems to be her objective prophetic charism. Such is also the position of Claudia Lee in "The Role of Mysticism within the Church."

20. Balthasar, *My Work*, 71; and *First Glance at Adrienne von Speyr*, 245. Cf. Speyr, cited by Balthasar in ibid., 187.

21. Moss, "The Saints," 81.

22. See Schrijver, *Le merveilleux accord*, 38. It bears mention that the extraordinary phenomena sur-

Balthasar as "the authentic interpreters of theo-drama."[23] They are not given to us so that we might simply admire "their heroic powers," Balthasar insists, but so that we might be "enlightened by them on the inner reality of Christ, both for our better understanding of the faith and for our living thereby in charity."[24]

Here, in other words, the emphasis is not upon the personality of the saint or mystic—including his or her subjective inner state and personal history—but, rather, upon the singularity of his or her mission in virtue of which he or she is given to participate in the saving act of Christian revelation: "In Jesus Christ […] the revealing of the triune God and the allotting of roles [that is to say, missions] to his human fellow actors are not separate functions. Since his role/person is central, those who have been personalized by the roles they have been given will also share in his function of revealing God."[25]

It follows that the "capital importance" that Balthasar attaches to Adrienne's spiritual and mystical experiences are *not* to be understood primarily from the perspective of his conviction—as Georges de Schrijver maintains—that the lived reality of the spiritual and mystical life is "far more important than systematic reflection, even more important than the literary study of the mystics."[26] While this is assuredly not untrue to Balthasar's thought, still more fundamental is, it seems to me, his conviction that the meaning of every human life is to be discovered within the context of a personal God-given mission. And, as Adrienne's mission was esteemed by Balthasar as a prophetic one, her teaching is judged by him as more important than attention to her person.

This conviction regarding the centrality of the mission explains, for example, Balthasar's particular focus, in his little book dedicated to Adrienne (*First Glance at Adrienne von Speyr*) upon her mission, not unlike the same focus within his presentation of Sts. Therese of Lisieux and Elizabeth of the Trinity.[27] It is likewise this conviction which accounts for my decision to

---

rounding Adrienne's life were numerous but they in no way assume a central importance in his biography of her. See Balthasar, *First Glance at Adrienne von Speyr*, 33–37 and 39–40. Adrienne's extraordinary gifts are also exposited in the three-volume diaries Balthasar kept and published in her name (*Erde und Himmel* I-III). The mystical nature of her work, which is obscure in many of her writings, is more apparent in many of the posthumous volumes which have not yet been translated into English, with the exception of the first volume of *Das Allerheiligenbuch* (*Book of All Saints*). See also *Das Allerheiligenbuch* II (*The Book of All Saints*), vol. 1.2 of *Die Nachlasswerke* (Einsiedeln: Johannes Verlag, 1977); *Das Fischernetz*, vol. 2 of *Die Nachlasswerke* (Einsiedeln: Johannes Verlag, 1969); *Kreuz und Hölle* I: *Die Passionen*, vol. 3 of *Die Nachlasswerke* (Einsiedeln: Johannes Verlag, 1966); *Kreuz und Hölle* II: *Auftragshöllen*, vol. 4 of *Die Nachlasswerke* (Einsiedeln: Johannes Verlag, 1972); *Das Wort und die Mystik* I and II; and *Geheimnis der Jugend*, vol. 7 of *Die Nachlasswerke* (Einsiedeln: Johannes Verlag, 1966).

23. Balthasar, *Theo-Drama* II, 14. 24. Balthasar, *Explorations in Theology* I, 204.
25. Balthasar, *Theo-Drama* III, 258. 26. Schrijver, *Le merveilleux accord*, 38.
27. See Hans Urs von Balthasar, *Two Sisters in the Spirit: Thérèse of Lisieux and Elizabeth of the*

focus not so much upon Adrienne's biography, as upon both her mission (especially as it is viewed by Balthasar) and her theology of mission, with a particular attention upon the correspondence between the two. To be sure, while one might object that my presentation of Adrienne's life and mission—precisely as coming from the perspective of Balthasar—is perhaps lacking in objectivity, one can hardly deny that beside Adrienne's own accounts of her life, which were either written or dictated in obedience to Balthasar and edited by him, the latter's accounts of her life and mission are the only written first-hand accounts that are readily available.[28]

One might hope that some Speyrian enthusiast might soon respond to Balthasar's challenge to seek additional details of her life and mission from her various friends, relatives, acquaintances, and former patients before the aforementioned are all deceased; although apparently none of them were aware of her mystical experiences nor, for that same reason, of the nature of her extensive collaboration with Balthasar. There furthermore remains the question of her "extensive correspondence" that Balthasar claimed in 1968 "will also need to be sorted through."[29] For the moment, however, most (if not all) of the numerous accounts of her life draw uniquely upon the above-named sources: those of Balthasar and those of Adrienne "exposing" herself, as it were, under his regard.[30] "I must be permitted to lay my entire soul in all

---

Trinity, trans. Donald Nichols, Anne Elizabeth Englund, and Dennis Martin (San Francisco: Ignatius Press, 1992).

28. Karen Kilby correctly intuits that Balthasar "is the channel through which she [Adrienne] is available; we have almost no access to von Speyr except through Balthasar" (*Critical Introduction*, 157). For Adrienne's accounts of her life, see *My Early Years*, trans. Mary Emily Hamilton and Dennis D. Martin (San Francisco: Ignatius Press, 1995), written in obedience to Balthasar; and *Das Geheimnis der Jugend*, dictated in obedience to Balthasar. For more explanation, see Balthasar, *Our Task*, 13–14n1; *First Glance at Adrienne von Speyr*, 17; and "General Introduction to the Posthumous Works," in Speyr, *Book of All Saints*, 17–18. For Balthasar's accounts of her life, see *First Glance at Adrienne von Speyr*; *Our Task*, 13–116; and the meticulous diaries he kept of his interactions with Adrienne, including her letters to him and his observation of the mystical experiences, which are published under her name in *Erde und Himmel* I-III.

29. Balthasar, *First Glance at Adrienne von Speyr*, 18. Adrienne's correspondence is again mentioned in ibid., 103. Barbara Albrecht confirms that "neither her family, nor the members of her community knew anything about it [her extraordinary mystical charisms]" ("Speyr (Adrienne von)" in *Dictionnaire de spiritualité ascétique et mystique, doctrine et histoire* XIV [Paris: Beauchesne, 1990], 1127). Cornelia Capol, an original member of the Johannesgemeinschaft and the personal secretary of Hans Urs von Balthasar, nonetheless admitted to me (in a private conversation) that she was aware of the mystical nature of Adrienne's experiences. She was after all responsible for typing all of the manuscripts dictated by Adrienne to Balthasar, including those which were obviously of a more mystical nature (the posthumous volumes). Capol nonetheless exercised a great deal of discretion regarding her knowledge of these events.

30. See, for example, Paola Ricci Sinoni, *Adrienne von Speyr: Storia di una esistenza teologica* (Torino: Società Editrice Internazionale, 1996); Elio Guerriero, *Hans Urs von Balthasar* (Milano: Edizioni Paoline, 1991), 109–32 and 195–200; Aidan Nichols, "Adrienne von Speyr and the Mystery of the Atone-

its depth transparent before you," Adrienne explained to Balthasar, "and you must not close yourself up (*zuschliessen*). Indeed, I must pray and contemplate before you, and that is possible only in perfect (*vollkommenen*) love."[31] It would thus be very difficult to simply dismiss the suspicion of certain of Balthasar's critics regarding his admittedly unconventional relationship with Adrienne.

What can, however, be objectively demonstrated—and what is therefore my intention to demonstrate in this chapter—is *first*, that Balthasar (however subjective or objective his regard: a judgment which certainly lies far beyond my expertise) claims to have recognized in the existence of Adrienne one in whom God's glory shown forth; *second*, that Adrienne's doctrine—which I will exposit in the pages and chapters which follow—is consistent with Balthasar's own insistence upon the unity of theology and sanctity; *third*, that there is a definite correspondence between the figure (or form, *Gestalt*)[32] of Adrienne as presented by Balthasar and her doctrine; and *finally and consequently* that Balthasar's own so-called kneeling[33] theology might well have been inspired not only by his perception of Adrienne's holiness, as measured by his own criterion of the unity of her person and mission (without, it bears repeating, judging the objectivity of his perception and the veracity of his claims) but also by what Adrienne taught in her own theology concerning the necessary unity between knowledge of God and committed service to him, between theology and holiness, between faith's object and faith's act. It is, however, most probably the correspondence between the two—Adrienne's life and her theology—that was most striking for Balthasar and most influential with regard to his own way of doing theology and thus also with

---

ment," *New Blackfriars* 73 (2007): 542–53 (543–46 are dedicated entirely to biographical material); Raymond Gawronski, *Word and Silence: Hans Urs von Balthasar and the Spiritual Encounter between East and West* (Edinburgh: T. & T. Clark, 1995), 210–13; Justin Matro, *Christian Suffering in the Spiritual Writings of Adrienne von Speyr*, 17–25; Schmitt, *The Sacrament of Confession as a "Sequela Christi" in the Writings of A. von Speyr*, 42–62; Berg, *Christian Marriage according to Adrienne von Speyr*, 19–42; Sutton, *Heaven Opens*, 1–36; Barbara Albrecht, "Speyr (Adrienne von)," as well as the following contributions to Balthasar, Chantraine, and Scola (eds.), *Adrienne von Speyr und ihre kirchliche Sendung*: Patrick Catry, "Spuren Gottes," 19–35 ("Des traces de Dieu," 19–37); Jean Léonard, "Geschmeidigkeit und Humor," 40–48 ("L'élasticité de l'esprit et humour," 45–52); and an anonymous Jesuit, "Arm um zu bereichern," 36–39 ("Pauvre pour enrichir," 38–42).

31. Speyr, *Erde und Himmel* II, no. 1595 (207).

32. For Balthasar, this is to be understood in the sense of Goethe, namely that of seeing a "'form' in its interconnected wholeness" (Balthasar, *Our Task*, 37). "What figure [*Ge-stalt*] does is attest to him who set it up [*der Stellende*]" (*The Glory of the Lord* VI, 87). See also *Epilogue*, 59; Oakes, *Pattern of Redemption*, 84–85 and 94; and Oliver Davies, "The Theological Aesthetics," in Oakes and Moss, *Cambridge Companion to Hans Urs von Balthasar*, 134.

33. Cf. Balthasar, *Explorations in Theology* I, 150 and 206; and David L. Schindler, "Preface," *Hans Urs von Balthasar: His Life and His Work*, xi–xiii.

regard to his "own" theological theory or "method," if we dare use the term with regard to his work.³⁴

A "Theodramatic" Hermeneutic: The Theologian's Openness to the Divine "Ever-More"

Although David Moss recognizes "the central task" of the theologian, as considered by Balthasar, to consist in his or her interpretation of revelation in the lives of the saints—what Moss calls the "exegesis of the saints' objective mission"—the theologian is in no way exempt from the burden of such a mission. For this "delicate task" necessarily presupposes, from Balthasar's point of view, "his or her own participation in the life of sanctity in some way."³⁵ The vocation of the theologian consists, more specifically, in "a theodramatic hermeneutic,"³⁶ characaterized by what Johann Roten identifies— and this with reference to what he perceives as the unity of Balthasar's own person and mission—as the ideal of "objective interiority" consisting in the complementary interaction between God's Word addressed in the form of a call to mission and the human person's obedient response.³⁷ By this ideal of objective interiority is meant, therefore, not simply that the theologian's personal or subjective inner state in no way "colors" or otherwise determines the divine "object" of revelation (including the "revelation" of Christ made visible in the Christian missions), but also that there is no such thing as a disengaged theology nor of a theologian who would work from a "neutral" position with regard to the faith.³⁸ Indeed, the Word of God makes demands upon its recipient who is thereby purified, as it were, of egoism and subjectivism—whence the Speyrian ideal of "anonymity"—and simultaneously commissioned to service.³⁹

---

34. "In a sense, it is almost inappropriate to speak of Balthasar in terms of method," explains Michelle A. Gonzalez ("Hans Urs von Balthasar and Contemporary Feminist Theology," 576). To do so would imply, she reasons, a systematic approach to the faith, and Balthasar profoundly objected to any "systematization." See, for example, Balthasar, *The Grain of Wheat*, 21–22; *My Work*, 105; *Explorations in Theology* IV, 333; *First Glance at Adrienne von Speyr*, 50; and (with Albus) "Spirit and Fire," 578.

35. Moss, "The Saints," 81.

36. Balthasar, *Theo-Drama* II, 91.

37. See Roten, "Hans Urs von Balthasar's Anthropology in Light of his Marian Thinking," 309. The term "objective interiority" is borrowed by Roten from Balthasar himself. See Balthasar, *My Work*, 71; cf. Speyr, *John* III, 118. The theme of the interaction between God's word and the human person's answering word will be developed in greater detail in chapter three of the present volume.

38. See Balthasar, *Explorations in Theology* I, 196 and 211. See also Matthew Sutton (*The Gate of Heaven Opens to the Trinity*, 63), who points to Adrienne's image of the burning of our subjective human word by the objective Word of God.

39. See, for example, Balthasar, *First Glance at Adrienne von Speyr*, 245. The ideal of anonymity, which will be more thoroughly addressed in chapters three and five, should be understood in terms of

This simultaneity of God's revelation and his commissioning to service is depicted with amazing clarity, as Balthasar notes, in the three stages of the dialogue between the Blessed Virgin and the angel Gabriel:

The Lord is with you, you shall bear a son (who will be called the Son of the Most High, and will rule the house of Jacob), the Holy Ghost will overshadow you (and behold, your cousin Elizabeth also …). Each successive revelation of the divine mystery is occasioned by a fresh demand on Mary and her assent to it: the Trinity emerges in the context of her obedience, her virginal state, and the New Testament contains no revelation of it that falls outside this context. Mary's attitude is, indeed, one of contemplation, but of a kind that is, at its source, one conjoined with the action of her loving response; it is a contemplation which "keeps all these things in her heart," only to bring forth what she has been given and contemplated and hand them on to the world.[40]

It is precisely this Marian attitude that Balthasar found lacking in neo-scholastic theology, which—as we have seen in chapter one—he perceived as failing to engage not only the experience of the contemporary world, but also and especially the lived encounter with the Word of God: an encounter requiring a true surrender of the self to the one (God) who is ever the first to surrender, or give, Himself.[41] Since the high Middle Ages there are few theologians, Balthasar points out, who are also saints—in contrast to the time preceding and including that era—wherein "the great saints […] were, mostly, great theologians."[42] Similar is the situation of the Christian mystic who, also since the Middle Ages, is increasingly identified, Balthasar observes, "in terms of his [or her] subjective experience of glory" so as to be considered the exception, "while the 'rule' is represented by the strictly logical and intellectualist metaphysics of the Church."[43]

This increasing decline of saintly theologians, and/or of theologians who are also mystics, accounts for the increasing separation of theology and spirituality, as Balthasar sees evidenced in the title of Henri Bremond's *La métaphysique des saints*.[44] "Do the saints," Balthasar rightly asks, "really need,

---

the Christian's increasing identification with his or her mission, such that the "personal" might be understood as "ecclesial." See also Balthasar, *Theo-Drama* III, 267; *New Elucidations*, 196; *Two Sisters in the Spirit*, 20–21; and Speyr, *John* III, 118. This ideal of anonymity is not, however, opposed to the "personal." See, for example, *John* IV, 310; and *Die katholischen Briefe* II, 170.

40. Balthasar, *Explorations in Theology* I, 197; cf. Lk 1:28, 31–33, and 35–36.

41. On the failure of scholastic theology to engage the contemporary world, see Balthasar, *Razing the Bastions*; and *My Work*, 40.

42. Balthasar, *Explorations in Theology* I, 181.

43. Balthasar, *The Glory of the Lord* I, 26.

44. Henri Bremond, *Histoire littéraire du sentiment religieux en France depuis la fin des guerres de religion jusqu'à nos jours*. Volumes VII et VIII: *La métaphysique des saints* (Paris: Bloud et Gay, 1928). See also A. N. Williams, "Mystical Theology Redux: The Pattern of Aquinas' *Summa theologica*," *Modern*

really demand a special metaphysics all their own?"⁴⁵ In thus posing the question, he does not mean to simply refute the failure of the metaphysician to address religious experience, for he also faults—as if to echo Adrienne—the tendency among the saints of modern times, which is also characteristic of this division between theology and spirituality, to describe the mode of their experience of God. The accent is typically placed more on the experiential state of the seer than on God who is thereby encountered, "for the nature of God is a subject [considered to be reserved] for the theological specialist."⁴⁶ Balthasar thus insists upon "the superiority of mission over 'psychology' so that the whole project becomes a concentric onslaught against modern subjectivism and 'personalism' in the religious sphere."⁴⁷ Of course, he does not intend thereby to propose "a devaluation of Christian interiority: all that is ever intended is to break open hollow human subjectivity to the clear fullness of the Church, which is the one Bride in whose mystery everyone who loves must participate."⁴⁸

As for these theological "specialists," they in turn are faulted by Balthasar for their apophatic (or negative) approach to theology, which he considers lifeless and—ironically enough, for such is directly contrary to their intention—delimiting of the Godhead.⁴⁹ To be sure, the important formula of the Fourth Lateran Council, "greater dissimilitude than similitude"⁵⁰ marking the analogical relation between the Creator and his creation as viewed by Balthasar, might also be understood as governing Balthasar's theological "method,"⁵¹ so profoundly influenced by the mystical intuitions of Adrienne, as we shall see. Because divine truth and life are much greater than our com-

---

Theology 13, no. 1 (January 1997): 53–74, esp. 53–56. This separation of theology and spirituality is attributed to the rise of nominalism by Servais Pinckaers; see his *The Sources of Christian Ethics*, 255–56.

45. Balthasar, *Explorations in Theology* I, 187; see also 191.

46. Ibid., 192; see also *The Glory of the Lord* V, 26. Cf. Speyr, *Das Wort und die Mystik* I, 171; and Balthasar, *First Glance at Adrienne von Speyr*, 50. Cf. Louis Bouyer, *The Christian Mystery: From Pagan Myth to Christian Mysticism*, trans. Illtyd Trethowan (Edinburgh: T. & T. Clark, 1990), 248–59. For a treatment of the role of experience in theology—particularly as it is brought to a head in the feminist debate—see Michele M. Schumacher, "Feminist Experience and Christian Experience" in Schumacher (ed.), *Women in Christ*, 169–200.

47. Balthasar, *My Work*, 31–32.

48. Ibid., 37.

49. See, for example, Balthasar, *Explorations in Theology* I, 175–76. Karen Kilby, in contrast, refers to the apophatic theology of St. Thomas Aquinas "as a kind of break against over-reaching, against the presumption of a God's eye view," which she recognizes in Balthasar's own theology (*Balthasar: A (Very) Critical Introduction*, 163). For a more general exposition of the debate between Balthasar and those of this opinion (including Kilby's criticism of this theological approach), see chapter seven and my general conclusion.

50. *DZ* 806. No less a specialist on St. Thomas than Jean-Pierre Torrell refers to this formula as "the golden rule" of theological analogy. See his *Pour nous les hommes et pour notre salut* (Paris: Cerf, 2014), 237.

51. Again, we use the term with caution, since Balthasar was uncomfortable with it.

prehension—because the content of revelation infinitely surpasses the vessel for whom it is destined—we must, Adrienne reasons, "allow for dimensions that we cannot master intellectually."[52] This accounts for the frequent reference throughout her works to such terms as "exploding" (*Sprengung*), "over-fulfillment" (*Übererfullung*), "over-flowing" (*Überborden*), and "over-stepping" (*Übersteigen*).[53] Similarly, although the Swiss mystic insists upon the validity and even the importance of striving after God by means of our inadequate human means and concepts,[54] she also warns against the temptation of limiting God's infinite word of revelation to human logic (to our "knowing better," as it were), of determining from the outset what God "can" say or do, or of analyzing and conceiving of him as we would "an earthly object."[55] "Every concept shatters against his fullness."[56]

From this perspective, Balthasar's adoption of the concept of "super-mutability"[57] in his own theology might be understood in terms of his conviction that God is always "ever greater," as he never tires of proclaiming, in unison with Adrienne. This Speyrian notion of the divine "ever-more," as it is adopted by Balthasar, does not however simply entail that the formula of "greater dissimilarity than similarity"[58] is considered as governing the "distance" (or difference) between God, as he is in himself (and in our conception of him), and thus also the distance (or difference) between what we know as change and the meaning of the term as it is analogically applied to the Trinity. While it is certainly true that God is "ever greater" with respect to our limited cognitive powers,[59] Balthasar and Adrienne also, and more

---

52. Speyr, *The Boundless God*, 24; cf. Balthasar, *Theo-Drama* II, 257. On the image of the content of revelation surpassing its vessel, see Balthasar, *A Theology of History*, 108.

53. See Balthasar, "Das literarische Werk Adriennes von Speyr" in Hans Urs von Balthasar Stiftung (ed.), *Adrienne von Speyr und ihre spirituelle Theologie. Symposium zu ihrem 100. Geburtstag* (Einsiedeln: Johannes Verlag, 2002), 130.

54. See, for example, Speyr, *World of Prayer*, 35. For Balthasar's accord with this principle, see *Explorations in Theology* I, 176; and *The Glory of the Lord*, 35–36.

55. Speyr, *John* I, 41; see also *Das Wort und die Mystik* I, 43. Cf. Balthasar, *First Glance at Adrienne von Speyr*, 50. Adrienne encourages us to proceed beyond "the finitude that we ourselves set to our insight and love," when, in the experience of limitations, we utter the word "impossible" (see Speyr, *Der Mensch vor Gott*, 12). This insight will be further developed in chapter three within the context of the "expansion" of human nature by grace.

56. Balthasar, *First Glance at Adrienne von Speyr*, 62. The Lord, after all, does not mediate concepts, Adrienne reasons, "but life" (Speyr, *John* III, 101).

57. By this term, Gerard O'Hanlon explains with respect to Balthasar's theology, is meant "that perfection and fullness of free inter-personal love, intrinsic to which are the receptivity of mutual exchange and that mysterious ontological comparative, the ever-more of self-giving" (Gerard O'Hanlon, *The Immutability of God in the Theology of Hans Urs von Balthasar* [Cambridge: Cambridge University Press, 1990], 169).

58. *DZ* 806.

59. See Speyr, *John* II, 79; *Handmaid of the Lord*, 94–97; and Balthasar, *Theo-Drama* II, 119.

fundamentally, hold to the teaching that God is "'ever-greater' even [with respect] to himself."[60]

By this idea (that God is "ever-greater to himself") is meant, in turn, not simply that God's "uniqueness embraces every kind of variety and difference" or that he is "greater than number and more than quantity."[61] Nor can we limit the meaning of the divine "ever more" to the fact that God is "utterly incomprehensible, intangible, colorless, timeless, forever beyond our grasp":[62] intuitions that might typify the kind of negative (apophatic) theology criticized by Balthasar as contradicting Christian revelation.[63] It also, and more profoundly, means that divine life is characterized by what he calls "superabundant vitality."[64]

Only the comparative, Adrienne and Balthasar claim—in contrast to the superlative, as in the scholastic formulation of God as the "highest good" or as "absolute immutability"—can capture the supremely dynamic nature of divine life.[65] Indeed, Trinitarian unity is, as Adrienne would have it, "never a finished fact, but always the miracle that fulfills itself and enriches itself beyond all expectation;"[66] for God is "constantly begetting in love the ever-greater in himself." The Father and Son thus give constant witness to "their own ever-more,"[67] while the Holy Spirit is "the eternal superabundance" in person, the "ever more, ever greater—the fountain of life."[68] Every question about God will therefore "always call forth the answer: I am greater. [...] I am more."[69]

This divine comparative has, in turn, particular consequences for the theologian, whose task is viewed by Balthasar as far more significant that that of simply, automatically, or mechanically proceeding from given premises of faith (namely, the Church's dogmas) in order to draw conclusions therefrom. Rather, "every step" of the theologian should be taken, Balthasar maintains,

---

60. Balthasar, *Theo-Drama* V, 78; cf. Speyr, *John* IV, 189. "Like John and Ignatius, like Anselm and the Greek Fathers, Adrienne is overwhelmed and as though possessed by the thought that God is the 'ever greater,'" Balthasar explains (*First Glance at Adreinne von Speyr*, 62).

61. Speyr, *John* I, 40.

62. Ibid., 17.

63. See, for example, Balthasar, *Explorations in Theology* I, 175–76.

64. Balthasar, *Theo-Drama* V, 79.

65. See ibid., 78; and *Unless You Become Like This Child*, trans. Erasmo Leiva-Merikakis (San Francisco: Ignatius Press, 1991), 46. This comparative is, however—Adrienne insists in a passage to which Balthasar refers in his own argument—"an eternal superlative," for God (it bears repeating) "is ever-greater" (Speyr, *John* I, 308). On the dynamic nature of the divine life, see, for example, Speyr, *John* II, 292.

66. Speyr, *John* II, 292.

67. Speyr, *Korinther* I, 412–13; cf. Balthasar, *Theo-Drama* V, 82n6.

68. Speyr, *John* I, 26. Balthasar refers to this passage in *Theo-Drama* V, 78.

69. Speyr, *John* I, 308.

"as a direct hearing and obeying of the living Spirit of Jesus Christ."[70] "True theology, the theology of the saints, with the central doctrines of revelation always in view, inquires, in a spirit of obedience and reverence, what processes of human thought, what modes of approach are best fitted to bring out the meaning of what has been revealed. That meaning does not involve teaching anything occult or abstruse, but bringing men [and women] and their whole existence, intellectual as well as spiritual, into closer relation with God."[71]

Similarly, Adrienne suggests—in an insight suited for every Christian, but perhaps most especially for the theologian—that the only way to appropriately approach the mystery of the divine Trinity is from within: "No mystery of the Trinity is so hidden in God that it is unnecessary to the Christian, so that he is absolved from trying to understand it: He is involved in it and must relate it to his life."[72] This means, more specifically, that while God's Word cannot be measured by human understanding, it does *measure us*: not so much by judging our weaknesses, as by pushing us beyond the limits that we set—in virtue most especially of our sin—to his power over our lives.[73] This power, as we shall see in chapter three, "stretches" our natural capacities and "expands" our consent so that God might accomplish his saving will in us and through us.

Faith: A Participation in the Revelatory Disposition of Christ

This expansion of the Christian's receptivity vis-à-vis God's Word occurs, Balthasar teaches, by way of the Christian's participation in the universal mission of Christ—a theme which will be treated more thoroughly in the following chapter—whereby he or she also participates in his revelatory function. The Christian (and thus also, in the case at hand, the Christian theologian) is called, more specifically, to receive Christ as Christ receives the Father; to obey Christ as Christ obeys the Father, to be transparent to Christ as Christ is transparent to the Father, and to surrender his or her life to Christ as he surrenders himself to the Father. This likeness of the Christian to Christ as regards the latter's relation to the Father is already apparent in Balthasar's presentation of the saints as "the authentic interpreters of theo-

---

70. Balthasar, *A Theology of History*, 108.
71. Balthasar, *Explorations in Theology* I, 196.
72. Speyr, *World of Prayer*, 46–47; cf. Balthasar, *Explorations in Theology* III, 44; and Mark McIntosh, *Christology from Within*.
73. On the impossibility of measuring God's word by our understanding, see for example, Speyr, *John* III, 164. On the setting of limits due to sin, see Speyr, *Wort und die Mystik* I, 42.

drama," as, that is to say, those who are called to enlighten us "on the inner reality of Christ."[74] It is also present in the typically Speyrian idea of "excessive demand" (*Überforderung*), which is integrated into Balthasar's work within the context of the mission wherein one is personally charged "*to give form and figure* to the 'ever greater' God."[75]

This task of giving form to God implies more specifically the act of rendering Him present—whence the theological idea of "representation" (*Stellvertretung*)—by putting oneself at his service as a docile instrument.[76] This role of representation, in turn, supposes a sort of "expropriation" of the subject in virtue of which he or she is personalized in his or her personal mission, as shall be developed more thoroughly in the following chapter. For "everything humanly personal is in some way finite" and must, Adrienne teaches, be expanded into the "transpersonalness" of divine love, so as also to be most unique.[77] In virtue of the Christian's fidelity to his or her mission, in other words, he or she may be said to take in, or take to heart, the Word of God, so as, in turn, to be taken in by the Word and employed for his purposes. Or, as Balthasar would have it, the Christian must be "incorporated" into the dogma of the Incarnation "down to the very foundation of his [or her] self," in his or her "innermost disposition," and "in every fiber and vibration of his [or her] sensibility."[78]

If, in fact, even in human communication the speaker may be said to be received by his listener, the Word of God should, Adrienne reasons, be so received by the Christian as to remain within him or her. This indwelling of the Word within the Christian causes, in turn, his or her incorporation into this same Word, that is to say, into the Lord himself.[79] "Whoever sees me ought

---

74. Balthasar, *Theo-Drama* II, 14; ibid., *Explorations in Theology* I, 204. See also Moss, "The Saints," 81–82.

75. Schrijver, *Le merveilleux accord*, 271. On the notion of excessive demand, see for example Speyr, *Mary in the Redemption*, 100; *They Followed His Call: Vocation and Asceticism*, trans. Erasmo Leiva-Merikakis (San Francisco: Ignatius Press, 1986), 16; and Balthasar, *First Glance at Adrienne von Speyr*, 45. This theme will also be developed more thoroughly in chapter three in our treatment of "The Expansion of the Christian's Consent to the 'Proportion' of God's Surrender."

76. See, for example, Balthasar, *Explorations in Theology* III, 45; *Theo-Logic* I, 237; and Speyr, *Light and Images*, 47. For the problems arising from this concept of representation within the context of the redemptive mysteries, see chapter five.

77. Adrienne von Speyr, *John IV: The Birth of the Church. Meditations on John 18–21*, trans. David Kipp (San Francisco: Ignatius Press, 1991), 356. For a development of the same in Balthasar's theology, see Christophe Potworowski, "Christian Experience in Hans Urs von Balthasar." On the uniqueness of one who is "expanded" to the dimensions of the mission, see for example Balthasar, *Theo-Drama* II, 270. See also Speyr, *John* IV, 310; *They Followed His Call*, 68–69; and *Mary in the Redemption*, 36–37.

78. Balthasar, *The Glory of the Lord* I, 254.

79. See Speyr, *John* I, 103; and *John* III, 342. On the image of the listener "receiving" the speaker and his word, see Speyr, *Theologie der Geschlechter*, 99.

by rights to see the Lord in me. He ought to see, not that I have received the Lord, but that I am one who has been received by the Lord."[80] Adrienne suggests that we ought, therefore, to understand ourselves as living "not in ourselves but in his word, the word in which we are created,"[81] and this by giving over even our powers to Christ to dispose of as he will. Indeed, the Lord takes possession of whatever 'space' the believer grants him, Adrienne explains, and he "will not rest until the Father's entire word [that is to say, the Son himself] has been introduced there."[82] It follows that the disciple of Christ can take no time off from hearing the Word so as "to become inebriated with the music of one's own words or to engage in a conversation just for the sake of talking."[83]

In precisely this way of remaining open for the Word, the Christian participates in Christ's mission of giving expression, or more correctly said to be the expression, or "the definitive 'interpretation' (Jn 1:18)" of God the Father.[84] Because even in eternity the Son is "the self-enunciation and self-revelation of the Father,"[85] what he reveals to us is not so much his own divine nature as the person of the Father. Similarly, Adrienne presents Christ as the Father's Word and witness, the expression of his glory, "the reality and the proof of what has been said and testified,"[86] and all of this in virtue of his perfect "transparency,"[87] or receptivity, vis-à-vis the Father. He is the truth, because he is obedient.[88] It follows from this logic that the incarnate Son's mission of revealing—giving form to and glorifying—the Father must not be understood as his own activity but rather, and in accord with his (Christ's) own affirmation, the "activity of the Father in him, of the Father who expresses and glorifies himself in the Son's form and word."[89] This in turn means that

---

80. Speyr, *John* I, 102.
81. Ibid., 36; cf. Balthasar, *Theo-Logic* I, 237. Similarly, Adrienne reasons that because Christ is "the Word, that makes us Christians," he is our "language of origin [*unsere Ursprache*]." "All of our remaining words and deeds must obtain their final and proper sense in him" (Speyr, *Das Wort und die Mystik* II, 42).
82. Speyr, *John* III, 321. On the identification of the Word and the Son, see ibid., 342.
83. Speyr, *They Followed His Call*, 60.
84. Balthasar, *Theo-Drama* III, 506; cf. *The Glory of the Lord* I, 612; and *Epilogue*, 112–13.
85. Balthasar, "God is His Own Exegete," *Communio* 4 (1986), 283. In a similar manner, Adrienne reasons that because "the Son is the Word of the Father, we hear the Father, too, in him" (*John* II, 372). See also Balthasar, *Theo-Logic* II, 160–61; *The Christian State of Life*, 82; and *The Glory of the Lord* I, 29.
86. Speyr, *John* III, 89.
87. For example, see ibid., 363: "He is pure openness, absolute mediation." See also Balthasar, *Theo-Logic* III, 443.
88. Cf. Speyr, *Das Buch von Gehorsam*, 39.
89. Balthasar, *The Glory of the Lord* I, 612. Balthasar makes reference to a whole series of Johannine texts to point out the extent to which Christ is dependent upon the Father and obedient to him. See, for example, Jn 5:19, 30; 6:38; 7:17; 12:49; 14:10; and 17:18. Cf. Balthasar, *A Theology of History*, 29–30; *The Glory of the Lord* I, 612–13; and *Theo-Logic* III, 443.

the Son's own "activity" (even in eternity) is more profoundly a willed (and in this sense active) "passivity," or what Balthasar calls a "passive *actio*" in relation to the Father's "active *actio*."[90] This is a letting go or a letting be, a receptivity, an availability, a transparency, an obedience, a surrender, a "making space." "In the one who makes space, in his whole conduct, one can see what fills him: the love of the Father. And the act of making space can itself be seen as love for the Father."[91]

Precisely as such—as surrendering himself to the Father, as obediently making himself available for the Father's action—Adrienne recognizes the Lord as the "prototype of faith." More specifically, in his relationship to the Father as the obedient, ever-available, fully surrendered Son, "he takes over the whole truth of the Father—not simply theoretically, but by living it, indeed by *being* it." Adrienne thus admits no "distance" between his acknowledging the Father's truth and his living it as his own, and it is precisely in "this full certainty between his receiving the Father's truth and living the truth," that "the Son is the archetype of faith."[92]

Not surprisingly, then, the unity of the Christian's life and mission—not unlike the unity of reception and progress, faith and knowledge—must, Balthasar and Adrienne teach in unison, be grounded in the very "self surrender of God in the attitude of Christ, who became obedient even unto death."[93] This means, more specifically, that Christ's own disposition is not merely the object of revelation; it is also actually given—precisely as the "prototype" of faith—to the Christian to have as his own (disposition = virtue), assuming that he or she is receptive of this (participated) receptivity. Communicated within the one self-revelation of God in Christ Jesus, in other words, is both the objective content of faith (*Glaubenslehre*) and the subjective disposition of faith (*Glaubenshaltung*), whereby the one is received in the other.[94] By

---

90. See Balthasar, *Theo-Drama* V, 86, where extensive reference to Adrienne's work is apparent.

91. Balthasar, *The Glory of the Lord* VII, 291; see also 248.

92. Speyr, *John* III, 90. This might well be the origin of the seemingly original insight of Balthasar expressed in his "*Fides Christi*: An Essay on the Consciousness of Christ," in *Explorations in Theology* II, 43–79; and *My Work*, 60–61. See also Donneaud, "Hans Urs von Balthasar contre saint Thomas d'Aquin sur la foi du Christ."

93. Balthasar, "Introduction," to Speyr, *Das Wort und die Mystik* I, 13. See also Balthasar, *Mysterium Paschale*, 90–91; *Theo-Drama* III, 225; *The Glory of the Lord* I, 479; *The Christian State of Life*, 37; and *A Theology of History*, 29–40. Cf. Ignace de la Potterie, *La vérité dans Saint Jean II: Le croyant et la vérité* (Rome: Biblical Institute Press, 1977), 769–70; and Michael Waldstein, "The Analogy of Mission and Obedience: A Central Point in the Relation between *Theologia* and *Oikonomia* in St. Thomas Aquinas's *Commentary on John*" in Michael Dauphinais and Matthew Levering (eds.), *Reading John with St. Thomas Aquinas: Theological Exegesis and Speculative Theology* (Washington, D.C.: The Catholic University of America Press, 2005), 92–112.

94. See, for example, Balthasar, *New Elucidations*, 44; and "*Fides Christi*: An Essay on the Consciousness of Christ."

"faith" is thus meant, as the *Catechism* teaches, both that which is received ("that which is contained in the word of God [...] which the Church proposes for belief as divinely revealed") and the means whereby it is received ("a personal adherence of the whole man to God who reveals himself").[95] And in both instances, faith remains, as Balthasar and Adrienne see it, a gift originating in the divine life of the Trinity and leading us into this life.[96]

If, in fact, we are to grasp God's revelation, we must, Balthasar explains, be "admitted to the sphere of the Holy Spirit, that holy intimacy between Father and Son; we must have been granted a share in the divine Spirit."[97] The Lord alone has received the Spirit "without measure" (cf. Jn 3:34) and this "ever more" is given to us along with the gift of faith, Adrienne teaches.[98] This, in turn, requires of us "the one thing necessary" (cf. Lk 10:42): "His answer can only be," Balthasar explains in an insight which is certainly Speyrian at the outset, "to permit God to be God in himself, to give God all the space to which he lays claim for his love."[99]

The only adequate response of the human person to the overwhelming power of God's word is, in other words, that of Christian readiness and availability or, as we saw in our introduction, that properly Trinitarian "disposition" of self-gift in the form of surrender. Contrary to our natural human tendency to let our light shine, to make our mark in the world, and to manifest our own personalities, we are thereby challenged by Adrienne's biblically inspired insight (cf. Jn 1:6–8) and in imitation of Christ, to "hide our light" in the Father, so that *he* might become our light. Indeed, Adrienne observes that it is precisely by concealing his light "in the Father" that Christ reveals both the Father and himself to the world; for this is precisely how he reveals his love for the Father, which is the meaning of his entire life, mission, and person.[100] It follows that we ought not to compel God to shed his light into our obscurity, "but allow his love to create clarity in us." Rather than suppose

---

95. *The Catechism of the Catholic Church*, nos. 176 and 182. Cf. Balthasar, *Prayer*, trans. Graham Harrison (San Francisco: Ignatius Press, 1986), 35–36, where these two dimensions of faith are presented as "an act and its content and object" or as "a holding as true and what is held-as-true."

96. See Speyr, *Korinther* I, 324. Cf. *The Catechism of the Catholic Church*, no. 179. On faith as originating within the Trinity, see Speyr, *World of Prayer*, 33–34; *John* III, 90; and Balthasar, *Theo-Drama* V, 97.

97. Balthasar, *Theo-Drama* III, 506; cf. Speyr, *Die katholischen Briefe* II, 160: "love allows itself to be recognized only by love," whence the importance of the theological virtues (faith, hope, and love), which Adrienne presents as "our participation in the relationship between the Father and the Son" (*John* III, 89–90).

98. Speyr, *Das Wort und die Mystik* II, 26.

99. Balthasar, *Explorations in Theology* III, 45.

100. See Speyr, *John* I, 69; *John* II, 102; *Theologie der Geschlechter*, 114; cf. Balthasar, *Explorations in Theology* I, 227–40; and *Love Alone Is Credible*, esp. 109–10.

that God should receive us as we are, Adrienne encourages us to "let happen" so as "not to be, but to become."[101]

Such, more specifically is the movement of making room within oneself for the whole of Christ and the Church, of being ready and available for God: a disposition which is also captured by the terms of Christological obedience or transparency, Ignatian indifference, the Marian attitude of "letting happen [*Geschehenlassen*]," the theological counsels of poverty, chastity, and obedience, and the particularly Speyrian stance of confession.[102] Such more fundamentally still is the human person's participation in the obedience of the Son, who is always perfectly transparent to the Father, even and especially on the Cross when he no longer perceives the Father.[103] This, we insist, supposes the work of the Spirit, whom Adrienne presents as both the objective gift of God and "the subject within our subject that receives him." In him, "we are open to God, acknowledge God and confess to God."[104] While it is the Son who offers us his body and word in the Eucharist, for example, Adrienne acknowledges "a sort of margin [*Spanne*]" between these saving graces and their effect (*Wirkung*) in us which is filled by the Spirit.[105]

Adrienne, the Mystic: Balthasar's Model "Theologian"

This same phenomenon of faith's twofold dimension is at the heart of Adrienne's mystical theory, for the emphasis here is upon the objective character of mysticism's content in virtue of which the subjective character of the mystic—his or her inner disposition of availability or inner transparency—is judged as important. Truth "acts with objectivity," Adrienne teaches, "free from any deceptive wrappings of subjective life. This naked objectivity affords the only possible access to true life."[106]

---

101. Speyr, *Theologie der Geschlechter*, 70. Cf. Balthasar, *Theo-Drama* V, 512.

102. On the Speyrian idea of "letting happen," see Jacques Servais, "The *Ressourcement* of Contemporary Spirituality under the Guidance of Adrienne von Speyr and Hans Urs von Balthasar." On the attitude implied by the vows, see Balthasar, "Adriennes Charisma," 176–77. As for the confessional stance, by this is meant the "nakedness" of the soul before God in imitation of Christ's nakedness before the Father on the Cross as he "confessed" the sins of the world. See Balthasar, *Our Task*, 27 and 63; *First Glance at Adrienne von Speyr*, 55–56, 72, 73, and 173; "Adrienne von Speyr et le sacrament de penitence," *Nouvelle revue théologique* 107 (1985): 394–440; Speyr, *Confession*, esp. 23; Georg Bätzing, "Homesickness for God: Adrienne von Speyr's *Confession*," *Communio* 31 (2004): 548–56; and Schmitt, *The Sacrament of Confession as a "Sequela Christi" in the Writings of A. von Speyr*.

103. See Speyr, *Wort und Mystik* I, 213; and *Das Buch vom Gehorsam*, 51–52; cf. Balthasar, *Theo-Drama* V, 123. For a development of the idea of Christ as transparent to the Father on the Cross, see chapter five of this volume.

104. Speyr, *John* I, 63 (see also 27); and *World of Prayer*, 282. Cf. Balthasar, *The Threefold Garland*, 30; and *Theo-Logic* III, 307–18.

105. Speyr, *Das Wort und die Mystik* II, 528.

106. Speyr, *John* III, 118.

The subjective character of the Christian is, on the other hand, what permits (or prohibits) a faithful, or "adequate," transmission of the divine message or content: that which assures (or hinders) true objectivity. Hence mysticism is, Adrienne insists, "always an expression of faith; it can only take place within faith. Faith loses its abstract, speculative character in order to take into itself an element of experience of divine reality. But one cannot use vision in order to take a rest from faith."[107] Indeed, even the most extraordinary experience of faith is at the service of faith's knowledge.[108]

Knowledge of God, in turn, grows in union with personal faith, Adrienne insists, "always, however, and solely *in him*, in his truth, which has an unshakable objectivity; the reception determines the progress but the progress on this walk, even today, never wanders from the reception."[109] And if this is true of the experience of faith in general, all the more is it true of mysticism: "the place of the mystic's union with God always lies in God himself; the human person only appears to be the place of the encounter."[110]

Far from a study of the psychological state of the mystic, Adrienne's presentation of the subjective aspect of mysticism is thus formulated in terms of obedience: "pure availability [*Verfügbarkeit*] for God."[111] This important disposition is nonetheless understood as a divine gift, perfective of the subject and corresponding to his or her objective charisma (that of mysticism, in this case). This is not to say that it is reserved for mystics, for the perfection of life to which all are called is contained therein. Balthasar nonetheless suggests that the authenticity of any mysticism might be tested thereby. Indeed, mysticism does not primarily "concern the difference of subjectivity, temperament and character," he explains, "but the grace of Christian instrumentality [*Werkzeuglichkeit*] in relation to the God-given content."[112]

---

107. Speyr, *World of Prayer*, 36; see also *Das Wort und die Mystik* I, 185. In his foreword to Adrienne's *My Early Years* (11), Balthasar explains that she "never made anything at all out of her supernatural experiences. Hence, when she comments on the theory of mysticism," for example, "one finds that she made no effective distinction between specifically mystical vision and experiences and the normal 'vision' of the mysteries of faith granted by grace and the indwelling Holy Spirit to anyone with living faith." See also Balthasar's foreword to Speyr, *Das Wort und die Mystik* I, 13.

108. See Balthasar, "Das literarische Werk Adriennes von Speyr," 127.

109. Speyr, *The Letter to the Colossians*, 71. Similar is the union of love and knowledge: love is "the way to God's omniscience," which in turn "is also a path to his love" (Speyr, *Three Women and the Lord*, 22).

110. Speyr, *Das Wort und die Mystik* I, 18. See also Balthasar's introduction to Speyr, *Kreuz und Hölle* I, 11. Extraordinary as this might seem, such is, in fact, the meaning of the divine filiation of the Christian: his or her "entrance" into the communion of persons, so as to live more in God than in him- or herself.

111. Balthasar's foreword to Speyr, *Das Wort und die Mystik* I, 12. To be sure, Adrienne's treatment of mysticism goes beyond the typical focus upon the subjective dimension of faith experience to include the objective content of the same. Hence her significant work on mysticism, *Das Wort und die Mystik*, is presented in two parts: I, *Subjektive Mystik*, and II, *Objektive Mystik*. See also Balthasar, *First Glance at Adrienne von Speyr*, 36 and 88.

112. See Balthasar's foreword to Speyr, *Das Wort und die Mystik* I, 13.

As is characteristic of the Christian life in general, gift encounters gift. To the one who lacks the strength of assent to God's call, for example, it is given to him or her along with the call, Adrienne teaches: "perhaps in a humbling of the person, who now knows that even his Yes has been taken over by God; perhaps, too, in a simple taking over of the answer, unknown even to the person."[113] In the particular case of mysticism, the objective charisma meets the subjective charisma, not so much as two instances in time, but as a single divinely-ordained reality: the Word of God who gives himself to be received into the open (Marian) heart. Marian consent is thus intelligible within this perspective only as "a secondary response to the primary word of God."[114]

It is precisely in light of this criterion of faith that Balthasar thinks it important that Adrienne's theology be perceived not only as a mystical one, but also as an existential (or lived) one: a theology which does not so much draw from her life experience as confirm it. Or, to put it in other terms, the same truth, which Balthasar presents as the motivating force of her life—Christ himself who is "the whole truth of the Father"[115]—is likewise at the heart of her theology. The Swiss theologian even seems to imply that the manner in which Adrienne approaches the mysteries of faith—that is, her own faith commitment—is for a serious, even scientific, study of her works of as much importance as her exposition of those mysteries.[116] In both, there emerges the central aspect of faith, by which is understood a committed engagement, a personal adherence to what is professed, a living relationship to Christ who is "the full truth, the fullness of truth" such that every "partial truth encountered in the world exists only if it has a place within his truth and is capable of opening to his truth, of rising to his truth."[117]

Balthasar observes, in other words—precisely in his united role as Adrienne's spiritual director and confessor, on the one hand, and as the editor of her works, on the other—a certain correspondence between the subjective and objective dimensions of her faith, between, that is to say, her faith's act and its content. "Man is in the truth," Balthasar explains in his effort to describe the unity between Adrienne's professional and contemplative life, "if being open himself he lives in the truth of God which has been opened and given over to him."

---

113. Speyr, *They Followed His Call*, 17.
114. Balthasar, *First Glance at Adrienne von Speyr*, 57.
115. Speyr, *John* III, 89.
116. See, for example, Balthasar, "Adriennes Charisma," 173.
117. Speyr, *John* III, 89–90. Cf. Pope John Paul II, *Veritatis Splendor*, no. 88.

That is above all the truth of the divine love, or, of the divine Trinity, which is the same thing. What Paul calls '*en Christô*,' existing in the sphere of Christ's being and life, is living with Christ in the triune love, walking with Christ on the paths between Father and Son in the Holy Spirit. With that, every artificially erected barrier between heaven and earth, this life and the life to come, collapses, something that Paul also says expressly: Christ has 'made both [worlds] into one and broken down the barrier of the dividing wall by destroying the enmity in his flesh' (Eph 2:14).[118]

Herein is described the relation between the objective and subjective elements of Adrienne's personal faith in the form of ready availability, on the one hand, and the truth, or content, of faith, on the other.[119] Indeed, what Balthasar considers as Adrienne's most "extraordinary" charisma—the "objective" gift of prophecy, that is to say, the "power to clearly pronounce in human concepts and words what God wills to reveal to her of his mysteries"[120]—might be characterized by a corresponding gift perfecting her character, whereby this primary gift is fruitful in her. The prophetic charism whereby Adrienne was—as Balthasar attests—"inspired from above and from within"[121] presupposed, in other words, what she herself considered the very "essence" of inspiration: namely, the "laying of everything in God [*In-Gott Hineinlegen*], so as to "allow God to think within oneself," or, more specifically, to "think from God and together with him."[122]

This act of allowing God to act within oneself supposes, in turn, the primary gift of obedient availability, or a "confessional attitude": a sort of transparency before God whereby one is so focused upon the Lord as to have forgotten oneself, as it were.[123] Hence, Balthasar is able to acknowledge as "the greatest gift of grace" bestowed on Adrienne her "special, anonymous, total availability,"[124] without thereby contradicting his earlier statement that her most "extraordinary" charisma was the "objective" gift of prophecy. After all, the one presupposes the other. It is in this sense that Balthasar dares to argue:

---

118. Balthasar, *First Glance at Adrienne von Speyr*, 245–46. Similarly: "Essentially, therefore, there is a simultaneous growth and integration of faith and experience, but in such a way that, while faith becomes experience by being lived, whatever is experienced in the Christian life acquires a faith-quality" (Balthasar, *The Office of Peter*, 299).

119. For a more thorough treatment of this theme, see Schumacher, "Feminist Experience and Christian Experience," esp. 184–96.

120. Balthasar, "Le charisme d'Adrienne," 188.

121. Balthasar's introduction to Balthasar, Chantraine, and Scola, *Adrienne von Speyr une ihre kirchliche Sendung*, 14; cf. Balthasar, *The Glory of the Lord* VII, 410.

122. Speyr, *Bereitschaft*, 68. This perhaps explains what she means when she says: "I was prayed [*Ich wurde gebetet*]" (Speyr, *Die Schöpfung*, 60).

123. See, for example, Balthasar, *First Glance at Adrienne von Speyr*, 170. On the confessional attitude as one of transparency, see ibid., 55–56 and 72; and Balthasar, *Our Task*, 27.

124. Balthasar, *First Glance at Adrienne von Speyr*, 72.

precisely because Adrienne lives such transparency before God—because he esteems that in her "service looks strait ahead to the [God-given] task"[125]—she is consequently suited, as it were, to "mediate" his truth in the form of her mystical insights. So "transparent" is Adrienne, as judged by Balthasar—so objective does he esteem her share in the mission of Christ—that the content of her dictations was, as he reports, immediately removed from her consciousness, and it would never have occurred to her, he claims, to go back and read any of them. This transparency is in no way clouded by the fact that she was able, as Balthasar reports, to engage in banal discussions during the dictations. Nor, on the other hand, could there be any question of disrupting her ordinary daily life and responsibilities—far less of escaping them—in order to fulfill her mystical mission.[126]

It is, on the other hand, in keeping with Adrienne's theological perspective that too much attention upon one's self, even upon one's own experiences of faith, might obscure the transmission of the divine message, which is given for that purpose (transmission). It is thus not surprising that Adrienne does not—except under strict obedience, Balthasar claims—write of her life and experiences, and it would in fact be very difficult to recognize in her existential theology any sort of introspection or reflection upon her own state before God. This too accords with her theological perspective, for she argues that when God "gives us a consciousness of ourselves, it is a consciousness through him, which is not caused by us but originates out of the grace that he places within us."[127] So objective is her work—again, as esteemed by Balthasar, although here room might be granted for the reader's own judgement—that Balthasar describes her personality "with her spontaneity and humor" as "only indirectly" implicated therein.[128] Similarly, he describes her work as distinct from that of many other mystics by its "generous sobriety," knowing "no exaltation [and] no subjective surge."[129]

It is perhaps not surprising, therefore, that he should claim that "the mystical," which is typically characterized "as unusual, original, personal," is simply not to be found in Adrienne's works.[130] This does not, however, pre-

---

125. Ibid., 53.
126. See Speyr, *Das Wort und die Mystik* I, 174.
127. Ibid., 173.
128. Balthasar, "Das literarische Werk Adrienne's von Speyr," 126.
129. Balthasar, "Le charisme d'Adrienne," 190. Oddly, this paragraph does not appear in the German edition.
130. See Balthasar's introduction to Speyr, *Das Wort und die Mystik* I, 13. This conviction stands in contrast to that of Fergus Kerr, for example, who holds that her four-volume commentary on the Gospel of John "betray[s] what look like cultural preconceptions and even personal obsessions" (Fergus Kerr, "Adrienne von Speyr and Hans Urs von Balthasar," *New Blackfriars* 79, no. 923 [1998]: 29).

clude that the images she uses are very personally colored. Those borrowed from her medical profession are, for example, particularly apparent, as in her description of blood in her commentary of John's Gospel.[131] The first-time reader of her *Theologie der Geschlechter* (Theology of the Sexes), to cite another example, might be taken aback by her often very candid presentation of the human body and the sexual sphere.[132] From this too is apparent her own experience of married life.[133] Similarly, her description of the woman of Apocalypse 12, about to give birth, is marked by her own expertise and experience in the delivery room (this time only professionally, since she miscarried all of the children whom she conceived).[134]

From these examples it is perhaps evident that far from obscuring the question of her distinct theological contribution, her unique—indeed extraordinary[135]—religious experiences, actually clarify it by enabling her to transcend what is subjective without destroying what is personal. It is, in fact, "precisely the personal element" in Adrienne's work, which Balthasar thinks "clearly reveals the stamp of her character, her way of thinking and expressing herself, or even of translating her inspiration—if such can be presupposed—into human words," which he also believes "clearly proves that the birth of these commentaries could only have taken place in an atmosphere of contemplative prayer."[136]

---

131. See, for example, *John* II, 67.

132. On the other hand, it is perhaps worth noting that, as Balthasar documents: "Despite the very crude and summary explanation of sexual intercourse which had been given in Leysin, even in medical school (where two good friends protected her from anything indecent) she did not really know much about the male organs, even though for a time she frequently had to fit men with catheters, which each time involved taking hold of the male organ. This [...] made not the slightest impression on her" (Balthasar, *Our Task*, 32, with reference to *Erde und Himmel* II, no. 1699 [274]).

133. Following the sudden death in 1934 of her first husband, the history professor and widower Emil Dürr, Adrienne married Werner Kaegi, who took over Dürr's chair at the University of Basel. Apparently (Balthasar tells us) the second marriage was never consummated. On her marriages, see Balthasar, *Our Task*, 30n38; and *First Glance at Adrienne von Speyr*, 28–30.

134. The scene is reported in Balthasar, *First Glance at Adrienne von Speyr*, 90–94. It is perhaps worth noting that she assumed the responsibility of mothering the two children of her first husband, whom she married after the death of his first wife, and she did experience a sort of mystical "pregnancy," which Balthasar describes in his diary, published under Adrienne's name as Speyr, *Erde und Himmel* II, no. 1645 (245).

135. Adrienne's extraordinary experiences are described by Balthasar in *First Glance at Adrienne von Speyr* (33–47) as the graces of visions, "transports," sudden, inexplicable cures; the experience of the passion of Christ every year during Holy Week, including her unusual experience of Holy Saturday, namely, Christ's descent into hell; the exterior stigmatization; and a series of mystical deaths. In his contribution to the Roman colloquium, *La mission ecclésiale d'Adrienne von Speyr*, Balthasar adds: emissions of light, encounters with the devil, and exorcisms ("Le charisme d'Adrienne," 190). Again, this paragraph is missing from the (presumably original) German version: "Adriennes Charisma." This absence is perhaps proof of how seriously he took what he wrote in the French edition: "But all of that [these extraordinary phenomena] had for her, and should likewise have for us, only secondary importance" ("Le charisme d'Adrienne," 190).

136. Balthasar, *First Glance at Adrienne von Speyr*, 97–98.

It is, furthermore, an important element of her own theory of biblical mysticism that each author received an inspiration, adapted to his personality, whereby he transmitted a unique aspect of the divine truth. Because the prophets "were men with their own character and personality," Adrienne reasons that the message that they were given to mediate "had to bear something of their personal character. This personal moment neither obscured nor concealed the message. Instead, God made use of it in order to make himself intelligible to men through men."[137]

This adaptation of the prophetic inspiration to the personality of the prophet ought not, however, to obscure the fact that the personal is—in Adrienne's life as in her teaching—judged by Balthasar as ecclesial: "whatever Adrienne experienced subjectively was meant," Balthasar maintains, "to bear objective, theological, and spiritual fruit for the Church as a whole. [...] All the various aspects of her charism are directed concentrically at a deeper interpretation of revelation."[138] On the other hand—and with this we stress again the personal, or subjective, element of her gift—"Adrienne's special, anonymous, total availability," which Balthasar recognizes as an outstanding grace, as indeed the "greatest" of the graces bestowed on her, is that which he likewise recognizes as enabling her "to put herself in the place of individual saints or other faithful in order to see and describe their prayer, their whole attitude before God, from this interior viewpoint."[139] This "knowledge of souls"[140] required, Balthasar believed, that her own soul "had to be comparable to a fully blank photographic plate, free for all that God willed to reveal to her, and through her, to us also."[141]

Far from a mere subjective state of consciousness, this extraordinary gift of availability, or surrender, is—Balthasar leads us to believe—that from which emerges the original Speyrian exposition of the communion of saints: the free exchange of all that is personal—not excluding the experience of prayer—among those who are given to Christ for the good of the Church. One might, in fact, argue that it is precisely because the saints are themselves marked by this so-called confessional attitude of absolute availability, readiness, obedience, or *indifferentia* that Adrienne is allowed to participate in their consciousness and prayer. It is nonetheless astonishing to recognize in

---

137. Speyr, *Mary in the Redemption*, 55.
138. Balthasar, *Our Task*, 9–10; see also "Adriennes Charisma," 174 ("Le charisme d'Adrienne," 189).
139. Balthasar, *First Glance at Adrienne von Speyr*, 72.
140. See, for example, Speyr, *Erde und Himmel* II, no. 1622 (222).
141. Balthasar, "Einleitung" in his co-edited volume, *Adrienne von Speyr und ihre kirchliche Sendung*, 15. See also his introduction to Adrienne's *Das Wort und die Mystik* I, 12–13.

her two-volume exposition of the saints that there are degrees of transparency, or self-abandonment, and thus of holiness, even among the saints.[142]

Similar to the correspondence between Adrienne's gift of self in the form of characteristically Marian availability and her charisma of entering into others' prayer is the correspondence between this same attitude of availability and her spiritual "transports." Balthasar reasons that "God took her at her word"[143] of fiat (that is to say, of generous availability) when transporting her in prayer, as Balthasar explains, to wherever he (God) deemed that her prayer and presence were needed: in concentration camps during the war years and then to convents where the life of prayer had become lukewarm, into churches emptied of piety, into confessionals where the stance of either priest or penitent was found lacking, into seminaries, and even into the Roman Curia.[144] It is thus not surprising that in his attempt to describe Adrienne's character, Balthasar admits an extreme difficulty in distinguishing the natural characteristics of her personality from the supernatural ones. This is especially the case because already in her youth "grace was so pronounced in her" that "the supernatural dimension in no way effaced her natural individuality: rather it underlined it."[145] Similarly, Adrienne's obedience, which Balthasar presents as characterizing her more than any other of her charismatic gifts, is described by him, in both "its extent and modes of application," as "completely rooted in grace."[146]

If in fact grace implies—as Balthasar and Adrienne teach and as shall be further apparent in chapter three—a participation in the mission of Christ, it is not surprising that there should be echoed in Adrienne's own life this same unity of grace and mission and thus also of theology and holiness. Nor is it surprising that Balthasar should seek to theologically sustain what he had for many years observed and experienced, we are told, in his interactions with Adrienne: the unity or inseparability of charis and charisma, of habitual grace and charismata, even to the point of disputing the scholastic argument that

---

142. See Speyr, *Das Allerheiligebuch*, Teil I and II. The first of these has been translated into English: *Book of All Saints* I. On the other hand, this observation points to the foundational and sustaining value of Christ's own yes, in which all others are formed, including the perfect yes of Mary. This theme will be thoroughly developed in chapter three of the present volume. See also Speyr, *John* I, 36–37 and 103; and *Handmaid of the Lord*.

143. Balthasar, *First Glance at Adrienne von Speyr*, 39. See, for example, Adrienne's prayer in Speyr, *Lumina and New Lumina*, trans. Adrian Walker (San Francisco: Ignatius Press, 2008), 28–29.

144. See also Speyr, *Erde und Himmel* II, no. 1622 (222), where mention is made of Adrienne seeing "all that was unaccomplished and untrue" in the confessions heard by Balthasar.

145. Balthasar, *First Glance at Adrienne von Speyr*, 47. For more detail, see her autobiographies: *My Early Years* and *Das Geheimnis der Jugend*.

146. Balthasar, *First Glance at Adrienne von Speyr*, 68.

the second—charismatic grace—may be given to sinners (as *gratiae gratis datae*).[147] Hence in his commentary of Aquinas's teaching on the charisms, for example—a commentary which he admits had its source "entirely" in his experience of Adrienne's charismatic gifts[148]—Balthasar argues that even if the ecclesial tradition maintains the possibility of an unworthy sinner bearing a particular grace for the community, the predominant and "normal" case should remain "that the existence of a charismatic grace be the expression and radiation of not only an ecclesial, but also a personal and sanctifying grace."[149]

The Fruits of Adrienne's Faith as a Gift for the Church

Because Adrienne's treatment of Christian anthropology is a theology of mission whereby the latter is presented as personalizing the human subject through a process of expropriation, as shall be made more explicit in chapter three, we would expect that her own mission should assume an important dimension in her existential theology.[150] This does not so much confirm the necessity of treating—as two poles of a single study—Adrienne's biography and her work, as of recognizing the expression within both her person and her theological work an important unity between the objective and subjective dimensions of faith. These two dimensions of faith are, of course, united in the theology of Adrienne, already and primarily in that hers is judged by Balthasar as a mystical theology: a theology that thereby bears a more "gifted" character than one drawing from the more "ordinary" experiences of faith. On the other hand, he also claims that is it "impossible to draw a distinct line" in her work between what is mystical and non-mystical.[151] "It

---

147. See Balthasar's introduction to *Das Wort und die Mystik* I, 10–11. See also Balthasar, "Charis and Charisma" in *Explorations in Theology* II, 301–14; "Understanding Christian Mysticism" in *Explorations in Theology* IV, 328–29; *First Glance at Adrienne von Speyr*, 88; *Theo-Logic* III, 310 and 312–18; and "Theology and Sanctity" (in *Explorations in Theology* I, 189–209)—which he admits, in *Our Task*, 103, was inspired by Adrienne who "united the two (theology and holiness) in a unique and almost unfathomable way." See also Sicari, "Hans Urs von Balthasar: Theology and Holiness."

148. See Balthasar, *Our Task*, 105.

149. Balthasar, *Besondere Gnadengaben und die zwei Wege menschlichen Lebens*, vol. 23 of P. Heinrich M. Christmann (ed.), *Die deutsche Thomas-Ausgabe* (Munich: Gemeinschaftsverlag, 1954), 271. See also Balthasar, *My Work*, 66; *Theo-Drama* III, 353; and *Explorations in Theology* IV, 328. It is worth noting that Balthasar's once "novel" position is implicit in the teaching of *The Catechism of the Catholic Church* (1994), wherein charity is presented as "the true measure of all charisms" (no. 800). Such is also the position of Jean-Hervé Nicolas with regard to the mystical charism, "whose progress always corresponds to an intensification of charity and of the action of the Holy Spirit," so as to "constitute a progress in the pure and simple Christian perfection" (*Dieu connu comme inconnu. Essai d'une critique de la connaissance théologique* [Paris: Desclée de Brouwer, 1966], 397).

150. On the personalization of the individual by his or her mission, see, for example, Adrienne's presentation of Magdalene in *Three Women and the Lord*, 28–29.

151. See Balthasar, *First Glance at Adrienne von Speyr*, 99.

goes without saying," for Adrienne as well as for Balthasar, "that the mystical experience neither replaces nor even weakens the act of faith; rather, it has faith as its basis in order to flow back into it renewed, enriched."[152]

In this sense too, it is important to recognize a unity between Adrienne's charismatic gifts and her ecclesial mission and even a unity between those more "objective" charismata (that of mysticism, for example) and the more personal perfection of her character—her spirit of obedience, her generous love of souls manifest in her willingness to endure great suffering for the sake of others, her willing practice of the evangelical counsels even in her married state, etc.—in virtue of which the former were put at the service of the Church.[153] Hence one might also observe the unity or correspondence (almost immediately evident to anyone who is at all familiar with the two) between her life as described by Balthasar and her teaching as transmitted by his tremendous stenographic and editorial efforts: between, that is to say, her experience and her doctrine, between her prayer and her theology.

To be sure, elements of her theology emerge in her biographies, not only because hers is a mystical theology, but also and especially because both are "measured" and directed by her God-given mission in virtue of which the personal is, as she teaches (in union with Balthasar), necessarily ecclesial.[154] An experience of faith which is thus more mystical than phenomenological, hers—Balthasar was utterly convinced—is an "objective" gift for the Church. As such it is an experience to be shared, which is to say, one that invites both reflection—of a spiritual and theological nature—and participation: an active response by way of commitment, or a sort of co-mission-ing. Indeed, Adrienne specially understood her mission as one of "revitalizing (personal as well as community) prayer," Balthasar explains.[155] It was thus also understood as "a service, not, to be sure, to a peripheral outgrowth of theology, not to enlarge 'side chapels' in the cathedral of existing dogma, but, on the contrary, as a service to its *central deepening and enlivening*."[156]

Indeed, if it be true, as Balthasar attests, that Adrienne practiced in an exemplary manner the virtue of obedience—which she also understood as ready availability, Ignatian indifference, inner transparency, and an open (expandable) fiat—then the gift of her life and teaching would follow according

---

152. Ibid., 86.
153. There are many examples of Adrienne's charity in the diaries kept by Balthasar, but published under Adrienne's name: Speyr, *Erde und Himmel* I-III.
154. See chapter five of the present volume for a thorough development of this theme in Adrienne's work.
155. Balthasar, *First Glance at Adrienne von Speyr*, 71.
156. Ibid., 57.

to her own theological argumentation. Like Mary, whom Adrienne describes as having so surrendered herself to her Son and his intentions that she "no longer possesses anything private that is not at the same time public and Catholic," Balthasar claims that Adrienne also allowed the Lord to dispose of "even the most secret things," namely, the "mysteries of her contemplation,"[157] for the renewal of the Church's own faith: "Her [Mary's] experience overflows [*überbordet*] her knowledge, and in this overflowing she simultaneously receives more insight and recognizes everything as more mysterious than she had thought. The mystery grows in her and becomes brighter and thereby becomes an open storehouse [*Vorrat*], a treasure, from which all generations of the Church might be nourished by penetrating more deeply into her mystery."[158] Might we not likewise view Adrienne's faith, Balthasar seems to suggest, as a treasury for the nourishment of the Church during our time and even for generations to come? How else indeed are we to understand her gift to the Church of more than sixty volumes of inspirational theology which, far from a product of speculative reason, are, Balthasar insists, a glimpse into the mysteries of her own mystical prayer?

Adrienne takes her readers with her on a journey as she "enters into" the lives of individual saints, scenes of the Gospel and other verses of Scripture.[159] As she does so, she opens up new perspectives for us based on her own (presumably) God-given knowledge. Hers is thus a perspective differing from that of the more "typical" experience of faith, whereby one might, for example, meditate upon the life of Mary Magdalene as it is revealed in the Gospel. Because Magdalene has, precisely as an object of revelation, "been handed over to the entire Church and to each one of us, we are free to imagine her life with the Lord," Adrienne reasons in a typically Ignatian manner, "in whatever way we wish." Such imagining is not, however, a matter of "guessing," Adrienne insists, but "a kind of shared experience within a given perspective and direction."[160]

Similarly—allowances being made for the difference between mystical knowledge and the "ordinary" knowledge of faith—Adrienne's reader might consider him- or herself free to imagine Adrienne's life with the Lord according to the descriptions provided by her autobiographies and by Balthasar's

---

157. Speyr, *Handmaid of the Lord*, 160; cf. Balthasar, *Razing the Bastions*, 94.
158. Speyr, *Das Wort und die Mystik* II, 26–27; cf. Balthasar, *Theo-Drama* V, 496. See also Speyr, *Das Wort und die Mystik* I, 28, where Adrienne explains that the missions of the saints lay seeds giving fruit to the Church's faith.
159. See Balthasar, *First Glance at Adrienne von Speyr*, 72.
160. Speyr, *Three Women and the Lord*, 20–21.

numerous accounts of her person and mission, including his detailed diaries (*Erde und Himmel* I–III) containing not only her many letters to him, but also his descriptions of her mystical experiences and other charismatic gifts, as well as his accounts of their continuous encounters and exchanges.

Beyond this and far more importantly, we have been given access to her spiritual life through her immense theological work. To be sure, this work reveals very little of her spiritual life, as such, but Balthasar is convinced that it is precisely the objective perspective of her theological work which points to her own inner transparency.[161] After all, Adrienne's work is not—at least not as Balthasar sees it—a work of research and deduction but rather a transmission of her mystical prayer. In this way, her unique experience of faith has—such was the unfaltering conviction of Balthasar—been surrendered to the Church for the edification of her (the Church's) own faith.

It nonetheless belongs to each of us to appropriate it at will: not, of course, by approaching her massive work as a sort of catechism; nor by critically studying it as one would a theological textbook or a systematic argument in defense of a certain ecclesial dogma (such as Christ's descent into hell, for example) or of an ecclesial practice (such as the voluntary taking on of penance for others). Rather, as Adrienne's self-consciousness has, according to Balthasar's description of the matter, given way to shared consciousness—a sort of personal participation in the consciousness of the Church, which in turn is a participation in the consciousness of Christ who is ever "turned" toward the Father—the student of Adrienne is invited to become an "*anima ecclesiastica*" or, in the spirit of St. Ignatius, to "*sentire cum Ecclesia.*"[162]

Analogical to the manner in which Adrienne was able—again, as testified by Balthasar—to enter into the prayer of the saints, the reader of Adrienne will profit best, he explains, by entering into her own attitude of prayer: that of inner transparency before God, of abandonment, and spiritual indifference. "Something that has grown out of slow meditation is also properly absorbed only slowly and meditatively."[163] Such an attitude, it must be grant-

---

161. This is also apparent in what Balthasar presents as her desire for anonymity. See, for example, Balthasar, *First Glance at Adrienne von Speyr*, 82 and 120–21.

162. "There is a point in each individual consciousness," Balthasar explains, "when thinking with the Church (*sentire cum ecclesia*) becomes *sentire ecclesiae,* the thinking of the Church, which is not ultimately separable from the thinking of the Holy Spirit, *sentire cum Spiritus Sancti*" (*A Theology of History*, 104). On Christ's consciousness as focalized upon the mission given by the Father, see, for example, Balthasar, *Explorations in Theology* II, 30–32 and 43–80.

163. Balthasar, *First Glance at Adrienne von Speyr*, 248; see also 71. See Joseph Fessio, "Comment lire Adrienne?" in Balthasar, Chantraine, and Scola, *La mission ecclésiale d'Adrienne von Speyr*, 172–83; and Balthasar's introduction to the same, 14 (French edition) and 14–15 (German edition).

ed, is a grace: a Christian perfection that, without losing its gifted character, is never "valuable and determined once and for all."[164]

The Christian's "measure" of open receptivity (*Hingabe*) never in fact matches that of Christ's own gift of self, which is to say that the Lord does not "adapt" the exuberance of his gift to the measure of the human person.[165] Adrienne's example and teaching point, however, to the "possibility of letting oneself be rounded out into the Church [...], of being brought to completion, through the community of saints."[166] Indeed, within the "boundary" of Mary's own unlimited (expandable) fiat, the Christian can, Adrienne teaches, truly be said to receive the Lord in all his fullness.[167] "In the end, everyone who truly lives in grace assumes a 'bridal' relationship to the Lord and participates in the grace of the Mother of God."[168] Hence, Mary-Church plays a very important, though hidden, role in the exchange of the gifts between the Lord, giver of all gifts, and the Christian from whom he asks the return of those gifts in the purest possible manner. She (Mary-Church) "mediates in both directions, loving water as the symbol of the purity of the bestowal in itself and of the cleansing of the gifts we intend to offer to the Lord."[169] In the final analysis, holiness is, according to Adrienne, "growth through grace into grace, a growth which divests a person increasingly of all that is his in order to allow him a participation in the unique holiness of God."[170]

---

164. Balthasar's introduction to *Adrienne von Speyr und ihre kirchliche Sendung*, 15 (14 in the French edition).

165. See Speyr, *John* III, 164; *Das Buch von Gehorsam*, 12–13; and Balthasar, "Das literarische Werk Adrienne's von Speyr," 130–31.

166. Balthasar, *First Glance at Adrienne von Speyr*, 84. The example refers to one of Adrienne's obviously more "mystical" works, *Das Fischernetz*. See also chapter five of this volume for a more complete exposition of this theme of the relationship between the individual and the community as exemplified in the communion of saints.

167. See Balthasar, *First Glance at Adrienne von Speyr*, 51; and Speyr, *Handmaid of the Lord* for examples of Mary's expanding fiat: a concept which will be developed at length in the following chapter.

168. Speyr, *Das Wort und die Mystik* I, 27. Hence, Adrienne's presentation of the saints as the "train of the Mother of God." See Balthasar, *First Glance at Adrienne von Speyr*, 72.

169. Speyr, *John* I, 221.

170. Speyr, *Handmaid of the Lord*, 23.

THREE

The Nature-Grace Difference-in-Unity

*The Expansion of Human Liberty to the
"Measure" of the Divine (Theological Persons)*

Introduction: The Question of Human Fulfillment

Given Balthasar's insistence, as we observed in chapter two, on the unity of theology and sanctity as an image of the fully receptive surrender of Christ to the Father—a unity which Balthasar saw exemplified in the figure of Adrienne von Speyr—it is not surprising that he should judge his own work of writing, editing, and publishing as ordered to this unity. Two years after the death of Adrienne, the Swiss theologian recognized the meaning of his work as, most especially, that of critically ordering the "treasures" of revelation, theology, and spirituality—including most especially, he notes, Adrienne's "vast literary estate"—around what he considered the "unifying midpoint of the Church": namely the link between the lay state and the life of the vows as expressed in the form of the secular institute. It is here, at the point where the tension between being a Christian and being like others in the world seems almost at its breaking point, or so tightly drawn as to appear "lacerating and 'psychologically' unbearable," that Balthasar recognized the center of the Church.[1]

This, more specifically, is the point of tension between the first Adam and the second and thus also the tension within each human being, who is called to break with his or her alliance with sin without—and this is critical to Balthasar's thought—leaving the world behind, so as to follow Christ

---

1. Balthasar, *My Work*, 58. See also Jacques Servais, "The Lay Vocation in the World according to Balthasar," *Communio* 23, no. 4 (1996): 656–76; and Henrici, "A Sketch of Von Balthasar's Life," 24–46. Henrici (ibid., 27) points out that the last twenty years of Balthasar's life were devoted "to getting Adrienne's mission recognized by the Church," and that the private printing of her works cost him at least 300,000 DM (roughly $200,000).

in the way of surrender.² This is also the point at which Balthasar recognizes the Christian's mission as joining—or rather participating in—that of Christ, who lives within himself the tension not only, nor foremost, between his divine and human natures, but also and especially (as we shall see more thoroughly in chapter five) between his filial and obedient surrender to the Father and his generous, life-giving surrender to mankind, in virtue of the same: his primary surrender of obedient love for the Father, as manifest on the Cross.

Herein, as elsewhere, might be perceived Adrienne's influence upon Balthasar, or at least the unity of their perspectives. This is evident, for example, in the primary importance that they both accord to their mission of co-founding the secular institute of St. John, whose own mission and spirituality can also be understood in these terms.³ Indeed, Balthasar understood all of his theological work, and thus also all of his writing, as "subordinated" to the task of promoting this form of community life. Even if his authorship were to be sacrificed to this end, "it would not seem as if anything had been lost," Balthasar argued; rather, "much would have been gained."⁴

This attitude—especially of one whose genius might easily be substantiated both qualitatively and quantitatively—can best be understood, as his commentators and biographers argue, in terms of his inner conviction that his entire person was to be taken into God's service. His vocation was, he firmly believed, first and foremost one of radical obedience, and thus not determined by himself.⁵ For this same reason, he believed his own mission to be so tightly bound up with those of others that "only a dry stem would remain" if one were to take from him what had been received from others.

---

2. See Balthasar, *My Work*, 51; *The Christian State of Life*; and *The Laity and the Life of the Counsels: The Church's Mission in the World*, trans. Brian McNeil and David C. Schindler (San Francisco: Ignatius Press, 2003). On the tension between the first Adam and the second, see *Theo-Drama* III, 33–34; *Theo-Drama* V, 33; and *The God Question and Modern Man*, 89–90. Cf. Speyr, *Korinther* I, 536. On the importance of remaining in the world as Christ's ambassador, see *Razing the Bastions*, 42.

3. See Balthasar, *Our Task*. On the Community of St. John, see Jacques Servais, "The Community of St. John," *Communio* 19 (1992): 208–19; Maximilian Greiner, "The Community of St. John: A Conversation with Cornelia Capol and Martha Gisi" in Schindler, *Hans Urs von Balthasar: His Life and Work*, 87–101; and "Kurze Darstellung der Johannesgemeinschaft," written by an anonymous member of the community, in Balthasar, Chantraine, and Scola, *Adrienne von Speyr und ihre kirchliche Sendung*, 49–57. See also Balthasar, *Explorations in Theology* III, 245–67, where the charism of secular institutes is explained.

4. Balthasar, *My Work*, 95. See also ibid., 43.

5. Balthasar explains the reception of his vocation in precisely these terms: "It was neither theology nor the priesthood which came to my mind at that time. It was simply this: You have nothing to decide; you are called. You will not serve; you will be taken into service. You have no plans to make; you are just a little stone in a mosaic which was already constituted" (Balthasar, "Pourquoi je suis devenu prêtre?" in Jorge Sans Villa [ed.], *Pourquoi je me suis fait prêtre: témoignages recueillis* [Tournai: Centre diocésain de documentation, 1961], 21).

"Even if nothing in my work were original"—and he adds that this would "not surprise" him—"there would still remain the passion to hand on what has been preserved to others (because it is unfamiliar to so many), together with the order to do this; for missions more than personal qualities are what individualize the Christian."[6]

With these words, and the entire content of chapter two, one is perhaps struck with the discrepancy between Balthasar's view of the fulfillment of the human person through fidelity to his or her God-given mission and the modern and contemporary obsession with self-realization: the dynamic frenzy of the human person in quest of him- or herself.[7] Presuming that human fulfillment is to be found in communion with the living God who reveals himself as "personified handing-over," Balthasar reasons that one can "know" and "possess" him "only when one is oneself expropriated and handed over."[8] Similarly, in the spirit of Adrienne, it is in the measure that the believer "decreases" to grant greater access to the Son (cf. Jn 3:30)—a "measure" that is infinitely surpassed by the Lord's "yes" to the Christian in which is contained (as we shall see) the latter's own more or less feeble "yes" to the Lord—that one belongs to the Lord, "who gives him [or her] to the community":[9] in, that is to say, the form of a mission. The share in Christ's sonship, which is central to the biblical, patristic, and Thomistic expositions of grace, is thus presented by both the theologian and the mystic who inspired him as a participation in Christ's own unique and universal mission.[10]

Without denying the teaching of the Second General Council of Constantinople, according to which we can speak of two generations (or births) of the divine Word—the one eternal, whereby he receives the divine nature

---

6. Balthasar, *My Work*, 19–20.

7. See Medard Kehl, "Hans Urs von Balthasar: A Portrait," in *The Von Balthasar Reader*, eds. Medard Kehl and Werner Löser (New York: Crossroad, 1982), 12–13; and Balthasar's foreword to Speyr, *The Mission of the Prophets*, trans. David Kipp (San Francisco: Ignatius Press, 1996), 9.

8. Balthasar, *The Glory of the Lord* VII, 400; see also *Theo-Drama* II, 258–59; and *Besondere Gnadengaben und die zwei Wege menschliche Lebens*, 458.

9. Speyr, *John* I, 102; and *Die katholischen Briefe* II, 179.

10. See, for example, Balthasar, *Unless You Become Like This Child*, 41. On the Thomistic presentations of grace as a participation in Christ's divine filiation, see for example: Luc-Thomas Somme, *Fils adoptifs de Dieu par Jésus Christ* (Paris: Vrin, 1997); Thomas Aquinas, *La divinization dans le Christ*, trans. Luc Somme (Geneva: Ad Solem, 1998); Jean-Pierre Torrell, *Saint Thomas Aquinas* II: *Spiritual Master*, trans. Robert Royal (Washington, D.C.: The Catholic University of America Press, 2003); *Christ and Spirituality in St. Thomas Aquinas*, trans. Bernhard Blankenhorn (Washington, D.C.: The Catholic University of America Press, 2011); *Encyclopédie, Jésus le Christ chez Saint Thomas d'Aquin. Texte de la Tertia Pars (ST IIIa) traduit et commenté, accompagné de données historiques et doctrinales et de cinquante Textes* (Paris: Cerf, 2008); Jean-Miguel Garrigues, "La doctrine de la grâce habituelle dans ses sources scripturaires et patristiques," *Revue thomistie* 103, no. 2 (2003): 179–202; and Jean-Hervé Nicolas, *Les profondeurs de la grâce* (Paris: Beauchesne, 1969). For a patristic presentation of the same, see Daniel A. Keating, *Deification and Grace* (Naples, Fla.: Sapientia Press, 2007).

from the Father; the other temporal, whereby he receives the human nature from his mother[11]—Adrienne recognizes that "being engendered and being created form a unity in the incarnate Son."[12] Hence, she reasons that the created world is assumed into the eternal generation of the Son. The "curve of man's life is [thus] enclosed within the curve of the Word made man,"[13] which means that Christ transforms us as he carries us within himself to the Father, who, in turn, "receives us as his children" and "perfects our childhood by allowing us to participate in the Son's mission."[14]

We cannot be children of God in the Lord without simultaneously being assigned a task and a corresponding empowerment. Otherwise our status as children would not be active, it would not really belong to us; it would be a mere title, not a truth. Implicit in our state of grace is a mission. But as the former has its place in the Son, so too our mission as children of God cannot be situated anywhere else but in the mission of the Son, in participation in it.[15]

Indeed, even the sacraments whereby we share in Christ's divine filiation are conceived by Adrienne as giving us a share in his mission.[16]

Herein might be perceived the most basic intuition of what Balthasar presents as "theological persons": the idea that human persons are "defined (in their theological relevance)" by reference to Christ, that is to say, "by reference to the unity of his person and his universal mission."[17]

In the acting area opened up by Christ, created conscious subjects can become persons of theological relevance, co-actors in theodrama. They cannot enter this acting area of their own accord; even less, once they are admitted, can they choose their own theological role. [...] But, [...] if man freely affirms and accepts the election, vocation and mission which God, in sovereign freedom, offers him, he has the greatest possible chance of becoming a person, of laying hold of his own substance, of

---

11. See *DZ* 422; cf. Thomas Aquinas, *Comp* 212 (= *Compendium theologiae seu brevis compilatio theologiae ad fratrem Raynaldum*, Leonine edition, vol. 42 [Rome: Editori di San Tommaso, 1979]; *Compendium of Theology*, trans. Cyril Vollert [London: Herder, 1952]).

12. See Speyr, *Die Schöpfung*, 11.

13. Speyr, *John* I, 34; cf. *Die katholischen Briefe* II, 66; and *Dienst der Freude*, 137.

14. Speyr, *John* I, 108; see *Handmaid of the Lord*, 47. Herein one might recognize an important influence upon Balthasar's profound little book, *Unless You Become Like This Child*.

15. Speyr, *The Letter to the Ephesians*, 31; see also *They Followed His Call*, 129; and *Theologie der Geschlechter*, 130. Cf. Balthasar, *Theo-Drama* V, 528; *The Christian State of Life*, 74; and *Unless You Become Like This Child*, 41.

16. See Adrienne von Speyr, *The Cross: Word and Sacrament*, trans. Graham Harrison (San Francisco: Ignatius Press, 1983), 10.

17. Balthasar, *Theo-Drama* III, 203; see also 149–229 and 270–71. Cf. *The Christian State of Life*, 72–83; "On the Concept of Person," *Communio* 13 (1986): 18–26; Marc Ouellet, *L'existence comme mission. L'anthropologie théologique de Hans Urs von Balthasar* (Rome: Pontifical Gregorian University, 1983); and Ellero Babini, "Jesus Christ: Form and Norm of Man according to Hans Urs von Balthasar" in Schindler, *Hans Urs von Balthasar: His Life and Work*, 221–23.

grasping that most intimate idea of his own self—which otherwise would remain undiscoverable.[18]

In an effort to exposit and develop this insight in what I believe to be its most original, although brute, form within Adrienne's mystical theology—and thus also and more specifically the Speyrian understanding of the delicate balance (or "tension": difference-in-unity) between nature and grace—this third chapter will begin by presenting a Thomistic understanding of human fulfillment in terms of the human person's unique assimilation to the Godhead by way of a participation in divine knowledge and love, before expositing Balthasar's own, particularly Ignatian, understanding of the human person as realized in his God-given mission. This will then be paralleled, as it were, by our exposition of Adrienne's presentation of the human being realized within the dynamic of his or her growing participation in divine communion: an exposition which will become the basis for our development of Adrienne's presentation of nature and grace in terms of the mutual indwelling of Christ and the Christian. Human nature will, more specifically, be presented as mysteriously surpassing its own limitations through Christ's indwelling in the Christian. A similar phenomenon will be studied in our presentation of the expansion of the Christian's assent within Christ's own obedient love for the Father. The reader who is already familiar with Balthasar's Christian anthropology will recognize in Adrienne's presentation of Mary the silhouette of what Balthasar calls a "theological person." Mary is presented there—as in Balthasar's *Theo-Drama*[19]—as the exemplar Christian, who is realized through her obedient and loving participation in Christ's mission. Finally, we will conclude with the Speyrian challenge to the Christian to accept Mary's maternity as a means of expanding his or her own surrender to the "measure" of God's self-gift in Christ.

St. Thomas on Human Fulfillment: Human Participation in Divine Knowledge and Love

To begin, we do well—within the specific goal of this volume—to place our investigation of Adrienne's understanding of human fulfillment, and more specifically her conception of the nature-grace tension of the human person and her influence upon Balthasar's perception of the same, within the context of the Catholic theological tradition as exemplified, once again, by the teaching of St. Thomas Aquinas.

---

18. Balthasar, *Theo-Drama* III, 263.
19. See especially ibid., 283–360.

Although the question of self-realization has been of central importance in western society—and thus also in much of western philosophy and psychology—since the Enlightenment era, it has been relegated by this (Catholic, especially Thomist) tradition to a place within the much broader question of God's governance of the world and the universe.[20] God governs all things, Thomas teaches, according to their natures, whereby they are "naturally" oriented to their proper ends. Since the human person has a rational nature, God governs this creature through his or her capacity to govern him- or herself.[21] Having the capacity to know the truth and to choose the good, we are naturally and supernaturally oriented to the true and the good, and thus to God himself; for "nothing is good and desirable except forasmuch as it participates in the likeness to God."[22] Hence, "everything seeks to be likened to God in its own way."[23] As for human beings, our *exitus* from the hands of the Creator, in whose image each of us is created,[24] is organically related to our *reditus*: our return to the Creator by the effective realization of this image, that is to say, through each one's voluntary adherence to God as to his or her last end. Hence, as Jean-Pierre Torrell observes, "Thomas puts all his thinking about human action under simultaneous considerations: image to be restored and end to be attained (image being restored when the end is rejoined). Thomas proposes a life program under the aegis of self-fulfillment, since the creature finds itself in finding its end."[25]

20. Similar is the pre-Christian context wherein Balthasar recognizes the question of the human being as posed uniquely "in connection with the question of the whole of being" (*Theo-Drama* II, 346). On the sense of self since the Enlightenment, see the now classic work of Charles Taylor, *Sources of the Self: The Making of Modern Identity* (Cambridge, Mass.: Harvard University Press, 1989), and, more recently, Jean Bethke Elshtain, *Sovereignty: God, State, and Self* (New York: Basic Books, 2008). It is perhaps of no little importance that Karen Kilby blames Karl Rahner's adoption of this Enlightenment perspective—at least as he is read by Balthasar—for the latter's repugnance of his work. See Karen Kilby, "Balthasar and Karl Rahner," in Oakes and Moss, *The Cambridge Companion to Hans Urs von Balthasar*, 256–68.

21. Cf. Thomas Aquinas, *ST* I-II, q. 91, a. 2; see also I-II, q. 114, a. 1.

22. Thomas Aquinas, *ST* I, q. 44, a. 4, ad. 3.

23. Thomas Aquinas, *ST* I-II, q. 109, a. 6.

24. Cf. Thomas Aquinas, *ST* I, q. 93. It is thus that St. Thomas presents the Son as "the first born of creation" (cf. Col 1:15): "For an artisan makes an artifact by making it participate in the form he has conceived within himself, enveloping it, so to say, with external matter; for we say that the artisan makes a house through the form of the thing that he has conceived within himself. This is the way God is said to make all things in his wisdom. [...] Now this form and wisdom is the Word; and in him all things were created, as in an exemplar" (*Super Col* I, lect. 4, no. 37 [= *Super Epistolam B. Pauli B. Pauli ad Colossenses*, in *Commentary on the Letters of Saint Paul to the Philippians, Colossians, Thessalonians, Timothy, Titus, and Philemon*, trans. Fabien R. Larcher, eds. John Mortensen and Enrique Alarcón, *Biblical Commentaries, vol. 40 of the Latin/English edition of the Works of St. Thomas Aquinas* [Lander, Wyo.: The Aquinas Institute for the Studey of Sacred Doctrine, 2012]). Cf. *SCG* IV, c. 13, 9–10; and q. 35, a. 2, ad. 3, where Thomas distinguishes the manner whereby the Son is considered the image of the Father and the manner whereby we are said to be the image of God.

25. Torrell, *Saint Thomas Aquinas* II: *Spiritual Master*, 82.

Within this emanation-return schema, the human person—so focal to the rugged individualism of contemporary western civilization—is necessarily de-centralized. For his or her accomplishment, or "self"-realization, and thus also his or her happiness,[26] is not achieved through the individual's own isolated action but by way of communion with other actors—human, angelic, and divine. These communitarian and self-perfecting actions are, moreover, also oriented towards communion as that in which each one's perfection consists: not because the self has so chosen it, but because God has so destined it. This means that the final (supernatural) end of the human person is most fundamentally and ultimately a gift received from another, with our part consisting in the willingness to receive and cooperate.[27]

Ours is thus an ecstatic nature[28]—a nature which is directed "out" of, or beyond (*ex-*), itself towards others—for one's personal good consists in the common good and one's own perfection is organically related to the good of all: the subjection of all beings to Christ as Head, who is himself perfectly subject to the Father.[29] Indeed, rather than the isolated human person, it is the divine person of Christ who is ultimately responsible for the human being's perfection, for Christ is both the instrumental and final cause of this perfection.[30] He is the instrumental cause of our perfection because it is through him and in him, the one mediator between God and man (cf. 1 Tim 2:5),[31] that the latter is accorded the grace of redemption and sanctification whereby the image of God is perfected in him (or her). Likewise, Christ is the final cause of our perfection, because it is to Christ, the Omega, that we tend as to our perfection: we are sons and daughters in the Son, in whose image we were created (the Alpha and predecessor of Adam).[32] The Incarnation thus "puts the finishing touch to the whole vast work envisaged by God. For man, who was the last to be created, returns by a sort of circulatory movement to his first beginning, being united by the work of the Incarnation to the very principle

26. See Thomas Aquinas, *ST* I-II, q. 3.
27. Cf. ibid., q. 62, a. 1.
28. See Peter A. Kwasniewski, "St. Thomas, *Extasis*, and Union with the Beloved," *The Thomist* 61 (1997): 587–603.
29. See Thomas Aquinas, *ST* III, q. 20, a. 2.
30. We nonetheless do well to note with Marie-Dominique Chenu that St. Thomas masterfully combines "the argument of fittingness (so despicable in Aristotelian epistemology, but so essential to theological epistemology) and the emination-return schema wherein divine freedom commands the rhythm of its development at decisive moments." (263). From this perspective, the divine Incarnation is a "contingent" event in a precise sense: "in the exitus-reditus cycle, it enters only as an absolutely gratuitous work of the absolute freedom of God. The predestination of Christ is capital from the fact that it does not enter by right into this economy; it is impossible to situate it *a priori* in the dialectical series of divine decrees" (*Introduction à l'étude de Saint Thomas d'Aquin*, 270).
31. See Thomas Aquinas, *ST* III, q. 26.
32. See ibid., q. 32, a. 3.

of all things."³³ As members of Christ, human persons are brought with him, in him and through him to the perfection of eternal glory.³⁴ Human nature is thus accomplished in the supernatural. We are given to participate in God's own beatitude.³⁵

The central importance that this tradition awards to the teleological movement of human nature is thus not entirely in contrast to the properly Ignatian perspective of Balthasar and Adrienne, wherein "God's elective will cannot be discovered and ascertained—neither in part nor as a whole—in and through human nature."³⁶ Indeed, Thomists would fully accord with this statement insofar as the natural desire to know God is, as Jacques Maritain would have it, "a desire which does not know what it asks, like the sons of Zebedee when they asked to sit on the right and on the left of the Son of Man."³⁷ On the other hand, St. Thomas teaches that the human person is

---

33. Thomas Aquinas, *Comp* I, 201. Gilbert Narcisse observes the central place of Christology in Aquinas's *Summa* in view of a twofold distinction: "The first is traditional, it concerns [the distinction between] 'theology' and 'economy'; the second has a philosophical origin: the return of a being to its principle" ("Le Christ selon Saint Thomas" in Serge-Thomas Bonino et al., *Thomistis ou de l'actualité de saint Thomas d'Aquin* [Paris: Parole et Silence, 2003], 116). See also Jean-Pierre Torrell, *Le Christ en ses mystères. La vie et l'œuvre de Jésus selon saint Thomas d'Aquin*, vol. I (Paris: Desclée de Brower, 1999); *Encyclopédie, Jésus le Christ chez Saint Thomas d'Aquin*; *Saint Thomas Aquinas* II: *Spiritual Master*, 73–74 and 125–52; *Christ and Spirituality in St. Thomas Aquinas*; and Gilles Emery, "The Personal Mode of Trinitarian Action in St. Thomas Aquinas," trans. Matthew Levering, in Emery, *Trinity, Church, and the Human Person: Thomistic Essays* (Naples, Fla.: Sapientia Press, 2007), esp. 129–34.

34. Cf. Thomas Aquinas, *ST* III, q. 69, a. 3. Jean-Pierre Torrell recognizes a "fundamental lacuna" in the reading of the *Summa* when the movement of the creature's return to God (*reditus*) is considered independently of Christ and his merit and "thus outside of the organic unity between the head and members" (*Pour nous les hommes et pour notre salut*, 95). "Thomas conceives the mystery of salvation in all of its aspects as that of a mystical unity between Christ and his [members]" (ibid., 93).

35. See, for example, Thomas Aquinas, *ST* I-II q. 5, a. 4, ad. 1; and III, q. 9, a. 2. Louis-Bertrand Geiger observes in Aquinas's treatise on man (cf. *ST* I, qq. 75–102) that "the *nature* studied in the first part of the treatise is the foundation of the aptitude in which his end consists, namely to be to the image of God. It is thus also common to all men. And because the knowledge and love by which God knows and loves himself constitutes his beatitude, one can say that man is naturally made to participate in the divine beatitude. That is to say, by his spiritual nature, he has proportionately the same beatitude as God" ("L'homme image de Dieu, à propos de *Summa Theologiae* I, 93, 4," in Geiger, *Penser avec Thomas d'Aquin. Etudes thomistes présentées par Ruedi Imbach* [Paris / Fribourg: Cerf / Editions universitaires Fribourg Suisse, 2000], 119). Of course, this is not to deny the central feature of grace, for "the true plenitude to which man is called is not that which he can obtain by his own efforts. It is the possession of God," as shall be made clear in what follows. (Marie-Joseph Nicolas, "L'idée de la nature dans la pensée de saint Thomas d'Aquin," 559). On the participation of human nature in the divine, see for example, *ST* I, q. 110, a. 4.

36. Roten, "Hans Urs von Balthasar's Anthropology in Light of His Marian Thinking," 317. Cf. Balthasar, *The Christian State of Life*, 75; *Prayer*, 26 and 41; and *Love Alone Is Credible*, 50. On the teleological orientation of human nature in St. Thomas, see Steven A. Long, *The Teleological Grammar of the Moral Act* (Naples, Fla.: Sapientia Press, 2007); *Natura Pura: On the Recovery of Nature in the Doctrine of Grace* (New York: Fordham Press, 2010), 10–51; and Georges Cottier, *Le Désir de Dieu. Sur les traces de saint Thomas* (Paris: Parole et Silence, 2002).

37. Jacques Maritain, *Approaches to God*, trans. Peter O'Reilly (New York / London: Macmillian Co. / Collier-MacMillian Limited, 1967), 97.

naturally capable of God (*capax Dei*): capable, that is to say, of knowledge of God and even of the vision of the divine essence,[38] although this capacity cannot be realized in the absence of grace.[39] "The beatific vision and knowledge are to some extent above the nature of the rational soul, inasmuch as it cannot reach it of its own strength," Thomas teaches, "but in another way it is in accordance with its nature, inasmuch as it is capable of it by nature, having been made to the likeness of God."[40] In short, "our intelligence is capable of the vision of the divine essence, but this vision "cannot be given by our intelligence to itself,"[41] and furthermore requires grace to receive it.[42]

Here, as elsewhere in Aquinas's synthesis, we might observe a profound unity between efficient and final causality with respect to God. In fact, when Aquinas invites us to consider divine love as a moving, or motivating [*primum motivum*] principle[43]—as that which sets all else in movement insofar as this love is the absolutely "First [or unmoved] Mover"[44]—he does not simply point to the divine efficient causality, that is, to that which sets everything into action by creating things and persons with natural forms and the inclinations that follow therefrom. He also points to the divine final causality: to the fact that God draws everything to himself by reason of his plenitude.[45] God is thus envisioned as a lover who woos his beloved creature, drawing her into his own "heart" in virtue of his supreme goodness.[46]

---

38. See, for example, Thomas Aquinas, *ST* III, q. 9, a. 2; I, q. 12, a. 1; *Comp* I, 104 and 201; and *SCG* IV, c. 54, 2. See also O'Neil, "L'homme ouvert à Dieu (Capax Dei)"; and Gilles Langevin, *"Capax Dei." La Créature intellectuelle et l'intimité de Dieu* (Paris: Desclée de Brouwer, 1966).

39. See Thomas Aquinas, *Comp* II, 9; and *ST* I, q. 12.

40. Cf. Thomas Aquinas, *ST* III, q. 9, a. 2, ad. 3.

41. Cottier, *Le Désir de Dieu*, 61–62. To be sure, St. Thomas explains that "man attains happiness [his last end] through his soul [*ex parte animae*]." But that which actually *constitutes* his happiness is "the thing itself which is desired as end. [...] Consequently we must say that happiness is something belonging to the soul; but that which constitutes happiness is something outside the soul" (*ST* I-II, q. 2, a. 7). Or, as Fergus Kerr explains by way of commentary, our beatitude is simultaneously "the uncreated good—God—who alone can fill the heart completely by his infinite goodness [*ST* I-II, q. 3, a. 1]" and "something created in the heart, since it is nothing other than our receiving God—our joy with God" (Fergus Kerr, *After Aquinas*: Versions of Thomism [Malden, Mass.: Blackwell, 2002], 130). Cf. Thomas Aquinas, *ST* I, q. 26, a. 3.

42. Cf. ibid., q. 38, a. 1.

43. Thomas Aquinas, *SCG* II, c. 28, 8; and *ST* I, q. 13, a. 2. On divine love as "the root of action" and "the aboriginal affection, reaching for the good, the principle of movement towards the beloved good," see Emery, *The Trinitarian Theology of Saint Thomas Aquinas*, 64–65.

44. See Thomas Aquinas, *ST* I, q. 2, a. 3.

45. Cf. Thomas Aquinas, *ST* I, q. 5, a. 2, ad. 1; ibid., a. 4, ad. 2; *De Ver* 21, 1, ad. 4 (= *Quaestiones Disputatae De Veritate*, Leonine edition, vol. 22 [3 volumes] [Rome: Editori di San Tommaso, 1975–1976]); *On Truth,* trans. James V. McGlynn and Robert W. Schmidt, ed. Robert W. Mulligan [Chicago: H. Regnery, 1952–1954; Indianapolis: Hackett, 1994]); and *SCG* I, c. 37.

46. Cf. Thomas Aquinas, *ST* I-II, q. 28, a. 2, ad. 2; and *SCG* IV, c. 54, 5. Williams recognizes desirability "as a prime factor in the Thomistic description of God" (*The Ground of Union*, 50). God's purpose of drawing us to himself is, in fact, one of the primary reasons that St. Thomas provides for explaining

The significance conveyed by this image of God drawing us into his heart—which, of course, assumes a certain importance in Balthasar's aesthetical and dramatic approach to theology[47]—is likewise expressed (less metaphorically) by St. Thomas in his observation that God draws all of creation into his own perfect goodness by way of its continuous assimilation to him, for "every beginning of perfection is ordained to complete perfection which is achieved through the last end."[48] The God of St. Thomas thus creates beings "for the purpose of finally assimilating things to himself. [...] The reason for creation is the union of creatures with God as their final end."[49]

Because, moreover, this assimilation presupposes nature, which Thomas presents as signifying "any intrinsic principle of motion,"[50] it follows that God "does not only create beings to participate in his essence, but also to participate in his operation; hence the reality of the causality exercised by the creature."[51] With regard to the human person, this means that beyond the persistent question dividing Thomists—whether there is only one final (supernatural) end of the human being or whether we might also admit one that is proportionate to our nature[52]—the encounter between human and divine nature must ultimately be resolved in such a way that God's purpose or intention in creating the human person (divine final causality) becomes the human person's purpose in willfully collaborating with God (human final

---

the fittingness of the Incarnation. See, for example, *ST* III, q. 1, a. 2, ad. 3; and *SCG* IV, c. 54, 4–7. See also chapter five of this volume for more explanation.

47. Cf. Hans Urs von Balthasar, *Heart of the World*, trans. Erasmo S. Leiva (San Francisco: Ignatius Press, 1979), 118; and *Love Alone Is Credible*, 146. See also Peter Henrici, "Response to Louis Dupré," in David L. Schindler (ed.), *Catholicism and Secularization in America: Essays on Nature, Grace, and Culture* (Huntington, Ind.: Our Sunday Visitor / Communio Books, 1990), 77.

48. Thomas Aquinas, *ST* I-II, q. 1, a. 6; *Comp* I, 124; and *SCG* I, c. 37, 2.

49. O'Rourke, *Pseudo-Dionysius and the Metaphysics of Aquinas*, 245; cf. *The Catechism of the Catholic Church*, no. 294.

50. Thomas Aquinas, *ST* III, q. 2, a. 1.

51. Marie-Joseph Nicolas, "Introduction à la *Somme théologique*," in Thomas Aquinas, *Somme théologique* I (Paris: Cerf, 1984), 40.

52. Unlike Balthasar, who follows Henri de Lubac's reading of St. Thomas, such that "[human] nature *de facto* has only one, single, supernatural end" (Balthasar, *The Theology of Karl Barth*, 287), certain Thomists insist that the human being also has an end proportioned to its nature. See, for example, Long, *Natura Pura*; and Lawrence Feingold, *The Natural Desire to See God according to St. Thomas Aquinas and His Interpreters* (Naples, Fla.: Sapientia Press, 2010). Meanwhile, other Thomists, such as Jean-Hervé Nicolas, reason that de Lubac is faithful to St. Thomas in refusing two ends to human nature: one supernatural, the other natural. To hold to such a position would be to conceive of grace as a second nature, Nicolas reasons; but "that is absurd" ("Les rapports entre la nature et le surnaturel dans les débats contemporains," *Revue Thomiste*, 95, no. 1 [1995]: 409–10). Meanwhile, Nicholas J. Healy denies that de Lubac grants only one end (namely a supernatural one) to human nature. The real point of contention between him and (certain) Thomists is whether the ultimate (supernatural) finality is inscribed in us by nature (the position of de Lubac) or added by grace (the position of certain Thomists, such as Long). See Nicholas J. Healy, "Henri de Lubac on Nature and Grace: A Note on Some Recent Contributions to the Debate," *Communio* 35, no. 4 (2008): 562.

causality).⁵³ Or to put it in terms specific to Thomas's *Summa* and the central place that question ninety-three of the *Prima Pars* plays therein,⁵⁴ God completes his production of man when man willingly and fully adheres to God with his spiritual powers of intellect and will.

St. Thomas thus distinguishes between two manners of conceiving God as the final cause of the human creature, which must nonetheless be brought into tandem: as, on the one hand, willed by God (that is to say, God has willed himself as the creature's end) and, on the other hand, as desired and chosen by the creature, whence Aquinas's consideration of human happiness from two inseparable perspectives.

On the one hand, our happiness is not less than God *ipse* (*ST* I.II. [q.] 2, [a.] 8 ad. 2). On the other hand, this happiness is a share in the divine happiness and something God creates in us ([*ST*] I.II. [q.] 3.[a.]1 resp.). This created happiness is a life of human activity in which human powers are ultimately fulfilled ([*ST*] I.II. [q.] 3, [a.] 2). Since, however, these are not two separate kinds of happiness, but one happiness considered from two different perspectives, Thomas is claiming that human beings not only become what they are meant to be only in union with God, but that specifically human activities are a form of participation in divine beatitude, in God's own self.⁵⁵

It is, in other words, by actually partaking of God's own knowledge and love of Himself that the human person is said by St. Thomas to be simultaneously most properly God-like, most properly human, and most properly one with God.⁵⁶

From this profoundly theocentric perspective, St. Thomas invites us to recognize a continuity between nature and grace based upon the human person's unique assimilation to God: by way of knowing God and loving Him. Hence, the image of God that the human being is *by nature* ("inasmuch as man possesses a natural aptitude for understanding and loving God") is oriented toward that act whereby he or she "actually and habitually knows and loves God," namely by grace.⁵⁷ The human soul is thus "naturally capable of grace [*naturaliter anima est gratiae capax*]," since it is naturally "fit to receive

---

53. "Creaturely action," which Gilles Emery specifies as "not only the natural action of beings lacking reason, but also the free and intelligent action of human beings—is attributed entirely to God and entirely to creatures, although according to different modes: God is wholly the source of the act insofar as He is the first cause (efficient, exemplar, and final), and the creature is wholly the source of its own act insofar as it is the second cause" ("Contemporary Questions about God," *Nova et Vetera* [English Edition], 8, no. 4 [2010]: 804).

54. See Geiger, "L'homme image de Dieu, à propos de *Summa Theologiae* I, 93, 4"; and O'Neil, "L'homme ouvert à Dieu [Capax Dei]"; Torrell, *Saint Thomas Aquinas*, II: *Spiritual Master*, 82–83; Williams, "Deification in the *Summa Theologiae*: A Structural Interpretation of the *Prima Pars*," *The Thomist* 61, no. 2 (1997): 219–55.

55. Williams, "Mystical Theology Redux," 61.   56. See Williams, *The Ground of Union*, 46.

57. Thomas Aquinas, *ST* I, q. 93, a. 4.

God by grace."[58] To be "capable of God" thus means, as Rupert Johannes Mayer reads St. Thomas, "orientation to and capacity for that which surpasses [*übersteigt*] man" and not "capacity for that which man is capable by nature."[59]

To say that the human person is the "image of God"—as differing from those creatures in whom there is a mere "vestige" (or "trace"[60]) of God—is, therefore, to admit more than that he or she provides a more fitting analogy for describing the mystery of God. It also means that although God is rightfully said to be the end of all creation, it is the prerogative of the rational creature alone to attain (*attingere*) him.[61]

God is in all things by His essence, power, and presence, according to His one common mode, as the cause existing in the effects which participate in His goodness. Above and beyond this common mode, however, there is one special mode belonging to the rational nature wherein God is said to be present as the object known is in the knower, and the beloved in the lover. And since the rational creature by its operation of knowledge and love attains to God Himself, according to this special mode God is said not only to exist in the rational creature, but also to dwell therein as in His own temple.[62]

The incorporation of human freedom into divine communion is thus presented by the angelic doctor in terms of the same psychological analogy that he uses to describe the Trinity of persons in one God: by way (as we saw in chapter one of this volume) of the procession of the intellect, which is that of the Word,[63] and the procession of the will, which is that of love, the name given to the Holy Spirit.[64] If, in fact, the human person is said to be the image of God in precisely this way—that in him or her "we find a procession of the word in the intellect, and a procession of the love in the will"[65]—it is also as such (as rational) that he or she is capable of being admitted into the Trinitarian processions. Indeed, the human person is said most properly to be the image of God not when he or she is at rest, but when, on the contrary, his or her spiritual powers are in act,[66] and still more properly when they are employed in knowing and loving God,[67] because God constantly knows and

---

58. Thomas Aquinas, *ST* I-II, q. 113, a. 10.

59. Rupert Johannes Mayer, "Zum *desiderium naturale visionis Dei* nach Johannes Duns Scotus und Thomas de Vio Cajetan. Eine Anmerkung zum Denken Henri de Lubacs," *Angelicum* 85 (2008): 755. The role of grace consists, from this perspective, in more perfectly determining (*näher bestimmt*) our natural end, rather than—as Cajetan would have it—as giving it another end; see 756. "According to Cajetan, nature is not perfected by grace, but destroyed [*zerstört*]" (760).

60. Cf. Thomas Aquinas, *ST* I, q. 93, a. 6: "*per modum vestigii*"; see also a. 2; and G. Rocca, *Speaking the Incomprehensible God* (Washington, D.C.: The Catholic University of America Press, 2004), 278–82.

61. Cf. Thomas Aquinas, *ST* I, q. 43, a. 3; I-II, q. 1, a. 8; q. 2, a. 7; and q. 3, a. 1.

62. Thomas Aquinas, *ST* I, q. 43, a. 3.

63. Cf. Thomas Aquinas, *ST* I, q. 27, a. 2.

64. Ibid., aa. 3–4; and q. 37, a. 1.

65. Ibid., q. 93, a. 6; cf. a. 1.

66. See ibid., aa. 4, 7.

67. See ibid., a. 8; *Comp* I, 106.

loves himself.⁶⁸ As such—as knowing God "truly" and loving God "rightly"—the human person is said by St. Thomas to be a "partaker of the divine Word and of the Love proceeding."⁶⁹

This, in fact, is what Thomas has in mind when he addresses happiness as man's final end. He is *not*, Anna Williams insists, "equating beatitude with human satisfaction per se, not even intellectual satisfaction." Far from "merely solipsistic personal fulfillment," the angelic doctor presents human happiness *theocentrically*. Our destiny is not to be obtained by what the human mind can know in and of itself, but rather—it bears repeating—from its participation in God's own self-knowledge: an idea altogether characteristic of Balthasar's teaching.⁷⁰ It follows, as Williams accurately reads Thomas—and in this we find again a strong similarity with Balthasar's doctrine⁷¹—that prayer and theology are both "theocentric activities and eccentric activities: means by which we are drawn towards God and beyond ourselves. Neither is a means of 'finding' ourselves in the contemporary sense, and certainly not a means of 'finding the god within.'"⁷²

In short, we might recognize in Aquinas's doctrine an important precedent for Balthasar's key insight as borrowed (such is my thesis) from Adrienne: that it is by way of the self-giving surrender, which constitutes the highest act of the spiritual creature, that he or she might be said to be integrated into divine freedom or communion.⁷³ However, the important question that Thomas seeks to resolve for his contemporaries within the perspective of their own language of *ontology*—the question, more specifically, of how to conceive of the union of the human and divine natures without destroying the former or reducing the latter⁷⁴—Balthasar seeks to resolve for his own

---

68. Thomas Aquinas, *SCG* III, c. 25, 8.

69. Thomas Aquinas, *ST* I, q. 38, a. 1; cf. q. 45, a. 7.

70. Williams, "Mystical Theology Redux," 62. "Strictly speaking, then, humanity does not [from Thomas's perspective] see the divine essence, but is granted a share in God's own self-knowledge" (Williams, *The Ground of Union*, 97). Cf. Balthasar, *Does Jesus Know Us?*, 52; *Theo-Drama* V, 425; and *Explorations in Theology* III, 44.

71. See Balthasar, *Prayer*; and Harrison, "Homo Orans: Von Balthasar's Christocentric Philosophical Anthropology."

72. Williams, "Mystical Theology Redux," 62. Cf. Balthasar, *Does Jesus Know Us?*, 57; Thomas Aquinas, *ST* III, q. 1, a. 8; ibid., I, q. 26, aa. 1–2; q. 12, a. 1; *SCG* III, c. 25, 8; *Comp* I, ch. 106; and ibid., II, ch. 9

73. See Balthasar, *Explorations in Theology* IV, 203 and 341; *Theo-Logic* I, 9; *Theo-Drama* II, 259; and Christopher Steck, *The Ethical Thought of Hans Urs von Balthasar* (New York: Herder / Crossroads, 2001), 78. Cf. Second Vatican Council, *Gaudium et Spes*, no. 24 (*DZ* 4324).

74. To admit with St. Thomas that we are most God-like when we are most united to God does not mean that the soul's union with God results in a leveling of differences, for "the soul that is beatified by the vision of God" is said by St. Thomas to be "made one with Him *in understanding*." When, therefore, the angelic doctor explains in this same passage that "the knower and the known must somehow be one" (*Comp* II, 9), this should not be read, Anna Williams explains, as implying some sort of "ontologi-

contemporaries within the context of their proper language of *freedom*. His, more specifically, is the uniquely modern question of how finite freedom can "fulfil itself in infinite freedom [...] without making infinite freedom somehow finite, without relegating it to one existent entity among others."[75]

A Balthasarian Understanding of Human Fulfillment: Human Surrender within Divine Surrender

In the era in which St. Thomas wrote, man still understood himself as "a 'nature' with its natural ambitions, needs and desires," Balthasar observes.

> He inferred God from the character of his capacities and "tendrils" which were natural, even though opening into the infinite. Yet there lurked a suspicion, that could never be wholly silenced, that the God who was thus visualized and desired had, after all, to correspond to the measure of the human demand for happiness, truth, or love. This [however] is no longer the case; though this does not mean that the natural aspect of the creature is being denied. It is there, but it does not anticipate the ultimate fact, which is freedom. Hence the cosmos can no longer be understood so completely without a break as the Fathers and the Schoolmen, following Plotinus, saw it; that is as an effulgence of the divine sun of grace (the good is by nature diffusive of itself). Today it is marked far more profoundly by the abysmal incomprehensibility of the divine decision arising from infinite freedom.[76]

From the perspective of this typically modern conflict between nature and freedom,[77] it is not surprising that Balthasar should characterize the human search for fulfillment not so much in terms of an Augustinian-styled restlessness,[78] nor of a Thomistic-styled striving for happiness in the terms laid out above, but rather, or most especially, by the Ignatian sense of *disposición*: the attitude of permitting "God to be God" in oneself, of giving God "all the space to which he lays claim for his love," not in the sense of a negative

---

cal melding, the absorption of one party into the other, or their joining to form a *tertia quid*." Rather, there is hereby addressed "a union in which two distinct entities are brought into a lasting relation that destroys neither" ("Mystical Theology Redux," 60). See also Emery, *Trinity, Church, and the Human Person*, 151.

75. Balthasar, *Theo-Drama* II, 228.
76. Balthasar, *The God Question and Modern Man*, 72–73.
77. See, for example, Michael Allen Gillespie, *The Theological Origins of Modernity* (Chicago: University of Chicago Press, 2008); and Louis Dupré, *The Enlightenment and the Intellectual Foundations of Modern Culture*, (New Haven, Conn.: Yale University Press, 2004).
78. "Qui fecisti nos ad te et inquietum est cor nostrum donec requiescat in te [You made us for yourself and our hearts find no peace until they rest in you]" (Augustine of Hippo, *Confessions* I, 1: Aureli Augustini, *Confessionum* [= *Bibliothèque Augustinienne*, vol. 13, trans. Eugène Tréhorel and Guilhem Bouissou, ed. M. Skutella (Paris: Études augustiniennes, 1992), trans. R. S. Pine-Coffin (Harmondsworth, Middlesex, England: Penguin Books, 1961, 1975), 21]). On Balthasar's distancing from this notion, see his *Two Sisters in the Spirit*, 302.

resignation but of a positive *indifferentia*, "for which it is the highest joy to do whatever is required, as it may be pleasing to the divine majesty."[79] As an "offer of *readiness*,"[80] indifference is "neither resignation, nor detachment but surrender alone."[81] Surrender, meanwhile, is employed by Balthasasr to emphasize the personal character of freedom such that "God's choice, accomplished in eternal freedom [...] is offered to man to choose for himself."[82]

Because human happiness must—from this properly Ignatian perspective—be subordinate to praise, reverence, and service of God, Balthasar reasons that "human nature, even when it is elevated by grace, cannot act as the guide for man in his praise, reverence and service of God; ultimately such guidance can only come from God and the revelation of his will."[83] Consequently, it is "no more possible, by simply assessing a man's nature, to predict God's gracious intentions for him. [...] Each one of us has to experience and grow attentive to God's sanctifying will in prayer and meditation."[84]

From what thus appears to be a "break with the teleological perspective,"[85] a dialogue between disciples of Balthasar and those of St. Thomas will inevitably entail the challenging confrontation between Ignatian spirituality, wherein obedience assumes such a central role that it is often presented (according to the interpreter) as preceding the act of reason—whence the term "blind" obedience—and the Dominican spirituality of the Thomistic tradition, wherein the act of the will necessarily follows upon the act of reason in accord with the principle that one can only love what one knows.[86] This, in turn, supposes the question of the nuance accorded to the subjective or the objective dimension of divine causality: the question of whether one would emphasize—as proper to Thomistic theology and perhaps slighted in

---

79. Balthasar, *Explorations in Theology* III, 45; see also *The Christian State of Life*, 82; foreword to Speyr, *The Mission of the Prophets*, 8; and Schrijver, *Le merveilleux accord*, 56. Cf. Speyr, *Erde und Himmel* I: *Einübungen*, vol. 8 of *Die Nachlasswerke* (Einsiedeln: Johannes Verlag, 1975), 84.

80. Balthasar, *Epilogue*, 36.

81. Balthasar, *Two Sisters in the Spirit*, 182. Cf. Thomas Aquinas, *ST* I-II, q. 5, a. 5.

82. Balthasar, *Two Sisters in the Spirit*, 302.   83. Ibid.

84. Ibid., 21.

85. Jacques Servais, *Théologie des exercices spirituels: Hans Urs von Balthasar interprète saint Ignace* (Bruxelles: Culture et Vérité, 1996), 135; see also "Freedom as Christ's Gift to Man in the Thought of Hans Urs von Balthasar," *Communio* 29, no. 4 (2002): 556–78, esp. 572–73; Balthasar, *God and Modern Man*, 73; Dalzell, *The Dramatic Encounter of Divine and Human Freedom in the Theology of Hans Urs von Balthasar*, 71; Marc Ouellet, "The Foundations of Christian Ethics according to Hans Urs von Balthasar" in Schindler, *Hans Urs von Balthasar: His Life and Work*, 231–49, esp. 244–45; and Harrison, "*Homo Orans*," 283–85. For Adrienne's perspective, see Balthasar's presentation thereof in "Adriennes Charisma," 174–75.

86. See Michael Sherwin, *By Knowledge and by Love: Charity and Knowledge in the Moral Theology of St. Thomas Aquinas* (Washington, D.C.: The Catholic University of America Press, 2005). This order is reversed, however, with regard to our final end of eternal beatitude, which consists in the vision of God. See *ST* I, q. 12, aa. 1, 5, and 6; and *SCG* III, c. 58, 4.

that of Balthasar—God's causal action as moving the creature *from within* by means of the creature's own desires[87] or—as is also characteristic of the Thomistic perspective, but also and especially of the aesthetic theology of Balthasar—*from without* (by reason of his supreme goodness, which attracts the creature to himself).[88] This question, furthermore, entails another: whether love is the very basis of all our desires,[89] which are thus to be affirmed as the most certain means to authentic love and ethical action—in which case the desire for happiness "is not only 'in order,'" as Josef Pieper insists with reference to Aquinas, but is also "the indispensable beginning of all perfection in love"[90]—or whether love requires (instead) that we renounce our desires, as typifies from Pieper's perspective a certain Protestant interpretation of love, as well as a Kantian, duty-based ethic.[91]

To be sure, most Thomists would assent to the basic principle of Ignatian indifference when by this is meant that "in all things we should desire and choose only those things which will best help us attain the end for which we are created,"[92] although there would likely remain the question of the nature

---

87. Cf. Thomas Aquinas, *ST* I, q. 105, a. 5; and *Supra Ioan* 1, lect. 5, no. 132.

88. Aquinas argues that "beauty adds to goodness a relation to the cognitive faculty: so that *good* means that which simply pleases the appetite; while the *beautiful* is something pleasant to apprehend" (*ST* I-II, q. 27, a. 1, ad. 3). On the Thomistic portrayal of love as "a living force that spurs the lover toward the beloved," provoking "a going out of the self (*amor facit extasim*)," see Torrell, *Thomas Aquinas* II: *Spiritual Master*, 91. As for Balthasar, although he follows Henri de Lubac in holding that historical human beings have but one final end, namely a supernatural one, he rejects, Peter Henrici explains, what the latter considers to be the characteristically anthropological perspective of de Lubac's theology: presumably one whose focus is upon the creature's natural desire for God, as is explicit in Balthasar's *Two Sisters in the Spirit*, 302. Instead, the Swiss theologian opts for what Henrici considers a more properly theocentric perspective emphasizing the objective "form [*Gestalt*]" of the glory of God, who makes himself "seen *as* God in a humanly perceivable and understandable appearance" (Henrici, "Response to Louis Dupré," 77). Grace is thus understood by Balthasar, Henrici concludes, in the properly biblical and patristic sense of the term: that of "a moving force, not as added to and competitive with man's natural abilities, but rather as a kind of attraction, adding love, urgency, and joy to a person's natural striving and acting" (ibid., 76).

89. Cf. Thomas Aquinas, *ST* I, q. 20, a. 1; q. 60, prologue; and *SCG* I, c. 4, 19.

90. See Josef Pieper, "On Love," trans. Richard and Clara Winston, in Pieper, *Faith, Hope, Love* (San Francisco: Ignatius Press, 1997), 223; see also 137–281, esp. 166, 208, and 222. See also Servais Pinckaers, *The Sources of Christian Ethics*; *The Pursuit of Happiness—God's Way: Living the Beatitudes*, trans. Sr. Mary Thomas Noble (Staten Island, N.Y.: St. Paul's, 1998); Albert Plé, *Par devoir ou par plaisir* (Paris: Cerf, 1980); David M. Gallagher, "Desire for Beatitude and Love of Friendship in Thomas Aquinas," *Mediaeval Studies* 58 (1996): 1–47; "Goodness and Moral Goodness," in Gallagher (ed.), *Thomas Aquinas and His Legacy* (Washington, D.C.: The Catholic University of America Press, 1994), 37–60; and Nicholas E. Lombardo, *The Logic of Desire: Aquinas on Emotion* (Washington, D.C.: The Catholic University of America Press, 2011).

91. Pieper reacts, most especially, to the Protestant ethic of Anders Nygren, *Agape and Eros*, trans. Philip S. Watson (Chicago: University of Chicago Press, 1982). See also Michael Sherwin, "Happiness and Its Discontents," *Logos: A Journal of Catholic Thought and Culture* 13, no. 4 (2010): 35–59; Pinckaers, *The Sources of Christian Ethics*, esp. 240–53 and 327–53; and (also by Pinckaers) *Morality: The Catholic View*, trans. Michael Sherwin (South Bend, Ind.: St. Augustine's Press, 2001), 65–81.

92. St. Ignatius of Loyola, *Spiritual Exercises*, trans. Anthony Mottola (New York: Image Books, 1964), no. 23 (48).

of that end: the question, more specifically, of whether, or to what extent, the Thomistic presentation of that end as human happiness, understood as the perfection of our intellectual nature by its participation in God's own knowledge of himself, is compatible with the Ignatian presentation of the end as rendering praise, reverence, and service to God.[93] Furthermore, Thomists would likely agree with the Ignatian concept of "indifference" when this is understood as serving either of these conceptions of the end: when, that is to say, indifference means being "free from any inordinate attachments"[94] or of settling for anything less than the perfect good, which is also the source of all authentic and lasting happiness.[95] More difficult to accept, however, is the Balthasarian interpretation of Ignatius's vision of the human person as one whose "center is not to be found in the aspirations and desires of the human heart, but in praise, reverence, and service of God and in readiness (*disposición*) vis-à-vis the divine will, which is never able—either in whole or part—to be read from [*abzulesenden*] or anticipated by [*vorauszuberechnenden*] human nature."[96]

From this perspective of human fulfillment as determined from on high, Balthasar might thus appear to reject a Thomistic ethic, wherein freedom is considered as "rooted in the soul's spontaneous inclinations to the true and the good,"[97] so as instead to espouse a duty-based ethic subscribing to what Servais Pinckaers presents as a modern idea of freedom: one claiming to be "'indifferent' to nature" whose inclinations are conceived "as the most insidious threat to the freedom and morality of actions"[98] or, at best, as what Pope John Paul II presents as "presuppositions or preambles materially necessary for freedom to make its choice, yet extrinsic to the person."[99] Hence there

---

93. See ibid., no. 23 (47); cf. Thomas Aquinas, *SCG* III, c. 120, 10.

94. Ignatius of Loyola, *Spiritual Exericses*, no. 179 (85): "I must have as my aim the end for which I am created, which is the praise of God our Lord and the salvation of my soul. At the same time I must remain indifferent and free from any inordinate attachments so that I am not more inclined or disposed to take the thing proposed than to reject it, nor to relinquish it rather than to accept it. I must rather be like the equalized scales of balance, ready to follow the course which I feel is more for the glory and praise of God our Lord and the salvation of my soul."

95. Cf. Thomas Aquinas, *Comp* II, ch. 9; and *ST* I-II, q. 2, a. 8. Sin, Aquinas teaches, is "a departure from the order to the end" (*ST* I-II, q. 21, a. 2; cf. a. 1; q. 75, a. 1; q. 109, a. 2, ad. 2; and *Comp* I, 120).

96. Hans Urs von Balthasar, "Exerzitien und Theologie," in *Orientierung: Katholische Blätter für weltanschauliche Information* 12 (1948): 231; see also *Two Sisters in the Spirit*, 302.

97. Pinckaers, *The Sources of Christian Ethics*, 333. "For St. Thomas," Pinckaers explains, "the natural inclinations to goodness, happiness, being and truth were the very source of freedom. They formed the will and intellect, whose union produced free will" (245).

98. Ibid., 333. This is a notion of freedom inspired by William Ockham, for whom "freedom dominated the natural inclinations and preceded them" (ibid., 245). See also Kerr, *After Aquinas*, 118.

99. Pope John Paul II, *Veritatis Splendor*, no. 48. "Their functions," he continues, "would not be able to constitute reference points for moral decisions, because the finalities of these inclinations would be merely 'physical' goods, called by some *premoral*" (ibid.).

arises the still more fundamental question of whether Balthasar would subscribe to what Pinckaers presents as a nominalist notion of freedom, namely that of *indifference* (or indetermination) with regard to two contraries (to good or to evil), or whether he would instead follow Aquinas's interpretation of freedom as one of *excellence*: "a freedom that presupposes natural inclinations and takes root in them so as to draw forth the strength needed for their development."[100]

The response to this question might be offered by Balthasar's enthusiastic endorsement of Maximus the Confessor's idea of freedom:

Freedom is not identical with the ability to choose between good and evil; otherwise, the fall of the creature could be expected to occur with a diabolical necessity! Christ's freedom reveals to Maximus the mistake in this concept of freedom—just as *our* freedom in Christ had revealed it to Augustine. Free self-determination toward every good thing by following the law implied in one's status as God's image, in obedience to the flow of one's own natural movement toward God: there, in Maximus' view, is where the personal freedom of the creature must come to its lived reality.[101]

Or, to put it still more straightforwardly in reference to Gregory of Nyssa: "[I]t is becoming clear from what we have said—contrary to Origen—that it is not 'indifference' that constitutes freedom of choice: the latter's innermost nature is the movement toward self-realization within infinite freedom. This is how finite freedom can be the 'image' of infinite freedom."[102] Its "path of self-realization" will necessarily be the path "toward absolute [that is to say, divine] freedom."[103] In other words, this path "is not imposed on the individual from without, but is developed from the deepest centre of his being."[104]

Not only might Balthasar thus be exonerated of the charge of voluntarism that Mark McIntosh lays upon him,[105] but he might also be more positively viewed as maintaining a Thomistic interpretation of human freedom: one which, it bears repeating, is "rooted in the soul's spontaneous inclinations to the true and the good."[106] In fact, it is precisely this notion of freedom which is foundational with respect to the transcendentals at the heart of

---

100. Pinckaers, *The Sources of Christian Ethics*, 357. Pinckaers draws upon the practice and perfection of the arts to illustrate this idea (355).
101. Balthasar, *Cosmic Liturgy*, 229; see also *A Theology of History*, 61–62.
102. Balthasar, *Theo-Drama* II, 237.   103. Ibid., 290.
104. Balthasar, *The Glory of the Lord* I, 221.
105. McIntosh nonetheless denies that Balthasar subscribes to a nominalist notion of freedom. See Mark McIntosh, *Mystical Theology: The Integrity of Spirituality and Theology* (Oxford: Blackwell, 1998), 107.
106. Pinckaers, *The Sources of Christian Ethics*, 333. "For St. Thomas," Pinckaers explains, "the natural inclinations to goodness, happiness, being and truth were the very source of freedom. They formed the will and intellect, whose union produced free will" (245). Cf. Balthasar, *Epilogue*, 17–18 and 69; and "Nine Propositions on Christian Ethics," 92.

his fifteen-volume trilogy.[107] Hence, "the Spirit breathes," as Balthasar would have it, "where every created freedom—whether open or closed to God—has its origin and its constitution: *in its orientation for the authentically good* and, through this, in its drive to realize itself as freedom."[108] "So there is a fundamental freedom (quite apart from all conscious or unconscious motives and compulsions) that enables us to affirm the value of things and reject their defects; to become involved with them or turn away from them."[109] Hence, "'Freedom from' (our egoistic drives and passions) is only the springboard for a 'freedom for' that issues from the innermost center of our freedom and our personal endowments."[110]

Such is also Balthasar's understanding of faith, which remains a theological virtue, not to be confused with the natural disposition of the human person.[111] Faith, he explains more specifically, is "allowing love to have its way: not only in what love does for me, but also in the goal of this act, which is affirmed and accomplished when I am seized by love."[112] In contrast to the Lutheran sense of faith, wherein—as Balthasar paraphrases—"everything lies in the Word that promises me salvation and that I allow in faith to be true in me," the Ignatian sense—adopted by Balthasar—regards "everything" as lying "in the call that introduces me into the following of Jesus' way (of the Cross)."[113] Whereas the first perspective of faith would render it "confidence" or "security," the second implies an expropriation whereby one is wholly centered (by obedience, or surrender) in Christ:[114] "Out of this very

---

107. See, for example, Balthasar, *The Glory of the Lord* VII, 398; and *Epilogue*.
108. Balthasar, *Epilogue*, 121.   109. Balthasar, *Theo-Drama* II, 211.
110. Balthasar, *Theo-Logic* III, 270.
111. On Balthasar's treatment of the faith of Christ as differing from the same concept in the theology of St. Thomas, see Donneaud, "Hans Urs von Balthasar contre saint Thomas d'Aquin sur la foi du Christ." The reduction of faith to a natural disposition is a criticism launched by various Thomists against Henri de Lubac. See, for example, Reinhard Hütter, "Aquinas on the Natural Desire for the Vision of God: A Reflection on *Summa Contra Gentiles* III, c. 25 *après* Henri de Lubac," *The Thomist* 73, no. 4 (2009): 575; Feingold, *The Natural Desire to See God according to St. Thomas Aquinas and His Interpreters*, 354; and Long, *Natura Pura*, 19.
112. Balthasar, *The Glory of the Lord* VII, 401; see also *Explorations in Theology* I, 168–69.
113. Balthasar, *Explorations in Theology* III, 89. Ironically, however, Lutheran faith in not a supernatural reality *in* the soul, a *habitus*. "What is emphasized here almost exclusively," notes Jean Borella, "is the human dimension of faith, faith as the human act, the human will within mercy. It is a faith *felt* by the believer, faith reduced to the subjective experience of faith and not properly a *theological* faith in which spiritual reality is by no means perceptible to ordinary consciousness" (Jean Borella, *The Sense of the Supernatural*, trans. G. John Champoux [Edinburgh: T. & T. Clark, 1998], 155). See also Gillespie, *The Theological Origins of Modernity*, 101–69.
114. See John O'Donnell, "Hans Urs von Balthasar: The Form of his Theology" in Schindler, *Hans Urs von Balthasar: His Life and Work*, 207–20, esp. 218–20. As for the notion of "expropriation," this concept is explained by Balthasar in terms of a God-given bestowal: "appropriation as expropriation; leadership, but from the last place" (Balthasar, *New Elucidations*, 196; see also *The Glory of the Lord* I, 219–22).

strongly emphasized *pro me* springs directly the question [for Ignatius, as observed by Balthasar]: *'Quid ego ... agere debeam pro Christo'* ["what should I do for Christ?"], which can be answered only where the call to imitation sounds forth incomprehensibly, that the useless sinner contrary to all expectations, would become usable for the Lord thanks to the pure grace of the Cross (and not to any synergism!)."[115] Faith, in short, "allows the truth of God's love to be true for us and in us (Gal 2:20; 1 Jn 5:1–4, 10–12). And since God's freedom is not formless but has a particular profile and is 'for us' (in the covenant fulfilled by Christ), our free readiness to enter his freedom also implies that we are ready to embrace a particular mission. Carrying out this mission is part and parcel of the gift of freedom: it is a duty and privilege."[116]

Balthasar's emphasis thus lies upon the experience of freedom as self-possession *and* universal openness: as, on the one hand, the capacity for self-movement, responsibility, and choice; and, on the other hand, as the capacity for assent, acceptance, and obedience—hence the two-fold dimension of faith: "opening to God and passing on the gospel, mission to the world."[117] The capacity of assent implies, moreover, the inescapable action of the (human and divine) other. "Suspended," as it were, "in the medium of God's freedom," the human being is, Balthasar explains, "anchored—objectively—solely in God's truthfulness—and subjectively—in his own attitude of trust."[118] Ours is thus an "existence in suspension."[119]

Angelo Scola thus reasons that the self-comprehension of the human being "cannot, by its nature, end," for Balthasar, "except in an open discussion":[120] in, that is to say, one's dialogue with the Trinitarian God, who is both Creator and Redeemer. What the human person is "by nature" is, in other words, necessarily related to his or her essential calling "as the complicated anatomy of the eye is related to the simple act of seeing." Just as this act, in other words, does not simply derive from the various physical, chemical, and physiological processes—which it nonetheless presupposes—so also the call to love, which is the proper end of the human person, cannot be derived from human nature, but only from God "who is love" (cf. 1 Jn 4:16). It follows, within Balthasar's logic—profoundly united to that of Adrienne—that we cannot grasp the "essence" of the human by looking "backward" to our "origin in the dust of the earth," but only by looking forward to our "calling

---

115. Balthasar, *Explorations in Theology* III, 96.
116. Balthasar, *Theo-Logic* III, 271.
117. Speyr, *John* III, 318. Cf. Balthasar, *Explorations in Theology* III, 349.
118. Balthasar, *Theo-Drama* II, 253.
119. Roten, "Hans Urs von Balthasar's Anthropology in Light of his Marian Thinking," 323.
120. Scola, *Hans Urs von Balthasar: A Theological Style*, 90.

to be the image and likeness of God."[121] In short, the relationship between nature and grace is examined by Balthasar (and Adrienne) not so much ontologically as vocationally: within, that is to say, the context of one's God-given mission.[122] "Man is not what he thinks himself to be but what God appoints him to be. He must apply all his strength to shift his personal center into what is implied by his new name ('for as his name is, so is he': 1 Sam 25:25)."[123]

Instead of presenting "a linear development of human capability" by way of growth in virtue, Balthasar thus presents human fulfillment in terms of what Christopher Steck calls a "narrative identity":[124] one whose emphasis is not so much on universal human nature as upon "the unique nature, strength and capacity of each individual."[125] As such, his perspective presupposes the important distinction that Guy Mansini makes between person and nature:

> I think it true to say that we are not who we are without the ordination to God, without the grace he has offered, without the promise of vision. Who we are is something dramatically constituted; it is something we become according as we are related to other persons, make moral decisions, and especially, according as we are engaged with the God revealed to us by Christ, whose Spirit dwells in our hearts. But what we are—that is another question. What we are can be the same, indeed, is the same, whether we are called to grace and glory or not. Sharing in the divine nature does not give us another nature. Deification does not make us no longer men.[126]

As for Balthasar, in responding to the question of how to resolve the "christological distinction between the human conscious subject" of Christ and his divine person, so as in turn to explain the "personal being of others in Christ,"[127] the theologian of Lucerne dismisses the utility of the nature-person distinction—so central for Boethius's definition of personhood—for

---

121. Balthasar, *The Christian State of Life*, 70. Similarly, Balthasar writes of Adrienne's perspective: "Nature is, and remains, clay in the hands of God, and no one but God knows just which forms he will bring forth out of you or me" ("Foreword" to Adrienne's *The Mission of the Prophets*, 8).

122. See, for example, Balthasar, *The Christian State of Life*, 64.

123. Balthasar, *Theo-Drama* III, 267.

124. Steck, *The Ethical Thought of Hans Urs von Balthasar*, 74. Herein Steck recognizes the influence of St. Ignatius of Loyola upon Balthasar's thinking; see ibid., 78. See also John O'Donnell, "The Form of von Balthasar's Theology" in Schindler, *Hans Urs von Balthasar: His Life and Work*, 219. Cf. Balthasar, *Explorations in Theology* IV, 15–28; *Theo-Drama* III, 284–87; and *Prayer*, 22–23.

125. Balthasar, *Two Sisters in the Lord*, 21. Meanwhile, Melanie Barrett argues that even in the absence of "the specific Aristotelian-Thomistic language of individual virtues and their distinctive operations," Balthasar can "be seen as working out of and contributing to the tradition of virtue ethics," namely by his emphasis upon contemplation "as a form of habituation, coupled with his conception of Christ as ethical norm" and by his conception of love "as the form of the virtues" (*Love's Beauty at the Heart of the Christian Moral Life: The Ethics of Catholic Theologian Hans Urs von Balthasar* [Lewiston: The Edwin Mellen Press, 2009], 199).

126. Guy Mansini, "The Abiding Theological Significance of Henri de Lubac's *Surnaturel*," *The Thomist* 73 (2009): 606–7.

127. Balthasar, *Theo-Drama* III, 218 and 220.

explaining the Creator-creature relation.[128] Likewise, he denies that the question can be answered with recourse to the typically modern comprehension of "person" as a conscious subject.[129] "Since God is essentially spirit, self-giving, receiving, and loving (that is, far beyond what Greek 'substance' philosophy understands as 'Being'), the relationship of this God to the creature whom he indwells should," Balthasar reasons, "be located beyond the opposition between physic-ontic and purely personal concepts."[130]

All the empirical approximations we use to try to describe the characteristics of the conscious subject within a species (man) are inadequate. Only God can define and designate such a subject in his qualitative uniqueness. And in the one, sole, archetypal instance, it is God who defines who this Subject is and why he is there; it is he who sets forth the meaning, the task, the vocation. In Jesus, the two are identical: this is what distinguishes him from other subjects.[131]

This identity of subject and mission in Jesus accounts for the archetypical value of his person, whom Balthasar presents as the "interior attunement, proportion, and harmony between God and man."[132] It is likewise in him, Balthasar recognizes, that "every man can cherish the hope of not remaining a merely individual conscious subject but of receiving personhood from God" by way, that is to say, of a personalizing "mission that is likewise defined *in Christo*."[133] Paralleling what Balthasar presents as the *a priori* union of person and mission in Christ is thus the analogy of unique personal missions synthesized *a posteriori*, whereby human persons realize their election to become what each one is "in God's sight."[134] As the universal mission of Christ is the "temporal modality" of his eternal procession,[135] the mission

---

128. These, he specifies, are the categories employed by Boethius in his famous definition of person: "*Persona est naturae rationalis individual substantia*" (Boethius, *Liber de Persona et Duabus Naturis*, c. 3: PL 64:1343 [*Patrologia Latina*, vol. 64: *Manlii Severini Boetii Opera Omnia*, ed. Jacques-Paul Migne (Paris, 1847)]; see also "Contra Eutychen et Nestorium," III, 1, in *Traités théologiques*, trans. Axel Tisserand [Paris: Flammarion, 2000], 74). Cf. Thomas Aquinas, *ST* I, q. 29, a. 1. See Balthasar, *Theo-Drama* III, 218. This is not to deny Balthasar's insistence upon Christology as the center of the nature-grace question; see Balthasar, *My Work*, 118.

129. See Balthasar, *Theo-Drama* III, 219–20; and Bernard Schumacher, "La personne comme conscience de soi performante au cœur du débat bioéthique. Analyse critique de la position de John Locke," *Laval théologique et philosophique* 64, no. 3 (2008): 709–43.

130. Balthasar, *Theo-Logic* III, 235. Gilles Emery meanwhile maintains that the metaphysical approach proper to St. Thomas "excludes neither the psychological, moral, and relational features of the person, nor the importance of action. Rather, it enables one to integrate these aspects, and it guarantees their foundation" (*The Trinity: An Introduction to Catholic Doctrine on the Triune God*, trans. Matthew Levering [Washington D.C.: The Catholic University of America Press], 104).

131. Balthasar, *Theo-Drama* III, 220; see also 207; and *Love Alone Is Credible*, 145.

132. Balthasar, *The Glory of the Lord* I, 477.

133. See Balthasar, *Theo-Drama* III, 222; see also *Theo-Logic* III, 271.

134. Ibid., 270.

135. Cf. Thomas Aquinas, *ST* I, q. 43, a. 1.

of each human person in Christ—his or her willing participation in Christ's own mission and form of existence as obedience—is, Balthasar teaches, the "temporal modality of his [or her] integration into the filiation-mission of the Word made flesh."[136] Hence, as if to echo his insistence, as we saw in chapter two, upon the unity of habitual (or sanctifying) grace and charismatic grace, Balthasar insists that every grace implies a mission.[137]

It follows—in accord with the demands of human freedom—that the identifying call from God must be "matched" by a personal response, which is itself—as will become increasingly apparent—also a grace.[138] Hence, from this properly Ignatian perspective of Balthasar—which is, as we shall see, likewise that of Adrienne who stood, since her youth, under the tutelage of the holy founder[139]—"participation in Christ's mission and in the form of his existence becomes possible, across the abiding difference between him and us, where a believer is ready to accept and to live his existence as mission in the Yes that faith utters."[140]

It is thus not surprising that by the same disposition of faith[141]—and again Balthasar uses the German term *Hingabe*, denoting both surrender and devotion, whence also the notion of obedience—the Christian is integrated into the divine communion. Such is Balthasar's understanding of a human

---

136. Marc Ouellet, "The Foundations of Christian Ethics according to Hans Urs von Balthasar" in Schindler, *Hans Urs von Balthasar: His Life and Work*, 237; cf. Balthasar, *Theo-Drama* V, 81, where reference is made to Speyr, *Die Schöpfung*, 11; and Balthasar, *The Christian State of Life*, 189. In this context it is perhaps also important to point out that even in that which concerns the person of Christ, we might distinguish, according to St. Thomas, two generations or births: the one (according to his divine nature) eternal, the other (according to his human nature) temporal. See *Comp* I, 212.

137. See, for example, *Theo-Drama* III, 349; *Theo-Drama* V, 528; *Engagement with God*, 28–29; *The Christian State of Life*, 74; and (with Ratzinger), *Mary: The Church at the Source*, 131. Cf. Speyr, *Ephesians*, 31–32; and *John* I, 108.

138. See Balthasar, *The Christian State of Life*, 141; and *Theo-Logic* III, 239–40 and 270. Cf. Speyr, *John* I, 125.

139. With regard to the influence of St. Ignatius, who appears throughout the diaries (Speyr, *Erde und Himmel* IIII) as SPN ("Sanctus Pater Noster"), Balthasar reports that she had visions of him throughout her youth and that he instructed her "far more" than did he (Balthasar). See Balthasar, *First Glance at Adrienne von Speyr*, 13. For an example of Ignatius's influence upon the common mission of Balthasar and Adrienne, see Balthasar, *Our Task*, 183; and Servais, *Théologie des exercices spirituels*, 42–54. Balthasar's personal secretary, Cornelia Capol, presents St. Ignatius as "a point of contact for them in which they met" (Greiner, "The Community of St. John," 94). See also Balthasar's foreword to Speyr, *Das Hohelied* (Einsiedeln: Johannes Verlag, 1972), 6.

140. Balthasar, "*Explorations in Theology* III, 349.

141. Balthasar appropriates the Speyrian insight according to which Christ, precisely in his relationship of loving obedience to the Father, is "the archetype of faith." See, for example, Speyr, *The Farewell Discourses*, 90; *Korinther* I, 138–41; and *World of Prayer*, 35. Balthasar's appropriation of this insight is particularly apparent in his famous essay, "*Fides Christi*: An Essay on the Consciousness of Christ" in *Explorations in Theology* II, 43–79 ; see also *Theo-Drama* V, 97; and *My Work*, 60–61. On Balthasar's treatment of the faith of Christ as differing from the same concept in the theology of St. Thomas, see Donneaud, "Hans Urs von Balthasar contre saint Thomas d'Aquin sur la foi du Christ."

freedom which is authentically free in virtue of its free subjection to the Son so as, in turn, to be subject in him to the One, "who put all things under him, that God may be everything to every one" (1 Cor 15:28).[142] Similarly, it is precisely in this sense that human freedom is considered as oriented to (and thus open to) divine freedom: by way of the Spirit's indwelling in the Christian, who willingly receives him.[143]

By the Spirit's mediation, the Son, who is the Father's gift to the world in both the Incarnation and the Eucharist, becomes "the norm" dwelling within believers.[144] The Spirit, who works upon the incarnate Son, also relates the resurrected Christ "to the historical Church of every age," particularly by means of the sacraments. He likewise, applies the life of Christ "to every Christian life and the whole life of the Church" by way of ecclesial missions.[145] It is also the Spirit who effects within the believer the Christ-like disposition of obedience: a disposition "that is bestowed as gift, and therefore more the im-pressing" of Christ's attitude "*upon* the believer than his spontaneous reproducing of such a feeling."[146] Meanwhile, the Christian who has received the Spirit of Christ seeks to be attuned (*sich-Einstimmen*) thereby "to the accord [*Stimmen*] existing between Christ and *his* mandate from the Father, in the context of salvation-history's assent [*Zu-stimmung*], which the Holy Spirit *is* in Christ and effects in him."[147]

In virtue of this Christic disposition mediated by the Spirit, the Christian is—like Christ and with Christ—simultaneously oriented to the Father and to the world (or, more specifically, to the world for love of the Father; cf. Jn 14:31) so as to become with Christ the Father's Eucharist: his love, and thus his 'glory,' poured forth as food for the world.[148] Indeed, the Christ of

---

142. See Balthasar, *Theo-Logic* III, 240.
143. See Balthasar, *Epilogue*, 119–22; and *Theo-Logic* III, 240. Similar is the manner in which Balthasar presents human history as expressed in salvation history. See Balthasar, *A Theology of History*, 62.
144. See Balthasar, *Epilogue*, 76; *A Theology of History*, 81; and "Nine Propositions on Christian Ethics," in Joseph Ratzinger, Heinz Schürmann, and Hans Urs von Balthasar, *Principles of Christian Morality* (San Francisco: Ignatius Press, 1986), 77–104. Cf. Pope John Paul II, *Veritatis Splendor*, no. 12.
145. Balthasar, *A Theology of History*, 82. Cf. Speyr, *John* I, 108; and *The Boundless God*, 43.
146. Balthasar, *The Glory of the Lord* I, 255. The Spirit is presented by Balthasar as being "antecedently present" within the believer to receive the impression and to "help it to become the ex-pression of the soul itself" (ibid.); see also *Theo-Drama* V, 485.
147. Balthasar, *The Glory of the Lord* I, 253. "The mandated task is divine, its execution human, and the proportion of perfect 'attunement' prevailing between them is both human and divine" (ibid., 469). See also ibid., 475; and *Theo-Logic* III, 239. The disposition of Christ is, Balthasar specifies, "the disposition of one who has become expropriated for God and for man: his subjectivity coincides with his mission" (ibid., 253–54). Cf. Speyr, *The Boundless God*, 19.
148. See Balthasar, *Theo-Drama* III, 38–39; *Theo-Drama* V, 484–85; and *You Crown the Year with Your Goodness: Radio Sermons*, trans. Graham Harrison (San Francisco: Ignatius Press, 1989), 128–34. See also chapter four of the present volume.

Balthasar is the image of the Father (cf. Col 1:15) not so much as the one in whom is *contained* the Father's glory, but rather as the one from whom this glory is *poured forth*, or communicated, as life-giving revelation for the world. This communication is most clearly manifest on the Cross, of course, but also in the Eucharist, wherein is united the grace of the Father, who gives the Son to the believer, and the grace of the Son, who gives the believer within himself to the Father.

A Speyrian Understanding of the Image of God: Nature and Grace

As is the ongoing thesis of this volume, the complementarity that might be discerned in the works of Balthasar and St. Thomas Aquinas implies the complementarity of both with the opus of Adrienne von Speyr. Hence, within the present context, it is in perfect harmony with the dynamic presentation of the image of God by the angelic doctor—that is to say by way of the ever-growing perfection of the human person in virtue of his or her spiritual capacities of intellect and will—that Adrienne presents this image as a natural birthright, whose fulfillment nonetheless supposes one's freely chosen communion with the triune God.[149] As such—as freely united to God—the image of God whom the person is by nature is invested, Adrienne teaches, with a supernatural quality.[150] Adrienne's commentary of the first creation story thus joins that of many Church Fathers (such as Irenaeus, Origen, Basil, and Maximus the Confessor) who recognize within the image-likeness (*selem-demut*) distinction of Genesis 1:27 the realization of Adam's rational nature in his assimilation to God by grace: the fulfillment of his natural aptitude to know and love in his actual knowing and loving of God.[151] "Imprinted" at the time of creation, it becomes "visible first with development": with, that is to say, one's actual (practical and contemplative) love of God and neighbor.[152]

Beyond this, Adrienne teaches, to say that we are created in the image of God means not only that we bear a "likeness to God's essence," but also that

---

149. Cf. Thomas Aquinas, *ST* I, q. 93, a. 4; and Balthasar, *The Glory of the Lord* VI, 87.
150. See Speyr, *Die Schöpfung*, 57.
151. See *The Catechism of the Catholic Church*, nos. 356–58. Abundant examples are also given by Balthasar in *Theo-Drama* II, 318 and 324–30; see also *Cosmic Liturgy*, 226; *Theo-Drama* V, 113 (with ample reference to Adrienne), and Matthias Joseph Scheeben, *Nature and Grace*, trans. Cyril Vollert (Eugence, Ore.: Wipf & Stock, 2009), 176–81.
152. Speyr, *Die Schöpfung*, 58. Hence, for example, Adam was not created within an actual relationship with Eve, Adrienne teaches, "but in the readiness for the meeting and in knowledge of the necessity of waiting and seeking until he had found her" (ibid.).

God has a certain idea of each of us that is present in God beyond time. In this second sense, the fact of being in the image of God is further understood as a challenge to "prove" ourselves: to correspond—"through the painful expansion of love"—to the particular image that God has of each one of us.[153] Because, moreover, we have no comprehensive overview of our divine likeness (our *Gottabbildlichkeit*),[154] our task is primarily to remain as God wishes us to be: to persist in a loving response to God whereby we reflect God's image and allow God to make use of us as he wills. Hence, the disciple John, for example, is presented by Adrienne as needed by the Lord "as he is" so as to be "used" by the Lord "as the one he is to become."[155] That is to say, his mission was eternally decreed and revealed in the womb "but only later did it become a mission consciously accepted."[156]

This dynamic presentation of the image of God, which the human person is by nature and by grace, is further described by Adrienne in terms of our participation in the divine communion, in virtue of which (*als Ergebnis*) we are equipped for service.[157] Hence God's image is given to the human person in the form of "three capacities": the capacity of *appropriating* the image (*Nehmen*); that of *abiding*, or persevering, in the image (*Verharren*); and that of *transmitting* the image (*Weitergeben*), especially by reflecting (*widerspiegeln*) it in the world through Christian service. The second and third capacities imply a "test" of authenticity with regard to the first capacity: a test determining whether God's image *in* each of us corresponds to God's image *of* each one of us.[158]

The image of God that we bear in the form of these threefold capacities—capacities which push us, as it were, toward fulfillment through a sort of "expansion" of our human nature by means of our own actions and divine grace, whence the idea of *becoming* as opposed to simply *being*—are contrasted by Adrienne to "the stamp and seal" of the Trinitarian life in us in virtue of cre-

---

153. Speyr, *Mary in the Redemption*, 42; cf. *John* I, 36–37; and *The Passion from Within*, trans. Lucia Wiedenhöver (San Francisco: Ignatius Press, 1998), 91–92. This theme of love's expansion is central to Balthasar's *The Christian State of Life*. Once again, we are not far from the perspective of St. Thomas, who teaches, as Marie-Joseph Nicolas summarizes, "This ordination of each nature to its end, to its accomplishment, is certainly inscribed in its very being, but this is so by the Cause of its being," namely, "the divine Reason" ("L'idée de la nature dans la pensée de saint Thomas d'Aquin," 548).

154. As we shall see, this likeness does not so much lie in us, Adrienne reasons, as it does in God. See Speyr, *Das Wort und die Mystik* II, 523. Cf. Balthasar, *Theo-Logic* I, 265–67; and *The Glory of the Lord* VI, 87.

155. Speyr, *John* I, 10. 156. Ibid., 145.

157. Cf. Thomas Aquinas, *ST* I, q. 62, a. 5, wherein it is argued that "grace perfects nature according to the manner of the nature; as every perfection is received in the subject capable of perfection, according to its mode."

158. Speyr, *Die Schöpfung*, 67. Cf. Balthasar, *Two Sisters in the Spirit*, 21. Adrienne's insight here might be compared to the patristic distinction explained above between image and likeness.

ation. This, she explains, is the threefold mark of lives characterized by a beginning (or origin), a middle (or center), and an end (or consummation). In each stage, we run up—at least within our actual, fallen state[159]—with our own finitude; for the beginning of our lives is "birth out of nothing," and our end is death: "a descent, not a completion," whence a center characterized by "flight" from a senseless beginning and dread of a meaningless end.[160] It is, however, precisely in this experience of living within "boundaries," Adrienne reasons, that we encounter God in faith as one granting us the possibility of emerging from this enclosed circle. God divests us of our limited and limiting center so that he might become—by his Word and his Eucharistic body in us—our "ever-greater center-point in the infinite open-angle of eternity."[161]

Viewed in this way, our limits or finitude, and thus also our craving for a "sure" or "certain [*gesicherten*]"[162] center, incline us, as it were, to grasp at the eternal life that Christ offered us, namely by living our temporal life "out of his eternity."[163] It is this eternal life, mediated by Christ, which enables us to transpose our beginning into the eternal and continuously new beginning of the Father, to surrender our center to Christ rather than to our own spirit, and ultimately to be "consumed in the flame of the Holy Spirit's love," which has no end.[164] Henceforth, our earthly life is "no longer a center [between beginning and end], but a line, whose middle has become God's Alpha and Omega."[165] Our unifying center becomes, in other words, the Trinitarian God with the result that—without ceasing to be human—we no longer need to be preoccupied with our selves: "our ego, our flesh, our concupiscence."[166]

---

159. In virtue of man's body, which implies form and space, boundaries are inherent to the human condition, Adrienne explains. In paradise, however, these boundaries were "set in the vast space of God's infinity," so as to be neither experienced nor measured. Only when man breaks off his relation with God by sin do they first become really apparent to man (Speyr, *The Victory of Love*, 32). "Man wants to be his own master within expanding limits" (*The Mystery of Death*, 18).

160. Speyr, *John* I, 27. Cf. Balthasar, *Epilogue*, 50; and *Explorations in Theology* I, 174.

161. Speyr, *Apokalypse*, 808–9; see also *Confession*, 16. On the role of the Word and the Eucharist in the fulfillment of the human person, see Speyr, *The Victory of Love*, 22, and my extensive treatment in chapter four of the Eucharist drawing us into Christ's own life and body.

162. I have taken the liberty here to propose my own translation, as "sure center," which seems more faithful to the original than the "safe center" proposed by the translator. See Speyr, *John* I, 27.

163. Each "excerpt" of Christ's temporal existence should not be viewed, Adrienne explains, as "some neutral middle between beginning and end," but as a middle containing both beginning and end within itself. See Speyr, *Apokalypse*, 808. Cf. Balthasar, *A Theology of History*.

164. Speyr, *John* I, 27 and 29. In a similar manner, Adrienne explains that the Christian must live from the innermost center of him- or herself which has become so occupied by the Word of God that it can no longer be possessed by him- or herself: "I [says the Christian] do not live; he [Christ] lives in me. He must grow, I diminish" (Speyr, *Theologie der Geschlechter*, 89). Cf. Gal 2:20 and Jn 3:30.

165. Speyr, *Apokalypse*, 808–9.

166. Cf. Speyr, *The Victory of Love*, 27–28. Not surprisingly, the sacrament of reconciliation plays an important role here; see Speyr, *Confession*, 18.

These are, as it were, surrendered in the act of loving obedience, which sets Christ's Spirit at the heart of our acting powers. This is, in fact, the meaning that Adrienne gives to Christ's final words on the Cross, "It is consummated": that our center of action is freed of these forces so as to become the force of the new law of the Spirit.[167] In contrast to the law of flesh, which is "closed in on itself" and which characterizes human life without Christ, the new law of Christ at the center of Christian existence is "a law of community, of church, of enlargement of life and ever-renewed union with God." It is "an opening, a beginning,"[168] into eternity.

From this perspective, the image of God in our finite nature is that whereby we are oriented toward fulfillment in divine communion, which, in turn, constitutes the realization of our likeness to God: the image that we are thereby corresponds (it bears repeating) to the image that God has of us. Because, in fact, each of us is the image of God, we are capable of contemplating God; but we are also required to do so. As image, we must look upon the "original," or archetype, so as to be thereby transformed into the image that God intends for us.[169] This image that God has of us—or intends for us—lies, in turn, within the eternal mystery of the Godhead, wherein it is ultimately realized. God's image is not—in the final analysis—realized in the human being, Adrienne explains, but in God, who desires that we be immersed in his Trinitarian life.[170] Such, of course, is a profoundly God-centered vision of the human person.

Human Perfection in Divine Communion as Viewed by Adrienne von Speyr

Foreshadowing, as it were, the Christological inspiration of the conciliar document *Gaudium et Spes* whereby Christ "fully reveals man to man himself and makes his supreme calling clear,"[171] Adrienne thus reasons in a manner opposite to the more traditional, especially Thomistic, anthropologies.[172] Rather than proceeding (by analogy) from general, abstract, or universal human nature to its particular concretization in any one individual human

---

167. Speyr, *The Victory of Love*, 24.   168. Ibid., 30.

169. See Speyr, *Light and Images*, 153; and *The Countenance of the Father*, 83. Cf. Balthasar, *Elucidations*, 64; and *Dare We Hope*, 234–35.

170. Speyr, *Die Schöpfung*, 67; cf. Jn 17.   171. *Gaudium et Spes*, no. 22; *DZ* 4322.

172. Whence the widespread criticism of this approach, as we shall see in chapter seven. See, for example, Thomas Joseph White, "The 'Pure Nature' of Christology: Human Nature and *Gaudium et Spes* 22," *Nova et Vetera* (English Edition) 8, no. 2 (2010): 283–322; and Long, *Natura Pura*, 22, 33, and 86–87. This criticism will be taken up more thoroughly in chapter seven within the context of the question of whether Balthasar adequately distinguishes between the human and divine natures of Christ.

being, she (like Balthasar) proceeds, as we saw in our general introduction, katalogically: from the concrete, individual being of the man-God, Jesus Christ, who manifests the universal significance of human nature within his own privileged relationship with the Father.[173] "Jesus is not 'anyone,' nor is he 'everyone': he is himself," Adrienne reasons. "And precisely as such a particular person is he the way to the Father."[174] In union with Balthasar, who presents Christ as the "concrete universal,"[175] Adrienne argues that Christ's uniqueness (*das Einmalige*) is the foundation of his universality.[176] The Lord is thus the norm of our humanity; he is "perfect and complete," unlike we, who are "barely indicated."[177] We have being only in the form of *becoming*, Adrienne explains, which is to say that we must "'become' what God 'is.'"[178] This, of course, does not mean that the Christian's movement toward God is simply a movement toward more being; nor is it simply a movement toward the source and goal of his or her being, except when this is understood as a movement toward ever more profound communion: the accomplishment of the human person—as we shall see throughout this chapter—by means of his or her participation in Christ's own filial relation to the Father, namely by way of a participation in his mission and by the grace of his Spirit.

From this perspective, the dynamic of Adrienne's anthropology is—like that of Balthasar, as we have seen—not so much that of the human being advancing toward God, who is presented as the "term" of his or her search for happiness, as that of God descending toward the human being to take him or her up into divine Trinitarian life. The "becoming," which constitutes the dynamism of the Christian life, is—for both Adrienne and Balthasar, not unlike the theological tradition as a whole—conceived as a continuation of the act of creation involving the human person not only as the object of the divine creative action, but also as an acting subject: "Coming from him, we are his handiwork, so that, returning to him, we may do good works"; works whose purpose is "to help us remain on the path that leads to God."[179]

Because God created us to freely participate in his divinity, our "being

---

173. "Christology (as sketched in its outlines by Chalcedon) gives an account of an event that cannot be made subject to any universal law but that subjects all other laws (regulating the relationship between God and the creature, that is) to its own uniqueness" (Balthasar, *Theo-Logic* II, 311); see also *A Theology of History*, 18–19, 21, and 70–71.

174. Speyr, *They Followed His Call*, 67; see also *John* II, 78–79.

175. See, for example, Balthasar, *Explorations in Theology* I, 170; *The Glory of the Lord* I, 147; *A Theology of History*, 118; "On the Task of Catholic Philosophy in our Time," 160; (with Albus), "Spirit and Fire," 593; and Babini, "Jesus Christ: Form and Norm of Man," 228–29.

176. Speyr, *Korinther* I, 323.   177. Speyr, *John* I, 40. See also ibid., 27.

178. Speyr, *Das Wort und die Mystik* II, 105; cf. Balthasar, *Theo-Drama* V, 512.

179. Speyr, *The Letter to the Ephesians*, 92; see also 21. On the similarities with the teaching of St. Thomas, see Nicolas, "L'idée de la nature dans la pensée de saint Thomas d'Aquin," 564–73.

here" is, Adrienne reasons, the beginning of our "being with God."[180] The dynamic of human fulfillment is—from this perspective—not understood as a discovery of the self from within the depths of one's own soul, unless these "depths" are understood as a place of encounter. Indeed, "If experience [...] even in a worldly sense is not a *state* but an *event* (and the very form of the word points to this with the prefix *ex*-), it follows," Balthasar reasons, "that it is not man's entry [*Einfahern*] into himself, into his best and highest possibilities, which can become an experience [*Erfahrung*], but rather, it is his act of entering into the Son of God, Christ Jesus, who is naturally inaccessible to him, which becomes the experience that alone can claim for itself his undivided obedience."[181] The "yes" of faith is initially directed, Adrienne explains, "to a being that is before me, above me, beside me. That is how we imagine the Son. [...] But our Yes is hardly uttered before it takes an altogether unexpected turn, it turns inward, it enters into us." By this, Adrienne explains—as if to echo a famous insight of St. Augustine of Hippo—that the Lord makes us thereby aware of his presence within us, "hidden in our inmost I."[182] It is not narcissism, therefore, that renders one fully human, in Adrienne's presentation, but communion within the "unity" of God, a unity which comprehends our own unity.

It follows that the interiorization symbolic of self-discovery is directed in Adrienne's theology towards an exteriorization: an ecstatic movement "out" of one's own self toward the divine other, who is always the first to surrender himself. "It is when we forget ourselves and rise above ourselves that we discover God's grace," Adrienne teaches, which is to say that grace is possessed only when one is confidently abandoned to it.[183] Such is also characteristic of the gift of redemption: it is never really "possessed" outside of the act of receiving it, which is to say that "we receive it continually as something new."[184] It is therefore not surprising that Adrienne presents the path to divine communion as more spiral than linear. Constantly mounting to higher vantage points, it simultaneously and continuously returns to the same reference point, or "overview," in con-

---

180. Speyr, *Korinther* I, 378; cf. Balthasar, *Theo-Drama* V, 113. Similarly, Adrienne notes that Paul, in his letter to the Ephesians, "is relating being to being holy" (*The Letter to the Ephesians*, 18): a remark which need not be understood as confusing nature and grace.

181. Balthasar, *The Glory of the Lord* I, 222.

182. Speyr, *John* I, 101; cf. Augustine, "*interior intimo meo et superior summo meo* [deeper than my inmost understanding and higher than the topmost height that I could reach]" (*Confessions* III, 6). See also Balthasar, *The Glory of the Lord* I, 430; *Theo-Drama* II, 410; and *Does Jesus Know Us?*, 98.

183. In contrast, "the more we concern ourselves with our being and our self, the further it eludes our grasp" (Speyr, *John* I, 41). Cf. Thomas Aquinas, *De Ver* q. 28, a. 8, ad. 6.

184. Speyr, *The Letter to the Ephesians*, 38; see also ibid., 30; *John* II, 64; and Balthasar, *Glory of the Lord* VII, 407 and 411.

templation.[185] The "action" of human perfection is thus primarily *contemplative* action, with primacy being awarded not so much to self-consciousness nor to objective knowledge, but rather to love— which is not to deny that the two might be harmoniously combined.[186] Adrienne recommends more specifically, as we saw in chapter two, a contemplation of the Trinity from within: in virtue, that is to say, of our graced participation in the divine nature (cf. 2 Pt 1:3–4).

Contemplating as God does, the Christian learns to contemplate. Observing how God lives with God, the Christian learns how to live with his fellow man. It is not enough for every action and every contemplation on earth to aspire to heaven in the vague hope of arriving somewhere and being accepted. Action and contemplation must also participate spiritually and cognitively in God's way, using it as a guide and a plumbline for earthly life in God. The human being is not only the observer of God: He contemplates God's contemplation, and he sees God's vision, a vision that embraces contemplation and action in a unity.[187]

The fullness of life that Christ wishes to give us is not, therefore, that "of *our* life, of our person, of our character, but unity in him." That which we regard as "our own unity, and perhaps endeavor to attain, can be won only by moving toward his unity."[188] This means that the "ever-more," whom God is— an image which we treated at length in chapter two—contains the "more" that he requires of us. However, unlike he who *is* more, "we must *become* more." In other words, we are to participate "in his *state of being* more" precisely by remaining "in the *life of becoming* more."[189]

Because Adrienne presents the triune God as the "ever-more," our apprehension of him is itself "a growing capacity to allow ourselves to be filled by the abundance of his light."[190] Of course, the Lord always remains "mysterious and beyond our grasp," she insists, but not in the manner of "an opaque mystery that one cannot get behind." Rather, it is precisely "through the very infinity and openness of his mystery itself"[191] that the Lord is overwhelming for us; for his mystery simultaneously lives within us, as a "parable of his grace" working "in hiddenness"[192] and drawing us into its own infinite space.

---

185. Speyr, *John* II, 304; see also *The Victory of Love*, 26, where the spiral image is also used to describe the life of the spirit.

186. Cf. Balthasar, *First Glance at Adrienne von Speyr*, 246. On the primacy of love even in this life, see also Georges Cottier, "Metaphysics and Mysticism," *Nova et Vetera* (English edition) 1 (2003): 269–82.

187. Speyr, *World of Prayer*, 46–47; cf. Balthasar, *Explorations in Theology* III, 44; and *First Glance at Adrienne von Speyr*, 245–46.

188. Speyr, *John* II, 72. This intuition is perhaps at the origin of the major thesis of Balthasar's *A Theological Anthropology*, whence the title in German: "The Whole in Part" (*Das Ganze im Fragment*). Cf. also Mk 8:35, and Adrienne's commentary thereof in *Markus*, 379.

189. Speyr, *John* I, 309.
190. Ibid., 48.
191. Speyr, *John* III, 364.
192. Ibid., 342.

The Mystery of Grace and Merit from the Perspective of the Mutual Immanence of Christ and the Christian

This movement (of becoming) toward unity (of being) in Christ—one which, as we saw in the general introduction to this volume, typifies Balthasar's integrative approach to theology—might thus be characterized, as he (Balthasar) explains, by a double movement: that of expropriation and that of appropriation. "Being carried out of oneself," which is the definition that Balthasar gives to faith, "is nothing else than a clearing of space in oneself for this love." It is "a determination of one's existence," whereby one is willingly "conformed to the existence of the crucified." Hence, "our inclusion in the life of Christ does not only give us an outward direction, but penetrates us from within."[193]

This, in other words, is accomplished by way of our continuous surrender to the one who integrates us into his life by means of his own (absolutely primary, that is to say, fully initiating) surrender to us.[194] In other words, the Christian receives the wealth of Christ's surrender—wherein is revealed the whole mystery of Trinitarian life and communion[195]—through his or her own surrender, which (as we saw in chapter two) is nonetheless the fruit of Christ's primary surrender to him or her. Human accomplishment thus implies a participation in divine communion: a participation in and by way of that which characterizes or is proper to this communion, namely the loving—and thus willing—surrender of the person as a gift to and for others.[196]

To help clarify the mode of this mediation, Adrienne calls upon the illustrative analogy of sexual love. Commenting, more specifically, upon Mark 10:1–9, in which reference is made to Genesis 2:24 ("So they are no longer two but one"), Adrienne recognizes the original unity of man and woman in God's creative plan as an analogy for the fruitful union between Christ and

---

193. Balthasar, *Glory of the Lord* VII, 407.
194. "God needs selfless vessels into which he can pour his essential selflessness" (Balthasar, *New Elucidations*, 44). This insight will be more thoroughly developed within the context of our treatment of the mystery of redemption in chapter five. See also Balthasar's foreword to Speyr, *Das Wort und die Mystik* I, 13; *First Glance at Adrienne von Speyr*, 59; *Mysterium Paschale*, 90–91; *The Christian State of Life*, 37; and *A Theology of History*, 29–40.
195. As we saw in chapter two, the terrestrial Lord is so perfectly transparent to the Father, so completely open to and receptive of his action, so fully submissive to his mandates, that he reveals the Father by allowing him (the Father) to act within him (the Son). See Speyr, *Das Wort und die Mystik* II, 523; and *John* II, 372. See also Balthasar, *Our Task*, 64–65; *First Glance at Adrienne von Speyr*, 60–61; and *Love Alone Is Credible*, 87.
196. See, for example, Balthasar's introduction to Speyr, *Das Wort und die Mystik* I, 13. This theme has already been treated in our general introduction to this volume and will be further developed in the pages which follow.

the Church, or Christ and the Christian: a union in virtue of which it is no longer possible for the latter to distinguish between that which is properly his or hers (and thus human) and that which is received as a supernatural gift: between that which is attributable to nature and that which is attributable to grace.

In the mutual gift of self (surrender) in the marital act, both man and woman experience self-forgetfulness: their personal distinctions appear less evident than the unity of their couple. The "boundaries between yours and mine disappear;" for the I is led, "without realization, into the You." Adrienne reasons that at a certain (culminating) point in the sexual act, self-forgetfulness is so great that it is no longer possible—at least on the experiential, or subjective, level—to determine whether the act takes place (or form) in the *I* or in the *You*. It is as if "the boundaries have fallen," she explains;[197] and in fact, the man does not bear fruit in himself, but in the woman. Similarly—or analogically—there is no clear boundary between the handing over (*Übergabe*) and taking on (*Übernahme*) of grace, between grace as given and grace as received, between the assent to and the exchange of absolute love in the form of grace.[198]

This exchange is effected by the indiscriminate manner in which the Lord hands himself over to the Church, such that it is no longer possible to distinguish between what the Lord gives and what the Church receives and gives back by way of her response.[199] She (the Church) is simply drawn into the Lord's "open space" with the result that "his openness becomes ours."[200] Giving and receiving are "one in love,"[201] which also means that love's expression is inspired by both the lover and the beloved in an "interplay of fulfillment and expectation."[202]

Despite possible impressions to the contrary, this is not to admit confusion between the natural and the supernatural realms, between God's always initiating action and our responsive action. Rather, Adrienne's intention in employing these images is to highlight both the generosity and the efficacy of grace, even to the extent that it might be said to call forth a positive response from the hardened human heart, as shall be addressed later in this chapter and still more thoroughly in chapter five. From within this perspective, the classic theological debate over the paradoxical relation between nature and

---

197. Speyr, *Theologie der Geschlechter*, 98; see also 100 and 104. On the other hand, Adrienne insists that the mutual transparency of lovers "does not violate their personhood or eliminate the boundaries that distinguish them" (Speyr, *Light and Images*, 18).

198. See Speyr, *Der Mensch vor Gott*, 53–54; *World of Prayer*, 4; and *Theologie der Geschlechter*, 140.

199. Speyr, *The Letter to the Ephesians*, 230–31.   200. Speyr, *John* III, 364.

201. Speyr, *Korinther* I, 427.   202. Speyr, *World of Prayer*, 40.

grace—guided, to some extent, by the Aristotelian principle, *ordo essendi est ordo agendi* ["the order of essence is the order of action"][203]—is presented in terms of the relationship of mutual immanence between Christ and the Christian, which follows upon the mutual immanence, or the circumincession, of the Father and the Son.[204] This explains the pivotal role assumed by the complementary concepts of mission and obedience, as is likewise to be found in Thomistic teaching,[205] and as we shall investigate more thoroughly in Adrienne's theology in the next section of this chapter.

Through Christ's presence in us—by means most especially of his Word and his grace—"we become him in us: we become children of God."[206] And, as there is "no boundary" in Christ "between his possessing the Father and his being possessed by the Father,"[207] so also (that is to say, analogically: allowing for difference on the level of substance)[208] our reception of the Son and his reception of us "can no longer be clearly distinguished: the border between the one received and the one receiving is obliterated."[209]

This mystery is also captured by Adrienne's presentation of Christ's life as an existence "in exchange": an idea altogether compatible with the patristic and Thomistic presentation of salvation as an *admirabile commercium*, a wonderful exchange.[210] Adrienne notes, more specifically, the movement in

---

203. See Nicolas, "L'idée de la nature dans la pensée de saint Thomas d'Aquin," 564–84.

204. See, for example, Speyr, *Mary in the Redemption*, 116–17; *John* III, 104; *John* I, 102; and *Die katholischen Briefe* II, 179. Similarly in the theology of Balthasar, as we shall see (especially in chapter four), the mediating role that Aquinas assigns to Christ's humanity—as the instrument of his divinity, it is both sanctified and sanctifying (cf. *ST* III, q. 34, a. 1, ad. 3 and a. 3; q. 48, a. 1; and I-II, q. 114, a. 6)—the Swiss theologian attributes to the divine personality of Christ. He is "the middle term of a double relation of reciprocal immanence" (*Does Jesus Know Us?*, 52): namely, his relationship of filiation to the Father in the unity of the Holy Spirit, and his relationship—for love of the Father—with the Church and mankind in the unity of the same Spirit.

205. See Waldstein, "The Analogy of Mission and Obedience."

206. Commentary of Jn 1:12 in Speyr, *John* I, 103. The Lord transforms our love, our expectations, and our efforts—as Adrienne comments on Jn 17:22—within his own love "until what is ours simply dissolves in what is his" (Speyr, *John* III, 364). "As ultimately we are unfit to dispose of our own Yes, we must give it to God in prayer so as not to live in ourselves but in his word, the word in which we are created" (*John* I, 36); see also *John* III, 342.

207. See Speyr, *John* III, 104. Similarly, Balthasar refers to the "identity" in Christ of the reception of his being from the Father and of his "adoring assent" to the Father, that is to say, "the identity between reception of one's being and adoring assent to the Father, between being and the act in which the whole of one's being is lovingly received" (*A Theology of History*, 32).

208. Hence, the Fourth Lateran General Council (1215) taught, for example, that when Christ prays "that they may be one in us as we also are one" (Jn 17:22), "the word 'one' as applied to the disciples is to be taken in the sense of a union of charity in grace but in the case of the Divine Persons, in the sense of a unity of identity in nature" (*DZ* 806).

209. Speyr, *John* I, 102; see also her commentary of 1 Jn 4:17 in *Die katholischen Briefe* II, 179; *Theologie der Geschlechter*, 98; and *Korinther* I, 390.

210. Such is the "exchange" realized by Christ in taking on our sinful humanity while simultaneously giving us to share in his divinity. The references are bountiful, as Balthasar notes. See his *Theo-*

John's Gospel from the presentation of Christ as having "all life" *in himself* to the presentation of Christians as having "all life" *through him*. It follows, Adrienne reasons, that Christian life is not static but occurs within the dynamic of the Son's movement to the Father. Because Christ *is*, in fact, both this movement and the life that he promises, he is also this movement and this life "in those who believe in him, love him and hope in him."[211] His being, received by us, brings about our becoming[212]—our growth in divine filiation, or the development of our baptismal grace—but always *in him*, with the result that our becoming is also rightfully described as remaining. "To remain means: to remain in movement, to hunger and to be fed, to thirst and to be given drink, to feel all the needs of the spirit and to experience their satisfaction, and all of this in a continuously intensifying sense, so that each satisfaction awakens a greater hunger, because it broadens out the soul, and love becomes ever more urgent and more burning."[213]

This biblical image of remaining in Christ (cf. Jn 6:56) opens still another dimension of the one mystery of our becoming (divinization; cf. Jn 1:12) within the Lord's "becoming" (Incarnation, Ascension, and all that follows therefrom):[214] the fact that Christ's dwelling within us—in virtue of our Eucharistic communions and of his word, or teaching, received by us—cannot be separated from our dwelling within him. The latter is a revealed reality that Adrienne admits is much more difficult to understand and visualize. Both of these mysteries of indwelling, common to Johannine and Pauline theology alike—Christ's dwelling in us and our dwelling in him[215]—are, however, so much a part of Christ's "essence,"[216] Adrienne explains, that they

---

Drama III, 237–45; and *Theo-Drama* IV, 246. Cf. *The Catechism of the Catholic Church*, no. 460; and Thomas Aquinas, *ST* III, q. 1, a. 2. This doctrine is complemented by the doctrine of the mystical body of Christ (cf. *ST* III, q. 48, a. 1; a. 2, ad. 1), as Torrell points out; see *Pour nous les hommes et pour notre salut*, 304. See also the selected passages on this theme from St. Irenaeus's *Adversus Haereses* in *The Scandal of the Incarnation*, 53–59.

211. Speyr, *John* II, 66; see also *The Letter to the Colossians*, 32.
212. See Speyr, *The Letter to the Colossians*, 71; and *John* I, 309.
213. Speyr, *John* II, 70–71; and *The Holy Mass*, 73, where reference is made to persevering in love.
214. See Adrienne von Speyr, *Passion nach Matthäus* (Einsiedeln: Johannes Verlag, 1957), 86; and Balthasar, *Theo-Drama* V, 519.
215. On the one hand, Paul addresses the mystery of "Christ [who] lives in me" or "in us" (Gal 2:19, 4:19; Rom 8:9–11; 2 Cor 4:16, 13:2–5); on the other hand, he presents Christians as living or being found "in Christ" (Rom 8:1; Gal 3:2b; Phil 3:9; etc.). In the Gospel of John, see, for example, 6:56; 14:23; 15:5, 7, 10; and 17:21–26. See also Balthasar's treatment of these "exchangeable formulae" in *The Glory of the Lord* VII, 407 and 411; on the formula "*en Christo*," see *Theo-Drama* III, 245–50; and *Theo-Drama* V, 520 and 528.
216. To be sure, this insight is more mystical than metaphysical or ontological, but again, the emphasis in Adrienne's "method" is upon the revealed reality, often formulated in terms of image and metaphor, both of which seek to clarify the mystery surpassing our human (and thus also our philosophical) concepts.

cannot be separated one from the other. By this, Adrienne means that we are not only "possessed" by him, but that we are also "comprehended in his person,"[217] so as to be incorporated into his filial relation to the Father, which is manifested in time as obedience to his mission.

This idea of being "in his person"—like that of being part of his essence—is assuredly not to be justified philosophically, for the insight it bespeaks is more biblical (or mystical) than philosophical (ontological or metaphysical). Within, more specifically, Adrienne's Johannine presentation of the person-mission identity of Christ[218]—wherein might well be the origin of Balthasar's apparently original concept of theological persons—the Swiss physician recognizes the possibility of a certain acquired perfection of the God-man. Beyond his growth "in wisdom and in stature, and in favor with God and man" (Lk 2:52), she, like Balthasar, notes a certain "fullness" attributable to Christ in virtue of his mission.[219] It is "his own self in fullness" that he offers the Father with the completed mission.[220] The mission, in turn, is achieved when his Incarnation (Jn 1:14) is achieved, or effected, *in us* (cf. Jn 1:12): by way, most especially, of the Eucharist.

The emphasis in Adrienne's theology is thus not upon Christ over and above the Christian, but upon the Christian within the total reality of Christ, who dominates both her anthropological and theological vision. He is everything, whereas we are "nothing." Nonetheless "his Everything would not be complete"[221]—for his mission would not be complete—if we were not to be found in him. Beyond the dialectic of nature or grace, Adrienne thus proposes the authentically Catholic unity of nature and grace,[222] or—more true to the thought of Adrienne—of the Christian and Christ. This formula, in turn, might be presented—so as to be more accurately accorded with her biblical insight—as the mystery of Christ in the Christian and of the Christian in Christ.

The Christian acts together with Christ, so as to act "with grace and by

---

217. Speyr, *John III*, 128. This incorporation is so extensive, Adrienne explains, that we are taken with him "everywhere that he is" (ibid.). See also ibid., 129; and *The Letter to the Colossians*, 71.

218. See, for example, Speyr, *John II*, 71 and 372; *John I*, 68 and 106; and *The Letter to the Ephesians*, 32.

219. For Adrienne's commentary on Luke 2:52, see Speyr, *Handmaid of the Lord*, 87–92. The theme of Christ's fullness will be treated more thoroughly in chapter four.

220. Speyr, *John II*, 373. This is not to deny—in a perspective altogether compatible with the notion of Christ as the sacrament in person from whom originate the sacraments of the Church, that Christ is "fullness in person: God and man, and both in a perfect, immutable manner" (Speyr, *The Letter to the Ephesians*, 166). Cf. Col 1:19; and Pope Pius XII, *Mystici Corporis*, June 29, 1943 (*DZ* 3813).

221. Speyr, *John III*, 128.

222. The saint, Adrienne explains, is a "graced human being [*ein Gnadenmensch*]" whose works contain the characteristics of both the human being and grace. See Speyr, *Der Mensch vor Gott*, 9.

merit."[223] This means that the Christian must have an "active faith" (which Adrienne qualifies as "merit") if he or she is to authentically experience the "grace of faith" (*Glaubensgnade*) in his or her life.[224] It is in this sense that Adrienne presents the grace of the Mass, for example, as "measured and proportioned to the individual believer," in virtue of which it is a real drama, moving "from person to person, from life to life."[225] Through the Mass, each individual Christian is given the grace to make of his or her life and suffering a part of the Lord's own life and suffering, and to the extent that he or she thus effectively participates in the Eucharistic mysteries—offering his or her life and sufferings—the Mass may be considered more "perfect" and "complete."[226] This participation is reckoned by Adrienne as part of the Church's faith, which is required of her in the celebration of the Eucharist; for it corresponds to the will of the Lord that he be received in faith, in virtue of which we may be said to live in him rather than in ourselves. Hence the efficacy of sacramental grace is determined, humanly speaking, by the extent of the believer's assent,[227] which, as we shall see, is fostered by the perfect assent of Mary, in whom the Church exists in plenitude.

By way of further explanation, Adrienne refers to the scene of the Cross, wherefrom—she explains, like the Church Fathers before her—the sacraments originate.[228] The Lord desires, she continues, that those witnessing his crucifixion take in and grasp as much as possible of what they observe and hear. His passion is not meant to be simply an *opus operatum*, happening to them in the absence of their knowledge. Rather, they are taken seriously in their humanity. By this is meant that they are expected *to accept* his self-surrender; and to the extent that they do, Christ's life is effectively "taken

---

223. Speyr, *The Victory of Love*, 23. Merit, understood as a human striving after God, is always a response to a divine grace, Adrienne explains; see *Das Wort und die Mystik* II, 529. Cf. *The Catechism of the Catholic Church*, no. 2008.

224. Speyr, *Theologie der Geschlechter*, 234.

225. Speyr, *John* I, 46.

226. Our suffering, Adrienne specifies, does not lighten the Lord's suffering in any way, but it does "feed" his joy: the joy experienced at his Resurrection and Ascension when he presents his perfected work to the Father. Our co-suffering is, Adrienne reasons, a sign and fruit of his work. See Speyr, *Erde und Himmel* III, no. 2259 (249). Similar is the theme, which we will treat in chapter four, of the "perfecting" of Christ's mission by the building up of his body, the Church.

227. See Speyr, *The Holy Mass*, 84; and *Das Wort und die Mystik* II, 497–98.

228. On the patristic theme of the sacraments of the Church coming forth from the side of Christ asleep on the Cross, see *The Catechism of the Catholic Church*, no. 766; St. Augustine of Hippo, *In Ioannis evangelium tractatus* IX,10, in *Homélies sur l'Évangile de Saint Jean*, trans. M.-F. Berrouard (Paris: Desclée de Brouwer, 1969), 474–76; PL 35:1463 (= *Patrologiae Latina*, vol. 35: *Sancti Aurelii Augustini Hipponesis Episcopi*, ed. Jacques-Paul Migne [Paris, 1842], English translation by William A. Jurgens in his *The Faith of the Early Fathers*, vol. III [Collegeville, Minn.: Liturgical Press, 1979], 117); Sabastian Tromp, "De nativitate ecclesiae ex Corde Jesus in Cruce," *Gregorianum* 13 (1932): 489–527; and Balthasar, *Explorations in Theology* II, 146. Cf. Speyr, *The Cross: Word and Sacrament*, 31.

from him" (cf. Jn 10:17–18), so as to be given to them.[229] The gift is only successfully given, in other words, when it is received: a point which is of no small importance for a Speyrian doctrine of redemption, as we shall see in chapter five. This acceptance of the Lord as redeemer also implies, in Adrienne's theology, an ongoing reception of the Eucharistic Lord, such that each communion might be understood as growth towards Christ: "we take what he gives us and give what he wishes to take from us."[230] In virtue of the Spirit's action and the believer's cooperation, the Eucharistic Lord thus presumes a certain "mutuality" of love: he not only obliges himself in our regard, "he obligates us, too, in his own regard."[231] This means, more specifically, that we are required to give ourselves to the one who gives himself to us.

Such is the power arising from Christ's own Spirit within us, who enables us to comprehend his grace and to give answer, not withstanding the mediation of the Incarnation, the Church, and the sacraments.[232] Hence, for example, the Spirit serves a double function in the sacrament of the Eucharist: he gives the sacramental form to the Son's body and he gives to believers the certainty of faith and hope. "The Son says, 'This is my body; it will work in you when you receive it.' But between the Son's word and its accomplishment, there remains a sort of margin in believers": a margin that is to say, between the prodigality of the Lord's surrender, which is at the origin of his gift, and the poverty or reserve of our surrender wherein that gift is received. It is this margin, Adrienne argues, that is "filled by the Spirit."[233]

With recourse (again) to the analogy of sexual love, Adrienne emphasizes the fact that grace is actualized by means of our cooperation. In other words, we really do surrender ourselves (especially by way of obedience, as we shall see) to the Lord, who is nonetheless always the first to surrender himself to us. It is his surrender of himself to the Church (and to the Christian) in the Eucharist that "opens" her to receive him in the readiness of love. This openness, which is also the attitude proper to confession, is thus comparable to the "nakedness" of spouses mutually offering themselves in the marital act.[234] Just as a woman must surrender herself to her husband if she is to be fecund with his seed, so also the Christian must give of him- or herself to the Lord so as to filled with his life and power.[235] "Only a naked soul can be

---

229. Speyr, *The Cross: Word and Sacrament*, 10; cf. Balthasar, *Theo-Logic* III, 310.
230. Speyr, *John* II, 73.   231. Ibid., 70.
232. See Speyr, *The Letter to the Ephesians*, 22–23; cf. (by the same author) *Isaias: Erklärung ausgewählter Texte mit einem Anhang zu den Visionen Daniels* (Einsiedeln: Johannes Verlag, 1958), 222–24.
233. Speyr, *Das Wort und die Mystik* II, 528.
234. See Speyr, *Theologie der Geschlechter*, 82–83 and 109; and *Das Wort und die Mystik* II, 514.
235. See Speyr, *Das Hohelied*, 43.

fruitful."²³⁶ If, in fact, the Church in each of her members were to receive the Eucharistic Lord with an openness matching his surrender to her, she would, Adrienne teaches, be formed fully in accord with his will.²³⁷ Every soul "can and must" be possessed entirely by the Lord, so as to be "pure devotion, pure surrender" in his regard.²³⁸

This means that the Christian's surrender is truly necessary for Christ's occupation of his or her soul. On the other hand, it is by "impregnating a soul," Adrienne reasons, that "the Lord renders it virginal," which is to say not only that the soul belongs henceforth to the Lord—as a bride belongs to her bridegroom²³⁹—but also that the Lord renders his beloved "unconditionally ready" to do all that he demands. Consequently, the soul is "fecund from *his* fecundity."²⁴⁰

It follows from this reasoning that the Eucharist is accomplished not in the changing of the bread and wine into the body and blood of Christ, but in the changing of the communicant who "rests" in the Lord during his or her prayer of thanksgiving before communicating the Eucharistic gift beyond him- or herself, namely by way of a participation in the universal mission of Christ and his Church.²⁴¹ Like all the sacraments, which connect believers with the Cross of Christ, it "both [shares] and give[s] a share in the Son's mission."²⁴² From the moment he is received, the Eucharistic Lord brings about in the communicant a movement *to the Lord*: not only an acceptance in faith of his Incarnation and life, but also of "everything he wants to do in us [...] a surrender, a taking on of new tasks."²⁴³ This he does not only by making more room in us for himself—expanding, as it were, our assent (amen) so as to prepare us in each Communion for the next—but also by making use of us, once we have received him, to give of himself to others. Indeed, he gives himself so radically that "in doing so he is given by us."²⁴⁴

236. Speyr, *Theologie der Geschlechter*, 123.
237. See Speyr, *Das Hohelied*, 43.
238. Speyr, *John* III, 364; see also *Letter to the Ephesians*, 225; and *Das Wort und die Mystik*, II, 27.
239. This, of course, implies that all members of the Church are in some sense "feminine" with regard to the Lord, as we shall see in chapter six of the present volume. See also Pope John Paul II, *Mulieris Dignitatem*, no. 29.
240. Speyr, *Theologie der Geschlechter*, 136. This is not to deny, however, the importance of human freedom, which is so great that each of us has the power, Adrienne explains, to determine whether he or she will be fecund or sterile vis-à-vis God. See ibid, 131; *Das Wort und die Mystik* I, 28 and 135; and *The Christian State of Life*, 174–75.
241. Speyr, *Theologie der Geschlechter*, 133. The miracle of the Eucharist occurs in those who eat this heavenly bread, Adrienne explains in *Markus*, 635; see also *The Letter to the Ephesians*, 48.
242. Speyr, *The Cross: Word and Sacrament*, 11.
243. Speyr, *The Victory of Love*, 23; see also *John* II, 64.
244. Speyr, *John* I, 83.

Breaking Boundaries from Within: The Expansion of Human Nature by Christ in the Christian

This mystery of our participation in Christ's fruitfulness is explained by Adrienne in terms of the Lord's presence within us, a presence in virtue of which we participate in his power and his possibilities. Christ does not, in other words, overcome the limitations of our nature from without—pushing us to excel beyond what we deem possible—but from within: by his power at work in us, namely, by faith and love, which he plants in our soul with the intention that they grow therein. Adrienne explains this phenomenon—within the context of her commentary on Paul's letter to the Ephesians—in terms not so much of grace and merit, as in the activity of the human person "meeting" the activity of God. Unlike the Son of God, who is eternally one with the Father, we must learn to become increasingly one with him. In so doing, we have the help of the Son, who assumes the most important part of our activity: from within us, he meets the Father "halfway."[245] This supposes, however, that Christ has already begun to accomplish his mission in us; for only when we are incorporated into his body may he be said to act in us and by us.[246]

In accord once again with what we have examined as a katalogical (as differing from an analogical) perspective—a perspective beginning with divine revelation so as to reason from the divine archetype to the human image rather than vice-versa—Adrienne's own emphasis is upon Christ and our incorporation into his life: a life of filiation. The thirty-three years of the Lord's terrestrial life are described as his continuous terrestrial "becoming,"[247] wherein is manifest—in a manner altogether compatible with the insights of St. Irenaeus, for example—"the mystery of our becoming within the becoming of the Lord."[248] The entire earthly existence of Christ is in service of our

---

245. Speyr, *The Letter to the Ephesians*, 22. See, for what follows, Speyr, *The Letter to the Colossians*, 56–57; and *Das Wort und die Mystik* II, 413.

246. See Speyr, *The Victory of Love*, 13; cf. *The Catechism of the Catholic Church*, no. 2011. See also chapter four of the present volume for a more extensive development of this theme.

247. Herein might be recognized his movement, or progression, toward the fulfillment of his mission on the Cross, including his growth to adulthood.

248. Speyr, *Die katholischen Briefe* II, 203; see also *John* I, 34. As for St. Irenaeus, he presents the Word of God as becoming man "to accustom man to seize God and God to dwell in man." (*Adversus Haereses* III, 20, 2; in *Contre les hérésies: édition critique d'après les versions arménienne et latine*, eds. Adelin Roussea and Louis Doutreleau [Paris: Cerf, 1974], 392; translated into English by John Saward in *The Scandal of the Incarnation* [San Francisco: Ignatius Press, 1994], 54). See *The Scandal of the Incarnation*, 53–93, for other passages of interest from Ireaneus on this theme, and see Balthasar, *Theo-Drama* II, 308–11, for examples of this theme among other patristic writers. More recently, Charles Journet has presented the Church as the continuous incarnation of the Son. See his *The Church of the Incarnate Word* (New York: Sheed & Ward, 1955).

incorporation, Adrienne argues, into his eternal life, with the result that we might be said to have life from him and even "to *live* and progress in him."[249]

This new life in Christ is so real and so radical that once it is received, "Christ means life." Christ, Adrienne specifies, as he is objectively and not as we imagine him to be; Christ, active and present in the Church, distributing his grace in the sacraments and revealing, through his teaching, the path to life, the path that leads to the Father.[250] On the other hand, Christ is both life and resurrection, which means that his life—the life that he gives to us—cannot even be considered apart from heavenly existence. The Lord did not become man so as simply to raise all of humankind up with him, Adrienne explains. He sought also to reveal a divine life within the mortal condition, and the resurrected life that he accords us from heaven might be understood as a manifestation of this truth.[251]

The Father does not simply deposit us in the world after this Resurrection but rather receives us into heaven together with his Son. Here, too, he does not separate us from the Son. In an infrangible unity with him, we enter the place reserved for him in the heavens. [...] Heaven and earth are bestowed upon us anew in him and the Christian can affirm from now on that in faith—that means, *in Christ Jesus*—he lives as much in heaven as on earth. The boundaries between the two have tumbled away.[252]

Given the radicalism of the Christian's life in Christ, it is not surprising that Adrienne presents our growth in faith, hope, and charity as a growing participation in the perfected virtue of Christ.[253] The theological virtues are, more specifically, presented by our author—following the lead of St. John the Evangelist—in terms of a bi-directional movement between heaven and earth, a movement which is "nothing other than the Son himself."[254]

It is in this sense also that we might understand Adrienne's claim that the Lord "needs" our works to fully "round off" his own,[255] for he wills to ac-

---

249. Speyr, *The Letter to the Colossians*, 71; see also 37; *John* II, 70; and *The Victory of Love*, 23.

250. Speyr, *Dienst der Freude*, 35. On Balthasar's development of this insight, especially with regard to the Spirit's role therein, see his *A Theology of History*.

251. See Speyr, *The Mystery of Death*, 67–68.

252. Speyr, *The Letter to the Ephesians*, 84–85.

253. Cf. Balthasar, *Explorations in Theology* I, 168–69. Such is also the perspective of the important encyclical of Pope John Paul II, *Veritatis Splendor*. See also Josef Pieper, *Faith, Hope, Love* (San Francisco: Ignatius Press, 1997); Torrell, *Saint Thomas Aquinas* II: *Spiritual Master*; and Romanus Cessario, *The Moral Virtues and Theological Ethics* (Notre Dame, Ind.: University of Notre Dame Press, 1991).

254. Speyr, *John* II, 64. "The essential content of grace is faith, love and hope," Adrienne teaches, which is given in the sacraments (*John* I, 75); see also *The Letter to the Ephesians*, 18–19.

255. Speyr, *Theologie der Geschlechter*, 234. Similarly, he needs the Church's fullness to manifest his own. See Speyr, *The Letter to the Ephesians*, 73–74; and also *Korinther* I, 389, where Adrienne reasons that the mystery of being one body (*Mit-Leib-Seins*) with the Lord, includes the mystery of the "co-working [*Mitwirkens*]" of each member with the whole body. The highest expression of this mystery is that of Mary's "co-redemption."

complish his mission in us and through us. Similarly, to admit that the Lord "needs [our] cooperation [*Mithilfe*]" means that "he needs [our] answer [of faith]" to the question that he always initiates.[256] By our answer, we nonetheless grant him a "place" within ourselves, so that he might accomplish his saving work therein. Christ's action is, in fact, so decisive in our "collaboration" with him that our merit consists in our readiness or availability for grace,[257] which—as we shall develop more thoroughly below—is also a graced participation in Christ's own receptive stance (or obedience) vis-à-vis the Father.[258]

Contrary to appearances, however, the believer's life in Christ is "infinitely more active," Adrienne insists, than the life which is not lived explicitly for Christ. Our "part" does not consist in simply allowing Christ to work in us, for we are also called at each particular moment "to the most intense, most vital participation."[259] For this reason, Adrienne reasons that one cannot address Christ as active with regard to the Church (or the Christian), who is passive; both are simultaneously active and passive, although—it bears repeating—the Lord is always the first to initiate.[260] It would be more accurate with respect to Adrienne's teaching to speak of a certain community of action between Christ and the Christian. In this sense, Christ's activity and ours form a single action, a "synergy of God's power with ours."[261] As a case in point, Adrienne explains that the Christian does not mediate grace in the manner of a sacrament—as a simple "canal"—but rather as something that is actually remaining *within* him or her without being *of* him or her.[262]

In virtue of our participation in Christ's power, we ought not, Adrienne reasons, to limit ourselves from the outset of any given task by esteeming our power and capacities as finite.[263] What we too often presume as "impossible—'I cannot walk or remain awake more than so many hours,' and so on—is already overcome in the Spirit of the Lord," Adrienne argues; for the incar-

---

256. Speyr, *Markus*, 248. Cf. Balthasar, *Theo-Drama* III, 35; *Epilogue*, 73; and *Theo-Drama* II, 253.
257. Cf. Thomas Aquinas, *ST* I-II, q. 109, a. 6.
258. Cf. *The Catechism of the Catholic Church*, nos. 2008–9.
259. Speyr, *John* I, 104. Mary is the most obvious example; see Speyr, *Die Apokalypse*, 820; and *Theologie der Geschlechter*, 63.
260. Speyr, *Theologie der Geschlechter*, 132; cf. Balthasar, *Theo-Drama* V, 85–91; and *Theo-Drama* III, 296. See also chapter six for a treatment of the active and passive qualities of love characteristic of both Christ and the Church, or of the Christian in the Church.
261. Speyr, *The Letter to the Ephesians*, 149.
262. See Speyr, *Erde und Himmel* I, 82; and *John* III, 365. On the other hand, Adrienne also insists that "grace comes solely from God." We can "only receive it," without ever possessing it as "our own property. [...] Grace is always with God, even though *we* transmit it, so that in spite of us it is he who transmits it" (*John* I, 121).
263. See, for example, Speyr, *Das Wort und die Mystik* II, 26; *Das Wort und die Mystik* I, 42–43; and *The Letter to the Ephesians*, 149. Cf. Balthasar, *Theo-Logic* I, 244; and *Heart of the World*, 117–18.

nate Lord included us within his own prayer[264] and unlimited obedience,[265] whereby the Father's all-powerful will is accomplished even (or precisely) in human weakness (cf. 2 Cor 12:10).[266] This, of course, presupposes a theology of substitution, but one which—as Angelo Scola and Karl-Heinz Menke[267] explain with regard to Balthasar's "own" theology—makes room for our participation in Christ's universal mission by liberating human freedom. "His Holy Spirit overcame all of the limitations of our own spirit, our being here, and not there; we are carried [*Mitgetragene*], taken along, no longer 'here and not there,' but 'simultaneously here and there.'" By this idea of being "here and not there," Adrienne addresses the limitations of our own understanding as constrained by human laws or principles. Such also is "our knowing better": "the finitude that we ourselves set to our insight and love," when, in the experience of boundaries, we utter the word "impossible."[268]

While one might be tempted to recognize within this reasoning a certain confusion of the natural and supernatural orders of human existence, of human nature and its elevation by grace[269]—a criticism which will be addressed in chapter seven of the present volume with regard to the two natures of Christ—Adrienne's purpose in the foregoing is precisely that of insisting upon the unlimited power of grace to elevate human nature. By grace, we live "in Christ" in whom every limit is overcome and every measuring rod banished.[270] To be sure, time remains as such, but it takes on a new meaning: that "wherein the eternal desires to find a place." Similarly, measure becomes that "wherein the immeasurable must find a home."[271] Adrienne thus invites her

---

264. This, for example, is the meaning that Adrienne recognizes in the Lord's forty-day fast in the desert (see Speyr, *Der Mensch vor Gott*, 11). Similarly, she recognizes the third petition of the Lord's prayer—"Thy will be done on earth as in heaven"—as originating out of the Lord's prayer on Gethsemane: "But not my will, but thine be done [Mk 14:36]" (*Markus*, 649). See also Speyr, *Bereitschaft*, 14; and *Das Wort und die Mystik* I, 21. Hence, although we have a tendency to regard prayer as "something that ascends from man to God," Adrienne presents it as descending from God to man, as permitting "a participation in the inner-Trinitarian prayer of God. In God himself lies the archetypes of all our modes of prayer." This accounts for the role of the Holy Spirit, who elevates us "into the sphere of inner-trinitarian prayer" (Balthasar and Scola, *Test Everything*, 89).

265. See Speyr, *Bereitschaft*, 70.   266. See Speyr, *Korinther* I, 53.

267. See Scola, *The Nuptial Mystery*, 236; and Karl-Heinz Menke, *Stellvertetung. Schlüsselbegriff christlichen Lebens und theologische Grundkategorie* (Einsiedeln: Johannes Verlag, 1991), 266–310, esp. 295–96, 300, and 310. Such, Balthasar claims, is a "vicarious suffering" that is "not exclusive but inclusive" (*Mysterium Paschale*, 133), for the "*one* sacrifice to the Father contains, from the very start, duality within itself: it is the sacrifice of the Head and of the Body, of the Bridegroom and of the Bride" (*A Theology of History*, 97–98). See also chapter five of the present volume for a thorough treatment of the complexities of the question regarding how human freedom is liberated by Christ's salvific act.

268. Speyr, *Der Mensch vor Gott*, 11–12.

269. See, for example, Speyr, *The Countenance of the Father*, 60.

270. See Speyr, *Victory of Love*, 13–14; cf. Balthasar, *Theo-Drama* II, 396.

271. Speyr, *Der Mensch vor Gott*, 75.

reader to remember that life on earth is a sort of exile (due to sin) not only with regard to time, but also with regard to the limitations of human being, acting, and possibilities (*Können*).[272] For the Lord, these "limitations" present no obstacle: for him every miracle is possible, not just the great ones, but also those concerning the minor details of our lives.

Adrienne explains that we are too theoretical in our thoughts concerning God's omnipotence. We disregard or fail to see the power that he has to change our lives so that they might be "useful" for him, to affect our acts so that they might really witness to his divine power, and to inform each of our thoughts so that they might accord with his all-powerful will. The Swiss physician invites us to extend the nature-grace balance beyond the limits imposed by our fragile intellects. The "measure" of this balance is, after all, she reasons, not the finite powers of human nature, but rather the infinite power of God, surpassing the limitations otherwise implied by human nature or imposed by sin. When human understanding is not continually nourished by divine meaning, it is dulled, Adrienne explains. Such is the case, for example, when certain limitations are automatically constructed by us precisely where God has spoken an infinite word. What God "can" say is then measured, as it were, by human comprehension; for the infinite is thereby subject to, or measured by, the finite.[273] In conceiving a thought, for example, we tend automatically to create a certain boundary: in acknowledging that an object is "so and thus," we simultaneously acknowledge that it is "not otherwise." When, in contrast, we acknowledge by an act of faith that something is "so," no negation is implied therein: "not because it is simultaneously so and otherwise, but because this 'so' lies open within the Lord's infinity."[274] Faith, as it is conceived by Adrienne, thus implies "stretching to God's measure,"[275] which is to say, no measure. "God's call knows only eternity as time and infinity as space."[276]

The Expansion of the Christian's Assent to the "Proportion" of God's Surrender

As shown above, the authentic gift of self proper to the divine persons is not only revealed by Christ in his self-surrender to the Church but is also communicated to us thereby—as a fruit of redemption, as we will see in chapter five of the present volume—so as also to be really required of us. Grace works

---

272. See Speyr, *The Passion from Within*, 44. 273. Speyr, *Das Wort und die Mystik* I, 43.
274. Ibid., 26.
275. Cf. Speyr, *The Letter to the Ephesians*, 149; *Der Mensch vor Gott*, 11–12; and *Korinther* I, 324. Cf. Balthasar, *Theo-Logic* I, 244; and *Heart of the World*, 117–18.
276. Speyr, *They Followed His Call*, 16.

in such a way as to render us increasingly capable of responding to God with a purity corresponding to the divine love.²⁷⁷ The strength of the Lord's power within us does not, however, lessen the force of his demands (*Forderungen*) upon us, which often appear as exorbitant or excessive (*Überforderungen*), Adrienne explains, because they do not account for the limitations of our nature.²⁷⁸ Hence, for example, when the Lord says to his disciples that for the human being it is impossible to be saved (cf. Mk 10:26), Adrienne insists with even greater intensity: "A human salvation [is] a complete impossibility,"²⁷⁹ even when one acts in conformity with "the rules" set forth by the commandments (cf. Mk 10:19–20), for example.

Far from leading us to despair, however, the acknowledgement that we are incapable of saving ourselves should lead us to salvation by encouraging us to live wholly by his grace, Adrienne argues. When we, like Martha, respond affirmatively to the ultimate question of faith—"Do you believe" that Christ is "the resurrection and the life"? (cf. Jn 11:26–27)—then our lives, like hers, "will be taken up into his life," with the result that "every anxiety we have, every attempt we make, every calculation—all is taken up into him and dissolved."²⁸⁰ Henceforth, it is his "ever-more [*Je-mehr*]"²⁸¹ that is determinative of our "limits." These he stretches from within us, so that the openness thereby accorded might match the extent of his unlimited grace: "His grace knows no barriers in itself, and therefore none in us."²⁸² "Who could measure the Lord, evaluate him, divide his work into partial achievements that can be counted up? His very origin negates every limiting measure."²⁸³ Simply speaking, the Lord will not adapt to our (human) measures.²⁸⁴

By this statement Adrienne would in no way deny the reality of the Incarnation. Her intention, rather, is to point us toward its purpose (as formulated by the Church Fathers): "The Son of God became man so that man might

277. See Speyr, *The Letter to the Ephesians*, 33–34.
278. See Speyr, *Mary in the Redemption*, 100; and *They Followed His Call*, 16. On the other hand, Adrienne explains that the Lord's demands "never come in a moment," because the individual's "yes" cannot be expected so quickly and requires a certain preparation. Hence Adrienne refers to "a beginning of the surrender" in which one "stands up, or does what is necessary, to open the door" (*Das Hohelied*, 60). On Adrienne's own experience of these "excessive demands," see Balthasar, *First Glance at Adrienne von Speyr*, 45.
279. Speyr, *Markus*, 473.
280. Speyr, *The Mystery of Death*, 66–67. Similarly, Adrienne explains that the Lord transforms our love, our expectations, and our efforts within his own "until what is ours simply dissolves in what is his" (*John* III, 364).
281. See Speyr, *Mary in the Redemption*, 100. See also our treatment of the comparative in chapter two.
282. Speyr, *John* III, 364.
283. Speyr, *The Victory of Love*, 14; see also *Gebetserfahrung*, 11.
284. Speyr, *John* III, 164.

become a son of God."[285] This means, more specifically, that God wants us to belong to him as he himself belongs to the Father: "unreservedly."[286] Indeed, when the Lord gives himself to us, he gives himself entirely: without restrictions, including those that would hinder our capacity to receive him. He is "ready for everything."[287] Coming to meet us in "the annihilation [*anéantissement*]" of the Eucharist—which is itself the fruit of his unlimited suffering[288]—he awaits a corresponding response from us in faith. As he, more specifically, "annihilates himself in the host," we must in turn "annihilate ourselves in him in order to receive him worthily and in faith."[289] Such shocking words can be properly understood only in the context—which follows—of Adrienne's conviction that the human person is fulfilled precisely in his or her willing identification with the personal and personalizing mission received from God: an identification which supposes a certain dispossession of one's self, or more correctly said, a true giving of oneself to the one who gives himself first and fully (without measure) in obedience to the Father's "command" (cf. Jn 14:31).

The divine person of Christ as revealed in John's Gospel—whence the emergence of these insights in the form of Adrienne's commentary—"constitutes himself in the mission and through the mission" from the Father. That is to say, he "is a Person in the mission."[290] This does not mean that the meaning of his divine person is to be understood primarily in terms of action, for the concept of mission is itself presented foremost in terms of obedience, from which proceed actions characteristic of the person.[291]

Obedience, in turn, points to the essentially *relational* quality of the divine person: "The Son is nothing more, and wishes to be nothing more, than the pure act of proceeding from the Father. He does not wish to be Son in

---

285. See the formulations of St. Irenaeus, St. Athanasius, and St. Thomas Aquinas in *The Catechism of the Catholic Church*, no. 460; in Balthasar, *Theo-Drama* III, 237–45; and selected passages of Irenaeus's *Adversus Haereses in Irenaeus*, in Saward (trans.), *The Scandal of the Incarnation*, 54–55. See also chapter four for a more thorough development of this theme in Adrienne's work.

286. Speyr, *John* III, 164.

287. Speyr, *Das Hohelied*, 70; cf. *John* III, 67: "It is a love that is ready to take everything on itself, even the Cross." On the Son belonging to the Father, see Speyr, *The Victory of Love*, 36.

288. See, for example, Speyr, *The Cross: Word and Sacrament*, 10.

289. Speyr, *The Holy Mass*, 71; see *Das Hohelied*, 70. Adrienne's presentation of Christ as "annihilated in the host" is in no manner a calling into question of the real presence, as is evident in the context. Adrienne argues there that confession "was instituted in order to make us worthy of receiving the Lord [in the Eucharist]" (*The Holy Mass*, 71).

290. Speyr, *John* II, 372. See also ibid., 71; *Achtzehn Psalmen* (Einsiedeln: Johannes Verlag, 1957), 69; *John* I, 68 and 106; and *The Letter to the Ephesians*, 32.

291. See Balthasar's foreword to Speyr, *The Mission of the Prophets*, 7–9; and Speyr, *The Letter to the Colossians*, 59. For similar insights in the theology of Aquinas, see Waldstein, "The Analogy of Mission and Obedience."

anything other than this; and he thanks the Father for permitting him to be this."²⁹² "Obedience," Balthasar explains with regard to Adrienne's theology, "is the innermost characteristic of Christ in relation to the Father, but it is also the innermost characteristic of the feminine Church in relation to Christ."²⁹³ As Christ might be said to be "fulfilled"²⁹⁴ in the obedient realization of his mission from the Father to draw all things to himself as head (cf. Eph 1:22–23; Col 1:18), the Christian is fulfilled in his or her effective participation in this same mission—the universal mission of Christ—by means of this same obedience: a participated obedience.²⁹⁵

Adrienne presents obedience as intensifying "human possibilities in a very vigorous way," even to the extent of "taking them into the supernatural." Obedience is "like a stimulant for the soul," significantly increasing one's "capacity for achievement," without recourse to one's own (passive) powers.

> I do not awaken a latent power within me because I want to obey. No, obedience brings it to me. It is *un apport de l'obéissance* [a contribution of obedience]. And it does not bring it to me personally. It is part of the obedience which the Son gave the Father. It is also somehow a proof of the truth of God that the Son, who brought this power into the world, should have made it accessible to the world, so much so, in fact, that we can avail ourselves of it today.²⁹⁶

This miracle (as it were) of obedience—the Christian's partaking of Christ's own obedience to the Father—is worked by the Lord's Spirit, who "guarantees the continuity between creation and redemption"²⁹⁷ and who is also so present to the disciple that he (the Spirit) "takes over in him, works in

---

292. Speyr, *John* II, 372.

293. Balthasar, "General Introduction to the Posthumous Works," in Speyr, *Book of All Saints* I, 5.

294. This idea of Christ being "fulfilled" will be explained and developed in chapter four within the context of Christ's mission to bring the Church, united with himself, "back" to the Father.

295. See Speyr, *The Letter to the Ephesians*, 225; *Das Word und die Mystik* I, 19; *John* I, 103; *The Letter to the Colossians*, 37; *The Victory of Love*, 22; *They Followed His Call*, 67; *Das Buch von Gehorsam*, 19–20 and 51–52; and *Bereitschaft*. Cf. Balthasar, *Theo-Drama* V, 123, and chapter three of Steck, *The Ethical Thought of Hans Urs von Balthasar*. Similar is the teaching of Pope John Paul II, who presents the new commandment of Christ as "holding fast to the very person of Jesus, partaking of his life and his destiny, sharing in his free and loving obedience to the will of the Father" (*Veritatis Splendor*, no. 19).

296. Speyr, in the appendix of Balthasar, *Our Task*, 192. See also Speyr, *John* I, 63.

297. Speyr, *John* I, 228. This continuity is due to the fact that he is the Spirit of the Son *and* of the Father. See Speyr, *World of Prayer*, 63; and *Mary in the Redemption*, 47. Even the incarnate Son "obeys the Father in the Holy Spirit, and the Holy Spirit is his rule, because he makes known the Father's will" (*Erde und Himmel* III, 193); see also *World of Prayer*, 63. After the Son's mission upon earth is completed, however, it is the Spirit who is obedient to the Son. "He is bound to the Son in a way that presents a mirror image of the Son's obedience to the Father" (*The Boundless God*, 43). This insight is also evident in Balthasar's presentation of the "Trinitarian inversion." See, for example, his *Theo-Drama* III, 183–202; and *A Theology of History*. On the Spirit's role in granting the Christian a participation in Christ's obedience to the Father, see Speyr, *The Victory of Love*, 17; *John* I, 63; *Das Wort und die Mystik* II, 26; *Confession*, 22; *John* II, 78–79; and *John* IV, 221–22.

him, transforms him, so that he [the disciple] is no longer aware of himself." The believer is, in fact, unable to draw distinctions between the Lord's Spirit within him- or herself and his or her own (human) spirit. To do so is hardly necessary, Adrienne argues, and potentially dangerous, for it could cause one to make reservations in his or her surrender—"or worse still, to measure the strength of his [or her] surrender." This "measure," Adrienne reasons, belongs to God alone, for in virtue of the divine indwelling the Christian belongs to the Lord "in the same way as the Lord belongs to the Father"[298]—in, that is to say, a manner known to God alone.

From this perspective, the Christian's growing identification with his or her mission might be understood in terms of what we investigated in the previous section of this chapter as a mutual self-gift: the Lord giving of himself to the Christian—especially in the Eucharist—in obedience to the Father (in accord with his mission), and the Christian's response in the form of an openness to receive. "To be Christian means this: to close nothing off as completed, but to open oneself up into the always-more of the Son's love for the Father. And if he is there for us as the one who brings us the always-more of faith, love and hope, then it is the Father who remains for him as the Always-More in love."[299]

Communion with the Eucharistic Lord—it bears repeating—does not only *presuppose* this openness, or "emptiness" in us; it also *creates* it. Every Communion is an exchange whereby we both receive the Lord, so as to approach him more closely, and simultaneously give him what he wishes to receive from us. Precisely as an exchange, it is not inhibited by our limitations, by our meager readiness for him, but breaks down the boundaries of our resistance according to the magnitude of the Father's love.[300] Within this context there can be no question of our measuring up, so to speak, "for the content [of his gift] far surpasses the container [whom we are]" (cf. 2 Cor 4:7).[301]

Because, on the other hand, his overabundant generosity really does provide for what is lacking in us, the Lord will permit nothing less than an unlimited engagement from us: an engagement matching, as it were, the extent of his own engagement in our lives and in our history. What is required of us, in other words, is an authentic and unconstrained "yes," a perfectly generous assent. While this "yes" is so faithfully given that it can never be withdrawn, this does not mean that we are no longer free, but only that our gift of self

---

298. Speyr, *The Victory of Love*, 36; see also *Light and Images*, 154.
299. Speyr, *John* IV, 77.
300. See Speyr, *John* II, 73–74; and *John* I, 83.
301. Speyr, *John* I, 102. Cf. Balthasar, *The Glory of the Lord* I, 114; *Love Alone Is Credible*, 76–77; and *A Theology of History*, 108.

is real. "God accepts the responsibility for his invitation in such a way that man remains jointly responsible and is able to form his answer, in faith out of a personal feeling of responsibility. He remains free to refuse."[302] When, on the other hand, we truly offer our assent, it can and must be expanded to meet the growing demands of the Lord; for he thereby draws us—by way of our personal missions—into his own unique and universal mission. "One can remain open for God only in a once-for-all total assent, not in a tentative, limited, cautious Yes."[303]

Adrienne takes the Christian's "yes" so seriously that she will admit of no "third" state of life within the Church. The disciple of the Lord cannot do otherwise than to give himself absolutely and thus irrevocably, whether in an indissoluble marriage or in the consecrated life, which is "as a matter of principle, equally irrevocable."[304] Those, on the other hand, who have already given of themselves once and for all must nonetheless guard themselves against complacency. Faith, Adrienne teaches, must be constantly exercised as something new, something living; it must be newly embraced every day so as to allow for no monotony. It corresponds, after all, to the vitality of God's Word: to, that is to say, the Lord himself.[305]

In this way, Adrienne cautions her reader against assuming the ultimate responsibility for his or her own fidelity. Recognizing that we are all really "unfit to dispose of our own Yes," she encourages us to surrender it to God in prayer, so as to live no longer in ourselves "but in his word."[306] This word, in whom we should strive to live, is also the word who lives in us: "the objective word which is proposed to my faith" and "the subjective word which prays in me," that is to say, God himself.[307] Thus guiding and ruling us from within and from without, the Word of God—who, in this capacity, is also the Spirit of God—is particularly efficacious in taking on our opposition to him.[308] And taking on our opposition is no small matter, for the Lord's "possibility"

---

302. Speyr, *The Boundless God*, 134–35. "For what God gives, he gives absolutely and entirely, giving us the right of ownership, though everything ultimately comes from him" (Speyr, *John* I, 125–26).

303. Speyr, *John* III, 261. On the demands of this "yes," from the first instant of the call, see Speyr, *Das Wort und die Mystik* I, 26.

304. Balthasar, *First Glance at Adrienne von Speyr*, 54; cf. *The Chrisitan State of Life*, 60–61. Balthasar explains (in *Our Task*, 99) that "Adrienne's doggedly maintained opinion" about there being no third state influenced his opinion on the matter; see also 29–30. Cf. Speyr, *Das Hohelied*, 61; and *Theologie der Geschlechter*, 114, 116, 180, and 186. Cf. Pope John Paul II, *Familiaris Consortio*, no. 11.

305. Speyr, *The Christian State of Life*, 146–47.

306. Speyr, *John* I, 36.

307. Speyr, *World of Prayer*, 282. God does not merely address us by his Spirit; he is also understood and received by us through his Holy Spirit; see Speyr, *John* I, 27 and 63. On the cooperation between the Holy Spirit and the Son, see *Theologie der Geschlechter*, 135; cf. Balthasar, *Prayer*, 35–36.

308. See Speyr, *Die katholischen Briefe* II, 179.

of changing us—of rendering us like himself—is, Adrienne maintains, determined by our openness to him.[309]

This is not to deny that our openness to God is always sharply limited: our "yes" to him is never full-hearted, Adrienne observes, and our reception of him is always tainted by selfishness. He must, therefore, constantly fight to destroy the boundaries we set up. The enemy here is us, Adrienne explains, with the result that the Lord "must continually be killing us to make us living in God."[310] He must, more specifically, fight for the entire space of our soul, and he prunes us from himself whenever we "apply measuring rods" and seek to "survey the whole."[311] Cutting away all that is not a generous unaccountable gift in us, the Lord clears not just a space for himself within us, but every space. Because, after all, the new life that he wishes to give "require[s]" every space within us, "every space must be emptied for it."[312]

Thrusting aside all that he considers incompatible with his presence, the Lord converts our half-hearted "yes" into "a whole" resounding "yes." No matter how feeble and uncertain our assent might be in its origin, when it is really given to the Lord, it is henceforth contained within his own superabundant "yes" to us. Therein it is carried, nourished, and fortified to the full stature of Christian faithfulness: the full surrender of the resurrected life.[313]

Even the most obedient of God's human creatures—and Adrienne calls upon the example of Mary and Joseph to bring clarity to the matter[314]—lack something of the plenitude required by God: a plenitude for which he is ultimately responsible.[315] Hence, the meaning of their obedience lies in their willingness to hand over their obedience, as it were, to entrust it to the Lord, who fills in "the empty spaces." They must, more specifically, be obedient "without strings attached" so as to be dispossessed of their own obedience. They must surrender it—along with every aspect of their persons—to God: as an act of love, of course, but also for his safekeeping, whereby the surrender is also an act of faith.[316] Christian obedience is thus purified, as it were, in

---

309. See Speyr, *Die Schöpfung*, 44.

310. Speyr, *John* III, 129–30; see also *John* I, 101–2.

311. Speyr, *John* III, 164. The context here is Jn 15:2: "Every branch of mine that bears no fruit, he takes away." See also Gal 2:20.

312. Speyr, *The Victory of Love*, 22; see also *Theologie der Geschlechter*, 89.

313. See Speyr, *John* I, 103; *The Letter to the Ephesians*, 18–19; and *John* IV, 77. On the full surrender in the life of the Resurrection, see *Markus*, 561.

314. This, more specifically, is not to say that their assent is not adequate, but only that it must be expanded at each step of the way, along with their missions. See Speyr, *They Followed His Call*, 60–61. On the correspondence between the persons of Mary and Joseph and God's intention for his creation, see Speyr, *The Countenance of the Father*, 64.

315. Cf. Speyr, *The Boundless God*, 134–35.

316. A similar thing happens, Adrienne explains, when the Lord surrenders his Spirit on the Cross:

its passage from active to passive obedience. In the latter case, it is as if Christ himself is obedient in us: by his Spirit.[317] On the other hand, Adrienne cautions her reader against thinking that everything might be left to God. Our faith in God is, in short, enclosed within his own faithfulness.

This mystery of our surrender to God's power over our lives is also explained by Adrienne as the act of depositing our "yes" with God in prayer, whereby it is actually his word more than our own. In giving it to him, we no longer have rights over it. "We do not say it of ourselves, by ourselves or in ourselves."[318] Having surrendered our word to God in faith, we must grow into his Word: the Son in whom we were created and in whom resides God's image of each one of us before the beginning of time, as we saw earlier in this chapter.

In the final analysis, Christian obedience is thereby transformed from a subjective gift of the human person offered to God to an objective gift accepted by God, in virtue of which it is also perfected, as if by fire.[319] In the one who dares to say "yes" to God, the perfect assent of Christ is "only imperfectly fulfilled." When, however, his "yes" is received and accepted by God, "it is fulfilled to utmost perfection in God."[320] His is a word of affirmation for which God himself offers the guarantee. It is an assent that is "formed from the very substance of his [the Son's] obedience to the Father."[321]

Mary-Church or Person as Response: An Anticipation of Balthasar's "Theological Person"

This mysterious encounter of grace and faith, of God's faithfulness and our assent, of his invitation and our response, and ultimately of the Spirit who is God's objective gift to us and the same Spirit who is "the subject within our subject that receives him,"[322] reaches a sort of climactic focus in Adrienne's presentation of the Church as a person in response to the person of the Lord. Anticipating Balthasar's presentation of a "theological person"[323]

"Weakness and death merely keep him from continuing to exercise an active kind of obedience, and in order to preserve it whole and total the Son hands it over to the Father" (Speyr, *They Followed His Call*, 64).

317. See Speyr, *The Letter to the Ephesians*, 19.   318. Speyr, *John* I, 36.

319. On the image of purifying fire, see Speyr, *John* I, 37 and 122.

320. Speyr, *They Followed His Call*, 62.

321. Ibid., 67; see also 122 with regard to sacramental grace as a partaking of Christ's obedience. On God's guarantee of our obedience, see Speyr, *The Mission of the Prophets*, 123. For an example of the perfection of a human being who surrenders himself in loving confidence to the Lord, see the example of St. John the Evangelist in as described in Speyr, *John* I, 7–14.

322. Speyr, *John* I, 63.

323. This concept which, in name, is attributable to him is undoubtedly inspired by Adrienne's presentation thereof in her *Theologie der Geschlechter*, 130: "The Church is in fact only a person insofar

by three decades, Adrienne presents a dialogical model of human fulfillment: "The word addressed by the Lord is the mission, and the response of the one commissioned to it is the 'person.'"[324] The project of human fulfillment from the Speyrian perspective thus consists, almost ironically, of being "depersonalized": of being, that is to say, so objective in one's orientation to the truth that one is purified of any subjective preferences which might lead one astray from God's truth. As such, one exists in total expectation and readiness for the Lord, whose grace is given in the form of a mission. "Being fully ecclesial means: to be so depersonalized [*entpersönlicht*] that one is as a whole readiness for the Lord."[325] Such is what Balthasar refers to as the assimilation of "our own 'I' more and more completely to our God-given mission" and the discovery "in this mission [of] our own identity, which is both personal and social."[326] Such, more specifically, is a participation in Christ's mission, which in turn is the constitutive element of his person, as we have seen.

The most obvious model of this mystery lies in the person of Mary, whose entire existence is presented by Adrienne—as is likewise the case in Balthasar's teaching—in terms of her all-encompassing and constantly expanding assent to the Lord.[327] Adrienne presents Mary as putting all the potentialities of her nature at God's disposal, without consciously or even unconsciously holding anything back.[328] In thus remaining open and continuously ready for the Son, to whom she is given to be used as he deems necessary for the accomplishment of his mission, she also realizes herself as the Creator intended her to be.[329] Her asset is "a malleable material out of which God can make whatever he will."[330] Having no particular image of herself, she concentrates all her energies upon the task of love, without wasting time reflecting upon the question of her own self-fulfillment.[331] She simply "lets happen [*geschehen lassen*] according to God's will so as to participate, as no other, in the Son's mission."[332] In so doing she simultaneously realizes herself in accord with the most intimate truth of her being.

---

as she is *response* to the person of the Lord." It bears mention that although Adrienne's *Theologie der Geschlechter* was published in 1969 (after her death), it was actually dictated in 1946 and 1947. Balthasar's four-volume *Theo-Drama* was published, shortly after being written, between 1973 and 1983 (in the original German).

324. Speyr, *Theologie der Geschlechter*, 130.   325. Ibid.
326. Balthasar, *Theo-Drama* III, 270–71.
327. See Speyr, *Handmaid of the Lord*, 7 and 9; *They Followed His Call*, 16–17 and 64; and Balthasar, *First Glance at Adrienne von Speyr*, 51. Cf. Balthasar, *You Crown the Year with Your Goodness*, 264–69; and Roten, "Hans Urs von Balthasar's Anthopology in Light of His Marian Thinking."
328. See Speyr, *Handmaid of the Lord*, 9; and *Das Wort und die Mystik* I, 19, 23, and 26.
329. See Speyr, *Mary in the Redemption*, 37.   330. Speyr, *Handmaid of the Lord*, 8.
331. See Speyr, *Das Wort und die Mystik* II, 517.
332. See Speyr, *The Mission of the Prophets*, 123; and *John* III, 266. On Adrienne's use of the term

She has remained willing to accept everything; she has lived in constant expectation of God's will and, as a result has received her Son, not as something foreign or as something imposed on her from outside, but rather as something of her own, something intended by God for her as her own. In remaining completely open for him, [...] she has realized herself as God had intended her most personal being for her. This is Mary's unity.[333]

In harmony with the constant tradition of the Church, Adrienne explains that all of Mary's extraordinary graces, including most especially her Immaculate Conception, are granted in view of her extraordinary mission to be the Mother of the Lord and thus also in some way to her human assent.[334] By her fiat, she determines the beginning of Christ's mission on earth, while he more profoundly determines her beginning in eternity.[335] Beyond this, or rather as part of the same mystery, Adrienne explains that her assent is itself a grace. It is, in other words, not only her word-gift to God—the determination of her own free will—it is also and more profoundly still God's gift-Word to her: the Word of God as faith and the Word of God in the most supreme sense, namely, the Son of God.[336] Hence, at the Annunciation it is as if she receives the Spirit "twice": once for the Son—who will become incarnate by the Spirit's action within her—and once for herself, so that she might respond with the open heart necessary to receive him.[337]

Hers, then, is not simply a human answer to God's invitation. It is also "the divine answer to her entire life," which Adrienne recognizes as united in her assent. It "accompanies her at every moment of her existence." To acknowledge it as a grace is thus not only to admit that it is realized by the assistance of the Holy Spirit, dwelling within her, so as to be "enclosed," as it were, "within the Yes of the Holy Spirit." It also means that this assent is authentically her own and thus human: "a true, free and independent word of her own spirit."[338] It is thus not surprising that Adrienne should present the

---

geschehen lassen (letting happen), see Servais, "The *Ressourcement* of Contemporary Spirituality under the Guidance of Adrienne von Speyr and Hans Urs von Balthasar."

333. Speyr, *Mary in the Redemption*, 37.

334. See Speyr, *They Followed His Call*, 70; and *John* III, 288. Cf. Balthasar, *Theo-Drama* III, 323–24; Pope Pius IX, Bull *Ineffabilis Deus* (DZ 2803); and *The Catechism of the Catholic Church*, nos. 491–92.

335. See Speyr, *Mary in the Redemption*, 24; cf. Pope John Paul II, *Redemptoris Mater*, no. 13.

336. See Speyr, *Mary in the Redemption*, 24; *Theologie der Geschlechter*, 99; and *The Mission of the Prophets*, 123. Cf. Balthasar, "Maria und der Geist," *Geist und Leben* 56 (1983): 175.

337. See Speyr, *Mary in the Redemption*, 107. In a similar manner, St. Thomas teaches that "the soul of the Blessed Virgin was so full of grace that it overflowed into her flesh thus fitting it for the conception of God's Son therefrom" (*Expositio Salutationis Angelicae*; in *The Three Greatest Prayers*, trans. Laurence Shapcote [London: Burns Oates & Washbourne, 1937], 32).

338. Speyr, *Handmaid of the Lord*, 7–8; see also *Mary in the Redemption*, 107; *John* III, 266; and *Das Wort und die Mystik* II, 19.

Lord as not simply seeking "empty room" for himself from Mary; for he wills that she be "his elevated daughter, mother, bride."[339]

In this encounter of Mary's word of surrender to God and of God's own Word surrendered to Mary, Adrienne thus recognizes a merging of obedience from which are formed the personalizing missions of both Christ and Mary. Here more specifically the Son's obedience to the Father meets that of Mary-Church in a common surrender to the Father's will.[340] The one relationship (Father-Son) is thus fruitful in the other (Son-mother/bride), with the result that there is more than an external likeness implied by the following comparison: "Just as the eternal and unique surrender between Father and Son flows out into the temporal and unbounded devotion of the Eucharist, so the unique virginal relation between Mother and Son flows out into the endless bestowal of her spiritual motherhood."[341]

Indeed, in the transformation and expansion of Mary's vocation as the mother of Christ to her vocation as the mother of Christians, Adrienne notes a sort of "suspension" of the limits between the "I" of Christ and the "thou" of Mary, such that "the one is fruitful in the other. [...] In receiving God's seed, she becomes fruit."[342] This occurs by way of Christ's redemptive action which "retroactively affects the Mother" so as to make of her the mother of all, beginning with John, the "son" born of their virginal love.[343] In this way, Mary assumes and accomplishes the mission of Eve to be the "mother of the living" by means of her ready willingness to give of herself to the Lord.[344]

This evolving relationship between mother and Son into that of bride and bridegroom, as we shall exposit more fully in chapter six—a relationship which Adrienne presents as "a new creation of human unity"[345]—thus becomes the paradigm of the relation between nature and grace, or between divine action and human cooperation, as they are united in the drama of human fulfillment.[346] In this exemplar relationship it is hardly possible—nor necessary, Adrienne tells us—to determine at what point the mother receives the Son and at what point the Son receives the mother. The whole is a con-

---

339. Speyr, *Das Wort und die Mystik* I, 63.
340. See, for example, Speyr, *Mary in the Redemption*, 13.
341. Speyr, *John* IV, 123–24.   342. Speyr, *Theologie der Geschlechter*, 99–100.
343. See Speyr, *John* IV, 123; and *The Cross: Word and Sacrament*, 34.
344. See Speyr, *Mary in the Redemption*, 52.
345. Ibid., 36. We might thus discern a certain similarity between Adrienne's teaching and that of St. Irenaeus of Lyons, who presents Mary as the new Eve beside the new Adam: "Just as Eve, by disobeying, became the cause of death for herself and the whole human race, so Mary, betrothed to a predestined man and yet a virgin, by obeying, became the cause of salvation for herself and the whole human race" (*Adversus Haereses* III, 22, 4; Saward [trans.], *The Scandal of the Incarnation*, 61).
346. See, for example, Speyr, *Korinther* I, 323.

stant, mysterious, reciprocal relationship in which it is equally impossible to ascertain who accomplishes what. Granted, Christ gives more to his mother than she gives to him, but we must not attempt, Adrienne warns us, "to reduce the mystery to a transparent proportion."[347] When Mary gives her assent, she gives herself entirely—body and soul—without attempting to determine how much she surrenders and how much God will take from her, nor how much he will give to her in return.[348] To speculate about such matters would, Adrienne explains, be potentially "deleterious to divine grace,"[349] for no earthly standard can be applied here; "the Spirit himself holds the standard in his hands."[350]

Similarly, it would be "perverse" to think of everything in Mary as attributable to a special grace, for Christ recognizes in his mother an authentic human good: a whole-hearted willingness to be united to him. This is, more specifically, "the human good that conforms to, nourishes, and, above all, makes possible his human form."[351] This is so much the case that Christ learns as a child to know love in the form in which his mother loves him, with the result that his love for the disciples is wholly penetrated with his mother's love: with, that is to say, the manner of loving that he learns from her. In this love, the divine and the human "are inseparably mingled. It is love that is heavenly as well as earthly."[352] As for Mary, she subjectively experiences her obedience as constant and living, with the result that she discovers therein "more far-reaching consequences and more energetic and inexhaustible life than she had suspected."[353] Hers is, under the Spirit's guidance, a "living, self-fulfilling perfection,"[354] as is manifest in the "perfect unity and harmony" between what Mary accomplishes in her mediation and what God accomplishes through her mediation.[355]

Ultimately this means not only that this holy mother (actively) realizes herself, or her person, in and through her mission, but also and more profoundly that she is realized (passively but willingly) in her mission. The mission stretches her, as it were, pushing her forward, and expanding her fiat and

---

347. Speyr, *Mary in the Redemption*, 38. On the question of Mary's merit in relation to the grace she has received, see *Das Wort und die Mystik* II, 430.
348. See Speyr, *Das Wort und die Mystik* I, 23; and *They Followed His Call*, 73.
349. Speyr, *The Mission of the Prophets*, 124.   350. Speyr, *They Followed His Call*, 63.
351. Speyr, *Mary in the Redemption*, 38.
352. Speyr, *John* III, 67. Cf. Balthasar, *Unless You Become Like This Child*, 67–75.
353. Speyr, *They Followed His Call*, 61. An obvious example given by Adrienne is the loss of the Christ child in the temple.
354. Speyr, *John* III, 266.
355. This unity and harmony is, Adrienne explains, ultimately founded in her graced participation in the Trinitarian life. See *Mary in the Redemption*, 45.

her other powers, without in any way alienating her from herself or from others.³⁵⁶ She does not fulfill her mission by simply becoming the Son's "vessel." More profoundly still, "she herself becomes [his] fruit,"³⁵⁷ for "God's action in her gradually outweighs her own action."³⁵⁸ This more passive, or obedient, form of human fulfillment points, moreover, to the fact that it is not so much her mission that is of significance, but rather Christ's mission, wherein she participates. Mary's mission "loses itself in, and is rounded off by, the Son's mission," which in turn is fulfilled "by merging with the Mother's mission."³⁵⁹ In the merging of their missions, the Lord "simultaneously fulfills his Mother," Adrienne continues, "and from that moment on, there exists an immutable state of being reciprocally bound together—the mother to the Son and the Son to the mother—which also provides the point of departure for all Christian missions."³⁶⁰

Drawn into Christ's mystery in this way, she becomes a significant part therein and actually helps him to realize his mission.³⁶¹ In receiving him into her womb, she simultaneously receives his mission; in carrying him, she also carries his mission; in praying, she carries his prayer; and in determining the hour of his public ministry, she gives birth to him again, this time "into his mission."³⁶² Accompanying him thereafter in her contemplation, she becomes his companion in the Spirit, in whom and through whom he accomplishes his every action,³⁶³ and in this capacity of helpmate, she "bears his fruit."³⁶⁴ Her mission throughout his public ministry is, in other words, conceived by Adrienne as "one extended pregnancy," impelling her toward the Cross, "the hour of birth."³⁶⁵ In this sense, she lives toward the Cross, together with her Son, but Adrienne also presents Mary as living most especially *from* the Cross: "She gives her consent at the foot of the Cross; the birth of the child in Bethlehem is the consummation of the sacrifice; and when the child was conceived in Nazareth she was already the victim, given to God."³⁶⁶

---

356. See ibid., 36–37.

357. Speyr, *Theologie der Geschlechter*, 99. Adrienne explains that 'being fruit' here means both that she becomes the Lord's mother and that she becomes his bride (ibid., 100).

358. Speyr, *John* III, 265.

359. Speyr, *The Mission of the Prophets*, 124. If Christ's mission were severed from that of Mary, it would be as it if he were severed from himself, Adrienne explains. See Speyr, *Mary in the Redemption*, 76.

360. Speyr, *The Mission of the Prophets*, 124; see also *John* III, 265. Cf. Balthasar, *Theo-Drama* III, 304–5.

361. See Speyr, *Handmaid of the Lord*, 38.

362. Speyr, *John* I, 167; see also *Mary in the Redemption*, 76, 103, and 122; and *Theologie der Geschlechter*, 118.

363. See Speyr, *John* I, 166; and *Mary in the Redemption*, 87. On contemplation as Mary's "new form" of accompanying her Son, see *Handmaid of the Lord*, 99; and *Mary in the Redemption*, 104.

364. Speyr, *The Handmaid of the Lord*, 37.   365. Speyr, *John* III, 265.

366. Speyr, *John* I, 53.

Although one would perhaps recognize in these words a reference to the Immaculate Conception—since the fruit of Christ's redemption is, as we have seen, at the origin of her maternal mission—Adrienne refers in the above citation to Mary's assent as uniting the events of Nazareth, Bethlehem, and Golgotha, such that the latter sacrifice is already implicit in the former.[367] This also means—especially given the prophecy of Simeon and Mary's knowledge of the Old Testament prophecies—that the Cross lies constantly in the shadow of her mind: Every manifestation of his glory and every task accomplished lead him closer and inevitably (by God's will) to the Cross.[368] It is there that she becomes the Mother of those to whom Christ gives his life, those who are entrusted to her in the person of John.[369]

It is within this context of Mary's universal maternity realized by the Cross that Adrienne recognizes her as having the express mission, and thus also the grace, to educate and nourish the faith and surrender of Christians: a mission earning for her the specific Speyrian title of the *"mediatrix of self-surrender."*[370] Mary realizes this mission by leading us along the paths of our lives—paths of joy and suffering, whence the importance of the rosary[371]—that she has already walked with her Son and in his Spirit. The strength of her faith encourages ours, even to the extent that her faith actually becomes our faith. By this is meant not only that the deposit of faith imparted to us by the Church and mediated by the apostles is first of all the faith of Mary: that "special heritage of God's revelation"[372] entrusted to the Church by the one who shared most closely in the redemptive mysteries. It also means that Mary's all-encompassing and unfailing assent, or surrender—wherein this deposit (beginning with the person of the incarnate Word) is received—strengthens and encourages our only too feeble assents to the Lord. Mary's "yes" is objectively so comprehensive that she becomes a "vessel for the whole of belief."[373] It is subjectively so comprehensive that it includes not only everything that the Lord might ask of her, but also everyone who wants to believe and to offer their assistance to the Lord in the accomplishment of his mission.[374] The unity of the objective

---

367. Speyr, *John* I, 53. Cf. Balthasar, *Theo-Drama* III, 332; *Mary for Today*, 62; *Unless You Become Like This Child*; and (with Ratzinger), *Mary: The Church at the Source*, 107–10.

368. Speyr, *John* I, 166.

369. Speyr, *John* IV, 124; see also *Handmaid of the Lord*, 165–66.

370. Speyr, *Handmaid of the Lord*, 170; emphasis added. See also Speyr, *They Followed His Call*, 72–73; *Mary in the Redemption*, 12; and *Mary for Today*, 41.

371. See Speyr, *Handmaid of the Lord*, 158–61; cf. Balthasar, *The Threefold Garland*.

372. Pope John Paul II, *Redemptoris Mater*, no. 27. Cf. Speyr, *Handmaid of the Lord*, 15 and 84; Balthasar, *The Threefold Garland*, 67; and *Mary for Today*, 35–45.

373. Speyr, *John* IV, 255; see also *Handmaid of the Lord*, 66–67.

374. See Speyr, *Mary in the Redemption*, 11. Cf. Balthasar, *First Glance at Adrienne von Speyr*, 51.

and subjective elements of her faith—realized in both cases by the intervention of the Holy Spirit, as we noted above—are apparent in that her "private" "yes" is, as Adrienne sees it, transformed by God into a "Catholic" one, so as to become "the cradle of all Christianity."[375] Like St. Thomas Aquinas, Adrienne thus recognizes Mary's consent as "besought in lieu of that of the entire human nature."[376]

As for our part, accepting Mary as a mother does not mean that we can simply resign ourselves to the power of her "yes." Rather, we must actually appropriate it as our own by generously surrendering and really entrusting ourselves "to these powers of growth which carry" us.[377] In so doing, we have Adrienne's assurance that this Mother lends her help in the expansion of our limited "yes" to the measure of the Lord's task, or mission, for us. "If anyone keeps faith with her, she will keep everlasting faith with him [or her]."[378]

Conclusion: Breaking the Boundary between Nature and Grace

Consonant with the traditional portrayal of the Church as the new Eve born of Christ "asleep" on the Cross and of Mary as pre-redeemed by her Son's merits is Adrienne's presentation of Mary-Church as the fruit of Christ's salvific mission in which she nonetheless has a real share. The "firstborn of the Redemption, just as Adam was the first-born of Creation," Mary corresponds to her Son's plan "by supporting him with love and faith all her life long."[379] This explains the importance of her Immaculate Conception, or her "pre-redemption [*Vorerlösung*]," as the necessary presupposition of her mission as the redeemer's mother and helpmate.[380] In virtue of this extraordinary grace, Adrienne recognizes Mary's faith as not only accomplishing but also preceding that of the prophets.[381] For this reason too, she is the "outline" and "germ" of the Church,[382] "the Una Sancta," which was founded

---

375. Speyr, *Handmaid of the Lord*, 66–67. It possesses the qualities of being "internally substitutive, social and eucharistic," Adrienne adds (67). Cf. Balthasar, *The Office of Peter and the Structure of the Church*, trans. André Emery (San Francisco: Ignatius Press, 1986), 208; see also *The Threefold Garland*, 34.

376. Thomas Aquinas, *ST* III, q. 30, a. 1.   377. Speyr, *Handmaid of the Lord*, 164.

378. Ibid., 171.

379. Speyr, *The Cross: Word and Sacrament*, 34; see also *Mary in the Redemption*, 36.

380. "The idea of 'co-redemption' is 'older' than that of pre-redemption: the latter is a consequence of the former, a means to the end" (Speyr, *Mary in the Redemption*, 19); see also *Handmaid of the Lord*, 8. Cf. *The Catechism of the Catholic Church*, no. 490.

381. See Speyr, *Mary in the Redemption*, 57. In the "conversion" of Old Testament faith to New Testament faith through the Incarnation (and thus also by way of the Virgin's consent), Adrienne recognizes a prefiguration of the reception of the Lord in holy communion. See Speyr, *Das Wort und die Mystik* II, 127.

382. Speyr, *The Cross: Word and Sacrament*, 34.

"with the first word [...], that he [the Incarnate Word] spoke on earth."[383] It is thus not surprising that Adrienne should present Mary as simultaneously revealing and realizing the dialogue of salvation to which we are all called: a dialogue between the Word of God who gives himself and the Church who (in her various members, beginning with Mary) receives him by the power of his grace.[384]

The example of the Mother of God demonstrates in archetypical fashion how one who surrenders him- or herself to the Lord is thereby drawn into his saving mission and may even help him to realize it.[385] At the same time, this example manifests how personal fulfillment is achieved precisely therein: by means of a real participation in Christ's universal mission and thus also in his obedience. Mary's surrender "goes beyond the measure of human surrender and includes, in its expansive opening-out, the Son's self-surrender to the Father." As such, it "represents the perfect distancing of the self from itself."[386] As God's gift, Mary's assent—to continue the example—is the highest grace. As a human response it is "the highest achievement made possible by grace: unconditional, definitive self-surrender."[387]

Adrienne thus teaches that the most personal and personalizing activities of the human being are not primarily of his or her own doing, but rather of one's allowing to be done to oneself (*geschehen lassen*). Requiring—contrary to appearances—an extraordinary exercise of the free will, such "actions" of allowing God to determine the direction of one's own accomplishment by grace consist primarily in the continued and generous perseverance of readiness and expectation. Like the fiat of the Blessed Virgin, this act of self-realization is, in other words, an act of obedience: a willing surrender of self—Adrienne uses the term *Hingabe*, denoting (it bears repeating) both surrender and devotion—which precisely as willed constitutes the highest form of personal freedom.[388]

It is certainly not in opposition to our freedom, then, that we should conceive of human perfection as consisting in being "burst apart,"[389] so as to

---

383. Speyr, *Theologie der Geschlechter*, 99. Adrienne argues that we are too accustomed to seeing the Church as an institution, but she lives "essentially in a movement from the Son [and] to the Son, as he lives from the Father and to the Father" (*Das Hohelied*, 51). Cf. Balthasar, *My Work*, 65.

384. See, for example, Speyr, *Das Wort und die Mystik* I, 24–25.

385. See Speyr, *Handmaid of the Lord*, 32; and *They Followed His Call*, 59.

386. Speyr, *Handmaid of the Lord*, 162.

387. Balthasar, *First Glance at Adrienne von Speyr*, 51.

388. As the Congregation for the Doctrine of the Faith aptly expresses it: "Mary is totally dependent upon God and completely directed towards him, and, at the side of her Son, she is *the most perfect image of freedom and of the liberation* of humanity and of the universe" (*Instruction on Christian Freedom and Liberation* [Washington, D.C.: United States Catholic Conference, 1986], no. 97). Cf. Pope John Paul II, *Redemptoris Mater*, no. 37.

389. See Speyr, *John* IV, 77; and *John* I, 103.

die perfectly open to (and thus fully receptive of) the Lord. Created in order to be fulfilled in Communion with the triune God, the human being is realized in a living relationship with God, Adrienne teaches, and more specifically, in a state of constant readiness to receive God according to God's desire to give of himself. This manner of remaining flexible, or of allowing oneself to be formed by God, is that which constitutes the "unity" of the human being.[390] In Mary, the new Eve, who remains fully open to God, permitting him to work within her as he pleases, it is perfectly realized: both in her complete readiness, or openness, which is already grace, and in the fulfillment of this readiness, that is to say, in her maternal mission: in the enfleshment of God's Word (and grace) within her.

Mary's genuine being and becoming is fulfilled through her acceptance of the Son. Even though she bears the Son within her and allows herself to be formed through him, she does not thereby alienate herself from other people or from herself; she experiences and performs her prime personal mission; she fulfils her task and adheres to becoming what God intended for her. Her unity is crowned by the Son.[391]

Like Mary, every Christian is challenged to let the Lord determine the conditions of his or her fulfillment by grace, with the result that it is the surrender itself that is decisive, humanly speaking, for the Christian's perfection. Just as the Lord's unlimited self-surrender on the Cross is the fulfillment of his life of love whereby death itself is destroyed and transformed into life, our own self-surrender to the Lord is that whereby our lives participate in the mystery of his ongoing Incarnation and thus also in his redemptive mission, which continues in the Church. It follows that our reception of the Lord and his reception of us—not unlike Mary's reception of Christ and his of her—cannot be clearly distinguished: "the border between the one received and the one receiving is obliterated."[392] To receive the Lord means quite simply to be received by him.[393]

As one body with the Lord, the Christian participates in this mystical marriage of Christ and the Church, in virtue of which it is impossible to distinguish between what the Lord gives and what the Church has received to give back in turn.[394] "In the reciprocal surrender the limit between yours

---

390. Adrienne calls it "keeping fluid," and she specifies: "within his essence and being" (Speyr, *Mary in the Redemption*, 35).

391. Ibid., 36.

392. Speyr, *John I*, 102. Similarly: "one can no longer say who received and who is received, where receiving begins and where being received ends" (ibid.). See also Speyr, *Theologie der Geschlechter*, 98.

393. Speyr, *The Letter to the Colossians*, 71.

394. Speyr, *The Letter to the Ephesians*, 231. The Church is "the fullness of Christ" without whom he cannot exist (*Theologie der Geschlechter*, 99).

and mine vanish; the *I*, without even noticing, is led into the *Thou*."[395] In this particular passage, Adrienne describes the act of human communication as a sort of dynamism between the word that is spoken and the word that is received in order to draw a comparison with the Word of God within his Church.[396] The analogy may also describe, however, the movement between Christ and the Christian in the Church. This specification—in the Church—is important, because the Christian's "measure" of open receptivity never matches that of Christ's own gift of self in virtue of which the former is enriched and fulfilled (cf. Jn 1:11–12). It is only in the "breadth" of Mary's own unlimited fiat that the Christian can truly be said to receive the Lord, such that his personal gift of surrender (*Hingabe*) takes the form of enriching receptivity precisely as received (*Hinnahme*).[397]

---

395. Speyr, *Theologie der Geschlechter*, 98.

396. Similar is Balthasar's presentation of woman (and thus also Mary-Church) as the "answer [*Antwort*]" to the "word [*Wort*]" of man (Christ/Logos). See Balthasar, *Theo-Drama* III, 281–360, and chapter six of this volume. Cf. Speyr, *The Letter to the Ephesians*, 240.

397. See Speyr, *Three Women and the Lord*, 27; and *Das Hohelied*, 43. Cf. Balthasar and Ratzinger, *Mary: The Church at the Source*, 113–14.

FOUR

The Body-Spirit Difference-in-Unity
A Speyrian Theology of the Body

Introduction to a Speyrian Theology of the Body

Given the central importance that Adrienne accords to the concept of surrender in her treatment of the so-called tension (or difference-in-unity) of grace and nature, as we saw in chapter three, it is perhaps not surprising that this same concept should emphatically reemerge in her treatment of the body-spirit relation of the human person, who in turn is understood within the mystery of the Trinity. Precedence is thus granted once again to God's surrender, namely the surrender of himself to humankind by way of the Incarnation: the mirror image, as it were, of the Son's eternal generation from the Father (God's surrender of himself to himself) and of the Spirit's proceeding from the Father and the Son. This surrender within the Godhead continues in the Church through the Eucharist whereby Christ might be said to become flesh in us: "God has introduced the world into the circulation of his eternal love, but he has taken it up in such a way that he has brought what is characteristic of a human being—being a soul in a body—to its perfect fulfillment in the Incarnation of the Son, for the Son has given to bodily life its complete, supernatural, divine meaning, and on his own body through the Eucharist he has bestowed continued, perduring existence, whereby he also grants to our body and to our whole humanity continuance in his body."[1]

Here again, we might recognize a certain similarity to the theology of Aquinas who, borrowing from Augustine and John Damascene, argues that the proper effect of the Eucharist is, as Gilles Emery summarizes, "the transformation (*transformatio*) of man into Christ by love, the transmutation (*transmutatio*) of the one who eats into the food that is eaten, our *conversion*

---

1. Speyr, *The Letter to the Colossians*, 33.

into Christ, a union or *adunatio* of man to Christ."[2] This incorporation, in turn, supposes—all in granting the absolute primacy of the divine surrender which, as we saw in chapter three, gives rise to our own—the surrender of our body-persons to Christ for the realization of our communion with him and, in him, with one another; whence the significant role of Mary in the theology of Aquinas,[3] as well as that of Balthasar and Speyr, as we shall see. Without diminishing the mystical doctrine of revelation, with its emphasis upon divine condescension (the descending mediation of the Word) and its presentation of Christ as the living sacrament of salvation, it is to Mary that is thus accorded—by Adrienne and Balthasar no less than by St. Thomas—the important role of receiving, within her whole body-spirit unity, the person of the Son, so that he might, in accord with his eternal will, take flesh in her and of her.

As differing, however, from the patristic and Thomistic presentation of Christ's humanity as the instrument of his divinity[4] and in keeping with her Christological focus as revelatory of the Trinity, Adrienne recognizes the role of Christ's flesh—indeed, of his entire human nature—as giving expression to his love for the Father. His body is the instrument (*Werkzeug*) of his obedient love for the Father,[5] and it is to this end that it might be understood as an "instrument" for our redemption. The Son accepts his body as proof of his willingness to redeem the world as an act of love for the Father, and throughout his earthly life he regards it—in "even the smallest actions"—as an "instrument" given by the Father for this purpose.[6] Far from promoting a certain spirit-body dualism, on the one hand, or a certain tri-theism—a charge which is taken up in chapter seven—on the other hand, Adrienne's intention is to thereby situate the whole of Christ's humanity (body and spirit) within the mystery of the Trinitarian union, which is not to deny that the Son alone is incarnate.

2. Emery, "The Ecclesial Fruit of the Eucharist in St. Thomas Aquinas," in *Trinity, Church, and the Human Person*, 159.

3. Cf. Thomas Aquinas, *ST* III, q. 30, a. 1.

4. Cf. Thomas Aquinas, *ST* I-II, q. 112, a. 1, ad. 1; III, q. 7, a. 1, ad. 3; q. 8, a. 1, ad. 1; q. 19, a. 1; q. 34, a. 1, ad. 3; q. 48, a. 6; and *Comp* I, 212. See also Torrell, *Pour nous les hommes et pour notre salut*, 50–57; and Theophil Tschipke, *Die Menschheit Christi als Heilsorgan der Gottheit: Unter Besonderer Berücksichtigung der Lehre des heiligen Thomas von Aquin* (Freiburg im Breisgau: Herder, 1940), wherein are traced the patristic roots of this doctrine leading up to Aquinas. This work has also been translated into French by Philibert Secrétan as *L'humanité du Christ comme instrument de salut de la divinité* (Fribourg: St. Paul, 2003).

5. See Speyr, *Theologie der Geschlechter*, 183; and *The Letter to the Ephesians*, 156.

6. Speyr, *The Letter to the Ephesians*, 36–37; see also 156. It follows for Adrienne that Christ's readiness to fulfill the Father's will in the body includes such ordinary actions as sleeping and eating, for these actions reveal his respect for the body's needs and thus also his profound respect for the Creator's intentions; see *Das Wort und die Mystik* II, 535.

What Adrienne regards as "the greatest mystery of Christianity," namely that Christ is one flesh with his Church, is realized, she argues, within the mystery of Christ's "being one with the Father and the Holy Spirit"[7]: a unity which is manifest in time as the obedience of the incarnate Son. Christ's obedience is corporal, Adrienne reasons, precisely because it is spiritual, and in both senses it is an expression in time—a revelation—of his eternal love for the Father (cf. Jn 14:31). It is, in other words, a revelation of his receptive partaking of the entire Godhead, and thus also of the one divine will.[8] Like the body of the first Adam, which was meant—as an "instrument of concrete obedience, [or] responsive grateful love"[9]—to express his likeness to God, the body of the new and definitive Adam is an expression of his concrete obedience: of, that is to say, his eternal responsive love. "The surpassing love of the Lord is the criterion of every possible relation between the spirit and the flesh." In other words, "his love is the norm of the relation between the spirit and the flesh in every particular instance."[10]

From this perspective, we might also recognize a likeness between Adrienne's theology of the body and that of Pope John Paul II, who presents the human body as possessing, in reason of our divine likeness, a "'spousal' attribute." By this term is meant the capacity of expressing love and more specifically "*that love in which the human person becomes a gift* and—through this gift—fulfils the very meaning of his being and existence."[11] As for Adrienne, she too recognizes the human body, precisely in its nudity, as "a being formed for love."[12] While this trait might be understood as a natural (typically human) one, the body also has a properly theological significance. Precisely as a "sacrament" of the person, it is—Pope John Paul II teaches—"capable of making visible what is invisible: the spiritual and the divine. It has been created to transfer into the visible reality of the world the mystery hidden from eternity in God [our redemption in Christ], and thus [to] be a sign of it."[13]

Strikingly similar, again, is the theology of Adrienne. Although she portrays the corporality of our first ancestors as expressing the unity of their

---

7. Speyr, *The Letter to the Ephesians*, 240–41.
8. See also chapter seven of the present volume, wherein I will present this argument more thoroughly within the context of certain challenges posed by Balthasar's appropriation of Adrienne's teaching.
9. Speyr, *Das Wort und die Mystik* II, 534.   10. Speyr, *John* I, 118.
11. Pope John Paul II, General Audience of January 16, 1980, in *Man and Woman He Created Them*, 185. Cf. Vatican Council II, *Gaudium et Spes*, no. 24 (DZ 4324). On the similarities between Adrienne's theology of the body and that of Pope John Paul II, see Berg, *Christian Marriage according to Adrienne von Speyr*, 208.
12. Speyr, *Theologie der Geschlechter*, 147.
13. Pope John Paul II, General Audience of February 20, 1980, in *Man and Woman He Created Them*, 203.

persons,[14] she does not recognize this unity as an end in itself. Rather, the experience of shared fecundity is, she explains, one of transcendence wherein man and woman might experience the surpassing not only of their personal limits, but also of the confinement marking their natural finitude.[15] It is thus not surprising that the Swiss mystic uses the same experience to describe, by way of metaphor, the incomprehensible mystery of Trinitarian love.[16] At the base of the likeness between these two very different personal unions—that of human persons in a physical, prolonged but nonetheless finite relationship of sexual love, and that of the divine persons in a spiritual, eternal communion of love)[17]—she notes "a certain unity between the mystery of the body and the mystery of God" whereby "the former is contained in the latter."[18]

Herein the progression of thought moves from the experience of the body as a means of communion to the knowledge of God as a Trinity of persons, but this movement is itself preceded, in Adrienne's thought, by the primordial "movement" of the Trinity "to" the body. The human body was created, she teaches, by the Father for the Son and the Spirit. The Son, in turn, incorporates us into his body as members by means of the Eucharistic mysteries, which he establishes in obedience to the Father and with the help of the Spirit who bears him. As for the Spirit, he takes residence in the body, as in a temple built by the Father and sanctified by the Son through the latter's Incarnation and Cross.

From this Trinitarian perspective, the human body is revelatory of Trinitarian love, especially within the context of the Eucharistic mysteries: "The Spirit causes [*bewirkt*] the Eucharistic existence of the body of Christ in the Church, as he already accomplished the Incarnation in the womb of Mary." For this reason, as we shall see, she is "the image and womb of the Church, to whom the Son surrenders himself in a spousal manner in the Eucharistic mystery"[19] and the "central point from which the Son's Eucharist can flow and spread forth."[20]

As is particularly evident in these passages, it is God's surrender—from

---

14. See Speyr, *Theologie der Geschlechter*, 159.

15. See ibid., 147. Similarly, Pope John Paul II argues for a bi-directional movement of analysis—arguing for a mutual clarification—between the mystery of redemption and the body-person with his or her conjugal significance. See his General Audience of October 13, 1982, in *Man and Woman He Created Them*, 510.

16. "So there results from our experience of the body in love a step towards the incomprehensible mystery of the Trinity" (Speyr, *Theologie der Geschlechter*, 143); Adrienne also compares the original unity of Adam and Eve in their nakedness to the unity of the divine persons (159). See also chapter six of the present volume for a more thorough development of these ideas.

17. Cf. *DZ* 806.
18. Speyr, *World of Prayer*, 190.
19. Speyr, *Korinther* I, 187–88.
20. Speyr, *World of Prayer*, 69.

the Trinity to the Incarnation, from the Incarnation to the Eucharist, and from the Eucharist to the Church—that explains and determines the meaning of the human body as "the instrument of a much more comprehensive surrender,"[21] and even—within the context of redemption—as "the instrument of a fundamentally unbounded obedience."[22] Combining, in some sense, the experiential approach, characteristic of phenomenology, with a properly theological approach proceeding from the data of revelation, Adrienne's unique mystical perspective invites her reader to so live the sacramental mysteries of the Christian faith that he or she might experience his or her own body as an "instrument" of obedience. As such, the Christian might also experience his or her body as an essential means of participating in the bridal mission of the Church, who in turn shares the filial mission of Christ: a mission, as we shall see, to be the Father's Eucharist for the world.[23] Hence also the role of mysticism, which Adrienne recognizes as having "an incarnate function in the Church."[24]

In an effort to expose Adrienne's very rich theology of the body within the larger context of her theology of mission, we will continue this chapter by briefly sketching Balthasar's own insights into this significant theme, bringing out most especially certain patristic themes which will provide the context for our demonstration of Adrienne's complementary approach. To this end, I will lead the reader through an examination of the meaning of the Incarnation as a Trinitarian act of love: the Father's love for the Son and the Son's love for the Father in and through their common Spirit. This conception of the Incarnation dominates, as we will see, her theological vision that I will present in terms of a corporal-spiritual unity. Because, moreover, Adrienne presents the Trinitarian love of God as founding both the Incarnation and the Eucharist, it is also the fundamental and final reference for her theological perspective. It is thus not surprising that she calls upon supernatural mysteries to illuminate and explicate natural and bodily realities. Hence, for example, the mystery of redemption is presented in terms of the one-flesh union of Christ and his Church, which in turn is explained from within the Eucharistic mysteries and still more fundamentally within the reciprocal

---

21. Speyr, *Theologie der Geschlechter*, 106.   22. Ibid., 183; see also *Erde und Himmel* II, 264.

23. See, for example, Speyr, *The Cross: Word and Sacrament*, 53; *The Passion from Within*, 118; and *The Holy Mass*, 65.

24. Speyr, *Theologie der Geschlechter*, 121; *Erde und Himmel* II, no. 1653 (253) and no. 1729 (295)—where mention is made of Adrienne's desire to "think" with her body and with her mystical wound, respectively—and Balthasar, *First Glance at Adrienne von Speyr*, 45. Balthasar thus fittingly notes that in contrast to those mysticisms inspired by Neo-Platonism, Adrienne's own mystical theory is characterized by the "key" importance awarded to the body. See Balthasar, *Our Task*, 39.

loving surrender of the divine persons of the Trinity. It is into this mystery that believers are incorporated, Adrienne also explains, by the humanity of Christ. Finally, by way of conclusion, we will see how Adrienne presents the Virgin Mary as the first "cell" of the Church and thus also as an archetypical member of Christ's body.

The Body-Spirit "Tension" in Balthasar's Work

Not unlike Adrienne's treatment of the first and most fundamental of the anthropological "tensions"—that of the human body and spirit, as will be more thoroughly exposited in the pages which follow—Balthasar's own treatment of this tension is marked not so much by the metaphysical question of the indisputable unity of the human body and soul, which dominates the approach of St. Thomas and Church doctrine.[25] For Balthasar and Adrienne, in contrast, the emphasis is upon the "rhythm" whereby "the body (nature) rises to spirit, and the spirit (which is the goal and rationale of 'evolution') descends into the body (nature)."[26] Indeed, despite the profound unity of the human person, "who originates from below and from above and extends both upward and downward" and whose highest operation of reflection requires his or her whole "physical-spiritual infrastructure,"[27] Balthasar notes the continuous temptation throughout human history of stressing either the descent of the spirit into nature (as in pantheism) or the ascent of the spirit by transcending the body (as in Platonism).

This bidirectional pull—upward and downward—betrays something of the dramatic structure of human existence, as Balthasar sees it,[28] but also the profound need of a transcendent answer to the question that the human person is to him- or herself. "If man is not to resign himself to a narrow Aris-

---

25. The Church's magisterium has definitively adopted the Aristotelian notion of hylomorphism, as apparent in her pronouncement by way of decree of the following: the human person is a unity constituted of body and soul (*DZ* 1440 and 3002); the soul is through itself and essentially the form of the body (*DZ* 902); and the soul is spiritual (*DZ* 372, 800, 1440, and 2812) and immortal (*DZ* 1440 and 2766). On the teaching of St. Thomas, see Marie-Joseph Nicolas, "Le corps humain," *Revue thomiste* 79, no. 3 (1979): 357–87; "Le corps humain et sa résurrection," *Revue thomiste* 79, no. 4 (1979): 533–45; "L'idée de nature dans la pensée de S. Thomas," 555–59; Gilles Emery, "The Unity of Man, Body and Soul in St. Thomas Aquinas," trans. Therese C. Scarpelli, *Trinity, Church and the Human Person: Thomistic Essays* (Naples, Fla.: Sapientia Press, 2007), 209–35. It is perhaps important to mention that Balthasar in no way calls this doctrine into question. He merely changes emphasis.

26. Balthasar, *Theo-Drama* II, 411.

27. Ibid., 359. In a similar manner, Jean-Pierre Torrell explains with regard to the theology of Aquinas: "The soul is not united to the body to spiritualize it, but indeed because the soul needs the body. For without the body, the soul cannot even perform its most noble operation, understanding" (*Saint Thomas Aquinas* II: *Spiritual Master*, 257).

28. See Scola, *Hans Urs von Balthasar: A Theological Style*, 90.

totelian 'middle'—in view of the destructiveness of extreme spiritualization and sensualisation—he must be given *Lebensraum* [living space] in the form of a concrete blueprint that will liberate him from this straitening 'middle,'" Balthasar argues. Such a blueprint must, more specifically he reasons, achieve both movements by descending into the flesh "from above" in order that the flesh itself might transcend toward God: *not* by a spiritualizing process that would deny, suppress, or surpass human corporality in an attempt to be God-like—an attempt which Balthasar recognizes as an inheritance of original sin—but by way of a "transfiguring"[29] or a "transformation of the bodily, which groans under the law of mortality, into the *soma pneumatikon* [spiritual body], into the spiritual, but explicitly incarnate, body (1 Cor 15:44)."[30]

Because, in fact, the Swiss theologian recognizes this bidirectional movement, or "rhythm" as integral to human nature, it is not destroyed by the Christian economy "but overlaid by the primacy of the descent," namely the Incarnation of God:

From the purely anthropological perspective, the spirit's rootedness in the flesh implies that the latter is permeated by spirit and lifted up into the sphere of the spirit; accordingly, in the new supernatural rhythm in which God becomes incarnate right down to the lowest depths and out to the farthest bounds, the physical is 'divinized,' permeated with God's Pneuma, transfigured and 'transferred' (Col 1:13) into the kingdom of the Son, and hence of God. The Platonic Eros, striving upward from the bodily to the spiritual and divine, is overtaken in the event of Agape and brought to share in a fulfillment that goes far beyond its own upward thrust; but this cannot take place unless it, too, is con-crucified together with the love of Christ.[31]

Herein Balthasar not only insists upon the primacy of God's movement toward the human person over and above any movement of the human person toward God, but he also argues that this unique path of descent is likewise that of the human person toward God. If God has humbled himself to come to us, we in turn must humble ourselves to come to him, sharing in his sufferings so as also to share in his glory (cf. Rom 8:17; Phil 3:10–11). Or, to put it in other words, the only true manner of Christian transcendence is to be found in the act of being "emptied" after the pattern of Christ, as in the famous hymn of Philippians 2:3–11. Balthasar thus argues against a simplistic reading of the "wonderful exchange" of salvation as it is formulated by the

---

29. Balthasar, *Theo-Drama* II, 364.
30. Balthasar, *Theo-Logic* II, 156. On the desire to deny or suppress the body as a result of original sin, see Balthasar, "The Fathers, The Scholastics, and Ourselves," *Communio* 24 (1997): 388–89. Because God willingly accepted to become incarnate "within the sphere of the finite, man does not draw near to him," Balthasar reasons, "by denying all that limits him" (*Explorations in Theology* I, 175).
31. Balthasar, *Theo-Drama* II, 412–13.

Church Fathers and taken up by St. Thomas—"God became man so that man might become God"[32]—for one is Christian "only in the exact imitation of Christ's movement." In other words, the law of the Incarnation as expressed by St. Paul—"He who descended is he who also ascended" (cf. Eph 4:10) is understood by Balthasar as "the law of the *one* Christ: Head and Body."[33] It follows that our participation in the divine nature (cf. 2 Pt 1:3–4) must not be thought of as overcoming or abolishing the distance between God and man. Indeed, any attempt to bridge the difference must always come up against this same law of the Incarnation wherein the "ever-greater" difference of the divine and human natures is presented as "the place and stage of union."[34]

The originality of Balthasar's thought with regard to the so-called tension between the human body and spirit does not, however, consist so much in his transposition of this tension to that of the presumably opposed movements of descent and ascent: a tension which he thus recognizes as indicating our share in Christ's own *kenosis* as the unique path to our share in his ascent. Far more "original" to Balthasar's presentation of the body-spirit tension—although here again we might recognize Adrienne's influence or at least a profound unity of perspectives—is his presentation of this tension as finding its original and final archetype in the Trinity, as revealed in Christ's bodily surrender of himself to the Father and to the Church, for love of the Father, throughout his earthly life and most especially on the Cross.[35]

In the man-God, Jesus Christ, Balthasar recognizes one who is "body and soul" a vessel surrendered to the divine activity, one who "not only speaks God's Word with body and soul, but *is* that Word. [...] Such an exhaustive taking possession of man on the part of God [...] is already as such an adaptation of man to the measure of God. For in this act of taking possession, man is not a merely passive vessel; he is what God has willed him to be: one who responds to the Word, one who corresponds to God's speech."[36] From this perspective, Christ's body—along with his entire human nature—serves the revelation of the Son's eternal surrender to the Father, which is expressed in time as obedience.[37] Hence Balthasar recognizes that he "seals his total spiritual-intellectual surrender to the (vanished) Father" on the

---

32. See Thomas Aquinas, *ST* III, q. 5, a. 4; The *Catechism of the Catholic Church*, no. 460; Balthasar, *Theo-Drama* III, 237–45; and the selection of passages from Irenaeus's *Adversus Haereses* in Saward (trans.), *The Scandal of the Incarnation*, 53–59.

33. Balthasar, "The Fathers, The Scholastics, and Ourselves," 361.

34. Ibid., 360.　　　　　　　　　35. See Balthasar, *Epilogue*, 112.

36. Balthasar, *The Glory of the Lord* I, 475. For this same reason, Christ is "the incarnate Covenant of humanity with God" (*Explorations in Theology* II, 78).

37. See my treatment of Christ's obedience in time in chapter three and the question of eternal, properly divine "obedience" in chapter seven.

Cross with the surrender of his completely expropriated body (*Körper*).[38] Or to put it in an other way, Christ's spiritual surrender—what we witness as obedience and what Balthasar recognizes as pointing to the inner-Trinitarian mystery wherein "every Hypostasis, in its own 'decline,' causes the Other to 'arise'"[39]—is both revealed and bodily bestowed in this sacrifice which is preserved in the Eucharistic mysteries.

Similarly, Christ's resurrected body (*Leib*) "expresses nothing other than his constant purpose of self-surrender," as vividly expressed in his ever-open wounds from which flow the "new fountain" of life for the Church and the world.[40] Hence, "none of these forms of descent [Incarnation, death, descent into hell, Eucharist] is revoked in the Resurrection on the third day and in the Ascension. Bodily Resurrection and Ascension are not dis-incarnation but a transformation of the entire human form, spirit and body, into the pneumatic mode of existence."[41] The particular concrete body of Christ thus takes on a universal significance through the surrender of his Spirit, giving rise to his body-bride the Church. She, in turn, is charged to continue Christ's mission of drawing others into the fruitfulness of his bodily surrender by means of the sacraments, especially the Eucharist, wherein each of her members is invited and empowered to give to his or her own life and body the meaning of love expressed as surrender.[42]

Such is the meaning of death which can be—even as a physical event—"assimilated in advance to that spiritual event" of handing over one's corporality to God as Creator and Redeemer. Indeed, Balthasar recognizes the Christian's regard for his or her body as "governed by this final sacrifice," namely death, which is to be lived as a conscious act. In other words, this final corporal-spiritual surrender should give "inner meaning" to all the actions of one's life.[43] In this way, Christ takes his members—"those who receive him" (cf. Jn 1:12)—"with him into his Cross," which requires that we "yield to the superior strength of love."[44] In this yielding, we have the help of the Spirit, who is responsible not only for the transformation of the resurrected body of Christ, manifest during the forty days between his Resurrection and Ascen-

---

38. Balthasar, *Theo-Drama* V, 476. The German distinction between *Körper* and *Leib* (both of which might be translated as "body" in English) expresses the distinction between that which is transitory as mortal, in the first case, and that which is living, in the second.

39. Ibid., 478.   40. Ibid., 476–77.

41. Balthasar, *Theo-Drama* II, 412.

42. See, for example, Balthasar, *Epilogue*, 112–15; *Theo-Drama* II, 410; and *Theo-Logic* II, 307–12.

43. Balthasar, *Theo-Drama* V, 476. Cf. Thomas Aquinas, *ST* I, q. 64, a. 2. Such is, for example, Balthasar explains, the meaning of Christian virginity, corporal penance, and mortification. In each case self-surrender and sacrifice are also related to a share in the fruit of Christ's sacrifice.

44. Ibid., 478–79.

sion, but also for relating the transformed body of Christ to the historical Church in every epoch, especially by way of the sacraments (the Eucharist foremost among them), and finally by creating the missions, which Balthasar presents as the "applications of the life of Christ to every Christian life and the whole life of the Church."[45] "As an earthly man, he is obedient to the Spirit; exalted, he breathes the Spirit into the world. So he can cause believers to share in both obeying the Spirit and communicating the Spirit, essential roles for members of the Church of Jesus."[46] Balthasar thus recognizes the movement (as it were) of God towards enfleshment as "completed by [his] becoming ecclesial, and even cosmic."[47]

Herein again we might recognize Balthasar's appreciation of the patristic theme of the *admirabile commercium*: the divine exchange whereby the Son of God becomes man so that human persons might become (by divine adoption) sons and daughters of God. One ought nonetheless to be on guard against a certain interpretation of this theme that would give the impression that Balthasar understands this exchange as occurring between the two natures of Christ. To be sure, no great connoisseur of the Church Fathers such as Balthasar would deny that this mystical doctrine of redemption, with its emphasis upon the divine condescension (the *descending mediation* of the Word), has its place within Church tradition, as attested to by St. Thomas.[48] Hence, for example, the important formula of Gregory of Nazianzus, "what is not assumed is not healed,"[49] or the highly influential insight of Pope Leo I that Christ's humanity is the instrument (*organon*) of his divinity.[50] The

---

45. Balthasar, *A Theology of History*, 82. Balthasar presents the Church as "an organism in which the Head no longer wants or is able to act in separation from his Body" (*Unless You Become Like This Child*, 39).

46. Balthasar, *Theo-Drama* III, 258–59; see also 38–39.

47. Balthasar, *Theo-Drama* II, 412; cf. Eph 1:23. See also Balthasar, *Explorations in Theology* I, 177; and "Introduction" to Speyr, *Light and Images*, 14. Balthasar explains that while the Church and her members are properly called the "body of Christ" by St. Paul (cf. Eph 1:23), such is not the case for the cosmos (*Theo-Logic* II, 308), which is not to deny the cosmic dimension of the Church. Indeed, Christ's passion has "broken" the resistance of the anti-divine powers ruling the cosmos (*Theo-Drama* II, 309–10 and 315). Balthasar presents the Eucharist as "liquefying" Christ's body, rendering it accessible to all times and places; see *Theo-Drama* III, 38–39.

48. See, for example, Thomas Aquinas, *ST* III, q. 5, a. 4.

49. Gregory of Nazianzus, *Episola 101: Ad Cledonium presbyterum*, in *Patrologiae Graeca*, vol. 37: *Sancti Patris Nostri Gegorii theologi vulgo Nazianzeni Archiepiscopi Constantinopolitani*, ed. Jacques-Paul Migne (Paris, 1857), 182–83: "*Nam quod assumptum non est curationis est: quod autem Deo unitum est, hoc quoque salutem consequitur* [What is not assumed is not healed; what is however united to God is saved thereby]." For the orginal Greek, see column 181. See also the numerous Church Fathers cited by the Second Vatican Council in its decree on the Church's missionary activity in *Ad Gentes Divinitus*, ch. 2, no. 3, note 4.

50. Building upon this insight, St. Thomas argues that as the instrument of his divinity, Christ's humanity is both sanctified and sanctifying. See *ST* III, q. 34, a. 1, ad. 3; a. 3; q. 48, a. 1; and I-II, q. 114, a. 6. Other examples of the mystical doctrine of salvation may be found in the works of Saints Irenaeus of

Swiss theologian nonetheless prefers to regard the mystery of salvation in terms borrowed from St. Thomas of an exchange between Head and members.[51] From this perspective, the mystical "marriage" of the two natures of Christ in the "wedding chamber" of the Virgin's womb—as it is presented by St. Augustine of Hippo[52]—is understood as ordered to the marriage between Christ and the Church: "For no man ever hates his own flesh, but nourishes and cherishes it, as Christ does the Church, because we are members of his body. 'For this reason a man shall leave his father and mother and be joined to his wife, and the two shall become one.' This is a great mystery, and I take it to mean Christ and the Church" (Eph 5:29–32).

Herein is emphasized the primacy of God's action, but this is a primacy—to emphasize our conclusion from the previous chapter and to likewise point ahead to chapter five—which grants a real place to human subjects who are nonetheless intimately related to him as members of his body and bride, the Church. She, in turn, is so intimately related to Christ that she is not to be perceived, Balthasar insists, as "set over against him as *another* subject." Rather, she is "his Body, animated and governed by his Spirit."[53]

There thus emerges still another patristic theme in Balthasar's corpus (which is also found in the doctrine of St. Thomas), namely that of the continued Incarnation of Christ as is implied in the threefold significance accorded by Scripture to the expression "Body of Christ" (*triplex modus corporis*): his fleshly body born of the Virgin, his sacramental body in the Eucharist, and his mystical body, the Church (**corpus natum, corpus eucharisticum, corpus mysticum**).[54] In each case, the body might be understood as

---

Lyons, Cyril of Alexandria, and Athanasius the Great. See Aloys Grillmeier, *Christ in Christian Tradition: From the Apostolic Age to Chalcedon (451)*, trans. J. S. Bowden (New York: Sheed and Ward, 1965), 466–67; and Tschipke, *Die Menschheit Christi als Heilsorgan der Gottheit*. See also Balthasar, *Theo-Drama* IV, 246–49.

51. Cf. See Thomas Aquinas, *ST* III, q. 8 and q. 7, a. 9. Aquinas teaches, more specifically, that the grace of Christ (as head) is communicated to us (as members) not by means of the humanity that we share with him in virtue of the Incarnation, but by means of his personal actions on our behalf. By this doctrine, the angelic doctor in no way denies that Christ's every action followed upon the hypostatic union (see q. 3, a. 11) in virtue of which his human actions are universally salvific. See *ST* III, q. 7, a. 1, ad. 3; q. 8, a. 1, ad. 1; q. 43, a. 2; q. 48, a. 6; and *De Ver*, q. 29, a. 5.

52. "*Verbum enim sponsus, et sponsa caro humana; et utrumque unus Filius Dei, et idem filius hominis: ubi factus est caput Ecclesiae, ille uterus virginis Mariae thalamus ejus, inde processit tanquam sponsus de thalamo suo* [The Word is the bridegroom and the bride is the human flesh, and one and the same is the Son of God and the Son of man; and when be became the head of the Church, the womb of the Virgin Mary was his room from which he came forth like a bridegroom from his (wedding) chamber]" (Augustine of Hippo, *In Johannis Evangelium*, VIII, 4; *Homélies sur l'Évangile de Saint Jean*, 474 and 476; PL 35:1452); the translation is my own.

53. Balthasar, *A Theology of History*, 114; see also 103–4.

54. For a thorough exposition of this teaching among the Fathers, see chapter seven of Jean Borella, *The Sense of the Supernatural* (Edinburgh: T. & T. Clark, 1998). See also Balthasar's homily, "The Three-

the "place" of a salvific exchange: not so much—to repeat—that of the two natures of Christ, but more profoundly of the person of Christ and the persons of each of his members, beginning first and foremost with the person of his mother who, as Aquinas teaches,[55] received him by her fiat for all of humankind. Her reception does not mean, assuredly, that we need not receive him ourselves, but precisely indicates that we might receive him (body, soul, and divinity) within the gift of our own persons (body and soul) to him.[56] "He is the living God, 'bodily present with and for man, and so he calls for an 'embodied' response: man, in the entirety of his existence as a hearer and answerer of the word."[57]

The corporal body of Christ thus assumes a capital importance as the point of union (cf. Eph 2:16) between the fullness of the Godhead (cf. Col 1:19) and the Church as the mystical body of Christ (cf. Eph 1:23; Col 1:18, 24).[58] Hence, in a manner altogether compatible with the teaching of St. Thomas[59] and that of the Second Vatican Council,[60] Balthasar presents Christ as the "primordial sacrament"[61] by which (or better: by whom) the grace of the Holy Spirit is communicated to the world. "In this way the divine life, which is manifested to the world through the humanity of the Son, is also imparted to this world, in the community of believers called the 'Body of Christ,' to be lived and shared by it."[62]

From this perspective, Christ's descending mediation (his assimilation of himself to humanity by way of the Incarnation) might be understood as ordered to the ascending mediation of his return to the Father along with his

---

fold Presence of Christ" in *You Crown the Year with Your Goodness*, 128–34; *Theo-Drama* II, 114; and Pope John Paul II, *Ecclesia de Eucharistia*, nos. 21–25. From a Thomistic perspective, see Emery, "The Ecclesial Fruit of the Eucharist in St. Thomas Aquinas."

55. Thomas Aquinas, *ST* III, q. 30, a. 1.

56. This possibility of really receiving him supposes, as we saw in chapter three, our participation in Mary's perfect receptivity.

57. Balthasar, *Prayer*, 36.

58. See Balthasar, *The Glory of the Lord* I, 433. Cf. Thomas Aquinas, *De Ver*, q. 29, a. 5.

59. Arguing from a Thomistic perspective, Emmanuel Perrier holds that what differentiates the exemplary value of Christ (and thus also his saving passion) from a sacramental sign is that the former "does not designate an invisible reality, but the person of Christ, in whom the invisible is united to the visible and by whom the invisible author of all mercy saves us in the visible flesh. From Christ's work arises an entirely new register of causality: one in which visible signs become cause of grace. Christ is, in reason of the mystery of his person, the source of sacramentality" ("L'enjeu christologique de la satisfaction (II)," *Revue thomiste* 103, no. 2 [2003]: 247).

60. "The Church is in Christ like a sacrament or as a sign and instrument both of a very closely knit union with God and of the unity of the whole human race" (Second Vatican Council, *Lumen Gentium, Dogmatic Constitution on the Church* [November 5, 1964], no. 1; *DZ* 4101). See also Peter Smulders, "L'Église sacrement du salut," in Guilherme Baraúna (ed.), *L'Église de Vatican II. Études autour de la Constitution Conciliaire sur l'Église* II (Collection *Unam Sanctum*, 51b) (Paris: Cerf, 1966), 313–38.

61. See Balthasar, *The Office of Peter*, 133.   62. Balthasar, *Theo-Drama* III, 259.

body-bride: his assimilation of humanity to himself.[63] This in turn supposes that this bride "without blemish" (cf. Eph 5:27) is not merely passively assimilated to the Lord, but becomes like him in the act of becoming one *with* him: in, that is to say, her bridal gift of herself (her self-surrender to the beloved) which is formed, as it were, from his absolutely primary surrender to her, as we saw in chapter three. This is in no way "an abstraction from the material creation and man's bodily reality; it is the transformation of the bodily, which groans under the laws of mortality, into the *soma pneumatikon* [spiritual body], into the spiritual, but explicitly incarnate, body (1 Cor 15:44)."[64]

The Heart of Adrienne's Theology of the Body: The Incarnation as a Revelation of Trinitarian Love

After treating the important theme of the body-spirit "tension" in Balthasar's theology, we now turn to the same in the theology of Adrienne. This theology is one in which the body is considered from the perspective of the divine Incarnation. As such, it is necessarily concerned with the most fundamental of all questions derived from Christian faith: *Cur Deus homo?* The response as formulated in the Nicene creed—*propter nos homines et propter nostram salutem*—is certainly not to be denied by Adrienne, for whom the entire human nature of Christ is "earmarked for the redemption."[65] From the moment of Christ's conception in the Virgin's womb until his descent among the dead, the body of Christ "is burdened with the task of redeeming the world."[66]

In this sense, redemption was already established in the Incarnation. "Already at that moment his blood was the blood of redemption. [...] He assumed it solely in order to be able to shed it, in order to give it to us as a gift."[67] Indeed, the Son willingly accepts this body as proof of his willingness to redeem the world as an act of love for the Father,[68] and throughout his earthly life he regards it—in "even the smallest actions"—as an instrument given by the Father for this end.[69] "He was ready to assume it but also to give it up again for the salvation of the world."[70]

The suffering humanity of Christ can therefore never be separated, in Adrienne's theology, from his divinity. It is not a "foreign body" that suf-

---

63. Cf. Speyr, *Victory of Love*, 16–17. 64. Balthasar, *Theo-Logic* II, 156.
65. Speyr, *The Letter to the Ephesians*, 36; see also *Confession*, 79.
66. Speyr, *The Letter to the Colossians*, 36. "The Incarnation of the Son is inseparably connected to the Cross" (*Die Schöpfung*, 39); "He came so as to redeem by dying" (*Markus*, 636).
67. Speyr, *The Letter to the Ephesians*, 35. 68. See ibid., 156.
69. Ibid., 36–37. See also *Das Wort und die Mystik* II, 535.
70. Speyr, *The Letter to the Ephesians*, 156.

fers here, but the Son's own body "fully integrated with his divine-human spirit."[71] His is "no indifferent flesh and blood" whose sanctification is determined "by right use or some blessing." Rather, it is "holy flesh and blood essentially and from all eternity."[72] Indeed, the designation of the Lord as redeemer in the flesh precedes the world's creation and even the question of whether or not Adam will fall, which is to say that the Son might have become man "only to recapitulate the whole creation in himself, to raze completely the boundaries between heaven and earth, to establish full unification between God and man, to introduce us into the vision of the Father through himself, not as redeemer, but as consummator."[73] Beyond all speculation about what might have been, however, Adrienne argues that the Son's mission is timeless: it is fulfilled before it has begun.[74]

Life thus takes on a richer meaning than that of being created by the Father; it also means, for the Christian, being "newly created through the Son."[75] It is not as if the Father simply leads fallen man back to the point from which he departed. Rather, he "unites him more profoundly with himself in his Son": the first Adam is included in the Second Adam's return to the Father.[76] The Son "destroys in himself the old Adam [...], yet he destroys only after having taken up into himself the thing to be destroyed. He destroys it by dying himself and by letting what he has assumed die together with him." With his resurrection, on the other hand, the world is "recreated" in the Son: "in his love made flesh," which in turn—precisely as Eucharist—is presented as "the substance of the vivification of the new man."[77] Adrienne thus notes in Pilate's words, "Behold the man!" (Jn 19:5), that without knowing it, this famous governor is referring to "*the* man, the archetype of man, man as God has always conceived of him."[78] "Adam destroys the image of God, and the Lord restores this image on the Cross."[79]

---

71. Speyr, *Theologie der Geschlechter*, 100–101. Herein is apparent the difficult challenge of simultaneously acknowledging the unity and the distinction of the two natures of Christ: a challenge which we will treat more thoroughly in chapter seven. See, on that subject, Thomas Aquinas, *Comp* I, 212.

72. Speyr, *The Letter to the Ephesians*, 36.

73. Ibid., 28. In contrast, St. Thomas prudently argues that because God's will is known to us uniquely through Scripture and "since everywhere in the Sacred Scripture the sin of the first man is assigned as the reason of the Incarnation, it is more in accordance with this to say that the work of the Incarnation was ordained by God as a remedy for sin; so that, had sin not existed, the Incarnation would not have been. And yet the power of God is not limited to this; even had sin not existed, God could have become incarnate" (*ST* III, q. 1, a. 3).

74. See Speyr, *John* I, 145.
75. See Speyr, *Dienst der Freude*, 35.
76. Speyr, *Das Wort und die Mystik* II, 261.
77. Speyr, *The Letter to the Ephesians*, 104–5.
78. Speyr, *John* IV, 78.
79. Speyr, *Die Schöpfung*, 39. "When Adam is sinless, the Son sees himself in him, but when Adam falls, he distances the Son from himself. On the Cross, he [the Son] once again takes up this image of Adam into himself" (ibid.).

In this way, Adrienne recognizes, as we saw in the general introduction to this volume, a profound unity between the work of creation and that of redemption as symbolized by the presence of the Cross in her mystical vision of creation.[80] The Son is present at the world's creation not merely in the foreshadowing of the Cross, however, for the image of God, restored to Adam by Christ also has its origin in him, as is also the case in the doctrine of St. Thomas Aquinas.[81] The birth of Christ presupposes the world's creation, but the meaning of creation is incomprehensible to one who has not "experienced" Christ's birth, Adrienne teaches.[82] The world and the human being are, in fact, created with regard to a fulfillment: the Son, who will become man.[83] And the Son brings all things to fulfillment in himself "by impressing upon them his stamp and character."[84] It is not surprising, then, that Adrienne recognizes the Father's eternal act of begetting the Son as the origin of his creative act of bringing forth the world and the human being in the world.[85]

A more fundamental motive for the Son's Incarnation in addition to our redemption is, however, in the Speyrian perspective, his love for the Father and the Spirit, which is revealed to us precisely in and through his incarnate existence.[86] To be sure, in her presentation of Christ's mediating role, Adrienne concentrates upon the dialogue of love between the Father and the incarnate Son, who loves the Father from within the world, so as to offer the world's response of praise and thanksgiving for the gift of the Father's love.[87] He who has adored the Father from all eternity thus recognizes in the creation of the human being still another form in which to adore the Father.[88] The Son becomes man so as to be the Father's Son on earth "as other men are his children." The desire to do so belongs to the particularity of his divine person—to the fact that he is the Son—and it reveals this particularity, Adrienne explains.[89] Indeed, the incarnate Son is the only human being to understand the depths of paternal love from which creation proceeds: as, namely,

---

80. See Speyr, *Apokalypse*, 385.

81. See Torrell, *Saint Thomas Aquinas* II: *Spiritual Master*, 125–52; *Christ and Spirituality in St. Thomas Aquinas*, 86–109.

82. Speyr, *Achtzehn Psalmen*, 16.

83. Speyr, *Das Wort und die Mystik* II, 50; see also *The Letter to the Colossians*, 31–32.

84. Speyr, *The Letter to the Ephesians*, 48; see also *Das Wort und die Mystik* II, 522; and *The Letter to the Colossians*, 33.

85. Speyr, *Das Wort und die Mystik* II, 525; see also 80. Obviously, we are not far from St. Thomas's presentation of "the processions of the divine Persons" as "the cause of creation" (*ST* I, q. 45, a. 6, ad. 1).

86. Ibid., 110.

87. See Speyr, *The Letter to the Ephesians*, 33; cf. Balthasar, *The Threefold Garland*, 29–30. Such is also Adrienne's understanding of the atonement of sin, which the incarnate Son experiences as an insult directed against the Father and the Spirit. See Speyr, *Das Wort und die Mystik* II, 110 and 261; and *World of Prayer*, 80.

88. See *Das Wort und die Mystik* II, 522.   89. Ibid. 82.

an act of love for the eternal Son. The latter, in turn, offers in the Eucharist not only his most perfect surrender, but also "the world's full response to the Father's extravagant love."[90] Of one will with the Father from all eternity, he accomplishes on earth what the Father had in mind for Adam at the moment of his creation[91]—namely, to respond to his love—and he does so precisely in the form of one of the Father's creatures.[92]

By assuming a human body and offering it "no longer as a finite, but as an infinite response of love to God,"[93] the Son accomplishes Adam's likeness to God, with which he was invested at creation (cf. Gen 1:26). In so doing, he not only assures the Father, expressly as a man, that creation really is good,[94] but he also invites each of Adam's descendants to share in his own response—his eternal Eucharist—arising out of Trinitarian love. "God created Adam just once; but he begets the Son, who becomes flesh and blood, in every Holy Mass. Adam, who was created at the beginning, sinned. God now creates the Son over and again in time, just as he perpetually begets him in eternity as the Son, who most certainly will never sin and whose sinlessness he communicates to us in the Eucharist."[95]

To summarize, Adrienne teaches that not only the creation of the world, but also the Incarnation of the Son of God and even the sanctification of believers in Christ are foreseen from all eternity for "the purpose of giving pleasure to the triune God."[96] Hence, the whole mystery of the Lord's terrestrial life stands, within Adrienne's theology, as testimony of the Son's love for the Father and his (the Father's) creation as well as to the Father's love for the Son

---

90. Ibid., 523.
91. See Speyr, *The Letter to the Ephesians*, 36; see also *Die Schöpfung*, 38.
92. See Speyr, *Die katholischen Briefe* II, 191.
93. Speyr, *Das Wort und die Mystik* II, 52; cf. Balthasar, *Theo-Drama* IV, 326.
94. See Speyr, *Das Wort und die Mystik* II, 261 and 523; and *World of Prayer*, 80.
95. Speyr, *The Holy Mass*, 83.
96. Speyr, *The Letter to the Ephesians*, 31. This, assuredly, is not an idea—when read literally rather than metaphorically—without certain consequences for the immutability of the Godhead. See, to that effect, my treatment of the criticisms launched at Balthasar's theology for his appropriation of this sort of language in chapter seven. Or, to express this insight in terms of St. Thomas's own teaching we might add the following precision: "To be loved by someone is identical to being pleasing to him. For he whom I love is pleasing to me. Now, since God loved us from eternity—he chose us before the foundation of the world in love, as has been said—how has he made us pleasing to himself in time? A reply is that those whom he loves eternally in himself, he renders pleasing in time according as they exist in their own natures. The former is from eternity and is not created, the latter happens in time and is said to come into being. Hence, the Apostle says that he has graced us, that is, made us pleasing that we should be worthy of his love" (Thomas Aquinas, *Super Eph* I, lect. 2, no. 15 [= *Super Epistolam B. Pauli ad Ephesios lectura*, in *Commentary on the Letters of Saint Paul to the Galatians and Ephesians*, trans. Fabien R. Larcher and Matthew L. Lamb, eds. John Mortensen and Enrique Alarcón, vol. 39 of the Latin/English Edition of the *Works of St. Thomas Aquinas* (Lander, Wyo.: The Aquinas Institute for the Study of Sacred Doctrine, 2012); the Latin text is based on the Marietti 1953 edition, prepared by Raffaele Ci, transcribed by Roberto Busa and revised by Enrique Alarcón]).

and this same creation: "testimony of a love within the Deity that in circulating has drawn into itself that creation which was created because the Son *is*."[97] As determinative of all creation, Trinitarian love is not only at the heart of the question most central to Adrienne's theology of the body—the question of why God took on a human body—but also of her Incarnation-based perspective, which in turn is essential to her theology of the body, as we shall see in what follows.

Adrienne's Incarnational Perspective: A Corporal-Spiritual Unity

As is perhaps already apparent from our treatment of the Incarnation as a revelation of Trinitarian love, Adrienne insists that far from being "hostile" to sexuality, Christianity imbues it with a new meaning: a meaning rooted, as we shall see, in the unity between Christ and his Church, which in turn is anchored in the eternal unity of the three divine persons.[98] This Trinitarian perspective ought not to be confused, however, with some sort of spiritualization that denies or ignores the concrete, bodily dimension of Christianity. If the concrete were not essential to Christianity, if the Lord were not truly flesh but "merely the product of an idea," then Mary might have been only spiritually pregnant, Adrienne reasons; but the reality of the Incarnation requires that she "feel his weight in her body and, after his birth, in her arms."[99] Indeed, the Son wills this authentically human—that is, corporal and spiritual—bond with his mother so as to be united to her as human children are united to their parents.[100]

It is thus not surprising that Adrienne cites the Marian doctrines—the Immaculate Conception, the virginal birth, and the Assumption—as evidence that the truth cannot be measured according to its degree of spiritualization.[101] In the case of each of these dogmas, the spiritual dimension implies, builds upon, and incorporates the corporal one without in any way denying or surpassing it. Adrienne recognizes, in fact, that it is precisely by way of the corporal dimension that Mary introduces us into the mysteries of the Christian faith: by way of her corporal experience of these mysteries or of her partaking therein, beginning with the experience of her virginal pregnancy.[102]

---

97. Speyr, *The Letter to the Colossians*, 30; see also *The Letter to the Ephesians*, 29. God created the world, Adrienne teaches, so that it might participate in his divinity, so that our "being-here" might be the beginning of our "being by God" (*Korinther* I, 378).

98. *Korinther* I, 319–20; see also 315.   99. Speyr, *Mary in the Redemption*, 67.

100. Ibid., 30.

101. See Balthasar, *First Glance at Adrienne von Speyr*, 247.

102. See, for example, Speyr, *Erde und Himmel* II, no. 1671 (261) and no. 1653 (253).

This profound unity of the spiritual and corporal is also to be found in Christ's mission of preaching, instruction, and admonishment. If the corporal dimension of Christ's mission was not important, then the mission of the prophets would, Adrienne reasons, have been sufficient. As it is, however, the Incarnation is a sort of testimony to the importance of "the bodily presence of God's fullness on earth," even to the extent that Christ's flesh "contains the whole mystery" of God.[103] Adrienne recognizes, in fact, that everything that Christ did for us—"whether he was being born, in order to take upon himself the burden of our guilt, or whether he was dying on the Cross under this burden"—he did "as much with his flesh as with his spirit."[104] It belongs to his mission, for example, "to feel," or experience, each of our failures "in his body"—especially, but not exclusively, during his passion—and to surmount them with his love for the Father.[105]

Our redemption is thus not merely "the content of an article of faith or of a celestial agreement between Father and Son, but one that the Son lives through and accomplishes" precisely as man: in the flesh. Similarly, the Christian is charged with the obligation of "finding his salvation in the body of the Son himself, in his blood shed on the Cross, in his entire humanity."[106] In short, corporality cannot be short-circuited in Christianity. It is "absolutely necessary for the explaining, grasping and apprehending" of our faith and thus also of our salvation.[107]

This very firm conviction regarding the corporal dimension of faith caused Adrienne to mourn what she judged to be "an artificial disembodiment" of the Church in her time. Any such disembodiment is, in fact, she argues, opposed to the divine intention of imbuing the flesh with the Spirit's truth.[108] As a case in point, Adrienne points out the significance of Christ's nakedness on the Cross. "The loincloth was the beginning of the Church's not-wanting-to-see." We should be conscious, she continues, that it is the

---

103. Speyr, *The Letter to the Colossians*, 83. Within the context of her commentary on Colossians, Adrienne argues that if the fullness of God resides in Christ in bodily form, then Christ's body obviously has an important part to play in this fullness.

104. Speyr, *The Letter to the Ephesians*, 103.

105. See Speyr, *The Passion from Within*, 41. Herein, we might recognize some elements of Balthasar's theology of vicarious representation, including what he presents as the "mystical incurring of guilt." (See my treatment of this in chapter five of the present volume). On the other hand, in this particular passage from Adrienne, the emphasis is more upon Christ's action than upon his "passion": "In him [Christ] lies the strength to overcome their [sinner's] failure; the effort comes from his innermost center" (ibid.).

106. Speyr, *The Letter to the Colossians*, 26.

107. Speyr, *Mary in the Redemption*, 68.

108. Ibid., 70; see also *Korinther* I, 532; and *Victory of Love*, 16–17. Cf. Balthasar, *Theo-Logic* II, 156; and *Theo-Drama* II, 412.

Church—and not the Lord—who covered up his nakedness. The Church may do so with good reason, Adrienne admits, "but she has too often forgotten that the Lord's nakedness exists."[109]

Even more drastic for Adrienne are the abstractions that she witnessed in her Protestant upbringing: "Protestants miss the ultimate seriousness of the Incarnation, the becoming flesh. That is why everything often remains so theoretical, speculative."[110] In contrast, Adrienne recognizes as highly significant the corporal dimension of the Catholic faith. Having assumed flesh as an act of love for the Father, the Lord is henceforth "so committed to it, it binds him so closely to the Father that he gives this *body* to the *Church.*"[111] As the incarnate Lord is completely and simultaneously spirit and flesh, so too is his Eucharist, Adrienne teaches. Hence his command to eat his flesh is "wholly unambiguous," allowing for no misunderstanding.[112] Because, moreover, the Church who administers this very real body of the Lord becomes herself the body of the Lord, it follows that the Church "is not an idea; she is perfectly concrete."[113] This mystery of embodying Christ's spirit is also true of the Christian in the Church: each one, in virtue of his or her corporality, embodies in some sense the teaching of Christ, which might otherwise remain abstract, giving it a "fleshly-concrete" existence.[114] In this way we are invited to regard our bodies as expressing our spiritual belonging to the Lord, who was obedient in his body even unto death.[115]

The things of this world cannot, therefore, "be valued in a stepwise progression from the corporal to the spiritual; common to all of them is that they are directed to the Son and have in him their continued being."[116] The Son, in turn, is oriented, as we have seen, to the Father. Despite the great significance of corporality within the Speyrian perspective, the "higher" (more obviously spiritual) mysteries dominate—in the sense of directing—the natural (corporal) ones; whence the specifically Christian challenge to give predominance to the spirit within one's concrete human existence.

The flesh and the spirit are—Adrienne notes with respect to Romans 8:5—

---

109. Speyr, *Theologie der Geschlechter*, 11.

110. Quoted by Balthasar in *First Glance at Adrienne von Speyr*, 247. See also Speyr, *Theologie der Geschlechter*, 162, where she also mourns the spiritualizing of the Catholic Church in her day to the neglect of the bodily dimension.

111. Speyr, *The Letter to the Colossians*, 34.

112. Speyr, *John* I, 65. On the other hand, Adrienne argues that precisely these words of the institution of the Eucharist, "This is my body," are "incomprehensible, even in the literal meaning." They are words that offer "an open, endless increase. Yet not an increase that could be traced in a line; rather right away there is a gulf, a wall, a break and a constant new beginning" (Speyr, *The Passion from Within*, 28).

113. Speyr, *The Letter to the Colossians*, 34.

114. Speyr, *Korinther* I, 376–77.

115. See ibid., 185.

116. Speyr, *The Letter to the Colossians*, 33.

"two poles apart" without ever being entirely separate, "for they meet as two poles within man," who is at once flesh and spirit. This polarization accords a certain importance to human freedom, which is charged to choose between the two, such "that either the one or the other will predominate." This freedom also explains the meaning of the Son's taking on of human flesh so as to condemn sin within the flesh and to "prove the predominance of the spirit," without denying the significance of the flesh and "without revealing God only in Heaven, as Spirit."[117] More positively, Christ takes on a human body so as to give us his Spirit. Because his entire corporal life is already a spiritual act (namely that of obedience, as we have seen) and a spiritual donation (a willing gift of self by surrender) it represents "a victory of the Spirit over nature" and of "the second, redeeming Adam order the first, sinning Adam."[118] It is also a triumph of the spirit over the flesh, or more properly, of the Holy Spirit "over any spirit that is not his [Christ's] Spirit."[119] This explains the significance of Adrienne's theory—which she attributes to a private revelation by Ignatius of Loyola—that "the more real the Incarnation, the more Spirit comes into the world."[120]

From this perspective, the Speyrian presentation of the human body as an instrument of obedience—far from promoting a spirit-body dualism—actually advocates the specific unity of the human being as body and soul—precisely as ordered to the larger unity of Christ's corporal-spiritual body, the Church—by way of his or her partaking of the sacraments. This ordering of the Christian to the Church, in turn, accounts for the further ordering of the unity of the human community within the Trinitarian communion, as we shall see.[121]

Sacraments as the Archetypal Form of Human Life: The Example of Christian Marriage

Without denying that the sacraments are determined by God "*for* the corporal human being," Adrienne recognizes them as being the original, or "archetypal," form (*Urform*) of the corporal life.[122] Because they connect us to God, they also lead us to the destiny he foresaw for each one of us at the moment of our creation. This is particularly true in Christian marriage, for

---

117. Speyr, *The Victory of Love*, 24.   118. Speyr, *Korinther* I, 535.
119. Speyr, *The Victory of Love*, 25. It is in this sense that one might understand Adrienne's statement that "in Christianity, the essential thing is no longer the body but the soul. [...] The soul is everlasting; what happens to the body makes little difference." Indeed, "the life of the soul no more comes to an end than does the life of the Christian teaching" (*John* IV, 151).
120. Speyr, *Erde und Himmel* II, no. 1681 (264).   121. Cf. Balthasar, *Theo-Drama* II, 412.
122. Speyr, *Theologie der Geschlechter*, 26.

example, which Adrienne recognizes as "primarily a supernatural thing,"[123] with the corporal dimension integrated within the larger realm of the supernatural and the spiritual fruitfulness of the sacrament considered as greater than bodily fruitfulness. Hence, for example, the "yes" to the Spirit precedes the "yes" to the flesh, which is to say that the final meaning of the physical act (marital consummation) is unity of spirit. Consent in the spirit also means consent to the flesh.[124] Adrienne thus recognizes within Christian marriage "an integration of the body into [the realm of] the Spirit; for the Spirit needs the body instrumentally, without forfeiting its spirit-being [*Geistsein*]."[125]

On the other hand, "whoever has not yet spoken a definitive word of consent [either to marriage or the consecrated life] can have no Christian relation to his [or her] body."[126] Indeed, the body's true significance is only really discovered when it is given to another: to Christ and/or to one's spouse.[127] In the marital embrace, for example, Adrienne recognizes that a man "awakens" his wife's body "to love," with the result that she does not really experience any one part of herself (her womb, for example) as given to the man; rather "her whole body belongs to her whole husband."[128]

Particularly important in these examples is the fact that the body be *given*, along with the whole of the person: not only to one's spouse, but still more fundamentally to the Lord, for carrying out his intentions or for making possible one's service to him. "God needs the entire man for the entire task; the response of man's spirit to God's Spirit demands the whole of him, body and soul."[129] Adrienne even goes so far as to argue that the body is really fruitful only when it is "assumed" within one's vocational decision for marriage or consecrated virginity.[130] This, in turn, follows from the fact that "we are created for what *God* wills, not for what *I* want. [...] Somehow the bodily aspect fits in with that."[131]

---

123. Ibid., 117.

124. Ibid., 135. This will be more thoroughly developed later in this chapter with connection to Mary's consent (in body and spirit) to the Incarnation.

125. Speyr, *Theologie der Geschlechter*, 102.   126. Ibid., 163.

127. To be sure, although the body cannot exist "without communion," this need not imply sexual communion. For the virginal, the experience of bodily communion is primarily that between child and mother. See Speyr, *Theologie der Geschlechter*, 165.

128. Ibid., 163. Similar is Pope John Paul II's commentary on *Ephesians* 5:21–33, wherein he argues that Christ, precisely as bridegroom, "is the one who loves," whereas the Church, his bride, is loved: "it is she who receives love, in order to love in return" (*Mulieris Dignitatem*, no. 29).

129. Speyr, *Light and Images*, 47.

130. Hence, as we saw in chapter three, Adrienne holds that from a Christian perspective there can be "no such thing as a 'third state'" between marriage and consecrated virginity.

131. Speyr, *Geheimnis der Jugend*, volume 7 of *Die Nachlasswerke*, ed. Hans Urs von Balthasar, published privately (Privatdruck) (Einsiedeln: Johannes Verlag, 1966), 241; cited in Balthasar, *Our Task*, 30.

The Christian wife, for example, knows that her husband is not the final goal (*letzter Zeilpunkt*) of her surrender, for in giving herself to him—precisely by way of their shared sacrament of marriage, as shall be more thoroughly developed in chapter six—she is still more profoundly surrendered to Christ.[132] Similarly, in Paul's exhortation to husbands to love their wives "as their bodies" (Eph 5:28), Adrienne perceives the specific challenge of drawing them (their wives) into their own "intimate love of the service of God."[133] It is unsurprising, therefore, that Adrienne should recognize the fecundity of the sexual act as realized "more in obedience than in the child."[134] The child born of a sacramental marriage, meanwhile, is also "born and begotten of the spirit," Adrienne teaches. "The spirit of marriage becomes flesh [with the birth of the child], which in turn becomes spirit,"[135] through the child's baptism and the other sacraments which follow therefrom. More profoundly still, Adrienne reasons that when a marriage is sacramentally determined, the sexual relations of the couple are "connected to the sacramental life between Christ and the Church" (cf. Eph 5:21–33). This in turn means not only that the latter relation becomes the archetype of the first (cf. Eph 5:32), but also that the one fecundity (that of the spouses) is assumed into the other (that of Christ and the Church): an insight also to be found in the corpus of Aquinas.[136] Adrienne thus recognizes the sacraments as "the rule and measure of the sexes" or (more generally) of "the entire corporal life of Christians."[137]

To summarize this incarnational perspective: the whole of the bodily person is viewed from the vantage point of Christ, whose flesh is the means by which he simultaneously communicates his Spirit and incorporates us into his human existence. The Christian's relationship to his or her body thus takes its lead from Christ's relationship to his body and that of Mary to hers: "What the Lord knew in the eternal divine decree of the Incarnation, what Mary learned through her motherhood, he [the Christian] has to learn through Christian stewardship of the body, perhaps best of all by practicing bodily penance: that the body, whatever use it is put to, will always have to be an instrument of the Christian's mission."[138] Far from "a de-incarnation, a flight into spirit," this sacramental approach is thus "a higher form of incarnation."[139]

---

132. Speyr, *Theologie der Geschlechter*, 17.
133. Speyr, *The Letter to the Ephesians*, 235.
134. Speyr, *Theologie der Geschlechter*, 24.
135. Speyr, *John* I, 119.
136. Cf. Thomas Aquinas, *SCG* IV, c. 78, 4.
137. Speyr, *Theologie der Geschlechter*, 26. Cf. Balthasar, *A Theology of History*, 96.
138. Speyr, *The Letter to the Ephesians*, 37; see also *Korinther* I, 185.
139. Balthasar and Scola, *Test Everything*, 81. Cf. Speyr, *Erde und Himmel* II, 264–65.

The Eucharist of the Father and the Son: Our Inclusion in Trinitarian Love

This properly sacramental vision of the body, so typical of Adrienne's perspective, is particularly evident in her very rich theology of the Eucharist as founded and likewise implied by the Incarnation, which in turn is continued by the Eucharist.[140] Adrienne presents Christ—already in his Incarnation—as a substantial Eucharist, the source of our Eucharistic Communion in him. He is the sacrament in person, from whom originate the sacraments of the Church and the sacrament which *is* the Church.[141] The "locus" or "embodiment of the sacraments," he is—in virtue of the Incarnation—"the predetermined connecting link between heaven and earth" with the result that all of his actions contain "the sign of his connecting being; [...] He connects, because he is himself connection": the perfect union not only of heaven and earth, but more profoundly of God and man and thus also of nature and grace. "He is connection so as to mediate; he possesses so as to give."[142]

Adrienne thus observes a development within the Gospels from the presentation of Christ as having all life in himself to that of believers having all life through him by way, most especially, of the sacraments. As such, he is also the source of the sacraments proper: "He binds us through every sacramental reception."[143] This means—to repeat what was mentioned in our cursory exposition of Balthasar's treatment of the body-spirit tension—that the mystical doctrine of redemption wherein Christ is portrayed as the salvific reality in person is understood as ordered to the salvific unity between Christ and the Church. Hence, for example, the substantial grace of the hypostatic union—the union of the two natures in Christ—is likewise viewed by St. Thomas as "capital" grace: that grace which belongs to Christ as head of the Church and thus the source or well-spring of all grace given to humankind.[144]

---

140. The Incarnation is "a foreshadowing of the Eucharist" (Speyr, *The Letter to the Colossians*, 33). See also Speyr, *John* IV, 339.

141. See Speyr, *The Letter to the Colossians*, 83; and *The Letter to the Ephesians*, 165–66. Cf. Balthasar, *The Office of Peter*, 133; and Second Vatican Council, *Lumen Gentium* I, 1 (*DZ* 4101). Adrienne recognizes the Church and the sacraments as "contained in the Word from the beginning" (Speyr, *John* I, 21); see also *Gebetserfahrung*, 13.

142. Speyr, *Markus*, 447. Hence, Christ's divine-human unity is portrayed by Adrienne as "the prototype for the unity of the Church," who is also divine and human, and also for the unity "of man and [ecclesial] office" (*Mary in the Redemption*, 34). In a similar manner, St. Thomas points to the profound unity between the ontology of Christ (cf. *ST* III, qq. 2–26) and his saving actions (III, qq. 27–59). See also the treatment by Emmanuel Perrier of this unity in both parts of his "L'enjeu christologique de la satisfaction."

143. Speyr, *Markus*, 447; see also *The Letter to the Colossians*, 83.

144. Cf. Thomas Aquinas, *ST* III, q. 2, aa. 10–12; q. 6, a. 6; and q. 7, a. 13.

From this perspective—that of Adrienne in union with the theological tradition of St. Thomas—the whole Gospel might be understood as situated between two movements of divine surrender: "In the Incarnation lies the promise of the Eucharist, and the Eucharist is a confirmation (or verification) of the Incarnation."[145] "The Son does not merely perform the work of redemption," Adrienne teaches. "He is as the beloved of the Father, the redemption in person; he contains it as he contains his blood, in order to communicate it to the world by shedding it and, by this shedding of himself, to give the world the holiness that is the holiness of God himself."[146]

As if to comment upon this image, Adrienne makes use elsewhere of still another: the distinction between Christ's body and blood in the Eucharist:

> When he speaks of the body, attention is focused chiefly on the personality of the incarnate Lord; when he appears in the blood, he does so in service of the Covenant that he brings. The body is, as it were, personal, whereas the blood is the depersonalized dimension of his mission. [...] The body is the Incarnation, whereas the blood is the reality of the Incarnation being poured out. The body is the one sent, whereas the blood is the sending that flows from the substance of the one sent into the Church he founded.[147]

This distinction in turn points to the paternal and filial qualities of the Eucharist. The Incarnation is, Adrienne teaches, "the Father's Eucharist," with the result that the Son's Eucharist is a sort of earthly reflection of the same: "In giving his body eucharistically, he does on earth the same as the Father in heaven when he gave his Word as seed to the Mother."[148] As the Father eternally begets the Son, the Son eternally begets the Church through his Eucharist.

To be sure, the Father also begets the Church, Adrienne teaches, but this he does through the Son. It is his will—as an expression of his love for the Son—"that the Church bear the Son's character [...] so [that] he will beget the Church in no other way except through the Son."[149] Adrienne similarly describes the Lord as the origin of the Church in two complementary ways: as the one who begets, that is, "as the original truth of Christian doctrine" and "as the one eucharistically distributed." These two forms—"the spirit-form as Word" and "the body-form as Eucharist"—are, however, "the double expression of one reality: that he is the incarnate Word of the Father."[150]

---

145. Speyr, *Das Wort und die Mystik* II, 529.
146. Speyr, *The Letter to the Ephesians*, 35. Holiness, she adds (29), is participation in God's life. Similarly: "*Holy* means: living his life" (28).
147. Speyr, *The Holy Mass,* 66.   148. Speyr, *Das Wort und die Mystik* II, 529.
149. Speyr, *The Passion from Within*, 43; see also *The Letter to the Ephesians*, 240; *John* IV, 339; *John* I, 91; and chapter six of the present volume for a more thorough treatment of this theme.
150. Speyr, *The Passion from Within*, 45.

In the theology of Adrienne—strongly influenced by St. John the Evangelist, as is herein evident—Christ is the Father's gift of eternal life to the world, precisely in virtue of his own self-gift to the Father for the accomplishment of his (the Father's) will. In virtue of the same—that is, in obedience to the Father's will—he is given without limit, as we shall see more thoroughly in chapter five of this volume, to the Church and the world alike. In the Lord's bodily surrender of himself to the Father for the world and to the world for the Father, Adrienne discerns both the receptive and generous aspects of his absolutely vulnerable—that is to say, unreserved and unlimited—self-gift.

With regard to the receptive aspect of his surrender, he gives himself as a sort of receptacle for sin, whereby he not only "feel[s] our failures in his flesh,"[151] but also "gathers up all sin and makes it visible in the absolute injury to the body."[152] With regard to the generous aspect of his surrender, he gives himself so as to live (sacramentally, that is, by the Eucharist) in other bodies, namely, the bodies of sinners, whereby he is willingly subject to us and eventually delivered to death.

This entire degradation of the Lord is, however, oriented to our enrichment. Redemption is not conceived by Adrienne as a sort of destruction of human nature with the goal of creating "a second natural life." It is, rather, the renewal of human nature:

> The Father made creatures come forth from nothing; the Son does not have to annihilate them in himself in order to recreate them in himself out of nothing. He destroys in himself the old Adam, the wall of separation and sin, yet he destroys only after having taken up into himself the thing to be destroyed. He destroys it by dying himself and by letting what he has assumed die together with him. He includes the act of destruction to enable resurrection with him out of the nothing of death. [...] The Son has recreated the world, in himself, in his love made flesh, which he offers in order to give to the destruction of sin and division the meaning of love.[153]

The Lord has, in other words, actually taken up our bodies with his to be "co-crucified" (cf. Gal 2:20) with the result that they have henceforth the quality of "being for him, living for him and dying for him."[154] For this reason the Christian is challenged to understand all of his or her suffering as "a burden

---

151. Ibid., 41.

152. Ibid., 45; see also *Confession*, 79. Such is similar to the exposition of Pope John Paul II of the salvific convincing of sin—"*mysterium iniquitatis*"—by the Holy Spirit in relation to the Cross of Christ. See his encyclical *Dominium et Vivificatem* (May 18, 1986) (Boston: Pauline Books and Media, 1986), no. 32.

153. Speyr, *The Letter to the Ephesians*, 104.

154. Speyr, *Korinther* I, 179. In this way, "the *communio eucharistica* becomes—'analytically,' as it were—the *communio sanctorum*," Balthasar explains (*Theo-Drama* II, 410).

that originally lay upon the Cross,"[155] such that he or she never suffers alone. This also means, to summarize, that redemption from a Speyrian perspective is nothing less than our inclusion—body and soul—in the Lord's own "accomplished corporality"[156] by means of his Resurrection, Church, and Eucharist. By this notion of accomplished corporality, Adrienne means more specifically that Christ is "whole" when his members are fully incorporated into his mystical body.[157]

"He, the Incarnate One, is the Bridegroom who does not leave his Bride [the Church, and thus also her members] when he returns to heaven."[158] Indeed, the entire earthly mission of Christ is viewed as a continuous Incarnation: a sort of assuming of all of humanity throughout the long history of the Church (even in its pre-figuration in the ecclesia of the Hebrew Bible) so as to present us to the Father in himself.[159] In precisely this way is realized his mission of recapitulating all of creation, and thus all of humanity, in himself.[160] There nonetheless remains our real participation, which is to say that the "corporeality of the Cross" and "the whole loving life of the Son of Man require a corporeal sharing of believers therein."[161] Or to put it otherwise, by giving us—his "members"—the possibility of becoming one body with him, the Lord also gives us the possibility of "fulfilling his humanity" with him: of realizing the fullness of his mystical body.[162]

The Eucharist of Believers: A Corporal-Spiritual Participation in Christ's Mission

This corporal sharing of Christ's members in his mystical body requires that we perceive our bodies as assuming a place "within the Lord's love for

---

155. Speyr, *Light and Images*, 46.
156. Speyr, *Korinther* I, 185.
157. See Speyr, *The Letter to the Colossians*, 33.
158. Speyr, *The Mystery of Death*, 73.
159. See, for example, Speyr, *John* IV, 339. Cf. Second Vatican Council, *Gaudium et Spes*, no. 22 (*DZ* 4322).
160. See Speyr, *The Letter to the Ephesians*, 48. Cf. Thomas Aquinas, *Comp* I, 201. St. Thomas thus observes a sort of reversal of the manner whereby original sin passed from the person of Adam to all human nature. "Christ in reverse order at first repairs what regards the person, and afterwards will simultaneously repair what pertains to the nature in all men" (*ST* III, q. 69, a. 3). This theme of recapitulating all things in Christ (cf. Eph 1:10) is of course a popular theme in the work of St. Irenaeus of Lyons. See the various selections from his *Adversus Haereses* in Saward (trans.), *The Scandal of the Incarnation*, 53–93. For the critical edition, see *Contre les hérésies: édition critique d'après les versions arménienne et latine*, trans. and eds. Adelin Roussea, Louis Doutreleau et al., volumes 1/1–5/2 (Sources chrétiennes 100, 152, 153, 210, 211, 263, 264, 293, and 294) (Paris: Cerf, 1952–74).
161. Speyr, *The Letter to the Colossians*, 26. Although Christ has already redeemed the world, the process of redemption still has need of us, Adrienne explains, that is to say, of the suffering and pain which bind us to the Lord's Cross. See Speyr, *The Victory of Love*, 70.
162. See Speyr, *Korinther* I, 390. Cf. Thomas Aquinas, *ST* III, q. 20, a. 2, ad. 3; Pope Pius XII, *Mystici corporis* (*DZ* 3809); and Second Vatican Council, *Lumen Gentium*, no. 7 (*DZ* 4116).

the Church."[163] To be sure, the Christian's body serves the reception of holy Communion so that this sacrament might work in his or her soul. Hence, the more "available" one is for this reception, the "more intimately and completely the Eucharistic Lord can work within him [or her]."[164] Although the Incarnation was achieved without the participation of our free wills—a fact which ought not to obscure the vital role of Mary's faith (and thus of her free will) on our behalf,[165] as we shall see later in this chapter—the incarnate Son of God offers to each believer the real possibility of becoming, precisely as his willing member (as, that is to say, a member of his body-bride, the Church), one body and one spirit with him (1 Cor 6:17).[166]

The body of Christ has, in fact, been given so radically to each of us that it has become our body, with the result that we become his. "Being flesh and spirit simultaneously, he reaches our spirit through our bodies and spiritually soaks our bodies through and through, so that what is spirit in us and what is *his* spirit in us may return to the Father."[167] Hence, the final consequence of the Incarnation—as expressed in his cry of fulfillment, "It is consummated"—is this: that the Son might have a center of action within us.[168] Henceforth, the Christian is called to live from this "center": one which has become so occupied by the Word of God that it can no longer be possessed by him- or herself.[169] Or, to put it otherwise, the Christian does not live in him- or herself "but in his [God's] word."[170]

From this perspective, redemption means being in Christ, and for Adrienne "this *in him* is as essential, as personal and as corporeal as one can possibly understand it to be."[171] At stake is, more specifically, our participation in Christ's humanity, precisely—it bears repeating—as members of his body.[172] Having created the Church without members, as it were, he grants us the possibility of being incorporated into his body (as members), and through us, he continues to exercise new functions in the Church and in her service.[173] Indeed, the function assumed by the fleshly body of Christ—namely, "to embody his spirit for us, to render it present, to make us aware of it, to

---

163. Speyr, *The Letter to the Ephesians*, 236.   164. Speyr, *Theologie der Geschlechter*, 113.
165. See, for example, Speyr, *Mary in the Redemption*, 56–57.
166. See Speyr, *Korinther* I, 390.
167. Speyr, *John* I, 117; emphasis added. See also Speyr, *The Letter to the Ephesians*, 102 and 105; and *Das Hohelied*, 50.
168. Speyr, *The Victory of Love*, 24.
169. See Speyr, *Theologie der Geschlechter*, 89. See my more thorough treatment of this theme in chapter three.
170. Speyr, *John* I, 36.   171. Speyr, *The Letter to the Colossians*, 26.
172. See Speyr, *Victory of Love*, 70.   173. See Speyr, *The Letter to the Ephesians*, 237.

communicate it"—is continued by his Church after him. She "shows us and presents the Lord to us," especially in the Eucharist.[174]

This incorporation of the Christian into Christ's body—not unlike the service that follows therefrom—is realized through the sacraments, especially the Eucharist which, far more than realizing the continuation of the Lord's terrestrial body, actually effects the inclusion of our bodies into his.[175] In transforming himself into a new state, the Lord seeks ultimately to transform us, drawing us, as it were, into himself. "At first he transforms as if from the inside out, by letting himself become Eucharistic, by shifting his center into the host. But because he can do that, he can also do the opposite: transform from the outside in, drawing things into his center."[176] By his passion and death, he not only made "room for us in himself," he has also made "himself to be this room."[177] He incorporates us, in other words, into himself precisely by giving himself to be incorporated into us; whence the Pauline formulas of mutual immanence, as we saw in chapter three.[178] "For it is not only he who communicates his Body and his Blood to us, who lives now in us, but we live in him."[179] Receiving him is, in this sense, "identical with being received by him."[180] Or, to repeat what we pointed to in chapter three, the Lord's being, received by us in the Eucharist, effects our "becoming," with the result that the unity of our lives and of our very persons ought no longer to be in ourselves but in him.[181]

Adrienne thus maintains—in a manner altogether compatible with the Christian tradition—that God did not create us once and for all, but that He continuously generates us anew by nourishing us with the Eucharist.[182] Such, more specifically, is the manner in which the Son draws us into his own eternal birth from the Father, or that whereby the Father "begets his Son 'into our hearts.'"[183] Indeed, the Lord is at the origin of the Church "as the one

---

174. Ibid., 73.

175. See Speyr, *The Letter to the Colossians*, 33.

176. Speyr, *The Letter to the Ephesians*, 48. Cf. Emery, "The Ecclesial Fruit of the Eucharist in St. Thomas Aquinas," 159.

177. Speyr, *The Letter to the Colossians*, 37.

178. On the one hand, Christ is "in me" or "in us" (Gal 2:19, 4:9; Rom 8:9–11; and 2 Cor 4:16, 13:2–5). On the other hand, we are, live, or are found "in Christ" (Rom 8:1; Gal 3:2b; Phil 3:9; etc.). Balthasar (*Theo-Drama* III, 247) identifies the first set of formulas as the effect of the second; see also *The Glory of the Lord* VII, 407–11; *Theo-Drama* V, 520 and 528; and *Does Jesus Know Us?*, 53.

179. Speyr, *John* II, 70.

180. Speyr, *The Letter to the Colossians*, 71.

181. See ibid., 72; *John* II, 66; *The Letter to the Ephesians*, 30 and 48; and *Das Wort und die Mystik* II, 106.

182. See Speyr, *The Letter to the Ephesians*, 104–5; and *John* IV, 339. With regard to the tradition, see the final encyclical of Pope John Paul II, *Ecclesia de Eucharistia*, in which this rich tradition is magnificently exposited.

183. Balthasar, *Unless You Become Like this Child*, 40.

eucharistically distributed,"[184] whereby it is possible to speak of a "one flesh" union (cf. Eph 5:29–32; Gen 2:24; Mk 10:8) of Christ and the Church, and thus also of Christ and the Christian. This fundamental and pivotal insight of Christianity, which Adrienne refers to—as we saw at the beginning of this chapter—as its "greatest mystery"[185] and which we will examine more closely in the chapters which follow, is also the meaning that she attributes to the Lord's entire terrestrial mission, including his whole passion and Ascension to the Father. Even as a child he was realizing this mystery, Adrienne reasons, because his entire terrestrial existence is lived as an exchange between himself and those to whom he is sent. It is thus impossible that he might exist without the Church, which comes forth from him. It is already present, Adrienne notes, in the form of the holy family.[186] Similarly, she explains that the real humanity of Christ is particularly evident in that he does not construct the Church alone but in association with Mary and the other saints.[187]

Christ's mission is thus achieved when his Incarnation (cf. Jn 1:14) is achieved, or effected in us (cf. Jn 1:12) by way, most especially, of the Eucharist. Indeed, the "infinite dissemination"[188] of the Lord in an unimaginable number of consecrated hosts serves our unity in him, Adrienne explains, and the dissemination is complete when all of his members have effectively received him. At that point his unity—that of his Church united to him as head—is again realized. While this image might spur objection as potentially leading to a misinterpretation of Catholic doctrine—notably a dividing of Christ into several (even innumerable) bodies[189]—Adrienne rightfully insists upon the central role of the Eucharist in mediating between the fleshly body of Christ, which he assumed at his Incarnation, and his mystical body, the Church, which is both formed from and nourished by the Eucharist.[190]

From this perspective, "the fullness of Christ" referred to by Paul (cf. Eph 1:23) is the Church present in each of her members who are personally

---

184. Speyr, *The Passion from Within*, 45.   185. Speyr, *The Letter to the Ephesians*, 240.
186. See Speyr, *Theologie der Geschlechter*, 99.
187. See Speyr, *The Countenance of the Father*, 99. This insight is similar to what Balthasar presents as Christ's existence within the context of "a human constellation." See, for example, *The Office of Peter*, 136–45.
188. Speyr, *John I*, 123.
189. Such, for example, is Anne Barbeau Gardiner's objection to what she (erroneously, I believe) perceives in another of Adrienne's works—*The Passion from Within*—as Christ "dividing himself up in two parts to elude death: The main part (all His power) is hidden in the Eucharist and in His followers who receive it, while the lesser part (His impotent flesh) goes to suffer and die" (Gardiner, "Correcting the Deposit of the Faith").
190. Adrienne thus solidly joins the biblical and patristic insight concerning the triple mode of the body of Christ, exposited above: his body born of the Virgin, his Eucharistic body, and his mystical body.

united to Christ. Similar to the idea, exposited above, of Christ becoming "complete" by means of our incorporation into his body, is thus Adrienne's portrayal of the reciprocal relation of fullness and fulfillment between Christ and the Church.[191] Of course, it is the Lord who has the priority in this relationship: he is the first to fill up, Adrienne insists. Indeed, he fills up *everything*, not least of all the Church, who is thus rightfully considered to be his fullness, as St. Thomas also teaches.[192] As such, he has need of her, namely to reveal his fullness and to transmit it.

It is thus also possible to say that Christ is filled up by the Church while simultaneously admitting that he is "fullness in person: God and man, and both in a perfect, immutable manner."[193] Adrienne observes that there exists "a reciprocal relationship of fullness and fulfillment between the Lord and the Church." To emphasize either partner in this relationship to the neglect of the other would, she reasons, be to obtain "a completely empty concept of fullness."[194] In a manner altogether compatible with the reasoning of St. Thomas, who argues that "it belongs to the essence of the highest good to communicate itself in the highest manner to the creature,"[195] Adrienne argues: any fullness "that could not deploy itself, could not pour itself out, could not fulfill itself, would not be a real fullness at all."[196]

As is typical of Adrienne's thought, she again points to the Father-Son relation as the archetype: "Even the fullness of the Father, in order to be itself, needs the Son to contain it, and for its part the fullness of the Son flows back to the Father." Similarly the Christ-Church relationship is one of reciprocal filling up, "even though the Lord, insofar as he is the all-transcending head, is the one who gives infinitely and the Church the one who receives infinitely." The divine bridegroom of the Church "is over the bride but draws her to himself, in order thereby to *fill her up in himself.*"[197] She is his body and bride; he, her bridegroom, who brings her with him to the Father when he ascends into heaven.[198] "The Son, who founded the Church, has this Church as his body and thus takes her fullness into himself, in order to let her be filled up in him. Thus, in the likeness of the body, the other likeness, that

---

191. Cf. Second Vatican Council, *Lumen Gentium*, no. 7 (*DZ* 4117); and Pope Pius XII, *Mystici Corporis* (*DZ* 3809).
192. See Thomas Aquinas, *Super Eph* I, lect. 8, no. 71.
193. Speyr, *The Letter to the Ephesians*, 165–66.
194. Ibid., 74. Cf. Pope Pius XII, *Mystici Corporis* (*DZ* 3805).
195. Thomas Aquinas, *ST* III, q. 1, a. 1; cf. I, q. 5, a. 4. Similarly, "the communication of being and goodness arises from goodness" (*SCG*, c. 37, 5).
196. Speyr, *The Letter to the Ephesians*, 74.
197. Ibid., 73–75. Cf. Balthasar, *Does Jesus Know Us?*, 98.
198. Speyr, *The Mystery of Death*, 73. Cf. Thomas Aquinas, *ST* III, q. 20, a. 2, ad. 3.

of bride and bridegroom, makes its appearance: the bridegroom is over the bride but draws her to himself [...] that he might fill himself up in her by pouring out his entire energy into her."[199]

The same theme of filling or completing is thus developed by Adrienne with regard to Christ and the Church, who "embodies" Christ's power as it is "efficacious and operative in us."[200] Such, more specifically, is the meaning of the Eucharist, whereby the Christian is equipped, as it were, to become "bread for the world," in imitation of the mysteries that he or she celebrates. Indeed, the Eucharist is illustrative of the mysterious "expansion" of human nature, as it was portrayed in chapter three, within the infinite dimension of divine life. The Christian who has eaten of the flesh of the Lord is impelled by a single and insatiable desire: "the striving, in intensifying yearning, to assimilate himself totally to the life of the Lord."[201]

The Eucharistic communion of believers is, therefore, "not only a communion with the Body of Christ, but also with his whole life."[202] We are all really "co-beings" with the Eucharistic Lord, Adrienne explains, "in whom God so allows his Trinitarian being to occur in the world that he squanders himself on [us] all."[203] Because, in fact, the Eucharist is "infinite distribution and communication," the consecrated host does not remain within the confines of the communicant. Bearing "visibly on his person that distinguishing something which the soldiers saw on the body of Christ," the communicant is earmarked for the apostolate: he or she is charged with the task of communicating the love that he or she has thus received.[204] Because, in other words, the communicant has been united with the Lord in one body, God's will should be realized *in the communicant's body*.[205]

To be sure, Adrienne acknowledges from her own objective experience as a physician and her subjective experience of bodily suffering, including her mystical share in the stigmata of Christ, that the human body is naturally opposed to sacrifice: it is, as it were, "installed in its function and does not want

---

199. Speyr, *The Letter to the Ephesians*, 74–75; cf. Eph 1:23 and Second Vatican Council, *Lumen Gentium* (*DZ* 4117). See also Balthasar, *Explorations in Theology* II, 143–91; and *A Theological Anthropology*, 310–14.

200. Speyr, *The Letter to the Ephesians*, 150. As such, she is a Church "who suits him" (cf. Eph 5:27): one whose suitability does not imply that every humiliation assumed by the Lord, in and through his Incarnation, need likewise be realized in her. We must, after all, allow for the distinction between God and his creature, Adrienne reasons. See Speyr, *Das Wort und die Mystik* I, 20. A similar claim is made by Balthasar in his article, "Kenosis of the Church?" in *Explorations in Theology* I, 125–38, esp. 133.

201. Speyr, *John* II, 67. 202. Ibid., 35.

203. Speyr, *Das Wort und die Mystik* II, 101.

204. Speyr, *John* IV, 140. On the Eucharist's power to surpass the confines of the individual to "be all to all," see Speyr, *Das Wort und die Mystik* II, 500; and *The Passion from Within*, 46.

205. See Speyr, *Korinther* I, 389.

to be disturbed."[206] She nonetheless recognizes in the demanding, burdensome, and painful nature of our corporality a preparation, ironically enough, for our supernatural end. The often very painful experiences of meeting up against the limit of our own corporality train us, more specifically, to be "God-seekers": to seek to surpass the constraints of this world and to enter the infinity of eternal life.[207] It does not belong to the body, therefore, to determine the boundaries of its own instrumental utility. Precisely because it is an instrument of the Christian's obedience, the body of the believer, like that of Christ, should be so radically enlisted in God's service that he (God) alone might determine how it is to be used.[208]

This is how Adrienne understands the vow of virginity: the placing of oneself entirely at God's disposal.[209] Similarly, the body of every 'accomplished' Christian must be characterized, she maintains, as governed by Christ's own Spirit.[210] To the extent that this is the case, the Christian's body is holy.[211] When, on the other hand, we disobey and misuse our bodies, it is not only our own bodies that are dishonored, but also that of the Lord.[212]

This example of bringing dishonor to Christ's body only really makes sense when the whole Christian—body and soul—is understood as a member of the one body of Christ, the Church. In other words, when he or she is surrendered (that is, willingly given) to Christ in a manner likened to—but also receptive of—Christ's sacrificial surrender to the Church and to each individual member of the Church; when, that is to say, the Christian is authentically united to Christ so as to form one body, one Spirit (cf. 1 Cor 6:17) with him. Hence, as we have seen in chapter three, the Eucharist is fittingly presented by Adrienne—in reference to and by way of commentary on the rich sexual im-

---

206. Speyr, *Theologie der Geschlechter*, 183.

207. See Speyr, *Korinther* I, 178; and *Victory of Love*, 70.

208. See Speyr, *Theologie der Geschlechter*, 183; and *The Letter to the Ephesians*, 236.

209. See Speyr, *Das Wort und die Mystik* I, 20. It is perhaps in this sense that we might best appreciate what Balthasar documents as the extraordinary phenomenon—unprecedented in the history of the Church, as he notes—of Adrienne's so-called restored virginity. In virtue of this—very frightening, as Balthasar notes—experience, she was to understand herself as "a toy ball in God's hand" and to learn that God can "wipe clean everything corporal just as the soul can be restored to its first purity by baptism" (Speyr, *Erde und Himmel* II, no. 1644 [243–46]). See also ibid., nos. 1644–45 [244–46]; and Balthasar, *Our Task*, 31.

210. See Speyr, *Korinther* I, 186. Hence Adrienne's reasoning that one must "know the world of grace (openness to God, to faith) so as to be able to properly correspond with his body" (*Theologie der Geschlechter*, 117).

211. "The holiness of every human body is measured by whether it is assigned a space within the Lord's mission of love, even if it is a mission of suffering, sickness, and death" (Speyr, *The Letter to the Ephesians*, 36).

212. "We, along with our body-members, *are* his body and therefore we truly dishonor his body when we misuse ours" (Speyr, *Korinther* I, 185).

agery in *The Song of Songs*—as the fruitful encounter of the Lord's sacrificial surrender of himself to the Church and of the Church's own reception of this sacrifice within herself by means of her own surrender to him. As a woman is surrendered to her husband in the marital act, "so also the Church through the Lord's Eucharist," Adrienne explains.[213]

The same analogy of a woman being awakened to love by a man—or, in this case, of a virgin "becoming a woman" through the sexual embrace of a loving man—is used by Adrienne to describe the mutuality of love between Christ and the Christian in virtue of which the Christian becomes the body of Christ and simultaneously contributes to his terrestrial mission. Such, we will see, is realized in a particularly striking manner in the relationship between Christ and his mother-body, Mary.

Mary-Church, the Body of Christ

The foregoing exposition of the Eucharistic communion between Christ and the Christian in one body is clarified for Adrienne in the lives of the saints. These, she explains, are those who realize—personally and collectively—the Church's act of surrender to the Lord, whereby she—due to *his* own prior surrender *to her*—is one body with him. "Each is a part [of the Church] and each is the whole."[214] As such, these matured Christians are "the practical exposition of the Eucharist," the proof that the Lord "takes us with into his love,"[215] by taking us into his body. Having been nourished by this heavenly bread, they are "in body and in soul bread for the fellowman."[216] Like the bread and wine offered at the altar of sacrifice, which initially are "nothing more than *good things*," Christians are transformed into Christ's body by his action and their 'contribution' of faith.[217]

This mystery of the Church and her saints, whereby "the whole [is] in each" and "each [is] in the whole," is concretized in the person of Mary: virgin-mother and bride of Christ, in whose "train" all the saints find their place beside Christ.[218] "Mary is in the name of all women the Mother of God, and the Church is in the name of all human persons the bride of Christ,

---

213. Speyr, *Das Hohelied*, 44; see also *Theologie der Geschlechter*, 135. Cf. Balthasar, *You Crown the Year with Your Goodness*, 133.
214. Speyr, *Das Wort und die Mystik* I, 266. Cf. Balthasar, *Theo-Drama* II, 416.
215. Speyr, *Die katholischen Briefe* II, 180.
216. Speyr, *Das Wort und die Mystik* II, 500; see also *John* IV, 121.
217. See Speyr, *The Holy Mass*, 84.
218. See Balthasar, *First Glance at Adrienne von Speyr*, 72; cf. *Threefold Garland*, 21 and 129; and (with Scola), *Test Everything*, 82–83.

whom she has become through Mary."[219] Every form of Christian fecundity—whether spiritual or physical, virginal or spousal—is recognized by Adrienne as "patterned on Mary."[220] Because she offered herself so completely to the Lord in body and in soul, she did not have to choose between marriage and consecrated life, Adrienne argues.[221] Her self-gift "goes beyond the measure of human surrender"[222] to include the Son's self-surrender to the Father, with the result that her vocation is that of virgin-mother *and* bride.[223] This means not only that Mary is simultaneously the mother of Christ and the spouse of Joseph, but also—and herein lies something of the genius of Adrienne—that she, the Mother of Christ, becomes his companion-bride.

As if to defend Adrienne's insights by embedding them within the tradition, Balthasar notes in the works of Ambrosius, Autpertus, and Paschasius Radbertus the linking of Mary's maternity with respect to the mystical body of Christ with her role as the bride of Christ. He also notes a tendency since the twelfth century of identifying the beloved woman of the Song of Songs and the woman of the Apocalypse with Mary. Without denying the "exaggeration" of those who would regard her as Christ's lover, whose beauty "entices" God to become man, Balthasar points to the legitimacy of "summing up" the Church's attributes in Mary. She is thus rightfully regarded, he argues, as "the kernel of the Church, in whom alone the whole idea of the Church is realized." Hence also the legitimacy of her title of Christ's "Helpmate" and that of the "New Eve."[224]

While this mystery of Mary's bridal maternity will be examined more thoroughly in chapter six, for the moment we might note that Adrienne recognizes in Mary's unbounded fiat at the Annunciation a sort of bridal gift of self, whereby she receives the Lord in a manner likened unto the reception of Eucharistic Communion.[225] Even the most basic Christian attribute of being a member of Christ's body is, Adrienne explains, a participation in the Marian quality of being the "body of Christ," a quality which is given to her in

---

219. Speyr, *Apokalypse*, 387; see also *The Letter to the Ephesians*, 225. Cf. Pope John Paul II, *Mulieris Dignitatem*, no. 27.

220. Speyr, *Handmaid of the Lord*, 170.   221. See Speyr, *Mary in the Redemption*, 15.

222. Speyr, *Handmaid of the Lord*, 162.

223. Both the religious and the married states were, Adrienne teaches, lived by and founded by Mary together with the Lord (*Handmaid of the Lord*, 123).

224. Balthasar, *Theo-Drama* III, 308–10. He therefore faults the mariology of the Second Vatican Council for its failure to more thoroughly emphasize Mary's role as Christ's "associate" (317); see also 323, where he links her twofold mission as mother and companion-bride with the Immaculate Conception. Cf. St. Irenaeus, *Adversus Haereses* III, 22, 4, in Saward (trans.), *The Scandal of the Incarnation*, 60–61.

225. Cf. Pope John Paul II, *Ecclesia de Eucharistia*, no. 55.

virtue of her divine maternity: through the "encounter, physical contact" and "fusion" of Christ's corporality with hers, not excepting her consent.[226]

Hence, for example, the beginning of the Mass "is a kind of embodied expectation and pregnancy of the Church, in union with the Mother." At the offertory, the Christian is invited by Adrienne to offer his "whole soul" as Mary offered hers, and the consecration "corresponds to the actual descent of the Son into the Mother's womb." When the Lord offers himself in the Eucharist, his surrender thus contains hers, "and it is she who teaches the Church to surrender herself according to the Lord's example." She therefore accompanies the Christian in his reception of the Eucharist, making up for his or her deficiencies, as it were, so that he or she might worthily receive the Lord within Mary's own spotless fiat.[227]

This Marian mission, as we observed it in chapter three, of nourishing and sustaining the assent of self-surrender in other Christians in view of their becoming members of his body is a consequence of Mary's spiritual maternity, which in turn is the fruit of her surrender not only at Calvary (cf. Jn 19:26–27) but also at the Annunciation. Through her faith, her body is willing, and indeed, this is the meaning that Adrienne accords to Mary's virginity: a "letting happen, even into her innermost flesh."[228] "Her whole essence—body, soul and spirit—is a single consent."[229] As if echoing Augustine of Hippo, who presents Mary as receiving Christ in her heart by faith before she received him in her womb, Adrienne presents Mary as receiving the Lord corporally precisely because she receives him spiritually.[230] Her fiat is the "first new corporal fecundity from the Spirit," characterizing the human race since the fall.[231] Her pregnancy is "a token" of the magnitude of her surrender implied within her contemplation.[232] The Spirit "will extend the

---

226. Speyr, *Mary in the Redemption*, 112.
227. See Speyr, *Handmaid of the Lord*, 151–54; on Mary's assistance to the Christian in "expanding" his soul to "meet" the demands of the Lord, see also 164.
228. Speyr, *Bereitschaft*, 68; see also *Handmaid of the Lord*, 8.
229. Speyr, *Bereitschaft*, 17; see also *Erde und Himmel* II, no. 2021 (482).
230. See Speyr, *Mary in the Redemption*, 36 and 115; *Korinther* I, 323; *Das Wort und die Mystik* I, 24 and 61–62; and *Handmaid of the Lord*, 8. Cf. Augustine of Hippo: "*Fide credidit, fide concepit* [With faith she believes, with faith she conceives]" (*Sermo* 25: "*De verbis Evangelii Matth.* XII, vers 41–50," PL 46:937); "*Angelius nuntiat, virgo audit, credit, et concipit. Fides in mente, Christus in ventre* [The angel announces, the virgin hears, believes and conceives. Faith in the mind, Christ in the womb]" (*Sermo* 196: "*In Natali Domini*, XIII," PL 38:1019); "*Virgo ergo Maria non concubuit et concepti, sed credidit et concepti* [Therefore the Virgin Mary does not conceive and believe but believes and conceives]" (*Sermo* 233, 3, 4, "*In diebus Paschalibus*, IV," PL 38:1114); and "*Christum prius mente quam ventre concipiens* [Christ is first of all conceived in the mind, then in the womb]" (*Sermo* 215, 4: "*In redditione symboli*," PL 38:1074). Cf. Pope John Paul II, *Redemptoris Mater*, no. 13 (note 35).
231. Speyr, *Erde und Himmel* II, no. 1681 (264).
232. See Speyr, *Handmaid of the Lord*, 157; see also *They Followed His Call*, 63.

Yes of her spirit to an assent of her body. He can do this because her assent is unbounded, a malleable material out of which God can make whatever he will."[233] This means that Mary's virginity is understood not only in terms of openness, surrender, and disclosure, but also and most especially of obedience,[234] which in turn is considered by Adrienne as the divinely-willed condition of her maternity. Precisely because she is so perfectly surrendered to God, Mary is the first human person to experience the Trinity corporally as well as spiritually.[235]

It is within Mary's school, then, that the Christian, precisely as a member of the ecclesial community formed by the Cross of Christ, will recognize his own body as an expression of his "spiritual belonging" to Christ. He, who was obedient in the body even unto death, does not cease to fulfill this obedience, Adrienne argues, when we, his members, are obedient to him. Taking this (our) obedience up into his own obedience to the Father, the Lord manifests the unity of our spirits with his own Spirit and thus also the power of his grace at work within our bodily existence.[236]

---

233. Speyr, *Handmaid of the Lord*, 8; see also *Erde und Himmel* II, no. 1682 (265); and *Mary in the Redemption*, 107.

234. Adrienne conceived of virginity "in a functional relationship to obedience" (Balthasar, *First Glance at Adrienne von Speyr*, 15). Cf. Speyr, *Theologie der Geschlechter*, 116; and Balthasar, *The Laity and the Life of the Counsels*, 24.

235. See Adrienne von Speyr, *Das Themenheft* (Einsiedeln: Johannes Verlag, 1977), 11; cf. Balthasar, *Explorations in Theology*, 197.

236. See Speyr, *Korinther* I, 185; see also *The Letter to the Ephesians*, 37.

FIVE

The Individual-Community Difference-in-Unity

The Trinitarian Face of Redemption and the Ecclesial Existence of the Christian

An Introduction to the Individual-Community Difference-in-Unity in the Works of Adrienne von Speyr and Hans Urs von Balthasar

The difference-in-unity or "tension" between nature and grace in the theologies of Adrienne von Speyr and Hans Urs von Balthasar has already been presented, in preceding chapters of this volume, in terms of the "tension" (difference-in-unity or unity-in-difference) between the individual and his or her mission, whence the notion of a "theological person," as Balthasar would have it, in reference to Adrienne's insights.[1] Particularly significant in this context is the correspondence that we noted between Christ's life-*giving* surrender and our own life-*receiving* surrender, such that the human person may be said to be fulfilled by his or her willing and ongoing appropriation of the unique God-given mission to which he or she is personally destined.

In this chapter we will examine the ecclesial or communitarian dimension of this mystery, such that what is designated by Balthasar (again, with reference to Adrienne's insights) as the basic human "tension" between the individual and the community (or, still more fundamentally, between the individual and the species)[2] might be understood in this light. Herein the tension is not so much between uniqueness and commonality, for—it bears repeating—the

---

1. Portions of this chapter first appeared under the title "Ecclesial Existence: Person and Community in the Anthropological Theology of Adrienne von Speyr" in *Modern Theology* 24, no. 3 (July 2008): 359–85.

2. See, for example, Balthasar, *Theo-Logic* I, 154–57; and *Theo-Logic* II, 82–83.

mission wherein the individual is adjusted, as it were, to the dimension of the community is precisely that which renders him or her absolutely unique.[3] Far from originating within the community as something that might be deduced from it, this personal and personalizing mission is presented by Balthasar as arising out of the very "uniqueness of God" for the distinct purpose of enriching the community. Hence the individual, in virtue of his or her unique mission, is understood as being "more profoundly drawn into the community" and even "expropriated for its [the community's] sake and obligated to it."[4]

Within this context and in light of the particular ecclesial identity of Mary—whom, as we saw in chapter four, is presented by Balthasar and Adrienne as the first cell of the Church, and even the Church in person—one can hardly help but raise the question that Balthasar succinctly poses for us:

> But who or what is the Church? What sort of interrelationship, what sort of encounter of human and divine sociology, where one and the same individual alternates between being member of the body and spouse of Christ, between his standing apart as a person and his absorption in a common identity? And, resulting from this, what is the mystery of the Christian life with the tension it involves between the claims of the person and those of the mission confided to him [or her], a duality deriving from and analogous with the double nature in Christ: 'As the Father has sent me so also I send you'?[5]

Within the very question, Balthasar points us in the direction of what he perceives as the solution. It is Christ who will reveal the meaning of the anthropological "tension" between the individual and the community. This tension—not unlike the others that we have examined in previous chapters—is, more specifically, presented by our authors as determined by the Christological tension between the love of the incarnate Son for the Father and his love for those to whom the Father has sent him. Because, more specifically, the incarnate Son is presented as identifying with his mission from the Father, his loving gift of himself to the Father simultaneously implies his obedient willingness to give himself to those to whom he is sent by the Father. Or, to put it another way, his love for the Father takes the form in time of obedience to his redemptive mission.

Here again, the important Speyrian concept of surrender emerges: this time as clarifying that Christological attitude in virtue of which the incarnate

---

3. See Balthasar, *Theo-Drama* II, 415; *Theo-Drama* III, 527; *Engagement with God*, 28–29. See also Speyr, *They Followed His Call*, 68–69; and *Mary in the Redemption*, 36–37.

4. Balthasar, *Theo-Drama* II, 415. Similar is Adrienne's equating of the personal and the anonymous. See, for example, Speyr, *John* IV, 310; and *Über die Liebe* (Einsiedeln: Johannes Verlag, 1976), 30–33.

5. Balthasar, *Explorations in Theology* I, 118–19.

Son is simultaneously disposed to receive the Father's gift of divine life and being and to bestow these gifts upon those to whom he is sent. As Adrienne would have it, the Son, who has been given to have life in himself (cf. Jn 5:26), accepts this life in a manner commensurate with his mission: "in view of his own distribution in the world."[6] Precisely because, in other words, he is receptive, available, and thus also obedient to the Father, it is also by the Father that he is surrendered, or bestowed, upon the world (cf. Jn 3:16).

Hence also, his generous gift of himself to the world in his Eucharist, passion, and death (cf. Jn 10:18) bespeaks (or reveals) the mystery of the Father's own generous gift of the whole divine life and being to him. "The Son's passive, suffering love becomes at once the upright and the inverted mirror-image of the Father's love,"[7] Balthasar argues in images that are assuredly Speyrian. This is possible because the Son's obedience is "so thoroughly love for the Father" that it is "by that very fact [...] altogether one (John 10, 30 [i.e., 10:30]) with the Father's own love."[8]

In a similar manner, the Christian's belonging to Christ implies, as we shall observe more closely in this chapter, that he or she is given, with Christ and in Christ, to the Church and the world. The incarnate Word gives to his disciples a share not only in his unique filial relation to the Father by grace, Balthasar explains, but also "in the unique surrender of his uniqueness 'for many,'"[9] in virtue of which the Church is built up throughout the ages. Hence the Christian's surrender to Christ "in favor of the divine life" simultaneously implies a willingness to be bestowed by Christ upon the community. He or she becomes a "*homo ecclesiasticus*," so as to be "universalized and fashioned after Christ"[10] and incorporated into the analogy of the Word-made-flesh.

Meanwhile, the community of saints is built up by such as these and lives by the mysterious law "whereby each can 'be for' others through prayer, initiative and suffering on their behalf."[11] All of this is moreover realized by way of love: the disciple who has been loved by Christ can hardly do otherwise than bestow this same love upon all of those to whom he is sent. "Every Christian who loves participates in the Son's attitude and is one whom the Son leads to the Father. The acts of his love are the steps he takes into this ever-greater triune love."[12]

It is thus not surprising that Balthasar should recognize, precisely with-

---

6. Speyr, *John* I, 284. 7. Balthasar, *Prayer*, 186.
8. Balthasar, *Mysterium Paschale*, 208–9; see also *The Glory of the Lord* VII, 249.
9. Balthasar, *Theo-Drama* II, 415; see also *Theo-Drama* III, 271.
10. Balthasar, *Theo-Drama* III, 527. 11. Ibid., 282.
12. Speyr, *Confession*, 151.

in this tension of love between the individual and the community rooted in Christ, a metaphor of the Trinity: "In the reciprocity between the uniqueness of the person and the uniqueness of his self-giving for the sake of the community, the Christian rhythm between the individual and the community becomes a concrete metaphor of Trinitarian life within God, inscribed in the very structures of the creaturely tension between individual and species."[13]

So far, so good. It would be sadly oversimplistic, however, if our treatment of the anthropological tension between the individual and the community were not to address the problematic theme of redemption by representation—and more specifically that of substitution (*Stellvertretung*)—as it is taken up by Balthasar in an attempt, I am convinced, to theologically sustain Adrienne's presumably mystically-gained insights into the paschal mysteries.

We will thus begin this chapter by expositing Balthasar's doctrine of redemption in light of Adrienne's mystical experiences, with a particular focus on the difficulties that it poses not so much to the doctrine of the immutability of the Godhead—a question to be addressed in chapter seven of this volume—as, rather, to the meaning of redemption itself and its implications for human freedom. Before arguing in my postscript for what I judge to be a more fitting interpretation of Adrienne's mystical experiences and of her doctrine as it is implicitly present throughout her works—one which does more justice to this Catholic meaning of redemption—I will exposit her treatment of the dynamic tension between the individual and the community as this mystery emerges within the context of Trinitarian love. In the new commandment of love, this mystery of our incorporation into divine communion is manifest by means of the very surrender that characterizes this communion. It is thus, Adrienne teaches, that the Lord draws his disciple into the mystery of his own love for and obedience to the Father: his generous and redemptive love for the world is the revelation of his eternal love for the Father and likewise of the Father's love for him and for the world to whom he has sent the Son. From this perspective, redemption might be viewed, I will argue, as a breaking of the barriers of our resistance so that we might receive the gift of divine love by the power of this same love. At the same time, it implies our participation in the ongoing mediation, or communication (surrender) of divine love, in virtue of which we might be considered, in accord with the Johannine insight, to abide in God's love (cf. Jn 15:10; 1 Jn 4:12, 16).

---

13. Balthasar, *Theo-Drama* II, 415; see also *Engagement with God*, 31; cf. Second Vatican Council, *Gaudium et Spes*, no. 24 (*DZ* 4324).

The Trinitarian Difference-in-Unity Revealed in "Alienation": Balthasar's Redemption by Substitution

As Balthasar would have it, all of Christian theology "depends" upon the "*pro nobis*" of our salvation, which in turn requires the whole truth of Chalcedon in its affirmation of the full and authentic humanity and divinity of Christ: "God alone can forgive sins, and so only he can 'bear sins'; and the way in which he actually bears them cannot be discovered through speculation but must be presented, for our belief, in the mystery of the Cross—which is a stumbling block to Jews and folly to Gentiles."[14]

Balthasar thus reads the doctrine of Chalcedon as providing the basis for his assertion that Christ's position as the new Adam alters the whole of human nature: he assumes the role of Head with regard to the rest of humanity, whom he makes to be his members.[15] This, in turn, is the basis of his presentation of Christ's mission as not only reconciling the world with God (cf. 2 Cor 5:18), but as also reconciling the anthropological tension between the individual and the species: a reconciliation which cannot, Balthasar reasons, be effected externally (for our benefit) but only internally: "in our place."[16]

Going one step further—in a move wherein we might discern his appropriation of the mystical insights of Adrienne, as shall be more apparent in what follows—the Swiss theologian reasons: "Let us assume that the whole of this nature finds itself to be in an explicitly negative place before God; then Jesus will appropriate to himself this negative position—in accord with his commission and his inner ability and freedom—in such a way that it will be transformed by him into what it is in truth: into the pain of alienation [*in den Schmerz der Entfremdung*] that now is experienced no longer simply by God [sic] but by man, too."[17]

---

14. Balthasar, *Theo-Drama* II, 120.

15. Balthasar, *Epilogue*, 120. Cf. Thomas Aquinas, *ST* I-II, q. 114, a. 6; III, q. 7, aa. 1 and 9; q. 8, aa. 1 and 5; q. 19, a. 4; q. 48, aa. 1–2, ad. 1; and q. 49, a. 3, ad. 3. See also Torrell, *Pour nous les hommes et pour notre salut*, 93.

16. Balthasar, *Theo-Drama* III, 240–41; see also *Does Jesus Know Us?*, 32. As for St. Thomas, he is, as Jean-Pierre Torrell points out, of the contrary opinion. Nowhere in his nineteen biblical commentaries treating the question of substitution and studied by Torrell does he suggest the idea of Christ substituting himself for sinners, whose fault he would be said to assume rather than the punishment following therefrom. Hence, for example, "in his reading of the the *Second Letter to the Corinthians* (5:21), he [the angelic doctor] so little entertains [the idea of] substitution that he comments in the preceeding verse that it is [rather] a matter of reconciliation: God has done his part, but it remains for us to do ours" (*Pour nous les hommes et pour notre salut* [Paris: Cerf, 2014], 259; see 255–97).

17. Balthasar, *Epilogue*, 120; on the "pain" of God caused by our refusal of his love, see *Theo-Drama* IV, 328 and 502; Pope John Paul II, *Dominum et Vivificantem*, no. 41; and Gilles Emery, "The Question of Evil and the Mystery of God in Charles Journet," trans. Robert E. Williams and Paul Gondreau, in Emery, *Trinity, Church, and the Human Person*, 237–62.

Balthasar's theology of redemption thus supposes a radical understanding of vicarious representation (*Stellvertretung*)—literally, "representation [*Vertretung*]" by assuming the other's "place [*Stelle*]"—such that Christ is said not only to represent the Father's love by freely giving himself to the disciples "to the end" (cf. Jn 13:1), but also to represent sinful humanity, precisely in our estrangement from God, before the Father.[18] From this point of view, he is said by Balthasar, in union with Adrienne, to personally endure the "conflict between God and man 'from both sides,'"[19] namely, that of God offended by the sinner—even to the point of "suffering"[20]—on the one hand, and that of the sinner subject to God's judgment, on the other. Or, to put it more succinctly, "God, taking manhood in Christ, becomes in one single Person both 'subject and object' of judgment and justification."[21] As such, he represents God among men and men before God; whence the unity of the katalogical and analogical aspect of Balthasar's theory of representation.[22]

The idea of solidarity is "much too weak to express the whole depth of identification taken on by Jesus"[23] of sinful humanity in its position of distance from God which, Balthasar further maintains, implies his mystical incurring of our guilt, or his internally bearing the burden of sin, so as to *subjectively* experience punishment for our sin.[24] To be sure, Balthasar specifies

---

18. See Antoine Birot, "'God in Christ, Reconciled the World to Himself': Redemption in Balthasar," *Communio* 24, no. 3 (1997): 263. This is but one of five motifs that Balthasar insists must be taken into account if a theory of redemption can be considered "truly ecclesial." In addition to this "changing of place" between the sinless one and sinners, which accounts for the second motif, Balthasar presents the following: "The Son gives himself, through God the Father, for the world's salvation"; the human being, in virtue of the substitutive act, is "set free (ransomed, redeemed, released)"; he or she is thereby initiated into the divine life of the Trinity; hence, the whole process is to be regarded as initiated by divine love. See Balthasar, *Theo-Drama* IV, 317. On the representative functions of Christ "from the world's point of view" and "from God's point of view," see *TheoDrama* III, 341.

19. Balthasar, *Theo-Drama* IV, 346. Reference is approvingly made to the theology of Karl Barth here. Cf. Speyr, *Confession*, 24–25; and *Die katholischen Briefe* II, 271. Such is also the conflict between the sinner's refusal of God and God's refusal of this refusal. See Balthasar, *Does Jesus Know Us?*, 35.

20. This is apparent in the citation above: "The pain of alienation that is now no longer experienced simply by God [sic]" (Balthasar, *Epilogue*, 120). See his presentation of the metaphorical value of this statement in ibid., 100; and our cursory treatment of the suffering in the Godhead in chapter seven. In contrast, St. Thomas reasons, "To sorrow, therefore, over the misery of others belongs not to God; but it does most properly belong to Him to dispel that misery, whatever be the defect we call by that name. Now defects are not removed, except by the perfection of some kind of goodness: and the primary source of goodness is God" (*ST* I, q. 21, a. 3).

21. Balthasar, *Mysterium Paschale*, 121.

22. See Karl-Heinz Menke, *Stellvertetung. Schlüsselbegriff christlichen Lebens und theologische Grundkategorie* (Einsiedeln: Johannes Verlag, 1991), 266–310; and Balthasar, *The Glory of the Lord* VII, 210.

23. See Balthasar, *Does Jesus Know Us?*, 35. Cf. Speyr, *Confession*, 24; and Schmitt, *The Sacrament of Confession as a "Sequela Christi" in the Writings of A. von Speyr*, 115. For a well-balanced interpretation of what Balthasar means by these images, see Norbert Hoffman, *Kreuz und Trinität. Zur Theologie der Sühne* (Einsiedeln: Johannes Verlag, 1982), 30–31.

24. On the mystical incurring of sin, see Balthasar, *Mysterium Paschale*, 101 and 134; *Does Jesus*

that objectively, Christ is not punished. He does not experience our sin, but the "hopelessness" of our resistance to God "and the graceless No of divine grace to this resistance."²⁵ Without himself sinning (cf. Heb 4:15), Christ is presented by Balthasar—again, following an important Speyrian insight—as "letting the sins of the world into the same space he had allowed the Father to fill, and to do so out of the love that God also fills, as the 'Lamb of God who takes away the sins of the world' (Jn 1:29)."²⁶ This, in turn, implies the work of the Spirit who gives to his body a universal significance in virtue of which it is made capable of containing our sin.²⁷

For this same reason, Christ is made capable of confessing—Balthasar explains, in defense of one of Adrienne's most fundamental intuitions²⁸—the world's sins to the Father upon the Cross so that they might be forgiven, presumably in accord with the eternal Trinitarian decision (cf. Rev 3:18) concerning how sin was to be repaired, namely by the infinitely superior force of the love of the God-man, Jesus Christ.²⁹ Before the "absolution" of Easter Sunday,³⁰ however—and in accord with this decision entailing his radical solidarity with sinners such that the incarnate Son refuses to distinguish himself from the sinner in the latter's position of distance from the Father—he simultaneously draws upon himself the judgment of God "like a lightning rod." By this image, Balthasar means—again following upon one of Adri-

---

Know Us?, 32; Guy Mansini, "Rahner and Balthasar on the Efficacy of the Cross," *Irish Theological Quarterly* 63, no. 3 (1998): 238; Alberto Espezel, "Quelques aspects de la sotériologie de Hans Urs von Balthasar," *Nouvelle revue théologique* 112 (1990): 80–92, esp. 87; and Thomas Rudolf Krenski, *Passio Caritatis: Trinitarische Passiologie im Werk Hans Urs von Balthasar* (Einsiedeln: Johannes Verlag, 1990), 292–320. On Adrienne's participation in Christ's experience of bearing sin, see, for example, Speyr, *Kreuz und Hölle* I, 26. On Christ's subjective experience of punishment, see Balthasar, *Theo-Drama* IV, 338.

25. Ibid., 349; see also *Does Jesus Know Us?*, 36.

26. Balthasar, *Love Alone Is Credible*, 99–100; for an affirmation that Christ does not sin, see *Theo-Drama* IV, 336.

27. See Balthasar, *Does Jesus Know Us?*, 49. Cf. Speyr, *Confession*, 57–58; *The Cross: Word and Sacrament*, 16; and *Kreuz und Hölle* I, 26, wherein is described Adrienne's mystical experience of bearing sin. Beyond the image of containing sin, Balthasar presents corporality as "an essential presupposition for someone being able to suffer vicariously for mankind as a whole" (*Epilogue*, 101). See also his *Explorations in Theology* IV, 415–22, esp. 419. Cf. Speyr, *Korinther* I, 52–53.

28. See Balthasar, *Does Jesus Know Us?*, 48; *Theo-Drama* IV, 180. Cf. Speyr, *John* III, 346; *The Cross: Word and Sacrament*, 15; *Confession*, esp. 50–55, 58, and 84–85; *Die katholischen Briefe* I, 332; and *Apokalypse*, 679. The event of redemption constitutes, as it were, Adrienne explains, "a primal confession [*Ur-beichte*]" (*Die katholischen Briefe* I, 331). See also Balthasar, "Adrienne von Speyr et le sacrement de pénitence," *Nouvelle revue théologique* 107 (1985): 394–403; and introduction to Speyr, *Die katholischen Briefe* I, 21.

29. See Balthasar, *Theo-Drama* IV, 329–30; *Mysterium Paschale*, 172; *A Theological Anthropology*, 129 and 240; Michel Beaudin, *Obéissance et solidarité: Essai sur la christologie de Hans Urs von Balthasar* (Montréal: Fides, 1989), 170; and Marc Ouellet "The Foundation of Christian Ethics according to Hans Urs von Balthasar," *Communio* 17, no. 3 (Fall 1990): 383. On the eternal Trinitarian decision, see Balthasar, *Mysterium Paschale*, 34; Speyr, *John* I, 144–45; and *Korinther* I, 345–46.

30. See Speyr, *Confession*, 86.

enne's insights gained through her presumably mystical experiences—that he literally experiences the mortal anguish "of being forsaken by God,"[31] whence his cry of despair upon the Cross (cf. Mk 15:34; Mt 17:45). Adrienne, in fact, changes the biblical formulation, "My God, my God, why have you forsaken me?" in her work on confession and in her commentary on John 11:33 to "Father, why have you forsaken me."[32] In her work on the sacraments, on the other hand, she explains that "here it is the *man*, the creature, who cries out to *God*. Father-to-Son here has become God-versus-human being. As Father he has disappeared. The 'Father' has forsaken him: he calls to 'God'—this is all that remains of their relationship."[33] And, in her commentary on Psalm 22, Adrienne recognizes the Lord as realizing David's prophetic cry by providing in his divine humanity (*Gottmenschlichkeit*) "representation [*Stellvertretung*] for all."[34]

As for the Father, he is said by Balthasar to unload "his wrath" upon the incarnate Son, and even—as if to follow through on the image above—to shatter and distribute him, "as by lightning" in the Eucharist, among sinners because of his solidarity with them.[35] While the Son is said to accomplish the work of redemption by means of his obedience to the Father's will,[36] the latter is said to accomplish it by turning upon him (the Son) "the face of his severity, and even anger, at the sinfulness of the world."[37] The Father's wrath,[38]

---

31. Balthasar, *Does Jesus Know Us?*, 32; and *The Glory of the Lord* VII, 224–25. This experience of being forsaken is so great that Balthasar finds it completely incompatible with the beatific vision. See, for example, Balthasar, *Truth is Symphonic: Aspects of Christian Pluralism*, trans. Graham Harrison (San Francisco: Ignatius Press, 1987), 40; and *Mysterium Paschale*, 101 and 125–26. See also Schmitt, *The Sacrament of Confession as a "Sequela Christi" in the Writings of A. von Speyr*, 119.

32. See Speyr, *Confession*, 52; and *John* II, 363.

33. Speyr, *The Cross: Word and Sacrament*, 39.

34. Speyr, *Achtzehn Psalmen*, 40; see also *Das Wort und die Mystik* I, 213; *Erde und Himmel* II, no. 1464 (154); and *Kreuz und Hölle* I, 207.

35. Balthasar, *Theo-Drama* IV, 345 and 348; and Mansini, "Rahner and Balthasar on the Efficacy of the Cross," 239.

36. Cf. Thomas Aquinas, *ST* III, q. 47, a. 2.

37. Balthasar, *The Christian State of Life*, 256; see also *Mysterium Paschale*, 123; *New Elucidations*, 233–34; and Schmitt, *The Sacrament of Confession as a "Sequela Christi" in the Writings of A. von Speyr*, 117. Among the graces obtained from the Father's "silence" is, Adrienne teaches, that of the mystical night of faith. See Speyr, *Das Wort und die Mystik* I, 92. In contrast, see Thomas Aquinas, *ST* III, q. 47, a. 3, ad. 1, wherein it is admitted that "it is indeed a wicked and cruel act to hand over an innocent man to torment and to death against his will. Yet God the Father did not so deliver up Christ, but inspired Him with the will to suffer for us." In the corpus for the same article the angelic doctor teaches that the Father delivered Christ up to the passion in three ways: "by His eternal will He preordained Christ's Passion for the deliverance of the human race"; "by the infusion of charity, He inspired Him with the will to suffer for us"; and "by not shielding Him from the Passion, but abandoning Him to His persecutors." See also *SCG* IV, c. 55, 18.

38. See the thorough exposition of both the exaggerations and a well-balanced interpretation of the anger of God by Jean-Pierre Torrell in *Pour nous les hommes et pour notre salut*, 230–47.

meanwhile, is but an image of his love, Balthasar maintains, because he does not remain unaffected by these events in some transcendent realm. Rather, he is truly present both in the Son's gift and in his earthly wanderings, notwithstanding the Spirit's mediating role.[39]

Proceeding from—as he would have it—the data of revelation provided by the Incarnation, Balthasar argues, more specifically, that this event implies still another: a "happening" or an "event" in God "that not only justifies the possibility and actual occurrence of all suffering in the world but also justifies God's sharing in the latter, in which he goes to the length of vicariously taking on man's God-lessness."[40] To be sure, it is the second person of the Trinity who alone, Balthasar admits, is incarnate and thus capable of suffering and death.[41] On the other hand, the Swiss theologian argues that Christ's actual death—precisely as an act of obedience to the Father and thus also of love for the Father—is "the human expression of a shared love-death in a supereminently Trinitarian sense: the One who forsakes is just as much affected (in his eternal life) as the One who is forsaken, and just as much as the forsaking and forsaken love that is One in the Holy Spirit."[42] Hence, the so-called distance—which Balthasar recognizes as implied by the "gulf of the Divine Persons' total distinctness,"[43] that is to say, their personal differences, in the immanent Trinity—is, he claims, most especially manifest in the "alienation between God and the sin-bearing Son" within the economy of our salvation.[44] Hence also, the sinner's alienation from God is resolved, as Balthasar would have it, within an intra-Trinitarian drama, so as to be "recapitulated" within the "infinite distance" between the Father and the Son in the union of the Holy Spirit.[45] From this point of view, the Balthasarian meaning of the *admirabile commercium* far exceeds, as he himself admits, the meaning given to it by the Fathers of the Church. For "even the sinner's alienation from God

---

39. See Balthasar, *Mysterium Paschale*, 30. This mediating role of the Spirit is presented by Balthasar—again, in virtue of a Speyrian insight—in terms of what he calls "a Trinitarian inversion." See Balthasar, *Theo-Drama* III, 183–91; and *Theo-Logic* III, 308. Cf. Speyr, *Erde und Himmel* III, 193; *World of Prayer*, 63; and *Confession*, 49. See also the pertinent criticism of this intuition in Jean-Noël Dol, "L'inversion trinitaire chez Hans Urs von Balthasar," *Revue thomiste* 100, no. 2 (2000): 201–38.

40. Balthasar, *Theo-Drama* IV, 324. Cf. Speyr, *The Countenance of the Father*, 8; and *The Passion from Within*, 61–62. The question of an "event" or "happening" in God will be examined in chapter seven of this volume in confrontation with Balthasar's critics.

41. See Balthasar, *Epilogue*, 100.

42. Balthasar, *Theo-Drama* IV, 501; see also 84; and *Theo-Drama* II, 120–21.

43. Balthasar, *Theo-Drama* IV, 326; see also *The Glory of the Lord* VII, 249.

44. Balthasar, *Theo-Drama* IV, 335; see also *Theo-Drama* III, 228; and Hoffmann, *Kreuz und Trinitität*, 53–84.

45. See Balthasar, *You Crown the Year*, 84–85; *Theo-Drama* IV, 324–35; and O'Hanlon, *The Immutability of God in the Theology of Hans Urs von Balthasar*, 35–36 and 67–68.

was taken into the Godhead, into the 'economic' distance between Father and Son."[46]

To be sure, any such novel view of our redemptive mysteries is not unproblematic, as Balthasar's critics have amply argued.[47] Beyond the problem highlighted above, however—namely that this vision of God's wrath tends to overshadow the revelation of his love, as Karen Kilby argues[48]—we are also faced with the obvious question of maintaining God's immutability. As Guy Mansini sums it up:

> If Balthasar moves from Christ's representation of us in bearing sin and the experienced alienation of the sinner from God, to Christ's bearing the wrath of God, to the Cross as inner-trinitarian event, to the mutability of God, and if this conclusion is to be rejected, where is he to be stopped? [...] If we stop him too soon, we face the serious danger of failing to recognize something essential to our appreciation of the passion, if Christ has indeed experienced the pangs of hell. On the other hand, if we do not stop him somewhere, we end up imputing a change to God that either destroys the divine transcendence, and thence the doctrine of creation itself, or that threatens theological discourse with incoherence.[49]

Mansini suggests that this predicament invites us to introduce the important distinction between what, in the redemptive mysteries, might be attributed to Christ in his human nature, as distinct from his divine nature.[50] That

---

46. Balthasar, *Theo-Drama* IV, 381.
47. See, for example, Pitstick, *Light in Darkness*; Levering, *Scripture and Metaphysics*, 120–32; Gilles Emery, "The Immutability of the God of Love and the Problem of Language Concerning the 'Suffering of God'" in James F. Keating and Thomas Joseph White (eds.), *Divine Impassibility and the Mystery of Human Suffering* (Grand Rapids, Mich.: Eerdmans, 2009), 27–76, esp. 48–52; Narcisse, "Participer à la vie trinitaire," 119–28; Mansini, "Rahner and Balthasar on the Efficacy of the Cross," 232–49; Richard Schenk, "Ist die Rede vom leidenden Gott theologisch zu vermeiden? Reflexionen über den Streit von K. Rahner und H. U. Von Balthasar," in Peter Koslowski und Friedrich Hermanni (eds.), *Der leidende Gott. Eine philosophische und theologische Kritik* (Munich: Wilhelm Fink Verlag, 2001), 225–39; Torrell, *Pour nous les hommes et pour notre salut*, 231 and 248–49; Thomas Joseph White, "Jesus' Cry on the Cross," *Nova et Vetera* (English Edition) 5, no. 3 (2007): 555–82; "Kenoticism and the Divinity of Christ Crucified," *The Thomist* 75, no. 1 (2011): 1–41; and Michele M. Schumacher, "The Concept of Representation in the Theology of Hans Urs von Balthasar," *Theological Studies* 60 (1999): 53–71.
48. See Kilby, *Balthasar: A (Very) Critical Introduction*, 122.
49. Mansini, "Rahner and Balthasar on the Efficacy of the Cross," 247–48.
50. Hence, the Third Council of Constantinople proclaims that Christ has "two natures that undergo no confusion, no change, no separation, no division; at no point was the difference between the natures taken away through the union, but rather the property of both natures is preserved and comes together in a single person and hypostasis; he is not parted or divided into two persons but is preserved and comes together in a single person and hypostasis" (*DZ* 555). "We likewise proclaim in him, according to the teaching of the holy Fathers, two natural volitions or wills and two natural actions, without division, without change, without separation, without confusion" (*DZ* 556). Hence, in "the same" incarnate Lord "we glory in proclaiming two natural actions, without division, without change, without separation, without confusion, namely, a divine action and a human action, as Leo [...] asserts with utmost clarity: 'For each of the two natures performs the function proper to it in communion with the other; the Word does what pertains to the Word and the flesh what pertains to the flesh' [*DZ* 294]" (*DZ* 557).

he might be said, more specifically, to experience the pain of abandonment, or even hell, "reveals his character of Son; it is an economic manifestation of whatever there is of 'mission' and 'obedience' that are to be verified supereminently in the eternal procession." As such, however, this manifestation remains a created reality: a reality nonetheless attributable to the common work "of the Three *ad extra*." To hold to this is *not*, however, to grant that a new "event" or "happening" might be found within the Trinity. To believe otherwise would, in fact, amount to confusing the two natures of Christ, Mansini argues. "And this, I think," he adds, "Balthasar does."[51]

Because this particular challenge to Balthasar's theology is addressed at length in chapter seven of this volume and briefly in my general conclusion within the context of the use of metaphorical expression in theological reasoning, here we will focus upon the second objection. This objection, more specifically, concerns—first of all—the dilemma of how the Father's abandonment of his only-begotten Son should be the greatest revelation of his love for those whom he wills to call his sons (and daughters) and, secondly (and not unrelated), how the latter are thereby truly restored in their dignity. Banishing from his presence the very one who patiently and lovingly bears the sins of the world, this "Father" is hard to embrace as the source of all love—the one who ultimately bids us to communion—especially when we consider that the "space" filled by sin within the Son (the space, which thus draws the Father's wrath upon him) had been willingly "emptied out" by him (the Son) as a place for the Father's love.[52] While the "man" Jesus thus bears our sins before the Father's wrath—an image that Jean-Pierre Torrell rightly qualifies as "a brutally anthropomorphic metaphor"[53]—the proper owners of those sins (we, human persons) are henceforth banished from the drama. "Outwardly it may seem that men cause Christ's Passion: they put him in chains, scourge and crucify him; they pierce his heart. But inwardly it is a Trinitarian action, in which God has the chief role and men are merely supernumeraries."[54]

"The difference of natures in that same and unique hypostasis is recognized by the fact that each of the two natures wills and performs what is proper to it in communion with the other. Thus, we glory in proclaiming two natural wills and actions concurring together for the salvation of the human race" (*DZ* 558). See also Thomas Aquinas, *Comp* I, 211.

51. Ibid., 248. Such is also the criticism of Bernhard Blankenhorn, as we will see and examine more thoroughly in chapter six of the present volume. See Bernhard-Thomas Blankenhorn, "Balthasar's Method of Divine Naming," *Nova et Vetera* (English edition) 1, no. 2 (2003): 245–67.

52. See Balthasar, *Love Alone Is Credible*, 100.

53. Torrell, *Pour nous les hommes et pour notre salut*, 231.

54. Balthasar, *Truth is Symphonic*, 42–43; see also *The Glory of the Lord* VII, 224–25. In contrast, Torrell rightly argues that "it is not the will of God that would have directly and expressly willed the murder of his Son. Nor is it the will of Jesus, who would have advanced [or chosen] his death, like one who commits suicide [...]. It is the bad will of those who refused the message of Jesus: it is the human

Almost imperceptible in Balthasar's portrayal of this event is the refusal *of* God by mankind, as is implied by our sins and as differing from God's refusal of mankind due to those same sins. From Balthasar's point of view, after all, this is a spectacle wherein "God is confronted with God; God is opposed by God."[55] To be sure, Balthasar would restore the image of this enraged and vengeful Father with the images cited above, images in virtue of which the entire Trinity might be understood as engaged for our salvation from all eternity. Precisely because the *kenosis* of the Incarnation (cf. Phil 2:7) is rooted, as Balthasar sees it, in a still more "primary kenosis"[56] wherein the Father hands over his entire being and substance to the Son—namely in the latter's generation from and by the Father—the Father may be said to give his very self in his gift of the Son for the world's salvation (cf. Jn 3:16). The Father only *appears* to remain a spectator of the drama; in reality, "he could not involve himself more profoundly."[57]

We are nonetheless left here with a very significant question: what is, in fact, revealed in the Son's passion? And what, more specifically, is the connection between sin and estrangement, on the one hand, and between the event of the Cross and the sinner's return to God, on the other? Christ's entrance into hell with a light illuminating the way to paradise is one thing; his death in total darkness is another. How, in other words, can Christ's apparent despair lead us to hope? Or, to phrase the question in Adrienne's own words, how is it that "by restricting his own vision as God, he expands us men in our faith"?[58] Or, again, to express it still more pointedly, how can his passion, death, and descent into hell lead us to conversion?[59]

---

freedom of certain of his adversaries that intervened to transform this contingent fact into a necessary state" (*Pour nous les hommes et pour notre salut*, 271). If, on the other hand, this event has become what we typically call "the sacrifice of the Cross," this is "in no way due to the killers [sacrificers] who have only committed an abominable crime [and] who are responsible in the measure that they knew what they were doing. Only the will of Jesus transformed this sacrifice in reason of the charity with which it was offered" (273). Cf. Thomas Aquinas, *ST* III, q. 22, a. 2, ad. 2; q. 47, a. 1; and q. 48, a. 3, ad. 3. In short, Torrell (232) argues that we must account for secondary causes.

55. Paul Althaus, *Die christliche Wahrheit: Lehrbuch der Dogmatik* (Gütersloh: C. Bertelsmann, 1952), 471, cited by Balthasar, *Theo-Drama* IV, 348. On sin as the refusal of God, see *The Catechism of the Catholic Church*, nos. 1850–51.

56. Balthasar, *Theo-Drama* V, 84; see also 123, where Balthasar addresses the "eternal kenosis of the Divine Persons to one another," and *Theo-Drama* IV, 323.

57. Balthasar, *Theo-Drama* III, 514. In a similar manner, St. Thomas, as read by Jean-Pierre Torrell, "fully values the human gesture of Jesus's passion, without failing to emphasize that this 'ascending' approach finds its origin in the absolutely primary 'descending' movement: that of the philanthropy of God, which is initially inclined with mercy toward human distress to provide the redemption that men are incapable of providing on their own" (*Pour nous les hommes et pour notre salut*, 50).

58. Speyr, *World of Prayer*, 81.

59. To be sure, Christ's satisfaction for sin obtains its effect in us, because we are incorporated, as St. Thomas teaches, as members of the head. It nonetheless remains for the members to "be conformed

Balthasar seems to imply that Christ's separation from the Father by love reverses the meaning of the sinner's separation from the Father by sin. Not surprisingly, the Swiss theologian thus points to the scandalous character of this event in virtue of which he attributes to it the characteristic of love.[60] If, however, we are not willing to fall prey to some Gnostic tendency—and thus remain unwilling, as is Adrienne in fact,[61] to separate love from knowledge—we might wish to confront this scandalous solution with a pertinent question: Does not this "solution" make sense only by way of a divine decree (God's eternal, and thus foreseen, plan for our salvation) having little, if any, significance with regard to its actual effect upon the sinner's free will? After all, is it not precisely therein—in the sinner's free will—that lies the actual separation between God and the estranged sinner?[62]

Given, furthermore, God's high regard for his own creation, he certainly will not—as St. Thomas teaches, and Balthasar presumably agrees[63]—force our wills. Hence, the idea of reversing the separation between God and the sinner—a separation caused by a perverted will—can only be overcome by a correction of that same (the sinner's) will: "The darkness had to become brighter; blind urge had to pass over into a love that sees; and the clever will to possess and develop had to be transfigured into the foolish wisdom that pours

---

to their head" (*ST* III, q. 49, a. 3, ad. 3), namely by way not only of suffering and death, but also and especially by virtue and sinlessness. Perhaps still more significant in the case at hand, although Christ is able to atone for his members, the latter are still responsible for their own confession and contrition. See ibid., q. 28, a. 2, ad. 1.

60. "Our inability to resolve this dogma into gnosis is the true scandal; it is a signal and a warning that this is where genuine faith begins. For it is precisely here, in this deed, that genuine divine love begins and ends, a love that overwhelms us and exceeds all capacity to think it—and thereby becomes completely evident as love" (Balthasar, *Love Alone Is Credible*, 100).

61. "Because [*indem*] this love is known to us, we have *believed*. This means that knowledge and faith form a unity: such a unity as is, in fact, realized by [*bewirkt wird*] love. [...] Without knowledge [*Erkenntnis*] and faith, love would not be received [*aufgenommen*]" (Speyr, *Die katholischen Briefe* II, 177); cf. 1 Jn 4:16. See also Michael Sherwin's very thorough work, *By Knowledge and By Love: Charity and Knowledge in the Moral Theology of St. Thomas Aquinas* (Washington, D.C.: The Catholic University of America Press, 2005).

62. Qualifying as "unbearable" (*insoutenable*) Balthasar's assimilation of Christ's distress in his agony and the distancing from God provoked by sin, Jean-Pierre Torrell rightly holds that there is only "one" thing that distances the human being from God: namely sin (see *Pour nous les hommes et pour notre salut*, 248.

63. "For men were not intended to lose that feedom of choice by which they are able to cleave or not to cleave to the incarnate God, lest the good of man be produced by coercion—a good without merit and without praise" (Thomas Aquinas, *SCG* IV, c. 55, 10). As for Balthasar, despite his own hope, he admits that no definitive statement can be made regarding whether "all men [will] be saved." See also Balthasar, *Dare We Hope*, 208; *Epilogue*, 119 and 122; "Jesus and Forgiveness," trans. Josephine Koeppel, *Communio* 11, no. 4 (1984): 229; *A Short Primer for Unsettled Laymen*, trans. Michael Waldstein (San Francisco: Ignatius Press, 1985, 1987), 86–87; *Theo-Drama* II, 123 and 253; *Explorations in Theology* IV, 416; *Theo-Logic* III, 234 and 270; and *The Threefold Garland*, 30–31.

itself out."⁶⁴ It is, however, difficult to discern in the so-called salvific act of Christ's estrangement from the Father—regardless of whether this estrangement is motivated by love⁶⁵—the means to our nearness to him: nearness, that is to say, in the specific form of a converted will, wherein lies the grace of salvation, as St. Thomas teaches.⁶⁶

It is with good reason, in fact, that Michel Beaudin recognizes Balthasar as insisting too unilaterally upon a resolution "from on high," that is to say, one wherein the eschatological perspective is almost exclusive. Everything leads back to a drama between the Father and the Son. Hence the risk, as Beaudin sees it, that the Trinitarian relation "expressed by the pre-existent obedience" might "substitute itself for the God-man relation rather than integrating it."⁶⁷ And this, I might add, would regretfully hinder the dialogue that I proposed in chapter three and that I will again touch upon in our general conclusion between Thomists and disciples of Balthasar based upon their common theme of the integration of human freedom into divine communion, whence Balthasar's analogy of reciprocal surrender.

In question here, more specifically, is not simply *whether* Balthasar would allow us a "place," as it were, within his saving mission, such that we might speak of an "inclusive representation [*Inklusive Stellvertretung*]"⁶⁸ in virtue of which Christ's mission is portrayed as opening up "a space of effective— that is, not predetermined—freedom for man," as we have seen in chapter three of this volume. Still more difficult is the important question of how "Jesus Christ's free availability (*disponibilità*) to die on the Cross *pro nobis* [in the particularly Balthasarian sense of vicarious representation] makes possible the liberation of human freedom": especially without recourse to the idea—which Angelo Scola denies as characterizing Balthasar's thought— that Christ's act of redemptive "substitution" might be understood as his "mechanically" taking our place, so as to fulfill what we could not do on our

---

64. Balthasar, *Heart of the World*, 40.

65. Balthasar follows Adrienne in arguing that the Father shows his love for the Son precisely by allowing the latter to realize his most profound desire to save us in precisely this manner. See, for example, *The Glory of the Lord* VII, 538.

66. "No one receives a suitable remedy against sin unless first he acknowledges his failure, so that man in his lowliness, not relying on himself, may put his hope in God, by whom alone sin can be healed" (Thomas Aquinas, *SCG* IV, c. 55, 12). Hence, "the flow of salvation from Christ to men is [...] through the zeal of good will in which a man cleaves to Christ" (ibid., c. 55, 30).

67. Beaudin, *Obéissance et solidarité*, 307. "God appears to occupy alone the human pole [of the Creator-creature relation], which for him [Balthasar] seems to serve only as a form of expression" (306). Cf. Balthasar, *TheoDrama* III, 535; *Prayer*, 57; and *Engagement with God*, 75.

68. See Karl-Heinz Menke, *Stellvertretung*, 278; and Tanguy Marie Pouliquen, *Libres en Christ. La liberté chrétienne selon l'anthropologie de Hans Urs von Balthasar* (Nouan-le-Fuzelier, France: Éditions des Béatitudes, 2008).

own.⁶⁹ In short, the question that I am raising is not only whether human freedom is—at least in Balthasar's mind—liberated by Christ's redemptive act,⁷⁰ nor even whether, once liberated, this freedom is charged to partake of Christ's mission.⁷¹ Rather, the question is how, by Christ's assuming our place of estrangement from God, our freedom can be liberated without violation. As the *Catechism* has put it so well:

> God's free initiative demands *man's free response,* for God has created man in his image by conferring on him, along with freedom, the power to know him and love him. The soul only enters freely into the communion of love. God immediately touches and directly moves the heart of man [without violating his freedom; hence, for example, by way of the powerful force of our attraction to his perfect goodness]. He has placed in man a longing for truth and goodness that only he can satisfy.⁷²

Hence, when it comes to freely choosing God over sin, the Church is also clear in proclaiming that "to do its work grace must uncover sin so as to convert our hearts and bestow on us 'righteousness to eternal life through Jesus Christ our Lord.' "Like a physician who probes the wound before treating it, God, by his Word and by his Spirit casts a living light on sin."⁷³ Balthasar, however, sadly remains ambiguous in responding to the question of the means to the end of conversion, although he does hold to the dignity of human freedom.⁷⁴

Far more consistent with Catholic (including, most especially, Thomistic) teaching and even with much of his own⁷⁵ and Adrienne's teaching is, I will argue, the image of Christ crucified calling forth from hardened hearts love in return for (or in response to) love. Hence Aquinas, for example, argues for the fittingness of Christ's passion in this: that "man knows thereby how much God loves him, and is thereby stirred to love Him in return, and herein lies the perfection of human salvation."⁷⁶ Similarly, "nothing so induces us to love one as the experience of his love for us. But God's love for men could be demonstrated to man in no way more effective than this: He willed to be united to man in person, for it is proper to love to unite the lover

---

69. Scola, *The Nuptial Mystery*, 236. See also Balthasar, *Explorations in Theology* IV, 418.

70. As Pope John Paul II has put it, "freedom itself needs to be set free" (*Veritatis Splendor*, no. 86).

71. See the excellent summary of this problem by Jacques Servais, "Préface" to Pouliquen, *Libres en Christ*, 15–18.

72. *The Catechism of the Catholic Church*, no. 2002. See also our treatment in chapter three of human perfection and our defense of Balthasar against the charge of voluntarism.

73. Ibid., no. 1848.

74. This ambiguity is particularly apparent in his relatively late essay "On Vicarious Representation" in *Explorations in Theology* IV, 415–22.

75. Cf. Schumacher, "The Concept of Representation in the Theology of Hans Urs von Balthasar."

76. Thomas Aquinas, *ST* III, q. 46, a. 3; cf. *SCG* IV, c. 55, 10.

with the beloved so far as possible."[77] It is thus not surprising that although Christ is recognized by the angelic doctor as meriting our salvation "from the beginning of His conception," he recognizes obstacles "on our side." These are said more specifically to hinder us "from securing the effect of His preceding merits," whence the "necessity" of Christ's passion: "to remove such hindrances."[78] "To be sure, the power of the divine Incarnation is equal to the salvation of all men, but the fact that some are not saved thereby comes from their indisposition: they are unwilling to take unto themselves the fruit of the Incarnation; they do not cleave to the incarnate God by faith and love."[79]

Christ's passion does not therefore merely free us from defect or deliver us from sin. More positively, it is said by the angelic doctor to provide an example of obedience, humility, constancy, justice, and the other virtues requisite for our salvation (cf. 1 Pt 2:21). Knowing, as a result of this striking manifestation of love, the price of our redemption (cf. 1 Cor 6:20), we are furthermore encouraged to refrain from sin and stirred to love God, who in the person of his Son "died for us while we were still sinners" (Rom 5:8).[80] Christ's passion is thus the proper cause of the forgiveness of sins not only by way of redemption (as head, he delivers his members) and efficacy (his humanity is the instrument of his divinity) but also and especially by inspiring our charity, in virtue of which we procure pardon.[81] Because, moreover, Christ willed that we be conformed to him chiefly in humility and meekness, these were the virtues "especially resplendent" in his passion.[82]

It follows, in Aquinas's logic, that Christ not only justifies us by *his* personal actions—namely his merit and atonement for us—but also by *our* operation in his regard: we are justified by faith in him.[83] Augustine's statement—"He who created you without you will not justify you without you"[84]—is

77. Thomas Aquinas, *SCG* IV, c. 54.

78. Thomas Aquinas, *ST* III, q. 48, a. 1, ad. 2. See also q. 46, a. 2, where St. Thomas clarifies the sense of the word "necessity" with regard to Christ's passion. In short, St. Thomas prefers to address the fittingness of the passion, rather than its necessity. See *ST* III, q. 1, a. 2. Torrell observes in this regard that Aquinas appeals "to the three predominantly popular reasons" accounting for the Incarnation: "the healing of the wound caused by sin (*remedium peccati*); the restoration (*reparatio*) of humanity to friendship with God; and satisfaction for sin," by which is meant the freeing of the human being from the slavery of sin (*Christ and Spirituality in St. Thomas Aquinas*, 81); cf. *ST* III, q. 1, a. 2. On the infinite value of every suffering of Christ, see *Comp* I, 231.

79. Thomas Aquinas, *SCG* IV, c. 55, 10.   80. Cf. Thomas Aquinas, *ST* III, q. 46, a. 3.

81. Ibid., a. 1.

82. Cf. Thomas Aquinas, *ST* I-II, q. 68, a. 1; and *Comp* I, 227. On the moral exemplarism of Christ, see, for example, *ST* III, q. 1, a. 2; q. 21, a. 1, ad. 1; q. 39, a. 2, ad. 1; q. 40, a. 1, ad. 3 and a. 2, ad. 1; and q. 41, a. 1. See also the important points of Perrier with regard to the exemplarity of Christ in "L'enjeu christologique de la satisfaction (II)," 247.

83. Thomas Aquinas, *De Ver*, q. 28, a. 8, ad. 6.

84. Augustine, *Sermo* 169, "*De verbis apostoli. Ephes, cap. VI, 23*," c. 11 (PL 38:923). Cf. Thomas Aquinas, *De Ver*, q. 29, a. 4.

thus interpreted by Thomas as meaning: "not without you disposing yourself to receive grace."[85] Or, as Pope John Paul II sets this profound intuition in vivid images borrowed from Scripture (cf. Apoc 3:20):

> Christ, precisely as the crucified one [...] stands at the door and knocks at the heart of every man, without restricting his freedom, but instead seeking to draw from this very freedom love, which is not only an act of solidarity with the suffering Son of man, but also a kind of "mercy" shown by each one of us to the Son of the eternal Father. In the whole of this messianic program of Christ, in the whole revelation of mercy through the cross, could man's dignity be more highly respected and ennobled, for, in obtaining mercy [in, more specifically, allowing himself to be moved by this magnificent display of love], he [the human person] is in a sense the one who at the same time "shows mercy" [to, that is to say, this divine "beggar," the suffering Son of Man, who seeks the love of humankind: "I thirst" (Jn 19:28)]?[86]

Or, again, in the words of St. Thomas: in order that the reconciliation between God and man realized by Christ might be meritorious for us, "it is necessary that reconiliation be made on our part, namely, in baptism and in penance. And then we cease from sins."[87] "In the spiritual life, consequently, there can be no opposition," as Pope Pius XII teaches, "between the action of God, who pours forth his grace into men's hearts so that the work of the redemption may always abide, and the tireless collaboration of man, who must not render vain the gift of God (cf. 2 Cor 6:1)."[88]

This chapter is thus an attempt—within the specific context of expositing the difference-in-unity of the individual and the community as still another analogy of the mystery of Trinitarian difference-in-unity—of demonstrating that the foundation for such an understanding of redemption: one that pierces hardened hearts (cf. Ps 81/80:13; Jer 7:24; Mk 3:5) with the arrow of Christ's burning love, provoking an authentic response of love. To be sure, we will not deny that many of the images that Adrienne employs to describe her mystical partaking of the paschal mysteries—experiences whose authenticity was "never doubted" by Balthasar, as he attests[89]—are at the origin of

---

85. Thomas Aquinas, *De Ver*, q. 28, a. 8, ad. 6; *Super Rom* III, lect. 3, 309 (= *Super Epistolam B. Pauli ad Romanus lectura*, in *Commentary on the Letter of Saint Paul to the Romans*, trans. Fabien R. Larcher, eds. John Mortensen and Enrique Alarcón, vol. 38 of the Latin/English Edition of the *Works of St. Thomas Aquinas* [Lander, Wyo.: The Aquinas Institute for the Study of Sacred Doctrine, 2012]). Cf. Balthasar, *Epilogue*, 119; and *Theo-Logic* III, 271.

86. Pope John Paul II, *Dives in Misericordia*, no. 8; see also *Dominium et Vivificantem*, no. 47.

87. Thomas Aquinas, *Super ad II Cor V*, lect. 5, no. 200 (= *Super II Epistolam B. Pauli ad Corinthios lectura*, in *Commentary on the Letters of Saint Paul to the Corinthians*, trans. Fabien R. Larcher, eds. John Mortensen and Enrique Alarcón, vol. 37 of the Latin/English Edition of the *Works of St. Thomas Aquinas* [Lander, Wyo.: The Aquinas Institute for the Study of Sacred Doctrine, 2012]).

88. Pope Pius XII, *Mediator Dei* (November 20, 1947); *DZ* 3846.

89. See his note to this effect in Speyr, *Kreuz und Hölle* I, 17.

the latter's controversial presentation of redemption. We will nevertheless argue that there are other images to be found in Adrienne's corpus (especially in her main corpus)[90] that might more readily lend themselves to a Catholic interpretation of redemption in harmony with Thomistic doctrine, by respecting her profoundly Trinitarian perspective. Such, more specifically, is an interpretation which—without usurping God's absolute freedom and his full prerogative to effect our salvation by his own initiative and infinite goodness[91]—accords a space for action not only to the human nature of Christ,[92] but also to human persons, who are held as a responsible agents.

This means taking seriously Balthasar's own requirement of a "sufficiently dramatic" theology of redemption: namely one in which the human being, "guilty as he is in God's sight," cannot simply "lie passive and anaesthetized on the operating table while the cancer of his sin is cut out."[93] At stake, in short, is the connection between the event of our salvation on Calvary—including "the greatest sin that man could commit," namely the refusal and even killing of "the Son of God, consubstantial with the Father"—and the grace of conversion: the condition *sine qua non* for both the granting of the grace of forgiveness and its reception.[94]

To be sure, "the greatest sin on man's part is matched in the heart of the Redeemer," to quote Pope John Paul II, "by the oblation of supreme love that conquers the evil of all the sins of man."[95] The actual forgiveness of sin does not, however, consist in an act of overweighing the balance, as it were: the magnificence of God's love overcoming even the worst of human sins.[96] Rather, as this same pope very aptly teaches, the Cross of Christ is efficacious in forgiving sin by opening human consciences to the action of the Holy

---

90. In question here are precisely the posthumous works, which are obviously of a more mystical nature, including, in the present case, the two-volume work—*Kreuz und Hölle*—wherein are recorded (in the first volume) Adrienne's mystical suffering during the passion-tide each year (from 1941 to 1965)—and her so-called "missions to hell [*Auftragshölle*]," wherein Adrienne was, as Balthasar explains, within a form of "being in the spirit [*Im-Geist-Seins*]" such that "the experiencing and speaking subject was reduced to a pure objective mission-subject" (Balthasar, introduction to Speyr, *Kreuz und Hölle* I, 7). The reader is to be reminded that while these are indeed revelatory of Adrienne's influence upon Balthasar, they are also to be read for what they are: accounts of presumably mystical experiences, which were, as Balthasar attests, "in no way enlarged, rounded off, set aside" (ibid., 12) by him.

91. See, for example, *The Catechism of the Catholic Church*, no. 2010.

92. As Balthasar would have it, "anthropology could be and ought to be treated as a function of Christology" (*Theo-Drama* II, 428); see also *Engagement with God*, 75. On God's free prerogative in realizing our salvation, see *The Catechism of the Catholic Church*, no. 2010.

93. Balthasar, *Theo-Drama* IV, 318; see also *Theo-Drama* II, 91 and 119; *The Office of Peter*, 134; and *Mysterium Paschale*, 133. The drama between divine and human freedom nonetheless appears for Balthasar as realized "in God" (see *Theo-Drama* II, 428).

94. Pope John Paul II, *Dominum et Vivificantem*, nos. 31, 42, and 46.

95. Ibid., no. 32.

96. Cf. Thomas Aquinas, *ST* I, q. 48, a. 3, ad. 2.

Spirit, who convinces the sinner not only of God's unfathomable mercy, but also of his own sin.[97] This he does precisely and "always in relation to the Cross of Christ"[98] and also therefore to "the sin of those who 'have not believed in him,' and who condemned Jesus Christ to death on the Cross."[99] By highlighting similar insights in Adrienne's work, I will seek in the remainder of this chapter to propose a more balanced (that is to say, Catholic) understanding of redemption: one that requires, as I have insisted throughout this work, that we read Balthasar in union with Adrienne von Speyr.

The Love Command at the Service of Divine Communion: Toward a More Adequate Theology of Redemption

Despite the problematic character of Balthasar's theology of redemption, as I have exposed it above, one of Adrienne's most central intuitions speaks in favor of a theology more true to the demands of both divine and human freedom: a theology, that is to say, wherein human freedom is incorporated into divine freedom by the very means that characterize the latter: the reciprocal and loving surrender of the divine persons to one another.[100] Such, I would propose, is the manner wherein we might best understand the mystery of our redemption: not so much in the identification of Christ with our sinful condition and the subsequent condemnation of sin in his flesh (cf. Rom 8:3), as in the super-generous and irrevocable surrender of God's own being to all of humankind in view of our incorporation therein (cf. Jn 17). This incorporation, Adrienne fittingly teaches, as we saw in chapter three, is achieved precisely by way of our reception of God's gift, which can be had in no other way than by the surrender of our very selves to him, who is always the first to surrender himself to us.

As Balthasar himself would have it, the fulfillment of finite freedom requires not only that the "Infinite take the finite into itself" but also that the finite "be capable of taking the Infinite into itself."[101] Far from denying the biblical data of revelation, this requires, as Balthasar would certainly agree, that we read it attentively with the mind of the Church, for whom divine

---

97. See Pope John Paul II, *Dominum et Vivificantem*, nos. 31 and 43.
98. Ibid., no. 44; see also nos. 32–33. From a Thomistic perspective, cf. Perrier, "L'eneju christologique de la satisfaction (II)," 247.
99. Pope John Paul II, *Dominum et Vivificantem*, no. 29.
100. See Balthasar, *Theo-Drama* II, 258.
101. Ibid., 201; see also 123. Or, as St. Thomas reasons, "every beloved is in a lover. Therefore, by the Holy Spirit not only is God in us, but we also are in God. Hence, we read in 1 John (4:16, 13): 'He that abideth in charity abideth in God, and God in him' and: in this we know that we abide in Him and He in us: because He hath given us of His Spirit'" (*SCG* IV, c. 21, 4)

justice is never set in opposition to divine mercy.[102] Indeed, the one is best understood in terms of the other: God's justice requires that hardened hearts "break" so as to receive from the abundance of his love, manifest as mercy. Such, in fact, is a love which is "more powerful than sin,"[103] precisely because it does not give up on even the most hardened sinner, but gives to the very end: and there is no end to infinity!

From the perspective of a human race hardened by sin and the effects of sin, however, divine love can hardly do otherwise than manifest itself in the very form that it has assumed: that of the suffering servant of God "despised and rejected by men; a man of sorrows, and acquainted with grief" (Is 53:3).[104] Biblical revelation thus sets us before a love which is "wounded for our transgressions" and "bruised for our iniquities" (Is 53:3–5). This need not mean—and this is hardly a moot point in this discussion—that love incarnate is *actually* "stricken, smitten by God," but only that it is so regarded by men (cf. Is 53:4). Hence Aquinas reads St. Paul (2 Cor 5:21: "Him, who knew no sin, he has made sin for us") with attention to an important distinction: a thing might be qualified in a certain manner "not because it is so, but because man considers it such." Hence, when we read "he has made sin," this means that he allowed him to be "regarded [as] a sinner: 'he was numbered with the transgressors' (Is 53:12)."[105] In short, to recognize Christ as "stricken, smitten by God" is an only too human interpretation of God's "scandalous" love (cf. 1 Cor 1:18) which refuses to defend itself from our rejection: "Like a lamb that is led to the slaughter [...] he opened not his mouth" (Is 53:7).

Far from being rejected by the Father, Christ is thus portrayed as one whose love for the Father is revealed in the act of communicating the superabundance of the Father's love for him (the Son) to those whom the Father wills to call his sons and daughters. Adrienne thus portrays the incarnate Son as saying to the Father: "You have given me such fullness as man that I cannot take it all in: It fills me to overflowing, and I must give it to others!"[106] Or to describe the same mystery from the perspective of the Father, this time in Balthasar's words: Christ is "the ecstasy of the divine eros flowing out of itself

---

102. See, for example, Pope John Paul II, *Dives in Misericordia*, no. 14. Cf. Balthasar, *The Glory of the Lord* I, 474.

103. Ibid.

104. "The death of Jesus was no accident but was the inevitable outcome of the clash between God's love and sinful humanity's refusal to accept that love" (John O'Donnell, "Hans Urs von Balthasar: The Form of His Theology" in Schindler, *Hans Urs von Balthasar: His Life and Work*, 211).

105. Thomas Aquinas, *Super ad II Cor V*, lect. 5, no. 200. Thomas teaches that Christ does not take on our sin but rather "the penalty due to sin" (*SCG* IV, c. 55, 22).

106. Speyr, *World of Prayer*, 81. Cf. Thomas Aquinas, *ST* q. 7, a. 1, 9; and q. 8, aa. 1 and 5.

in which God hands himself over and entrusts himself to the world."[107] Such indeed is a gift which is given so radically, so irrevocably, so "recklessly,"[108] that it refuses to be withdrawn, even when it meets the most extreme form of human resistance: that of death by crucifixion.[109] "The Father's Word, made flesh, is definitively given and distributed by him and is never to be taken back."[110]

Precisely as such—as absolutely, even recklessly vulnerable and limitless in its patience and mercy—this (divine) love "conquers by total self-surrender."[111] In other words, in this particularly vulnerable form, God's love is efficacious in breaking down our resistance: of drawing forth love from our hardened hearts in return to love. Or, as Balthasar would have it, "the self-fulfilling Word of God, that is, his perfect self-giving, must elicit a perfect answer from and in the free creature; absolute freedom must not force or overpower the creature's freedom."[112]

As for Adrienne, she explains that when one comes to understand that the Lord has "personally suffered and died for our sins," his or her soul is "blasted open [*aufgesprengt*]"[113] so as to be receptive of the gift of the Eucharist and the sacrament of reconciliation, which, of course, are fruits of the Lord's passion. Or, as John Paul II would have it: "Conversion to God always consists *in discovering His mercy*. [...] Authentic knowledge of the God of mercy, the God of tender love, is a constant and inexhaustible source of conversion, not only as a momentary interior act but also as a permanent attitude, as a state of mind. Those who come to know God in this way, who 'see' Him in this way, can live only in a state of being continually converted to Him."[114]

Ultimately this means that a Christian doctrine of substitution can never—as St. Thomas rightly insists[115]—consist simply in Christ taking our place

---

107. Balthasar, *Explorations in Theology* II, 78. Reference here is made to Dionysius. See also Balthasar, *The Glory of the Lord* I, 673; and *The Christian State of Life*, 234. Cf. Speyr, *Theologie der Geschlechter*, 132; and *John* II, 69. This image might be understood as compatible with the Thomistic presentation of redemptive grace as proceeding from the grace that filled the human soul of Christ. See *ST* III, q. 8, a. 5; and *De Ver*, q. 29, a. 5.

108. Cf. Balthasar, *Theo-Drama* IV, 328.

109. Cf. Thomas Aquinas, *ST* III, q. 47, a. 1.

110. Balthasar, *New Elucidations*, 117; see also *Theo-Logic* II, 148.

111. Balthasar, *Theo-Drama* II, 161.

112. Ibid., 123; see also *The Threefold Garland*, 30–31.

113. Speyr, *Die katholische Briefe* II, 178.

114. Pope John Paul II, *Dives in Misericordia*, no. 13.

115. Torrell suggests that rather than speak of substitution—an idea which is easily misleading—we might join St. Thomas in his presentation of a mystical solidarity based upon the doctrine of the mystical body of Christ (cf. *ST* III, q. 48, a. 1; and a. 2, ad. 1), an idea which Torrell regretfully observes to be lacking in much contemporary theology of redemption, although he praises Balthasar for the impor-

without our willingness to take our place within Christ. This conviction, in fact, is at the origin of the distinction between objective and subjective redemption: a distinction which nonetheless supposes that Christ infuses his "exact obedience"[116] of filial love, as we shall see, into the Church and each of her members. Such a portrayal of redemption as an integration of human freedom within divine freedom by way of a mutual surrender—God's absolutely primary surrender of himself, in the person of his Son to the human person, and the latter's responsive surrender of him- or herself to God—nonetheless presupposes, from Adrienne's perspective, the profound unity of divine love as paternal and filial.

There would be no redemption through the Son for the world and for each individual if the Father had not permitted and bestowed this work of love. This is why every distinction between justice and love disappears in God. The Father is very far from embodying justice above the Son's love: on the contrary, he stands at the origin of the entire work of love that the Son carries out. The love of the Son is not in the least directed against the justice of the Father, and still less does the Father have a love distinct from the Son's love. [...] There exists only one single love of the Father for the Son and of the Son for the Father, and God's love for the man is given its place in this love.[117]

This mystery of love's unity is poignantly portrayed in Adrienne's exposition of the love commandment: "This is my commandment, that you love one another as I have loved you" (Jn 15:12). In issuing this command just before his imminent death, Christ does not intend to exclude himself from the disciples' love, as might be gathered from his words, "where I am going you cannot come" (Jn 13:33). Rather, his intention is, Adrienne teaches, to give them "a possibility of living in him without seeing him." This he does because "the *one another* of this new love [of the disciples for one another] proceeds from the *one another* between the Father and Son," which always supposes the Spirit's presence.[118]

---

tance that he accords to it in his *Theo-Drama*; see Torrell's *Pour nous les hommes et pour notre salut*, 251, 265–66, and 308–9. Similar is the patristic theme of the "wonderful exchange" (304), an idea which is, of course, also very present in Balthasar's theology. In offering himself as a sacrifice for our sins, Christ certainly did not think of us, Torrell argues, as "passive beneficiaries." Instead, he invistes us to participate (289). "Only Christ merited, say Protestant theologians, and they can then push to a limit the idea of substitution even to the point of denying any active role to the human being." So too Catholics, he admits, recognize that Christ alone merited. "But we add, he asks us to merit in turn and he gives us the means to do so: not so that we might add to his merits, but so that we might freely colllaborate in his work of salvation" (266).

116. Balthasar, *Theo-Drama* III, 123. Cf. Speyr, *John* IV, 292; and *Das Buch der Gehorsam*, 51–52. See also our treatment of this mystery in chapter three of this volume.

117. Speyr, *John* II, 443. Cf. Thomas Aquinas, *ST* III, q. 47, a. 3.

118. Speyr, *John* I, 66; on the Spirit's presence, see *Theologie der Geschlechter*, 96.

By this statement, Adrienne means not only that Christ—precisely as "the form of one of the Father's creatures [*die Gestalt eines väterlichen Geschöpfs*]"—is the "meeting place" of the love of God and the love of neighbor: in loving him, we love both God and neighbor, because he, the God-man, is both.[119] It also means that the incarnate Lord, the new Adam (cf. Rom 5:12–18), is the first to obey the very command that he himself lays down for his disciples. In other words, Adrienne understands this command as implying the participation of Christ's disciples within Christ's own obedience to the Father.[120] As such, her insight is fully compatible with that of St. Thomas in his commentary on John 10:10: "He [Christ] adds an example when he says, *as I have kept my Father's commandments and abide in his love.* For just as the love which the Father has for him is the model or standard of Christ's love for us, so Christ wants his obedience to be the model of our obedience. By saying this Christ shows that he abided in the Father's love because in all things he kept the Father's commandments."[121] As for us, "keeping the commandments is an effect of divine love," Aquinas teaches. "For from the fact that God loves us, he influences us and helps us to fulfil his commandments, which we cannot do without grace; in this is love, not that we love God but that he loved us first (1 John 4:10)."[122]

As for Adrienne, she holds that even in commanding the disciples, the Lord acts in obedience to the Father through the Spirit's mediation.[123] In other words, he does not simply bring to earth a command "which would be the formula and result of his life," for he actually lives it through and through "not for himself, but for the Father and for mankind. His whole life was the expression of the obedience of love [...] that he had stamped as the quintessence of his life."[124] By the same disposition of loving openness, or vulnerability, the incarnate Son is observed by Adrienne as thus given, without reserve, to the Father and to the world alike, so as to set a precedent for the formula expressed in the first epistle of John: "he who loves God should love his brother also" (4:21). All of this follows, for Adrienne, as a consequence of the fact that God's love for us not only derives from his love for the Son, but is also inseparable from this love, as St. Thomas also teaches.[125] So too we

---

119. See Speyr, *Die katholischen Briefe* II, 165 and 191.
120. See, for example, Speyr, *The Boundless God*, 124; *John* III, 133; and Balthasar, *Unless You Become Like This Child*, 40–41.
121. Thomas Aquinas, *Super Ioan* 15, lect. 2, no. 2003.
122. Ibid., no. 2002.
123. See Speyr, *The Countenance of the Father*, 61–62.
124. Speyr, *Die katholische Briefe* II, 271–72; see also *Das Buch der Gehorsam*, 51; cf. Balthasar, *A Theology of History*, 51–60.
125. "We are loved by God, not for what we are in ourselves, but in him who by himself is beloved of

are included in the Son's love for the Father.[126] In fact, the incarnate Son is, Adrienne teaches, love itself in the form of man.[127]

By this expression "love in the form of man," the Swiss mystic means, first of all, that Christ's life reveals the very love that motivates the Incarnation: the Son's love for the Father and the Holy Spirit, as well as their love for him.[128] Because, however, love in God is not only transitive but also "intransitive,"[129] it also means that Christ manifests this love as "love on the whole [*die Liebe überhaupt*]," as love which "essentially incorporates everything into its sphere." This is possible, Adrienne maintains, because the Father loved us, his creatures, as his children "from the start" within the "unity of love [*in der Liebeseinheit*]" that he shares with the Son and the Holy Spirit.[130] The Father loves us, more specifically, with the same love that he has for his Son,[131] and it is this love that is communicated to the disciples through Christ's ministry: Christ's love for us *is* the love with which the Father loves him, and this love also includes the Holy Spirit, who has "the function of love" in the Trinity.[132] Indeed, in the words of Balthasar, inspired by St. John, Jesus is "the love that flows from God the Father to men."[133]

It is this Trinitarian character of God's love for us that Adrienne recognizes as the basis of the love command: the Son's revelation and mediation of the Father's love, a love "in which we are all to have a share"[134] as sons and

---

the Father. Thus the Apostle adds 'in his beloved Son' [cf. Eph 1:6] on account of whom he loves us and to the degree that we are like him. For love is based on similarity [...]. By his own nature, the Son is similar to the Father, he is beloved before all else and essentially. Hence he is naturally, and in a most excellent way, loved by the Father. We, on the other hand, are sons through adoption to the degree that we are conformed to his Son; in this way we enjoy a certain participation in the divine love" (Thomas Aquinas, *Super Eph* I, lect. 2, no. 16). See also *ST* I, q. 37, a. 2, ad. 3; and Torrell, *Saint Thomas Aquinas* II: *Spiritual Master*, 175–78.

126. Speyr, *The Letter to the Ephesians*, 29. See also *Die katholischen Briefe* II, 271. Cf. Balthasar, *Theo-Drama* V, 123.

127. Speyr, *Korinther* I, 401. Similarly, Balthasar presents salvation as an outpouring of love. "The Son does not call himself the eternal product of this outpouring; rather, he is within it and he himself pours out—his outpouring is the 'truth' that reveals the Father's outpouring" (Balthasar, *You Have the Words of Everlasting Life: Scripture Meditations*, trans. Dennis Martin [San Francisco: Ignatius Press, 1991], 70).

128. See Speyr, *The Letter to the Colossians*, 30. See my more thorough treatment of this theme in chapter four of the present volume.

129. See Speyr, *Das Wort und die Mystik* II, 108; cf. Balthasar, *Theo-Drama* V, 122.

130. Speyr, *Das Wort und die Mystik* II, 110; see also *The Letter to the Ephesians*, 27; Cf. Balthasar, *Mysterium Paschale*, 79.

131. Speyr, *Die katholischen Briefe* II, 164. Christ's obedience to the Father—precisely as the revelation of his eternal love for the Father—is also the revelation of the love of the Father. See Balthasar, "General Introduction to the Posthumous Works" in Speyr, *Book of All Saints*, 5.

132. Speyr, *Theologie der Geschlechter*, 96; cf. *John* II, 292.

133. Balthasar, *The Glory of the Lord* VII, 454.

134. Speyr, *The Letter to the Ephesians*, 47; see also *John* III, 133.

daughters of the Father in and through the only-begotten Son. The filial obedience of Christ, which is the manifestation of the paternal command,[135] is of essential importance here, for it reveals the salvific *pro nobis* ("for us men an for our salvation") of the Nicene Creed[136] as a revelation of the even more profound *pro Patre* (*"for the Father"*).[137]

In the first instance, this means that the incarnate Son does everything out of love for the Father, even to the extent that he identifies with his mission from the Father.[138] Capable of understanding, as no other human being can, the depths of paternal love from which creation precedes, and desiring to offer the Father a love far greater than the offence it has shown him,[139] the incarnate Son offers "the full response of the world to the Father's extravagant love."[140] This he does in the form of his most profound surrender, that of the Eucharist, as inseparable from the passion. In this total surrender, he "loves and suffers without differentiation between the Father and mankind. He no longer differentiates and cannot even differentiate, for the Father's commission [*Auftrag*] has mankind as its content."[141] Hence, the terrible event of Calvary is understood as the fulfillment—in time—of the Son's eternal surrender to the Father.[142] What is revealed in the Son's exorbitant suffering on the Cross, for example, is a revelation of the manner in which the Son has always given himself to the Father in response to the Father's own infinite love for him.[143]

From this perspective, Christ's historical sacrifice and surrender are not only, nor simply, the revelation of a love which does not stop short of any

---

135. Cf. Thomas Aquinas, *SCG* IV, c. 55, 17. Christ's mission and obedience are so perfectly coordinated that what comes from the Father as a "command" (Jn 10:18 and 12:49) returns to him as the Son's entreaty: "May they all be one; even as thou, Father, art in me, and I in thee" (Jn 17:20). One might observe in John's Gospel, for example, a perfect parallelism between the objective and paternal perspective of redemption (Jn 3:16–19) and the subjective and filial one (Jn 12:46–49). This accord between the Father's command and the Son's obedience is, according to Balthasar, "the economic form of the common spiration of the Spirit" (Balthasar, *Theo-Drama* III, 188) who are, as the fruit of their mutual love and as the "seal" of their common "yes," witnesses to their eternal unanimity.

136. Cf. *DZ* 125: "Credimus in unum Deum [...] Et in unum Dominum nostrum Iesum Christum [...] qui propter nostram salutem descendit, incarnatus est et homo factus est et passus est et resurrexit tertia die [...] [We believe in one God [...] and in one Lord Jesus Christ [...], who for us men and for our salvation came down and became flesh, was made man, suffered, and rose again on the third day [...].").

137. Cf. Thomas Aquinas, *ST* III, q. 47, a. 2, ad. 1.

138. Speyr, *The Letter to the Ephesians*, 32; cf. *John* I, 106 and 145.

139. Speyr, *John* III, 311; and *The Countenance of the Father*, 61–62.

140. Speyr, *Das Wort und die Mystik* II, 523; see also 101 and 510; *Theologie der Geschlechter*, 133; and *The Letter to the Ephesians*, 33. Cf. Balthasar, *The Threefold Garland*, 29–30.

141. Speyr, *John* III, 70; see also *John* II, 49.

142. See Speyr, *Das Wort und die Mystik* II, 53.

143. The Son, Adrienne argues, "is both an expression of and a response to the Father" (Speyr, *Confession*, 22). See also Balthasar, *A Theology of History*, 32.

obstacle, of eternal divine love which gives without counting the cost and, still more specifically, of this same love as it is extravagantly poured out in the presence of an unbelieving and unreceptive world.[144] More profoundly still, it is a revelation of the Son's eternal heavenly "will to offer and surrender [*Opfer- und Hingabewillen*] in an inseparable union with the love of the Trinitarian God."[145] Indeed, in contemplating the Son—whether in the Incarnation, the hidden life, the public mission, the passion and death, the descent into hell, or the Resurrection—one must never abstract from the Trinity, Adrienne teaches.[146] Hence, she presents the Son as "committed to the Father's will, the Father to the path the Son has set before him, and the Spirit to both."[147] Not surprisingly, then, it is especially on the Cross—when the Father's will is most apparent in the dying Son—that Adrienne recognizes the Trinity as most clearly revealed.[148]

On the other hand, it is precisely at this same moment that the Father withdraws "in absence," leaving the Son alone in view. Adrienne calls this "the revelation of the Father in his absence": "The revelation of the Son is such that it not only includes presence, but also exceeds presence because it is so truly presence that it no longer comes out as presence. For it is now that the infinity of the Father becomes really visible in this abandonment."[149] Meanwhile, the Son is said to be only an object of obedience "which he no longer knows," or which he "can no longer reflect upon." Because his experience of abandonment is so "complete," he cannot even remember his eternal consent to the passion. Even his memory is "submerged [*untergegangen*] in the night."[150] Although the Trinitarian union remains fully intact, the distinction between

---

144. See Speyr, *Das Wort und die Mystik* II, 113; cf. Balthasar, *Theo-Drama* IV, 328.

145. Speyr, *Korinther* I, 345. Cf. Thomas Aquinas, *ST* III, q. 46, a. 12; and q. 48, a. 5. In his commentary on Gal 2:19–21, St. Thomas points to three manners of being deliverd to death: "the Son delivered himself and the Father delivered his Son: he spared not even his own Son, but delivered him up for us (Rom 8:32). Judas, too, delivered him up (Mt 26:48). It is all one event, but the intention is not the same, because the Father did so out of love, the Son out of obedience along with love, but Judas out of avarice and treachery" (*Super Gal* II, lect. 6, no. 110 [= *Super Epistolam B. Pauli ad Galatas lectura*, in *Commentary on the Letters of Saint Paul to the Galatians and Ephesians*, trans. Fabien R. Larcher and Matthew L. Lamb, eds. John Mortensen and Enrique Alarcón, vol. 39 of the Latin/English Edition of the *Works of St. Thomas Aquinas* [Lander, Wyo.: The Aquinas Institute for the Study of Sacred Doctrine, 2012]).

146. See Speyr, *Das Wort und die Mystik* II, 115.

147. Speyr, *World of Prayer*, 28. Cf. Balthasar, *Theo-Drama* V, 517.

148. See Speyr, *The Boundless God*, 79; *Erde und Himmel* II, 228; and *Handmaid of the Lord*, 38.

149. Speyr, *The Boundless God*, 79. Balthasar specifies (in an editor's note) that this is "the mode of suffering [*Leidens-Modus*] of his [the Father's] presence" (ibid.); see also *The Countenance of the Father*, 84.

150. Speyr, *Das Wort und die Mystik* I, 91. It is as if, Adrienne explains, Christ were to say, "I once said Yes and this belongs to that [Yes]" (ibid.). "The Lord's time has from all eternity been loaned from the Father's eternity, and apart from his abandonment on the Cross, he always beholds time from the angle of eternity" (Speyr, *John* I, 145).

the divine persons has never been so clearly manifest as in the relationship between the "abandoned" Son and the Father "who abandons him."[151]

Ironically, it is precisely here, at the moment of this "abandonment"—the point at which the Father is said, in accord with biblical revelation (cf. Jn 3:16), to hand over the Son as proof of his love, that it is particularly difficult to recognize the Father's love, as Adrienne willfully acknowledges in reference to Romans 8:32:

> God did not spare his Son *but gave him up for us all.* For love of us he did something that we could never interpret as love, for love spares. The Father, however, not only did not spare the Son, he handed him over, turned away from him, betrayed him and cast him out into loneliness, allowed him to die in forsakenness. The cry on the Cross gives witness to this abandonment. And the whole is the sign of love for us who are unworthy, who do not understand it at all, who are weak in faith and in deeds of faith.[152]

Here the scriptural data sets us before the paradox of a love whose logic escapes us. At the heart of this mystery is, however, not only the revelation of human freedom in the form of sin—and thus also the "challenge,"[153] as Balthasar sees it, that this created freedom presents to divine freedom—but also and especially the specifically dogmatic challenge of simultaneously acknowledging the essential union of the divine persons, which cannot be separated from their reciprocal love, and the distinction of the divine persons, each of whom is, from Adrienne's perspective, a real agent of love, despite the fact that "in the world the Divine Persons work in common."[154]

As Adrienne puts it, the "outrageous" statement of St. Paul that God "did not spare his own Son but gave him up for us all" (Rom 8:32), together with the whole reality of Christ's violent death and suffering, actually attests to the unity of this love.[155] Combining the Johannine prologue and the parable of the wicked husbandmen who kill the vineyard owner's son (cf. Jn 1:10–11,

---

151. Speyr, *The Countenance of the Father*, 84; see also *John* III, 128; and *Apokalypse*, 523. Cf. Balthasar, *Epilogue*, 120–21; and *Prayer*, 169.

152. Speyr, *The Victory of Love*, 94.

153. See Balthasar, *Theo-Drama* V, 506. Balthasar argues that one should avoid the notion of the Trinity as somehow entangled in sin (an idea for which he faults process theology), but also the idea of the Trinity as hovering unmoved above the event of the Cross (an idea that he attributes to the doctrine of the beatific vision). See ibid., 333; and *Explorations in Theology* IV, 416.

154. Speyr, *The Letter to the Ephesians*, 21. The distinction of the divine persons, in turn, supposes the question of the unity between the immanent and the economic Trinity. For Adrienne, this means that "the meaning of the Cross is only complete in God; it is in God that the Son's eternal self-surrender, which integrates his sacrificial death in time and the Church's Eucharist, attains its full meaning" (Speyr, *Korinther* I, 345). See also Speyr, *Die Bergpredigt: Betrachtungen über Matthäus 5–7* (Einsiedeln: Johannes Verlag, 1948), 229; and *The Mystery of Death*, 74.

155. See Speyr, *The Victory of Love*, 96; cf. Balthasar, *Theo-Drama* V, 517.

Mk 12:1–12, Mt 21:33–43, and Lk 20:9–19), the Swiss mystic argues that it is in gifting the Son with the vineyard—those whom the Father had given him before the creation of the world[156]—that the Father hands him over to his enemies. The Son, meanwhile, loves and suffers for mankind "out of love for the Father" and thus also "because the Father loves mankind."[157] Such is the motivation behind his willingness to hand himself over (cf. Jn 10:18).[158]

Precisely at this point where the love of the Father and that of the Son appear particularly distinct, the pendulum swings in the other direction, revealing again the essential unity of this love.[159] For the Son loves us as one "compelled by the Father's love for mankind," but also as one experiencing this love "as if it were not his own love, but the love wholly belonging to the Father," so as to love mankind "in the Father," even unto death on the Cross.[160] Even his suffering is so completely committed to the Father, along with every aspect of his being, that it is as if he no longer possesses it. The Father alone is "the unlimited master of the suffering, the Son is only the one who carries it out, who surrenders himself up." This surrender is, more specifically, abasement: the beginning of the final descent of *agape*—including not only the Cross, but also the experience of abandonment and the descent into hell—whereby the Son is so purely human that Adrienne recognizes him as having "deposited his divinity with God." By this she suggests not only that his "magnificence" is "fully concealed and withdrawn from him," but also that he is "so naked" that "he no longer possesses even his destiny, but has left it in God's hands and goes denuded into the darkest night of suffering."[161]

Assuredly, this is not to deny the divinity of the dying Son, for it is precisely in his "bare" humanity, as it were, that Adrienne—faithful to the Johannine influence so apparent throughout her works (cf. Jn 17)—recognizes the clearest manifestation of his divinity: in that is to say, the specific form of his obedient realization of the Father's will.[162] "What he [the Father] bequeathed

---

156. See Speyr, *John* I, 99.

157. Speyr, *John* III, 133.

158. See, for example, Speyr, *John* II, 279–80; and *The Passion from Within*, 62.

159. "What is Two here can be shown only in unity: what is One here can be shown only in duality. There is no possibility of seeing the Son without the Father, or the Father without the Son. For, together, they form love" (Speyr, *John* II, 166).

160. Speyr, *John* III, 133. Indeed, he is said by Adrienne to be, even at the moment of the abandonment, radically "in the Father" (128). Cf. Thomas Aquinas, *SCG* IV, c. 55, 17.

161. Speyr, *John* IV, 78; cf. Balthasar, *Theo-Drama* V, 517.

162. Adrienne argues that the moment of the abandonment, which constitutes the point of the highest veiling of Christ's divinity—the point at which "only now [his] humanity [*Nur-noch-Menschlichkeit*]" is apparent—is precisely the point at which his divinity becomes again apparent in the form of his purity and absolute obedience (*Apokalypse*, 523). See also *Korinther* I, 53; *John* III, 311; and *The Passion from Within*, 61–62. On the depositing of his divinity, see *Bergpredigt*, 145.

to the Son—his mission with its path through the world—has now become fully the Son's possession, something the Son has accomplished so utterly that the Father's will has been fully realized and made apparent in the Son; while the Father himself withdraws into absence, so as to enable all the light to fall upon the Son."[163]

Precisely this explanation of love's unity—and thus also the unity of the divine will[164]—points again, however, to the distinction of the persons in the form of the Son's solitude: "The Son receives no praise from the Father, no thanks from the Spirit, no appreciation from mankind. He has to recognize this accomplishment in dry objectivity, in loneliness, without any encouragement, in deepest desperation and extreme anguish."[165] Indeed, in the hard objectivity of the Cross, Adrienne recognizes the Lord's love for the Father in the form of his obedience to an order.[166] His eternal resolve "to show the Father his whole love," despite every possible obstacle invented by the freedom of mankind, is manifest in precisely this way.[167]

This in turn supposes that divine love has, as it were, invented for itself precisely this mode of revealing itself, which is also to again admit the unity of the immanent and economic Trinity.[168] As Adrienne puts it, "Not only to the Father but also to himself as God in heaven he says, 'If it be possible, let this chalice pass from me'—like a man who has made a big life-decision in his youth that with the years becomes extremely difficult to maintain, and now he once again talks with the self that made the decision at the time."[169]

Having been, as it were, "discussed and agreed between them both [the Father and the Son]" this (divine) resolve nonetheless lies beyond his (human) reach, as the passion precedes. During the solitude of the Cross, it lies "entirely in the hands of the Father" for safekeeping.[170] For to be able to recall this resolution would, Adrienne argues, somehow detract from his "perfect suffering,"[171] and the Son does not wish to allow for even the slight-

---

163. Speyr, *The Countenance of the Father*, 84.
164. See Speyr, *The Boundless God*, 79; and *The Countenance of the Father*, 84. See also chapter seven of the present volume, wherein the question of a single divine will is more thoroughly addressed within the context of responding to critics of Balthasar's theology.
165. Speyr, *The Cross: Word and Sacrament*, 54.
166. See, for example, Speyr, *Das Wort und die Mystik* I, 91. Cf. Balthasar, *Theo-Drama* III, 188 and 225.
167. Speyr, *John* III, 159; see also *Korinther* I, 345; and Balthasar, *The Christian State of Life*, 256.
168. See, for example, Speyr, *John* I, 144–45; *John* III, 364; and Balthasar, *Theo-Drama* V, 123, where ample reference is made to Adrienne.
169. Speyr, *The Passion from Within*, 63.
170. Speyr, *John* III, 159; see also 178; and *John* II, 279. The Spirit's role of guaranteeing the "common will" of the Father and Son is of particular importance in Balthasar's theology. See, for example, his *Theo-Drama* III, 188, 511, and 522.
171. Speyr, *John* III, 159; translation slightly altered. See also ibid., 68. Similarly, Balthasar records

est relief to his suffering. "A suffering that could see its own outcome would still have a point of view, a standpoint. But here the Son must hang [on the Cross], completely naked, in the pure resolve of the Father."[172] Meanwhile, the Father and the Spirit are said by Adrienne to respect the Son's wish to suffer without limit as a form of their love for him.[173]

This, it must be insisted, is not to admit suffering for the sake of suffering, nor even for the sake of atonement thus understood (namely, as suffering); rather this is a willingness to suffer for the sake of love, wherein atonement principally resides.[174] Here, in other words, in the most extreme of all suffering, is revealed the willingness to endure everything—even the worst effects of sin[175]—out of love and for the sake of love as governed by the Spirit of love.[176] Hence in Christ crucified it is no longer possible to discern the Son's love as other than that of the Father whom he loves in this way and who loves us in the dying Son. "While the Son is separated more and more all the time from the Father in his journey into suffering, he is at the same time united more and more to the Father in this separation, until he is nothing more on the Cross than the revelation of the will of the Father."[177]

Here, in his desolation on the Cross, the Son acknowledges the fulfillment of his mission not as something that *he* has done, but as an objective fact; hence the objective formulation, "*it* is accomplished" (Jn 19:30), which reveals the subjective distance between the Son and his mission.[178] Balthasar explains this "distance" in terms of Christ's priestly office, which he accomplishes "by submerging all subjectivity" (cf. Mt 26:39, Jn 12:27–28, and Lk 22:42). Meanwhile, the Father is said to accomplish the priestly office "by turning upon his Son the face of his severity, and even anger, at the sinfulness of the world" (cf. Mt 27:46); whence "*the synthesis between the activity of offering and the passivity of being offered*" which the theologian of Lucerne

---

that Adrienne herself wished to die in fear and agony (*in der Todesangst sterben, mit einem wahren Todeskampf*) so as to be freely offered (*hingegeben*) for sinners. See Speyr, *Erde und Himmel* II, no. 1628 (223).

172. Speyr, *John* III, 159; translation slightly altered. See also ibid., 68; and *Mary in the Redemption*, 88.

173. See Speyr, *Erde und Himmel* II, no. 1636 (229); and *The Boundless God*, 50–51. Cf. Thomas Aquinas, *ST* III, q. 48, a. 2.

174. Cf. Thomas Aquinas, *ST* III, q. 14, a. 1, ad. 1; and a. 2. "It is truth's paradox that the Son separates himself from the Father in order to show him the extent of his great love. [...] But this paradox is the truth, and this whole movement has only one meaning: that there be more love" (Speyr, *Die katholischen Briefe II*, 324–25); see also *The Passion from Within*, 116. Similarly, "the best obedience is always perfect [*vollkommene*] Love" (*Erde und Himmel* II, no. 1688 [267]).

175. It bears repeating, as mentioned in the first part of this chapter, that these "effects" include, for Adrienne, Christ's experience of abandonment by the Father on the Cross and of hell.

176. See Speyr, *Theologie der Geschlechter*, 96. Cf. Balthasar, *Elucidations*, 82.

177. Speyr, *John* II, 166; see also *The Countenance of the Father*, 84.

178. Speyr, *The Cross: Word and Sacrament*, 52. Cf. Balthasar, *Theo-Drama* III, 182.

recognizes as characterizing the New Testament priesthood.[179] Similarly, Adrienne recognizes the obedient Son as so submissive to the Father, so "compliant with everything that God makes out of him," that he is rightfully considered the objective gift of the Father.[180]

On the other hand—and here the pendulum swings back again in the other direction—although the Son is expropriated, as it were, out of obedience, he is "not repressed as [a] person," so as to become something like "a hollow space or a thoroughfare." This is so precisely because everything is accepted out of love, even to the extent that "love comes to occupy every space in him and through him, attains its every effect."[181] By this attaining of love's "every effect" is meant that the very world "that will know nothing of him" is the one that he is charged "to transform into a world that is really and inwardly his own." What he brings back to the Father—as the fruit of his accomplished mission—is "a world no longer without access to God, in which there is a mustard-seed of hope that God may be received."[182]

This hope supposes, more specifically—and this is hardly a moot point, since this is precisely what I pointed to at the beginning of this chapter as apparently lacking to Balthasar's theology of redemption—that Christ's supreme act of love (cf. Jn 15:13) is particularly effective in opening hearts to its reception. Such, for example, is the state of one after confession: that of a "liberated surrender [*befreiter Hingabe*]" so as to be "free for God."[183] Such is also the state of humility, which Adrienne presents as particularly effective in removing the barriers separating us from the grace of God.[184] In order to clear the way for divine love in the world, to forge a place within human hearts for its indwelling, this love must, more specifically, "first clear away all the hindrances blocking the path." It does this, she reasons, by taking these hindrances on itself, by living through "loneliness, forsakenness, fear, shame and death."[185]

Adrienne specifies that this statement means, in the first instance, that Christ overcomes the boundaries of fallen human nature—sickness, fatigue,

---

179. Balthasar, *The Christian State of Life*, 256.
180. See Speyr, *John* IV, 78.
181. Speyr, *They Followed His Call*, 68–69. "God's Son became obedient unto death," Adrienne further clarifies, "and this neither from passivity nor from resignation and a hollow sense of *lassez-faire*, but from love. It is love that lets things happen, that puts up with and even accepts passively those things it must" (58). See also Speyr, *The Holy Mass*, 73.
182. Speyr, *John* I, 97–98.
183. Speyr, *Markus*, 561.
184. See Adrienne von Speyr, *Das Allerheiligen Buch* II, vol. 1.2 of *Die Nachlasswerke* (Einsiedeln: Johannes Verlag, 1977), 103.
185. Speyr, *John* III, 68.

and death—from the power of his human obedience to the Father and not from the exercise of his divine nature which would, as it were, *de facto* destroy these boundaries.[186] "He bore more than others, because he loved more; supported more, because he was more obedient."[187] This, it is important to insist, however, is not to admit that the incarnate Son is merely passive.[188] Indeed, he actively gives himself fully and willfully to both the Father and humankind (cf. Jn 10:18), as if without distinction.[189]

For us, he is the path to God. But for him himself, there is no other path back to God than that of being sacrificed by men. He not only becomes the path for us; he will make use of us as the path upon which he returns to the Father. In this abasement, he has fallen from himself and into our hands, into a state of utmost self-surrender, in which he is now nothing more than something that is controlled by us. He allows himself to become an object of men to such a degree that he wants to lead men back to the Father through the [consecrated] host [of the Eucharist].[190]

Such is the proof of his fully confident surrender to the Father in whose hands his life and Spirit are entrusted, and such is also the proof of his divine sonship, which is manifest precisely in this form of confidence, surrender, and thus obedience.[191] His confidence is, moreover, well-founded, for he does not only suffer "because of his own weakness, but also through the grace of the Father and the Holy Spirit." Meanwhile the Father and the Spirit realize their "renunciation [which consists in permitting the Son to suffer in this terrible way] in the Son's grace."[192]

This admittedly is a very shocking statement, but precisely its shocking

---

186. See Speyr, *World of Prayer*, 79; and *The Countenance of the Father*, 60–62. By the absolute "overexertion" of his suffering with merely human strength, Adrienne sees Christ freeing for us the divine power of grace. See *Korinther* I, 288; and *John* IV, 78. For this reason, she recognizes that "the completion of the work [...] lies in his human nature being stretched beyond its limits in a night of suffering in which no word to the Father will be possible any longer" (*John* III, 311).

187. Speyr, *Der Mensch vor Gott*, 11.

188. See Torrell, *Pour nous les hommes et pour notre salut*, 205; Thomas Aquinas, *Comp* I, 230; *ST* III, q. 47, aa. 1–2; and a. 3, ad. 2.

189. "Demands are constantly made of him from both sides; he is plundered from both sides" (Speyr, *Die katholischen Briefe* II, 272). Adrienne nonetheless admits (ibid.) that this fact of being given over "without distinction" to the Father and to mankind is the precise expression of his love for the Father; see *Confession*, 24–25. Similar to the idea of being given without discretion (or differentiation between the Father and humankind) is the parallel withdrawal of the disciples and the Father. Both are pictured as abandoning the incarnate Son. See Speyr, *The Passion from Within*, 65.

190. Speyr, *John* IV, 339.

191. See Speyr, *Theologie der Geschlechter*, 133. Cf. Balthasar, *Theo-Drama* V, 516–17. The theme of Christ's confidence might also be perceived in Balthasar's presentation of Christ as the exemplar of the faith. See his essay: "*Fides Christi*: An Essay on the Consciousness of Christ" in *Explorations in Theology* II, 43–79, esp. 78.

192. Speyr, *Die Schöpfung*, 63. The Father and the Spirit led the Son throughout his entire earthly life, Adrienne teaches, and this accompaniment is revealed "in the unity on the Cross" (Speyr, *Erde und Himmel* II, no. 1635 [228]).

effect points (again) to the unity of the divine will, as paternal and filial. In fact, ultimately and fundamentally, Christological obedience is presented by Adrienne in terms of the Son's union with the Father in the Holy Spirit, whence the Speyrian understanding of redemption as our introduction into the Trinitarian communion.[193] As the "fulfillment of his perfect surrender to the Father,"[194] the Lord's surrender to sinners is the means whereby he admits them—and the whole reality of sin, understood as willful distancing from God—into "what is most central and intimate to him," namely his relationship with the Father.[195]

The Redemptive Gift of Surrender

It is precisely this attitude of obedient abandonment or surrender—characterizing Christ's divine filiation—that is communicated to us, Adrienne teaches, as the grace of redemption so that we might not unceasingly "stumble over our boundaries."[196] This is not to say that redemption is primarily a communication of grace enabling us to surpass the human limits originating out of sin and punishment for sin. Nor is it to be understood simply as Christ's offering on our behalf and precisely as man the love that is rightly due the Creator, a love that we have denied him by our sin.[197] Without denying either of these aspects of Christian redemption, more profoundly and fundamentally, Adrienne presents Christ as really offering us his own filial love with which to love the Father and thus also his receptivity of the Father's love in the form of his filial surrender.

Such, in fact, is the meaning that Adrienne accords to Christ's experience, on our behalf, of the Father's presence in "absence," or his "dark night" of faith: that he might thereby accord to us a share in his eternal and loving fidelity for (or surrender to) the Father.[198] This offer in turn means both that we love the Father and our neighbor (that we surrender ourselves to them) *in Christ*—that is to say, as incorporated into his body by the Spirit—and that Christ also loves the Father and our neighbor *in us*: in virtue of his Spirit within us.[199] Christ's offering also explains the sense of our earlier remark

---

193. See, for example, Speyr, *Das Buch der Gehorsam*, 51.
194. Speyr, *Das Wort und die Mystik* II, 53.   195. Speyr, *The Passion from Within*, 41.
196. Speyr, *Der Mensch vor Gott*, 11.
197. See, for example, Speyr, *Das Wort und die Mystik* II, 101, 510 and 523; *Theologie der Geschlechter*, 133; *The Letter to the Ephesians*, 33; and *The Countenance of the Father*, 61–62.
198. See for example, Speyr, *Bergpredigt*, 145; *Das Wort und die Mystik* I, 92; *World of Prayer*, 79; and *The Cross: Word and Sacrament*, 46–47.
199. See Speyr, *Confession*, 151. On the Spirit's role in our incorporation in divine love, see *Korinther* I, 373; and *John* III, 117 and 134. Cf. Balthasar, *Theo-Logic* III.

that he overcomes the boundary between his own generous self-gift and the disciple's only too-limited gift of self in virtue of which he or she is receptive of God's gift.[200] Indeed, redemption requires that it be received by those to whom it is offered, and it is herein that resides the terrible "challenge" to divine love that is posed by human persons.

To be sure, the rejection of Christ by the accusative chief priests and officers is magnified, as it were, by his own fragility: by, that is to say, his "impotence" before them, which "affords them an unexpected opportunity for intensified sin."[201] By this commentary Adrienne suggests, more specifically, that the absolute love of the Lord in the form of total vulnerability manifests the truth of human hearts and calls for a decision: that of love or its refusal.[202]

On the other hand, by our resistance we "force" God, as it were, to provide ever greater proofs of his love for us. This need not imply that creatures have a real power over their Creator: a position which would *de facto* entail a certain potency in God.[203] Rather, the emphasis here is upon God's respect for the human freedom that he has created.[204] Christ "does not flee from suffering into prayer to the Father, into the thought that it will soon be over, that everything is useful for the world. He opens himself to pain; he measures the offense to the Father by the offense offered to himself."[205] Hence, far from forcing our love, he invites it by means of his own ingenious and supergenerous love, revealed in the form of his bloody sacrifice. This sacrifice is, in fact, the origin of what John Paul II presents as "*a double gift*: the gift of the truth of conscience and the gift of the certainty of redemption."[206]

In the revelation of the Cross one is, in other words, simultaneously confronted with the knowledge of one's own sin[207] and the knowledge of God's unfailing mercy, for precisely this event is the occasion whereby God grants the forgiveness of sin: "Father, forgive them; for they know not what they do" (Lk 23:34). Such, John Paul II explains, is the mystery of Christ's "blood [that] purifies the conscience" (Heb 9:14) by opening it to the Holy Spirit, who

---

200. For a development of this theme within the Christian tradition, see Michele M. Schumacher, "Towards a Spirituality of Poverty," *Nova et Vetera* 3, no. 2 (Spring 2005): 217–30.

201. Speyr, *John* IV, 79.

202. See Speyr, *John* III, 51. Cf. Pope John Paul II, *Dominium et Vivificantem*, no. 55.

203. This question will be examined in the seventh and concluding chapters of this volume.

204. See Thomas Aquinas, *SCG* III, c. 112. This explains the importance of secondary causes in accounting for evil, as Torrell points out (see *Pour nous les hommes et pour notre salut*, 232). As a case in point, Aquinas teaches, "Christ indeed willed His Passion just as the Father willed it; yet He did not will the unjust action of the Jews" (*ST* III, q. 47, a. 6, ad. 3).

205. Speyr, *The Passion from Within*, 118; cf. Balthasar, *Does Jesus Know Us?*, 49.

206. Pope John Paul II, *Dominum et Vivificantem*, no. 31.

207. As we saw in chapter four, Adrienne portrays Christ during his passion as making sin "visible" by way of its "absolute injury" to his body (Speyr, *The Passion from Within*, 45).

brings about authentic conversion. This opening to the Spirit, in turn, consists in an acknowledgement of sin, which John Paul II equates with a rejection of God,[208] and "a sincere and firm purpose of amendment."[209] Or, as Adrienne would have it, such is the exuberant power of divine love, even and especially as it encounters the most extreme forms of resistance: it reveals itself as capable of calling forth from hardened hearts an authentic reciprocity in love.[210] Precisely because the Father's "command" to the Son (cf. Jn 10:18) is made without any "calculating spirit" which would include "the ulterior motive of enriching himself through the answering love," it has a particular power of "awakening" the love of the disciples. It is that whereby Christ "brings home to the Father the harvest of love."[211]

From this perspective, Christ is the image of the Father (cf. Col 1:15) not primarily as one in whom is contained the Father's glory, but as one who constantly communicates this glory by generously pouring it forth into an unbelieving world. Hence, although the Son surrenders everything to the Father from the very beginning of his earthly mission, it is as if more and more is actually taken from him until, in death, he is "in the condition of *being withdrawn*." Hence, the wound of the soldier's lance is presented by Adrienne, in union with the patristic tradition, as the origin of the sacraments, whereby the Lord is "exposed" beyond his nakedness: exposed, because he is "no longer just the bestower, but the bestowed. Through it [the wound], he is what is poured out, the offered sacrifice."[212]

In the final analysis, the redemptive surrender of Christ is thus ordered to a bestowal: he is fullness which overflows; as a complete gift of self, he is fully receptive of the Father's life and goodness and fully generous in offering the same to the world.[213] Even as freshly incarnate, he is already "distributed," Adrienne explains; for he is "already Eucharistic in his essence."[214] Combined in the theology of Adrienne is thus the idea of Christ as a substantial Eucharist—he is "objectively" the Father's gift of eternal life to the world, precisely as one who is "subjectively" given, fully and unreservedly, to the Father for the accomplishment of his will—and the total emptying, or pouring out, of

208. See Pope John Paul II, *Dominium et Vivificantem*, no. 29.
209. Ibid., no. 42.
210. See Speyr, *Die katholischen Briefe* II, 186; and *John* III, 68.
211. Speyr, *John* II, 280; see also *John* I, 106; and *The Letter to the Colossians*, 32. On the awakening of love, see Balthasar's image of the mother's smile awakening love in her child, in *Love Alone Is Credible*, 76; *The Glory of the Lord* V, 615–18; and *A Theological Anthropology*, 87–88. Cf. Speyr, *Über die Liebe*, 12.
212. Speyr, *John* IV, 141. On Christ as bestowed and bestower, see also 337.
213. See Speyr, *The Countenance of the Father*, 63.
214. Speyr, *Die katholischen Briefe* II, 191. This also manifests how much the Eucharist is also the Father's gift to us. See, for example, *John* IV, 436; and Balthasar, *Theo-Drama* V, 123.

this gift of life in the form of his bloody bodily sacrifice, whereby the Church is born in the form of the sacraments.[215]

What is "accomplished" on the Cross is, therefore, "the substance of his mission,"[216] which Adrienne describes as setting free the path to eternal life offered in baptism and of thereby drawing believers into the mystery of his love.[217] This in turn means not only that Christ's surrender becomes the gift of life that cleanses and nourishes us as blood poured forth for the multitude, but also that it evokes a response of generous love in us, a response in virtue of which we are drawn into Trinitarian communion and draw others into the same.

This [is] the essence of the Lord's gift of self: it is a full gift, knowing no measure, poured out extravagantly. And when the Lord shows this gift of himself to people, he awakens in them the understanding of such a gift of self, he makes it possible for them to imitate him. He awakens in them the yearning to give more than they themselves possess. He draws forth from them an inclination to pass beyond all boundaries.[218]

The first of the "boundaries" overcome by the extravagant gift of Christ's love to his disciples is, it bears repeating, the boundary between what Christ gives and what we receive, between his *generous* surrender and our *receptive* surrender.[219] Coming to us out of his eternal, reciprocated love for the Father, the incarnate Son is prepared for "nothing other than this continual exchange."[220] What he awaits from us is, quite simply, a gift of self that—by the power of his grace—knows no boundaries. This implies, as we saw in chapter three, that his surrender actually conditions ours: it is graced receptivity.[221]

In reason of this received receptivity, God's love *for us* becomes God's love *in us*. Because God "*is* love, he causes [*bewirkt*] believers to *become* love."[222] By

---

215. See Speyr, *John* II, 35–36 and 167; *John* IV, 136; *The Cross: Word and Sacrament*, 47 and 53; and *Theologie der Geschlechter*, 133. On the Son as the Father's Eucharist, see also Speyr, *Das Wort und die Mystik* II, 533; and Balthasar, *New Elucidations*, 115. For a more extensive development of these ideas in Adrienne's theology, see chapter four of the present volume. For an exposition of the same theme in Balthasar's theology, see Nicholas J. Healy and David L. Schindler, "For the Life of the World: Hans Urs von Balthasar on the Church as Eucharist" in Oakes and Moss, *The Cambridge Companion to Hans Urs von Balthasar*, 51–63.

216. Speyr, *The Cross: Word and Sacrament*, 52.

217. The "content" of the sacraments is love, Adrienne explains: the indivisible love of God and neighbor. See Speyr, *John* I, 93. Not surprisingly then, the double commandment of love becomes possible in a new way through the Eucharist; see *The Passion from Within*, 44–45.

218. Speyr, *John* II, 278–79. It is the Spirit, Adrienne teaches, who resolves "the unattainability of our inborn impulse toward perfection, toward expansion of our boundaries, toward universal life." Proceeding from the "fidelity between Father and Son," he "also mediates this fidelity" (*John* III, 117; see also 134).

219. See Speyr, *John* I, 102; *Die katholischen Briefe* II, 179; and *Korinther* I, 390.

220. Ibid., 177; see also *The Letter to the Ephesians*, 33 and 203–4; and *World of Prayer*, 28–33.

221. See Speyr, *Das Buch vom Gehorsam*, 13; and *John* II, 61.

222. Speyr, *Die katholischen Briefe* I, 178.

this is meant not only that Christ's love becomes "an objective state of grace in the soul," for love has a subjective element as well; and this subjective element, corresponding to the "objective perfection of sanctifying grace in us," is the perfection of the love of God and of neighbor.[223] Or, as Balthasar puts it with reference to Adrienne's teaching: in Christ, God "surrenders his love, which is both 'transitive,' focusing on the other, and 'intransitive,' since God's entire being 'is love.'"[224] "The saying, 'God is, we become,' perhaps sounds too theoretical. Its practical complement lies in the Lord's love of neighbor (*Nächstenliebe*). When one considers the two sayings together, then the primacy of Christ's love (which is divine) simultaneously becomes clear [as does the fact] that we must entrust ourselves to him in order to acquire love. Love makes the distance (between God and man) clear by bridging it."[225]

Adrienne does not merely argue, therefore, that the norm for Christian love is Christ's love for us (cf. Jn 15:13), although this idea is not lacking in her teaching.[226] More profoundly still, she maintains that Christ's love for us is actually a revelation and a mediation of the Father's love: the Father's love for us (cf. Jn 3:15–16), but also his love for the Son (Jn 17:23–24, 26) who, in turn, mediates this paternal love—the Father's love for him, the only-begotten One—to us (cf. Jn 15:9). Because, moreover, the Son's revelation of this love is an act of filial obedience, it is also a revelation and a mediation of the Son's love for the Father (Jn 13:41), which always also implies the Spirit of love. "God is not a lover; God is love, and this love has a threefold form."[227] Hence, in Christ, the love of neighbor is truly one with the triune love of God.[228] This also means that the love of Christ *is* the love of the Father: a love that despite its particular paternal and filial qualities remains a "consubstantial" love.[229] It follows that there is only one love worthy of the name: the mutual love of Father and Son, wherein the human person is given a place through the redemption accomplished by this same love.[230]

---

223. Speyr, *The Letter to the Ephesians*, 34.
224. Balthasar, *Theo-Drama* V, 122; see also 82. Cf. Speyr, *Das Wort und die Mystik* II, 108 and 113.
225. Speyr, *Das Wort und die Mystik* II, 108.
226. "God is, of course, love, and thus God's love is the general norm for all love" (ibid., 356–57).
227. Speyr, *John* I, 27.
228. "God loves God, because God has God as his neighbor. When the God-Man loves his fellow man, than he also loves his neighbor, but [he does so] with the same love (he is God after all) with which he loves God the Father and the Spirit" (Speyr, *Das Wort und die Mystik* II, 108).
229. See Speyr, *The Letter to the Ephesians*, 33; and *John* I, 26–27. Cf. Balthasar, *Theo-Logic* III, 441. On the particular qualities of divine love as it is associated with each of the divine persons, see Speyr, *Das Wort und die Mystik*, 114. Cf. Thomas Aquinas, *Super Ioan* 17, lect. 5, no. 2240: "There is a twofold unity of the Father and the Son: a unity of essence and of love. In both of these ways the Father is in the Son and the Son is in the Father."
230. See Speyr, *John* II, 443; *Das Themenheft*, 8; and *The Letter to the Ephesians*, 230.

Abiding in Love: Communicating Love Received

While the emphasis in the previous section was upon the redemptive gift of receptivity which enables us to partake of the Lord's plenty—by, for example, hindering us from "draw[ing] back from this torrent" of love so as instead to be "covered by love"[231]—this same gift of redemption also supposes our willingness to communicate Christ's love beyond ourselves. The Christian, Adrienne argues, possesses only what he "squanders."[232] His life is characterized by the constant reception of grace "that allows him to give himself away."[233] In other words, the divine revelation of love in the Lord's terrible passion suffered for us is not only an invitation to love; it is also "a bestowal" of love.

The wound in Christ's side is thus portrayed by Adrienne as "a symbol of the apostolate," for what the Lord gives through this wound "does not stop at its recipient, but transforms itself in him at once into a wellspring for his neighbor."[234] Such, in other words, is "the constant receiving of the grace that allows him [the Christian] to give himself away."[235] The love of God is the most communicable of all his gifts, Adrienne teaches, "and what the Lord demands, he demands out of his love."[236] In other words, we receive from the Lord what he requires of us: "love as charity [*Nächsteliebe*] and love as adoration [*Anbetung*]."[237] The reciprocity that is established by redemption is, therefore, one which simultaneously expands beyond the 'I-thou' relationship of Christ and the Christian to include the other for whom Christ has also given his life out of love for the Father. Hence, the commandment of love is "a challenge to the same obedience that the Son exercises towards the Father,"[238] but it also supposes a participation in the same abundant love that makes this obedience possible.

"Because," in fact, "everything is pure superabundance [*Überfluss*] in the Trinity," Adrienne reasons that "there is nothing calculating [*Berechnendes*] in God's love." This is an absolutely unconditional love: one which constantly surpasses itself and its object. When, for example, the Son loves the Father,

---

231. Speyr, *John* III, 178.　　232. Ibid., 101; see also *John* IV, 352.
233. Speyr, *They Followed His Call*, 118.
234. Speyr, *John* IV, 140. The Spirit's role here is particularly significant. Just as he acts on the Father's behalf in the Incarnation, so also does he whenever the Son comes to us in the Eucharist. "He is not less active," Balthasar notes with reference to Adrienne's teaching, "in communicating the Son's sacrificial mind and heart to those who receive him so that they can make sacrifice together with the Son to the Father" (Balthasar, *Theo-Drama* V, 485).
235. Speyr, *They Followed His Call*, 118.　　236. Speyr, *Korinther* I, 400.
237. Speyr, *Die katholischen Briefe* II, 167.
238. Speyr, *Das Buch vom Gehorsam*, 12. Cf. Pope Benedict XVI, *Deus caritas est*, nos. 13–14.

he simultaneously loves the Spirit in an ever-surpassing, overflowing plenitude. Analogically, the Christian's "love for *one* fellow human being always includes love for *other* human beings and, in the last analysis, for *all* human beings." Beyond this analogy, Adrienne insists that precisely because authentic love of neighbor stems from God, it "must go beyond our neighbor, namely back to God." By this she means that we necessarily take our neighbor with us on our way to God, especially by stimulating him or her to love God.[239] In short, precisely because we are united to the triune God by God's own initiating love, we are, so to speak, equipped to love our neighbor: our love of neighbor is authentic, because it is divine.

Despite, therefore, the comparison employed by the Lord in his commandment in John 13:14 ("as I have loved you, you should love one another")—in virtue of which "one might be tempted to understand this as a measure, as his measure," with the Lord there is, in fact, "no measure."[240] His is a love that is ready to assume everything, even the Cross.[241] Such should also be the love of Christ's disciples: their love cannot be measured, because its origin is divine and thus infinite.[242] As is already evident in the original Greek, the word "as [*kathos*]" employed by the evangelist in the above passage (Jn 13:34) refers not simply to an *imitation* of Christ's love, but to a real *participation* therein and thus also to the impossibility of differentiating between love of God and love of neighbor.[243]

By employing this term (*as*), the Lord assumes our love, Adrienne reasons, "into the measure and mode of his own."[244] Because, moreover, the "measure" of Christ's love is limitless, the demands of his love in us are likewise limitless: they exceed the constraints of our fragile humanity, like grace in earthen vessels (cf. 2 Cor 4:7). "The Lord gives to us of his own infinity and unshakability in love; he pours, as it were, this love into us" so that we might share "through him, in the love between Father and Son."[245]

Ultimately this means that the disciple must be configured to the Lord in such a way that his or her own personal destiny takes on the dimensions of the Lord's infinite mission and thus also his superhuman suffering. The

---

239. Speyr, *Das Wort und die Mystik* II, 113–14; see also 101 and 523; and *The Boundless God*, 44–45.
240. Speyr, *John* III, 69.
241. See ibid., 67.
242. See ibid., 66; and *John* IV, 121. This is accomplished by the infinite power of the Holy Spirit, whose work is "implicit" in the Lord's own mission. In virtue of this same power, the Spirit requires of the disciples "more than they possess" (*John* IV, 221).
243. See Olivier de Dinechin, "*Kathos*: La similitude dans l'évangile selon Saint Jean, " *Recherches de Science et Religion* 58 (1970): 195–236.
244. Speyr, *John* III, 70.
245. Speyr, *John* IV, 365–66.

disciple's own human suffering, which as such knows a particular limit, is caught up into the Lord's own suffering with the result that the limit of human possibilities "is overstepped, not into emptiness, but into the infinity of the Lord's suffering."[246] Adrienne recognizes the possibility of participating in even "his most personal suffering" such that the "boundaries between his suffering and ours might momentarily disappear," for "in the excess of suffering, we really suffer in his name, by him, with his strength, and in the love which unites him to the Father."[247] Such, Adrienne explains, is a fruit of the Lord's dereliction on the Cross.[248]

The Cross reveals "what God desires for man, what man receives as a gift, but also what he must be and do."[249] In fact, Adrienne recognizes as "implicit" in "the complete will of the Father [which is] in the complete surrender of the Son" the "demand on us to be co-involved in that surrender."[250] The Son "needs" our suffering, Adrienne reasons, like that of his mother at the foot of the Cross, so as to "show the Father that he is not suffering alone."[251] Again, it is important to insist that it is not suffering as such that is significant, but the "vulnerable" gift of self that is characteristic of love and, in the present case, compassion for the suffering Christ, whose unlimited suffering is the fruit of his unlimited love.[252] As compassion for Christ, our suffering, moreover, is truly a form of participation in Christ's suffering. Or, as Balthasar puts it, in union with Adrienne, "his *one* sacrifice to the Father," belongs not only to the head but also "contains, from the very start," the sacrifice of his body-bride. "This one marriage in blood contains within itself in advance not only every bodily approach of the Lord to his Church until the end of the world but also every response on the Church's part: the Church whom the Lord had already drawn into his liturgy of the Cross by the liturgical con-celebration of the Last Supper."[253] Meanwhile, the suffering of those who authentically share in Christ's sorrowful lot is purified of its subjective character so as to be truly ecclesial in nature. Mary Magdalene, for example, becomes so much "an

---

246. Speyr, *John* III, 72; see also *Erde und Himmel* II, no. 1736 (306). For the Christian's participation in Christ's suffering, see Speyr, *The Victory of Love*, 70.

247. Speyr, *Die katholischen Briefe* I, 381.

248. The reader is to be reminded that the Lord's dereliction is the origin of the dark night of faith, as Adrienne sees it. See Speyr, *Das Wort und die Mystik* I, 91–92; and *The Passion from Within*, 66–67.

249. Speyr, *Light and Images*, 27.

250. Speyr, *The Countenance of the Father*, 84.

251. Speyr, *Three Women and the Lord*, 27. On the theological significance of Mary's co-suffering at the Cross, see also *Das Wort und die Mystik* II, 517.

252. See Speyr, *The Passion from Within*, 115–16; *Erde und Himmel* III, no. 2259 (249); and Balthasar, *Mysterium Paschale*, 132–36.

253. Balthasar, *A Theology of History*, 97–98; cf. Speyr, *The Passion from Within*, 119. Such, Balthasar explains, is an "inclusive" form of vicarious suffering. See Balthasar, *Mysterium Paschale*, 133.

entity of the Church" that she grieves "in an "apostolic sense." By this Adrienne suggests that Magdalene grieves more for sinners "from whom the Lord has been taken away" than for herself.[254]

Something of this mystery of loving surrender, even to the point of self-effacement in imitation of Christ, is realized in one whose humility is such that "the unimpeded view of the Father" might be visible in him or her.[255] Such, in fact, is the fulfillment of the redemptive mysteries. The Son lovingly surrenders himself to the Father, who, meanwhile, also surrenders the Son to us in the Incarnation. The Son, in turn, surrenders himself to us in the Eucharist—and in his redemptive suffering implied therein. He does so, however, in such a way that he gives himself to us to be given by us.[256] He reckons so much with the reciprocity of our love, Adrienne explains, "that he makes use of us when he needs us [...]. In us and through us, he lives his life of the Eucharist and makes the gift of himself through us to others."[257]

It is the Eucharist, in fact, that mediates in Adrienne's theology not only between the divine and the human, the spiritual and the corporal, "the finiteness of sin" and the infinity of Trinitarian life and love, but also between the love of God and the love of neighbor.[258] An "interior nourishment of love,"[259] the Eucharist causes the communicant to become a form of the Eucharist: "He bears in himself the wordless apostolate, the outflowing of love as such, which simply communicates itself."[260] Upon receiving the Eucharist, we must therefore mediate its graces through fidelity to what is received. We ought not to sin with our bodies, nor with our speech; for in so doing, we cause "the word of Christ, the word that is Christ" to lose its "Eucharistic content" in us. Because the Eucharist is the Lord's Word lovingly poured forth as redemption for all, those who have received these Eucharistic graces must communicate them beyond themselves. "As Word of God's love," this word necessarily "has a claim on my word of love of neighbor."[261] Because, in other words, the Lord's "state" in the Eucharist is, as Adrienne observes, that of persevering in love, the same is expected of us: we who are nourished thereby should persevere "in a *state* of love"[262] without ever being able to boast of having attained "the definitive state of having arrived."[263]

From a Christian perspective it is thus meaningless, Adrienne teaches, to

---

254. Speyr, *John* IV, 182.
255. Speyr, *They Followed His Call*, 68–69. This theme is developed more thoroughly in chapter two of the present volume.
256. See Speyr, *John* I, 83.
257. Speyr, *John* II, 70.
258. See Speyr, *The Passion from Within*, 44.
259. Speyr, *John* II, 72.
260. Speyr, *John* IV, 140.
261. Speyr, *The Passion from Within*, 46.
262. Speyr, *The Holy Mass*, 73.
263. Speyr, *The Letter to the Ephesians*, 30.

speak of personal existence other than "with" the world in the Trinitarian communion of love. "Every thought that I squander on my 'I' is—in a Christian sense—a lost thought when the sense of this 'I' does not lie in union, surrender, service to the whole."[264] Indeed, because the Church is a communion of the saints with the Lord, it is also the communion of saints with one another.[265] This means that the Church cannot be understood as a sort of "massing" of individuals. Any such thing would be "non-ecclesial." Instead, "She" is an almost organic unity of persons existing, each and all, in the Eucharistic Lord, who, in turn, is one in all. "Each is a part and each is the whole of the body in the eyes of the Lord."[266] It is this unity of all in Christ—and of Christ in all—that also explains the reconciliation of Jews and Gentiles in the early Christian community (cf. Eph 2:16). "It is not as if he reconciled them in himself in order then to release them again from himself," Adrienne explains in her commentary of this passage. Rather, "they remain in his one body in order to remain reconciled to one another."[267]

All of this implies that the Eucharistic Lord not only gives himself to be given by us to others, but also that he gives us to others in virtue of our communion with him. There is, in fact, no such thing as an exclusive relationship of a human being with God, Adrienne insists.[268] It is certainly possible to have a "personal" relationship with the Lord, but never a "private" one.[269] In other words, the Lord's love for the individual overflows into his love for all of humanity, not withstanding the fact that this love for humanity as a whole is always manifest as love for individuals.[270]

The particular mission of the mother of God, for example, demonstrates how even the most profound intimacy with the Lord "is disposed of for the benefit of others."[271] The most "secret" mysteries of Mary's life become the "public mysteries of the Church, her concealed thoughts the laws of the faith, her relationship to her Son a standard to which every believer is subject."[272] "[E]verything ecclesial was preformed in Mary,"[273] Adrienne explains, by

---

264. Speyr, *Das Wort und die Mystik* II, 101; cf. *Light and Images*, 30; *The Boundless God*, 28; Pope Benedict XVI, *Deus caritas est*, no. 14; and Balthasar, *Explorations in Theology* II, 170–71.
265. Speyr, *Das Wort und die Mystik* I, 266.
266. Ibid.; see also *Das Wort und die Mystik* II, 531.
267. Speyr, *The Letter to the Ephesians*, 106.
268. Speyr, *Die Schöpfung*, 56. Cf. Pope Benedict XVI, *Deus caritas est*, no. 14.
269. Speyr, *John* I, 102; see also 75. Similarly, Adrienne explains that in "all Christian things" may be found the personal and the general, "full surrender and full discretion" (*Theologie der Geschlechter*, 137).
270. Speyr, *John* IV, 326.   271. Speyr, *Handmaid of the Lord*, 161.
272. Speyr, *The Countenance of the Father*, 99.
273. Speyr, *Mary in the Redemption*, 104. Hence, for example, Balthasar's presentation of the mysteries of the rosary as the Church's partaking of the mysteries of Mary's life. See Balthasar, *The Threefold Garland*. Cf. Pope John Paul II, *Rosarium Virginis Mariae* (Boston: Daughters of St. Paul, 2002).

which is meant not only that Mary is an archetypical disciple and an *anima ecclesia*, as we saw in chapter three, but also that she is the first cell of the Church and the bride of Christ *par excellence*,[274] as we saw in chapter four.

This also means that the mystery of love that God realized in Mary's life and with her willing cooperation, he realized for us all.[275] It is in virtue of Mary's universal motherhood—itself a consequence of her privileged relation with the Lord, that is to say, of her divine maternity—that we are all capable of becoming "mothers" of Christ by doing the will of the Father (cf. Mt 12:48).[276] All the graces that Mary receives, even the most apparently 'personal' ones, are not retained for herself but are communicated to others. They are, in other words, meant to be dispersed throughout the Church and, by means of the Church, throughout the world. Her absolute openness, which is receptivity in relation to God's bounty, is at the same time generosity in relation to her neighbor.

In the Speyrian formulation, the grace that Mary receives in the person of her Son is not an end in itself (*Endziel*) but a gateway (*Durchgang*), as is apparent in the visitation to Elizabeth. The grace of the Incarnation is mediated almost immediately by Mary to both Elizabeth and to the child within Elizabeth's womb. Because her relation with God and neighbor are experienced as a single grace, she mediates in a simple and unproblematic manner.[277] In this way, she accomplishes the mission that God had in mind for the first woman: to be, in virtue of her "permanent proximity to God and to Adam,"[278] a mediator of grace for her husband and the mother of the living. It is not surprising, then, that Adrienne recognizes her as teaching us "to see her Son in our neighbor and to grasp the fulfillment of his greatest commandment, in our little everyday love for each other."[279]

Conclusion: Redemption as a Mystery of Reciprocal Surrender

It is this commandment of love for one's neighbor as a manifestation and proof of one's love for God and of God's love "in us" that is, in many respects, the focal point of Adrienne's treatment—in accord with the Johannine in-

---

274. See, for example, Speyr, *They Followed His Call*, 75; *The Countenance of the Father*, 98–99; *Mary in the Redemption*, 34; *Apokalypse*, 387; *Das Wort und die Mystik* I, 24; and Balthasar, *First Glance at Adrienne von Speyr*, 72. For a description of an "*anima ecclesia*," see ibid., 52–53; *Explorations in Theology* II, 160–72; and (with Ratzinger), *Mary: The Church at the Source*, 135. In his introduction to Speyr, *Book of All Saints* I, Balthasar likens this concept to that of Ignatius's "*sentire cum Ecclesia*" (23).

275. See Speyr, *Mary in the Redemption*, 113.   276. See Speyr, *Handmaid of the Lord*, 40.
277. See Speyr, *Mary in the Redemption*, 41–45.   278. Ibid., 48.
279. Speyr, *Handmaid of the Lord*, 167.

sight that inspires her—of the Christian relation between the individual and the community, between the disciple of Christ and the Church. This, in turn, is the case precisely because it is illustrative of the Eucharistic meaning of Christ's life: a life which is poured forth in absolute and unrelenting generosity for the multitude as a form of his absolute and unrelenting love for the Father, who in turn, loves the Son and all of us in the Son absolutely and unrelentingly. The Son's eternal and loving surrender to the Father, in response to the Father's continuous outpouring of love to the Son, makes of him a fitting receptacle and revelation of the Father's love and glory.

This same loving surrender takes the form of a generous bestowal of the Father's love—that is to say, the Father's love for him, the only begotten one—upon the world to whom he is sent by the Father. The disciple of Christ, who has been touched by the incarnate Son's generous self-gift, is introduced into this prodigal movement of love: receiving the love of Christ, he is immediately charged to communicate it beyond himself so as to abide therein, for Christian love is preserved precisely in its mediation. In so doing, he or she is likened unto Christ, who by his Incarnation likened himself unto us. This "likening" is, moreover, not simply a matter of imitation but also and especially of participation, for the disciple of Christ actually participates in Trinitarian love: love in the form of receptivity and love in the form of generosity. In both forms our share originates within "the superfluity of love that comes from the Lord's Passion and from the Holy Spirit set free through the Cross" as well as from "the superfluity of love in the Mother of God's consent."[280]

Because the Son is the image of God from all eternity (cf. Col 1:15)—that is to say, the image of the Father—and because he continues to bear this image precisely in his humanity, that is to say in his economic mission, it is by becoming like him, through an active participation in his life and mission, that we—like Mary and with the help of her maternal mediation—bear the divine image. Or, to put it in other words, our status as children of God—our state of grace—supposes a mission in virtue of which our divine adoption in Christ is active: it is not a mere title, but a fact implying a part in his own mission to communicate the Father's love to all of mankind.[281]

To the extent that we really accept and live this mission, God "experiences the love of men as something that he has not simply created but that

---

280. Speyr, *John* I, 105.
281. See Sepyr, *The Letter to the Ephesians*, 31; and *The Christian State of Life*, 186 (this book should not be confused with Balthasar's book of the same title). This same theme is to be found throughout Balthasar's work. For more detail, see chapter two of this volume.

he has poured forth from within him, so that throughout all transient time, proofs of this love will pour back to him as guarantees that created love will remain creative for all eternal time through the sacrifice of the Son."²⁸² We, in turn, might experience in our love of neighbor a love that is "not only filial, but also paternal and spiritual [that is to say, of the Holy Spirit]."²⁸³ In the last analysis, there is only one Love: the Trinitarian love of God manifest in the love with which Christ has loved us (cf. 1 Jn 4:9–10).²⁸⁴ In virtue of this love, we live in the triune God, God lives in us (1 Jn 4:16), and we are one with all who share in this same divine life.²⁸⁵ Ours is an ecclesial existence.

Postscript: An Alternative Interpretation of Christological "Abandonment"

This focal emphasis upon the love of surrender as revealed by Christ in his relation with the Father is obscured when attention is granted instead to the idea of abandonment (*Verlassenheit*) or estrangement from God (*Gottentfremdung*).²⁸⁶ One can hardly blame Balthasar for having been preoccupied by Adrienne's terrible experiences, which he was presumably granted to partake of by way of his spiritual accompaniment during her visions. As for us, we are likewise set before the same challenge of interpreting not only the biblical revelation of Christ's cry "of dereliction" on the Cross (Mk 15:34; Mt 17:45; cf. Ps 22:2) but also of Adrienne's presumably mystical experience of feeling herself estranged from God and more specifically of partaking, as Balthasar attests, of "the interior states"²⁸⁷ of Christ during the passion event and beyond. To be sure, Adrienne's dictations might be considered as interpretations of her own experiences,²⁸⁸ such that the first interpretative phase has—as it were—already been performed for us. Hence, Balthasar, for example, seems often enough to take her doctrine at face value, drawing directly upon it without seeking to first interpret the metaphorical images contain

---

282. Speyr, *The Boundless God*, 49; see also *Confession*, 151.

283. *Das Wort und die Mystik* II, 114. Similarly, Adrienne teaches that the Father gives the Christian and the Church a share of his potency (*Können*), the Son a share of his will (*Wollen*), and the Spirit a share of his understanding (*Fassen*) in the form of charity. See *Erde und Himmel* II, no. 1635 (228).

284. Balthasar, *Heart of the World*, 40–41.

285. "The final, heavenly shape of the communio, as the reciprocal openness of the redeemed is so much a part of the mystery of the Trinity," Balthasar argues, "that there are hardly words and concepts to describe it" (Balthasar, *Theo-Drama* V, 485). See also Speyr, *John* I, 108.

286. See, for example (among so many others), Speyr, *Erde und Himmel* II, no. 1736 (305).

287. See Balthasar's foreword to Speyr, *Passion From Within*, 7.

288. Unlike many other mystics, Adrienne's mission is esteemed by Balthasar as "not only one of experience, of the dark night and other Christological states, but also quite expressly one of interpretation" (Balthasar, *Our Task*, 18–19). See also Balthasar, "General Introduction to the Posthumous Works" in Speyr, *Book of All Saints*, I, 13.

therein: images which his critics (myself included) often consider misleading or even in error with regard to a Catholic interpretation of the redemptive mysteries.

Hence the question might be raised, especially in the present case, of whether we might otherwise interpret Adrienne's presumably mystical share—and let us, at least for the sake of argumentation, give her the benefit of the doubt—in Christ's terrible experience of "God-forsakenness." Is it possible, for example, that instead of being abandoned by the Father because of his bearing of our sin—as goes not only Balthasar's interpretation of Adrienne's doctrine, but also that of William Schmitt[289]—Christ might be understood to be so radically given, or "handed over," by the Father to us sinful creatures that there can be no interruption of his generous outpouring, no drawing back of the gift?

What I am proposing, more specifically—and this in light of insights drawn from within Adrienne's main corpus and exposited throughout this chapter—is that Christ's experience of dereliction might serve our understanding of the radical nature of his gift to us: not only from the "objective" perspective of the Father who gives the Son (cf. Jn 3:16), but also from the "subjective" perspective of the Son, who experiences himself as a gift—indeed as *the* gift of the Father—which is given so radically that it cannot be withdrawn by the Giver: not even when the gift is refused (cf. Jn 1:11).

In this sense, the incarnate Son might indeed be understood as "abandoned" by the Father into the hands of those who will crucify him.[290] Here, in other words, is not so much the revelation of the Son's "abandonment" by his Father (a revelation of "justice" done the one representing sinners), as the revelation of the rejection of God, in the person of his incarnate Son, by those whom he came to save. In fact, this interpretation is not altogether foreign to Balthasar, who explicitly writes: "We can even say that, in the cry of dereliction on the Cross, Jesus reveals how God is forsaken by sinners."[291] Because the Father does not intervene—because, in other words, his gift of the Son to the world is irrevocable even before the most extreme forms of hu-

---

289. See Schmitt, *The Sacrament of Confession as a "Sequela Christi" in the Writings of A. von Speyr*, 119. Schmitt refers to Adrienne's commentary of Psalm 22:2, wherein she explains: "Both the psalmist and the Son live out this abandonment [*Verlassensheit*], which comes from the Father, and [they] find in it not only their own feelings of being abandoned, but also something objective, common [*Gemeinsames*], a sort of determination [*Gestimmtheit*] by the Father" (Speyr, *Achtzehn Psalmen*, 40). Similarly: "the Son does not merely think himself to be forsaken [*verlassen*]; he is really forsaken. He recognizes a fact when he says, 'Why have you forsaken me?'" (*Erde und Himmel* II, no. 1464 [154]); see also *Kreuz und Hölle* I, 207.

290. Thomas Aquinas, *ST* III, q. 47, a. 3.

291. Balthasar, *Theo-Drama* III, 225. Similarly, Pope John Paul II recognizes that "in Christ there suffers a God who has been rejected by his own creature: 'They do not believe in me!'" (*Dominium et Vivificantem*, no. 41).

man resistance—Christ might well experience himself as "abandoned" by the Father both within his own human consciousness and within his members whom he has admitted therein: in, that is to say, his human consciousness and thus also in his psychological suffering.[292]

In fact, this solution actually coincides well with Balthasar's presentation of what he calls the "mission consciousness" of Christ:

> Now, the disposition of Christ is the disposition of one who has become expropriated for God and for man: his subjectivity coincides with his mission (this is the truth of the 'functional Christology' of Karl Barth and Oscar Cullmann). There is in him no unaffected residue of subjectivity which has not been assumed into his task as redeemer: everything down to the foundation of his person has been put at the disposal of his ministry and made available for his work. For this reason, in him the exalted feeling of his filial mission can coincide with the most extreme feeling of humiliation of the servant of Yahweh.[293]

From this point of view, we need not regard Christ as assuming our separation, or "distance," from God: as if such an act might mysteriously (almost "magically"[294]) bring us nearness. Instead, we are invited to focus upon Christ's eternal fidelity to the Father, which takes the concrete form in time of the irrevocable gift of himself to those to whom he is sent by the Father (cf. Jn 10:18; 14:31).[295] Hence also, as Balthasar fittingly puts it: "[T]his Body [of Christ] is given up through divine love more than through the world's hatred."[296] The Cross of Christ thus reveals God as "the One who conquers by," it bears repeating, "total self-surrender."[297]

It follows from this perspective that the mystical experience of the dark night is not simply one (as traditional spiritual theology teaches) of entering into the upper echelons of human perfection: of being more perfectly united to God through the passive purification of the soul by way of the "removal" of the effects of God's presence—effects which render union with him so delightful—in order that the mature soul might love God for himself

---

292. See McIntosh, *A Christology from Within*.

293. Balthasar, *The Glory of the Lord* I, 253–54; see also *Theo-Drama* III, 225, 254, and 509–11.

294. Balthasar acknowledges that his own proposition—that "the sinner is liberated to his own freedom by Christ's taking his place (Gal 5:1)"—"could border on magic: How is someone from outside of me to manipulate my freedom without my becoming aware of it and without my consent to or refusal of it?" He is nonetheless content acknowledging that "Paul, of course, does not seem to shy away from such an aporia when he maintains that 'Christ has died for us sinners at just the right time,' namely, 'when we were still powerless' and could not help ourselves (Rom 5:6)" (Balthasar, *Explorations in Theology* IV, 418).

295. Cf. Thomas Aquinas, *ST* III, q. 47, a. 2.

296. Balthasar, *Theo-Drama* V, 477; cf. Jn 10:18. See Thomas Aquinas, *ST* III, q. 37, a. 3, ad. 3; and *Comp* I, 231.

297. Balthasar, *Theo-Drama* II, 161.

alone.²⁹⁸ Without denying this important doctrine of spiritual perfection, I am proposing (at Adrienne's heel) that personal spiritual perfection be complemented by missionary zeal, such that even the experience of darkness might be understood in its light: not, to be sure, in the sense that the mystic might take the "place" of the estranged sinner in order that the former might thereby (by way of exchange) experience divine friendship.

Assuredly, the spiritual darkness of holiness (that of true mysticism) ought in no way to be thought of as a participation in the consciousness of sinners, as implying, for example, their repugnance for God: an idea absolutely foreign to the doctrine of both Balthasar and Adrienne, not to mention St. Thomas.²⁹⁹ Nor, however, should it be interpreted—and this idea is less foreign to their doctrine—as a participation in, or as a "taking on" of, their separation from God as caused by the sin of refusing God.³⁰⁰ Rather, precisely as a share in the spiritual suffering of Christ, the "dark night" of the Christian mystic is more appropriately interpreted—or so it seems to me—as that suffering caused by the knowledge that the sinner's rejection of Christ necessarily implies a *de facto* rejection of the Father (cf. Jn 8:19; 10:38; 14:10, 24; and 15:23–25) and, indeed, of salvation itself (cf. Jn 14:6, 17:3; Acts 4:12; and 1 Tim 2:5). As Balthasar would have it, "Jesus was aware that he was God's final Word of salvation to mankind."³⁰¹ Hence, "in Jesus judgment is actually present precisely because he is making love's last offer."³⁰² "Behind it, there is no greater

---

298. The most obvious example comes from St. John of the Cross in his classic, *Dark Night of the Soul*: "A description of this suffering and pain, although in truth it transcends all description, is given by David, when he says: 'The lamentations of death compassed me about; the pains of hell surrounded me; I cried in my tribulation' [Ps 17:5–7]. But what the sorrowful soul feels most in this condition is [...] that God has abandoned it, and, in His abhorrence of it, has flung it into darkness; it is a grave and piteous grief for it to believe that God has forsaken it. [...] For indeed, when this purgative contemplation is most severe, the soul feels very keenly the shadow of death and the lamentations of death and the pains of hell, which consist in its feeling itself to be without God, and chastised and cast out, and unworthy of Him; and it feels that He is wroth with it. All this is felt by the soul in this condition—yea, and more, for it believes that it is so with it for ever" (*Dark Night of the Soul*, trans. E. Allison Peers [New York: Image Books, 1959], II, ch. 4, 104–5). This is the example provided by Torrell in *Pour nous les hommes et pour notre salut*, 253–54. See also Teresa of Avila, *The Interior Castle*, trans. and ed. Edgar Allison Peers (New York: Image Books, 1989).

299. Torrell has good reason to argue that not only is the distancing due to sin impossible to Christ, but even that we must admit to the very contrary: that which approaches us to God is loving obedience, and Jesus gave the most supreme evidence of this throughout his passion (cf. Mk 14:36). See *Pour nous les hommes et pour notre salut*, 249. We thus do better to hold with St. Thomas that although Christ suffers on account of the flesh that he assumed which was "subject to pain," he does not suffer from the guilt of sin. See Thomas Aquinas, *ST* III, q. 15, a. 5, ad. 2.

300. It bears insisting that sin alone separates us from God. See Thomas Aquinas, *ST* III, q. 48, a. 4, ad. 1.

301. Balthasar, *The Glory of the Lord* VII, 163.

302. Balthasar, *Does Jesus Know Us?*, 83; see also 81; *Love Alone Is Credible*, 76 and 91; *Theo-Logic* II, 148; and Pope John Paul II, *Dominium et Vivificantem*, nos. 46–48.

love to call upon and to turn to (Heb 6:4–8; 10:26–31)."[303] This also explains Balthasar's very bold statement, "On the Cross, man's fear of God has become God's anxiety for man."[304]

Meanwhile, the one who is thus surrendered to the Lord within the Lord's own surrender is simultaneously given to share in his human experience of suffering love for all who reject him.[305] This suffering furthermore implies, Balthasar suggests, that the dark night of faith is to be lived with hope "against hope," as it were, that all men might be saved.[306] In this sense, it might be admitted that Christ suffered more *for* sinners (psychologically) than *in* himself (in his corporal members).[307] This suffering for sinners includes, moreover, Adrienne recognizes, a suffering for those who will share in his redemptive suffering for others and thus also in his own dark night. As such, it is proof that far from abandoning sinners, he actually takes upon himself the pain caused by our willing separation from him. Adrienne thus recognizes the Son's prayer, "My God, my God, why hast thou forsaken me?" (Mt 27:46) as implying a suffering for all who will in some way be initiated into his own salvific suffering.

> The entire premonition of the coming Passion lies entirely in this compassion with the others [his members]. It is not so much the mirror image of his own suffering in the others that troubles him as the fact that others—sinners, guilty persons—share his own suffering. And he fears that, because they are sinners, their insight into love could be much shorter and smaller than his own, that they could perish in this night. He knows that he himself will be at the end of his powers; but this excessive demand will nevertheless remain within perfect love, and, until the very moment of abandonment, he will always know that he has deposited everything with God. But how are the others, the sinners, to know this? They have their own personal experience of sin, and they will no longer be able to distinguish their own sin from that of others when they are in the night. Their own experience of sin will be used in their suffering to fill out the suffering [cf. Col 1:24]. He sees them as separated from themselves, as snatched away from themselves in their suffering through this experience of sin, and sharing, in this mode of separation, in his own separation from the Father.[308]

If such is the suffering of the dark night that the Lord endured for his members, such also—in, of course, a far lesser degree—is the suffering of those who share intimately therein. When, in other words, the dark night of the soul is lived authentically, it is lived—and Adrienne would hardly deny this—as in-

303. Balthasar, *Love Alone Is Credible*, 93.
304. Balthasar, *Theo-Drama* IV, 502.
305. See, for example, Balthasar, *Dare We Hope?*, 26.
306. See Balthasar, *Dare We Hope?*
307. Cf. Thomas Aquinas, *ST* III, q. 46, a. 6, ad. 4.
308. Speyr, *John* II, 363–64.

tercession for the world: "Forgive them, for they know not what they do!" (Lk 23:34; cf. Acts 7:60).

Where "abandonment" is granted a place in this scenario, it is not to be understood primarily in the negative sense as abandonment *by* God, but rather in the positive sense of abandonment (that is, surrender) *to* God, who has first of all abandoned himself to us: even to the point of suffering in advance what we will suffer *in him* for the salvation of the world, including our own salvation. "He [the Lord] alone has given the participation, and it is he who shudders and suffers here, by suffering the suffering of the others: he shares in suffering the other's share in suffering, he suffers in the others their suffering for him and with him."[309] Ultimately "Jesus' death in the sinner's estrangement from God means that no sinner can now attain to a perfect 'autonomous' loneliness." Instead, Christ accompanies the one who willfully refuses the Father's love all the way to the threshold of his or her definitive refusal. It is there—at the moment of the definitive "Yes or No of finite freedom" to God—that the Spirit of Christ, who is "exhaled in death" (the Son's "ultimate surrender to the Father and to us"), solicits finite freedom "at the very roots of freedom." As Balthasar writes:

> We do not know whether a human freedom can deny to the very end this offer of the Spirit to give it his own true freedom. If it could do so definitively, then it would be fully conscious in doing so and would be committing the sin against the Holy Spirit, an 'eternal sin' that 'never has forgiveness' (Mk 3:29). There is only room for hope at this point, where we simply can know nothing more. For a Christian, this is no arbitrary hope but one that makes, according to Jesus' command of love, no exception of any of our fellow human beings and lets none of them travel but halfway to the goal and then falter. 'J'espère en Toi pour nous' (Gabriel Marcel: I hope in Thee for us). We have the *obligation* to hope for the salvation of all.[310]

---

309. Ibid., 364.
310. Balthasar, *Epilogue*, 122. On the "'eternal sin' that 'never has forgiveness,'" cf. Thomas Aquinas, *ST* II-II, q. 14, a. 3.

SIX

The Man-Woman Difference-in-Unity
A "Trinitarian" Theology of the Sexes

Introduction: Sexual Differentiation Viewed from the Perspective of Christ's Assumption of Human Nature

The mysterious polarity of the sexes, intrinsic to the human condition, has already been addressed in our treatment (in chapter four) of Adrienne's theology of the body—wherein we investigated the spiritual-corporal unity of the human being from a sacramental perspective—as well as in our treatment of the relation between the individual and the community from an ecclesial perspective (in chapter five). Our desire to treat it more directly in a separate chapter not only confirms its importance within Adrienne's theological anthropology (as pointing, once again, to the Trinitarian difference-in-unity), but also reaffirms the interpenetrating nature of these tensions.[1] As for Balthasar's "own"[2] anthropology, the mysterious polarity of the sexes is so fundamental to human nature that it cannot, he maintains, go unexamined in his *Theo-Drama*. At the same time, in keeping with the overall theme of this volume, it represents—especially within the context of the love that animates it—"a concrete metaphor of Trinitiarian life within God."[3]

This fundamental significance of sexual difference revealed by Christ entails more than the simple "unfolding of what is latent in, and deducible from, the 'natural' datum," however. As Balthasar sees it, the ultimate, Christian, meaning of sexual differentiation "will *at least* bring what is human to its perfection (and superabundantly so)."[4] "The Incarnate Word, who is the

---

1. "For the man/woman relationship can stand as a paradigm of that community dimension which characterizes man's entire nature" (Balthasar, *Theo-Drama* II, 365).
2. In question, of course, is the unity of his anthropology with that of Adrienne.
3. Ibid., 415.   4. Balthasar, *Theo-Drama* III, 283.

ground and cause of everything, enters into the narrow limitation of sexual difference. He becomes human in one mode of being human and not in the other. With this passing of the whole into the fragment, the limitation of being able to live only in one sex becomes apparent in all its implications for the first time."[5]

In other words, the meaning of sexuality in its whole metaphysical dimension is—as Adrienne will also argue in her own exposition of the natural tension between the sexes—revealed by Christ. It is he, more specifically, who assumes the original meaning of sexuality implicit in the Father's creation by making himself dependent upon a woman and by associating her in his redemptive mission, just as he assumes everything that is human: as an act of love for the Father and with respect for the Father's creative intentions.[6] That he does so necessarily follows from the reality of his Incarnation, which Adrienne presents as the divine intention and goal of the whole relation between the sexes spanning the period between old and new covenants: "Men enable women to become fecund so that, at last, the Word might become flesh and the Church might issue from the Word-made-flesh."[7] He assumes this meaning, however, only after having first *established* this meaning within his eternal, divine will and with respect to his 'coming' Incarnation.

Adrienne, to explain, recognizes Christ as giving a new "fullness" to the relation of man and woman: a fullness which is "altogether heavenly" while remaining utterly connected to human sexuality.[8] This in turn means that whatever complementarity and mutually perfecting interaction might be said to exist between man and woman—as, for example, in their mutual receptivity and their complementary manners of self-giving[9]—might be understood as a sign or sacrament of the difference-in-unity, or unity-in-difference, of nature and grace. Hence, for example, the natural realm will be understood as revealing the supernatural, which will, in turn, reveal the most profound meaning of the natural. For "it is not the spiritual which is first but the physical, and then the spiritual. The first man was from the earth, a man of dust; the second man is from heaven" (1 Cor 15:46–47).

Similar is the teaching of St. Thomas, who recognizes a unity between the order of creation and the Incarnation of Christ such that he grants to

---

5. Balthasar, *A Theological Anthropology*, 308.
6. On the Son's willing dependency upon his Mother, see Speyr, *Handmaid of the Lord*, 39. Similarly, Balthasar argues: "For being in-the-flesh always means receiving from others" (*Theo-Drama* III, 177); see also *Elucidations*, 101–13, esp. 108; and *The Threefold Garland*, 31.
7. Speyr, *Theologie der Geschlechter*, 155.   8. Speyr, *Korinther* I, 324; cf. 1 Cor 11:12.
9. See Michele M. Schumacher, "Feminism, Nature and *Humanae Vitae*: What's Love Got To Do with It?" *Nova et Vetera* (English Edition) 6 (2008): 879–99.

Adam—even in the absence of his foreknowledge of his own sin—not only "an explicit faith in the Incarnation of Christ" but also a certain knowledge of "the great mystery" of Christ's love for the Church within his [Adam's] love for Eve.[10] This unity between the order of creation and the order of grace, between the first Adam and the second—so central to Balthasar's presentation of sexual differentiation[11]—is further evident in the still more recent presentation by Pope John Paul II of the Pauline analogy comparing the love of Christian spouses, on the one hand, and the love of Christ and the Church, on the other (cf. Eph 5:25–32), as *bi-directional*: "The covenant proper to spouses 'explains' the spousal character of the union of Christ with the Church," while the latter—precisely as a "great sacrament [*sacramentum magnum*]" (Eph 5:32)—"determines the sacramentality of marriage as a holy covenant between the two spouses, man and woman."[12] It could hardly be otherwise since, as Aquinas would have it, Christian spouses are "included in the union of Christ and the Church."[13]

It is thus in accord with recent and medieval tradition that Balthasar argues, as if to express the mind of Adrienne:

> The reciprocal fruitfulness of man and woman is surpassed by the ultimate priority of the 'Second Adam,' who, in suprasexual fruitfulness, brings a "companion," the Church, into being. Now the "deep sleep" of death on the Cross, the "taking of the rib" in the wound that opens the heart of Jesus, no longer takes place in unconsciousness and passivity, as in the case of the First Adam, but in the consciously affirmed love-death of the Agape, from which the Eucharist's fruitfulness also springs. [...] The first account of creation is over-fulfilled here, for in the mind of God the incarnate Word has never existed without his Church (Eph 1:4–6).[14]

What is unique, however, to the Speyrian-Balthasarian presentation of the mysterious "tension" of love between the sexes—not unlike that of the other "tensions" (differences-in-unity) that we have observed in previous chapters, and not unlike Balthasar's "own" approach, as we shall see later in this chapter—is the metaphorical description of the Trinitarian relations in terms of the relation between the sexes: the mutual giving and receiving of the divine persons to one another in what Adrienne presents as their reciprocal and archetypical surrender.

---

10. Thomas Aquinas, *ST* II-II, q. 2, a. 7.

11. See, for example, Balthasar, *Theo-Drama* II, 373–74; *The Christian State of Life*, 226–29; and *Elucidations*, 105–7.

12. Pope John Paul II, *Mulieris Dignitatem*, no. 23. Cf. Balthasar, "A Word on *Humanae Vitae*," *Communio* 20, no. 3 (1993): 437–50; and *Theo-Logic* I, 15.

13. Thomas Aquinas, *SCG* IV, c. 78, 4.

14. Balthasar, *Theo-Drama* II, 413. Cf. Speyr, *Das Wort und die Mystik* II, 534. See also Balthasar, *The Christian State of Life*, 103; and (with Scola), *Test Everything*, 81.

From this perspective, it is important to insist that although Adrienne draws from her experience of relating as a woman to men—her experience, that is to say, of relating in her whole physical-psychological-spiritual unity *qua feminine*, especially within her marital relationships but also in a nonsexual (by which I do not mean asexual) manner with Balthasar (within the context of what they perceived as their shared mission), her intention is not primarily nor especially that of "explaining" Trinitarian relations in terms of human ones: of "sexing the Trinity,"[15] as it were. Rather, she seeks within the fundamental communion of man and woman (whether within the marriage bond or within the state of consecrated virginity) an image to describe her mystical insight into the unity-in-difference of the divine persons: "a likeness [*Gleichnis*] of the unending love of the Father and Son, of Christ and the Church."[16]

This likeness observed by Adrienne—to repeat what I have already argued in chapter one—does not mean that her anthropology (as consistent with that of Balthasar) proceeds transcendentally from human persons to God. Rather, precisely because Adrienne recognizes human relations as patterned (however distantly) after Trinitarian ones, she has recourse to the former to explain (by way of metaphor or distant analogy) the latter. In other words, precisely this method of seeking, within human experience and human relations, images of Trinitarian life supposes the archetypical character of the latter. From this primacy of the divine archetype, it follows that human persons are enabled by grace—in accord with the important insight of the Second Vatican Council in *Gaudium et Spes*, no. 24—to pattern their relations with one another after the revealed relations of the Trinity.[17] This in turn presupposes not only the continuity of the original meaning of male-female relations as revealed in Genesis 2:23–24 and the redeemed relation of the same, as revealed in Ephesians 5:25, 29–32—but also the real mediating role of the Holy Spirit, who both animates the relation between Christ

---

15. Such is the accusation of Gerard Loughlin with regard to Balthasar's theology. Such is also more explicitly the project of Gavin d'Costa, who borrows from the works of the French feminist psychoanalytical philosopher, Luce Irigaray. See Gerard Loughlin, "Sexing the Trinity," *New Blackfriars* 79 (1998): 18–25; and Gavin d'Costa, *Sexing the Trinity: Gender, Culture and the Divine* (London: SCM Press, 2000).

16. Speyr, *Korinther* I, 320; see also, for example, Speyr, *Das Wort und die Mystik* I, 96. Cf. Balthasar, *TheoDrama* III, 340.

17. "Furthermore, the Lord Jesus, when praying to the Father 'that they may all be one ... even as we are one' (Jn 17:21–22), has opened up new horizons closed to human reason by implying that there is a certain parallel between the union existing among the divine persons and the union of the sons of God in truth and love. It follows, then, that if man is the only creature on earth that God has wanted for its own sake, man can fully discover his true self only in a sincere giving of himself" (*Gaudium et Spes*, no. 24). Cf. Balthasar, "A Word on *Humanae Vitae*," 443.

and the Church and resides within the faithful, enabling our relationships to reflect, or mirror, those of the Trinity, while simultaneously respecting the "ever-greater" difference[18] implied in any relation of created likeness to the Trinity.[19]

Before expositing Adrienne's presentation of the complementarity of the sexes within the order of redemption in light of this higher (most sublime) mystery of Trinitarian life and the mediating role of Christ and his Spirit, I will briefly exposit, in what follows, Balthasar's "own" treatment of the "tension-in-union" of the sexes from the perspective of, and in response to, his critics. Here, more specifically, I will highlight the fact that Adrienne's "vision from above" is likewise typical of Balthasar's treatment of sexual difference. The reader will then be invited to reconsider the so-called natural tension between the sexes, which Adrienne presents in terms of what she judges to be characteristically masculine and feminine manners of surrender. These, in turn, will be observed as archetypically existing within the revealed relation between Christ and the Father, on the one hand, and between Christ and Mary—his mother and "bride"—on the other. Finally, these archetypical relations will serve to clarify the question of masculine and feminine relations within the ecclesial missions.

Balthasar's Regard from Above in His Treatment of the Difference-in-Union of the Sexes

Turning, as we have done throughout this work, to Balthasar's treatment of the theme at hand before focusing on the amazing correspondence to the work of Adrienne—whence the constant question of their reciprocal influence—we might begin this chapter with still another challenge posed by Balthasar's critics: one which was in some sense already adumbrated in our introduction to this chapter. This challenge concerns, more specifically, the "ever-greater" difference between the Creator and his creation alluded to above. This principle of "ever-greater" difference, which Balthasar rightfully insists upon throughout his enormous corpus, is not, Gerard Loughlin argues,

---

18. Cf. *DZ* 806.

19. This, in turn, requires an active or dynamic assimilation of human relations to Trinitarian ones, an assimilation which both requires and respects our liberty. On the Spirit's role of mediating the love of Christ, with which Christians are challenged to love one another, see Balthasar, *Explorations in Theology* III, 173–83. It is worth noting that the Fourth Lateran Council makes reference in its formulation above to the very scriptural passage cited by the Second Vatican Council to draw comparison between the communion of human persons and that of the divine persons (Jn 17:22). Commenting on this passage, the earlier council (1215) teaches: "the word 'one' as applied to the disciples is to be taken in the sense of a union of charity in grace, but in the case of the Divine Persons in the sense of a unity of identity in nature" (*DZ* 806).

adequately respected in Balthasar's reference to the divinity in "supra-" sexual terms. Hence, for example:

> In Trinitarian terms, of course, the Father, who begets him without origin, appears primarily as (super-) masculine; the Son, in consenting, appears initially as (super-) feminine, but in the act (together with the Father) of breathing forth the Spirit, he is (super-)masculine. As for the Spirit, he is (super-)feminine. There is even something (super-)feminine about the Father too, since, as we have shown, in the action of begetting and breathing forth he allows himself to be determined by the Persons who thus proceed from him; however, this does not affect his primacy in the order of the Trinity.[20]

The prefix "supra" hardly compensates, Loughlin maintains, for Balthasar's description of the Trinitarian relations "in resolutely sexual terms" which "parody" an ancient biology, wherein "man gives to the woman, who is but an extension of himself."[21] To be sure, Balthasar elsewhere explicitly rejects these ideas.[22] Meanwhile, Loughlin refers to "parodies rather than metaphors, symbols or analogies," with the intention "not so much [...] to deny the propriety of these terms, as [rather to] disturb the ease with which theology uses them."[23] As for Corinne Crammer, she discerns a contradiction between Balthasar's insistence that sexuality and sexual difference cannot be applied to God, and his description of divine activities as "vividly reminiscent of sexual reproduction."[24] Hence, not unlike Laughlin who recognizes in Balthasar's theology a Trinity which is "parodied as a self-inseminating, self-fertilizing womb,"[25] Crammer observes in Balthasar's presentation of the Trinity that the "divine Persons penetrate each other. The Holy Spirit is the fruit of the love between the Father and the Son, who together generate the Spirit in an act of communal love. Christ's giving of himself in the Eucharist is compared to a man having intercourse, and in the act of procreation, a man 'represents only a distant analogy to this Trinitarian and Christological event' of the generation of the Son."[26]

From this point of view it is perhaps not surprising that Tina Beattie should

---

20. Balthasar, *Theo-Drama* V, 91.
21. Gerard Loughlin, "Sexing the Trinity," 24.
22. "The husband [...] encounters his wife as a separate person, with her own freedom and her own act of surrender to him—a freedom and a surrender that he does not create. The husband also realizes that [...] his wife possesses a feminine fruitfulness that is her own and stems even less from him" (Balthasar, "A Word on *Humanae Vitae*," 443). On Balthasar's faulting of ancient biology and his endorsement of the insights gathered from modern biology, see ibid., 442.
23. Ibid., 18.
24. Corinne Crammer, "One Sex or Two? Balthasar's Theology of the Sexes," in Oakes and Moss, *The Cambridge Companion to Hans Urs von Balthasar*, 101. Cf. Balthasar, *Theo-Drama* V, 91; and *Theo-Drama* II, 368.
25. Loughlin, "Sexing the Trinity," 23.
26. Crammer, "Balthasar's Theology of the Sexes," 101; she cites Balthasar, *New Elucidations*, 217.

judge Balthasar's "muddling of biological and spiritual categories" as "indefensible" from the perspective of the Catholic tradition.[27] By this critique she does not mean to deny the legitimate reference to, for example, the traditional symbol of Christ giving birth on the Cross, wherein she recognizes "a fluidity of meaning that invites a certain sense of playfulness and perhaps even irony and mimicry in the way we relate to sexual symbolism." She does not, however, find this fluidity of meaning respected in the Balthasar's appropriation of these symbols. For him, they become "clogged together with biological glue."[28]

These important objections are developed more thoroughly by Lucy Gardner and David Moss who esteem "the burden which sexual difference will be made to carry" in Balthasar's theology as perhaps "too much for it to bear."[29] By this they mean, more specifically, that sexual difference will be found responsible for providing "a space and a time between Christ and Mary, between Christ and the Church, analogous always to the difference, the *diastasis*, of creature from Creator."[30] To be sure, Gardner and Moss explain that it is impossible to consider the latter relation (that of the creature and the Creator) "before or apart" from our experience of inner-worldly difference.[31] Furthermore, they note as proper to Balthasar's thought the idea that "sexual difference is *more like* 'something like (the) sexes' [i.e., the Trinity] than that something [the Trinity] is 'like' sexual difference, or the sexes."[32] In other words, creation reflects the Creator, who—Balthasar would maintain in union with St. Thomas Aquinas—is *not* the reflection of creation.[33]

If, then, the Swiss theologian is to be faulted by Gardner and Moss, the fault lies *not* in his recourse to the analogy of sexual difference, but rather in his introduction within this same analogy of the themes of necessity, order, and number which "threaten violence [to women] in the reductive logic of a phenomenological account of sexual difference."[34] Here, more specifically, they recognize Balthasar's second (soteriological) portrayal of woman, as differing

27. Tina Beattie, "A Man and Three Women—Hans, Adrienne, Mary and Luce," *New Blackfriars* 79, no. 927 (1998): 104. In contrast to this accusation, see Balthasar, *New Elucidations*, 196.
28. Beattie, "A Man and Three Women," 103.
29. Gardner and Moss, "Something Like Time; Something Like the Sexes," 84; see also "Difference—the Immaculate Concept? The Laws of Sexual Difference in the Theology of Hans Urs von Balthasar," *Modern Theology* 14, no. 3 (July 1998): 377–401; and Kilby, *Balthasar: A Very Critical Introduction*, 146.
30. Gardner and Moss, "Something Like Time; Something Like the Sexes," 83.
31. See ibid., 128.   32. Ibid., 125; see also 117–18.
33. Cf. Thomas Aquinas, *ST* I, q. 4, a. 3, ad. 4
34. Gardner and Moss, "Something Like Time; Something Like the Sexes," 124. Cf. Crammer, "Balthasar's Theology of the Sexes," 107. From the contrary standpoint—that Balthasar's theology "threaten[s] violence"—see Aristotle Papanikolaou, "Person, *Kenosis* and Abuse: Hans Urs von Balthasar and Feminist Theologies in Conversation," *Modern Theology* 19, no. 1 (2003): 41–65. Papanikolaou argues that "Balthasar's understanding of *kenotic* personhood is the most adequate way to account for the healing of abused victims" (ibid., 42).

from his first (anthropological) portrayal of the same, as fundamentally unequal to man.[35] Not unlike Simone de Beauvoir's classic observation of woman as "the second sex,"[36] Balthasar's woman is "chronologically, temporally, historically, accidentally second,"[37] while his "man is the normative center."[38]

Picking up on this criticism, Corinne Crammer argues that the metaphors employed by Balthasar to describe sexual difference—namely the presentation of woman as "answer [*Antwort*]" and "answering gaze [*Anlitz*]"[39]—are "explicitly or implicitly hierarchical and incompatible with equality." This tendency toward inequality is furthermore advanced—or so it is argued—by Balthasar's presentation of Mary as "the archetype of the feminine" in relation to the male Christ and his arbitrary assumption that "whoever is hierarchically superior is masculine."[40] Still more objectionable to Gardner and Moss is Balthasar's phenomenological presentation of woman as answer, wherein she threatens to disappear, for she occupies a place in the *Theo-Drama* which "is more about Christ and the *Mensch* [that is to say, the normative male] than it is about woman."[41] "Woman cannot really act [therein] but only react, whereas Man can act—and it is his nature to do so."[42]

In short, Balthasar is accused of superimposing a theological vision of the

---

35. On the first (anthropological) portrayal of women, see Balthasar, *Theo-Drama* II, 365–82; on the second (soteriological) portrayal, see *Theo-Drama* III, 283–92. Moss and Gardner recognize this second account as "phenomenological." Inspired by the second creation account (in Gen 2), this account is, however—or so it seems to me—more exegetical (by which I mean specifically theological) than phenomenological, although his exegesis is undoubtedly inspired by Balthasar's Ignatian training, in virtue of which the human person is invited to enter, as it were, with all of his imaginative (and thus sensory) capacities into the biblical text. Unlike the project of Pope John Paul II, whose famous theology of the body might more properly be characterized as a phenomenological reading of the second creation account, with the intention of developing a theological anthropology of the sexes, Balthasar's work is governed—as much in the second volume of his *Theo-Drama*, as in his third—by the intention of developing a theological anthropology clarifying the relation between the human creature and the Creator in terms of the former's participation in the unique mission of Christ. See, to this effect, our presentation of Balthasar's "theological person" in chapter three of this volume. In contrast, see Pope John Paul II, *Man and Woman He Created Them*.

36. "Thus humanity is male and man defines woman not in herself but as relative to him; she is not regarded as an autonomous being. [...] She is defined and differentiated with reference to man and not he with reference to her; she is the incidental, the inessential as opposed to the essential. He is the Subject, he is the Absolute—she is the Other" (Simone de Beauvoir, *The Second Sex*, trans. H. M. Parshley [New York: Vintage Books, 1989], xxii).

37. Ibid., 86; cf. Crammer, "Balthasar's Theology of the Sexes," 103.

38. Gonzalez, "Hans Urs von Balthasar and Contemporary Feminist Theology," 573.

39. See Balthasar, *Theo-Drama* III, 283–92.

40. Crammer, "Balthasar's Theology of the Sexes," 105–6. See also Loughlin, "Sexing the Trinity," 24; and d'Costa, *Sexing the Trinity*, 31.

41. Gardner and Moss, "Something Like Time; Something Like the Sexes," 88. Balthasar's "Woman" appears to belong *to* man "as an object of property, not as a proper subject," they argue. She is "a word, and then a face, a vessel, a delight and even encounter—almost anything but herself, anything but woman" (88–89).

42. Crammer, "Balthasar's Theology of the Sexes," 106. Why, moreover, Crammer asks (ibid.), if woman's gaze is directed to man is not his gaze, in turn, directed to her?

relation between Christ and Mary (who is also the archetype of the Church)[43] upon the relation between the sexes, such that man (Christ) is always and necessarily prior to woman (Mary/Church), despite the possibility of granting her a certain *relative* priority in virtue of her maternal role.[44] Hence, although he insists upon the equality of the sexes, Balthasar also grants—or so it is maintained—"primary status" to the male, who is associated with the divinity, while woman is an image of the created order.[45] This association results, as Crammer sees it, in the "theological justification for [the] social inequality"[46] of—and even violence toward—women. Perhaps more to the point at hand, however, the "increasing over-determination"[47] of woman in relation to man is considered by Gardner and Moss as leading to a rigid fixation of sexual differentiation. Hence the very image that Balthasar employs to describe the *diastasis*—or to what we have referred to throughout this volume as difference-in-unity: "the dynamic movement of that which properly belongs together—a distance which gives unity"[48] between the Creator and the creature (namely, the image of sexual differentiation) is in fact, "conceived not so much as graceful unity but as a fixed distance or measure."[49] There thus arises the question of whether the difference-in-unity, or "tension-in-unity," of the Trinity, which finds an echo, or image, in the abiding difference between the Creator and his creation,[50] is in fact appropriately represented by the concept of sexual difference: at least, that is to say, as the latter is conceived by Balthasar.

In response to the first of these criticisms—that of theologically justifying social inequality—we do well to acknowledge that Balthasar, not unlike

---

43. Balthasar presents Mary as "Type of the Church" and "Bride of the Lord." See chapter four of the present volume and Balthasar, *Theo-Drama* III, 300–312; cf. Second Vatican Council, *Lumen Gentium*, no. 63 (*DZ* 4177).

44. As the child of Mary, Christ is issued from the "Church" of Israel; see Balthasar, *Explorations in Theology* II, 191.

45. Gonzalez, "Hans Urs von Balthasar and Contemporary Feminist Theology," 570. Cf. Balthasar, *Theo-Drama* II, 373. See also Gardner and Moss, "Something Like Time; Something Like the Sexes," 82 and 87; Crammer, "Balthasar's Theology of the Sexes," 107; and Agneta Sutton, "The Complementarity and Symbolism of the Two Sexes: Karl Barth, Hans Urs von Balthasar, and John Paul II," *New Balckfriars* 87, no. 1010 (July 2006): 433. On Balthasar's insistence upon the equality of the sexes, see his *Theo-Drama* III, 338; "Die Würde der Frau," *Internationale katholische Zeitschrift: Communio* 11, no. 4 (1982): 346–52; Susanne Greiner, "Die Würde der Frau: Ihre Bedeutung in der Theologie Hans Urs von Balthasar" in Karl Lehmann and Walter Kasper, *Hans Urs von Balthasar. Gestalt und Werk* (Köln: Communio, 1989), 285–97; and Anton Strukelj, "Man and Woman under God: The Dignity of the Human Being according to Hans Urs von Balthasar," *Communio* 20, no. 2 (Summer 1993): 377–88.

46. Crammer, "Balthasar's Theology of the Sexes," 107. Cf. Balthasar, *Mary for Today*, 56; *Theo-Drama* III, 287–88; "A Word on *Humanae Vitae*," 422; and "Die Würde der Frau," 350.

47. Gardner and Moss, "Something Like Time; Something Like the Sexes," 87.

48. Ibid., 85.

49. Ibid., 86; see also their "Difference—the Immaculate Concept?", 386. In contrast, see Balthasar, *Theo-Drama* III, 293.

50. Ibid., 340.

Adrienne as we shall see, is not primarily preoccupied, in the passages alluded to above, with the question of male-female differences and equality, which is not to admit that these are of no concern to him. Indeed, given, on the one hand, his caution with regard to "omnipresent danger" of equating the male with "the heavenly," or the spiritual, and the female with "matter" or "nature" and, on the other hand, his explicit rejection of certain "misogynistic utterances of the Fathers and Scholastics," we have reason to believe—contrary to the assertion of Gavin d'Costa—that he would have rejected any subordination of woman's freedom to that of man.[51] This, in fact, he explicitly acknowledges when—within the specific context of addressing sexual differentiation—he explains: "the freedom of the 'thou' cannot be mastered by the 'I' using any superior transcendental grasp—since in its proper context, all human freedom only opens up to absolute divine freedom."[52]

Hence, rather than addressing sexual differentiation in his *Theo-Drama* from the perspective of defending the unjust subordination of women or of encouraging the equality of women and of their rights within the Church and society—however much he might have supported these goals in principle—Balthasar addresses this subject as one preoccupied with what Gardner and Moss point to as *"theological* difference."[53] He is, more specifically, driven by the key insight that has concerned us throughout the many pages of this volume: that of the relation between the creature and the Creator as it images the Trinitarian relations revealed by Christ.[54] Hence, he warns us, for example, against promoting Mary to equal rank, as Christ's helpmate. This

---

51. Balthasar, *Theo-Drama* II, 367. Because the "archetype" for both the "masculine" and the "feminine" are to be found "together" in the eternal Logos, Balthasar reasons that it is impossible that we might regard one sex as "overpowering" the other; see "Die Würde der Frau," 350. On the other hand, in imitation of Mary's attitude vis-à-vis Christ, a woman ought to comply, Balthasar suggests, to her husband's wishes even "when she does not understand them" (Balthasar, *Mary for Today*, 56). As for d'Costa's criticism, he maintains that woman is depicted by Balthasar "as *primarily* passive, purely an instrument of a greater will and force" (*Sexing the Trinity*, 31).

52. Balthasar, *Theo-Drama* II, 366; see also "A Word on *Humanae Vitae*," 440; and "Die Würde der Frau," 350.

53. Gardner and Moss, "Something Like Time; Something Like the Sexes," 78; "Difference—the Immaculate Concept?," 386. See also Gonzalez, "Hans Urs von Balthasar and Contemporary Feminist Theology," 568–69.

54. This goal is particularly evident in "Die Würde der Frau," esp. 349; and *Elucidations*, 105–6. See also Balthasar, *Theo-Drama* V, 477–78; *A Short Primer for Unsettled Laymen*, 91; "Women Priests?" in *New Elucidations*, 195–96; John O'Donnell, "Man and Woman as *Imago Dei* in the Theology of Hans Urs von Balthasar," *Clergy Review* 68, no. 4 (1983): 117–28; Robert A. Pesarchick, *The Trinitarian Foundation of Human Sexuality as Revealed by Christ according to Hans Urs von Balthasar: The Revelatory Significance of the Male Christ and the Male Ministerial Priesthood* (Rome: Editrice Pontificia Università Gregoriana, 2000), esp. 173–212; David L. Schindler, "Catholic Theology, Gender, and the Future of Western Civilization" in his *Heart of the World, Center of the Church: "Communio" Ecclesiology, Liberalism, and Liberation* (Grand Rapids, Mich.: Eerdmans, 1996), 237–74; and Gardner and Moss, "Something Like Time; Something Like the Sexes," 75–76.

would have "dire consequences in Mariology if the man/woman polarity is allowed to obscure the distance between God and the creature."⁵⁵ "There is no original 'collaboration' between God and the creature," Balthasar explains, but "the creature's 'femininity' possesses an original, God-given active fruitfulness."⁵⁶ It follows that Mariology and ecclesiology are "functionally dependent on Christology."⁵⁷

It is to this end—that of explaining the analogy between the creature and the Creator—that Balthasar employs what Crammer refers to as the important nuptial metaphor that she rightly recognizes as "so central to Balthasar's theology."⁵⁸ However unpopular this comparison is in the eyes of his critics,⁵⁹ it can hardly be attributed to Balthasar's misogynist intentions, for example. Indeed, as Tina Beattie correctly acknowledges, it is not of his invention at all, but is, rather, of biblical and patristic origin, so as to be theological in the true sense of the term.⁶⁰ The Swiss theologian is, furthermore, careful to note (already at this stage, for his Christology is the central piece of his bi-directional analogy between the Trinity, on one hand, and the Creator-creature relation, on the other hand)⁶¹ not only the likeness that is to be implied by this comparison, but also the unlikeness that might lead astray those who would apply the image too literally:

Christ does something that a husband can in no way do: Christ brings forth the Church from himself as his own fullness, as his body, and, finally, as his Bride. By his self-surrender, he confers upon the Church the form and structure he desires, the

---

55. Balthasar, *Theo-Drama* III, 310; see also 287; and *Heart of the World*, 39–40.
56. Balthasar, *Theo-Drama* III, 296.
57. Ibid., 290.
58. Ibid., 100. Cf. Balthasar, *Explorations in Theology* II, 143–66; *A Short Primer for Unsettled Laymen*, 92; *Theo-Drama* V, 462; *Theo-Logic* II, 62; *Elucidations*, 67; *A Theological Anthropology*, 313; and (with Scola), *Test Everything*, 81. See also Strukelj, "Man and Woman under God," 387; Kerr, *Twentieth-Century Theologians*, 121–44; Kilby, *Balthasar: A (Very) Critical Introduction*, 123–46; and Raymond Gawronski, *Word and Silence*.
59. See, for example, Fergus Kerr, "Discipleship of Equals or Nuptial Mystery?", *New Blackfriars* 75, no. 884 (July/August 1994): 344–54, esp. 349.
60. See Beattie, "A Man and Three Women," 103–4. In the Old Testament this image is used to describe the relation between Yahweh and Israel (Hos 1–3; Is 54:1–17, 62:5; Jer 8; and Ez 16), whereas in the New Testament Christ is presented as the bridegroom of his Church, the bride (Mt 9:15; Mk 2:19–20; Lk 5:34–35; Jn 3:29; 2 Cor 11:2; Eph 5:27; and Apoc 19:7–8, 21:2–9). On the patristic imagery, see, for example, Balthasar, "A Word on *Humanae Vitae*," 440–41; and *Explorations in Theology* II, 146–48. See also *The Catechism of the Catholic Church*, nos. 757, 766, and 772. Karen Kilby, meanwhile, criticizes Balthasar for "arguing *from* his nuptial scheme rather than *to* it in relation to tradition" (*Balthasar: A (Very) Critical Introduction*, 144). "Gender and sexuality become for Balthasar something of a framework uniting many of the loci of theology, a key in light of which Scripture is organized and interpreted, a norm by which tradition is sifted" (ibid., 146). My own thesis is that this theme is only *one* of the metaphors and analogies that he uses to explain the Trinitarian relations, which in turn is the fundamental concern dominating his vast theological project.
61. See Balthasar, *Theo-Drama* II, 413–14.

life of the Holy Spirit that is a counterpart to his own life. The husband, on the other hand, encounters his wife as a separate person, with her own freedom and her own act of surrender to him—a freedom and a surrender that he does not create. The husband also realizes that, as we have seen, his wife possess a feminine fruitfulness that is her own and stems even less from him.[62]

It is, moreover, precisely this archetypical surrender of Christ which is the key moment of Balthasar's reasoning whenever this (nuptial) comparison is applied by him (or Adrienne, as we will see) to the relation between the sexes.[63] After all, the importance which he does indeed accord to woman as "answer" and "face"—both of which, as his critics rightfully point out, imply secondary or responsive action based upon "male" (that is, "Christic") initiative—serves to highlight the fact that this woman of Genesis 2 is *the* woman. Simultaneously Eve, Mary, the Church, and the Christian, "She" is, in other words, the archetypical theological person whom we exposited in chapter three. Balthasar admits to this explicitly when, in his exposition of "Woman's Answer," he presents her as "the prototype who fulfills everything said in the previous volume [*Theo-Drama* II] concerning the relationship between finite and infinite freedom."[64] This, more specifically, is the relationship resulting from Christ's always initiating surrender, which awakens and enables our own surrender, such that our "yes" of fidelity is not only provoked by, but also taken up into, his own. Our self-gift is, in other words, introduced into his own gift of self to the Father for the salvation of the world. Or as Balthasar puts it: "This is finite freedom that hands itself over and entrusts itself to the sphere of infinite freedom, which, through grace, stands wide open."[65] From this perspective we might agree with Balthasar's critics that his view of sexual differentiation is perhaps limited by his particular cultural context and that it should not be applied as a measure of the "correct" "distance" between the sexes, especially when that means prioritizing the male and conceiving of women in terms of her role of responding—or of *being* (rather than of *speaking*) a response—to male initiative.[66]

---

62. Balthasar, "A Word on *Humanae Vitae*," 443. Similarly: "For God and man are related in a manner far different from man and woman: in no way do they complete one another" (*Heart of the World*, 39–40). On man's dependence upon woman, see *Theo-Drama* II, 369.

63. See, for example, Balthasar, *A Short Primer for Unsettled Laymen*, 92 and 95; *New Elucidations*, 193 and 196; *Glory of the Lord* I, 673; *Mysterium Paschale*, 132; *Theo-Drama* III, 332, 334 and 357; "A Word on *Humanae Vitae*," 446; and Healy, *The Eschatology of Hans Urs von Balthasar*, 152–55.

64. Balthasar, *Theo-Drama* III, 299; see also 341; and (with Ratzinger) *Mary: The Church at the Source*, 102–14.

65. Balthasar, *Theo-Drama* III, 299.

66. This is a particular concern of Gardner and Moss; see their "Difference—the Immaculate Concept?", 383; and "Something Like Time; Something Like the Sexes," 88–92. See also Rachel Muers, "A Question of Two Answers: Difference and Determination in Barth and von Balthasar," *Hethrup*

On the other hand, and more importantly, it might be maintained that Balthasar recognized in this (possibly culturally-determined)[67] view of sexual difference a particularly appropriate expression, analogy, or metaphor of the Creator-creature relation.[68] In that case, it might also be true—as Gardner and Moss propose—that it is not so much his *culture* that influences Balthasar's perception of sexual difference as it is his *theology*: "we trace the fixing of sexual difference—in the over-determination of woman as essentially second and dual, and ultimately as body—as *a difference in which the God-creature differential is to be secured*."[69] This, in other words, is an important example of how, for Balthasar, "anthropology could be and ought to be treated as a function of Christology,"[70] which in turn, we have seen, he anchors in Trinitarian theology. In the words of Gardner and Moss: "In order to represent Origin in the world (and this is his procession from the Father) the one who appears to be quasi-feminine must nevertheless be a man. In addition, in order to establish him *as man*, the feminine will be made to proceed from him. And, to 'reassure' still further, we are guaranteed that there can be no question of parthenogenesis—of feminine from feminine—here."[71]

From this perspective, the danger posed by Balthasar's presentation of sexual difference is not simply nor primarily the threat of "violence" to women, as many of his critics (including Gardner and Moss)[72] point out. More fundamental still, they suggest, is the danger that this particular manner of viewing sexual difference—what Gardner and Moss present as "a distortion

---

Journal 60 (1999): 276; and "The Mute Cannot Keep Silent: Barth, von Balthasar, and Irigaray, on the Construction of Women's Silence," in Susan Frank Parsons (ed.), *Challenging Women's Orthodoxies in the Context of Faith* (Sydney: Ashgate, 2000), 109–20. As for the accusation that Balthasar is subject to his cultural context, this seems—ironically enough—to be the case when he writes, for example: "Prescinding from any and every social system (patriarchal or matriarchal) and from all theories of procreation (ancient, scholastic, or modern), it always remains true that in sexual intercourse it is the man who is the initiator, the leader, the shaper, while the woman's love—even if it is not passive, but just as active in its own way—is still essentially receptive" (Balthasar, "A Word on *Humanae Vitae*," 443–44). This affirmation seems to make sense only if by "sexual intercourse" Balthasar refers uniquely to the moment of penetration: an understanding which I view as a reduction of this particular act of love. For a more holistic (metaphysical) presentation of the love between the sexes, see Balthasar, *New Elucidations*, 196.

67. This he denies when, for example, in the context of arguing that a woman (in imitation of Mary's submission to Christ) ought to comply with her husband's wishes even when she does not understand them, he writes: "We should not speak too easily of this view being sociologically outdated. Mary is not a feminist" (Balthasar, *Mary for Today*, 56). On the other hand, in referring to the "matriarchal" and "patriarchal" dimensions of the Church, he writes that "these sociological categories can be applied only in a very loose sense to the Church" (Balthasar and Ratzinger, *Mary: The Church at the Source*, 140).

68. This is explicit, for example, in his *A Theological Anthropology*, 313.

69. Gardner and Moss, "Something Like Time; Something Like the Sexes," 78; emphasis added.

70. Balthasar, *Theo-Drama* II, 428.

71. Gardner and Moss, "Something Like Time; Something Like the Sexes," 131; cf. Balthasar, *Theo-Drama* III, 283–84.

72. See, for example, "Difference—the Immaculate Concept?" 379.

of the truth of the mutuality and exchange and undecidability of the relationships between the sexes"—might influence our manner of viewing the relation between the Creator and the creature and ultimately of the Trinitarian relations *as fixed*.[73] What Gardner and Moss observe in Balthasar's theology, in other words, is not only that sexual difference is employed as a distant analogy or metaphor to describe the inner life of God (*"something like* something in the life of God") but also—and herein lies their critique—that this difference is itself "forced," or "fixed in advance," in such a way as "to order and similarly over-determine the whole of Balthasar's thought," including most especially his understanding of the Creator-creature relation and even of the intra-Trinitarian relations.[74]

We are thus again confronted, from still another angle, with the critique of Balthasar's theology that dominated chapter five. In his presentation of the conflict between divine and human freedom, the Swiss theologian is accused, to be more exact, of insisting too unilaterally upon a resolution "from on high."[75] Hence, the question is asked whether the human person is indeed granted a place (or "voice"[76]) within this drama or whether instead everything is realized within the "space" of divine freedom: between the Father and Son in the union of the Spirit. In short, we are faced again with the question of whether the "distant analogy"[77]—this time, that of sexual difference—employed by Balthasar to describe the *diastasis* between the Creator and the creature calls into question one of the most fundamental presuppositions of Balthasar's *Theo-Drama*: that God has given to human persons "a genuine, spiritual freedom which, because it has been really *given*, cannot be 'upstaged' by God's infinite freedom but has to fulfill itself in its proper area (in God, where else?)." In other words, the question is being raised whether "the primal drama" is indeed—as Balthasar claims—"played between divine and human freedom,"[78] or whether instead it is played out not only *within* divine freedom, but also *between* divine freedom, namely that of the Father and the Son in the union of the Holy Spirit. The latter proposition moreover would not only call into question the role of human freedom, it would also

---

73. Gardner and Moss, "Something Like Time; Something Like the Sexes," 129; see also 78–79.
74. Ibid., 132–35.
75. Michel Beaudin, *Obéissance et solidarité,* 307.
76. Cf. Gardner and Moss, "Something Like Time; Something Like the Sexes," 136–37.
77. "A distant analogy […] but it is an analogy nonetheless" (Balthasar, "A Word on *Humanae Vitae,*" 444).
78. Balthasar, *Theo-Drama* II, 428. "In brief, we must see on the theodramatic stage the same magnanimity and generosity on God's part as that which caused him to allow created reality to enjoy free partnership with him" (*Theo-Drama* III, 341).

seem to entail, as we will see at length in chapter seven, that there are several wills within the Godhead: a doctrine that would in turn call into question the unity of divine nature.

It is, however, among the goals of this chapter to demonstrate that if Balthasar is read—as he himself insisted that he ought to be read—in union with Adrienne's doctrine, then the nuptial symbolism that does indeed dominate much of his work might be interpreted in such a way as to more congruently support his thesis that "the divine act whereby Christ provides himself with a vessel, a Bride (Eph 5:26), is not simply one-sided, for the divine-human Agent has himself been brought into the world by a woman. Her cooperation, the work of her who serves both as a woman *and* as a creature, is not forgotten: it is integrated into his."[79]

In, for example, Adrienne's presentation (appropriated by Balthasar)[80] of the oscillating character of woman, who is—precisely in relation to man, but also in virtue of her free and personal surrender—both mother and bride, we approach the solution of Gardner and Moss to the so-called fixation of sexual differentiation in Balthasar's thought, or to what they consider his spatial and temporal ordering of the sexes in such a way as to grant "persisting priority"[81] to the male. This, in turn—it is argued—leads to the fixation of an analogy between the sexes and the divine Persons: an analogy which ought to remain—or, again, so it is argued—fluid.[82]

The solution of Gardner and Moss is, in fact, amazingly similar to that of Adrienne, as we have seen in chapter three, where Mary is considered as the primary theological person: "Person as Response."

Mary is not only *dual*—bride (to one *Mensch*) and mother (to others)—but also *first* bride, bride in her *fiat*, in order, at the last (that is, eschatologically) to become again

---

79. Balthasar, *Theo-Drama* III, 351; see also *Explorations in Theology* IV, 340; and (with Ratzinger), *Mary: The Church at the Source*, 114.

80. Woman, Balthasar maintains, "cannot be summed up in a neat definition. She is a process that oscillates (from the Virgin Bride to the Mother of the Church, from the answering Person to the Source of the race); it is the theorizing of men that attempts to make this flux and flow into a rigid principle" (Balthasar, *Theo-Drama* III, 293; see also 338).

81. Balthasar, *Theo-Drama* II, 373. This would follow, more specifically, as a consequence of the fact that: "Every true human stance toward the Absolute can only be an answer to the prior 'deed-word' of God: by hearing and following it by proceeding along God's way" (Balthasar, *Explorations in Theology* IV, 324; see also 342).

82. "For analogy would, at first glance, appear to be a relation between two. And yet, repeatedly, there seems to be (at least) three in play: world and God—and Christ; man and woman—and child, or God, or Christ; before and after—and now; sexual difference and time—and God, or space; Christ and Mary—and Church; giving and receiving, doing and letting happen—but three Persons; and perhaps most puzzlingly, the hypostatic union (two) as the concrete *analogia entis* and also as an image of the relationships of the three Persons of the Trinity" (Gardner and Moss, "Something Like Time; Something Like the Sexes," 127).

his bride. And so we might suggest that she is at once his bride and his mother, whilst also being (becoming) his bride in order to become his mother, and then his mother *in order* to become his bride. Indeed, she is—becomes—first his bride in order to become his bride (at the last).[83]

Such, more specifically, it is argued, are the implications of the doctrine of the Immaculate Conception, which Gardner and Moss regard as "an unbreakable circle in which effect is cause of cause."[84] Meanwhile, this formulation is also amazingly similar to that of Balthasar, who regards the Immaculate Conception in view of Mary's "twofold mission: as a Mother, she has to mediate—in the requisite purity—everything human that her Child needs; as her Son's 'companion' and 'bride,' she must be able to share his sufferings in a way appropriate to her."[85]

Still more significant is the oscillating character of Christ himself, who—Adrienne will argue, and Balthasar will echo[86]—is the "archetype" and "primal image [*Urbild*]" of both masculinity and femininity, for Christ is said—already in his eternal relation to the Father—to image what Adrienne presents as typically feminine and masculine forms of surrender. Or, as Balthasar explains, in terms which echo those of Adrienne, the eternal Son is simultaneously "passive" in his "self-reception [*Selbstempfang*]," and thus "feminine," and "affirmative-active" in his "self-thanking [*Selbstverdankung*]," and thus "masculine."[87] While these characterisations might—to return to the concern of Balthasar's critics—be said to be culturally determined, it is once again evident that the primary concern is theological. His purpose in employing these images is, more specifically, that of guarding the distance between the Creator and his creation.

Hence, while the Son might be said to be *both* "masculine" and "feminine" in relation to the Father,[88] all in respecting the necessary ("unchangeable" or *unumkehrbare*) order in the Trinity, in the world he is—precisely as the representative of the Father who is the "absolutely primal"[89] origin—nec-

---

83. Ibid., 133.
84. Ibid; cf. Balthasar, *Theo-Drama* III, 97 and 352; *Mary for Today*, 56; and *Explorations in Theology* II, 190–91.
85. Balthasar, *Theo-Drama* III, 323.
86. See, for example, his "Die Würde der Frau," 50–51; *Theo-Drama* III, 283–84 and 341; *New Elucidations*, 193; John O'Donnell, "Man and Woman as *Imago Dei* in the Theology of Hans Urs von Balthasar"; and Pesarchick, *The Trinitarian Foundation of Human Sexuality*, 173–78.
87. Balthasar, "Die Würde der Frau," 350–51.
88. It is thus not surprising that Gardner and Moss should argue that "Trinitarian differencing seems at once to establish and to question an ordering of 'primacy'" ("Something Like Time; Something Like the Sexes," 127).
89. Hans Urs von Balthasar, *Credo: Meditations on the Apostles' Creed*, trans. David Kipp (San Francisco: Ignatius Press, 2002, 2005²), 30.

essarily masculine. This logic follows from his association (borrowed from Adrienne, as we shall see)—whether by reason of biology, of culture, or of a more metaphysically-founded meaning—of *the masculine* with the giving, or "dispensing," form of (self-) surrender and his association (also to be found in the works of Adrienne) of *the feminine* with the receptive form of (self-) surrender.[90]

"In no way" can the Son of God be said, Balthasar reasons, to be primarily receptive (*Empfangende*) vis-à-vis creation and the Church. Rather, he is necessarily "the one who produces [*Hervorbringende*]": even when he wills himself to be "won-back [*zurückgewinnen*]" from the Church and creation so as to fulfill his terrestrial mission.[91] Hence, "The Woman (the 'Immaculata' of Ephesians 5:27) who comes forth from the Man as he slumbers on the Cross is not so much a gift to him in his need as the product of his own fullness."[92] In this way, Balthasar reasons, Christ's generosity vis-à-vis the Church and creation, which is reflected in the Marian and Petrine dimensions of the Church,[93] might be likened to that of God the Father, who, although he remains the "absolutely primal"[94] origin of the Trinity, nonetheless accords to the Son and the Spirit, within his begetting act, the possibility of (passively) receiving and of (actively) thanking the Father for the gift of the whole divine essence. In a similar manner, God "always entrusts something of his creative power to the responsibility of his creature, and man [that is to say, man *and* woman] is not giving thanks properly when he freezes, as it were, in the act of looking backward in reverent thanksgiving. No, he must show that he has understood God's gesture of gift-giving by taking it over and becoming a giver: not only in the generation of children, but in every kind of human communication and fruitfulness."[95]

The Complementarity of the Sexes within the Sublime Order of Redemption as Viewed by Adrienne von Speyr

It is among the purposes of this chapter to demonstrate that Balthasar's primary concern of proposing—precisely within the "open, perfected ten-

---

90. See ibid. As Corinne Crammer sees it, for example: "For Balthasasr, the feminine is characterized by receptivity (*Emphfänglichkeit*), obedience, disponibility, and willing consent to the action of another, or letting be (*Gelassenheit*). Although he regards these characteristics as appropriate for all people in relation to God, he describes these qualities as specifically *feminine*." ("Balthasar's Theology of the Sexes," 98).

91. Balthasar, "Die Würde der Frau," 351. 92. Balthasar, *Theo-Drama* III, 338.

93. See Balthasar, *Explorations in Theology* II, 158; *Elucidations*, 101–13; and (with Ratzinger), *Mary: The Church at the Source*, 111, 140, and 167–76.

94. Balthasar, *Credo*, 30.

95. Balthasar and Ratzinger, *Mary: The Church at the Source*, 128–29.

sion and fruitfulness"[96] of the sexes—a fitting image of the dynamic tension of love marking both the Creator-creature relation and the relation of the divine persons,[97] is shared (if not inspired) by Adrienne von Speyr. Not unlike Balthasar's insistence upon the irreducible difference between the sexes,[98] for example, Adrienne maintains that neither man nor woman can—in the absence of the other—represent the whole of humanity. And, in that which concerns Christ, he is man, not woman. "As the new Adam he needs the new Eve," Adrienne reasons. It is after all precisely in his interaction with Mary and not as an isolated man, nor as a man among other men, that he reveals the divinely intended meaning of sexuality.[99] This also explains the importance of Mary's role in the whole economy of redemption. "Man alone should not be the one who is redeeming and redeemed: woman, too, should be the first redeemed and therefore co-redeeming. Just as Adam and Eve have sinned with one another, so, too, must the Son and Mother, at another level, redeem with one another; they put the work of redemption into place where the fall from sin [sic] occurred. Eve drew Adam into sin, and Christ draws Mary into redemption."[100]

Given (as we have seen in the general introduction to this volume) the place of the Cross in Adrienne's visions of creation, it is not surprising that Mary—precisely as "co-redeemer" and thus also as "pre-redeemed," or immaculately conceived—is somehow mysteriously present at the world's creation: by way, that is to say, of her place of precedence within the divine intentions.[101] Adrienne admits "of course," that Mary is not actually present on the first day of creation, but the mystic reasons that she "co-creates" in the work of "correcting" creation: in the rectification of Eve.[102] The "first-born of Redemption," Mary realizes "the idea of the perfect human being" that God had in mind in creating the first woman.[103] Eve willingly distanced herself from this divine idea, but it is effectively realized in Mary, who does not succumb

---

96. Ibid., 140.
97. See, for example, Balthasar, *New Elucidations*, 195–96; and *Theo-Drama* V, 91.
98. See, for example, Balthasar, *Theo-Drama* II, 365–66; and *Elucidations*, 105–6.
99. See Speyr, *Handmaid of the Lord*, 37; cf. Balthasar, *Theo-Drama* III, 338. For an application of this logic within the context of the feminist debate, see Michele M. Schumacher, "The Nature of Nature in Feminism, Old and New: From Dualism to Complementary Unity" in Schumacher, *Women in Christ*, 17–51.
100. Speyr, *Mary in the Redemption*, 65; cf. Balthasar and Ratzinger, *Mary: The Church at the Source*, 114. We are not far from the insight of St. Irenaeus: "the knot of Eve's disobedience was untied through the obedience of Mary. For what the virgin Eve tied through unbelief, the Virgin Mary set free through faith" (Cf. St. Irenaeus, *Adversus Haereses* III, 22, 4; Saward (trans.), *The Scandal of the Incarnation*, 60–61).
101. See Speyr, *Mary in the Redemption*, 18–19.
102. Cf. ibid., 64.
103. Speyr, *The Cross: Word and Sacrament*, 34; and *Mary in the Redemption*, 20.

to temptation.[104] She is "the true creation, as it goes forth from the Creator's hands and as it returns to God without distancing itself, without dispersing its unity." As such, she is not simply a natural creature, but one enjoying "a new impulse" of grace through her corporal and spiritual bond with her Son, who is also the Son of God. By means of this authentically human bond, the Son acknowledges and affirms in Mary's graced humanity "the essence of human nature as the Father desired it."[105] Hence, she is "in fact not the second but the first Eve," the one "who did not fall," who looks on as the second Eve does fall.[106] Adrienne thus insists upon a certain priority of Mary over Eve: "Christ is not just Adam regained: he is God. Mary is not just the reintegration of Eve: she is the Mother of God."[107]

Faithful to this inspiration of regarding the Christ-Mary bond as preceding, within the divine intention, the bond between Adam and Eve, Adrienne recognizes the former relationship as embodying not simply the meaning of sexuality in general—the 'original' meaning of sexuality as it was intended by the Creator but also "all the later relationships between man and woman in the Church." This original meaning concerns, more specifically, "the first bond between man and woman" so as to be "decisive for all later bonds."[108] It is thus not surprising that Adrienne's theology of the sexes draws its inspiration here. In contrast to the popular tendency of explaining the spiritual fruitfulness of virginity in terms of the corporal fruitfulness of marriage, for example, Adrienne takes as her starting point the "pre-eminent" fecundity of the virginal, consecrated life—the life chosen by Christ and upheld by the Church as a means of following him "more nearly"[109]—to explain the fecundity and sacramental significance of marriage.[110]

It is, more specifically, the mystery of the spousal relationship between Christ and Mary-Church[111] and that of the maternal-filial relationship also between Mary and Christ and later between Mary and John that found and explain the original, created meaning of sexual relations and thus also of marriage. The latter relation, in turn, is a sort of revelation of—based upon a par-

---

104. See Speyr, *The Cross: Word and Sacrament*, 42.
105. Ibid., 30; see also 38 and 43.   106. See ibid., 20.
107. Ibid., 64.
108. Speyr, *Handmaid of the Lord*, 85. Cf. Balthasar, *A Theology of History*, 96.
109. See *The Catechism of the Catholic Church*, no. 916.
110. Such is also the perspective of Balthasar. See David S. Crawford, "Of Spouses, the Real World, and the 'Where' of Christian Marriage," *Communio* 33 (Spring 2006): 100–116. As an example of studying the fruitfulness of virginity in light of the natural fecundity of marriage, see for example Pope John Paul II, *Mulieris Dignitatem*, no. 20.
111. See our treatment of the identification of Mary with the Church in chapters three and four of the present volume.

ticipation in—the former relations.[112] Within this perspective, sacramental marriage is—as we saw in chapter four—"primarily a supernatural thing"[113] such that the corporal dimension is integrated within the larger realm of the supernatural and the spiritual fruitfulness of the sacrament is considered greater than bodily fruitfulness. Such, of course, is the mystery of consecrated celibacy wherein spiritual fruitfulness is deemed more significant than natural fecundity. This, however, is not in any way to deny or otherwise downplay both the natural *and* supernatural significance of human sexuality, as we shall see. Married persons are also called to spiritual fruitfulness, and consecrated virgins—whether male or female—must embrace their sexuality as a gift offered to God for bearing fruit according to God's own measure, that is to say, as "a participation in the mystery of fruitfulness of the Divine Persons."[114]

From this perspective, the ultimate source and archetype of fecundity in both the marital and the virginal vocations is the Trinitarian love of God: as the Son lives constantly from the Father and to the Father, the Church lives essentially from the Son and to the Son.[115] As if to clarify that this "as" implies a continuation between the one relationship and the other rather than an external likeness between the two, Adrienne explains that the Son's fruitfulness in the Church stems from the Father, rather than from himself, so as to also reveal the Father. As such, it is, Adrienne insists, necessarily virginal.[116] It follows that the "law" governing both the religious and married states of life is that of remaining within the "circulation" of Trinitarian love: from God to God.[117]

The Natural "Tension" between the Sexes and Their Reciprocity in View of Grace

This "higher" vision of sexuality should in no way be confused with a sort of shunning, belittling, or overlooking of the natural difference between the sexes. In fact, Adrienne opens her *Theology of the Sexes* with these telling

---

112. Adrienne argues, for example, that in giving himself corporally to the Church in the Eucharist, the Lord simultaneously elevates the man's "surrender [*Hingabe*]" to his wife within the marital act. See Speyr, *Theologie der Geschlechter*, 132.

113. Ibid., 117; see also *Das Wort und die Mystik* II, 534.

114. See Speyr, *John* IV, 125.   115. See Speyr, *Das Hohelied*, 50–51.

116. See Speyr, *John* IV, 125. Cf. Balthasar, *Unless You Become Like This Child*, 64; and *The Christian State of Life*, 234. The connection between the one relationship (Christ-Church) and the other (Father-Son) is, Adrienne teaches, the Eucharist. Hence, whoever rejects the Eucharist "is without access to the Trinitarian fellowship" (*World of Prayer*, 72).

117. Ultimately Adrienne argues, as we saw in chapter three, that there can be no "third" state of life, because unlike marriage and the consecrated life, the single (non-consecrated) state could not procure the fruit arising from sexual difference, which in turn lies within the mystery of Trinitarian love and divine fecundity. See also Speyr, *Theologie der Geschlechter*, 116.

words: "Look at reality head-on: no flight [*Flucht*] from the sexual."[118] Similarly she argues that the virginal men and women of the community of St. John that she co-founded with Balthasar, far from shunning the flesh, should be truly thankful to God for the gift of their sexuality so as to better offer it to Him: not so much in sacrifice as in service.[119] Making oneself into a eunuch is the very contrary of Christian virginity, Adrienne insists. "The eunuch is wholly sterile; the Christian is fruitful to the highest degree."[120] More surprising still, she—a physician—recommends that every priest, precisely as a confessor, be present, at least once, at the birth of a child. When, she reasons, he observes the price that a woman "pays for her surrender [in the sexual act]—such that her surrender to the man becomes a symbol of the surrender in giving birth—then the entire sexual sphere appears in an entirely different light": namely that of self-surrender in view of conception. "The act becomes a prelude; the emphasis lies in the child."[121]

It is this positive and realist perspective, as much as her deeply spiritual insight, that Adrienne brings to her theological study of human sexuality. She recognizes, for example, a certain "tension [*Spannung*]" as well as a certain "commonality [*Gemeinsame*]" between the sexes and thus also a difference-in-unity, which she attributes not only to their common (human) nature, but also to their particular mutual interaction and exchange. This exchange, which is perhaps most evident in the sexual act, can also include, Adrienne explains, everything that differentiates them as man and woman, including that which is most spiritual.[122]

Created "beside one another [*nebeneinander*]"—each one for his or her own sake—man and woman must learn "to grasp within one another [*ineinandergreifen*]" such that the man's gravitational point might be found within the woman and the woman's within the man. Even their sexual organs witness to their mutual orientation, as is evident in the amazing correspondence between them: the orifice and cervix of the uterus form, the Swiss physician notes, the exact counterpart to the penis, such that each is, as it were, the "mirrored image [*Spiegelbild*]" of the other in accord—she continues—with the Creator's intention.[123]

Because the emphasis here is upon a real reciprocity (*Gegenseitigkeit*) be-

---

118. Ibid., 10.
119. See Speyr, *Erde und Himmel* II, no. 1646 (247).
120. Speyr, *Theologie der Geschlechter*, 15.
121. Ibid., 10. As differing from the "private" act whereby the child is conceived, Adrienne recognizes the child's birth as a "public" act which follows the "law of promulgation [*Veröffentlichung*]" or "dispossession" which, in turn, is the guiding principle of the Christian life (see 196, 211, and 226).
122. See Speyr, *Das Wort und die Mystik* I, 20.
123. See Speyr, *Theologie der Geschlechter*, 148–49 and 221.

tween man and woman, this is far from a polarized approach to sexual difference which would set one sex over against the other in a divisive sense.[124] Rather, Adrienne's theological anthropology recognizes sexual differences as existing within and actually permitting the necessary "tension" of love that characterizes an authentic communion of persons, as shall become increasingly evident. Authentic unity is possible "precisely when both partners (Father and Son, Man and Woman) act in the greatest possibly polarity [*Polarität*], not in the most similar manner possible," Adrienne holds. "In polarity is the equal value of love (or, in God, of essence) guaranteed."[125] Within the unity of being and of will that characterizes such a communion, there can be no elimination of the boundaries distinguishing the individuals as persons, Adrienne insists. "Man remains man and woman remains woman." The fundamental mystery of each of their persons "is not laid bare; indeed, their reciprocal revelation to one another serves only to deepen and quicken this mystery."[126]

Such, Adrienne notes—to return to her purpose of finding a suitable analogy for her theology—is the relationship between Christ and the Church which, to repeat, is the original image (*Urbild*) of the union between man and woman. The reciprocal fruitfulness of man and woman—whereby the first woman comes forth from the first man (cf. Gen 2:21–23), whose descendants are born of woman—is therefore, as Balthasar puts it in terms characteristic of Adrienne's perspective, "surpassed by the ultimate priority of the second Adam, who in suprasexual fruitfulness, brings a 'companion,' the Church, into being."[127]

On the other hand, Adrienne recognizes in the mutual self-giving love of husband and wife prototypical characteristics of the sacraments based upon the mystery of love between Christ and the Church.[128] In both cases—in the union of man and woman, as in the union of Christ and the Church—it is the Holy Spirit who creates and maintains mutual love as well as the unity of love.[129] The Church lives in a continual movement from the Son to the Son, as he himself lives from the Father to the Father. Hence, the relationship between the Lord and the Church is never simply established "once and for

---

124. On the real reciprocity of man and woman, see, for example, Speyr, *Das Hohelied*, 44.
125. Speyr, *Theologie der Geschlechter*, 23; see also 79; and *Korinther* I, 322 and 427.
126. Speyr, *Light and Images*, 18; see also *Theologie der Geschlechter*, 143 and 159; and *Korinther* I, 322.
127. Balthasar, *Theo-Drama* II, 413.
128. See Schmitt, *The Sacrament of Confession as a "Sequela Christi."*
129. See Speyr, *Das Hohelied*, 51. For the same reason, Adrienne presents the fruitfulness of man and woman in paradise in terms of Trinitarian love. The Father and the Son need not concern themselves with the spiration of the Spirit. "It suffices that they love one another, and he is there" (*Theologie der Geschlechter*, 148; see also 24).

all" but issues ever anew. "It is full inversion and mutuality, coming together and then separating again."[130] It is this reciprocity in the love between Christ and the Church, as characterizing the reciprocity of love between the Father and the Son—as we shall see—which should, therefore, never be forgotten when addressing the reciprocity of man and woman in Adrienne's theological anthropology.

Within this context it is perhaps not surprising that Adrienne should share with Pope John Paul II one of the profound intuitions marking his pontificate: namely that being in the image of God means not only that both man and woman, precisely as rational and free beings, are "capable of knowing God and loving him," but also that, in virtue of the same, they are capable—and herein we also recognize an insight of St. Thomas[131]—of "existing in a relationship, in relation to the other 'I.'"[132] Far from denying the importance of rationality in our imaging of the Godhead, as Fergus Kerr argues,[133] this vision thus presupposes rationality as that which enables the reciprocal self-gift that creates and constitutes the communion of persons. In this communion of persons, in turn, Pope John Paul II recognized "a prelude to the definitive self-revelation of the Triune God: a living unity in the communion of the Father, Son and Holy Spirit."[134] As for Adrienne, she too insists upon the personal aspect of the image of God (namely human rationality), which serves as the foundation for her exposition of the relational or communitarian dimension of the image of God.

We have already treated Adrienne's presentation of the human being as an image of God in chapter three of this volume within the context of the human person's dynamic movement toward communion with God. There we observed this movement as realized not so much by way of a natural or supernatural desire for transcendence, but rather or most especially—and herein lies a constant and distinctive feature of Adrienne's perspective—by way of both a natural and graced aptitude to surrender (*Hingabe*) in virtue of which

---

130. Speyr, *Das Hohelied*, 51; see also *Korinther* I, 320.
131. See Thomas Aquinas, *ST* I, q. 93, a. 5.
132. Pope John Paul II, *Mulieris Dignitatem*, no. 7.
133. Kerr incorrectly reads *Mulieris Dignitatem*, no. 6, as maintaining (within the context of the Congregation for the Doctrine of the Faith's letter *On the Collaboration of Men and Women in the Church and in the World*, nos. 5–6) that "it is not in our rationality but in sexual difference that we image God—in our genitalia, not in our heads, so to speak" (*Twentieth-Century Theologians*, 194). "What makes man like God is," however, we read in *Mulieris Dignitatem*, no. 6, "the fact that—unlike the whole world of other living creatures, including those endowed with senses (*animalia*)—man is also a rational being (*animal rationale*)."
134. Pope John Paul II, *Mulieris Dignitatem*, no. 7; see also *Familiaris Consortio*, no. 11; Pope Benedict XVI, *Deus caritas est*, no. 2; *The Catechism of the Catholic Church*, no. 1702; and Balthasar, *The Christian State of Life*, 103.

one is simultaneously receptive and generous. The emphasis is thus upon personal likeness to God, for it is in virtue of our spiritual nature that human beings are said by Adrienne to be created in the image of God. Precisely as rational, we are, more specifically, capable of communion with God: capable of hearing God's word, of receiving and understanding it, and of responding to it.[135] Both man and woman are created as personal essences, Adrienne teaches in her commentary of Genesis 1, by which she means that they do not combine to form a single essence. "Each is for him- [or her-] self an image [*Bild*] of the unity of God"[136] and each—precisely as a person—is different from all others: "an image [*Abbild*] of the one, unique God."[137]

It follows from this personal uniqueness of man and woman that each directly enjoys intimacy with God so as to be free with regard to other's mediation. On the other hand, each is not simply an image of God in himself or in herself; for Adrienne also teaches that each is also an image of God for the other. Because, more specifically, we cannot see God, he has given us "as his image" our brother or sister, in whom we discover and learn what we cannot learn about the divine in ourselves.[138]

Beyond, moreover, each one's personal likeness to God, Adrienne maintains that the image of God, precisely as Trinitarian, is more "impressively" apparent in the man-woman relationship. In their mutual love, man and woman may be said more specifically to create an opening, or a "space," for God wherein his Spirit can "burst forth" to expand their otherwise limited human love to the infinite "proportion" of divine love.[139] In virtue of their reciprocal gift of self, each is for the other "an open space," which Adrienne insists is a new beginning rather than a barrier up against which the *I* is buffeted.[140] Of course, the Swiss mystic recognizes that we constantly come up

---

135. On the word-dimension of both human and divine life, see Speyr, *Das Wort und die Mystik* II, 21. Cf. *ST* I, q. 93, a. 4, corpus; ibid., ad. 2.

136. Ibid., 56.   137. Speyr, *Das Wort und die Mystik* I, 20.

138. See Speyr, *Die Schöpfung*, 55; and *John* I, 65. We thus love ourselves as mirrored images of our neighbor; see Speyr, *Markus*, 567.

139. It is the Spirit, Adrienne teaches, who "realizes (*bewirkt*) the exchange in God and also in sex (*im Geschlecht*)" (*Theologie der Geschlechter*, 23). To clarify the way in which the Spirit might be said to work the exchange of persons in God, see Thomas Aquinas, *ST* III, q. 37, a. 2: as "we say that a tree flowers by its flower, so do we say [...] the Father and the Son love each other and us, by the Holy Spirit, or by Love proceeding." Again, it is important to insist that Adrienne is seeking analogies by which to illuminate the mystery of the Trinity. See also Speyr, *John* III, 117 and 134. On the "expansion" of human love, see Pope Benedict XVI, *Deus caritas est*, no. 6; and chapter five of the present volume for a treatment of this mystery within the context of redemption. On this point, Adrienne's theology might be enlightened by the Thomistic insight according to which the human being is ordered to a supernatural good which surpasses man's natural powers to attain it; hence the importance of the supernatural virtues of faith, hope, and charity. See chapter two of the present volume.

140. Speyr, *Theologie der Geschlechter*, 113–14. Such, more specifically, is the mystery of the mutual

against barriers within ourselves and others, due to both our finite natures and sin, which preclude the fulfillment of our longing for perfect love.[141] In this is evident not only our fallen nature but also the fact that the love between man and woman cannot be limited to their corporal-spiritual unity.

The experience of this unity ought, in fact, to lead to an ecstatic estrangement of the self toward transcendence: "I no longer know who I am; you no longer know who you are, but together we are something that belongs to the joy of the Lord."[142] Similarly, the circle between the couple, which might otherwise threaten to close in upon itself, is torn open with the apparition of the child, who is not only the fruit of their love but also and especially God's gift.[143] Like the Holy Spirit who reveals the "eternal movement" of love between the Father and the Son, the child is revelatory of the transcendent dimension of love and of the divine origin of grace.[144]

Precisely as the fruit of the marital union and as God's gift to the couple, the child thus points to the fact that more than an extrinsic likeness is implied between the human communion of persons, on the one hand, and the Trinitarian communion of persons, on the other.[145] Creation in the image of God thus means, for Adrienne—and this will be more fully developed in what follows—that the human being is "complete [*vervollständigt*]" only through the human "other"—in, that is to say, the communion made possible by the reciprocal surrender of two persons—which in turn is only possible, as we shall see, in each one's opening to God.[146] This—it bears repeating—is not to say that man and woman are like two "halves" or "fragments" that together form

---

complementarity of man and woman. Cf. Pope John Paul II, *Letter to Women*, in *Origins: CNS Documentary Service* 25, no. 9 (July 27, 1995), nos. 7–8.

141. See Speyr, *John III*, 364 (on sin precluding the fulfillment of love); *Victory of Love*, 14; *John IV*, 157; and *Markus*, 446. Similar are the insights of Edith Stein, who argues that it is the deepest longing of every woman "to belong to another, and to possess this other being completely". Unless, however, this 'other' is God, her surrender will be a "perverted self-abandon and a form of slavery" (Edith Stein, "The Ethos of Women's Professions" in her *Essays on Women*, 52).

142. Speyr, *Theologie der Geschlechter*, 102; see also 143; and *World of Prayer*, 73. For a similar treatment of this theme elsewhere in the tradition, see Peter A. Kwasniewski, "Solitude, Communion, and Ecstasy," *Communio* 26 (Summer 1999): 371–92; and "St. Thomas, *Extasis*, and Union with the Beloved," *The Thomist* 61 (1997): 587–603.

143. Speyr, *Theologie der Geschlechter*, 22. Hence, as we saw in chapter four, the fecundity of the sexual act is recognized by Adrienne as realized for Christians more in obedience than in the child (see ibid., 24).

144. See Speyr, *John I*, 28–29. The child also reveals the meaning, as it were, of the mutual surrender of the couple; see *Theologie der Geschlechter*, 192 and 226.

145. See, for example, Speyr, *Theologie der Geschlechter*, 147. To be sure, a metaphorical likeness is not lacking in Adrienne's theology, for she refers to the differentiation of the sexes as corresponding—in virtue of their creation in the divine image—to the difference of the persons in the Trinity (see ibid., 115) and the unity of their nature and of their exchange as similarly corresponding to the unity of the Godhead (see *Das Wort und die Mystik* I, 29).

146. Speyr, *Die Schöpfung*, 57. Cf. Pope Benedict XVI, *Deus caritas est*, no. 11.

a whole.[147] Nor is it the case that their bi-unity serves exclusively as an end in itself. Rather, this properly human unity is presented by Adrienne as an integral part of their common unity with God. The human being is "realized," or fulfilled, within a marital union precisely so that he or she might thereby be initiated into the mystery of God who, precisely as a Trinity of persons, has created humankind as a communion of persons: male and female.

Authentic spousal communion supposes communion with God, but authentic union with God also requires "co-human community [*mitmenschliche Gemeinschaft*]." The unity of these two communities is "constitutive for the human person,"[148] which is to say that we exist and are fulfilled only within a tri-polar unity: I-You-God.[149] In their mutual relation of distance and nearness, or of difference and attraction, man and woman come to know, Adrienne argues, something of the absolute love of God wherein alone their own love can be realized.[150] More profoundly still, human persons are fulfilled as images of God by means that are characteristic of the divine communion of persons: the loving—and thus willing—surrender of themselves as gifts for others.[151] This, however, as we saw in chapter five, is a redemptive grace in view of the restoration of God's original intention for humanity: in accord, that is to say, with the image of the Father in the person of Christ, who is "the archetype of man, man as God has always conceived of him."[152] Between the first Adam and the second there thus "lies the whole Trinitarian love, which resolves to bridge the distance between earth and heaven, and the whole filial love which, together with the Spirit, does everything for love of the Father."[153]

"Masculine" and "Feminine" Forms of Surrender

Before turning to the Trinitarian relations as the archetype of the relation between the sexes, it might be helpful to observe what Adrienne presents as characteristically male and female manners of surrender, which will

---

147. See Balthasar, *Theo-Drama* II, 366; cf. *The Catechism of the Catholic Church*, no. 372.
148. Speyr, *Die Schöpfung*, 54; see also *Theologie der Geschlechter*, 151; and *Markus*, 446. On the implications for those in the consecrated state, see Pope John Paul II, *Mulieris Dignitatem*, no. 21.
149. Speyr, *Die Schöpfung*, 58. One could actually argue—while remaining faithful to Adrienne's thought—that the human being is fulfilled in the polarities: I-you-we and I-you-God. The Holy Spirit, symbolized by the child, binds the "we" with God, so as to hold the two polarities together. See, for example, Speyr, *Theologie der Geschlechter*, 24; and *Das Hohelied*, 51.
150. See Speyr, *Die Schöpfung*, 55; *Korinther* I, 320; and *World of Prayer*, 22.
151. See, for example, Speyr, *World of Prayer*, 213; *Apokalypse*, 64; and *Theologie der Geschlechter*, 79. Cf. Balthasar, *Theo-Drama* II, 259; *Theo-Drama* III, 340; *Theo-Drama* V, 485; *A Theology of History*, 32; and *Explorations in Theology* IV, 125–38.
152. Speyr, *John* IV, 78; see also *The Letter to the Colossians*, 30; and *Das Wort und die Mystik* II, 50. Cf. Balthasar, *My Work*, 118.
153. Speyr, *Korinther* I, 536.

serve later in this chapter to illustrate the difference-in-unity of the divine persons. For the Swiss mystic—it is essential to note—both the ontological and behavioural differences between men and women only make sense "as the expression of their mutual love and surrender."[154] Far from Gertrud von le Fort's formulation that woman *is* surrender (*Hingabe*),[155] Adrienne's logic thus precludes that this vital concept—which in her theology is first of all divine before it is human, as we have seen in previous chapters and as shall be further developed here—be thought of as the prerogative of any one sex. Rather, the ideal of surrender is necessarily attributable to *both sexes*, each in his or her own manner.

This ideal is, however, attributed to each only as conditioned by the other. As such, surrender is conceived as characterizing the mutual exchange and communion of the sexes: especially, but not exclusively, that of spouses. Hence, the notion of surrender takes on two complementary dimensions: one corresponding to what Adrienne presents as the typically masculine form of generative, or initiating, self-giving (a sort of generous outpouring, or giving of oneself to the other); and one corresponding to what she regards as the typically feminine form of receptive self-giving (a generous openness, docility, or readiness for the other).[156]

Of course, it might be argued—to repeat what was said in our brief exposition of Balthasar's treatment of the subject at hand—that these so-called characteristically male and female modes of surrender, or self-gift, run the risk of falling into stereotypes or clichés or of perpetuating culturally determined patterns of behavior, as certain strands of feminism have sought to argue. Adrienne does, however, rightfully insist upon real metaphysical differences between the sexes in virtue of which they really are naturally (that is to say, with divine intent) oriented to one another in their whole physical, psychological, and spiritual unity.[157] Hence, without denying the real influence of culture upon our manner of conceiving sexual differences—whence the original feminist distinction between sex and gender[158]—Adrienne argues

---

154. Speyr, *Theologie der Geschlechter*, 79–80; cf. *Korinther* I, 322.

155. See Gertrud von le Fort, *The Eternal Woman*, trans. Placid Jordan (San Francisco: Ignatius Press, 2010).

156. Cf. Balthasar, "Die Würde der Frau," 350; and *Explorations in Theology* IV, 341.

157. See *The Catechism of the Catholic Church*, no. 2332; and Michele M. Schumacher, "Feminism, Nature and *Humanae Vitae*: What's Love Got To Do with It?". On the culturally determined manners of looking at sexual difference exposited by feminism, see my treatment in "The Nature of Nature in Feminism, Old and New."

158. See my treatment thereof in Michele M. Schumacher, "A Women in Stone or in the Heart of Man? Navigating between Naturalism and Idealism in the Spirit of *Veritatis Splendor*," *Nova et Vetera* (English Edition) 11, no. 4 (2013): 1249–86. See also Beatriz Vollmer de Marcellus, *The Ontological Differentiation of Human Gender: A Critique of the Philosophical Literature between 1965 and 1995* (Phila-

that this natural orientation of each sex to the other serves each one's willful surrender to the other. This mutual surrender is that whereby they realize their communion of persons—their unity-in-difference, or their "dual unity," as Balthasar would have it—which, in turn, serves as a fitting metaphor to describe, as was previously mentioned, Adrienne's mystical insights into the divine life of the Trinity.[159]

In other words, Adrienne's primary intention within her *Theology of the Sexes*—like that of Balthasar, as we have seen—is not so much that of developing an anthropology based upon theological insights and Trinitarian relations, but rather of seeking a fitting image of both the Creator-creature relation and ultimately of the relation of the divine persons within the dual-unity of the sexes: not as they represent certain fixed, unchanging, or eternal essences,[160] but as together they form a dynamic unity characterizing the constant movement of love.

From within this intentional framework and from the perspective of her own experience of relating, within the parameters of her own particular cultural context—as a woman to men, especially but not exclusively in marriage and as a physician[161]—Adrienne argues that it is the man who initiates the mutual surrender of the couple by risking love first of all. Despite his later sexual maturity, a young man is sexually stimulated or "awakened" much sooner than is a young woman, Adrienne explains, whereby he is also more apt, or likely, to be sexually active.[162] The mystic of Basel notes in her commentary of Ephesians 5:31, wherein reference is made to the original unity of man and woman in Genesis 2:24, that it is he who clings to the woman, rather than she to him. Only after he has assumed the risk of humiliation, even rejection, in his courtship of her, so as to prove "the unbreachable strength of the bond,"[163] should the woman consider subjecting herself to him.

---

delphia: Xlibris, 2004); "New Feminism: A Sex-Gender Reunion" in Schumacher, *Women in Christ*, 52–66; and Sylviane Agacinski, *Femmes entre sexe et genre* (Paris: Seuil, 2012).

159. See Speyr, *Korinther* I, 320; and *Das Wort und die Mystik* I, 96. Cf. Balthasar, *Theo-Drama* V, 91; and *The Christian State of Life*, 227. On the dual unity of the sexes, see *Theo-Drama* II, 365–66 and 373. Similar is the formulation of Pope John Paul II, who explains that in their "interpersonal community," husband and wife form a "unity of the two," a "uni-duality," which preserves the "specific diversity and personal originality" of both. See his *Letter to Women*, nos. 7–8; and *Mulieris Dignitatem*, nos. 7, 10.

160. Again, by this I do not mean to imply that Adrienne would deny a metaphysical dimension to human sexuality, but rather that she recognizes the relations between the sexes in terms of dynamic giving and receiving characteristic of love.

161. On Adrienne's marriages, see Balthasar, *Our Task*, 30n38; and *First Glance at Adrienne von Speyr*, 28–30. As for Adrienne's experience as a physician, it might be added that hers was a cultural context unfavorable to women. On the difficulties that she suffered throughout medical school, see Balthasar, *First Glance at Adrienne von Speyr*, 27–28, and Speyr, *My Early Years*, 264.

162. See Speyr, *Theologie der Geschlechter*, 66.

163. Speyr, *The Letter to the Ephesians*, 239. On the risk of non-reciprocated love, see Kenneth

What might thus appear as an old-fashioned or nostalgic ideal of courtship—with the male assuming the initiative in wooing—follows as a logical consequence of Adrienne's conviction that a man seeks to surrender his spirit to the woman he loves, as distinct from a woman whom he simply uses for his own sexual pleasure,[164] *before* he surrenders his body, whereas a woman tends to surrender her spirit *with* her body in a single, comprehensive gift of herself.[165] For this reason, Adrienne mourns young women who have had premarital sex before entering the religious or consecrated life: they, unlike most young men who have also had premarital sex and for whom the bodily surrender is not a *de facto* surrender of the spirit, are often spiritually—and not just corporally—marked by the experience. It is consequently very difficult for young women—the case is different, Adrienne maintains, for young men—to be "freed" of the experience of a first encounter so as to give themselves anew.[166] The woman gives *all* of herself; the man "gives his demand [or challenge: *Forderung*]."[167] He is, in other words, more likely than the woman to take without giving. It is for this reason—that a woman is typically engaged *spiritually*, as well as physically, in her self-surrender to the man, for whom the same is not necessarily true—that a young woman should test a man, Adrienne maintains, before submitting to him in marriage; hence the importance of a betrothal period.[168]

Schmitz's excellent analysis of a gift that is not received: *The Gift: Creation* (Milwaukee, Wis.: Marquette University Press, 1982), 48–49.

164. The precision is important, because a man may "give" himself corporally to many women without necessarily giving himself spiritually: without truly loving them. See Speyr, *Theologie der Geschlechter*, 252. "If," on the other hand, "a man loves a woman, he will do everything he can to be transparent to the one he loves and to grant her an insight into him" (Speyr, *Light and Images*, 18). In this case, the man's corporal surrender is, as it were, a sign of his having already given himself spiritually to her.

165. See Speyr, *Theologie der Geschlechter*, 252. Regrettable, then, is the bride of the Song of Songs who, despite this typically feminine unity, belongs to the bridegroom "more corporally than spiritually." The bridegroom has left her, Adrienne argues (in her commentary of 5:5–6) "because his masculine spirit stands over his masculine body," whereas in her case, the body is foremost. See Speyr, *Das Hohelied*, 58. Of course, we must not forget that this biblical symbol of the bride represents both women and men, that is to say, the creature before the Creator. See, to that effect, Pope John Paul II, *Mulieris Dignitatem*, no. 25.

166. See Speyr, *Theologie der Geschlechter*, 168–69; and *Kreuz und Hölle* I, 39. According to Adrienne's reasoning, men who engage in premarital sex do not give their spirits at all: there is merely a bodily encounter, which has no deeper meaning for them. This does not necessarily contradict her observation (see *Theologie der Geschlechter*, 66) that a man cannot engage in sexual intercourse without his spirit participating in the act—unlike a woman, who, in the case of a rape, for example, might be spiritually absent—for the spiritual presence of a man in the act does not necessarily imply the surrender of his spirit to the woman in the act. Of questionable consequence to this logic, however, is Adrienne's observation of the de-spiritualization, or reduction, of the sexual act to something purely physiological: for the man, it is simply a means of releasing tension or of showing protest; for the woman, it is a means of imitating her peers. When, moreover, the first experience occurs on this purely physical plane, it is very difficult, Adrienne notes, to elevate the act to a higher level of significance: one expressing a spiritual commitment. See ibid., 14. Adrienne's own theology of the body aims at a spiritual-corporal unity.

167. Speyr, *Theologie der Geschlechter*, 69.   168. Ibid., 81.

On the other hand, despite this presumably "natural" tendency among young men to separate body and soul within their self-surrender to a woman, Adrienne recognizes that they tend to reunite the two within the marital context. Holding to a very different thesis than that of her contemporary, the phenomenological philosopher Edith Stein,[169] Adrienne reasons that because a man is always "one with his task, with his official position [*Amt*]," his spiritual and corporal capacities are integrated within his commitment to marriage. When a man marries he is thus less likely to separate his professional life from his private life.[170] Despite, therefore, the real possibility of a man giving himself, spiritually *or* physically, to *many* women—unlike the woman whose predilection for the corporal over the spiritual unveiling of her person tends to limit her to *one* man—the man who actually surrenders himself fully (body and soul) to one woman, is able to recognize himself fully within her and thus also to recognize monogamy as corresponding to God's will.[171]

This example also demonstrates that the man, all in assuming the initiative in courtship, must nonetheless learn to surrender himself to a single woman, namely, by means of her comprehensive and trusting surrender to him. It is her surrender which makes his own surrender possible; but it is his challenge (*Forderung*)—the challenge, for example, that comes with his expectation of good from her[172]—that invites her surrender. It follows that although Adrienne really does insist upon male initiative in courtship, as in the sexual act, her intention is obviously not to usurp the woman's equally significant role of shaping the love of a couple. She too can "invite" the man, out of a desire that is "fully in order, when it is from God."[173] Indeed, the love between a couple "can be inspired and shaped" from both sides: not by each planning independently, "but in mutual accommodation" through an "interplay of fulfillment and expectation," whereby their love is "self-renewing" and in "continual motion."[174]

---

169. For Stein, "the relationship of soul and body is not completely similar in man and woman. In the case of woman, the soul's union with the body is naturally more intimately emphasized. [...] This is closely related to the vocation of motherhood" (*Essays on Women*, 95). For this same reason, Stein recognizes woman as "better protected by nature against a one-sided activation and development of her faculties than man is" (96). Man, by contrast, tends to be more focused on one aspect of his life (his profession, for example), to the possible detriment of the rest of his life (such as his family life). Stein concludes that a woman "protects man from his natural one-sidedness by her own harmonious development" (72).

170. See Speyr, *Theologie der Geschlechter*, 67.

171. See ibid., 252–53 and 67. On the man's recognition of himself in the woman to whom he has surrendered himself, see also Balthasar, *Theo-Drama* II, 373.

172. See Speyr, *Theologie der Geschlechter*, 62. Cf. Balthasar, *Convergences*, 128–29.

173. Speyr, *Theologie der Geschlechter*, 81; see also *World of Prayer*, 74.

174. Speyr, *World of Prayer*, 40.

It is in virtue of his characteristically initiating love in the sexual act, for example, that the man consequently invites or provokes the woman's characteristically responsive surrender in the form of loving availability: he "takes the lead by surrendering and losing himself."[175] Her surrender, in turn—which Adrienne qualifies as her part in love[176]—is necessary for his own, which is to say that his surrender presupposes hers. His is "always a response to the feminine surrender," which in turn is a response to his initiating call or invitation, his "challenge [*Forderung*]."[177]

What might otherwise appear as a form of circular logic in Adrienne's teaching—that the man initiates the mutual surrender, or "mutual subordination" (cf. Eph 5:21) of the couple, on the one hand, and that his surrender is formed out of hers, on the other hand—might thus be explained in terms of the reciprocity of love.[178] Such is the nature of Adrienne's insight, which we addressed in chapter three, regarding the "breaking" of the boundaries separating what is "mine" from what is "yours" within a couple. Arguing by analogy to explain the interaction of nature and grace, or of God's action and ours, Adrienne explains that at a certain climactic point within the marital act, husband and wife are no longer capable of discerning between, on the one hand, each one's self and his or her personal action and, on the one hand, his or her spouse and the spouse's action. That is to say, it is no longer possible to determine whether the act occurs "in the *I* or in the *You*, because the boundaries have fallen."[179] Similarly, Adrienne observes—presumably from her own experience—that at a certain point within the sexual act, what occurs "in" her husband, is more important to a woman than what occurs within herself, with the result that she "forgets herself in her husband."[180] So too,

---

175. Speyr, *World of Prayer*, 41. Cf. Balthasar, *Theo-Drama* II, 373; and *Theo-Drama* V, 475. On the availability that is characteristic of female surrender, see for example Speyr, *Theologie der Geschlechter*, 252. It is important—it seems to me—to insist upon such an initiating love as characteristically male (as differing from a characteristically female love as responsive and receptive) need not be thought of as defining what is male and female. For an excellent presentation of specifically feminine character types within the philosophy of Edith Stein, for example, see Sibylle von Streng, "Woman's Threefold Vocation according to Edith Stein" in Schumacher, *Women in Christ*, 105–38, esp. 108.

176. See Speyr, *World of Prayer*, 191; *The Passion from Within*, 89; cf. Balthasar, "A Word on *Humanae Vitae*," 443–44.

177. Speyr, *Theologie der Geschlechter*, 65.

178. Similarly, Pope John Paul II interprets the Pauline exhortation that "wives be subject to your husbands" (Eph 5:22)—some forty years after Adrienne—in terms of a "mutual subjection out of reverence for Christ" and "not just that of the wife to the husband" (*Mulieris Dignitatem*, no. 24). Cf. Balthasar, "A Word on *Humanae Vitae*," 440; and *Paul Struggles with His Congregation: The Pastoral Message of the Letters to the Corinthians*, trans. Brigitte L. Bojarska (San Francisco: Ignatius Press, 1992), 47.

179. Speyr, *Theologie der Geschlechter*, 98.

180. Ibid., 140; cf. *Das Wort und die Mystik* I, 173. A woman's love is perfect (*vollkommen*), Adrienne teaches, when she no longer reflects upon herself, but awaits only what the man desires; see *Theologie der Geschlechter*, 113.

the man is said to forget himself when he is no longer the one who invites (or who challenges: *der Fordernder*) but is rather the one who "is surrendered [*der Hingegebener*]."[181]

From this perspective, any initiative that is accorded to the man in the sexual love of the couple is that—it bears repeating—of surrender: he takes "the lead by surrendering and losing himself."[182] He is passive, Adrienne observes, precisely at the moment in which he appears the most active, namely the moment in which his sperm ascends: "It *is* given, before he *has* given it."[183] At this moment—the moment, more specifically, in which he forgets himself in the sexual act—he *is* "full surrender."[184]

This might explain the meaning of Adrienne's claim that the "truth" of the male person—what the Swiss mystic identifies as his potency—is realized outside of himself, namely within the female person. Her "truth," by contrast, is realized, by the man's agency, within herself. "She contains man's truth and thereby becomes true, because she now realizes her determination [*Bestimmung*]":[185] her life has been marked or enriched by the meaning of love. Hence, the "final meaning" of man's challenge, or invitation, to woman is recognized by Adrienne as lying within her (the woman): her surrender reveals what was "contained" in his demand.[186] For this same reason the woman is said by the Swiss mystic to represent her husband after their sexual encounter: not just corporally but also spiritually, that is to say, "fully."[187] His potency is, in other words, actualized within her, with the consequence that every member of her body, one after another, is "awakened" to an effective response.[188] Far from being surrendered to him in such a way as to forfeit her own self-determining power, however, it is precisely this power of self-determination which enables her—especially when it is reinforced by the "power" of his demand, or challenge—to be willingly responsive to him. As for the man, he actually experiences his being more intensively, Adrienne explains, in his "possession" of his wife in the sexual act, whereas she is said to receive, in virtue of her own surrender, "a share in her husband's nature."[189]

---

181. Speyr, *Theologie der Geschlechter*, 64. Similarly, Balthasar argues: "In genuine sexual love, the man's part, which seems to be pure 'action,' is really self-surrender only if the loss of its own substance is seen as a gain and a possibility of further development in the other (the woman)" (Balthasar, *Theo-Drama* V, 475).

182. Speyr, *World of Prayer*, 41.   183. Speyr, *Erde und Himmel* II, no. 1683 (265).

184. Speyr, *Theologie der Geschlechter*, 231. Before this point, he is simply "demand [*Forderung*]," Adrienne explains.

185. Speyr, *Erde und Himmel* II, no. 1683 (265).   186. Speyr, *Theologie der Geschlechter*, 64.

187. Ibid., 67. Cf. Balthasar, *Theo-Drama* II, 373.   188. Speyr, *Theologie der Geschlechter*, 93.

189. Ibid., 140. As an application of these ideas in union with the patristic tradition, see Gertrude Gillette, "Augustine and the Significance of Perpetua's Words: 'And I was a man,'" *Augustinian Studies* 32, no. 1 (2001): 115–25.

By this share in his nature, Adrienne obviously does not mean that a woman becomes masculine. Rather, precisely that which was previously qualified as masculine is appropriated by the woman in virtue of her surrender to him. It is, in other words, as if that which was formerly appropriated to the man *qua* masculine or to the woman *qua* feminine is now shared by the opposite sex in virtue of the intimate communion of their persons.[190] As if to explain, Adrienne draws again upon the analogy of the sexual act and its effect upon the man and the woman:

> The man opens the woman from outside; he penetrates inward in order to initiate the woman's movement (in giving birth) from inside outward. The two belong together; each is both an end and a beginning. We see here a dialectic of unilateral and bilateral roles: a man addresses the woman's ability to conceive and bring to birth in order to act generatively in her; by exercising his male role in the conjugal act, he shows the woman her power, while the woman, in conceiving and giving birth, shows the man his power. In the conjugal act the man is active, the woman contemplative, whereas in giving birth the situations are reversed.[191]

In this way, receptivity—which might better be understood as a welcoming or a willing accepting of the other—conditions giving, and vice versa.[192] As such, receptivity is not strictly feminine; nor is it attributable to woman in an essential manner, as in the case of biological reductionism. Rather—and herein lies the analogical significance of the sexual realm—it is a strictly co-relative term, one that can only be properly understood within the light of the positive relationships of men and women, including the reciprocal exchange or communication of all that differentiates man from woman and woman from man, namely, that which suits each one for communion with the other.[193]

Here, more specifically, we have recourse to the important notion of natural and freely appropriated, or accomplished, complementarity. As such, this notion of complementarity is not to be understood in merely physical terms, with sexuality being reducible to the physical differences of man and woman and their communion being reducible to their physical union.

---

190. This might be explained by what Pope John Paul II observes as a harmonious "integration of what is 'masculine' and what is 'feminine'" based upon the "principle of mutually being 'for' the other" (*Mulieris Dignitatem*, no. 7).

191. Speyr, *Achtzehn Psalmen*, 113–14, cited by Balthasar in *Theo-Drama* V, 475–76.

192. Hence, Pope John Paul II refers to "self-donation" and "the acceptance of the other as a gift" as "two functions of the mutual exchange [which are] deeply connected in the whole process of the 'gift of self' [implied in the marital act]: giving and accepting the gift interpenetrate in such a way that the very act of giving becomes acceptance, and acceptance transforms itself into giving" (*Man and Woman He Created Them*, 196). On receptivity as the act of welcoming, see Balthasar, *Theo-Logic* I, 44–45.

193. See Schumacher, "A Woman in Stone or in the Heart of Man?" and "Feminism, Nature and Humanae Vitae."

Rather, all dimensions of the human person might be said to come into play in their interactions as specifically male and female persons: the sensual, of course, but also the intellectual (and thus the volitional), the psychological (and thus also the imaginative), the spiritual, etc. Balthasar thus rightly recognizes that what Adam "misses" in relating to the animals and what he finds in Eve (cf. Gen 2) "is the relationship in which bodily things are communicated spiritually and spiritual things bodily."[194] It is, therefore, the *whole* person who is sexual, and not just his or her physical constitution.[195] For this same reason, it is also the whole person who is given to the other within the sexual act (and not just the body) and the whole person who receives this gift within him- or herself, as Pope John Paul II has so aptly argued in his theology of the body.[196] More fundamentally still, the Creator's entrusting of each to the other requires, he also teaches, that both man and woman be responsible for the other's self-gift.[197]

From this perspective, receptivity is neither objectively nor subjectively reducible to its physical dimension. This is so not only because the gift that is given—or surrendered, in view of its reception—is the person-self in his or her whole metaphysical dimension, but also because this person-gift can only be fittingly received by another person: again, in his or her whole metaphysical dimension, that is to say, as a whole of body, soul and spirit.[198] Hence, Adrienne explains that the personal "exchange" between the sexes "obtains a physical-concrete expression in the [sexual] act, but can include everything that differentiates man and woman, even that which is most spiritual."[199]

This insight—that receptivity is a metaphysical quality of the person in view of, or corresponding to, another person (precisely as given) in his or her whole corporal-spiritual unity—is so essential to Adrienne's own theology of the sexes that it should never be forgotten or otherwise overshadowed by her apparent emphasis upon the sexual act. While the latter has an undeniable significance in the construction of her analogy between human love and

---

194. Balthasar, *Theo-Drama* II, 366.
195. On this issue, see Vollmer de Marcellus, "New Feminism: A Sex-Gender Reunion"; and *The Catechism of the Catholic Church*, no. 2332.
196. See Pope John Paul II, *Man and Woman He Created Them*; and Michele M. Schumacher, "John Paul II's Theology of the Body on Trial: Responding to the Accusation of the Biological Reduction of Women," *Nova et Vetera* (English Edition) 10, no. 2 (Spring 2012): 463–84.
197. See Pope John Paul II, *Mulieris Dignitatem*, no. 14.
198. As Pope John Paul II would have it: "Only a person can love and only a person can be loved. This statement is primarily ontological in nature, and it gives rise to an ethical affirmation. Love is an ontological and ethical requirement of the person. The person must be loved, since love alone corresponds to what the person is" (ibid., no. 29).
199. Speyr, *Das Wort und die Mystik* I, 20.

divine love, this significance should not lead the reader to conclude that the mystery of human persons is reducible to the sexual union between them, especially when this union is itself understood—in necessarily non-Speyrian terms—as a merely physical encounter. Rather, Adrienne reasons that this union actually reveals a more profound truth about each of their respective persons: namely that each is fulfilled by means of his or her self-gift to the other.[200]

This fact—that man and woman are each fulfilled in their self-gift to the other—in turn, does not mean that this reciprocal surrender might be considered as an end in itself, but (more profoundly) as that which gives rise to a still greater capacity of self-gift and communion, as is apparent in the new life that originates thereby.[201] Hence, the bodily communion of man and woman in the sexual act is, it bears repeating, "only a symbol and prelude" of their unity in the child.[202] When this child is held for the first time, a woman sees "incarnated what remained invisible in the man's act." In the child born to her, she is, in other words, able to observe—as through a veil—both the significance of her own surrender (its "measure"), and the significance that she herself holds for her husband.[203] As if to echo Adrienne, Balthasar observes that the man "is hardly aware of the extent of his self-surrender; it becomes clear to him only through the woman's pregnancy, the birth of the child and his own responsibility for bringing up the child."[204] In short, both man and woman recognize within the child the image of themselves and of their encounter, and in so doing they also recognize marriage as a fruitful expansion of the *I* and the *We* within the community of the family.[205]

When, therefore, Adrienne argues that woman's surrender "incarnates"[206] man's challenge, or demand, this is not simply to admit that his power exists passively within her (*Potenz*, "potency"), but also to acknowledge that it becomes active (*Kraft*, "power") in her. This, in turn, is not merely to recognize that his sperm are received by her in such a way as to be—in union with her own life-bearing potency—the source of new life (at least potentially) within her. More fundamentally still, his love, which is expressed as a gift of his

200. Cf. Balthasar, *Theo-Drama* II, 373.
201. On this point, see Speyr, *Theologie der Geschlechter*, 248.
202. Ibid., 196; see also 10.
203. One might also argue that the man's surrender is also visible in the child, although the personal "cost" of that surrender is obviously much less significant for the man. See on this subject Balthasar, "A Word on *Humanae Vitae*," 442; and Pope John Paul II, *Mulieris Dignitatem*, no. 18.
204. Balthasar, *Theo-Drama* V, 476.
205. Speyr, *Theologie der Geschlechter*, 226. The reference here is to the experience of the woman, because she is the subject addressed within this particular context of childbirth.
206. Ibid., 64.

entire person, invites hers (the gift of her whole person), as we have already seen in the preceding chapter. His love is effectively communicated when "he awakes the lover in his beloved."[207] There is also a sense in which, precisely as a mother—at least in potency—and thus in virtue of what has been confided to her (namely his sperm)—she is enabled to assume a more active, initiating role in love, which is not to deny that she might also initiate the sexual act itself. This initiating role might be symbolized, as Adrienne observes, in the contraction of a woman's uterus in the days after she has given birth and the corresponding expansion of her breasts: the child who was nourished by her passively from within must now be nourished by her actively from without.[208] Precisely that which is a distinguishing mark of the woman with regard to the man—the fruitful nature of her breasts[209]—might thus be seen, from still another perspective, as likening her to him: in nurturing the child outside of her own body, the woman's role as mother is less clearly a passively generous (or receptive) one and more distinctly an actively generous (or initiating) one.

Because Adrienne observes that woman's surrender is not only characteristically receptive but also responsive, woman herself is presented—and here we observe an amazing similarity between Adrienne's teaching and that of Balthasar, who certainly draws from Adrienne's insight—as oscillating between both forms: her surrender, in the form of receptive responsiveness to the man's call, differs from her surrender in the form of generous, initiating love vis-à-vis the child born of their mutual self-gift, although the one is a natural consequence of the other. A woman's "yes" to a man implies a sort of "yes" to the child, which is also a "yes" to herself: to the wife and mother who she is and becomes. Both the child and the man leave a physical mark upon her—the man from without, the child from within[210]—which is symbolic of the spiritual change, or transformation, that they effect within her. Together they make of her a mother, in both the fully human and Christian sense of the term.[211]

---

207. Speyr, *World of Prayer*, 38; cf. Balthasar, "A Word on *Humanae Vitae*," 444. This idea is closely related to Pope John Paul II's teaching concerning the "order of love" in *Mulieris Dignitatem*, no. 29. For a developed presentation of the concept, see Michele M. Schumacher, "The Prophetic Vocation of Women and the Order of Love" in *Logos: A Journal of Catholic Thought and Culture* 2, no. 2 (Spring 1999): 147–92.

208. See Speyr, *Theologie der Geschlechter*, 244.

209. Through her breasts, a woman remains a sort of "bridge" to paradise, Adrienne recognizes, because she alone is fruitful where man apparently had also once been fruitful (he too has "breasts" that remain undeveloped). See ibid., 66.

210. See ibid., 243; cf. *Achtzehn Psalmen*, 113–14.

211. The same might, of course, be said of the man, who—in the keen insight of Pope John Paul II —"in many ways […] has to *learn* his own '*fatherhood' from the mother*" (*Mulieris Dignitatem*, no. 18).

It is the man, however, who invites the response of love from her first of all (that is to say, before the child does), with the result that her maternal self-giving—without denying its typically feminine dimension—is a sort of mirroring of man's active, initiating love in her regard. As Balthasar notes, in a sort of echoing of Adrienne's insights, the woman gives the man "the fully formed child that the seed can only indicate." As his helpmate, she "does all the work, which he only, as it were, proposes and stimulates."[212] Similarly, Adrienne argues that woman's willingness to accept the pain of childbirth as implied by her "yes" to the man who has chosen her as his bride—her becoming "entirely body" (through pain) for love of him—is the "mirrored image [*Spiegelbild*]" of that same man who, for love of her, becomes "entirely body" (through pleasure) in the act of their marital union.[213] Whereas his peak experience of surrender, lies "in pleasure," however, hers is to be found in childbirth when her spirit and soul are immersed "in pain and forgetfulness."[214] Herein Adrienne recognizes both a punishment (for original sin) and a sort of redemptive substitution (*Stellvertretung*) of the woman for the man. In Adrienne's consideration of the connection between the Virgin's suffering of childbirth and Christ's suffering on the Cross, by contrast, the second Adam is said to assume all of woman's suffering, as shall be apparent in what follows.

A similar "imaging," or reflecting, of man's behavior by woman is observed by Adrienne in a woman's "self-control" during childbirth: her refusal to succumb to the pain in screams of torment with the helpful assurance of her husband's love for her. This, Adrienne explains, is a counter-image (*Gegenbild*) of the man's self-control during his wife's pregnancy: his confident surrender to her of all that lies outside of his control with regard to this fragile new life. "So is everything between the sexes constantly complemented: question and answer, image and counter-image, ever emerge in a constant oscillating of stages."[215] Hence, for example, the changing role of the woman, who is first of all bride and then mother, so as to be dually oriented: on the

---

212. Balthasar, *A Theological Anthropology*, 313; see also *Explorations in Theology* II, 158. This reflection might well have originated out of his conversation on July 12, 1941, with Adrienne concerning "man and woman in the kingdom of God," during which they were both on their knees: "Carrying is indeed a thing of the woman, but the man nonetheless cares for her and remains at her side. And the child, for all of that, is not only hers but also his" (Speyr, *Erde und Himmel* I, no. 122 [93]).

213. Speyr, *Theologie der Geschlechter*, 213. Similar is Adrienne's observation, noted above, that man "is surrendered" or is "full surrender" at the peak experience of sexual pleasure. See, for example, ibid., 64 and 231; and *World of Prayer*, 41.

214. Speyr, *Theologie der Geschlechter*, 212. On the pain of childbirth, whereby a woman "lives wholly in the present pain," see Speyr, *John* III, 264.

215. Speyr, *Theologie der Geschlechter*, 225.

one hand, she is oriented to her husband; on the other hand, she is oriented to the child who is born of their love. The distinction and unity between the two is of capital importance in Adrienne's theological anthropology, which, in turn, is an image of Trinitarian love, as we shall now see.

The Transition between the "Feminine" and "Masculine" Qualities of Love in Christ

This dual orientation of woman (toward her husband and toward their child) assumes particular significance in Adrienne's theology precisely because it is founded in and therefore reflects—so as to be a fitting analogy for—the dual orientation of the Son of God: his most primary orientation, by way of submissive surrender, to the Father and for love of the Father, on the one hand, and his orientation to the Church and to the world in the form of generous, initiating surrender, on the other. It is, in fact, in this sense that Adrienne recognizes Christ as possessing both masculine and feminine qualities.[216] The Son is "feminine" in his contemplation of the Father and "masculine" when he acts in the world with the purpose of bringing it back to the Father. The Father, for his part, is "masculine" in his generation of the Son and in his spiration of the Spirit together with the Son. He too is "feminine," however, in that he "incessantly, immediately loves."[217]

Because even the Father has feminine qualities, there can be no question of one sex—presumably the masculine[218]—co-opting the divine likeness for itself, to the negligence of the other. To be sure, there is a definite association in Adrienne's theology—as in Balthasar's—of the contemplative and the feminine, the active and the masculine, but this association is transferred from one sex to the other at precisely the moment in which the communion of persons is effectively realized.[219] It is as if an exchange is affected in their communion, with the woman sharing her femininity with the man in the

---

216. The Father, Adrienne specifies, is "masculine," the Church and Mary are "feminine," and the Son is "feminine-masculine" (Speyr, *Erde und Himmel* III, no. 2255 [246]). Cf. Balthasar, *New Elucidations*, 193; and "Die Würde der Frau," 350–51.

217. Speyr, *Theologie der Geschlechter*, 22–23. Adrienne recognizes in Christ the crossroads (*Treffpunkt*) and middle point of both action and contemplation; see *Erde und Himmel* III, no. 2155 (111).

218. Such is Corinne Crammer's argument against Balthasar; see "One Sex or Two?", 107. While Balthasar does indeed regard creation as feminine with respect to God (see for example Balthasar, "A Word on *Humanae Vitae*," 442), he also recognizes that "the archetype of both sexes" exists in the Son of God. As such, they are of "eternal and of equal value [*gleich würdig*]" ("Die Würde der Frau," 350). See the more positive feminist response to Balthasar's portrayal of the sexes by Margaret A. Farley, "New Patterns of Relationship: Beginnings of a Moral Revolution," *Theological Studies* 36, no. 4 (1975): 627–46.

219. See Adrienne von Speyr, *Achtzehn Psalmen*, 113–14. Cf. Balthasar, *Theo-Drama* V, 91; and *Explorations in Theology* IV, 341.

form of her contemplation and the man sharing his masculinity with the woman in the form of his activity. Hence the woman becomes, for example, the principal actor during her pregnancy, while the man is passive.[220] Analogically, the Church becomes active precisely at the moment in which, through Christ's passion, she is created. He, on the other hand, having entrusted his "seed" to her in the Word and the Eucharist, assumes a certain "passive" role in the world with his Ascension to the Father.[221] In this transitional relationship between Christ and the Church is mirrored the most basic relationship between the Son and the Father.

The whole of the Son's fruitfulness in this world stems from his relation with the Father, and *is*, at the same time, a revelation of the relationship itself. That is why the Son must be virginal. If he were not, then there would be moments at which he would reveal and mirror himself rather than the Father.[222] That, however, is quite impossible. His fruitfulness is completely bound up with the Father beyond. But both the Mother and the disciple John participate in this fruitfulness of the Lord.[223]

In the eternal generation of the Son by the Father, the former rests "fully in the feminine observation of the Father,"[224] leaving all activity to the Father, even to the extent of being comparable to a child begotten in his or her mother's womb: "pure letting-be, pure obedience." In that which concerns the generation of Christians, however, the Son assumes an active part in the "generative activity of the Father."[225] As the Father eternally begets the Son, the Son, in turn, begets the Church.[226] He does so "in a sort of dependence upon the Father's generation."[227] It is thus not surprising that the Lord—precisely in his mission of bringing the Father to the Church and the Church to the Father—represents the Father for her and assumes a paternal role in her regard.[228] In his "feminine" readiness for the Father and his "feminine" obedi-

---

220. Similarly, Mary is presented as "incarnating" action insofar as her "yes" affects the "act of the Incarnation." See Speyr, *Erde und Himmel* III, no. 2155 (111). On the other hand, Adrienne holds that "bearing [*Gebären*] is more contemplative than engendering [*Zeugen*]" (no. 2255 [247]).

221. Speyr, *Theologie der Geschlechter*, 69; see also 132.

222. He reveals the Father, in other words, precisely as receptive vis-à-vis the Father, and directly mediates the Father's fecundity to the Church and, through the Church, to the world.

223. Speyr, *John* IV, 125.

224. Speyr, *Theologie der Geschlechter*, 23.

225. Speyr, *The Letter to the Ephesians*, 21. Cf. Balthasar, "Die Würde der Frau," 350; and "A Word on Humanae Vitae," 444. On the other hand, Adrienne argues that one might recognize in the Incarnation "the Lord's masculine act" and in the Eucharist his "feminine act"; see *Das Wort und die Mystik* II, 530.

226. Speyr, *The Passion From Within*, 43 and 45; cf. *John* IV, 339.

227. Speyr, *The Letter to the Ephesians*, 240; see also *John* IV, 125. Similarly, Balthasar presents the Son as allowing himself throughout his early existence "to be led and 'fertilized' by the Father; but in such a way that, at the same time, as a man, he represents the originally generative force of God in the world" (Balthasar, *Credo*, 78); see also *Unless You Become Like This Child*, 64.

228. Speyr, *The Letter to the Ephesians*, 140. Cf. Balthasar, *Short Primer for Unsettled Laymen*, 91.

ence to the Father's will throughout his earthly mission,[229] he sets the paternal will into action, so as to fulfill the petition of the Lord's prayer, "thy will be done on earth as in heaven."[230] In precisely this way—in fulfilling the Father's will of bringing the world back to the paternal embrace—the Son, Adrienne argues, is "masculine" vis-à-vis the Father.[231] The Father, meanwhile, assumes a contemplative—and thus, in Adrienne's perspective, feminine—stance with regard to the Son, in whom he has entrusted the paternal task of redemption and in whom he recognizes the perfectly accomplished human being.[232]

In this way, Adrienne recognizes a turning point (*Wendung*) between Christ's "feminine" obedience and his "masculine" activity occasioned by this same obedience: the Father "shows the Son all that he does," not unlike a man who, certain of his wife's fidelity, invites her to share in all of his projects and plans.[233] Hence, there is in Christ a sort of "transition [*Übergang*]": "He is first of all together with the Father so as later to be together with his Church. He is first of all (like a boy) born wholly in the Father's will, so as then (like a man) to emerge in his own right [or "achievement": *Leistung*] and thereby beget the Church and be 'one flesh' together with her."[234]

It is thus also logical to recognize, as do both Adrienne and Balthasar, that as the second Adam, Christ has, at one point, the second Eve within himself: the Church who exists in Mary—immaculately conceived—as its first cell. At that point, he is "more the second Eve than is Mary [or even the Church] herself."[235] When, however, Mary-Church emerges from the side of Christ, "asleep" on the Cross,[236] there is still another transition in Christ's mission, which is nonetheless so oriented to the Cross that all of his words and actions find their significance therein.[237] At this key moment, when the Lord is most

---

229. Adrienne explains, for example, that the Lord's preparation for his preaching consisted in "readiness." See Speyr, *Theologie der Geschlechter*, 101. Adrienne also explains (in *Erde und Himmel* III, no. 2255 [246]) that "the Son's attitude with regard to the Father is characterized by the fact that he awaits his entire fruitfulness from the Father."

230. Speyr, *Erde und Himmel* III, no. 2255 (247).

231. Speyr, *Theologie der Geschlechter*, 23.

232. Speyr, *Erde und Himmel* III, no. 2255 (247).

233. On this point, see Speyr, *Handmaid of the Lord*, 38; and *John* I, 168.

234. Speyr, *Theologie der Geschlechter*, 69. Cf. Balthasar, "A Word on *Humanae Vitae*," 444. In giving his body in the Eucharist—which Adrienne identifies as a "feminine" act—the Lord does on earth what the Father does in heaven when he gives his Word as "seed" to Mary (see *Das Wort und die Mystik*, II, 529). Here Adrienne identifies the Incarnation as a "masculine act" of the Lord and the Eucharist as a "feminine act" (see ibid., 530). On the mediating role of Christ and Mary in terms of action and contemplation, see also *Erde und Himmel* III, no. 2155 (111).

235. Speyr, *Erde und Himmel* III, no. 2255 (246). Cf. Balthasar, *A Theological Anthropology*, 312–13.

236. Cf. *ST* I, q. 92, a. 3; *The Catechism of the Catholic Church*, no. 766; and Augustine of Hippo, *In Ioannis evangelium tractatus* IX, 10 (*Bibliothèque Augustinienne*, 71: 528 and 530; PL 35:1452). Cf. Balthasar, *Explorations in Theology* II, 146–47; *Mysterium Paschale*, 132–33; and *Epilogue*, 114.

237. See Speyr, *They Followed His Call*, 115; and *The Cross: Word and Sacrament*, 5–6.

clearly the new Adam and thus masculine, Adrienne observes an oscillation within his activity from what she considers as typically masculine to what she considers as typically feminine:

> On the Cross, the Lord does not beget the Church but gives birth to her. Or better: begetting and giving birth fall together. [...] We grasp the begetting of the Church more easily at the moment when the Son gives up his spirit on the Cross. This handing over is the begetting. The act of begetting is a more spiritual act than that of giving birth, in as much as it is left to the free will of the begetter. The words of the Lord on the Cross are acts of begetting, male begetting, each time the Holy Spirit is the great begetter. After giving this Spirit back into the Father's hand, the Son can only give birth. The power of begetting returns from the Son to the Father: it is the Father who now begets with the word of the Son.[238]

It is the Father's "masculine" power that is particularly evident in the crucifixion, for the Son could not be "so powerless and surrendered on the Cross," Adrienne reasons, "if the Father were not so powerful and challenging." At this moment—a historical moment, which nonetheless spans the course of all time so as to affect all of creation—the Son is like a vessel in relation to the Father's "overabundance," with the result that here, as in the eternal begetting of the Son by the Father, he allows the Father to be "predominant" in him and even "holds himself back" so that the Father might be "everything in him."[239]

The comparison between the act of allowing himself to be begotten and his allowing himself to be sacrificed on the Cross are of supreme importance, for Adrienne recognizes redemption as the integration—through the obedience of the second Adam—of the Father's act of creation within his eternal act of begetting the Son. The latter's suffering for the fallen world is presented as "birthing pains, through which he brings the child, the world, back intact to the begetting Father."[240] On the other hand, it is thereby—namely, "by bringing the Father to his Church and bringing his Church back to the Father on the Cross"—that the Lord assumes a paternal role in her regard. He furthermore allows her to participate in this fatherhood, precisely by placing "his Cross in the midst of the Church," which is to say, by giving her a share in his suffering.[241]

In this is also apparent the redemptive meaning of woman's own birthing pains which are incorporated into Christ's suffering and which are biblically

---

238. Speyr, *The Passion from Within*, 47; cf. *Achtzehn Psalmen*, 113–14.
239. Speyr, *Theologie der Geschlechter*, 23. Cf. Balthasar, *Unless You Become Like This Child*, 64.
240. Speyr, *Das Wort und die Mystik* II, 261.
241. Speyr, *The Letter to the Ephesians*, 140.

portrayed in the birthing cry of the woman of the twelfth chapter of Apocalypse, whom Adrienne mystically witnessed during the retreat marking the foundation of the Community of St. John.[242] Adrienne presents her as "the woman, every woman, a woman."[243] The woman's anonymity, which is apparent in that even Adrienne was not certain (during her vision) of the woman's identity,[244] lies within the mystery of the second Eve: the woman who fulfils "the meaning and law of every woman, so as to fall back into the anonymity of the Church," the universal bride of Christ.[245] Because "Mary is in the name of all women the Mother of God, and the Church is in the name of all human persons the bride of Christ, who she has become through Mary," Adrienne reasons that Mary is exemplary of two forms of anonymity, so as to confer "meaning and direction" upon them both: that of the woman in general and that of the fruitful bride of the Lord.[246] As the prototype of Christ's bride, for example, she is presented by Adrienne as participating, in an archetypical manner, throughout her pregnancy and delivery of Christ, in his own birthing pains on the Cross. "In suffering, he gives birth; in giving birth, she suffers. Her sufferings are included in his."[247] Rather than crying out because of her own pain, "she cries out in anticipation, in the distinct awareness of her Son's pains," even to the extent that "she suffers in advance a portion of her Son's suffering."[248] For other women, the cry of childbirth is related to the past: it unites them to the punishment of Eve. For Mary, this cry extends to the future, wherein lies the terrible suffering of her Son.[249]

When, therefore, the Lord explains that "the hour is coming" (cf. Jn 16:21), Adrienne imagines that he speaks not only for himself, but also for his mother. And just as his agony—due to his tremendous capacity for spiritual suffering—is far more intense than that of any other man, including those who have died

---

242. Balthasar describes the experience in *First Glance at Adrienne von Speyr*, 90–93. See also Speyr, *Theologie der Geschlechter*, 212; *Erde und Himmel* II, no. 1594 (207); and *Apokalypse*, 39, where Adrienne explains that every birthing cry has the meaning of atonement through the Lord's suffering. Cf. Pope John Paul II, *Mulieris Dignitatem*, no. 19; and *Redemptoris Mater*, no. 18.

243. Speyr, *Apokalypse*, 386; see also *Korinther* I, 323, where Adrienne argues that Mary's originality is the basis of her universality.

244. Balthasar explains: "Suddenly she looked at me, deathly afraid, 'Who is this woman? Is she ... the Mother?'" (Balthasar, *First Glance at Adrienne von Speyr*, 91). On "the woman" as the second Eve, see also Speyr, *Apokalypse*, 394, wherein Adrienne presents the child as masculine, so as to be related to the woman as Adam to Eve. For the Marian identity of the woman of the *Apocalypse*, see Speyr, *They Followed His Call*, 75.

245. Speyr, *Apokalypse*, 387. Cf. Balthasar, *Theo-Drama* III, 338; *Elucidations*, 101–13; and (with Ratzinger), *Mary: The Church at the Source*, 141–43.

246. Speyr, *Apokalypse*, 387.   247. Speyr, *Theologie der Geschlechter*, 217.

248. Balthasar, *First Glance at Adrienne von Speyr*, 92–93. This, Balthasar argues, is already the case during her pregnancy, that is to say, before the birth; see *Mary for Today*, 24–25.

249. Speyr, *Apokalypse*, 389; cf. Balthasar, *Theo-Drama* III, 332 and 334.

by crucifixion,[250] so also Mary's pain of childbirth is, for the same reason, far greater than that of any other woman: already at the beginning of her Son's earthly mission, she shares both corporally and spiritually in his agony. Indeed, the suffering of her "virginal birth" is necessarily related, Adrienne argues, to the suffering of "the virginal Son."[251] This explains how Adrienne might recognize Mary as assuming Eve's birthing pains into her own pain under her Son's Cross. "Mary takes from Eve the pain of fecundity" but in so doing she also gives to Eve a "new, supernatural fecundity" that is born by way of this suffering.[252] Mary's virginal share in her Son's mission is not, however, limited to her bearing and giving birth to him, for she shares as none other in Christ's destiny "not least because her Son will also be a virgin." Adrienne argues, more specifically, with reference to John 16:21—wherein the Lord compares his approaching passion to the pains of childbirth—that Christ is celibate because Mary is celibate, and Mary is a virgin because Christ is also. "Together they form the first virgin couple."[253]

This virginal unity of Mother and Son means that Mary is fruitful with Christ's "seed." Already during her pregnancy she bore, together with the Son, "his divine-human, objective and unchanging office" within her.[254] The years of her Son's earthly mission are, moreover, presented by Adrienne as "one extended pregnancy" advancing towards Calvary, where she gives birth again; "and on the next day she will hold the Child in her arms."[255] Hence like a man who is not satisfied with a wife who simply surrenders herself to him "without sharing his masculine thoughts and plans," Christ seeks in Mary a partner to (spiritually, and thus virginally) "fructify" his work. Hence "this second, spiritual motherhood becomes perfect actuality" in her.[256] It is she who, by the Spirit's prompting, determines the hour in which the Son's mission is revealed, and it is thus—as "the immediate cause that sets his mission in motion"—that she gives birth to him again: this time "into his mission."[257] In so doing, she accompanies him along the way to Calvary, for she is keenly aware—in virtue of Simeon's prophecy and her own knowledge of scripture—that every miracle, every glorification, "drives him inexorably into the Passion."[258]

250. See Thomas Aquinas, *ST* III, q. 46, aa. 5–6.
251. Speyr, *Theologie der Geschlechter*, 217; cf. Balthasar, *Mary for Today*, 25.
252. Speyr, *Erde und Himmel* II, no. 1594 (207).
253. Speyr, *John* III, 266. Precisely as a virgin, Adrienne recognizes Mary as having a large part in the mystery of the sexes; see *Theologie der Geschlechter*, 8.
254. Speyr, *Mary in the Redemption*, 100; cf. Balthasar, *Mary for Today*, 24.
255. Speyr, *John* III, 265; cf. Balthasar, *Theo-Drama* III, 332.
256. Speyr, *Handmaid of the Lord*, 38; cf. Balthasar, *Theo-Drama* III, 338.
257. Speyr, *John* I, 167; cf. Balthasar, *Mary for Today*, 62–63.
258. Speyr, *John* I, 166. Similarly, Adrienne recognizes the "power" of the Lord's miracles following

Adrienne thus presents the Mother's presence at the wedding feast of Cana as initiating her into his approaching passion, whence his rather harsh words to her: "O woman, what have you to do with me? My hour has not yet come" (Jn 2:4). Adrienne understands this to mean that he "neither may nor wants to cover up the pain of [their inevitable] separation through accommodating words."[259] Hence while he, at this point in the Gospel, becomes increasingly occupied with his mission of preaching and healing, she already lives her properly spousal share in his suffering. She, in other words, precisely as the Mother of the redeemer, is charged to participate in his redemptive mission, whereby he becomes the bridegroom of the Church (cf. Eph 5:21–32).

Already in Simeon's prophetic words (cf. Lk 2:34–35), Adrienne recognizes Mary as receiving a portion of Christ's suffering: a portion corresponding "to her womanly and maternal concomitant path." Hers is, Adrienne teaches, a "feminine mission" composed of two parts, which must nonetheless be integrated: her particular mission of taking the Son's mission "into herself" must be "fitted" into "the womanly mission of pregnancy and birth."[260] This integration is realized in virtue of her original, unlimited fiat wherein she accepts, even in the absence of understanding, everything implied within that mission. This same fiat is thus confirmed again and again in her surrender of herself to the Son and to his mission. In precisely this way, she—whom the tradition presents as the new Eve, the one who by her obedience unties the knot of Eve's disobedience—accompanies her Son throughout his long route towards Calvary:[261] a destination which becomes increasingly apparent to her as she meditates upon the prophecy of Simeon and the events of her child's life in light of the Jewish Scriptures. She is thus portrayed by Adrienne as living "with the Cross constantly at the back of her mind," while he, "because he is a man, lives toward the Cross ahead of him."[262] Indeed, already at the moment of the presentation, the sword "pierced her soul," while Christ, on the other

---

the institution of the Eucharist as originating out of the "power" of his surrender therein; see *Theologie der Geschlechter*, 133. On Mary's knowledge of her Son's future suffering, see Speyr, *Handmaid of the Lord*, 76.

259. Speyr, *John* I, 168.

260. Speyr, *Handmaid of the Lord*, 82.

261. This accompaniment, Adrienne teaches, occurs precisely in her separation from him; see Speyr, *Handmaid of the Lord*, 108. On the new Eve undoing the knot of the sin of the first woman, see Irenaeus of Lyons, *Adversus Heareses* III, 22, 4 (SC 211: 438–44); Saward (trans.), *The Scandal of the Incarnation*, 60–61; cf. *The Catechism of the Catholic Church*, no. 494; and the Second Vatican Council, *Lumen Gentium*, no. 63 (*DZ* 4177).

262. Speyr, *John* I, 167. The Lord's entire life is, Adrienne teaches, oriented to the Cross "in such a way that all his words and deeds had a continuous significance and interconnection by which the uniqueness of the Cross was borne, a significance which gave meaning to the Cross and interpreted it" (*They Followed His Call*, 115). See also the introduction to Speyr, *The Cross: Word and Sacrament*.

hand, "is only now [when he works the miracle at Cana, cf. Jn 2:1–11] marching toward his 'hour.'"[263]

A sharp distinction is thus made between what Adrienne presents as the specifically male and female modes of suffering, originating out of the distinction between Christ's and Mary's respective ways of carrying out the Father's will: that of actively representing the Father, as his Son—the Son's self-gift *is* the Father's gift of redemption for the world, as we saw in chapter five—and that of willingly letting-it-happen (that is to say, the Father's will). As the one who shares intimately in Christ's suffering, Mary "fulfills the destination of woman: she is the Mother as such, the Mother of all, the Mother for all."[264]

Parallel to the distinction between male and female modes of suffering is what Adrienne presents as characteristically male and female missions originating out of the mystery of Mary's share in Christ's self-gift "from the time of Christ's virginal conception up to his death"[265] on Calvary: the summit of his life lived as a gift of self-surrender. Her self-gift thus meets his in a holy sacrifice to God for the redemption of the world: "In obedience to God she had given the first assent to the angel and, through him, to the Spirit. Now she gives the new assent to the Son, to fulfill the will of the Son who is suffering wholly in the will of the Father. Thus, at the Cross, the Father receives the Son together with his Mother in a new, inseparable surrender."[266]

The example of Mary and her particularly feminine manner of suffering—of carrying in her contemplation the painful agony of her Son, already long before its realization, namely by way of her meditation on Simeon's prophecy (cf. Lk 2:34–35) in conjunction with the Jewish Scriptures—does not, therefore, serve merely to illustrate a certain likeness to her Son's own archetypically feminine surrender vis-à-vis the Father. It also serves to explain how the one relationship—that of mother and Son—is, as it were, integrated

---

263. Balthasar, *Mary for Today*, 62; cf. Speyr, *Handmaid of the Lord*, 82.

264. Speyr, *John* IV, 117. Mary is not the only woman who suffers at the foot of the Cross, however, for she is joined by the wife of Clopas and Mary Magdalene (cf. Jn 19:25). "Together they circumscribe the possible modes of womanly suffering." Whereas, Mary, more specifically, "embodies everything that makes possible the Son's mission (and thus his suffering)," Magdalene suffers in the form of penance and gratitude, thus embodying the fulfillment of Christ's mission, whereas the wife of Clopas "embodies any woman in particular. [...] She is distinguished by no special holiness, her calling is not special participation in the Passion; she only demonstrates the possibility that someone can stand by the Lord in his hour of death, wordlessly, wholly veiled in the unobtrusive" (ibid., 118–19).

265. Second Vatican Council, Dogmatic Constitution on the Church, *Lumen Gentium* (November 5, 1964), no. 57; in *Vatican Council II: The Conciliar and Post Conciliar Documents*, ed. Austin Flannery (Collegeville, Minn.: The Liturgical Press, 1975, 1979⁴), 416 (the passage does not appear in *DZ*); cf. *The Catechism of the Catholic Church*, no. 964.

266. Speyr, *Handmaid of the Lord*, 117.

into the other: that of Father and Son. This is so precisely because the Son's relationship to his mother follows as a "fruit" of his relationship with the Father: he who is "feminine" in relation to the Father is "masculine" in relation to Mary (and, in her, to the Church). Concretely this means that "his doing the will of the Father" implies that he observe the Father's "authority over the Mother."[267] This in turn supposes that Mary's own relationship with her Son evolves from that of mother to that of "Spouse" (again, in archetypical, non-sexual—which is not to say asexual—terms) which in turn supposes that his suffering on the Cross gives "birth" to the Church, whom she *is*.[268] Indeed, Adrienne teaches in union with the Church herself that the latter's bridal relationship with Christ "proceeds from the Mother's relationship to the Son."[269]

"Masculine" and "Feminine" Missions

Something of this mystery of the mediating role of Christ's surrender and that, in turn, of Mary-Church continues in the mystery of the Church's mission. "That place within the Son where he possesses a dual countenance—one turned toward the Father and one toward the world—that place which is most characteristic of the Son, does not become empty with his Ascension to the Father. On the contrary, it remains in existence," Adrienne reasons, namely in the persons of Mary and the beloved disciple: "those whom he has put in that place in his stead."[270] Both Mary and John participate—each in his or her own particular manner, corresponding to their respective missions—in the Lord's fruitfulness.[271] This more specifically is a fruitfulness that overflows from the wound of Christ's open heart, from which (it bears repeating) the Church is born in the form of her sacraments.[272] Their place at the foot of the Cross assures the future of the Church, which is to say that together they form the "primordial cell of the Church"[273] and "[the] simple incarnate Body of Christ."[274] They do so as "an original couple like Adam and

---

267. Speyr, *Das Wort und die Mystik* I, 24.
268. "It was at the same time, at the Cross, that the Mother and the church became the Bride of Christ" (Speyr, *John* IV, 172). Cf. Balthasar, *Mary for Today*, 53.
269. Speyr, *Mary in the Redemption*, 111. Cf. *The Catechism of the Catholic Church*, no. 507, wherein Mary is presented as "the symbol and the most perfect realization of the Church," and the Second Vatican Council, *Lumen Gentium*, no. 63 (*DZ* 4177).
270. Speyr, *John* IV, 135.   271. Ibid., 125.
272. See Speyr, *The Cross: Word and Sacrament*, 8.
273. Balthasar, *Our Task*, 66. As Adrienne sees it, the Church's very structure is established by the Lord's entrusting of John to Mary and of Mary to John. See Speyr, *The Cross: Word and Sacrament*, 34; cf. Balthasar, *The Threefold Garland*, 103.
274. Speyr, *Theologie der Geschlechter*, 253.

Eve,"[275] whom both Adrienne and Balthasar present as fruitful without intercourse:[276] a couple "created by the Lord's word from the Cross," in whom "human relationships are refashioned by the dying Son."[277]

As such, they (Mary and John) represent all who are virginal, but also all who live the grace of the sacrament of marriage originating from the Cross, in virtue of which we might again recognize a continuity between the so-called natural and supernatural relations between the sexes.[278] In uniting this "couple," the Lord establishes the Church's structure, but he also establishes that primary human community from which the family is born and which, according to the original Speyrian insight as we have seen, is illuminated by this virginal relationship. Indeed, the Cross forms "every human relationship; in this case it yields the word which brings together Mary and John, Church and mankind, woman and man."[279]

This is not to deny Adrienne's profound insight, alluded to earlier, that the bond between Christ and Mary is "first" and "decisive" for all later bonds between man and woman, which is to say that in God's intention the second Adam (Christ) and his female companion (Mary-Church) precede the first couple, as St. Thomas Aquinas also argues in light of Ephesians 5.[280] Indeed, the relationship between Mary and the beloved disciple is—precisely as a fruit of the Cross—a fruit of this more fundamental relationship between Christ and Mary.[281] Together, Christ and Mary found both the religious and the married states.[282] This also means that John stands in a two-fold relation to Mary, as he is both her son and the custodian of the mystery that Christ confided to her. Because—to explain the latter relationship—she is "open and transparent" to John in what Adrienne recognizes as an archetypical manner of confession, "he has her fruitfulness at his disposal."[283] This

---

275. Speyr, *The Cross: Word and Sacrament*, 31; see also *John* IV, 130.

276. See Speyr, *Theologie der Geschlechter*, 149; and Balthasar, *The Christian State of Life*, 93.

277. Speyr, *The Cross: Word and Sacrament*, 31.

278. On Mary and John as representing those who are virginal, see Speyr, *John* IV, 146. Together they are the "founders of a new lineage: that of his priests and monastic people" (ibid., 130). See also ibid., 133; and *Handmaid of the Lord*, 123–32. On their representation of those who receive from the Lord the sacrament of marriage, born as a fruit of grace from the Cross, see Speyr, *The Cross: Word and Sacrament*, 33.

279. Speyr, *The Cross: Word and Sacrament*, 35.

280. See Thomas Aquinas, *ST* II-II, q. 2, a. 7; and Speyr, *Handmaid of the Lord*, 85. Adrienne presents Christ and Mary as forming "a pair in the same way that Christ as Bridegroom and the Church as bride form a pair" (*Mary in the Redemption*, 93); see also *World of Prayer*, 69–70.

281. See Speyr, *Mary in the Redemption*, 105.

282. "Both states were lived by Mary and were founded by her together with the Lord" (Speyr, *Handmaid of the Lord*, 123); see also *John* III, 266.

283. *John* IV, 147. With regard to this archetypical surrender, Adrienne writes: "She exists in that state at which true confession aims" (ibid.; see also 171).

fruitfulness, which is her share in Christ's own fruitfulness from the Father, is bound up with the whole mystery of her spiritual maternity, but also with the mystery of her real bodily bearing of the Son, which cannot be separated, as we have seen in chapter four, from her spiritual bearing of his destiny: not only during the pregnancy, but more profoundly still throughout his entire public mission, trial, and death, wherein Adrienne recognizes that her role is more apparently that of spouse than of mother.[284]

In her consent to the Incarnation, Adrienne recognizes that the mother, without understanding, but with a generous openness that knew no limits from the outset—a generosity that was able to include all that was implied within the Messiah's mission—"parenthetically gave her consent to the transubstantiation."[285] For this same reason, she received his entire fruitfulness at the foot of the Cross. This reception of his fruitfulness was, in turn, prepared by "her acceptance of the Son's life and suffering," which is to say that "a ground" was created in her heart for the coming tradition.[286] The mysteries which Christ eventually reveals to the world are, in other words, first of all laid in the heart of Mary, who willingly receives them along with the person of her Son.[287] Hence the growth of the Church is already contained in her self-surrender.[288] In this way, Mary is recognized by Adrienne as uniting within herself the two properly feminine missions of natural and spiritual (virginal) motherhood.[289]

These are the mysteries to which John has special access by means of his privileged relationship with Mary in virtue of the Lord's entrusting act from the Cross (cf. Jn 19:26), but also in virtue of her "complete virginity" expressed by way of her total self-gift to God: her absolute surrender which is both openness and transparency vis-à-vis Christ and his mysteries, on the one hand, and vis-à-vis the Church in the person of John, on the other.[290] This means that what she receives from her Son is further and completely mediated to the Church in what Adrienne recognizes as a typically "feminine" manner: that of sharing the fruits of her contemplation, not by way of proclamation, but by a simple generous surrender, which is also the basis of

---

284. On her changing role, see for example Speyr, *Handmaid of the Lord*, 108, and my development of this theme in chapter four.

285. Speyr, *Theologie der Geschlechter*, 224; cf. *Mary in the Redemption*, 118.

286. Speyr, *Handmaid of the Lord*, 85; cf. Balthasar, *The Office of Peter*, 212.

287. See Speyr, *Handmaid of the Lord*, 83.

288. Ibid., 164.

289. Such are, similarly, the "two dimensions of the female vocation" recognized by Pope John Paul II (*Mulieris Dignitatem*, no. 17): namely, motherhood (in both its physical and spiritual dimensions, see nos. 18–19) and virginity, wherein a woman's "prerogative" for motherhood is not deprived but lived "'*according to the Spirit*' (cf. Rom 8:4)" (ibid., no. 21). Precisely as mother, Mary is said by Adrienne to fulfill the destiny of woman as such; see Speyr, *John* IV, 117.

290. On Mary's self-surrender, see Speyr, *John* IV, 147.

the Marian and thus the ecclesial mediation of Christ's mysteries and love. "Her love is her office."[291]

John, for his part, receives these Marian (and thus Christological) mysteries and this Marian (and Christological) love by means of his own virginal surrender to the Lord, who in turn gives him to Mary, as her son and guardian. While all the apostles are commissioned to administer the sacraments, John has gained "special insight"[292] into the origin of baptism and the Eucharist, through his vision of the Lord's pierced side, which the tradition presents as the origin of the sacraments. Similar is his insight into the sacrament of reconciliation, whose efficacy "originates in the Cross."[293] From within his looking into the Lord's side, "he is initiated into looking into men"[294] and most especially "into the opened soul of the sinner."[295] This, in turn, supposes that John partakes of the Lord's mediating role, whereby he is simultaneously oriented to the Father and to the world. As for the confessor, he stands in the position of "conscious representativeness in two directions" and this "in a mediatory way, by taking the sinner up into himself and presenting him, in himself, to the Lord. Correspondingly, the Lord lives in him through his office, and the priest mediates the Lord to the sinner."[296]

It is, therefore, precisely within each one's transparency and "immediacy"[297] to the Lord that Mary and John are transparent to one another in what Adrienne presents as a mutual "relationship of disclosure." Because in "the spirit of virginity" they are open in service, each within his or her respective mission, they are also "disclosed to one another within that mission."[298] Hence, for example, Mary discloses herself to John "as does a penitent to his father confessor."[299] In precisely this way, John is given a share in the fruits of Mary's self-disclosure: in, that is to say, the whole deposit of revelation entrusted to the Church through Mary, but also in the whole sacramental economy that was born of the Cross and of Mary's "yes." When the Lord offers his body in the Eucharist, for example, "he gives us the body his mother conceived and bore, formed and nourished."[300] It is also she who bore not only the Messiah, but also his entire office within herself: the office that he will hand over to the Church through her.[301] Precisely as the "primordial cell" of the Church,[302] Mary is not

---

291. Ibid., 174.
292. Speyr, *Mary in the Redemption*, 118.
293. Speyr, *John* IV, 146.
294. Ibid., 191.
295. Ibid., 148.
296. Ibid., 224.
297. Ibid., 127.
298. Ibid., 148.
299. Ibid., 171.
300. Speyr, *Mary in the Redemption*, 116.
301. Ibid., 103 and 105.
302. See ibid., 119. Cf. Balthasar and Ratzinger, *Mary: The Church at the Source*; and the Second Vatican Council, *Lumen Gentium*, no. 63 (*DZ* 4177).

meant to begin "something new, alone and for herself," Adrienne argues. Rather, she is given by the Lord to the priesthood present in the person of John, who further mediates the fruit of the Cross—especially the fecundity of love—to Peter, who is absent at the moment of the Church's birth on Calvary.[303]

Not surprisingly then, Mary is "closely linked to the officiating priest"[304] who nevertheless renounces "any potency"—namely his own sexual potency—"which is oriented towards [*zugekehrt*] woman."[305] This renouncement is, more specifically, realized in view of a positive orientation: that of the representative role that he assumes during the Mass and most especially at the moment of the transsubstantiation. At that instant, he must rely entirely upon *God's* potency.[306] At each transsubstantiation a new form of Mary's "officiality" arises within the Church, Adrienne explains, "through the uniting of her being represented in the body of the Lord," that is to say, in the Eucharist, "with that which represents her in the priest," namely the word of consent that realizes the fleshly becoming of the Son (in the Eucharist as in the Incarnation).[307]

In the example provided by Mary's archetypical femininity, Adrienne also recognizes a woman's contemplation as feeding a man's predication: "Woman will hear and receive more of the divine word than man," Adrienne maintains. "But the woman does not reveal what is heard; she lets the man reveal it."[308] While Adrienne gives no reason for this silence on woman's part, this likely follows from her conviction that it is to a masculine priesthood that the Church has entrusted the mission, as the *Catechism* teaches, of being "authentic teachers" of the faith, "endowed with the authority of Christ" and thus also with "the charism of infallibility":[309] a charism, which Adrienne nonetheless recognizes as originating out of the purity of Mary's faith.[310] Because Adri-

---

303. Speyr, *Handmaid of the Lord*, 129; see also *The Boundless God*, 128; and *John* IV, 356. The whole male-female complementarity that Adrienne observes in the relationship between Mary and John is further developed in her explanation of the relationship between Mary and Peter.

304. Speyr, *Mary in the Redemption*, 117.

305. Speyr, *Theologie der Geschlechter*, 224. The sexual power is always "something which is realized together [*etwas Zusammengerafftes*]" (ibid.).

306. Ibid. Because Christ's fecundity is "explicitly divine, it cannot be bound to any specific female body," Balthasar reasons, "but can have as its body only the universality of the Church of all the redeemed." His is a "completely virginal" fecundity (Balthasar, *The Christian State of Life*, 234). This is not, however, to deny the identity of Mary as the new Eve in union with the new Adam, for precisely as a virgin she is also the principle, or first cell, of the Church, or even the Church in person.

307. See Speyr, *Mary in the Redemption*, 118.

308. Speyr, *Handmaid of the Lord*, 84.

309. *The Catechism of the Catholic Church*, nos. 2034–35. This, it is important to insist, is not to deny the collaboration of the lay faithful, including women (see no. 2038).

310. "Her belief is in the same position as the infallibility of the Church" (Speyr, *John* IV, 172); see also *Handmaid of the Lord*, 142.

enne recognizes Peter's office as derived from the unity of the Church embodied in Mary, she also recognizes the "outward" infallibility of his office as deriving from the "inner" infallibility of the immaculate virgin.[311]

From this perspective, Adrienne's characterization of women might be regarded as very positively emphasizing, in accord with the Marian mysteries explained above, the so-called feminine role of bearing the word of God within one's very self, and of even personifying the Church as a whole. On the other hand and far less positively, it might also fuel the feminist concern over the alleged denial of a voice and an active place to women within the visible structure of the Church[312] or of feeding what Michelle A. Gonzalez disapprovingly regards as Balthasar's "gendered understanding of the theological task": an understanding wherein "the male is seen as the active, intellectualizing force" and the woman is characterized "as mystic."[313] Still others—such as Tina Beattie[314]—interpret Adrienne's words as witnessing to the oppressive power of the man (Balthasar) over the submissive woman (Adrienne), at best, or even as a less than successful attempt to defend the unconventional (presumably suspect) relationship between this presumed mystic and her confessor, the priest-theologian.

In responding to these concerns and without entering into the debate of women's prophetic voice and ministry within the Church—a subject whose scope lies beyond our intentions here[315]—I might point out first of all that

---

311. See Speyr, *Handmaid of the Lord*, 142; cf. Balthasar, *The Office of Peter*.

312. See for example Rachel Muers, "The Mute Cannot Keep Silent," 109–20, and in a more general sense, the now-classic work of Elisabeth Schüssler Fiorenza, *In Memory of Her: Feminist Theological Reconstruction of Christian Origins* (New York: Crossroad, 1984).

313. Gonzalez, "Hans Urs von Balthasar and Contemporary Feminist Theology," 581. Gonzalez recognizes Balthasar as living out this "gendered theological method" in his relationship with Adrienne, whose role "as mystic was to provide the data which he in turn would shape with his intellectual background into theological reflection." While there is certainly some truth to this point, I dispute Gonzalez's claim that Balthasar presents his relationship with Adrienne as "a model for gendered theological activity," for nowhere does he present himself as a model to be imitated. I likewise dispute (as I indirectly argued in chapter two) her claim that Balthasar did not regard Adrienne's work as properly "theological" (ibid., 582).

314. See for example Beattie, *New Catholic Feminism*, esp. 163–67, 170, and 194. For a much more positive portrayal of their relationship within the context of their particular male-female charisma, see Roten, "Two Halves of the Moon." Similarly, but more pragmatically, Peter Henrici argues: "If Adrienne von Speyr had a mission in the Church (and ecclesiastical statements of recent years seem to point in that direction), then, to carry it out, she needed the mediation of a priest like von Balthasar who could accept her visions with theological knowledge and a childlike simplicity of faith" ("Hans Urs von Balthasar: A Sketch of His Life," 23). Balthasar makes a similar claim in *Our Task*, 18–19, and in (with Scola), *Test Everything*, 88.

315. For a treatment of the theme within other contexts, see Michele M. Schumacher, "Towards a New Feminist Theology of the Body" in *Women in Christ*, 201–31; "Feminine Experience and Religious Experience" in *Women in Christ*, 169–200; "Therese, Woman in the Church," *Logos: A Journal of Catholic Thought and Culture* 3, no. 3 (Summer 2000): 122–51; and "The Prophetic Vocation of Women and the Order of Love."

these objections fail to take into account Balthasar's humility in assuming the role of stenographer and editor of Adrienne's more than sixty volumes, which were almost entirely dictated to him. As Johann Roten aptly puts it, "God's own Prometheus—the author of the monumental *Apokalypse der deutschen Seele*, 1937–39—will become the humble stenographer, taking down God's word transmitted to him by Adrienne, and the proud and self-conscious aristocrat will eventually have to leave his spiritual homeland, the Society of Jesus, following thereby the will and call of God, again expressed in the visions and words of Adrienne."[316]

Of course, one can hardly deny the correspondence between the actual relationship of this (admittedly) unconventional couple—as it is recorded in the diaries (*Erde und Himmel* IIII), for example—and Adrienne's theological presentation of the relation between the sexes, including their respective, but nonetheless shared, missions.[317] Both the diaries and Balthasar's *Our Task* reveal the conscious appropriation by both Adrienne and Balthasar of what they perceived as a "double mission,"[318] wherein they also understood themselves—precisely as man and woman—as complementing each other "like the 'two halves of the moon.'"[319] There is, furthermore, good reason to believe that they understood this mission as entailing the formulation of their actual experience of serving the Lord and the Church together as sexually paired,[320] wherein sexuality, as we have seen, is in no way reduced to the physical dimension.

Adrienne, for example, was conscious of being called precisely as a woman and more particularly as a sort of "mystical bride"[321] to accompany Balthasar in his own "masculine" priestly mission: to suffer for him,[322] to visibly bear his

---

316. Roten, "Two Halves of the Moon," 84.

317. Such is the observation of Roten in "Two Halves of the Moon" with regard to Balthasar's own theological presentation of the sexes.

318. See, for example, Speyr, *Erde und Himmel* III, no. 1645 (246); and Balthasar, *Our Task*, 16. On the nature of a "double mission," see also Speyr, *The Mission of the Prophets*, 124–25; and *Handmaid of the Lord*, 63.

319. Balthasar, *Our Task*, 16; see also *My Work*, 89.

320. In at least one passage (in the diaries, which were not meant to be circulated as properly theological works), their shared mission is presented as comparable to that of spouses. Adrienne's suffering is presented as "birthing pains" which she, the woman, must bear alone, in bringing forth "the child" (i.e., the Community of St. John). To Balthasar, the man is however entrusted the task of caring for and accompanying her. See Speyr, *Erde und Himmel* I, no. 122 (91–94).

321. See Speyr, *Erde und Himmel* II, no. 1656 (253–54); cf. *Theologie der Geschlechter*, 176–77. It bears repeating that Adrienne viewed her extraordinary friendship with Balthasar within the context of what they both perceived as their common mission, wherein was situated her mystical charism. See for example Speyr, *Erde und Himmel* II, no. 1994 (458); cf. Balthasar, *Our Task*, 17–19.

322. See for example Speyr, *Erde und Himmel* I, no. 47 (34) and no. 122 (93); and *Erde und Himmel* II, no. 1680 (263), where it is explained that the man's "spiritual fecundity is laid in the woman's flesh so that

"mark" in the form of a wound above her heart and under her left breast,[323] and to bear his—that is to say, their common—spiritual children.[324] Balthasar, on the other hand, understood that he was meant to provide clarification and calm, to stand beside her and to care for her: a role which her own husband was presumably unable to do—or not divinely commissioned to do—given what seems to be his complete ignorance of her mystical visions.[325] Undoubtedly these mystical experiences—especially that, in the present case, of a so-called virginal pregnancy[326]—were significant to her mission of transmitting, by way of her dictations, the mysteries entrusted to her for the Church.[327] It

---

it might be fruitful: for the man." In addition to the wound that she understood herself as bearing for Balthasar (see ibid., no. 1642 [242]) and which she likewise understood as a visible "mark" of her spiritual relation to him, Adrienne actually suffered a series of mystical "deaths" for him. Balthasar describes her as "giving herself up more and more to the inner core of my mission" (Balthasar, *Our Task*, 21).

323. This wound, which Adrienne compares to a woman's menstruation, is given to Adrienne at the moment of her first vision of Mary, and she later comes to know Balthasar as the one for whom she has been called to suffer in this way: the one whose "mark" she bears virginally within herself, as a woman is physically marked by her first sexual encounter with a man. See Speyr, *Erde und Himmel* II, no. 1645 (245–46); cf. *Das Hohelied*, 43; and *Korinther* I, 390.

324. Adrienne typically referred to the community that she co-founded with Balthasar (the Johannesgemeinschaft, or Community of St. John) as "the child," and she recognized herself as bearing and nourishing it with her suffering (see Balthasar, *Our Task*, 88; and Speyr, *Erde und Himmel* I, no. 122 [93]). Beyond this, the diaries witness to her presumably mystical experience of giving birth to three "children" whom she understood as having her husband (presumably her first, as the second marriage was not consummated) as their natural father and Balthasar as the father of their "angel-like essence [*engelhaftes Wesen*]." The identity of these children is revealed by St. Ignatius, in a vision to Adrienne, as signifying the two communities (male and female) of the Johannesgemeinschaft and their common (presumably theological) work. See Speyr, *Erde und Himmel* II, no. 1654 (253) and no. 1650 (249–50); and Balthasar, *Our Task*, 34–35, where reference is made to Adrienne's three miscarriages as spiritually linked to Balthasar's priestly vocation.

325. Barbara Albrecht claims that none of her family members, nor any of the members of her community, were aware of Adrienne's mystical charisma. See Albrecht, "Speyr (Adrienne von)," 1127. Again one exception is Balthasar's personal secretary, who was also an original member of the community, Cornelia Capol. On Balthasar's understanding of his mission at Adrienne's side, see Speyr, *Erde und Himmel* II, no. 1646 (248); and *Erde und Himmel* I, no. 122 (93).

326. See Speyr, *Erde und Himmel* II, no. 1644 (243). Balthasar explains in his introduction to Speyr, *Theologie der Geschlechter*, 9, that although the reader might be tempted to laugh at Adrienne's account of the virginal birth (cf. ibid., 217–19), he or she should remember that this is "not the product of a speculation, but of an 'experience'" in the mystical sense. Balthasar's comment resonates with Adrienne's own mention of "thinking" with her body (cf. *Erde und Himmel* II, no. 1653 [253]) or of "thinking" with her wound (no. 1729 [295]). Balthasar's diary presents Adrienne's mystical experience of, on the one hand, a so-called "restored virginity" (Speyr, *Erde und Himmel* II, no. 1664 [258]; cf. Balthasar, *Our Task*, 31)—that is to say, the closing of the hymen (*Gebärwege*) (*Erde und Himmel* II, no. 1649 [249])—and of "an undeniable pregnancy" (no. 1651 [251]), on the other hand, as "significant with regard to what she will later have to write or otherwise transmit to the Church" (no. 1646 [247]). As such, these experiences are analogical to those of Mary, whose own experience of the virginal pregnancy was given over to the Church as a sort of treasury of her (the Church's) faith. See ibid, no. 1653 [253] and no. 1671 [261]; and *Das Wort und die Mystik* II, 26–27. See also Balthasar, *Our Task*, 41; and Servais, "Per una valutazione dell'influsso di Adrienne von Speyr su Hans Urs von Balthasar," 74.

327. See Speyr, *Erde und Himmel* II, no. 1646 (247) and no. 1671 (261). Worth noting is that her *Theology of the Sexes* (*Theologie der Geschlechter*) consists of dictations which occurred between Decem-

was, moreover, the experience of their shared mission, as reflected upon in a discussion over "man and woman in the reign of God"[328]—a discussion which Balthasar records as taking place while they were both on their knees—that Adrienne claims inspired her thoughts on Christian marriage and motivated the writing of a book on the subject: "Its [the book's] coming about lies in a very particular moment of our stammering on Friday and arises out of our communion [*Verbundenheit*], our reciprocity deeply rooted in God, but also out of our embodiment as man and woman."[329]

The analysis here, as is typical of Adrienne's method, proceeds from the concrete, particular, experiential, and personal—which, as I pointed out in chapter two, is not opposed to the objective and thus the mystical—to the abstract, theoretical, and universal. On the other hand, Adrienne never loses sight, as I have repeatedly argued, of the higher Trinitarian vision of reality, and it is this higher vision which also dominates her relationship with Balthasar: already from the very beginning and consistently throughout their long collaboration. It follows—at least for those who are willing to regard their theology for its objective content—that there is no question in the present case of what Tina Beattie claims to recognize as a distorted sexual attraction between this married laywoman and the celibate priest. Rather, their writings and the diaries point to a serious and prolonged reflection on the mysteries of the Christian faith, wherein they also reflected upon the meaning of human sexuality. This reflection, in turn, was fueled not only by their own experiences of faith—including, most especially, Adrienne's extraordinary mystical experiences—but also by their shared relationship, founded upon that faith and oriented to what they recognized, it bears repeating, as their "double" mission.

In this particular mystical method of experiencing what one is entrusted to share with the Church is also evident Adrienne's personal appropriation of her own counsel to those in the consecrated state: that they ought not to flee from relationships with members of the opposite sex. By this advice, she explicitly states that she does not seek to endorse erotic relationships nor, we might add, would she encourage subliminal ones. Rather, the Swiss mystic proposes a sort of mastery of the sexual sphere which, far from denying sexual attraction, is better expressed as a "letting-be [*Sein-lassen*]" of the gift—a sort of acknowledgement that does not seek to incite or provoke—and that grows out of obedience: "as when one knows the contents of a box, which

---

ber 8, 1946, and mid-January 1947, which corresponds to the time of her mystical experience of a "virginal" pregnancy, as mentioned above.

328. Speyr, *Erde und Himmel* I, no. 122 (93).

329. Speyr, letter of July 13, 1941, to Balthasar, in *Erde und Himmel* I, no. 123 (95).

one does not open."³³⁰ This counsel also means, however, that the gift of sexuality must be embraced by those in the virginal state, as much as by those in marriage; for the virginal man or woman, far from renouncing the fruitfulness of his or her sexuality, offers it—along with his or her body—to the Lord, so as to be fully (corporally and spiritually) in God's service.³³¹ Only as such, may he or she be said to enjoy a greater share in God's mystery.³³²

This belonging to the Lord does not however exempt one from simultaneously belonging to the Christian community, without which no Christian mission can be fruitful.³³³ This is not to deny the more immediate presence of the consecrated man or woman to the Lord. In contrast to the married person for whom the family "stands in a sense, between him and the Lord," the celibate man or woman is, Adrienne reasons, "immediate to the Lord, and his [or her] relationship to his [or her] neighbor is one of commission and mission from within that immediacy."³³⁴ On the other hand, it is from within this immediacy—like that of both Mary and John to the Lord, and through the Lord to one another—that might best be understood the cooperation of the sexes within the various missions of the Church.

Just as man and woman are together fruitful in marriage, so also—Adrienne reasons—does "the celibacy of man and woman enhance one another in pairs" according to the likeness of "the first virginal couple, Christ and his Mother."³³⁵ The whole Marian accompaniment of Christ throughout his terrestrial mission and of his priests throughout the history of the Church is, for example, analogically paralleled by the religious woman who carries in her prayer the missions of the male religious and the priest.³³⁶ Adrienne regards it as "superficial [*oberflächliche*]" or otherwise unnecessary for a male religious to ask a religious sister to pray for his intentions, because a profound truth,

---

330. Speyr, *Theologie der Geschlechter*, 177; see also *John* IV, 131; and *Erde und Himmel* II, no. 1646 (247).

331. This is particularly significant insofar as the supernatural vocation to virginity serves to explain or illuminate the natural vocation of marriage, as we saw in chapter four. For a presentation of virginity as belonging—body and soul—to God and for his service even in the act of martyrdom, see Speyr, *Bereitschaft*, 68; and *Theologie der Geschlechter*, 116 and 237–38. The male religious, who lives his virginity as a positive gift to God, has a "higher understanding" of this mystery, Adrienne argues, than is the case of the secular priest for whom it is considered a renunciation. See ibid., 176.

332. Speyr, *Das Wort und die Mystik* I, 20.

333. See Speyr, *Handmaid of the Lord*, 123; cf. Balthasar, *The Threefold Garland*, 31.

334. Speyr, *John* IV, 126–27.

335. Speyr, *John* III, 266. Adrienne explains that "because the priest is celibate, the nun can be so, and vice versa. Far from alienating themselves through virginity, they rather enhance each other as a couple that corresponds to the first virgin couple, Christ and his Mother" (ibid.). See also Speyr, *Theologie der Geschlechter*, 116.

336. The latter is presented by Adrienne as related, precisely within the context of his official ministry (*Amt*), to the Church as man is related to woman. See Speyr, *Theologie der Geschlechter*, 223.

corresponding to her feminine vocation, is expressed in this request: "She offers her feminine power of prayer for his masculine action and prayer,"[337] and she assumes the task of bearing fruit.

Of course, some readers might recognize in this perspective a cultural stereotype of male and female roles based more upon practice or even oppressive intentions—presumably under the influence of male pressure—than upon real metaphysical differences of the sexes reflecting the Creator's will. More importantly, however, the emphasis here, as elsewhere in Adrienne's theology of the sexes, lies upon the important analogy of sexually paired fecundity—both within the natural and the supernatural realms, and thus also within both the married and the virginal states of life—to describe the supreme fecundity of Trinitarian love.[338] This means not only that femininity and masculinity are so essential to what it means to be human that they cannot be overlooked within the virginal state of life, but also that their meaning—the meaning of human sexuality—is essentially relational. The male, in other words, is radically oriented to the female, just as the female is radically oriented to the male: not in a simple vis-à-vis, but in a transcendence of each one's personal limits in a fecundity that surpasses the sum of their natural sexual powers. This explains Adrienne's reasoning that the virginal woman—as much as, if not more than, the married woman—"belongs to man,"[339] which implies that she is "burdened" by her surrender to him—perhaps a man whom she has never met—so as to carry his mission toward fecundity.[340] Mary, Adrienne explains, is "virginal for the man, who is her Son." Similarly, every woman who has chosen virginity for love of Christ does not so much *renounce* a man as *receive* him—especially within his hierarchical, or official, position (*Amtlichkeit*)—in a manner "determined by the Church."[341]

Conclusion: Sexual Differentiation and Divine Differentiation

In Adrienne's presentation of sexual relations, not unlike that of Balthasar, we might—to conclude this chapter—observe an important principle that,

---

337. Ibid., 177.
338. See ibid., 116.
339. Ibid., 237. The man's virginity, on the other hand, is presented by Adrienne as derived from that of woman, for virginity is characteristically "feminine" (see ibid., 223), notably, as derived from Christ's attitude vis-à-vis the Father. See *John* IV, 125.
340. See Speyr, *Theologie der Geschlechter*, 177.
341. Ibid., 237. Hence, Adrienne reasons (ibid.) that it is "impossible" from an ecclesial perspective to speak of "private" virginity. See also Speyr, *Mary in the Redemption*, 101, where Mary is presented as carrying Christ's messianic mission together with Christ himself, whence she becomes "the prototype of the church, the perfect bride in the ecclesial sense."

as we have seen, is constant in her anthropology. The human—and thus also the corporal and the sexual—reveals the divine, but only because the human itself is patterned after and predestined to union with the divine in the person of Christ, who incorporates all of humanity into his filial relation with the Father through their common Spirit, and all of this by way of the key notion of surrender.[342] This means that if, as St. Paul proposes (cf. Eph 5:21–33), the relationship between the spouses is to be patterned upon the relationship between Christ and the Church, then both will ultimately and necessarily be patterned after the relationship between the Father and the Son in the unity of their one Spirit. It is this same Spirit, moreover, who unifies the Christian with Christ and simultaneously unites Christians (including most especially man and woman) in Christ.[343]

This unity of Christians in Christ and by his Spirit accounts for the significance of the analogy, so prevalent in Adrienne's theology as we saw in chapters three and four, between sexual intercourse and the Eucharist.[344] This analogy is rooted within what she regards as the "Eucharistically conceived" origin of sexual relations. The mystic of Basel maintains, more specifically, that the Eucharist models the "giving and receiving and giving back of the body as the concretisation of love—as, that is to say, the 'I' finding itself in the 'Thou'— and as 'apostolic' fruitfulness in the child."[345] Similarly and more fundamentally, Adrienne speaks of the "Trinitarian Eucharist of the divine Persons," or "their going-into-one-another," which in turn "presupposes their reciprocal, fully-realized disclosure," or their archetypical "surrender" whereby "each is everything to each": the Father's essence belongs to the Son, whose essence belongs to the Spirit, etc. In this way, the divine persons—all in being vis-à-vis one another—are also "fully in one another."[346]

Because it is the Son, moreover, who founds the Eucharist, he is characterized, Adrienne reasons, even within the Trinity by an eternal "Eucharistic attitude," which is at the origin of his "Eucharistic surrender." This surrender is, more precisely, his filial "response" to the Father's begetting act.[347] Hence

---

342. See for example Balthasar, *New Elucidations*, 196; and (with Scola), *Test Everything*, 81.

343. See for example Speyr, *Korinther* I, 315 and 319–20.

344. See for example Speyr, *Theologie der Geschlechter*, 113, 127, 132, 141, and 248; *The Holy Mass*, 69; and *Das Hohelied*, 43–44. The same analogy of sexual intercourse, which we exposited in chapter three, is also employed by Adrienne to explain the mystery of mysticism in the Church; see *Das Wort und die Mystik* I, 22.

345. Speyr, *Das Wort und die Mystik* II, 534; see 113 for the original meaning of love at the time of creation in precisely these terms.

346. Ibid., 524; see also 101.

347. Ibid., 525; cf. Hans Urs von Balthasar, *Theo-Drama* V, 87, where ample reference is made to Adrienne.

the mystery of Christ's union with the Church through his Eucharistic surrender is effected "within the mystery of his being one with the Father and the Holy Spirit."[348] In the final analysis, "the Adam-Eve reciprocity, which was itself an image of Trinitarian love, is fulfilled in the Christ-Church reciprocity in the Eucharistic mystery, whereby the divine archetype prevails over the created image."[349]

This, it is important to insist, is not to admit that "the temporal sexual relationship between man and woman is replaced" in Adrienne's theology, as Tina Beattie incorrectly claims to be the case in Balthasar's theology, by "the original, 'absolute,' suprasexual relationship between the sexes," such that the value of human (especially female) sexuality is necessarily called into question.[350] After all, not only is the "suprasexual (and not sexless) relationship between the incarnate Word and his Church" viewed by the Swiss theologian as a "genuinely human one," but the natural, sexual fruitfulness of man and woman is also presented by him as a fitting image of the spiritual fecundity of this Word in the Church.[351]

As for Adrienne, she argues that the tension between the sexes is marked simultaneously by the tension between the natural and the supernatural. By this she means, more specifically, that one can never categorically separate the married state from the Christian mysteries of redemption, nor the celibate state from the natural orientation of man to woman and woman to man. One must therefore choose between these two states of life with one's eyes open: to choose "the state of marriage without ignorance of the tension between the Incarnation and the Eucharist" or to choose the state of the counsels without ignorance of the man-woman tension."[352]

From this perspective, the mystic of Basel opposes what she regards as the "tendency" of the 19th- and early 20th-century Church to have hidden the lower body and to have thus "handed over to Freud the complex ensuing therefrom." As a countermeasure, she recommends that "the whole question be seized openly and without timidity today" (that is to say, more than

---

348. Speyr, *The Letter to the Ephesians*, 241.
349. Speyr, *Das Wort und die Mystik* II, 534.
350. Beattie, *New Catholic Feminism*, 105; cf. Balthasar, *Theo-Drama* III, 325. "In Balthasar," Beattie maintains, "sexual difference is denied through a complex and often contradictory theological symbolics in which woman becomes a projection of man, and the particularity and revelatory potential of female sexual embodiment is denied" (*New Catholic Feminism*, 94). Cf. Loughlin, "Sexing the Trinity."
351. See Balthasar, *Theo-Drama* II, 413; see also *Epilogue*, 112–13; and *Theo-Drama* III, 325.
352. Speyr, *Das Wort und die Mystik* II, 531. It bears repeating that Adrienne, not unlike Balthasar, argues that there can be no "third" state, because "the serious Christian gives himself irrevocably so that he can no longer take himself back" (Balthasar, *First Glance*, 54). See also Speyr, *Theologie der Geschlechter*, 114 and 180; and Balthasar, *Our Task*, 29–30.

70 years ago, when these words were dictated): "not in the isolation of the sexual sphere," wherein the question is "unanswerable, but in the integration in the whole human, Christian, ecclesial, Christological and Trinitarian."[353] This is why Tina Beattie's claim that Balthasar's theology—whom she (falsely, I am convinced)[354] recognizes as influenced more by his "psychological struggle"[355] with the temptation posed by Adrienne's body-person than by her theology—is characterized by the "looping together of sexual difference and creaturely difference in an elliptical relationship"[356] is, precisely as inspired by Adrienne's mystical insights, true only insofar as both are more profoundly looped together, as it were, in the most fundamental difference of all: the infinite difference of the Father, Son and Holy Spirit.

From this perspective, far from seeking (at least unconsciously) to eliminate sexual differentiation by regarding both man and woman as "feminine" before God, as Beattie claims is fundamental to Balthasar's teaching,[357] the

---

353. Speyr, *Theologie der Geschlechter*, 11. As noted above, although Adrienne's *Theologie der Geschlechter* was published in 1969, it was actually dictated between December 8, 1946, and mid-January 1947, as Balthasar reports in his foreword to the volume (8).

354. Balthasar's theology, it seems to me, speaks for itself: particularly in its accord with the long tradition of Church teaching, as differing from Beattie's explicit attempt to override that tradition in favor of a female priesthood. The so-called "pornographic" images that Beattie reads into Balthasar's *Heart of the World*—with the nuptial love between Christ and the Church being "represented as a sado-masochistic 'blood-wedding' consummated in an act of rape during which the woman's body is conquered by the Bridegroom" (Beattie, *New Catholic Feminism*, 174), is, in fact, entirely of her inventing. This is evident in the fact that—despite her certainty that her readers will be nauseated by her interpretation of his writing—she explicitly notes "no evidence of such nausea among his devoted readers" (ibid., 176). I, as well, have found no such nausea among any of his other readers for the simple reason that none of them interpret his writing as she does. It is, incidentally, of no little significance to Beattie (see ibid., 170) that this same work by Balthasar—*Heart of the World*—is recognized by Andrew Louth as "an uncanny crystallization of the vision of Adrienne von Speyr" (Louth, "The Place of *Heart of the World* in the Theology of Hans Urs von Balthasar," in John Riches [ed.], *The Analogy of Beauty: The Theology of Hans Urs von Balthasar* [Edinburgh: T. & T. Clark, 1986], 148) and that Peter Henrici describes it as "the first thing to be written entirely under the influence of Adrienne's visions" ("A Sketch of von Balthasar's Life," 31).

355. Beattie, *New Catholic Feminism*, 167. "Balthasar's desire for Speyr/Christ becomes Christ's violent desire for the Church/the body. But Christ's violent rape of the Bride is masked by her sexual transgressions: she was asking for it; she deserved it; it was for her own good" (ibid., 203). See also ibid., 170–78, esp. 177–78.

356. Ibid., 92.

357. "How can the first human be male, if all human creatures are woman in relation to God? [...] Balthasar's 'woman' is the body of Christ, while 'man' is the headship and divinity of Christ. 'She' is the community of the Church, while 'he' is the representative of the one and only true man, Jesus Christ. 'She' is the woman, identified with humanity, creation, derivation. 'He' is the man, identified with God, creator, origination. But he is not God, and in order to become other than God, in order to establish the diastasis that marks the separation between 'man' and God and to experience the desire that draws 'man' to God, he must become what he is not—he must become 'her'" (ibid., 114–15); see also 196–97. Meanwhile, Beattie's reading of Balthasar that all of humanity is "feminine" before God is not far from the official teaching of the Church. Although the Church is "*a collective subject and not an individual person*," in her every human being is called to become the bride of Christ, Pope John Paul II teaches, by accepting the gift of his redemptive love and by responding to it "with the gift of his or her own person" (*Mulieris*

Swiss theologian might better be understood—particularly insofar as his voice is consonant with that of Adrienne—as seeking in sexual difference an important biblical image for describing the unity-in-difference of Christ and the Church, as well as the difference-in-unity of the Creator and the creature and ultimately the difference-in-unity of the Trinity of Persons in God. Hence, for example, the mystery of the reciprocity of man and woman in the sexual act serves as a Speyrian analogy or metaphor for describing the manner in which Christ and the Church are revealed through their reciprocity.[358] Or, the reciprocal "possession" of Adam and Eve in their nakedness serves to explain how the Father and Son might be said to "possess" one another without disappearing as persons.[359]

This reciprocity of man and woman is in no way compromised by Adrienne's commentaries on the Pauline texts concerning hierarchy in marriage (cf. Col 3:18–19; Eph 5:19). Fundamental to her interpretation of these passages is the place that the second Adam assumes in relation to the Church, of course, but still more primarily in relation to the Father. This means, more specifically, that the relationship between man and woman in marriage is based not simply nor primarily upon an external likeness between two relationships—the one human, the other divine—as is the case in the above example regarding the Adam-Eve relationship, on the one hand, and the relation between Father and Son, on the other. Rather, the reciprocity between man and woman, not unlike the hierarchical relationship between them, is profoundly marked—by way of participation—in the reciprocal relationship of love between the Father and the Son in the Holy Spirit.

Both man and woman, Adrienne specifies in her commentary of 1 Corinthians 11:11,[360] have equal title to redemption in Christ, just as both have sinned before God. Insofar, however, as the Lord himself stands under the Father's headship, the hierarchy between the sexes is not obliterated. Indeed, it is precisely his submission to the Father along with the willing surrender of his body and his members for the crucifixion that renders him the head of the Church. The Church, for her part, must surrender herself—and each of her

---

Dignitatem, no. 25). For this reason, the "very essence of the Church" is symbolically present in women, especially faithful women. Theirs is an "inherent 'prophecy' [...], a highly significant 'iconic character,'" which finds its full realization in Mary" (Pope John Paul II, *Letter to Women*, no. 11).

358. See Speyr, *Erde und Himmel* II, no. 1684 (266); cf. no. 1683 (265). Similar insights might be gathered from the famous theology of the body of Pope John Paul II (see *Man and Woman He Created Them*). See also Agneta Sutton, "The Complementarity and Symbolism of the Two Sexes: Karl Barth, Hans Urs von Balthasar and John Paul II," *New Blackfriars* 87, no. 1010 (July 2006): 418–33.

359. See Speyr, *Theologie der Geschlechter*, 143 and 159.

360. "Nevertheless, in the Lord woman is not independent of man nor man of woman." See Speyr, *Korinther* I, 322 for what follows.

members within her—to Christ. To the extent that she does so, she permits Christ to die within her and to become, expressly as resurrected, her head.[361] "She receives his seed, which she must bear; his word, which she must carry forth, while the Son (in his Ascension) draws back in a sort of passivity."[362]

Similarly, the woman who "fully" loves her husband is ever ready for him, Adrienne explains. Out of love for him, she is given to him in such a way as to realize the meaning of Paul's words (cf. Eph 5:23) that "the husband is the head of the wife."[363] The husband, meanwhile, is expected to love his wife in a way that reflects (by way of participation) the Lord's generous, initiating love towards him (cf. Eph 5:25) so as to lead her—precisely through her surrender to him as her husband—towards an ever greater surrender to the Lord.[364] This, in turn, requires that the "roots of his challenge [or demand: Forderung] [to his wife] remain in God"[365] and thus also that he himself—precisely as a member of Christ's body and thus as one under Christ's headship—must assume a passive, receptive, and thus "feminine," attitude vis-à-vis the Lord.[366] He must, more specifically, allow the Lord to take him "entirely to himself," so as to be permanently handed over to the Lord and to imitate him, not merely in an exterior fashion, "but by having the same attitude toward him [the Lord] that he [the Lord] has toward the Father."[367]

When, by contrast, a man's likeness to God is disturbed by sin such that he is no longer conscious of being in God's image, he can also no longer be conscious of the specifically Christian character of his relation to his wife. She consequently falls out from under his headship, Adrienne explains, and can no longer be considered his "glory" (cf. 1 Cor 11:7).[368] If, therefore, man is to remain properly ordained to a woman in accord with the Christian sense of headship, his initiating self-surrender to her must be animated by his more fundamental self-surrender to Christ, who in turn, is surrendered to the Church out of his submissive love for the Father.[369] It follows that the Christian woman never recognizes her husband as "an absolute head," since he himself is submitted to Christ. The submissive woman, meanwhile, is en-

---

361. Speyr, *Erde und Himmel* II, no. 1636 (229); cf. *Das Wort und die Mystik* II, 531: "The unity of the Church is built out of individual believers, bound together through the body of Christ, who is in them."

362. Speyr, *Theologie der Geschlechter*, 69; see also *Das Wort und die Mystik* II, 529.

363. Speyr, *Erde und Himmel* III, no. 2255 (248).

364. See for example Speyr, *Theologie der Geschlechter*, 117–18 and 248. The corporal surrender in paradise would only have been possible, Adrienne argues, with a simultaneous surrender to God; see *Theologie der Geschlechter*, 132.

365. Ibid., 69.

366. See Speyr, *The Letter to the Ephesians*, 225.

367. Ibid., 232.

368. Speyr, *Korinther* I, 318.

369. See Speyr, *Handmaid of the Lord*, 127–28. On the primacy of man's surrender in imitation of Christ, see *World of Prayer*, 41; cf. Balthasar, *Theo-Drama* II, 373.

nobled by her own likeness to Christ, who willingly stands under the Father's headship.[370] Her subordination to her husband "leads to the Lord, an ordering into his order."[371]

This order—to repeat—is Trinitarian, which means that God has granted to human beings a true participation in his own divine love and fruitfulness, as we saw in chapter five. From Adrienne's perspective, the "opposition" of man and woman within both the married and consecrated states of life "leads into the circulation of Trinitarian love" so as to draw upon the infinite fecundity of this same love.[372] For Christian couples and for religious men and women who live their virginity in accord with the profound meaning of their sexuality, there is, Adrienne teaches, "a fresh and unsuspected richness, with all possible transformations and ways of complementing and corresponding to one another, which are an expression of the 'greater-than' of supernatural love."[373]

370. Speyr, *Korinther* I, 315.
371. Speyr, *The Letter to the Colossians*, 134.
372. Speyr, *Theologie der Geschlechter*, 116; cf. Balthasar, *The Christian State of Life*, 228.
373. Speyr, *World of Prayer*, 47–48; see also *Korinther* I, 319–20.

SEVEN

A Critical Appraisal of the Trinitarian Anthropology of Adrienne von Speyr as Appropriated by Hans Urs von Balthasar

To bring Adrienne's "Trinitarian-shaped" anthropology to conclusion is certainly no easy task, for Adrienne is, as Hans Urs von Balthasar fittingly describes her, "a world."[1] To be sure, she is no world unto herself. Rather, her thought is so Catholic that her theological anthropology can only be expressed as "Catholic" in the sense of integral, and thus simultaneously ecclesial, sacramental, Christological and—above all and explicit in all the rest—Trinitarian.[2]

Certainly the greatest novelty of Adrienne's theology is, in fact, her Trinitarian approach, which in turn supposes the novel articulation of the unity of the divine will and the unity of the divine operation despite (or, better said, precisely *in*, or due to) the personal distinctions: a unity which is expressed in terms of the perfect surrender of the divine persons to one another. This key concept (surrender) of Adrienne's theological anthropology connotes—even more in the original German (*Hingabe*) than in its English translation—an active letting go (or letting be) by way of a generous outpouring, as it were, or a passive but nonetheless willful letting be or letting go by way of availability, consent, and receptivity. Hence, in her description of the Trinitarian relations, upon which her anthropology is constructed, both the Father's act of begetting the Son and the Son's reception of this gift of the Father's being as his own can be described by this term with recourse to this concept. What is described in each case is however different so as to be likewise complemen-

---

1. Balthasar and Scola, *Test Everything*, 88.
2. "Trinity, Christology, and Church form an indissoluble unity both theoretically and practically, theologically and ethically" (Balthasar, *Elucidations*, 79). On the integrality of Catholicism, see Balthasar, *My Work*, 10.

tary. The paternal action implies the filial "passion,"[3] as it were, and vice versa in what the Swiss mystic describes as a perfect correspondence. "The Son lets himself be begotten [...] as if to contribute toward his own fashioning"[4] and likewise "makes himself available" to the Father "for the generation of the Spirit."[5] Similar is their combined action of spirating the Spirit and the passive action of the Spirit's proceeding from both. "Because the Son is God, the perennial generation of the Son is at the same time the Son's always being in existence already."[6] Thus, "right from the outset there is a reciprocal closeness. For the distance—implied by his being begotten—embraces the closeness—implied by his return to the Father; his filial relation to the Father is the constant result of the Father's paternal relation to the Son."[7]

These insights into the mystery of the intra-Trinitarian life are made accessible for Adrienne, as we have seen, through the incarnate Son, who is simultaneously (but consequentially) the revelation of the mystery of the human person, created in his image.[8] From this perspective, the Son's salvific earthward descent mirrors, as it were, the Father's own primal begetting of the Son, which is the origin of the responsive and total self-giving of the Son and, in turn, the Spirit. Similar is Balthasar's presentation of the Son as receiving from the Father not only his entire divine being, but also his mission to give himself to the world as an act of obedience to the Father—who, it is important to add, communicates his commands "by way not of precept but of generation"—and even his ability to send forth the Spirit with the Father.[9] "The crux of the matter"—not only in Balthasar's appropriation of Chalcedon as read by Nicholas Healy, but also in his appropriation of Adrienne's theology—is the idea that "the Son does not actualize the integrity of his human nature outside of, or apart from, the act of receiving his entire being

---

3. By this is meant the fundamental sense of the term: that of being acted upon, rather than in the derived sense of his life given *pro nobis*. On the relation between passion and action, see *ST* I, q. 28, a. 3, ad. 1. We nonetheless do well to recall with Gilles Emery that when we speak of the procession of a divine person, this does not imply any "passivity." "To proceed is an act." Hence, "when we consider the generation of the Son and the procession of the Holy Spirit, it is necessary to avoid any idea of passivity. [...] It is by one operation that the Father begets and that the Son is born form all eternity, but this one operation is in the Father and in the Son under distinct relations: paternity and filiation" (*The Trinity*, 150).

4. Speyr, *World of Prayer*, 59; see also 30 and 65. Cf. Balthasar, *Theo-Drama* V, 85 and 93; *Theo-Logic* II, 136; and *Theo-Logic* III, 236.

5. Speyr, *World of Prayer*, 61.   6. Speyr, *The Letter to the Ephesians*, 21.

7. Speyr, *Die katholischen Briefe* II, 238.

8. See Balthasar, *First Glance at Adrienne von Speyr*, 60–61.

9. Balthasar, *The Christian State of Life*, 36; cf. Speyr, *World of Prayer*, 61; and Emery, *The Trinitarian Theology of St. Thomas Aquinas*, 365. On the Son receiving his mission from the Father in obedience, see Balthasar, *Mysterium Paschale*, 35–36; *Theo-Drama* III, 186; and *Explorations in Theology* IV, 141–53. On the Son receiving the possibility of communicating the Spirit, see *Theo-Drama* III, 190; *Theo-Drama* V, 75; and *Theo-Logic* III, 119.

and existence from the Father."¹⁰ This accounts for Balthasar's caution with regard to the doctrine of Chalcedon, which he recognizes as slighting the Trinitarian union in accounting for the personhood of Christ.¹¹

The Trinitarian Dynamic Called into Question: Analogical and Metaphorical Descriptions of the Godhead

Balthasar, meanwhile, is himself faulted by his critics for "a kind of human psychologicalism" whereby he risks leading his readers "in the direction of tritheism."¹² This is apparent, they argue, for example, in his reference—again following Adrienne—to an "unanimous salvific decision on the part of the Trinity"¹³ to send the Son into the world, and thus also to the Son's pretemporal or even "hypostatic"¹⁴ obedience whereby he "permits in full consciousness and with full consent [...] to be used as the Father wishes."¹⁵ Beyond even this, both the mystic and the trained theologian present the Son as consenting to the act whereby he is himself begotten.¹⁶ Indeed, "his human obedience can be explained," Balthasar specifies (with qualification), "only in terms of his divine obedience," which is an expression of "Trinitarian love."¹⁷

Balthasar would explain this in Speyrian terms: namely of "one freedom of the divine Essence [...] possessed by each Hypostasis in its own specific way."¹⁸ Hence, more specifically, "the unity of the divine will is *also* the result of an integration of the intentions of the Hypostases,"¹⁹ by which we might understand that "the hypostases determine in their *circumincessio* what God

---

10. Healy, *The Eschatology of Hans Urs von Balthasar*, 116; cf. Balthasar, *A Theology of History*, 34. This is not, however, to grant that the Son's obedience is merely passive. See Balthasar, *Theo-Drama* III, 186.

11. See Balthasar, "On the Concept of Person," 22; and Healy, *The Eschatology of Hans Urs von Balthasar*, 133.

12. Bertrand de Margerie, "Note on Balthasar's Trinitarian Theology," *The Thomist* 64 (2000): 128; and Kilby, *Balthasar: A (Very) Critical Introduction*, 105n31.

13. Balthasar, *Theo-Drama* III, 187; see also (with Speyr) *Au cœur du mystère rédempteur* (Paris: CLD, 1980), 37–40. Cf. Speyr, *Das Allerheiligen Buch* II, 104–8. See also Beaudin, *Obéissance et solidarité*, 90; Birot, "The Divine Drama," 420–21.

14. Balthasar, *Theo-Logic* II, 354.

15. Balthasar, *Credo*, 45–46; see also *Theo-Drama* III, 186 and 226; and *Explorations in Theology* IV, 141–46. Cf. Speyr, *Das Buch von Gehorsam*, 36.

16. See Balthasar, *Theo-Logic* II, 136; *Theo-Logic* III, 236; *Theo-Drama* III, 186; *Theo-Drama* II, 256; and *Theo-Drama* V, 88 (with extensive references to Speyr, including her *World of Prayer*, 59) and 425. Similarly with regard to the Spirit: "we can and must think of the Persons who proceed, the Son and the Spirit, as 'letting themselves be brought forth'" (Balthasar, *Theo-Logic* II, 136).

17. Balthasar, *Theo-Logic* II, 354; see also *First Glance at Adrienne von Speyr*, 61.

18. Balthasar, *Theo-Drama* V, 485 and 517; cf. Speyr, *World of Prayer*, 57–71.

19. Balthasar, *Theo-Drama* V, 485.

is and wills and does."[20] Balthasar's critics nonetheless insist that he comes dangerously close to proposing multiple wills within the one divine nature,[21] a criticism that we will address below. It might thus be admitted that the very hinge of this original theological perspective, so profoundly influenced by Adrienne—namely, the presentation of Christ's love as revealing the eternal dynamic "event" within the Godhead of begetting and being begotten, of breathing forth and proceeding, of giving and receiving—is the origin not only of potential misunderstanding but even of a certain disrepute in which Balthasar's theology is held by his critics.

To be sure, a number of Balthasar's commentators argue that his "almost unrestrained"[22] appropriation of the images and metaphors used by Adrienne to address the Godhead in terms of a dynamic "happening" or "event" should be read as an attempt to surpass the constraints of a negative theology in an approach similar to that of Scripture. Karen Kilby, on the other hand, judges that Balthasar's theology does not "hold itself accountable to Scripture, tradition, or its readers, but somehow soars above them all."[23] By this she means that Balthasar adopts a "God's eye view," a "sense of [...] privileged access," or an "insider's view" into the inner life of the Trinity, so as to write "from a position above his materials—above tradition, above Scripture, above history—and also, indeed, above his readers."[24]

Defenders of Balthasar, in turn, maintain that his characteristically dynamic concepts do "more justice" to God's greatness than those describing the Trinity as "static perfection," precisely because the divine processions should not be conceived as having occurred "once and for all." Rather, the self-giving

---

20. Balthasar, *Theo-Logic* II, 148; see also 164; *Theo-Logic* III, 163; and *Theo-Drama* II, 256 and 258.

21. Commenting on the passage above in which Balthasar argues for an "unanimous salvific decision on the part of the Trinity" (Balthasar, *Theo-Drama* II, 187), Alyssa Pitstick argues: "Now a single will may make a resolution, but in no case is the decision of a single will said to be 'unanimous.' [...] Multiple individual intentions and their integration are simply not possible if there is but one simple divine will" (Pitstick, *Light in Darkness*, 291–92). See also Bertrand de Margerie, "Note on Balthasar's Trinitarian Theology," 130. Antoine Birot ("The Divine Drama," 421–22n23), far from defending Balthasar on this point as he proposes to do, actually comes close to the same critique when he judges as incompatible with Balthasar's perspective the Thomistic teaching that the Son assumed the human nature without depositing the divine nature. Cf. Thomas Aquinas, *Super Phil* II, lect. 2, no. 57 (= *Super Epistolem B. Pauli ad Philipenses lectura*; in *Commentary on the Letters of Saint Paul to the Philippians, Colossians, Thessalonians, Timothy, Titus, and Philemon*, trans. Fabien R. Larcher, eds. John Mortensen and Enrique Alarcón, vol. 40 of the Latin/English edition of the *Works of St. Thomas Aquinas* [Lander, Wyo.: The Aquinas Institute for the Studey of Sacred Doctrine, 2012]).

22. Thomas G. Dalzell, *The Dramatic Encounter of Divine and Human Freedom in the Theology of Hans Urs von Balthasar* (Frankfurt: Peter Lang, 1997), 191.

23. Kilby, *Balthasar: A (Very) Critical Introduction*, 40; see also 162.

24. Ibid., 13 and 112. Kilby does *not* attribute this "insider's view" to Balthasar's direct access to Adrienne's presumably mystical experiences. See ibid., 157 and 160.

and self-receiving that mark these processions—as Adrienne would have it—are "eternally actual" and infinite: not in the sense of an "endless extension," but that of "an ever-greater intensity."[25] This explains, as we saw in chapter two, Balthasar's tendency—in union with Adrienne—of employing the comparative, which alone is, Balthasar argues, "open to the 'ever-greater'" characteristic of God's infinite fullness of Trinitarian life.[26] "The divine unity is one of fullness," he reasons, "and not of bare abstraction."[27]

We could hardly be closer to the Thomistic presentation of God in terms of pure act, so as to be more adequately described, as Fergus Kerr observes, by a verb than a noun: "more event than entity."[28] Or, as Marie-Joseph Nicolas would have it:

> The 'Pure Act' is certainly not a being in becoming [*un être en devenir*]. But he is also not [from the perspective of St. Thomas] an immobile being, stopped. The entire dynamism attributable to the idea of nature is infinitely present here, [as is] everything that is in act and in the state of becoming, but without potentiality. God is not a being that is made, nor is he an achieved being: he is a totality that gushes forth; he is an eternal spring. In him being is act, and it is *action*, that is to say, primarily thought, love, life and then creation.[29]

Nevertheless, the continuous alteration in Adrienne's perspective, adopted by Balthasar, between the unity of the divine essence and the difference of persons, as well as the unity of the immanent and the economic Trinity—although serving the tension of the mystery, especially the mystery of love—are faulted by critics as leading to confusion or at least ambiguity, especially when terms like 'distance' and 'separation' are ascribed almost indistinguishably from one to the other. Indeed, St. Thomas argues that terms such as 'separation' and 'division' should be avoided in speaking of God so as not to challenge the simplicity of the divine substance.[30]

To be sure, there are other images employed by Balthasar and Adrienne which seek to clarify that however "infinite" the distance between the divine persons, there is no rupture in their unity.[31] Foremost among these is, ironi-

---

25. Dalzell, *The Dramatic Encounter of Divine and Human Freedom*, 187; cf. Speyr, *World of Prayer*, 30 and 40. Dalzell describes this as a "razor's edge method" (ibid., 192; and "The Enrichment of God in Balthasar's Trinitarian Eschatology," 8). See also O'Hanlon, *The Immutability of God in the Theology of Hans Urs von Balthasar*; and López, "Eternal Happening: God as an Event of Love."

26. See Balthasar, *Theo-Drama* V, 78 (including his reference to Speyr, *John* I, 308) and 82n6; *Theo-Drama* II, 259; *Does Jesus Know Us?*, 97; *The Glory of the Lord* VII, 213; and Palakeel, *The Use of Analogy in Theological Discourse*, 106. Cf. Speyr, *John* I, 10 and 13; and *Korinther* I, 412–13.

27. Balthasar, *Explorations in Theology* I, 224.

28. Kerr, *After Aquinas*, 188; see also 187.

29. Nicolas, "L'idée de nature dans la pensée de saint Thomas d'Aquin," 554–55.

30. Cf. Thomas Aquinas, *ST* I, q. 31, a. 2.

31. See, for example, Balthasar, *Truth is Symphonic*, 40; and *Mysterium Paschale*, 101 and 125–26.

cally enough, that to which is likewise attributed the idea of Trinitarian "distance": namely surrender. Precisely because this term can express both the generosity that holds onto nothing as one's own and the perfect willingness to let happen, to allow, or to otherwise receive and respond, it is possible to imagine that what is so radically given (even "abandoned") is never lost but received and even returned with the same generous spirit of self-giving surrender, thanks also, as we shall see, to the third person of the Trinity. Hence for Balthasar, "the glorification of the Son by the Father is already contained by virtue of its total truth in the glorification of the Father by the Son."[32]

On the other hand, the image of surrender in the form of receptivity leads to still other objections from Balthasar's critics.[33] They question, more specifically, whether his attribution of receptivity to the Godhead—despite his obvious attempts to distance this concept from its Aristotelian association with passive potency and thus also with neediness and imperfection—creates more confusion and even error than clarification of the Trinitarian mystery. Such is particularly apparent in the arguments of Nicholas Healy and Gerard O'Hanlon offered, ironically enough, in Balthasar's defense.[34] Maintaining, more specifically, that receptivity is a positive characteristic in human persons, they argue that it should also be ascribed, albeit analogically, to God with respect to his creatures. Hence, Healy reasons, for example: "Insofar as the 'potencies' of the finite order are intrinsic to the form and content of the gift and not simply negative in relation to God's simple perfection, God must contain supereminently all the *diverse perfections* that, *at the creaturely level, are saturated with potentiality* and finitude."[35] To reason in this way is, however, it seems to me, to miss the very point of the objection: namely, in what sense we can speak of potency as even a *creaturely* perfection.

Throughout most of the western philosophical tradition this concept was in fact understood—even in the more novel sense noted by Norris Clarke as "a positive disposition to be actively open"[36]—as implying the very absence of the perfection to which it is naturally and/or supernaturally ordered. In other words, any such "positive" disposition can only be understood in terms of this orderedness, which is not to deny that it (the positive disposition) is

---

32. Balthasar, *The Glory of the Lord* I, 476.
33. See, for example, De Margerie, "Note on Balthasar's Trinitarian Theology"; Guy Mansini, "Balthasar and the Theodramatic Enrichment of the Trinity," *The Thomist* 64 (2000): 499–519; and Narcisse, "Participer à la vie trinitaire," 119–28.
34. See O'Hanlon, *The Immutability of God in the Theology of Hans Urs von Balthasar*; and Healy, *The Eschatology of Hans Urs von Balthasar*.
35. Healy, *The Eschatology of Hans Urs von Balthasar*, 89; emphasis added.
36. Norris Clarke, "Response to Long's Comments," *Communio* 21 (1994): 167. Clarke is cited by Healy (*The Eschatology of Hans Urs von Balthasar*, 75) in support of his defense of Balthasar.

unable by its own power to bring about the circumstances of its own perfection. Rather, in keeping with the traditional meaning of the concept, it would thus seem that the circumstances of perfection must be gratuitously offered (*donum*) or otherwise given (*datum*).

This is not to deny, of course, that every created entity is, as Healy rightly points out, already good in virtue of its form, whereby it is nonetheless in potency with regard to its proper perfection.[37] "[T]he form which makes a thing actual is a perfection and a good," St. Thomas reasons, "and thus every actual being is a good; and likewise every potential being, as such, is a good, as having a relation to good. For as it has being in potentiality, so has it goodness in potentiality."[38] From this idea of goodness in potentiality we cannot conclude, however, that potency might be considered a good in itself, nor that a thing is good insofar as (to the extent that) it is in potency. Indeed, it is not potency but act that is the measure of perfection for Aquinas, who could hardly be clearer on this point: "To be in act, therefore, constitutes the nature of the good"; "By nature, the good of each thing is its act and perfection."[39] If, therefore, a natural potency might be taken as good, this is the case precisely insofar as it implies an orientation to act, and thus (consequently) to the good, or to its own perfection; for "good has the nature of an end,"[40] and "nothing except a good thing desires the good."[41]

In this sense, it would seem that the concept of potentiality, or receptivity understood in this sense, is of its very nature proper to the creature, which might explain De Magerie's accusation that the Swiss theologian fashions the Trinity "in the image of man."[42] Balthasar, meanwhile, maintains the same with regard to the Thomistic tradition and likewise argues that it is God himself who has chosen, in virtue of the Incarnation, to "represent in human form (anthropomorphically) God's sovereignty and lowliness." With reference to Schelling, he asks: "if God should want to be human, [...] who would dare to make objections?"[43] Still more to the point, Healy argues that

---

37. See Healy, *The Eschatology of Hans Urs von Balthasar*, 89.
38. Thomas Aquinas, *ST* I, q. 48, a. 3. 39. Thomas Aquinas, *SCG* I, c. 37, 4 and 5.
40. Thomas Aquinas, *ST* I, q. 103, a. 2. 41. Thomas Aquinas, *SCG* III, c. 20, 5.
42. De Margerie, "Note on Balthasar's Trinitarian Theology," 130. See also Richard Schenk, "Ist die Rede vom leidenden Gott theologisch zu vermeiden? Reflexionen über den Streit von K. Rahner und H. U. Von Balthasar," in Peter Koslowski and Friedrich Hermanni (eds.), *Der leidende Gott: Eine philosophische und theologische Kritik* (Munich: Wilhelm Fink Verlag, 2001), 225–39; and Schumacher, "Representation in the Theology of Hans Urs von Balthasar."
43. Balthasar, *Theo-Logic* II, 70; see also 84; and *The Glory of the Lord* I, 84. With regard to the Thomistic tradition, Balthasar asks whether, as stated in chapter one of this volume, the ordering of knowledge over love, according to the principle that something can be loved only when it is known (cf. *ST* I, q. 27, a. 3, ad. 3), "is not in the end merely read off of the created *imago* and thence elevated to a

the Aristotelian conflating of receptivity with passive potency begs the very question at hand: namely, what is the meaning and perfection of act?[44]

To be sure, Thomists are concerned with maintaining what Gregory Rocca observes to be essential to Aquinas's use of analogy: his "unwavering [...] dismissal of any kind of analogy that he thinks will compromise God's excellence and superiority,"[45] whence his insistence that no perfection can accrue to God from creatures.[46] Precisely as the supreme good and as complete act—in whom nothing is in potency, because in him nothing can be perfected—God acts, Thomas teaches, not by reason of, or for desire of, an end to be attained, but only by love for an end which he wishes to communicate.[47] God, in other words, loves without desire, or passion.[48] As such, his love can be considered identical with his will,[49] whereby he causes all things[50] and wills some good "to every existing thing."

Hence, since to love anything is nothing else than to will good to that thing, it is manifest that God loves everything that exists. Yet not as we love. Because since our will is not the cause of the goodness of things, but is moved by it as by its object [cf. *ST* I-II, q. 27, a. 1; q. 25, a. 2] our love, whereby we will good to anything, is not the cause of its goodness; but conversely its goodness, whether real or imaginary, calls forth our love, by which we will that it should preserve the good it has, and receive besides the good it has not, and to this end we direct our actions: whereas the love of God infuses and creates goodness.[51]"

Or, to put it in the words of St. Augustine of Hippo, that St. Thomas repeats in various contexts, "because God is good, we are."[52]

---

metaphysical principle" (Balthasar, *Theo-Logic* II, 164). Similarly: "Might not this ranking of knowledge before love be an importation from the created order into the divine world?" (ibid., 162).

44. Healy, *The Eschatology of Hans Urs von Balthasar*, 75. Cf. David C. Schindler, *Hans Urs von Balthasar and the Dramatic Structure of Truth: A Philosophical Investigation* (New York: Fordham University Press, 2004), 68.

45. Gregory Rocca, *Speaking the Incomprehensible God*, 143. Cf. Balthasar, *Theo-Drama* II, 261.

46. Thomas Aquinas, *ST* I, q. 19, a. 2, ad. 3.

47. Cf. Thomas Aquinas, *SCG* III, c. 18, 5; and *ST* I, q. 44, a. 4. See also Bernhard-Thomas Blankenhorn, "The Good as Self-Diffusive in Thomas Aquinas," *Angelicum* 79, no. 4 (2002): 803–37; O'Rourke, *Pseudo-Dionysius and the Metaphysics of Aquinas*, esp. 249; Nicolas, "L'Idée de nature dans la pensée de Saint Thomas d'Aquin," 554–55; and Cottier, *Le Désir de Dieu*, 192.

48. Cf. Thomas Aquinas, *ST* I, q. 20, a. 1, ad. 1; and *SCG* I, c. 91, 12. See also Lombardo, *The Logic of Desire*, 82–83.

49. Cf. Thomas Aquinas, *ST* I, q. 20, a. 1; and *SCG* I, c. 91, 1.

50. See Thomas Aquinas, *ST* I, q. 19, a. 4.

51. Thomas Aquinas, *ST* I, q. 20, a. 2; cf. *Super Ioan* 5, lect. 3, no. 753; and *ST* I-II, q. 110, a. 1.

52. Augustine, *De doctrina christiana* I, 32 (Œuvres *de Saint Augustin*, vol. 11/2, trans. Madeleine Moreau, eds. Isabelle Bochet and Goulven Madec [Paris: Etudes Augustiniennes, 1997], 120; translated into English as *Teaching Christianity, The Works of Saint Augustine: A Translation for the 21st Century* I/11, trans. Edmund Hill, ed. John E. Rotelle [New Haven, N.Y.: New City Press, 1996, 1997], 121). Cf. *SCG* II, c. 28, 8; and *ST* I, q. 13, a. 2.

All created perfections are thus recognized by St. Thomas in reference to God, "who alone is good essentially"[53] and who creates for the simple reason of communicating his goodness: by way of the creature's continuous assimilation to Him. "God loses no dignity no matter how closely a creature draws near to Him, although this makes the creature grow in dignity. For He communicates His goodness to creatures in such wise that He Himself suffers no loss."[54] It follows that "the divine nature is only communicable according to the participation of some similitude,"[55] and "whatever has existence by way of participation is traced back, as to its cause, to that which exists in virtue of its own essence; for example, what is on fire has, in some way or other, fire as the cause that ignited it. Since God alone is good by His very essence, and all other things receive their complement of goodness by some sort of participation, all beings must be brought to their complement of goodness by God."[56]

This important and central insight of the angelic doctor accounts for his insistence upon the fact that creatures are like their Creator, but the Creator is in "no wise" like his creatures;[57] whence also Aquinas's constant teaching that the Creator-creature relation is entirely one-sided, or "asymmetrical."[58] Since "God is outside the whole order of creation, and all creatures are ordered to Him, and not conversely, it is manifest that creatures are really related to God Himself; whereas in God there is no real relation to creatures, but a relation only in idea, inasmuch as creatures are referred to Him."[59]

This teaching regarding the asymmetrical relation between the Creator and his creation, which is fully affirmed by Balthasar,[60] should be kept in mind when interpreting his teaching that "the diverse forms of potentiality in creatures cannot be considered as sheer *dissimilitudines* opposed to the divine actuality."[61] Balthasar does *not* thereby mean that God is in potency with regard to his creation so as to receive some perfection from his creatures. In fact, he is not making a direct comparison between God and his creation at all. Rather, the comparison that is signified here—not unlike the

53. Thomas Aquinas, *ST* I, q. 6, a. 3; cf. *SCG* I, c. 38; Lk 18:19; Mk 10:18; and Mt 19:17.
54. Thomas Aquinas, *SCG* IV, c. 55, 3.
55. Thomas Aquinas, *ST* I, q. 13, a. 9, ad. 1; see also q. 9, a. 2, ad. 2.
56. Thomas Aquinas, *Comp* I, 124; cf. *ST* I, q. 4, a. 2; q. 8, a. 1; q. 104, a. 1; and *SCG* I, c. 37–38.
57. Thomas Aquinas, *ST* I, q. 4, a. 3, ad. 4.
58. See Torrell, *Saint Thomas Aquinas* II: *Spiritual Master*, 77. See also Emery, "*Theologia and Dispensatio*," 525; "The Immutability of the God of Love and the Problem of Language Concerning the 'Suffering of God,'" 70–72; and "Contemporary Questions about God," *Nova et Vetera* (English edition) 8, no. 4 (2010): 799–811; and O'Rourke, *Pseudo-Dionysius and the Metaphysics of Aquinas*, 258.
59. Thomas Aquinas, *ST* I, q. 13, a. 7; cf. q. 45, a. 3, ad. 1; and q. 6, a. 2, ad. 1.
60. "The absolute, infinite God cannot be compared with the finite creature who is entirely dependent on him" (Balthasar, *Theo-Drama* III, 222).
61. Balthasar, *Theo-Logic* II, 83.

many that we have studied throughout these pages—is what Balthasar calls, in terms borrowed from St. Thomas, "a *proportionalitas*: a 'proportional relation between proportional relations,' that is, between the relation of difference between God and creature and the relation of difference between Father, Son, and Spirit."[62] Hence "what matters," Balthasar explains with regard to this specific term (*proportionalitas*), "is the functioning not of the proportionate members themselves [the Creator and his creation], but only of the two proportions,"[63] that is, the difference-in-unity of the Trinity, on the one hand, and (on the other) the difference-in-unity of God and man, the body and the soul, the individual and the community, man and woman, etc.

As serving to enlighten his attribution of receptivity to the Godhead, Balthasar thus invites us to distinguish between this notion as it is ascribed to the immanent life of God—an idea which is altogether compatible with Thomistic teaching[64]—and this notion as it is attributed to God with respect to his creatures: an idea which is far more problematic from a Thomistic perspective, which is why Balthasar is careful to avoid it. "God does not need the world to confirm him as God or to provide him with a series of stages to go through and so perfect himself; indeed, he does not even need the world to reveal to himself the possibilities of his omnipotence."[65] Hence, while we might agree with Healy's presentation of created receptivity as having "an analogical foundation in the fullness of actuality itself" and even that this proposition might constitute a "creative retrieval and development of Aquinas's achievement,"[66] the same can *not* be said of Healy's proposition, which he falsely attributes to Balthasar, that "God can 'receive' something from the creature."[67] This meanwhile is not to deny God of that "unqualified perfection of being" attributable to the spiritual creature that Balthasar refers to, as we saw in chapter one, as receptivity in an analogical sense: "accessibility to another's being, openness to something other than the inner dimension of one's own subjectivity, the possession of windows looking out on all being and truth," in short, "the power to welcome and, so to say, host another's being in one's own home."[68] Indeed, God may be said to do this precisely within the context of generously conferring his grace, as we saw in chapter three, without being himself enriched thereby. "For as the sun is said to enter

---

62. Ibid., 316.
63. Balthasar, *The Glory of the Lord* IV, 409n379.
64. Cf. Thomas Aquinas, *Super Ioan* 14, lect. 8, no. 1971; and *ST* I, q. 42, a. 1, ad. 3.
65. Balthasar, *Theo-Drama* II, 261.
66. Cf. Thomas Aquinas, *ST* I, q. 42, a. 1, ad. 3.
67. Healy, *The Eschatology of Hans Urs von Balthasar*, 25–26.
68. Balthasar, *Theo-Logic* I, 44–45.

a house, or to go out, according as its rays reach the house, so God is said to approach to us, or to recede from us, when we receive the influx of His goodness, or decline from Him."[69]

As for the first of Healy's propositions—that there is an analogical foundation for created receptivity within the Godhead—Edward Oakes fittingly reasons, in Balthasar's wake, that because the divine persons "have no self-subsistent substance but are definable only in terms of their mutual relations," we cannot do otherwise than to speak of passivity and receptivity in God.[70] In so doing, however, we need not deny, Oakes also insists, that God is necessary being and pure act: a fact which is necessarily called into question by the proposition that God receives something from his creatures,[71] but not by the proposition that we might speak of receptivity within the Godhead, namely as implied by the doctrine of the circumincession of the divine persons.

Oakes argues more specifically that Balthasar's tendency of grounding all that might be understood as possibility and change—including the possibility of the world itself—within the Godhead does not imply that the Swiss theologian perceives God's nature in worldly terms, or that, in other words, he reads "back the nature of God *from* the world."[72] On the contrary, Balthasar follows Aquinas[73] in insisting upon biblical revelation as the one and only inroad to the intra-Trinitarian mystery, whence the re-emergence of this same concept of receptivity, especially with regard to the Son's terrestrial mission and obedience (cf. Jn 10:18, 14:31, etc.) and to the mutual indwelling of the divine persons (cf. Jn 14:10, 17:21, etc.).[74] As for Adrienne, she joins Aquinas[75] in rightfully insisting upon the central importance of the humanity of Christ in the revelation of the divinity:

69. Thomas Aquinas, *ST* I, q. 9, a. 1, ad. 3.
70. Oakes, *Pattern of Redemption*, 286. Cf. Balthasar, *Theo-Drama* V, 85.
71. "Again, that which is can participate in something, but the act of being can participate in nothing. For that which participates is in potency, and being is an act. But God is being itself, as we have proven [cf. *SCG* I, c. 22]. He is not, therefore, by participation good; He is good essentially" (Thomas Aquinas, *SCG* I, c. 38, 5).
72. Oakes, *Pattern of Redemption*, 285. Oakes thus insists upon the essential distinction between the ontological and the epistemological realms, such that the former "is blocked by the epistemological": "we cannot know the 'what' or the 'how' directly. [...] All we know is *that* God is the precondition for creation and all its attributes" (ibid., 295).
73. Cf. Thomas Aquinas, *ST* I, q. 36, a. 2, ad. 1.
74. On biblical revelation as the only inroad to the intra-Trinitarian mystery, see Balthasar, *Theo-Drama* IV, 324; *Our Task*, 64–65; *Theo-Drama* II, 161 and 229; *Love Alone Is Credible*, 87; *Prayer*, 164; *First Glance at Adrienne von Speyr*, 60–61; Speyr, *Das Wort und die Mystik* II, 523; and Waldstein, "The Analogy of Mission and Obedience." On the importance of receptivity, see Balthasar, *Theo-Logic* II, 137; *The Glory of the Lord* I, 463–535; *Theo-Drama* III, 250–58; and *The Christian State of Life*, 79.
75. See, for example, Thomas Aquinas, *SCG* IV, c. 54–55; and *ST* III, q. 1. It is perhaps important to insist that Thomas prefers to speak of the "suitability" (*convenientia*) of the Incarnation, rather than its necessity.

Since the Lord is at the same time man [*Mensch*] and God, the [human] person understands that he is, as it were, looking to two sides: the one face turned to the man [*zum Menschen*],[76] the other face turned to God. Thereby, the Lord himself becomes the movement of the human spirit from the man [*Menschen*] to God. He can see and understand the human side of the Lord but not the divine side; by means of the human side, he can sense something of the divine life, of the love between Father and Son, and so he is led to understand the incomprehensible dimension of God *in* the human dimension itself and to move in its direction. Through what is comprehensible in the Son, the human being is initiated into the incomprehensible dimension of the Father, without being able to grasp this, and thereby his yearning grows, that is to say, his spirit and his life.[77]

As if to defend Adrienne's insights, Balthasar rejects both the psychological analogy of the Trinity proposed by Augustine and Aquinas and the intra-subjective analogy of Richard of St. Victor. Instead, he argues that the only valid access to the mystery of the Trinity is the revealed archetype, Jesus Christ.[78] This does not mean—contrary to what Matthew Levering seems to imply as proper to Balthasar's thought—that the hypostatic union is an analogy of the Trinitarian union. Indeed, Balthasar reasons in much the same way as Levering: the relation between the two natures of Christ in his one divine person are incomparable to the relationship among the three divine persons in their one divine nature.[79] Nor, Balthasar insists, is it the case that the incarnate Son represents his own divine nature, although the Swiss theologian does admit that the Son makes no personal statement "that is not at the same time a statement of the one divine nature!"[80] "Although he is God,

76. I have taken the liberty to alter the official translation from "person" to "man" to translate *Mensch*. This avoids the inevitable misunderstanding that the person of Christ might be thought by Adrienne to be human.

77. Speyr, *John* II, 79. Adrienne thus addresses the "appearance [*Erscheinung*] of the Trinitarian fullness" in Christ's human being [*Menschendasein*]" (*Das Wort und die Mystik* II, 106); see also *The Letter to the Ephesians*, 240–41; and *Das Buch vom Gehorsam*, 37–38. Cf. Balthasar, *Prayer*, 162–64 and 193.

78. See Balthasar, *Theo-Logic* II, 132–33 and 178–79; and Buckley, "Balthasar's Use of the Theology of Aquinas," *The Thomist* 59, no. 4, (1995), 517–45. Buckley recognizes Balthasar as preferring the model of "interpersonality" (cf. *Theo-Drama* III, 340 and 457–60), but Balthasar is also critical of this model. Cf. Speyr, *Mary in the Redemption*, 34 and 116–17; *The Mystery of Death*, 74; *Dienst der Freude*, 69–71; *Theologie der Geschlechter*, 183; *Das Wort und die Mystik* II, 106, 108, and 115; *John* II, 71; *Korinther* I, 53; and Balthasar, *First Glance at Adrienne von Speyr*, 61.

79. See Balthasar, *Theo-Drama* V, 86; and *Theo-Logic* II, 133 (cf. Thomas Aquinas, *ST* I, q. 28, a. 2; and a. 3, ad. 1). Levering reasons, more specifically, that to address the divine *being* (the "*ente*" of the *analogia entis*) is to refer to that which is *one* in God; hence, the analogy of being cannot be 'Trinitarian,' "because the divine being is (necessarily) conceptually distinct from the [personal] relations in the divine being." God's being is not a communion, Levering concludes, "because being is not what relates in God" (Levering, *Scripture and Metaphysics*, 228). On this point, cf. *ST* I, q. 28, a. 3: "Boethius says (*De Trin.*) that in God *the substance contains the unity; and relation multiplies the Trinity*." By extrapolation, we might reason (as Balthasar does) that it is not the natures in Christ that relate, but the person of Christ who relates to the persons of the Father and the Spirit.

80. Balthasar, *The Glory of the Lord* I, 612; see also 437.

he does not exposit himself in his humanity. Rather, he exposits the Father in the Holy Spirit, with whom he is identical as divine nature, but not as hypostasis."[81] In short, what is of primary signficance for Balthasar's understanding of Trinitarian revelation is the relation of the incarnate Son to his heavenly Father.

This explains the "fundamental" importance that Balthasar and Adrienne accord to the "Trinitarian contemplation of the Son," for "in contemplating the Son we must not for a moment abstract from the Trinity."[82] Christological revelation is, in other words, primarily Trinitarian: "Jesus does not speak about God in general but shows us the Father and gives us the Holy Spirit. Thus it is on the basis of Jesus's Trinitarian relationship with God that we should construct a picture of the divine 'essence' and 'being.' The latter manifests itself, in the historical 'happening' of Jesus himself, as an eternal 'happening.'"[83] Again, this is not a happening that need imply movement or change within the immanent Trinity, which is denied by St. Thomas,[84] but merely receptivity, as he is willing to admit. Or, to put it in still other words expressing the mystery from the perspective of the Trinity, the incarnate Son "translates his eternal relationship with the Father into the terms of time and creatureliness."[85]

Confusion of the Divine and Human Natures in Christ?

Precisely this move from the only "too" human Jesus to the divine Trinity is, meanwhile, the origin of still another important criticism of Balthasar's theology, as Bernhard Blankenhorn, Steven A. Long, and Guy Mansini point out.[86] More specifically, in Balthasar's adoption of Adrienne's presentation of the Incarnation as permitting that an element of "surprise"[87] be introduced within the Godhead, the Swiss theologian is himself found guilty of the following contradiction summarized by Blankenhorn: "[The] divine Persons

---

81. Balthasar, *Theo-Logic* II, 312.
82. Speyr, *Das Wort und die Mystik* II, 115, cited by Balthasar in *Theo-Drama* V, 122. Cf. Balthasar, *Prayer*, 193.
83. Balthasar, *Theo-Drama* V, 67; see also *You Crown the Year With Your Goodness*, 142–43.
84. See Thomas Aquinas, *ST* I, q. 9.
85. Balthasar, *Theo-Drama* IV, 120; cf. *A Theology of History*, 31; and *The Glory of the Lord* I, 613.
86. See Blankenhorn, "Balthasar's Method of Divine Naming," 263–64; Long, *Natura Pura*, 52–109; and Guy Mansini, "Rahner and Balthasar on the Efficacy of the Cross," *Irish Theological Quarterly* 63 (1998): 248.
87. See, for example, Balthasar, *Theo-Drama* V, 79, 90, and 516; *Theo-Logic* III, 237; and *Theo-Drama* II, 258. Herein—it is worth insisting—is also particularly evident the influence of Adrienne. See Speyr, *World of Prayer*, 28–74, esp. 49; and *Das Wort und die Mystik* II, 82–83. It is nonetheless important to add that for Adrienne this element of "surprise" does not entail that knowledge of one divine person might be hidden, as it were, from another. See Speyr, *John* III, 364; and *The Countenance of the Father*, 101.

[are those] who always fully know one another and yet keep a secret to themselves in order to reveal it to the other, resulting in the surprise and joy of the other. This surprise includes the Son's 'decision' to answer the Father's incredible gift of self with thanksgiving. The Son is so filled with this gratefulness that he wants to be able to give the Father something 'of his own.'"[88]

Balthasar reasons that precisely in order to "prove" his love to the Father and "to present a new gift to the Father"—one that is "not already in the divine essence"—Blankenhorn incorrectly maintains as proper to the teaching of Balthasar (as derived from Adrienne) that the Son "gives up his divinity" and becomes incarnate.[89] To be sure, although Balthasar does follow Adrienne in teaching that the Son "deposits" his divinity with the Father when he becomes incarnate,[90] this does not mean for Balthasar, as I explained in chapter five, that the Son is no longer divine. On the contrary, both Balthasar and Adrienne present the extreme humility of the incarnate Son (cf. Phil 2:6–8) as revealing his divine Sonship in the mode of radical receptivity, as we will see more thoroughly in what follows.

Blankenhorn's critique of Balthasar, meanwhile, focuses upon the latter's method of divine naming as employing three notions, each of which the Dominican theologian calls into question: Balthasar's presentation of Christ as the concrete *analogia entis*, which is standard for every other analogy;[91] his presentation of Christ as revealing his relationship to the Father;[92] and his use of modes of potentiality such as surprise and suffering to describe the Godhead.

While we have already examined the third objection—namely the ascribing of potentiality to God—this follows, Blankenhorn argues, upon what he esteems to be a faulty understanding of the *analogia entis*. When, more specifically, Balthasar addresses Christ as the concrete *analogia entis*, he no longer distinguishes the content of Christ's revelation from his humanity, with the result that it becomes impossible to distinguish between the divine and the created in Christ. "The very notion of Christ's humanity presumes,"

---

88. Blankenhorn, "Balthasar's Method of Divine Naming," 263–64; cf. Balthasar, *Theo-Drama* V, 516.
89. Blankenhorn, "Balthasar's Method of Divine Naming," 265. The quotation marks refer to Blankenhorn's interpretation of Balthasar (cf. *Theo-Drama* V, 516), rather than to direct citations of the latter's work, which is somewhat misconstrued in this passage. Cf. Speyr, *Die katholischen Briefe* II, 25: "He must do this [become incarnate] so that he can possess something, so that he can have something to give away."
90. See Speyr, *John* IV, 78; *Passion nach Matthäus*, 153–54; *Bergpredigt*, 145; and *John* II, 364. Cf. Balthasar, *Theo-Logic* III, 174; *Theo-Drama* V, 517; and *Explorations in Theology* IV, 138.
91. See, for example, Balthasar, *A Theology of History*, 69; *Theo-Drama* II, 222; and *Theo-Logic* II, 314.
92. The references are bountiful. See, for example, Balthasar, *The Glory of the Lord* VII, 409; *A Theology of History*, 29; *Unless You Become Like This Child*; etc. Similarly, the theme is popular in Adrienne's works, as is evident, for example, in Speyr, *John* III, 341; and *World of Prayer*, 83–84.

Blankenhorn argues, "a pretheological understanding of what humanity is, some of which would be recognized as perfections, others as limitations."[93] Precisely because, moreover, Balthasar is faulted (incorrectly, I will argue) for not admitting this pretheological understanding of humanity,[94] Blankenhorn states—and herein consists his second objection—it becomes impossible to distinguish the manner in which Christ relates to the Father in his human condition from the manner in which he relates to the Father in his divine condition.[95]

To be sure, this objection is of no little significance, as Balthasar well knows: "Every suggestion that underplays the genuine humanity of Christ (Gnosticism) and his genuine divinity (Arianism), as expressed by the formula of Chalcedon, threatens and actually destroys the full meaning of the 'pro nobis' upon which all Christian theology depends."[96] Perhaps for this same reason, Balthasar finds it important to insist that the Son "accepts all that is involved in adopting human nature [...] including no doubt, existing in relation to God in the analogy of being."[97] On the other hand, it is "only because the Son in very truth possesses the 'form of God' (*morphe theou*, Phil 2:6), and hence the divine pole of the *analogia entis*, that he can 'empty himself' and take 'the form of a servant.'"[98] Hence the following paradox, which for God is, Balthasar insists, "no paradox":[99] "Anyone who confesses the full humanity of Jesus must necessarily allow that, having 'become' man, he stands within the *analogia entis*. And anyone who professes to believe in the full divinity of a person will have to admit that the person simultaneous-

---

93. Blankenhorn, "Balthasar's Method of Divine Naming," 266. A similar argument is offered in Long, *Natura Pura*, 52–109, esp. 96; and (without direct refutation of Balthasar) in White, "The 'Pure Nature' of Christology."

94. See Fergus Kerr, "Forward: Assessing this 'Giddy Synthesis,'" in Gardner et al., *Balthasar at the End of Modernity*, 13. So too, Steven A. Long recognizes Balthasar's presentation of nature in terms of a "vacuole for grace"; such is the title ("A Criticism of Nature as Vacuole for Grace") that he gives to his second chapter (52–109) of *Natura Pura*, which is largely a criticism of Balthasar's treatment of nature. Cf. Scola, *Hans Urs von Balthasar: A Theological Style*, 102; and Balthasar "Current Trends in Catholic Theology," 82–83.

95. See Blankenhorn, "Balthasar's Divine Naming," 266–67. Similar is the critique of Pitstick: "In the context of Balthasar's theology, *as man* does not mean *by virtue of or in the human nature of Christ rather than by virtue of His divine nature*. It means instead *the divine Person in the form of human nature* [...], i.e., that the Word has emptied Himself of the divine attributes and assumed those of humanity" (*Light in Darkness*, 296). Or, from the analogical (rather than katalogical) perspective, Pitstick reads Balthasar thus: "We get the following chain of reasoning that illustrates Balthasar's peculiar Christology in which the filial hypostasis has human attributes and expresses Himself in them: Jesus *as man* = His task = His mission = the procession of the Word *as divine*" (ibid., 297).

96. Balthasar, *Theo-Drama* II, 120. Cf. *DZ* 300–303; and Thomas Aquinas, *Comp* I, 211.

97. Ibid., 407; see also *Theo-Drama* III, 203; *Explorations in Theology* I, 185; and *Epilogue*, 65.

98. Balthasar, *Theo-Drama* II, 268; see also *A Theology of History*, 30.

99. See Balthasar, *Love Alone Is Credible*, 87n1.

ly transcends the analogy or, more precisely, that he stands on both sides of the analogy, that the analogy goes right through the center of his consciousness."[100]

In this passage might be discerned an important element of Balthasar's Christology, which likewise sheds light on his presentation of Christ as the "concrete *analogia entis*": Christ's human words, acts, and even his human knowledge and consciousness—which Balthasar presents as profoundly marked by his eternally willed mission—are a revelation "of his divine existence in the mode of Sonship,"[101] whence our return to Blankenhorn's objection. In fact, for Balthasar—and here again we find him echoing Adrienne, as we saw in chapter four—the humanity of Christ is presented not so much as an instrument of his divinity or of the Godhead but rather (or most especially) as an instrument of his obedient love for the Father.[102] Jesus willingly reveals God "at the behest, not of the Trinity," Balthasar argues, "but of the Father." Hence, although he may be said to reveal God "of his very *essence*," he does so "in the *personal* mode [*qua* Son]" not excepting that he is "driven by the Holy Spirit."[103]

While one might already discern herein something of the idea of a properly divine obedience—an important objection which we will address below—for the moment we might consider whether Balthasar's theology—precisely in its overarching concern to preserve the Trinitarian nature of Christian revelation—might rightfully be judged as lacking in its exposition of the two distinct natures of Christ. Or, to phrase the question differently, we might ask whether Balthasar has reason to maintain that the humanity of the Son—which is proper to him in as much as he alone is incarnate—might nonetheless and even "necessarily" express "the total triune essence of God."[104] Can the Son of Man correctly be said to represent, in Balthasar's words, "the entire trinitarian love in the form of expression"?[105]

---

100. Balthasar, *Theo-Drama* II, 407; see also *Theo-Drama* III, 220 and 230n68.

101. Healy, *The Eschatology of Hans Urs von Balthasar*, 109; see also Balthasar, *Theo-Drama* III, 225. Cf. Speyr, *Das Wort und die Mystik* II, 82 and 92; *Erde und Himmel* III, 193; and *Die katholischen Briefe* II, 213–14. On Balthasar's presentation of Christ's knowledge and consciousness as determined by his mission, see, for example, *Theo-Drama* III, 254–55 and 510–11; and *The Glory of the Lord* I, 469. Cf. *The Catechism of the Catholic Church*, no. 475.

102. Cf. Speyr, *The Letter to the Ephesians*, 36–37; *Das Wort und die Mystik* II, 522–23; and *Das Buch vom Gehorsam*, 36. On the other hand, Balthasar does present "the Son's humanity as a mediation between the Trinity and us" (*Theo-Drama* V, 482). Cf. *ST* III, q. 7, a. 1, ad. 3; q. 8, a. 1, ad. 1; q. 19, a. 1; and q. 34, a. 1, ad. 3.

103. Balthasar, *Theo-Drama* III, 225.

104. Balthasar, *The Glory of the Lord* I, 458; see also *Explorations in Theology* I, 117 and 176. Cf. Speyr, *Das Wort und die Mystik* II, 94–95 and 98; and *The Boundless God*, 20.

105. Balthasar, *Theo-Logic* II, 154; see also *Theo-Drama* V, 75.

In seeking a response to these important questions, we might keep in mind, as the *Catechism* teaches: "Everything that Christ is and does in this [human] nature derives from 'one of the Trinity.' The Son of God therefore communicates to his humanity his own personal mode of existence in the Trinity. In his soul as in his body, Christ thus expresses humanly the divine ways of the Trinity."[106] Or, as Balthasar would have it, "the form of revelation does not present itself as an independent image of God, standing over against what is imaged, but as a unique, hypostatic union between archetype and image."[107]

This revelation of the Godhead in the human nature of Christ requires, in turn, that there be allowed no oppression nor compromise of the human nature of Christ, but that on the contrary this nature, including most especially the self-determining will, must be integrally maintained as a conjoint and animate instrument of the divine Logos.[108] As such we might (indeed, we must) admit a distinction of operations while simultaneously acknowledging a single principal agent: the eternal Son of God.[109] In Balthasar's words, "God does not use human nature like an external instrument in order to articulate, from the outside and from above, the wholly other which God is; rather, God takes on man's nature as his own and expresses himself from within it through the expressive structures of that nature's essence."[110]

In precisely this passage we might, however, discern still another question implicit in Blankenhorn's objection: how might we distinguish, within Balthasar's Christology, the humanity of Christ as simply human from the

---

106. *The Catechism of the Catholic Church*, no. 470; see also no. 473, where reference is made to St. Maximus the Confessor: "The human nature of God's Son, *not by itself but by its union with the Word*, knew and showed forth in itself everything that pertains to God."

107. Balthasar, *The Glory of the Lord* I, 432; see also *Prayer*, 184; cf. Speyr, *Das Wort und die Mystik* II, 106 and 108.

108. The precision—"conjoint and animate" is important because although the humanity of Christ is an instrument of God, it is not an extrinsic or separate instrument as would challenge the reality of the Incarnation. Furthermore, the humanity of Christ, precisely as an instrument animated by a rational soul, is not merely passive: it simultaneously moves itself as it is moved. See *ST* III, q. 18, a. 1; ibid., q. 7., a. 1, ad. 3; and *SCG* IV, c. 41, 11. Balthasar is, in fact, concerned that we not interpret the instrumentality of Christ's humanity extrinsically. See, on that subject, *The Glory of the Lord* I, 437; and *Does Jesus Know Us?*, 69. On the self-determining will of Christ's humanity, see Speyr, *The Countenance of the Father*, 61.

109. Such is Thomistic teaching, as appropriated from the Greek Fathers and in response to the various heresies touching upon the unity of the divine and human natures in Christ. See, for example, Thomas Aquinas, *Comp* I, 212. See also Paul G. Crowley, "*Instrumentum Divinitatis* in Thomas Aquinas: Recovering the Divinity of Christ," *Theological Studies* 52 (1991): 451–75; Gilles Emery, "A Note on St. Thomas and the Greek Fathers" in his *Trinity, Church and the Human Person: Thomistic Essays* (Naples, Fla.: Sapientia Press, 2007), 198–204; and Tschipke, *Die Menschheit Christi als Heilsorgan der Gottheit*. For an objection to Balthasar's appropriation of this teaching, see Pitstick, *Light in Darkness*, 293.

110. Balthasar, *The Glory of the Lord* I, 459; see also 432 and 474–75; and Schrijver, *Le merveilleux accord*, 291.

humanity of Christ as a revelation of the Trinity? The question is a good one, for Balthasar argues that Christ's created nature is drawn into the act of his eternal generation with the result that it is "entirely the expression and property of his divine Person."[111]

The Jesus of the Gospels does not simply absorb the total otherness of God, whom he exposits in truth, into the difference between divinity and humanity within himself. Rather, this very difference has in truth passed entirely into the 'language' of his humanity. [...] Both his sovereign lordship and his lowliness are human, just as they represent in human form (anthropomorphically) God's sovereignty and lowliness. Jesus' exposition is in a specific, positive sense anthropomorphic.[112]

Such is, in fact, the specific challenge of faith: to recognize Christ's "divine form [*theomorphie*] in his human form [*anthropomorphie*]."[113]

Beyond, however, what we might recognize in the above passage as a certain importance that Balthasar accords to the real humanity of Christ and thus also to the fact that Christ acts in a properly human manner, we might also discern what Nicholas Healy points to as "the novelty" of Balthasar's position: namely, that "the seemingly 'human' aspects of Jesus' existence, such as sorrow, hunger, suffering, obedience [...] reveal via the principle of hypostatic union interpreted in terms of the identity of person and mission, the very nature of God and of man."[114]

To be sure, Balthasar is concerned—again, within the context of his primary intention of founding his Christology within a Trinitarian theology as inspired by Adrienne—that we preserve the personal identity of the incarnate Son. This means, more specifically, that we not "split the Son of God in the exercise of his mission into the one who carries out his mission on earth and the one who remains unaffected in heaven, looking down at the 'sent' Son."[115] More specifically still, the Swiss theologian seeks to present the constant identity of the Son, in time and in eternity, in terms of his uninterrupted relation of filiation vis-à-vis the eternal Father.

We should misunderstand everything if we saw this as heteronomy; heteronomy is excluded because of the identity of person and mission affirmed at the very outset. And both are experienced as springing in unity from the source that is the Father; both owe their existence to him and give him thanks for the "autonomy" they have been given. "For as the Father has life in himself, so he has granted the Son also to have life in himself" (Jn 5:26). But the more the Son unites himself with the Ground

---

111. Balthasar, *Explorations in Theology* I, 176.   112. Balthasar, *Theo-Logic* II, 70.
113. Ibid., 71.
114. Healy, *The Eschatology of Hans Urs von Balthasar*, 106; see also 89–91 and 110.
115. Balthasar, *Theo-Drama* III, 228; see also *The Glory of the Lord* I, 437.

from which his person and mission simultaneously spring forth, the better he understands both his mission and himself. It is only in connection with his origin in the Father that he can utter the "I am" that corresponds exactly to the "Abba," that is, both utterances belong to the context of Jesus' prayer to the Father.[116]

Proceeding from the Thomistic insight according to which the Son's mission is a form of his eternal procession,[117] Balthasar argues that the Son's "mode of being here on earth will simply be the manifestation in the created sphere, the translation into creatureliness, of this heavenly form of existence: existence as receiving, as openness to the will of the Father, as subsistent fulfillment of that will in a continuous mission."[118]

It follows, Balthasar reasons from his typically Trinitarian perspective, that just as the eternal Son "is not in the first instance a person for himself, only subsequently undertaking to place himself at the disposal of the Father," so also the Son throughout his earthly pilgrimage "is not in the first instance a man for himself, only subsequently opening himself to the Father to hear and do his will."[119] Or, to put it in Speyrian terms, "there is no further distance between the Son on earth and his relation to the Father and the Spirit than between the Son in heaven and his relation to the Father and the Spirit. The harmony is the same."[120]

Indeed, the incarnate Son "constantly refers to the Father," Adrienne observes. "He speaks of him so as to reveal him to men, but also so as to manifest how *he* is related to the Father, how much he is the Son." His "filial being [*Sohnsein*]" is evident in that wherever the Father is named, the Son's "fully affirming obedience" is simultaneously expressed.[121] This means more specifically, Balthasar explains with specific reference to Johannine theology, that the Son who reveals the Father is himself known primarily in negative terms:

The Son can do nothing of himself (Jn 5:19); he cannot speak on his own authority (7:17; 12:49; 14:10). And so he does not do his own will (5:30; 6:38), although he has

---

116. Balthasar, *Theo-Drama* III, 169; cf. *The Christian State of Life*, 78; and *Explorations in Theology* I, 93.

117. Cf. Thomas Aquinas, *ST* I, q. 43, a. 1; and a. 2, ad. 3. On the other hand, Thomas is careful to distinguish two generations or two "births" of Christ, in accord with his two natures: one eternal, the other temporal. See *Comp* I, 212; cf. Speyr, *Die Schöpfung*, 11.

118. Balthasar, *A Theology of History*, 31; see also *Theo-Drama* III, 226 and 228; *Theo-Drama* IV, 326; *Theo-Drama* V, 81; *The Christian State of Life*, 189; *Explorations in Theology* I, 176; and Turek, *Towards a Theology of God the Father*, 61.

119. Balthasar, *A Theology of History*, 31; cf. *The Glory of the Lord* I, 478; *The Threefold Garland*, 29–30; *Theo-Drama* III, 185; and John Randall Sachs, *The Pneumatology and Christian Spirituality of Hans Urs von Balthasar*, PhD Diss., Universität Tübingen (1984), 148–49; and Healy, *The Eschatology of Hans Urs von Balthasar*, 106. Cf. Speyr, *World of Prayer*, 58.

120. Speyr, *Die Wort und die Mystik* II, 106; see also *The Boundless God*, 20; and *Markus*, 646.

121. Speyr, *Das Buch vom Gehorsam*, 38–39.

a will of his own (5:21; 17:24; 21:22) and so cannot be described as a vacuum in which God exists. He utters, as subject, an abundance of things about himself, he possesses an explicit self-consciousness as ego and person, rising to that tremendous, unpredicted 'I am he' (8:24, 58; 13:19); but always he is what he is on the basis of 'not my will,' 'not my own honor' (17:18).[122]

In precisely this manner of being bent entirely on revealing the Father and perfectly accomplishing *his* (the Father's) will—Christ secondarily, or consequentially, reveals himself as the eternal Son who receives everything—both in time and in eternity, including his very essence and thus also his divine and human wills and his mission—from the Father, and who might thus be understood as deferring all things to the Father. Christ, in other words, reveals himself, within his revelation of the Father, as a person turned entirely toward the person of the Father in an eternal act of receptivity. With reference again to John's Gospel, Balthasar explains:

> It is of his essence as Son to receive life (5:26), insight (3:11), spirit (3:34–35), word (3:34; 14:24), will (5:30), deed (6:9), doctrine (7:16), work (14:10) and glorification (8:54; 17:22, 24) from another, from the Father. He receives it, indeed, in such a way that he has it all *in himself* (5:26) and disposes of all that he receives as of his own (10:18, 28); yet never with any denial of that receiving, but affirming it always, eternally, as the ground of his very being. If in him 'having' were for one moment to cease to be 'receiving,' to become a radically independent disposal of himself, he would in that moment cease to be the Father's Son, would have forfeited all claim to be believed, and would have to call upon men not to believe him (10:37).[123]

Similarly, Adrienne argues that the incarnate Son "does not obey a foreseen plan; he personally obeys the personal Father."[124]

Balthasar is thus concerned that we avoid the "danger" of interpreting "the Son's act of revelation—by giving form and glorifying—as his own activity and no longer, as he himself affirms, as the activity of the Father in him, of the Father who expresses and glorifies himself in the Son's form and word."[125] "It is God himself who reveals and glorifies himself when the appearing Son

---

122. Balthasar, *A Theology of History*, 29–30; see also *The Glory of the Lord* I, 612–13.
123. Balthasar, *A Theology of History*, 30.
124. Speyr, *Das Buch von Gehorsam*, 36; see also *The Boundless God*, 20; and *John* III, 341. The latter reference is cited by Balthasar in *Theo-Drama* V, 121–22.
125. Balthasar, *The Glory of the Lord* I, 612; see also 614. Cf. Aquinas, *In Ioan* 14, lect. 2, no. 1874: "And just like one of us who wants to be known by others by revealing to them the words in his heart, clothes these words with letters or sounds, so God, wanting to be known by us, takes his Word, conceived from eternity, and clothes it with flesh in time. And so no one can arrive at knowledge of the Father except through the Son." Balthasar notes a word of caution regarding the word "form" as applied to the incarnate Son: "Like all other words that are applied to Christ and his revelation, the word 'form' too must be used with care, which means that its abstract and general conceptual content must be held *in suspenso* in view of the uniqueness of this particular application" (Balthasar, *The Glory of the Lord* I, 432).

glorifies the non-appearing Father—the Father who appears in the Son. This assertion of the identity of nature between Father and Son leads us without fail, if we pursue its personal aspects, to the existential paradox of the Son, in whose servant form is manifested—really manifested—the Father's form of lordship."[126]

This, of course, does not mean that we might discern two divine actions—one attributed to the Father and one to the Son, even if the latter is understood as "acting" by moving aside, as it were. Balthasar, after all, follows Adrienne in insisting upon the unity of the one divine nature and thus also the unity of the divine action. "What one [divine] Person does corresponds respectively to the Trinitarian will," Adrienne explains.[127] Hence, "Every divine action is always equally rooted in the other Person[s]."[128] Nor, on the other hand, would Balthasar deny that the incarnate Son acts in a properly human manner. Rather, as typifies the largely Johannine-inspired thought of both Balthasar and Adrienne, the Son's human will always accords with the Father's command (cf. Jn 10:18). Because, in other words, the incarnate Son wills to accept what the Father wills (cf. Jn 4:34; 6:38), he may be said to accomplish the Father's work (cf. Jn 7:16).

Because, however, Balthasar is aware of certain dangerous Arian interpretations of his position,[129] he again insists upon the common nature of the Father and Son: "Only the identity of nature between Father and Son, in union with their personal opposition (which is expressed in the opposition of God and man), can make the expressive relationship between God and man an expressive relationship in God himself."[130] Here again, the emphasis is not upon the revelation of Christ's divine nature via his human nature, but upon the revelation of the divine person of the Father by his incarnate Son: true God and true man. Christ is "what he expresses—namely, God—but he is not *whom* he expresses—namely the Father."[131] This explains the meaning of the statement: "The two natures cannot be separated in his exposition of the Father."[132] Or, as Adrienne would have it: "Everywhere we try to penetrate

---

126. Balthasar, *The Glory of the Lord* I, 612.
127. Speyr, *Das Wort und die Mystik* II, 80.
128. Speyr, *World of Prayer*, 50; see also *The Letter to the Ephesians*, 21; and *John* II, 166.
129. Hence he specifies in the context of the above citation: "the humiliation itself is already in essence the glorification of the Father and, hence, also of the Son himself, as John's statements underline and confirm (Jn 3:14; 12:28; 17:4; 18:6), and the Son's external glorification through his Resurrection can only ratify the extent to which a love that goes unto death has already glorified itself interiorly" (*The Glory of the Lord* I, 613). Cf. Thomas Aquinas, *Comp* I, 212.
130. Balthasar, *The Glory of the Lord* I, 613.
131. Ibid., 29; emphasis added.
132. Balthasar, *Theo-Logic* II, 70; see also "God is His Own Exegete," 283.

into his humanity we encounter the mystery of his being more than a man; that is his divine sonship."[133]

As a case in point, Balthasar explains that when the incarnate Word addresses the Father as "Thou" in his high priestly prayer (Jn 17), this is "a human vocable, but it must also be the expression of an eternal relation in God himself—a relation in which the Son turns to the Father in knowledge, love, adoration, and readiness for the Father's very wish."[134] Balthasar argues, more specifically, that the "'exposition' or 'setting out' (*exegesis*) of God the Father by the Son," although he performs this "in the flesh" for us to see, is not simply an economic act, for it is "proper to the Logos." It "coincides with his essence as 'Word' and 'Son.'"[135] The eternal Logos *is*, in other words, "the 'exegesis' of the Father (Jn 1:18)."[136] Hence, as Thomas Joseph White might well have summarized the theology of Balthasar, the revelation of Christ "occurs by virtue of the hypostatic union," whereby the "obedience of the Son made man not only exists in God, but also subsists *hypostatically* so as to reveal that Jesus is *personally* relative to the Father."[137]

Fair enough, one might admit, but have we really made any progress in responding to Blankenhorn's objection? Can we really assent to the proposition highlighted by Healy above that *everything* human in Christ can be taken as an expression of the divine? Certainly we cannot argue from the fact that Christ sleeps and eats to the conclusion that God, in his divine nature, also sleeps and eats. Or, more to the point in Balthasar's theology, we might ask: can we really conclude from the fact that Christ suffers for love of us that the three divine persons also suffer in their divine nature? Or again, because the incarnate Son shows signs of delightful surprise in the bountiful evidence of the Father's goodness, might we hold that each of the divine persons is also "surprised" by the beloved "other" within the intra-Trinitarian mystery?

To be sure, there are certain correctives in Balthasar's accounts, as when

---

133. Speyr, *Confession*, 147; see also *Das Wort und die Mystik* II, 21.
134. Balthasar, *Theo-Logic* II, 125–26.
135. Ibid., 160–61.
136. Balthasar, *The Glory of the Lord* I, 612; see also 29; *Epilogue*, 89–91; and "God is His Own Exegete." Cf. Speyr, *John* III, 90; and Thomas Aquinas, *In Ioan* 14, lect. 2, no. 1874.
137. Thomas Joseph White, "Intra-Trinitarian Obedience and Nicene-Chalcedonian Christology," *Nova et Vetera* (English edition) 6 (2008): 401. White refers this remark to the Christology of Barth rather than that of Balthasar. I quote him because of the pertinence of his remark to the Christology of Balthasar, which nonetheless differs from that of Barth, as Georges de Schrijver points out. Balthasar has much more recourse to the humanity of Christ in the work of redemption. See Schrijver, *Le merveilleux accord*, 288–96. As for St. Thomas, he teaches in opposition to the Nestorian heresy that Christ's humanity is "an instrument belonging to the unity of the hypostasis" (Aquinas, *ST* III, q. 2, a. 6, ad. 4). Cf. Balthasar, *Theo-Logic* II, 354; *First Glance at Adrienne von Speyr*, 59; and *Explorations in Theology* I, 168–69.

he admits, for example, that "suffering of soul in the human sense is possible only because of our bodiliness. Even if this pain has purely mental causes, it is still provoked by the body: the way we understand suffering recognizes that spiritual suffering is made possible precisely because the soul is thoroughly and completely entissued [*Eingesenktheit*] in the body. [...] That is why we can speak only analogously when we talk about the suffering of God or the suffering of pure spirits."[138]

Beyond the distance implied by his use of analogy, Balthasar might, furthermore, be thought of as responding to the important questions above within the context of an important precision that is sadly overlooked by Healy. When he writes, more specifically, that "in Christ there is nothing human [...] that is not the utterance and expression of the divine," he adds: "we speak of course of the *actus humani* and not the *actus hominis*."[139] He thereby makes the important distinction, at the heel of St. Thomas,[140] between acts that are properly and specifically human—acts that suppose a rational nature—and acts that the human being shares with sub-rational beings, such as sleeping or eating. Balthasar thus implies that while the former necessarily serve Christ's revelation of the triune God, the same is not true of the latter.

Of no little importance for understanding Balthasar's reasoning at this junction is the argument of St. Thomas regarding the fittingness of human nature for the divine Incarnation in virtue of its dignity: "because human nature, as being rational and intellectual, was made for attaining to the [divine] Word to some extent by its operation, viz. by knowing and loving Him."[141] Indeed, it is precisely in those acts whereby Christ is revealed as knowing and loving the Father—and thus most especially in his acts of obedience—that Balthasar recognizes the heart of his revelation.

Of course, this is not to exclude the important insight of Adrienne according to which Christ's readiness to fulfill the Father's will in the body is evident not only in the extraordinary signs that he (Christ) works, but even in the very ordinary actions of his life, such as eating and drinking. After all, it is precisely in his respect for the needs of his human body that Adrienne recognizes "how much he is in communion with the Father, how much he

---

138. Balthasar, *Epilogue*, 100.
139. Balthasar, *Explorations in Theology* I, 57; cf. Karol Wojtyla, *Person and Community: Selected Essays*, trans. Theresa Sandok, OSM (New York: Peter Lang, 1993), 189.
140. Cf. Thomas Aquinas, *ST* I-II, q. 1, a. 1.
141. Thomas Aquinas, *ST* III, q. 4, a. 1. See also *SCG* IV, 41; and *ST* III, q. 20, a. 1, where St. Thomas exposits the three manners in which human nature may be said to be subject to God, including most especially (with regard to our argument here) its submission "through its proper act, inasmuch as by its own will it obeys His command."

does his will and observes the laws that he gave to nature in creating it."[142] Similarly, Balthasar's "great insight," as Nicholas Healy would have it and which he expressly attributes to Adrienne's influence, is that the obedience of Christ is not simply an expression of "the true posture of the creature before his Creator," but also that of "the Son's eternal reception of the Godhead from the Father."[143]

This means more specifically, Balthasar reasons, that the Son is predestined to the redemptive Incarnation and all that it entails by reason of his "place in the mystery of the Trinity," for he is "the first to receive totally from the Father, just as, in breathing forth the Spirit together with the Father, he is the one who consents, responds and collaborates up to the last."[144] It thus follows for Balthasar that in virtue of the Son's one and same disposition—that of loving surrender or availability which is manifest in time as obedience—the Son both becomes incarnate and, precisely as incarnate, exists "on both sides" of the analogy of being: to be concomitantly the one who speaks and acts "with divine power" and the one who suffers and dies "with human impotence."[145]

Of course, this so-called great insight of Balthasar is also of no little significance as far as his critics are concerned, for it is precisely herein—in what might be considered the hinge upon which Balthasar's argument rests—that also lies the heart of Blankenhorn's criticism. What, in other words, Blankenhorn might ask—and he would certainly be joined by Alyssa Pitstick, Gilbert Narcisse, Karen Kilby, and Jean-Noël Dol,[146] among others—justifies Balthasar's move from the obedience of the incarnate Son to the surrender of the eternal Son vis-à-vis the Father? Or, to put the objection in still other terms, is it possible that Balthasar's own insistence upon the important formula of the Fourth Lateran Council to describe the relation between the Creator and his creation—namely that of "greater dissimilitude" than similitude[147]—is not adequately respected with regard to his own presentation of the two natures of Christ?

142. Speyr, *Das Wort und die Mystik* II, 535.
143. Healy, *The Eschatology of Hans Urs von Balthasar*, 107. Cf. Balthasar, *Theo-Logic* II, 354; *A Theology of History*, 31–32; *The Christian State of Life*, 78; *The Glory of the Lord* I, 478; and Dalzell, *The Dramatic Encounter of Divine and Human Freedom*, 157.
144. Balthasar, *Theo-Drama* II, 267.
145. Balthasar, *The Glory of the Lord* I, 478. Cf. Speyr, *The Countenance of the Father*, 61. On the Son's incarnate obedience as an expression of his eternal love, see Balthasar, *The Glory of the Lord* VII, 248.
146. See Pitstick, *Light in Darkness*, 293; Narcisse, "Participer à la vie trinitaire," 128; Kilby, *Balthasar: A (Very) Critical Introduction*, 101; and Jean-Noël Dol, "L'inversion trinitaire chez Hans Urs von Balthasar," *Revue thomiste* 100, no. 2 (2000): 230–35.
147. *DZ* 806.

To be sure, Balthasar is not unaware of this objection: "The crux" of the matter, as he sees and expresses it, "is that it is extremely hard to see how the Son, who 'receives' Godhead, and hence eternal freedom, from the Father (and so seems to be closely related to the creature), can nonetheless possess this infinite freedom in the same sovereign manner (albeit in the mode of obedience) as the Father."[148] This difficulty is, in fact, particularly pronounced within Balthasar's Christology in that which touches upon the question of Christ's consciousness and (it bears repeating) obedience.[149] Balthasar is explicit on this count:

> We cannot ascribe a twofold consciousness to the Logos-made-man. The mission of which Jesus is aware is the mission of the only Son. He knows that, as man, he freely does what, as Logos, he wills to do. Or—which is the same thing—the man Jesus knows that what he freely does is done by the Son of God. He is not the executor of a project decided upon by someone else; even in his temporal existence he is always the One who offers himself to the Father to carry out the work of the world's redemption. [...] There is no question of Jesus as man obeying himself as God; nor does he obey the Trinity: as Son, in the Holy Spirit, he obeys the Father.[150]

Balthasar thus holds, more specifically, that the Son's consciousness in time is determined by his mission, which in turn—as the temporal form of his eternal procession from the Father—has an eternal dimension: it is eternally willed by the triune God. "If we are to understand this," Balthasar explains, then "we must first start with the purely human conscious subject. This purely human subject cannot surmise and seize his mission, or God's will for him, or the idea God has of him, through his own ('autonomous') power: man must open up to something that is infused into him from above, something that is laid upon him as a task." It is for this reason that Jesus prays: to open himself, Balthasar explains, to the operation of the Spirit, who presents the Father's will—that is to say, his mission—to him. The Spirit thus mediates to the Son what Balthasar presents as the "economic form of the eternal unanimity between Father and Son," namely the eternal divinely willed mis-

---

148. Balthasar, *Theo-Drama* II, 267.

149. The delicate nature of this question is, Jean-Pierre Torrell notes, evidenced by succession of authorities cited in contrary sense (*sed contra*) to the solution that Aquinas offers to the question, "Whether Christ is Subject to Himself?" (*ST* III, q. 20, a. 2). Here, more specifically, we find the authority of Augustine against that of St. Cyril and the Greek Fathers, the latter refusing to speak of Christ's submission to himself out of fear of the heretical affirmation (cf. Nestorius) of two persons in Christ. Although St. Thomas sides with Augustine here (in his *Summa*) by admitting that the Word of God in his human nature is subject to the Word of God in his divine nature, the angelic doctor avoids any such formulation, Torrell notes, in his homiletic discourses. See Torrell, *Encyclopédie: Jésus le Christ chez Saint Thomas d'Aquin*, 308–10.

150. Balthasar, *Theo-Drama* III, 227. It is precisely with regard to this passage that Pitstick poses an objection; see her *Light in Darkness*, 299.

sion of our redemption.[151] Indeed, although the eternal Son in heaven "possesses an overall grasp of the whole drama—Incarnation, Passion, Resurrection," the same cannot be said "in the same sense of the Incarnate One who lives out his earthly mission."[152]

Despite the accusation of certain critics recognizing "tritheism" in Balthasar's doctrine, it is thus possible to discern therein the unifying role of the Spirit, who is simultaneously the Spirit of the Father and the Spirit of the Son, "in personal unity." As such, he is both "the heart of the Father's command and the heart of the Son's obedience."[153] It follows that in the revelation of the God-man there is simultaneously revealed "the inner-trinitarian event of his procession; there appears the triune God, who, as God, can command absolutely and obey absolutely and, as the Spirit of love, can be the unity of both."[154]

It is thus not surprising that Balthasar recognizes—in what likely originates out of a Speyrian insight—that the opposition of "my will" and "thy will" in Gethsemane serves to reveal not so much the opposition of the divine and human wills of Christ—although this theme is not lacking in Adrienne's corpus[155]—as (most especially) the opposition (or distinction) of the divine persons.[156] "When he prays on the Mount of Olives, 'Not my will but thine be done,'" Christ—as viewed by Adrienne—is merely "repeating in a new way the request already uttered in his eternal origin."[157] Hence, despite Balthasar's explicit acknowledgement that "a 'personal will' destroys the very notion of the divine nature,"[158] there inevitably arises the question—at least

---

151. Balthasar, *Theo-Drama* III, 510–11; cf. Speyr, *The Passion from Within*, 63. See also the critique of this notion of "Trinitarian inversion" by Dol, "L'inversion trinitaire chez Hans Urs von Balthasar." On the idea of intra-Trinitarian "prayer," see Balthasar, *Theo-Drama* V, 122–23; cf. Speyr, *World of Prayer*, 28–74.

152. Balthasar, *Theo-Drama* III, 254.

153. Balthasar, *A Theology of History*, 62; cf. Speyr, *John* II, 292.

154. Balthasar, *The Glory of the Lord* I, 479; see also 409; *Theo-Logic* II, 354; and *Mysterium Paschale*, 82. Cf. Speyr, *World of Prayer*, 83–84.

155. It is thus that Adrienne presents the scene of Gethsemane. See Speyr, *The Passion from Within*, 63–64; and *Bereitschaft*, 15. On the two wills of Christ, see *The Catechism of the Catholic Church*, no. 475; and Thomas Aquinas, *ST* III, q. 19, a. 1.

156. See, for example, Balthasar, *Theo-Logic* II, 69–70; *Convergences*, 98; and *Explorations in Theology* IV, 143. Hence, for example, John Milbank's criticism that "Balthasar substitutes a rupture between Father and Son for a tension between Christ's divine and his human nature" (*The Suspended Middle*, 75). As for Adrienne, she recognizes in Christ's prayer in Gethsemane the petition of the "Our Father": "Your will be done on earth as it is in heaven." See Speyr, *Markus*, 649. Similarly, she recognizes the "Suscipe" of St. Ignatius of Loyola ("Take Lord, receive all my liberty") as inspired by this same prayer (of Gethsemane), but also by the Lord's prayer upon his entry into the world: "Lo, I have come to do thy will, O God" (cf. Heb 10:5–7). See Speyr, *Bereitschaft*, 14; and *The Countenance of the Father*, 61.

157. Speyr, *World of Prayer*, 68; see also *The Passion from Within*, 63–64.

158. Balthasar, *Cosmic Liturgy*, 214.

when these authors are taken out of context[159]—of whether Balthasar and Adrienne do not propose the idea of a properly *divine* obedience, whence the re-emergence of the question of multiple wills in the Godhead.

Thomas Joseph White, for example, objects that Balthasar ignores Maximus's understanding of Gethsemane as a mystery of "natural *human* repugnance in the will of Christ to the onslaught of moral evil, and evil that *the man* Jesus knows is permitted but not willed by the Father."[160] He concludes that for Balthasar the event of Gethsemane is a revelation of the "'*divine* will' of the Son, obedient to the Father, and therefore as expressive of an eternal 'intra-Trinitarian' obedience which preexists the creation."[161] Balthasar meanwhile insists, with explicit reference to Maximus's teaching, that "we cannot read the Agony in the Garden as if Jesus' human will had first balked at the eminent Passion and had then been overpowered and brought back into line by the divine will, but that, on the contrary, it was none other than this human will that had to give its free consent to the Father's plan."[162] Hence, although the Son's divine will must be the same as that of the Father—with the result that Christ struggles with his own divine will in the garden of Gethsemane—"as a man he does the will of someone else. Both wills stand over and against each other."[163]

To better understand this reasoning, we do well to call upon Balthasar's presentation of Christ as revealing the Father "in the personal mode," especially when we recall that this person is *not human*, but divine, although having assumed a human nature.[164] Hence, in his treatment of Christ as "the

159. To be sure, Adrienne adds an important point to the citation above, namely that "human nature and his office of representing sinners give it [i.e., "the request uttered in his eternal origin"] new aspects of obedience and submission" (*World of Prayer*, 68).

160. Helpful, within this context, is the distinction that St. Thomas makes between Christ's act of willing *ut natura* and willing *ut ratio*: "Now it is clear that the will of sensuality [*voluntas sensualitatis*] naturally shrinks from sensible pains and bodily hurt. In like manner, the will as nature [*voluntas ut natura*] turns from what is against nature and what is evil in itself, as death and the like; yet the will as reason [*voluntas per modum rationis*] may at time choose these things in relation to an end [...]. Now it was the will of God that Christ should undergo pain, suffering, and death, not that these of themselves were willed by God, but for the sake of man's salvation. Hence it is plain that in His will of sensuality and in His rational will considered as nature, Christ could will what God did not; but in His will as reason He always willed the same as God" (*ST* III, q. 18, a. 5).

161. Thomas Joseph White, "Von Balthasar and Journet on the Universal Possibility of Salvation and the Twofold Will of God," *Nova et Vetera* (English edition) 4, no. 3 (2006): 633-666, (cf. Balthasar, Mysterium Paschale, 80–82, 105–7). See also Thomas Joseph White, "Kenoticism and the Divinity of Christ Crucified," *The Thomist* 75 (2011): 1–41, esp. 36–39.

162. Balthasar, *Theo-Logic* II, 69–70. Balthasar makes reference at this juncture to F.-M. Léthel, *Théologie de l'agonie du Christ: la liberté humaine du Fils de Dieu et son importance sotériologique mises en lumière par Saint Maxime le Confesseur* (Paris: Beauchesne, 1979).

163. Dalzell, *The Dramatic Encounter of Divine and Human Freedom*, 156n1.

164. See *The Catechism of the Catholic Church*, no. 466; cf. the First Council of Nicaea (*DZ* 126 and 130).

concrete *analogia entis,*" Balthasar holds that it is possible "to apply qualities and attributes of the one nature to the other" precisely because "both are united in the one person of the Logos."[165] The divine personality of Christ helps to account, more specifically, for the fact that his human nature—including his human will, especially as obedient—is an expression, or revelation, of his divine person. "No matter what he [Christ] does in his human nature, he does it as a Divine Person," Adrienne reasons.[166]

This divine person is, in turn—and herein resides the particularity of Balthasar's contribution, as borrowed from Adrienne—entirely turned toward the Father in an act of receptivity.[167] In virtue, more specifically of the properly Speyrian concept of surrender, letting-happen, or availability,[168] the Son is said by Balthasar to receive everything—in time as in eternity—from the Father and to accomplish the paternal will (that is to say, the one divine will) which he (the Son) has received, along with the entire divine nature, as his own. "As man he only does what, as God, he has done from eternity," Adrienne explains. "In order, as God, to be man, he must also know all aspects of his relationship, as God, with the Father; he must have lived in eternity in free subordination to the Father, although this subordination already had its basis within the divine necessity."[169] Similarly, in the theology of St. Thomas, each of the divine persons "exists and acts in accordance with his relation to the other persons," Gilles Emery explains, whence the importance of the order of origin within the Trinity for founding the personal distinctions.[170]

It follows from this particular manner of thinking that Christ's human words and gestures manifest, as Thomas Joseph White explains with regard to the Christology of Karl Barth, "his *filial* relation to the Father, *and* the presence in Jesus of a divine *will* received from the Father."[171] This is also explicit in Balthasar, with direct reference to Adrienne: "the Son, in being begotten,

165. Balthasar, *Theo-Drama* III, 222. Cf. *DZ* 555.
166. Speyr, *The Countenance of the Father*, 60.
167. See, for example, Balthasar, *The Christian State of Life*, 78; *Theo-Drama* II, 267; and *Theo-Drama* IV, 326. Cf. Speyr, *Das Buch von Gehorsam*, 36; *The Boundless God*, 20; and *John* III, 341. The latter reference is cited by Balthasar in *Theo-Drama* V, 121–22. Or as Gilles Emery puts it, from a properly Thomistic perspective, "When he acts in the world, the Son does not cease to receive himself from the Father by generation: the Son is turned toward the Father who begets him. The proper mode of existence of divine persons does not disappear when these persons act in the world; rather, this proper mode remains present as a constitutive feature of each person's action." (*The Trinity*, 163).
168. It bears repeating that the same German word (*Hingabe*) implies all the foregoing.
169. Speyr, *World of Prayer*, 67–68; see also *Korinther* I, 53; *The Letter to the Ephesians*, 21; *John* III, 90; *Erde und Himmel* III, 193; *Das Wort und die Mystik* I, 21; Balthasar, *A Theology of History*, 34; *Theo-Drama* V, 88, 517; *Theo-Logic* III, 308; and Healy, *The Eschatology of Hans Urs von Balthasar*, 106–7.
170. Emery, *Trinity, Church, and the Human Person*, 136.
171. White, "Intra-Trinitarian Obedience and Nicene-Chalcedonian Christology," 400. Cf. Thomas Aquinas, *Super Ioan* 5, lect. 5, no. 798.

admits 'the fullness of the Father's necessary will [...] in no way intervening with the free will with which he was begotten, as if to contribute toward his own fashioning.' On the other hand, however, *'the Father has given the Son everything,' including his will.*"[172] Or as Adrienne would have it: he "proclaims his filial will" by accomplishing the Father's will entrusted to him.[173]

So as to avoid misunderstanding on this point, we might cite Adrienne in still another context, wherein she insists that Christ's specifically "filial characteristics" must be considered "only within the wholeness of the divine nature, as belonging equally to the Father and the Spirit within the one nature, which will, however, always remain a mystery for us."[174] On the other hand, Adrienne holds that it is possible to observe within the revelation of Christ "the complete will of the Father in the complete surrender of the Son."[175] Or, as Balthasar would have it: "Insofar as he is God, he is eternal, infinite freedom; insofar as he is the Son of the Father, he is this freedom in the mode (*'tropos'*) of readiness, receptivity, obedience and hence of appropriate response: that is, he is the Father's Word, image and expression."[176] Indeed, the Son "cannot *be* and *possess* the absolute nature of God except in the mode of receptivity."[177]

It follows that the Son does not possess a divine will that is "other" than that of the Father. Rather, as is the case in the Christology of Karl Barth, so also in that of Balthasar: the divine obedience of the incarnate Son is "a figurative expression of his eternal reception of the divine will from the Father."[178] Or, in Balthasar's own words, "In the selfsame act in which he receives himself (and hence his divine understanding) he receives, too, the entire will of the Father concerning God and the world, and assents to it as his own."[179]

A Distortion of the Catholic Balance between Philosophy and Theology?

A similar logic—that of surrender—is at work in Balthasar's presentation of Christ as the concrete *analogia entis*. It is, more specifically, by reason of his "place" within the Trinitarian mystery—that of the *second* person, who

---

172. Balthasar, *Theo-Drama* V, 88; emphasis added. Cf. Speyr, *World of Prayer*, 59.
173. Speyr, *World of Prayer*, 63; cf. Balthasar, *Prayer*, 189.
174. Speyr, *Mary in the Redemption*, 116.
175. Speyr, *The Countenance of the Father*, 84; see also *The Boundless God*, 79; *Handmaid of the Lord*, 117; and *John* II, 166.
176. Balthasar, *Theo-Drama* II, 267; see also *My Work*, 118.
177. Balthasar, *Theo-Drama* IV, 326.
178. White, "Intra-Trinitarian Obedience and Nicene-Chalcedonian Christology," 402. See also Healy, *The Eschatology of Hans Urs von Balthasar*, 106–7.
179. Balthasar, *A Theology of History*, 31; see also *The Threefold Garland*, 32.

receives everything from the Father—that Balthasar (again following Adrienne)[180] presents Christ as the archetype of all of creation and thus also as the "concrete analogy of being." It is, in other words, precisely in his revelation of the Father and his love—to draw upon an important insight from the Second Vatican Council, although for Balthasar this is understood in terms of the Son's making "space"[181] for the Father in his filial disposition of receptivity—that is also illuminated the truth of the human person "as God sees him."[182] Lest there be any misunderstanding regarding the modality of this revelation, however, Balthasar adds an important clarification: "Jesus does not live in order to exhibit himself as the highest example of the human species but solely to fulfil the Father's will."[183]

Assuredly—to draw out still another element implied within Blankenhorn's criticism—this properly Speyrian-Balthasarian perspective entails a certain regard from above, as it were: a certain preference for a theological perspective not so much over and above a philosophical one, as under and sustaining it, whence Balthasar's respectful insistence upon the integrity of philosophy—as well as the whole natural realm—as distinct but inseparable from theology and grace.[184] Hence, as Angelo Scola adequately describes Balthasar's view: "natural law is assumed in Christ and in the new law. And that which is assumed is not abolished: *quod est assumptum est servatum.*"[185] On the other hand, not only do philosophical concepts lose nothing of their content in being taken up "as part of the *assumption humanae naturae* in Christ," but they are also "transfigured" by this assumption so as to become—not unlike the humanity of Christ—"wholly a function and expression of his divine person and truth."[186] This explains the danger—as Balthasar sees it—of approaching theology with "preconceived concepts" whose elevation to a higher level—namely that of biblical revelation—requires "the highest degree of maturity,

---

180. See, for example, Speyr, *Das Wort und die Mystik* II, 82.

181. Balthasar presents the obedience of the incarnate Son as proof of "his eternal love for the Father, a love that itself was nothing but the act of making space for the eternal love of the Father for the Son" (*Glory of the Lord* VII, 250–51); see also *Theo-Drama* IV, 324 and 326; and "Christian Prayer," *Communio* 5 (1978): 21.

182. Balthasar, *Theo-Drama* III, 225; see also *Explorations in Theology* I, 168–69; Speyr, *The Countenance of the Father*, 101; and Balthasar's introduction to Speyr, *Light and Images*, 14. Cf. *Gaudium et Spes*, no. 22: "Christ, the final Adam, by the revelation of the mystery of the Father and his love, fully reveals man to man himself and makes his supreme calling clear" (*DZ* 4322).

183. Balthasar, *Theo-Drama* III, 225.

184. See "The Theological *A Priori* Element in Metaphysics," in Balthasar, *The Glory of the Lord* V, 628–34; *Theo-Drama* II, 192; "On the Task of Catholic Philosophy in Our Time," 187; and *The Glory of the Lord* VII, 408.

185. Scola, *Hans Urs von Balthasar: A Theological Style*, 106; cf. Balthasar, *Explorations in Theology* I, 195.

186. Balthasar, *Explorations in Theology* I, 185.

of genius allied with holiness": an alliance that Balthasar judges lacking in much neo-scholastic theology.[187] Balthasar's theological understanding of human nature is not, therefore, a denial of the philosophical-ontic one. Rather, the two are so interrelated—without being thereby confused—that the latter is conceived as included in the former and thus as best understood within that realm.[188]

This tightly related synthesis of creation and revelation is, meanwhile, the origin of Steven A. Long's objection that Balthasar makes of created nature a simple "vacuole for grace"[189] and thereby "cripples the doctrine of the *analogia entis* and renders it something like a musical composition with no notes, leaving it to be treated as a blank space to be filled by something like theological intuition."[190] Healy, on the other hand, understands Balthasar as treating the analogy of being as "an inner requirement of christocentric theology." In other words, the authentic union of the divine and human natures in the person of Christ "presupposes an order of creation with a relative autonomy, and by analogy, a relatively autonomous philosophy,"[191] a difference which "cannot and will not" be abolished.

To be sure, Balthasar does hold that the hypostatic union of the two natures in the one divine person of Christ "must constitute the final proportion [or better: the final *measure* (*Mass*)] between the two [natures] and hence must be the 'concrete *analogia entis*' itself."[192] On the other hand, he also holds that "the inner-worldly analogies [...] have their ultimate measure in the analogy of creation." Indeed, "God's revelation at the level of creation [...] is the ground of every inner-worldly analogy."[193] The two affirmations can be held simultaneously because God is entirely outside of the order of his creation so as also to be incomparable to the finite creature "who is entirely dependent on him."[194]

It is thus "impossible," Balthasar reasons, "to subsume the relation of participation and manifestation that obtains between God and the creature

187. Ibid., 186.
188. See Balthasar, *The Glory of the Lord* VII, 409.
189. Long, *Natura Pura*, 52. It is, he maintains, "a mere limit or remainder concept of a content-less *minimum natura* for the reception of grace, but lacking any ontological character, density, or dynamism in its own right" (80). In contrast, see Balthasar, *The Glory of the Lord* I, 29.
190. Long, *Natura Pura*, 95. See also White, "The 'Pure Nature' of Christology."
191. Healy, *The Eschatology of Hans Urs von Balthasar*, 100n21. As a case in point, Healy cites Balthasar's critique of Barth's rejection of philosophical reflection "concomitant to theology" as "self-destructive." See Balthasar, *The Theology of Karl Barth*, 393; see also *Theo-Logic* II, 173.
192. Balthasar, *Theo-Drama* III, 222.
193. Balthasar, *Theo-Logic* I, 232.
194. Balthasar, *Theo-Drama* III, 222. Cf. Thomas Aquinas, *ST* I, q. 4, a. 3, ad. 4; Emery, "La rélation de création," esp. 25.

under some (univocal) category, as if it were a 'case,' one distinctive form of participation and revelation among many." Hence also the Creator-creature analogy, which is "established by creation is congruent with every other analogy *only in an analogous way*."[195] When addressing the revelatory function of Christ's humanity, however, we do well to recall with Balthasar that "it is the Creator who is at work, and that he does not misuse his own creation for a purpose alien to it, but rather, by his becoming man, he could only honor it and crown it and bring it to own most intimate perfection."[196] Similarly, from the opposite perspective: "as the Son in God is the eternal icon of the Father, he can without contradiction assume in himself the image that is the creation, purify it and make it enter into the communion of the divine life without dissolving it (in a false mysticism)."[197]

Helpful for clarifying this delicate balance between nature and grace, and thus also between philosophy and theology, are the important remarks of Cardinal Ratzinger with regard to the theology of Karl Barth: "Karl Barth was right to reject philosophy as the foundation of the faith independent from the faith. If it were such, our faith would be based from the beginning to the end on the changing philosophical theories. But Barth was wrong when, for this same reason, he proposed the faith as a pure paradox that can only exist against reason and totally independent from it."[198] To be sure, Balthasar himself is not without criticism of Barth's position, particularly with regard to the latter's refusal of the *analogia entis*. On the other hand, he was in perfect agreement with Barth's Christocentrism and sought to rework the doctrine of analogy from this perspective.[199]

We could describe this thought as a kind of hourglass, where the two contiguous vessels (God and creature) meet only at the narrow passage through the center: where they both encounter each other in Jesus Christ. The purpose of the image is to show that there is no other point of contact between the two chambers of the glass. And just as the sand flows only from top to bottom, so too God's revelation is one-sided, flowing from his gracious decision alone. But of course the sand flows down into the other chamber so that the sand there can really *increase*. In other words, there *is* a countermovement in the other chamber, but only because of the first movement, the initiative of the first chamber.[200]

---

195. Balthasar, *Theo-Logic* I, 232; emphasis added.
196. Balthasar, *The Glory of the Lord* I, 459.
197. Balthasar, *My Work*, 118.
198. Joseph Ratzinger, "Relativism: The Central Problem for Faith Today," *Origins* 26, no. 20 (October 31, 1996): 316.
199. See Balthasar, *The Theology of Karl Barth*, 55.
200. Ibid., 197.

Balthasar's point—which he shares with Barth—is that "God's immanencing into the world in Jesus Christ can be neither constructed (Hegel) nor postulated (Baius) starting from the world." It can only be "received as pure 'grace' (Jn 1:14, 16–17)." When, however, the incarnate Word "comes into 'his own property' (Jn 1:11)," he "does not travel merely into a foreign land (as Karl Barth says) but into a country whose language he knows." This language, more specifically, is "not only the Galilean variety of Aramaic that he learns as a child in Nazareth, but more profoundly, the ontological language of creatureliness as such. The logic of the creature is not foreign to the logic of God."[201] Nor, Balthasar maintains, is the logic of God entirely foreign to the logic of the creature.[202] Similarly, the theologian of Lucerne explains:

> [All worldly being is] spoken of as Being only in a secondary, analogous sense [as is already implied within the *analogia entis*] which is determined by the first sense of this term. And as the one infinite Being of God reveals itself through the fullness and manifold character of the form of worldly Being, which is in itself held in tension, contradictory and mutually determinative in a polar relationship, so too the infinite truth of the Trinity is portrayed only through innumerable forms of expression of worldly truth, which can of course come more or less close to the ideal of the divine truth.[203]

It follows, for Balthasar, that far from relativizing or otherwise calling into question worldly truth, it is taken seriously in the one truth of Christ, who is himself the perfect expression not only of the created domain in general and of the human being in particular, but also and still more fundamentally of the Trinitarian mystery. "Jesus is not a distorted image but the pure truth," Balthasar explains, "because he gives the adequate exposition of the Father in worldly figure [*Gestalt*]."[204]

We are not far from a profound insight of St. Thomas Aquinas: "In God the Word conceived by the intellect of the Father is the name of a Person: but all things that are in the Father's knowledge, whether they refer to the Essence or to the Persons, or to the works of God are expressed by this Word [...]. And among other things expressed by this Word, the eternal law itself is expressed thereby."[205]

---

201. Balthasar, *Theo-Logic* II, 84.

202. If one is capable of hearing and understanding God's self-revelation, then "man must in himself be a search for God, a question posed to him," Balthasar reasons. "Thus there is no biblical theology without a religious philosophy. Human reason must be open to the infinite" (*My Work*, 114).

203. Balthasar, "On the Task of Catholic Philosophy in Our Time," 157–58; cf. his *The Theology of Henri de Lubac: An Overview*, trans. Joseph Fessio, Michael Waldstein, and Susan Clements (San Francisco: Ignatius Press, 1991), 15. Similarly, "God's revelation at the level of creation [...] is the ground of every inner-worldly analogy" (*Theo-Logic* I, 232).

204. Balthasar, *Theo-Logic* II, 84. 205. Thomas Aquinas, *ST* I-II, q. 93, a. 1, ad. 2.

A "Loss" in the Godhead?

Not unlike Blankenhorn's criticism regarding Balthasar's invoking of an element of "surprise" in the Godhead, other critics of Balthasar object to his tendency of passing beyond the communication of idioms outlined at the Council of Chalcedon—the predication of the attributes of both natures to the one divine person of Christ[206]—so as to attribute directly to the Godhead certain "super"-human traits.[207] Hence the ascribing of something like pain and suffering to the Father, notwithstanding what Balthasar—following Sergei Bulgakov more than Adrienne—presents as a "primary kenosis" whereby the Son's generation from the Father is presented as the Father's giving not simply something "that he *has* but all that he *is*," even to the extent that his paternal "womb" is left "empty."[208] This explains how it is then possible, according to Balthasar, for the Father—without revoking his omnipotence and his omni-benevolence—to "'pitilessly' hand over this All to the world."[209] "What is called 'God's *kenosis*' is certainly acute in the unique life and suffering of Jesus, but it is also in this context the revelation of God's own way of eternal being: it is according to God the Father's very mode of being to 'abandon' his Son, 'to pour out' his Pneuma, in order that he might be his own 'divine form' (Phil 2:6) in this act of self-surrender."[210]

To be sure, the *kenosis* described in Philippians 2:7—which Balthasar equates with the Son's *kenosis* of obedience—is rooted, he argues in union with Adrienne, "in the eternal kenosis of the Divine Persons to one another,"[211] and more fundamentally still in the *Ur-kenosis* "that underpins all subsequent kenosis."

For the Father strips himself, without remainder, of his Godhead and hands it over to the Son; he 'imparts' to the Son all that is his. 'All that is mine' (John 17:10). The Father must not be thought to exist 'prior' to this self-surrender (in an Arian sense): he is this movement of self-giving that holds nothing back. This divine act that brings forth the Son, that is, the second way of participating in (and of *being*) the identical

---

206. Cf. *DZ* 301 and *The Catechism of the Catholic Church*, no. 467. Balthasar's intention to hold to this defined truth is explicit in *Theo-Drama* III, 222.

207. This is explicit in, for example, Balthasar, *Theo-Logic* II, 137. See also O'Hanlon, *The Immutability of God in the Theology of Hans Urs von Balthasar*, 43.

208. Balthasar, *Theo-Drama* V, 84. Cf. Sergei Bulgakov, *Le Verbe incarné: Agnus Dei* (Paris: Aubier, 1943), esp. 291.

209. Balthasar, *Theo-Drama* III, 518–19. 210. Balthasar, *Explorations in Theology* IV, 59.

211. Balthasar, *Theo-Drama* V, 123. The Son's *kenosis* in time is, therefore, "*one* of the infinite aspects of eternal life" (ibid.). Cf. Speyr, *John* III, 90; and *Korinther* I, 138–41. See also Balthasar, *Mysterium Paschale*, 35. This intra-Trinitarian "*kenosis*" (as it were) is described by Balthasar as "a kind of 'death,' a first, radical 'kenosis' [...] a kind of 'super-death' that is a component of all love'" (*Theo-Drama* V, 84). See also Turek, *Towards a Theology of God the Father*, esp. 108–9.

Godhead, involves the positing of an absolute, infinite 'distance' that can contain and embrace all the other distances that are possible within the world of finitude, including the distance of sin.²¹²

It might be granted to Alyssa Pitstick—if, that is to say, one were to isolate this passage from those cited above to demonstrate the constant tension (that is to say difference-in-unity) in Balthasar's theology between essential identity and personal difference in the Trinity—that this kind of language does not necessarily accord with Balthasar's own insistence, following the teaching of the Fourth Lateran Council, that "the Giver (whose act of giving is eternal) does not lose what he gives, that is, himself."²¹³ Pitstick recognizes, more specifically, in Balthasar's presentation of the divine nature a sort of "glass (the self-subsisting relational *ratio*)" in the absence of "a necessary content (namely the divine attributes)." Hence, the divinity does not, she maintains as proper to Balthasar's thought, bespeak *what* God is, "but *how* He is, i.e., His self-giving, which constitutes the personal relations."²¹⁴

As differing from Pitstick's metaphorical image of the glass, however, Balthasar's own metaphorical language—largely borrowed from Adrienne—seems compatible with the Thomistic rejection of a supposit that "could be thought in a pre-relational or essential manner (as subsisting essence) independently of his constitution as a person—independently of his personal relation." Hence the person of the Father can never be posed, as Gilles Emery has fittingly argued, "without the relation of paternity which constitutes it" so as to be identified with "the essence of divinity in a stage preceding the deployment of the doctrine of relation."²¹⁵ Similarly, Adrienne reasons that "the Son, by proceeding from the Father, and the Spirit, by proceeding from Father and Son, both cause the Father to be Father. [...] All the Persons define each other reciprocally."²¹⁶ As for Balthasar, he suggests that there is nothing to retain (or to "contain," draw upon on Pitstick's image) the divine being, which exists only within the processions: "[Divine] Giving does not retain what it has but contains what it gives."²¹⁷ There is, in other words, no "room" for a glass in this imagery.

212. Balthasar, *Theo-Drama* IV, 323; see also 325.
213. Balthasar, *Theo-Drama* V, 85; cf. *DZ* 805. Hence, Balthasar continues in his reasoning: "We need to hold the two things simultaneously and affirm their identity: the genuine, active giving that involves the entire Person who gives, and the eternal Being of the Person that remains constant throughout this act of self-giving" (ibid., 86). See also his *Theo-Drama* II, 257; and *Theo-Logic* III, 226.
214. Pitstick, *Light in Darkness*, 154–55.
215. Emery, *Trinity in Aquinas*, 192 and 198. For an important presentation of Balthasar's understanding of the relation between God's essence and the divine hypostases in light of the tradition, see his *Theo-Logic* II, 128–49; and *Epilogue*, 93.
216. Speyr, *Das Wort und die Mystik* II, 104; see also Balthasar, *Theo-Logic* III, 225–26.
217. Klaus Hemmerle, *Thesen zu einer trinitarischen Ontologie* (Einsiedeln: Johannes Verlag, 1976),

This is not to deny that in the absence of frequent recourse to the philosophical concepts of essence and hypostasis to describe the life of the triune God, Balthasar often risks significant misunderstanding. On the other hand, even these important philosophical terms are—as Emery rightfully explains—impoverished in explaining the divine reality:

> In our language about God, we signify the essence as if we were referring to a form: we *signify* 'that through which' God is God, even though, in the divine reality itself, the divine essence is nothing other than the person (there is in God none of that composition of form and suppost which characterizes corporeal creatures). And we *signify* the person as the divine essence itself. Our words cannot do any better than this.[218]

To return to Pitstick's primary objection: while we must admit that Balthasar presents the *kenosis* as "God's very own secret" whereby he "reveals and communicates his own nature to the world,"[219] we might also point out that he explicitly denies that this concept (*kenosis*) implies a diminution in the Godhead.[220] The Father, Balthasar explains, "does not extinguish himself by self-giving, just as he does not keep back anything of himself either. For, in this self-surrender, he *is* the whole divine essence."[221]

In reading this, we ought not to follow Alyssa Pitstick in believing that Balthasar would identify the divine essence (understood as substance) with self-surrender, for he is careful to distinguish the divine substance (which is one and the same in all three divine persons) from the relations (which distinguish the divine persons as such), while nonetheless insisting that we cannot conceive of the one without the other.[222] When, in fact, Balthasar presents the Father—in the passage to which Pitstick refers—as "the whole divine essence" in his surrender, he does not mean to identify the divine essence (understood as being or substance) with self-surrender.[223] If, after all, such were the case, he would surely not continue: "It follows that the Son, for his part, cannot *be* and *possess* the absolute nature of God except in the mode of receptivity."[224]

47; cited in Balthasar, *Theo-Drama* V, 74. See also Balthasar, *Theo-Logic* II, 130 and 136; and *Theo-Logic* III, 158.

218. Emery, *The Trinitarian Theology of St. Thomas Aquinas*, 146–47. To be sure, Emery points out both the importance of philosophical precision and the impossibility of ever being precise enough, as it were; see *Trinity in Aquinas*, 158–59.

219. Balthasar, *Theo-Drama* IV, 333; cf. *The Catechism of the Catholic Church*, no. 221.

220. With specific reference to this concept (*kenosis*), Balthasar maintains: "Those who are reluctant to import such concepts into God (preferring to stay at the level of the equation *relation = persona*) ought to remove these imperfect likenesses from the world" (*Theo-Logic* III, 241).

221. Balthasar, *Theo-Drama* IV, 325; see also *Theo-Drama* II, 256. Of particular importance in comprehending this notion of fatherhood is thus reference to filiation, for as Balthasar rightly expresses it: "To think in any other way would be Arianism" (Balthasar, *Epilogue*, 93).

222. See, for example, Balthasar, *Theo-Logic* II, 130; and *Theo-Logic* III, 130.

223. See Pitstick, *Light in Darkness*, 287 and 290–91.

224. Balthasar, *Theo-Drama* IV, 325–26; see also *Theo-Drama* II, 129–31; and *Epilogue*, 93.

From this perspective, we do well to consider with Marc Ouellet that the "ever greater difference" implied in the formula of the Fourth Lateran Council to describe the relation between the Creator and the creature might also be applied to the relation between the *kenosis* of the Cross and that of the inner life of the Trinity: the self-giving of the divine persons within the Godhead. This means, more specifically, that "the analogy between the intratrinitarian '*Ur*-Kenosis' and the soteriological kenosis allows us to conceive of something like suffering in God, which does not express a 'lack' comparable to the creature's experience, but rather the infinite superabundance of divine love, capable of linking itself also in this free and willing way to the suffering of its creature."[225] It is furthermore important, Balthasar maintains, to insist upon the freedom of God to express himself beyond the limits of human understanding.[226]

The Center of the Whole: Descent or Surrender?

This "ever greater difference" between the *kenosis* of the Cross and the intra-Trinitarian life should also be kept in mind when evaluating Pitstick's estimation of "the descent" as that which is most central to Balthasar's theology.[227] While the same is argued by Wilhelm Maas, whom Pitstick cites to drive home her point, I strongly disagree with her—as differing from his—interpretation of this concept as it is employed by Balthasar and Adrienne: in terms, namely, of the Christological, and thus Trinitarian, movement toward hell. Maas adds, in fact, an important corrective overlooked by Pitstick, namely that the entire "dimension of God-forsakenness and the descent into hell" is grounded within "the intra-divine dimension of unlimited surrender."[228] From Balthasar's perspective, as consonant with that of Adrienne, this means that "the one single total truth," or the "one single dogma"—including Christology, Trinitarian theology, and soteriology—is *not* the descent, as Pitstick claims with reference to this very passage, but rather, in Balthasar's

---

225. Marc Ouellet, "The Message of Balthasar's Theology to Modern Theology," *Communio* 23 (1996): 293. Within this context it bears repeating the insight offered by Gilles Emery (cf. note 65) that rather than speak of divine "suffering"—a notion which risks introducing a lack, or defect, into the absolute perfection of divine being—we should speak instead of God's infinite and unchanging love. Hence, the Pauline formulation that nothing "will be able to separate us from the love of God in Christ Jesus our Lord" (Rom 8:39). See Emery, "The Question of Evil and the Mystery of God in Charles Journet," 261, and Thomas Aquinas, *ST* I, q. 21, a. 3.

226. See Balthasar, *Love Alone Is Credible*, 87n1.

227. See Pitstick, *Light in Darkness*, 244.

228. Wilhem Maas, *Gott und die Hölle. Studien zum Decensus Christi* (Einsiedeln: Johannes Verlag, 1979), 247; cf. Balthasar, *Explorations in Theology* IV, 35–36. For an exposition of the Trinitarian dimension of hell in the theology of Adrienne as incorporated into Balthasar's own work, see his *Theo-Logic* II, 352.

own words therein, "*trinitarian love*":[229] especially Trinitarian love expressed as surrender.[230] Indeed, even the divine *kenosis* is to be interpreted in this light, as Gilbert Narcisse remarks when, within the context of presenting the primacy of love in Balthasar's theology, he explains: "every love contains a kenotic expression, hence a gift that integrates renouncement, even a quasi-annihilation."[231]

Only from this perspective—that of the overriding significance of Trinitarian love—might one argue for the centrality of *kenosis* in Balthasar's theology, as does Christophe Potworowski, for example, when he explains that Christ's self-emptying and obedience unto death (cf. Phil 2:6–11) "reveals a new image of God":[232] one which manifests not only God's love *for us*, but also and more fundamentally still, the divine love *in itself*.[233] The incarnate Son's obedience is, Balthasar observes, "so thoroughly love for the Father" as to be by that very fact [...] altogether one (Jn 10:30) with the Father's own love."[234] "In other words, the love that is, in the Son, a mission received 'by way of generation' [...] is the expression of a love that is, in the Father, a mission to generate. [...] When, therefore, the Son reveals to us his love for the Father in the transferred mode of obedience, this revelation is, at the same time, a revelation of the love of the whole Trinity."[235]

The obedience which determines that whole existence of his [Christ's] is not simply a function of what he has *become* [...]. It is also a function of what, in his self-emptying and self-abasement, he *willed* to become. By letting go of the "form of God" that was his (and so his divine power of self-disposal) he willed to become the One who, in a remarkable and unique manner, is obedient to the Father—in a manner, namely, where his obedience presents the kenotic translation of the external love of the Son for the "ever-greater" Father. [...] This constitutes the expression of the fact that all of his existence is ordered, functionally and kenotically, to the Cross. Even those great affirmations which begin with the word "I" are not the language of "self-consciousness" but of mission.[236]

---

229. Balthasar, *Convergences*, 93; emphasis added. See also *Epilogue*, 93. Cf. Speyr, *The Birth of the Church*, 266; and *Das Wort und die Mystik* II, 92.

230. "All these mysteries are ones of love and therefore of self-surrender" (Speyr, *John* IV, 141). Cf. Balthasar, *Theo-Drama* II, 256; and *Mysterium Paschale*, 153.

231. Narcisse, "The Supernatural in Contemporary Theology," 302.

232. Christophe Potworowski, "Christian Experience in Hans Urs von Balthasar," *Communio* 20 (Spring 1993): 114.

233. See our treatment of this theme in chapter one.

234. Balthasar, *Mysterium Paschale*, 208.

235. Balthasar, *The Christian State of Life*, 79; see also *Theo-Logic* II, 154.

236. Balthasar, *Mysterium Paschale*, 90–91; see also 80–81; *The Glory of the Lord* I, 479; and *Explorations in Theology* IV, 141–42. Cf. Speyr, *Das Buch vom Gehorsam*, 36. The "ever-greater" designation need not be understood as implying that the Son is inferior to the Father, but only that he proceeds from the Father, as from his origin. Cf. Thomas Aquinas, *ST* I, q. 43, a. 1, ad. 1.

As is herein evident, the primacy of descent that Pitstick accords to Balthasar's theology is correct only insofar as all theological reasoning necessarily proceeds from "on high": from the free revelation of God in the person of his incarnate Son. Hence, while Balthasar often employs a bi-directional analysis (from image to archetype and from archetype to image), his reasoning by analogy—his argument from image to archetype—always presupposes what he calls *katalogy*: the reasoning from archetype to image.[237] From this point of view, the revealed mysteries of our faith obviously "cannot be deduced from the perspective of a necessary analogy between worldly being and its origin." Rather, they arise out of God's free self-revelation, including his revelation of himself as the Creator of the world, which—as we have attempted to exposit throughout this volume—is therefore known to contain "within itself traces and images of the intradivine difference."[238]

This typically Balthasarian method of reasoning from "on high" should, it seems to me, be kept in mind when evaluating Pitstick's interpretation of the descent as "the center" of Balthasar's theology. In fact, the passage that Pitstick cites to defend her thesis is, ironically enough, situated within the context of a subchapter entitled "The Transcendence of Jesus Christ," whose purpose is to demonstrate the centrality of obedience in the life of Christ. This (Christ's obedience) in turn is responsible for what Balthasar calls a "breakthrough upward to God and downward to death and hell."[239] As for this bi-directional "breakthrough," it presupposes what Balthasar presents as a "Trinitarian analogy" permitting the Son, "without abolishing the *analogia entis*" to simultaneously represent God to the world—"but in the mode of the Son who regards the Father as 'greater' and to whom he eternally owes all that he is"—and to represent "the world to God, by being, as man (or rather as the God-man), humble, lowly, modest, docile [...]. It is on the basis of these two aspects, united in an abiding analogy, that the Son can take up his one, unitary mission."[240]

From the perspective of this unitary mission, "the 'distance' of the *kenosis* is a mode of intra-trinitarian nearness and of the circumincession of the divine hypostases"[241] and, as such, "part of the absolute positivity of the divine life."[242] In fact, "Without this personal distance in the *circumincessio* of the Persons it would be impossible to understand either the creature's distance

---

237. See for example Balthasar, *Theo-Logic* II, 312–13.
238. Balthasar, *Epilogue*, 86; see also *Theo-Drama* II, 119; and *Theo-Logic* I, 232.
239. See Balthasar, *Convergences*, 91.
240. Balthasar, *Theo-Drama* III, 230n68.
241. Balthasar, *Explorations in Theology* IV, 138.
242. Balthasar, *Theo-Drama* II, 261.

from God or the Son's 'economic' distance from the Father—a distance that goes to the limit of forsakenness."[243]

As differing from Pitstick's interpretation of the whole of Balthasar's theology as colored by Christ's descent into hell, my own suggestion, therefore, is that we join a large number of Balthasar's commentators in reading his theology—including the doctrine of the redemptive *kenosis*—as centered within the intra-divine relations of loving mutual surrender, as revealed in the obedience of Christ.[244] Far from founding the intra-Trinitarian relations within the economic *kenosis*, as Pitstick would have it, we would thus read Balthasar as founding the economic *kenosis* within the intra-divine relations of loving surrender. "Here we clearly see the Son's 'economic' death as the revelation, in terms of the world, of the *kenosis* (or selflessness) of the love of Father and Son at the heart of the Trinity."[245] This interpretation has, moreover, the particular advantage of contextualizing Balthasar's theology within what he esteems the "locus" of Adrienne's mysticism: "Christological (and thereby soteriological) obedience, which—according to the ancient theological tradition—is the revelation in human form of the eternal love of the divine Son for his eternal Father, who has eternally begotten him out of love."[246]

To be sure, the intra-Trinitarian relations are much more central to Adrienne's theology than her mystical experiences of Christ's descent into hell, which explains why this descent has not assumed a more prominent place in these pages. In fact, despite Adrienne's notoriety for these experiences and the theology of Holy Saturday which Balthasar developed therefrom (for example, in his *Mysterium Paschale*), these experiences are only indirectly—if at all—apparent in her works, with the exception of the two-volume diaries, kept and edited by Balthasar and published under Adrienne's name, which record her mystical experiences of the paschal mysteries and her so-called missions into hell.[247] Indeed, even hell itself is "enclosed in the mystery of

243. Balthasar, *Theo-Drama* V, 98; cf. Thomas Aquinas, *ST* I, q. 42, a. 5; and q. 32, a. 1, ad. 3.
244. Such is the interpretation of, for example, Pascal Ide, *Une théologie de l'amour. L'amour, centre de la* Trilogie *de Hans Urs von Balthasar* (Bruxelles: Lessius, 2012); *Être et mystère. La philosophie de Hans Urs von Balthasar* (Bruxelles: Culture et Vérité, 1995), 173; Schrijver, *Le merveilleux accord*, 4, 45 and 57; Levering, *Scripture and Metaphysics*, 124–25; John O'Donnell, *Hans Urs von Balthasar* (Collegeville, Minn.: Liturgical Press, 1992), 7; Nichols, *No Bloodless Myth*, 197; Angela Franz Franks, "Trinitarian *Analogia Entis* in Hans Urs von Balthasar," *The Thomist* 62, no. 4 (1998), 533–59; Lochbrunner, *Analogia Caritatis*; McIntosh, *Mystical Theology*, 107; Sachs, "Hans Urs von Balthasar," 499–500; Gonzalez, "Hans Urs von Balthasar and Contemporary Feminist Theology," 566–95; Papanikalaou, "Person, *Kenosis* and Abuse," 42; and David L. Schindler, postscript to, "Modernity and the Nature of a Distinction," in Rodney A. Howsare and Larry S. Chapp (eds.), *How Balthasar Changed my Mind*, 255–58.
245. Balthasar, *Theo-Logic* III, 300.
246. Balthasar, *First Glance at Adrienne von Speyr*, 59. See also Balthasar's many citations of Adrienne's *Kreuz und Hölle* I in his *Theo-Logic* II, 354–55; and (with Albus), "Fire and Spirit," 581.
247. See Speyr, *Kreuz und Hölle* I and II. See also Balthasar, *First Glance at Adrienne von Speyr*,

the Trinity," as Adrienne "sees" it,[248] which means that it can in no way be reckoned anthropologically; it has no place "in our understanding, nor in our life experience, nor in our need."[249] Nor, we might add with Adrienne and Balthasar, are we able to follow Christ there, except perhaps through the dark night of the faith, wherein the question of God "can no longer be answered."[250]

In short, Christ's descent into hell finds its rightful place in the theology of Adrienne and Balthasar only within the mystery of self-giving love (surrender) in the immanent Trinity, for it is this mystery which grounds the Son's entire redemptive *kenosis*: the Incarnation, passion, death, descent into hell, and Eucharist.[251] Hence, while there is, in fact, very little that the theologian can actually affirm with regard to Christ's actual descent into hell, Balthasar has good reason to present the redemptive *kenosis*, at the center of New Testament revelation, as the privileged manifestation of the intra-Trinitarian mystery of self-giving love.

64–68; "Theologie des Abstiegs zur Hölle" in Balthasar, Chantarine, and Scola (eds.), *Adrienne von Speyr und ihre kirchliche Sendung*, 138–46; *Explorations in Theology* IV, 401–14; *Our Task*, 65–66; Wilhelm Maas, "Das Geheimnis des Karsamstags"; Marc Ouellet, "Adrienne von Speyr et le Samedi Saint de la theologie" in Hans Urs von Balthasar Stiftung, ed., *Adrienne von Speyr und ihre spirituelle theologie*, 31–56; Gérard Rémy, "Le merveilleux et la nuit divine: Un aspect de l'expérience mystique d'Adrienne von Speyr" in Patrick Dondelinger (ed.), *Faut-il croire au merveilleux? Actes du colloque de Metz* (Paris: Les Editions du Cerf, 2003), 133–34; Aidan Nichols, "Adrienne von Speyr and the Mystery of Atonement," *New Blackfriars* 73 (1992): 542–53; Juan M. Sara, "*Descensus ad Inferos*, Dawn of Hope. Aspects of the Theology of Holy Saturday in the Trilogy of Hans Urs von Balthasar," *Communio* 32 (Fall 2005): 541–72; and John R. Sachs, "Current Eschatology: Universal Salvation and the Problem of Hell," *Theological Studies* 52 (1991): 227–54.

248. See Speyr, *Kreuz und Hölle* I, 207.

249. Ibid., 348; see also the commentary of Wilhelm Maas, "Das Geheimnis des Karsamstags," 136. As Marc Ouellet puts it, there is "no speculative Good Friday" nor a "speculative Holy Saturday," precisely because these events point to "a rational hiatus where human logic must die so as to rise up beyond itself" ("The Message of Balthasar's Theology to Modern Theology," 292–93).

250. Speyr, *Das Wort und die Mystik* I, 107. See also Balthasar, "Theologie des Abstiegs zur Hölle," 146; and "General Introduction to the Posthumous Works" in Speyr, *Book of All Saints* I, 13. Cf. Speyr, *Kreuz und Hölle* I, 262, 304, and 332.

251. See Balthasar, *Mysterium Paschale*, 35; and *Theo-Drama* IV, 324. This is not to deny the centrality of the concept of the theology of satisfaction in Balthasar's theology of redemption and thus also Balthasar's downplaying of Aquinas's soteriology as lacking "any inner connection [*jede innere Berührung*] between Jesus and the reality of sin as such," precisely because the Christ of St. Thomas continues to enjoy the beatific vision throughout his suffering (Balthasar, *Theo-Drama* III, 243–44). Bernhard Blankenhorn, meanwhile, calls upon the authority of Jean-Pierre Torrell to point out that Christ's constant beatific vision in via is hardly "a settled teaching of 'the tradition.'" After all, the "scholastic consensus [...] followed a real diversity of patristic positions" (Bernhard Blankenhorn, review of Alyssa Lyra Pitstick's *Light in Darkness*, in *Nova et Vetera* [English Edition], 6 [2008]: 954). Cf. Jean-Pierre Torrell, *Le Christ en ses mystères. La vie et l'œuvre de Jésus selon saint Thomas d'Aquin*, I (Paris: Desclée, 1999), 135–42; and "Saint Thomas d'Aquin et la science du Christ. Une relecture des questions 9–12 de la 'Tertia Pars' de la 'Somme Théologie,'" in his *Recherches thomasiennes* (Paris: Vrin, 2000), 198–213.

Jesus proclaims himself with his teaching, he is essentially "handed over" (*traditus*) in it; without conditions and without reservations [...]. The indissoluble connection between word and act of suffering thus points back at every moment to one who commissions [...]. He never speaks of his self-surrender in tones of ecstatic eros, but rather uses almost deadpan words that point to his obedience: without ever denying his own responsibility, he refers all the initiative and the ultimate responsibility (and therefore the glory of this consummate plan) back to the Father. Obediently identifying himself with his mission, he himself is his mission in person, and therefore, in his kenosis as the "servant of God," he becomes the manifestation of God's eternal love for the world."[252]

This kenotic attitude of Christ, which is "paradigmatic" of the creature's rightful attitude before his Creator, is, Balthasar explains, more profoundly still "the radiant paradigm of divine love itself," for "precisely in—and *only* in—the kenosis of Christ, the *inner* mystery of God's love comes to light, the mystery of the God who 'is love' (1 Jn 4:8) in himself and therefore is 'triune.'"[253] Hence, the entire kenotic existence of the incarnate Son of God is for Balthasar, not unlike Adrienne, a revelation of the immanent Trinity.[254] "Not only is it true that God appears *only* in man (as the Wholly Other), but he moreover appears in that dimension of man that is most dissimilar to God. But the sign of contradiction that covers this mystery like a veil is in fact a contradiction only for man in his natural and sinful reason, not for God; and if God in his sovereign freedom chooses this sign as his mode of expression, there can be none more adequate—for him, it is no 'paradox.'"[255]

This does not mean, then—as Pitstick seems to imply and Balthasar openly refutes—"that God's essence becomes itself (univocally) 'kenotic,' such that a single concept could include both the divine foundation of the possibility of Kenosis, and the Kenosis itself."[256] Rather, "the exteriorsation of God (in the Incarnation) has," as the Swiss theologian explains, "its ontic condition

---

252. Balthasar, *Love Alone Is Credible*, 85–86.

253. Ibid., 87; see also *Theo-Drama* IV, 324; *Theo-Logic* II, 352–55; and Healy, *The Eschatology of Hans Urs von Balthasar*, 107.

254. See Balthasar, *The Glory of the Lord* VII, 248–49; and *Prayer*, 193. Cf. Speyr, *Das Wort und die Mystik* II, 106 and 108; *John* II, 71; *Korinther* I, 53; and *The Countenance of the Father*, 60. Cf. The International Theological Commission, "Theology, Christology, Anthropology" (1981), in its *Texts and Documents, 1969–1985* (San Francisco: Ignatius Press, 1989), 212. Even the descent into hell is described by Balthasar and Adrienne in terms of divine love: "Nowhere," writes Balthasar of Adrienne's teaching, "is the difference of the divine persons more evident than in hell, but also nowhere is the unity of the divine love more visible during the Son's terrestrial life than in this final work of redemption, which the inseparable [*unzertrennliche*] Trinitarian God realized" (Balthasar, "Theologie des Abstiegs zur Hölle," 146); see also *Explorations in Theology* III, 410; "Vorwort des Herausgebers" in Speyr, *Das Wort und die Mystik* I, 12; *Epilogue*, 90–91; and Oakes, *Pattern of Redemption*, 269.

255. Balthasar, *Love Alone Is Credible*, 87.

256. Balthasar, *Mysterium Paschale*, 29.

of possibility in the eternal exteriorisation of God—that is, in his tripersonal self-gift."[257] And it is precisely this that is revealed—to repeat—in the obedient love of the incarnate Son: "[On] the far side of the boundaries of earthly existence, Jesus' authority and poverty, but also his self-abandonment, exist no more, but are comprised within his obedience; but this is possible only if the whole structure of his being and his time is built upon the foundation of the free act of obedience [i.e., the filial surrender] that is his kenosis."[258] The divine *commercium* of salvation is thus regarded by both the theologian and the mystic who inspired him as "firmly based on [...] *the Son's self-surrender, insofar as the latter is the 'economic' representation of the Father's Trinitarian, loving self-surrender.*"[259] Only as such is this surrender a source of transcendence for all of humankind. Indeed, the obedient Son returns "to God with the whole human 'accomplishment,' and the human accomplishment is precisely the 'complete faith,' pure obedience."[260]

From this perspective, even the Eucharist is presented as a sort of "descriptive summary," as Adrienne puts it, "of the whole being-there [*Dasein*] of the incarnate God," whereby it is also a description of "the Triune God's manner of being-there [*Daseinsweise*]: namely, so to be, that this being—in its very foundation—is the always-there of the ever-now occurring *ascent* [*Aufgang*]"—not *descent*—"of Trinitarian love."[261] More fundamental than the Son's surrender of his bodily gift of himself in the Eucharist is thus the "Trinitarian Eucharist of the divine Persons," by which Adrienne addresses the mystery of "their going-into-one-another," which in turn "presupposes their mutual, fully realized disclosure."[262] Hence, Christ's union with the Church by means of his Eucharistic surrender is effected "within the mystery of his being one with the Father and the Holy Spirit."[263] Taking up this Speyrian insight as his own, Balthasar reasons that in the Eucharist is revealed "the innermost law of triune love" in virtue of which "every Hypostasis in its 'decline,' causes the Other to '*arise*.'"[264] Descent (and thus *kenosis*) never has the final word.

---

257. Ibid., 28; see also *Epilogue*, 93.
258. Balthasar, *The Glory of the Lord* VII, 231; see also *Theo-Drama* V, 517.
259. Balthasar, *Theo-Drama* IV, 332.
260. Balthasar, *Convergences*, 91.
261. Speyr, *Das Wort und die Mystik* II, 101; emphasis added.
262. Ibid., 524.
263. Speyr, *The Letter to the Ephesians*, 241.
264. Balthasar, *Theo-Drama* V, 477–78; emphasis added.

The Grounding of the Analogy between Creator and Creature: The "Distance" Implied in Surrender

It is precisely this manner of placing God's self-surrender "in God himself"—of even recognizing this surrender as *expressing*[265] the "very essence"[266] of the Godhead—which avoids, Balthasar argues, "the 'perilous' idea that God is somehow dependent upon the world for his self-revelation." On the other hand, "this becomes real *as* love only when the act of divine surrender simultaneously calls forth one who receives himself in this surrender and replies to it, necessarily, as one who receives [*Empfangenhabender*]."[267]

"This mutuality of surrender, in which all other acts of surrender find meaning, is in God absolute surrender as such: this mutuality is the proper product of the divine process of giving and receiving: the Spirit of love, the quintessence, as it were, of God."[268] Or, to put it in other words, the "counterpart" of the Father's active self-giving "in the Son (and in the Spirit vis-à-vis Father and Son) is a letting be that is just as eternal as the act by which he is brought forth; it is implicit in this act." Balthasar even goes so far as to admit—in a bold insight gained from Adrienne—that the "'passive *actio*' is a condition of the 'active *actio*' and imparts to the latter a certain quality of 'letting go.' Thus the Father causes the Son to be, to 'go'; but this also means that the Father 'lets go' of him, lets him go free."[269]

This idea of allowing him to "go free" does not, it bears repeating, mean that the begotten Son is given a will of his own—a will, that is to say, that would be in contradistinction to the Father's will—for Balthasar follows Adrienne in speaking analogically (even metaphorically), as is apparent in what follows: "So too, in the act of begetting, a man causes his seed to go on its way while he himself retires into the background."[270] Or, to put this same

---

265. The verb "expressing" is significant in this context, for Balthasar does *not* maintain that surrender is itself the essence of the Godhead (as Pitstick maintains in *Light in Darkness*, 287 and 290–91), but rather a revelation thereof. Balthasar's intention, I have argued throughout these pages, is precisely to demonstrate that we cannot separate the divine essence from the divine relations.

266. Balthasar, *Explorations in Theology* IV, 35.

267. Ibid. The official translation reads: "as one whose essence is to *receive* being," which I judge imprudent in the context. That is to say, it risks conveying the idea that Balthasar confuses the divine essence, common to the three divine persons, and the persons themselves who are distinguished uniquely by their relations to one another. This possible misunderstanding is in no way apparent in the original German text: "*der Akt der göttlichen Hingabe zugleich den hervorbringt, der sich in dieser Hingabe empfängt und sie deshalb, als Empfangenhabender, auch notwendig erwidert*" (*Skizzen zur Theologie* IV: Pneuma und Institution [Einsiedeln: Johannes Verlag, 1974], 32).

268. Ibid.; see also *Theo-Drama* IV, 324; and *Theo-Drama* V, 87, where ample reference is made to Adrienne.

269. Balthasar, *Theo-Drama* V, 86.

270. Ibid. A similar reading is found in Adrienne's *World of Prayer*, to cite just one of her works,

insight more straightforwardly, "the divine hypostases know and interpenetrate each other to the very same degree that each of them opens up to the other in absolute freedom [that, is to say, absolutely: without any form of limitation]."²⁷¹ Balthasar concludes: "Each subsists by being *let*-be."²⁷²

From this perspective, Emmanuel Durand—although opposing Balthasar's notion of a paternal *kenosis*—argues for the validity of Balthasar's language of hierarchical "distance,"²⁷³ borrowed, as is now evident, from Adrienne—for describing the distinction of the divine persons, the opening of the Trinity to the world, and "the intra-trinitarian possibility of salvation." Balthasar's merit consists, Durand argues, in conceiving of the relation between otherness and communion "in a manner open to the world."²⁷⁴ Without recourse to the idea of *kenosis* in God, Durand suggests that we might nonetheless retain the "salvific value" of Christ's obedience and abandonment *to* (and not *from*) the Father, whose "intra-divine archetype" exists not in the form of the Son's *kenosis*, but as his eternal reception of, or consent to, his own generation by the Father; whence our return to the still more fundamental concept (from my perspective) of surrender.²⁷⁵ Indeed, Balthasar explains the significance of the former term (distance) as "materially identical with the 'kenosis' mentioned in the Philippians hymn" but as presupposing "an explicit Trinitarian thinking," which "merits a terminology that makes this distinction plain."²⁷⁶

Here, spanning the gulf of the Divine Persons' total distinctness, we have a correspondence between the Father's self-giving, expressed in generation, and the Son's thanksgiving and readiness (a readiness that goes to the limit of forgiveness). It is a profound mystery of faith. Thus the absolute is manifest as 'We' in the identity of the

---

although Balthasar also makes reference to Speyr, *The Letter to the Ephesians*, 21, and *Die katholischen Briefe* II, 238.

271. Balthasar, *Theo-Drama* II, 259. In response to the objection of Alyssa Pitstick, who argues with regard to this passage that the "Trinitarian perichoresis is limited precisely to the extent to which surprise exists among the divine Persons" (*Light in Darkness*, 283), it is obvious that Balthasar's intention here is to highlight the absolutely unlimited, or infinite, surrender of each of the divine persons to the others, in virtue of which each Person's surrender is also fully received.

272. Balthasar, *Theo-Drama* II, 259.

273. "In God no spatial separation is possible or necessary. It is replaced by the hierarchical distance of the processions" (Speyr, *World of Prayer*, 66). Cf. Balthasar, *Theo-Drama* V, 88.

274. Emmanuel Durand, "L'image créée et sa destination trinitaire. Discernement sur les fondements de l'eschatologie chez Balthasar," *Transversalités* 104 (2007): 239. Cf. Speyr, *Light and Images*, 23. On the other hand, Durand points to a certain risk associated with the image of "distance": namely, that of conceiving of the mystery of salvation in terms of "a kind of fundamental Trinitarian automatism" or as a "geometrical miracle" in which "the (created) distance always remains included in a given (divine) space" (Durand, "L'image créée et sa destination trinitaire," 243). On the question of the use of image and metaphor in theology, see my general conclusion to this volume.

275. Durand, "L'image créée et sa destination trinitaire," 241.

276. Balthasar, *The Glory of the Lord* VII, 249n5.

gift-as-given and the gift-as-received in thanksgiving, which can only be such by attesting, maintaining and fuelling the infinite distinction between Father and Son.[277]

It follows that for all its "novelty,"[278] Balthasar's presentation—so greatly influenced by Adrienne's insights—of the perfect correspondence between the Father's begetting act and the Son's receiving of the whole divinity of and from the Father, as viewed from the perspective of the terrestrial Son, need not, as Durand seems to agree, "separate" us from this tradition.[279] It is, in fact, these notions of reciprocity and exchange in the Trinity which found, for both the theologian and the mystic, their presentation of the world—in light of the Incarnation—as an *imago Trinitatis*: "the creaturely 'other-than-God' is plunged into the uncreated 'Other-in-God' *while maintaining* that fundamental 'distance' [or otherness] which alone makes love possible."[280] Echoing, as it were, in virtue of these metaphorical images a fundamental insight of the Second Vatican Council according to which there exists "a certain likeness [*aliquam similitudinem*]" between the divine persons, who are revealed in Christ's priestly prayer (cf. Jn 17:21–22) as existing within a circumincession, and human beings who are realized as such "through a sincere gift of himself,"[281] Balthasar argues that "we cannot conceive of a person as otherwise than holding himself within himself in order to give himself."[282]

Of course, one might object that Balthasar (not unlike Pope John Paul II)[283] fails, in the context of this insight, to respect the distinction between the divine persons, who are unique in that they exist as substantial relations, and human persons, whose relationality—as Gilles Emery points out in reference to the development of the Christological doctrines—is a characteristic of their rational nature rather than their personhood.[284] It is in virtue

---

277. Balthasar, *Theo-Drama* IV, 326.
278. Without acknowledging Balthasar's indebtedness to Adrienne's mystical insights, Durand presents Balthasar's theology as having "recourse to the secondary resources of the imagination" ("L'image créée et sa destination trinitaire," 242) and as fashioned "of images, audacities and novelties" (245).
279. Similarly, Adrian J. Walker argues that Adrienne's account of the relationship between the Father and the Son "clearly [...] re-states, and attempts to develop in terms of 'gift,' the classical theology of the Son's consubstantiality with his paternal source" ("The Gift of Simplicity: Reflections on Obedience in the Work of Adrienne von Speyr," *Communio* 34 [2007]: 575).
280. Balthasar, *Theo-Drama* V, 105; cf. *The Glory of the Lord* VII, 409; *Explorations in Theology* II, 191; and *Theo-Logic* II, 315; and Speyr, *John* II, 166 and 292.
281. Second Vatican Council, *Gaudium et Spes*, no. 24 (DZ 4324).
282. Balthasar, *New Elucidations*, 119; cf. *Elucidations*, 92–93; *Credo*, 30–31; and *Mysterium Pachale*, 28.
283. In the form of a commentary on the important passage from *Gaudium et Spes*, cited above (no. 24, paragraph 3), he explains that this creature "is thus a person. Being a person means striving towards self-realization (the Council text speaks of self-discovery), which can only be achieved 'through a sincere gift of self'" (Pope John Paul II, *Mulieris Dignitatem*, no. 7).
284. Cf. Thomas Aquinas, *ST* I, q. 1, a. 39, a. 1, ad. 1.

of their personhood that they are said to subsist "in themselves" and not in another.[285] On the other hand, the Swiss theologian continually insists that "the great 'similarity' between God and the creature [...] does not abolish the greater dissimilarity," which in this case "consists in the fact that the created persons remain individual substances, each of which is an image and likeness of the Absolute Substance."[286]

It is, furthermore, with good reason that Balthasar argues, by way of analogy based upon the Incarnation, that "Christ does not alienate man from himself when he raises him from the apparently closed substantiality of his personal being (in which he thinks that he definitively stands over against God) into the open relatedness of the life within the Godhead." On the contrary, the human person is thus brought into "the genuine truth of his origin" in virtue of which he or she is "a distant image of this [*imago trinitatis*] in the love between human persons."[287] In pointing to the image of the Trinity in the communion of human persons as "distant," moreover, Balthasar reminds us once again—in terms borrowed from the Fourth Lateran Council—that we must respect the ever-greater difference between the Creator and his creation and thus also between the "unity of identity of nature," characterizing the divine persons, and the "union of charity in grace," characterizing human persons.[288]

When, however, this difference is both acknowledged and respected, we do well, as Emmanuel Durand pointed out above, to highlight the important likeness between the divine persons, who live always in what Adrienne calls "perfect, self-surpassing correspondence,"[289] and the mystery of our incorporation into the divine life by means of a graced reception thereof: our

---

285. See Gilles Emery, "La Trinité, le Christ et l'homme: Théologie et métaphysique de la personne," in François-Xavier Putallaz and Bernard N. Schumacher, *L'humain et la personne* (Paris: Cerf, 2008), 175–93; "The Dignity of Being a Substance: Person, Subsistence, and Nature," *Nova et Vetera* (English Edition) 9, no. 4 (2011): 991–1001; *The Trinity: An Introduction to Catholic Doctrine on the Triune God*, 109–10; "Personne humaine et relation: la personne se définit-elle par la relation?" *Nova et Vetera* 87, no. 1 (2014): 7–29; Matthew Levering, "Essence, Persons, and the Question of Trinitarian Metaphysics," in his *Scripture and Metaphysics*, 197–235; Narcisse, "Participer à la vie trinitaire," 120 and 124; Papanikalaou, "Person, *Kenosis* and Abuse," 42; and Harriet A. Harris, "Should We Say that Personhood is Relational?", *Scottish Journal of Theology* 51 (1998): 214–34. As differing from the analysis of these other authors, Harris's argumentation is based upon philosophical—especially ethical—difficulties posed by a relational understanding of personhood. Meanwhile, Balthasar, who is not ignorant of this distinction (see his *Theo-Logic* II, 130), argues that Boethius's definition of person—"*persona est naturae rationalis individua substantia*" (PL 64:1343; *Traités théologiques*, 74)—is "extremely difficult" to apply to God. See Balthasar, "On the Concept of Person," 22; and *Theo-Drama* V, 76.

286. Balthasar, *Theo-Drama* II, 416.

287. Balthasar, *The Glory of the Lord* VII, 409; see also 400. Cf. Speyr, *Die Schöpfung*, 11.

288. DZ 806.

289. Speyr, *World of Prayer*, 35. Similarly, Balthasar—quoting Adrienne—argues: "'The divine processions occur in eternal simultaneity,' so that the Father's very act of begetting 'is an act of surrender to the Son, to which the Son replies with his surrender'" (*Theo-Drama* V, 87). Cf. Speyr, *World of Prayer*,

participation in the Son's own perfect receptivity.[290] Indeed, it is precisely in the act of self-surrender that the human person is said by Balthasar, in union with Adrienne, not only to be most like the divine persons, but also to be actually incorporated into their divine life by the reception of grace that grace itself prepares and accomplishes.[291] It is thus not surprising that we might conclude with Aquinas that "to be the image of God by imitation of the Divine Nature does not exclude being to the same image by the representation of the Divine Persons: but rather one follows from the other."[292]

Of course, only the divine archetype "can fully achieve this identity between reception of one's being and adoring assent to the Father, between being and the act in which the whole of one's being is lovingly received," Balthasar explains. "This is what is meant by being 'from above' (Jn 3:31)." By grace, however, Balthasar acknowledges, human persons "may participate in this Trinitarian love and surrender."[293] This, he suggests, is what it means to an image (*eidos*) of God, for it is that which enables us to be "stretched to the measure of the transcendent Head."[294] An image of God is "something which is to know God, respond to him in freedom, and welcome him with love."[295]

In short, the analogy between human and divine persons is expanded by Balthasar and Adrienne in such a way that the divine life by grace is understood as a participation in the mutual indwelling of the Trinity: a share in the Son's love for the Father and the Father's love for the Son in their common Spirit of love.[296] Or, to put it in biblical terms, this participation—"That they

---

213 and 245. Pertinent in this regard are the insights of Norris Clark: "The higher we go [up the scale of life], the more receiving, as well as giving, becomes an integral part of the very perfection—not imperfection—of our love relations. The balance becomes more perfect and equal as we approach slowly ... the perfectly balanced status in God" (Norris Clarke, "Response to Long," *The Thomist* 61 [1997]: 620).

290. Such, for example, is the argument of the International Theological Commission, *Communion and Stewardship: Human Persons Created in the Image of God* (2002), no. 53, in *International Theological Commission. Texts and Documents*, Volume II: 1986–2007 (San Francisco: Ignatius Press, 2009), 336. See also chapter three for an exposition of this theme in the works of Adrienne and Balthasar.

291. See for example Balthasar, *The Glory of the Lord* VII, 400; *Theo-Drama* II, 258–59; *Theo-Drama* V, 89; and *Explorations in Theology* IV, 203 and 341.

292. Thomas Aquinas, *ST* I, q. 93, a. 5. He concludes in the same article: "We must, therefore, say that in man there exists the image of God, both as regards the Divine Nature and as regards the Trinity of Persons; for also in God Himself there is one Nature in Three Persons."

293. Balthasar, *A Theology of History*, 32–33; see also *Elucidations*, 64. This participation in Christ's receptivity is particularly apparent in the doctrine of the Immaculate Conception of Mary, in virtue of which Balthasar speaks of her "pre-redeemed consent" (Balthasar, *The Glory of the Lord* VII, 94); see also *You Crown the Year with Your Goodness*, 264–69; and *First Glance at Adrienne von Speyr*, 51. Cf. Speyr, *The Cross: Word and Sacrament*, 33–34. It is not surprising, then, that Mary is presented as "the prototype who fulfills [...] the relationship between finite and infinite freedom" (Balthasar, *Theo-Drama* III, 299).

294. Balthasar, *Elucidations*, 118; see also *The Glory of the Lord* VII, 400 and 409.

295. Balthasar, *The Glory of the Lord* VI, 87.

296. See Balthasar, *The Threefold Garland*, 30; *Convergences*, 93; and Speyr, *World of Prayer*, 47–48.

may be one in us as we also are one" (Jn 17:22)—is accomplished by way of the mutual indwelling of the Christian and Christ, who is always one with the Father and the Spirit: "I in them and you in me" (Jn 17:23). This means, in the final analysis, that the Spirit, whom Adrienne presents as taking over and continuing the Son's mission in the Church,[297] also "takes over" in the Christian, "works in him, transforms him, so that he is no longer aware of himself. Nor does he need such awareness because he is allowed to belong to the Lord in the same way that the Lord belongs to the Father in an analogy that God alone can analyze."[298] In the final analysis, the human being is thus realized more in God than in him- or herself.[299]

297. See Speyr, *The Boundless God*, 43; and Balthasar, *Theo-Logic* III, 271.
298. Speyr, *The Victory of Love*, 36. "For the Spirit, by giving us this gift to be our very own, achieves a free will acceptance of it (*voluntaria susceptio*) and hence an appropriate response" (Balthasar, *Theo-Drama* V, 478).
299. Cf. Speyr, *Die Schöpfung*, 67.

GENERAL CONCLUSION

Difference-in-Unity

*An Invitation to Dialogue in the
Spirit of Catholicism*

Analogical and Katalogical Reasoning:
Balthasar and St. Thomas

Despite Adrienne's telling phrase which concluded our last chapter—that the Christian's relationship to Christ is comparable to the latter's relationship to the Father "in an analogy that God alone can analyze"[1]—neither the mystic of Basel nor the theologian who directed her would discourage us from analyzing the important likeness between the divine life of the triune God and the graced participation of human persons therein. Balthasar nonetheless invites us to heed what he considers an important warning: that analogy is misused when God's revelation "with its own form" is simply subjugated and subordinated "to the laws not only of metaphysics and of private, social, and sociological ethics but also of this-worldly aesthetics."[2]

By this admonition, the Swiss theologian points us in turn toward one of his most fundamental convictions: that this likeness is mediated both ontologically and epistemologically by Jesus Christ, true God and true man. Hence, "the 'analogy' that occurs as event in *Verbum-Caro* becomes the measure of every other analogy, whether philosophical or theological."[3] This, of course, does not mean—as we argued in chapter seven—that the distance between the divine and human in Christ is somehow leveled. Rather, as Balthasar explains: "What *does* remain within the Christological analogy is the original, always infinite, distance between God and the creature, which

---

1. Speyr, *The Victory of Love*, 36.
2. Balthasar, *The Glory of the Lord* I, 37; see also *The Glory of the Lord* V, 656.
3. Balthasar, *Theo-Logic* II, 314; see also *Theo-Logic* I, 232.

the creature can never measure and so cannot bridge in the form of analogy, but which nevertheless—and this is the other side of the question—endures only within the recapitulation of the creation in Christ and, therefore, is not nullified; rather, it is *transfigured* into the infinite distance between the divine Persons in the identity of the divine nature."[4]

Proceeding from the fundamental insight that the "measure of worldly being, considered as a whole, lies in God," Balthasar thus invites the human creature to give over "its own measure [namely its own knowledge and will] to God," so as to thereby "correspond to the measure meted out to it by God's knowledge and will."[5] Hence, "the correct attitude" implied by this relationship of analogy, as it is recognized by the Swiss theologian, is that of allowing God to make use of oneself as "an instrument for his purposes" by way of a "deathlike" surrender in virtue of which one is, ironically, "most alive."[6]

This, in fact, is precisely how finite freedom "can be," as Balthasar sees it, "the 'image' of infinite freedom."[7] "Infinite freedom provides it with law [*Gesetz*] and instruction [*Weisung*], not imposed externally but inscribed internally."[8] Finite freedom cannot therefore simply "set off in just any direction," as Balthasar sees it. Rather, it "must pursue the path of self-realization," that is to say, the path "toward absolute freedom. Its coming forth (*egressus*) from its origin is the beginning of its return (*regressus*) there."[9]

This return, we have seen throughout this volume, is presented by Balthasar in terms (borrowed from Adrienne, as goes my thesis) of *surrender*. Likewise, it is the concept of surrender that unifies—by holding in a positive "tension"—each of the differences that we have investigated in this volume: nature and grace (or person and mission), body and spirit, individual and community, man and woman. In fact, all of created being is understood by Balthasar, with reference to this important concept, as directed beyond itself, so as to simultaneously exist in itself and proceed out of itself. As such, it is intrinsically self-showing (beautiful), self-bestowing (good), and self-expressive (true).

Because, moreover, Balthasar recognizes the self-showing, self-bestowing, and self-expressive character of worldly being as arising not out of need but as belonging "to their essential ontological perfection," he simultaneously rec-

---

4. Ibid.; cf. Speyr, *John* II, 79.

5. Balthasar, *Theo-Logic* I, 244; see also *The Christian State of Life*, 82. Herein we might recognize the truth of Joseph Palakeel's claim that Balthasar's understanding of analogy assumes a mediating role between Przywara's *analogia entis* and Barth's *analogia fidei*; see Palakeel, *The Use of Analogy in Theological Discourse*, 119.

6. Balthasar, *Theo-Logic* I, 237.   7. Balthasar, *Theo-Drama* II, 237.
8. Ibid., 285; see also *Epilogue*, 76.   9. Balthasar, *Theo-Drama* II, 290.

ognizes these qualities as having their "archetype in divine Being."[10] Hence, "what seems to be structured as a polarity in the world could be established in thought as identical in God."[11]

Here 'To Be,' as perfect self-expression and as self-surrender within the identity, will be the personal difference of Father and Son, a difference that must, as love, have its fruitfulness as Holy Spirit. 'Son' is therefore at the same time 'Word' (as self-expression). He is 'expression' (as the One who shows himself). He is also, and equally, 'child' (the One lovingly begotten). And this personal difference must be overtaken in the personal unity of the different Persons, a unity that does not abolish these differences but rather unites them in the unity of the fruitfulness transcending the differences.[12]

From this perspective of the circuminsession of the transcendentals, which David C. Schindler presents as the "fundamental ordering principle"[13] of Balthasar's thought, there can be no question of his choosing between the *De Deo uno* and the *De Deo trino*. In fact, unity "is in a sense the transcendence that makes the circumincession of the three possible," Schindler reasons, "and this is why it cannot be simply included among them. It is the most hidden in Balthasar's work, one might say, because it is in a sense the deepest."[14]

Such is also—indeed foremost and primarily—the profoundly unified vision of St. Thomas Aquinas, as he is read by Gilles Emery:

The wholly original concept of *transcendental multitude* (a concept that is truly nonsensical for a strict neo-Platonist) expresses, through Aquinas's pen, a radical Christian novelty in understanding the relations between the One and the Many. The introduction of the multitude (*multitudo*) among the transcendentals clearly comes as the expression of the eminent status of the *plurality* that the Christian faith recognizes in God. In the sweep of this thesis Aquinas can express the eminently positive status of created plurality: Intra-Trinitarian relation (distinction) is the cause, the reason, and the exemplar of distinction in creatures. The Trinitarian distinction is, for Aquinas, the cause not only of the distinction of creation (distinction between God and the world), but also of the plurality of creatures: "Relation in God surpasses in causality what in creatures is the principle of distinction; for it is through the procession of distinct divine persons that the whole process of creatures as well as the multiplication of creatures is caused" [1 Sent d. 26, q. 2, a. 2, ad. 2]. With Thomas Aquinas, medieval thought bears witness to an astounding effort to promote plurality on the metaphysical plane, to wed Trinitarian theology to creation theology: Plurality re-

---

10. Balthasar, *Epilogue*, 85; see also *The Glory of the Lord* IV, 374; and *My Work*, 115–18. Cf. Thomas Aquinas, *ST* I, q. 13, a. 3.
11. Balthasar, *Epilogue*, 92; see also *Theo-Logic* II, 178. Cf. Thomas Aquinas, *ST* I, q. 13, a. 4.
12. Balthasar, *Epilogue*, 85–86.
13. Schindler, *Hans Urs von Balthasar and the Dynamic Structure of Truth*, 368.
14. Ibid., 369; cf. Balthasar, *My Work*, 115–17.

ceives the eminent status of a transcendental, while Trinitarian relation exercises a creative causality that establishes created plurality and confers on it the value of an expression of the Trinitarian mystery.[15]

This simultaneity of the one and the many, which Emery insists is essential to the perspective of St. Thomas despite Karl Rahner's celebrated claim to the contrary,[16] is a mystery that is echoed, as it were, in the works of Adrienne and Balthasar in terms of unity-in-difference or difference-in-unity. As such, it is a mystery that marks both the Trinity and creation, so as to serve the analogy between them.[17] It is not surprising, then, that this key notion of unity-in-difference also describes the mystery of our incorporation into the Godhead, with the result that our supernatural elevation must in no way be perceived as the obliteration of our otherness or difference with respect to God.[18]

Indeed, Balthasar presents the perfection of the creature's own truth (and thus also its proper goodness and beauty) as lying within the all-encompassing truth of God: the divine *Logos*, who is also the archetype of all creation.

Because the archetype in God, that is, the higher reality into which the creature is elevated and that counts as its definitive truth before God, is a progeny of love, the creature knows that it is *kept safe* in this archetype. To be sure, it has an existence and an essence in itself, and this existence and essence is a reality in and for itself that is not identical with God; but even this reality of its own is something that it has inside of God. It has this reality only insofar as it is in God, is generated by him, and is protected and embraced by his all-encompassing essence. There is no way that it can consider and understand itself outside of God. [...] It cannot even think independently of the thought with which God thinks it. The thought of the image is measured by the thought of the archetype, the first passes continuously into the second. [...] Only when the creature looks at itself does the tension in its being between its total contingency and the eternal archetype that is its idea seem to exceed all measure. In looking to God, it opens its relativity to the absolute in the primordial attitude of abandonment [*Hingabe-surrender*].[19]

---

15. Emery, *Trinity in Aquinas*, 31; cf. Balthasar, *Theo-Logic* II, 173–86. On the role of the transcendentals in the thought of St. Thomas, see also the important work of Jan Aertsen, *Medieval Philosophy and the Transcendentals: The Case of Thomas Aquinas* (Leiden: Brill, 1996).

16. See Karl Rahner, "Remarks on the Dogmatic Treatise 'De Trinitate'" in his *Theological Investigations* IV, trans. Joseph Donceel (New York: Crossroad, 1998), 79–102, esp. 83–84. Gilles Emery masterfully defends Aquinas against this charge in his "Essentialism or Personalism in the Treatise on God in St. Thomas Aquinas."

17. "If there is an insurmountable distance between God and his creature, but if there is also an analogy between them that cannot be resolved in any form of identity, there must also exist an analogy between the transcendentals—between those of the creature and those in God" (Balthasar, *My Work*, 115).

18. See Balthasar, *Theo-Drama* V, 83; *Theo-Logic* II; 180–81; *Theo-Drama* III, 340; and *Epilogue*, 35. Such is also the profound conviction of St. Thomas. See Williams, "Mystical Theology Redux," 60; and Emery, *Trinity, Church, and the Human Person*, 151.

19. Balthasar, *Theo-Logic* I, 266–67; see also *Theo-Drama* III, 222 and 261. Cf. Speyr, *Light and Images*, 152–53.

With this insight, we are obviously not far from the exemplar causality of the divine Word in the theology of St. Thomas, as we saw in chapter one. Nor are we far from the profound unity of ontological and analogical discourse in Aquinas's thought, as we likewise saw in chapter one, and which Fran O'Rourke further summarizes in the following terms:

> God is present in all things not according to his essence but through a participation of his created likeness. Through creation, God 'transfuses' into beings a likeness to himself. [...] Diffusion, similitude, participation—these notions are integral to a proper understanding of creation and the relation of creatures to God: their total presence within God, God's infinite intimacy within them; their utter separation and his infinite transcendence. Diffusion leaves God untouched in his nature; it safeguards the divine presence within beings without entering into relation with creatures. Creatures participate in God's presence but God is not participated. Beings share in the similitude of God while God in no manner resembles them.[20]

Of course, this reading of St. Thomas presupposes—as O'Rourke is eager to acknowledge, along with Balthasar—that his Neo-Platonism is not overshadowed by his Aristotelianism, with the result that we might consider the creature's perfection according to what Georges Cottier presents as a "double reference": that of its proper, or specific, perfection, on the one hand, and that of its "participated, transcendental perfection," on the other hand.[21] The latter is qualified by Gregory P. Rocca as "a kind of shorthand" for Aquinas's "Christian outlook on how God is the cause and goal of the hierarchical structure and order of the universe."[22] Because, St. Thomas reasons, "every creature intends to acquire its own perfection, which is the likeness of the

---

20. O'Rourke, *Pseudo-Dionysius and the Metaphysics of Aquinas*, 258. O'Rourke concludes: "Beings do not share in divine essence but in the illuminative effusion of divine Being which emanates from him" (257). Cf. Thomas Aquinas, *ST* I, q. 9, a. 1, ad. 2; q. 104, a. 1; and *Comp* I, 124. See also Rocca, *Speaking the Incomprehensible God*, 284 and 286; and Stephen L. Brock, "Harmonizing Plato and Aristotle on *Esse*: Thomas Aquinas and the *De hebdomadibus*," *Nova et Vetera* (English edition) 5, no. 3 (2007): 465–94, esp. 480.

21. Cottier, *Le désir de Dieu*, 213–14. See also Rocca, *Speaking the Incomprehensible God*, 286. As we saw in chapter three, Aquinas also understands human happiness from two perspectives; cf. *ST* I-II, q. 5, a. 5; q. 62, a. 1; and *Comp* I, 109. O'Rourke holds that the perspectives of Plato and Aristotle complement each other: "communication of act and diffusion of goodness; goodness gives of itself and act is expansive. Aquinas is able to synthesize the Aristotelian and Platonist theories of causality. Moreover, in *esse*, the duality of Aristotle's principles is overcome: it belongs to act to fulfill itself by actualizing others, and the good is what all things desire: act as expansive or communicative and act as desirable are identical in the act of existing" (O'Rourke, *Pseudo-Dionysius and the Metaphysics of Aquinas*, 248–49). Cf. Balthasar *Theo-Logic* I, 14. As for Louis-Bertrand Geiger, he notes, with reference to Aquinas's *exitus-reditus* schema, that "if one considers the final cause of movement, the movement of return can be joined without difficulty to Aristotle's thought. The same cannot be said for the movement of return which consists for each creatures in realizing itself in conformity with its nature." The reason is that "its nature is none other than the realization of a divine idea: itself participation in the plenitude of the perfection of God." ("L'homme image de Dieu," 131n32).

22. Rocca, *Speaking the Incomprehensible God*, 286.

divine perfection and goodness," it follows that "the divine goodness is the end of all things."[23]

Gilles Emery thus observes that there are "two orders, two relations"[24] in the creature as considered by St. Thomas: "First, an order toward God, and second, an internal ordering of the created universe. Neither one suppresses the other, but the first provides the foundation for the second."[25] Or, as Jan Aertsen beautifully summarizes the profoundly unified perspective of St. Thomas:

> The *same* beings are *per se* (the Aristotelian model of predication) and *per participationem* (the Platonic model). They are real substances and independent natures; and they are the emanation and deficient likenesses of a first, perfect Principle. Between these two viewpoints there is no contradiction, because they are no longer on the same philosophical level. Aristotle's viewpoint applies whenever created beings are considered on a horizontal level, without concern for their relation to the first Being.[26]

Just as Aertsen thus recognizes no contradiction between Thomas's Aristotelianism and his Neo-Platonism, so also Balthasar recognizes no contradiction between what he (short-sightedly)[27] considers Thomas's preference for *ana*logical (bottom-up) reasoning and his own (Balthasar's) preference for *kata*logical (downward) reasoning: "Looking from below upward, as St. Thomas likes to do, we can say the human virtues and habits (*habitus*) are transformed, whereas, looking from above downward, it is more that the divine qualities express themselves in the created spiritual being. It is impossible to squeeze these two ways of viewing the mystery of God's indwelling in the creature into a single comprehensive system."[28] Nor, on the other hand, Balthasar holds, must

---

23. Thomas Aquinas, *ST* I, q. 44, a. 4; cf. q. 103, a. 4.
24. Cf. Thomas Aquinas, cf. *ST* III, q. 6, a. 1, ad. 1.
25. Emery, "Contemporary Questions about God," 804. Emery makes reference here to *De Pot* q. 7, a. 9; *SCG* I, c. 78; *ST* II, q. 103, a. 2; and *Commentary on the Sentences* II, dist. 1, a. 2, a. 3 (*Scriptum super libros Sententiarum*, vols. 1–2, ed. Pierre Mandonnet [Paris: Lethiellieux, 1929]). Emery's summary of St. Thomas reads almost as an echo of what we noted in chapter seven as Balthasar's own "preference for a theological perspective not so much *over and above* a philosophical one, as *under and sustaining* it."
26. Aertsen, *Nature and Creature*, 129.
27. Jean-Pierre Torrell has good reason to argue that St. Thomas is often wrongly accused of neglecting the primacy of the divine gift in his theology of redemption, for example (although the same is said of other aspects of his theology), by focusing upon the ascending mediation of Christ to the detriment of the descending action of the Godhead. To read the *Summa* in this way is, however, Torrell insists, "to commit a monumental error of interpretation," namely that of isolating certain parts of this important work from the whole; see his *Pour nous les hommes et pour notre salut*, 41. The unity of ascending and descending mediation in Thomas's theology is contextualized within his treatment of the Incarnation: "We may consider a twofold order between creatures and God: the first is by reason of creatures being caused by God and depending on Him as on the principle of their being [...]. But the second order is by reason of things being directed to God as to their end" (*ST* III, q. 6, a. 1, ad. 1).
28. Bathasar, *Theo-Logic* III, 234–35; see also *Theo-Logic* I, 14–15.

we think "that there is a gulf separating the descending methods [...] from the ascending ones."[29]

In fact, Marc Ouellet has good reason to argue that Balthasar's own theological point of view "is neither purely ascending [...] nor purely descending." Rather, "it is a perspective of integration beginning with the Covenant concluded in Jesus Christ at the center of the history of the world. It is an integration of nature and grace, an integration of human freedom into divine freedom which leaves the necessary room (the analogy of being) for an autonomous and authentic 'play' of human freedom that is interior to the 'dramatic action' of the divine freedom."[30]

As for the perspective of St. Thomas, not everyone would agree with Balthasar's conviction that he is "more of a philosopher than a theologian":[31] as one who, in Thomas's own words, "considers creatures in themselves and leads us from them to the knowledge of God, the first consideration is about creatures; the last, of God"—as differing from the theologian, who "considers creatures only in their relation to God." In that (second) case, "the consideration of God comes first, that of creatures afterwards."[32] Gilles Emery, for example, clearly regards St. Thomas as a theologian, who "guides us toward a reunion of Christian thought around the central mystery of God considered either in Himself, or insofar as He is the source and end of His creatures."[33]

However, Aquinas's consideration of God as source and end of creation is, as we saw in chapter one, based upon his consideration of God in himself. Hence, "the doctrine of God does not begin by examining the relationship between God and the world, but by studying God in His divine being": an option, Emery adds, which safeguards the divine transcendence.[34] Similarly, Jean-Pierre Torrell observes:

In passing from one part of the *Summa* to another, the theologian does not abandon God as a subject in favor of man. The subject of *sacra doctrina* always remains God. But now he will not be directly considered in himself, nor as the absolute beginning of man and the universe, but rather as its culmination—its end, equally absolute, final—which attracts all things to itself by the radiation of its supreme goodness and raises, in response and in a special ways, the rational creation's free action.[35]

---

29. Balthasar, *Theo-Logic* II, 188.
30. Ouellet, "Foundations of Christian Ethics," 233. Cf. Balthasar, *Theo-Logic* I, 15; *The Theology of Karl Barth*, 197; and Scola, *Hans Urs von Balthasar: A Theological Style*, 86 and 90.
31. Balthasar, *The Glory of the Lord* III, 9.   32. Thomas Aquinas, *SCG* II, c. 4, 5.
33. Cf. Thomas Aquinas, *ST* I, q. 1, a. 7.
34. Emery, "Contemporary Questions about God," 800.
35. Torrell, *Saint Thomas Aquinas* II: *Spiritual Master*, 82.

It is thus not surprising that Torrell presents Aquinas's *Summa* as "theological from one end to the other, and its author [Thomas himself] above all a theologian, who makes use of philosophical doctrines as needed, but whose authority [that of philosophy] he recognizes as 'extrinsic and merely probable.'"[36]

As for Fergus Kerr, although he acknowledges as "the standard understanding of Thomas" that he is "primarily a philosopher,"[37] the Scottish Dominican would persuade us to follow the interpretation of Anna Williams:

> Mostly, in standard approaches, we think of Thomas in the *Summa Theologiae* as laying down the foundations ('God exists'), proceeding to build up his great system. The simple move that shapes Williams's interpretation is to start, so to speak, from the end. She argues, and no reader could disagree, that the *Summa* situates everything *sub ratione Dei* (ST 1 [q]. 1 [a].7). Everything is focused on God as *principium et finis*. In the end, everything culminates in our 'seeing God as He is' (1 John 3:2)—in the beatific vision (ST 1 [q]. 12). The *Summa*, Williams argues, is concerned above all to spell out the conditions for participation by graced human beings in the life of the blessed Trinity. [...] Thomas's theological project no doubt begins by establishing God's existence but his thinking is thoroughly teleological, indeed eschatological; to paraphrase Williams, the *Summa Theologiae* is a study of the transcendental conditions of beatific vision; not foundationalist apologetics but a set of practices for receiving the gift of beatitude.[38]

In short, as St. Thomas is understood by these Thomists, his emphasis is not only, nor primarily, upon the creature with its natural form and the inclinations which follow therefrom in view of its perfection, but also and most especially upon the Creator in whom every perfection of creation pre-exists in a "more eminent way."[39] Hence, although "we can name God only by taking creatures as our starting point, and in accordance with our limited human ways of knowing and thinking,"[40] Aquinas encourages us to treat all things "under the aspect of God [*sub ratione Dei*],"[41] or from a properly theocentric perspective: one—it bears repeating—in which the creature is studied in terms of his relation to God as his source and end.

Therefore, although St. Thomas acknowledges that our knowledge of the divine perfections proceeds from creatures to God, the perfections themselves proceed, he likewise acknowledges, in the reverse sense.[42] This is why

---

36. Jean-Pierre Torrell, *La Somme de Saint Thomas* (Paris: Cerf, 1998), 171.
37. Kerr, *After Aquinas*, 120.
38. Ibid., 160–61. Cf. Williams, *The Ground of Union*, 41.
39. Thomas Aquinas, *SCG* I, c. 30, 2; cf. *ST* I, q. 49, a. 3; and q. 6, a. 1, ad. 2.
40. *The Catechism of the Catholic Church*, no. 41. Cf. Speyr, *World of Prayer*, 35.
41. Thomas Aquinas, *ST* I, q. 1, a. 7.
42. Cf. ibid., q. 13, a. 6.

the angelic doctor insists upon a strictly one-directional form of analogy between the Creator and his creation: "Although it may be admitted that creatures are in some sort like God, it must nowise be admitted that God is like creatures [...]. For, we say that a statue is like a man, but not conversely."[43]

There is thus good reason to call into question Balthasar's consideration of St. Thomas as founding his doctrine of God upon the knowledge of creatures, rather than vice-versa. In fact, even Balthasar himself calls upon the doctrine of St. Thomas at several occasions to justify his own preference for a theology from on high.[44] As Thomas writes:[45]

The knowledge of the divine persons was necessary [...] for the right idea of creation. The fact of saying that God made all things by His Word excludes the error of those who say that God produced things by necessity. When we say that in Him there is a procession of love, we show that God produced creatures not because He needed them, nor because of any other extrinsic reason, but on account of the love of His own goodness. [...] In another way and chiefly [knowledge of the Trinity is necessary] so that we might think rightly concerning the salvation of the human race, accomplished by the Incarnate Son, and by the gift of the Holy Ghost.

Indeed, and in short, "God's 'transitive acts' (creation, providence, salvation) find their source and explanation," from St. Thomas's point of view, "in His 'immanent acts': God knows Himself and us by one and the same wisdom; God loves Himself and each one of His creatures with one and the same love."[46]

Again, we are not far from Balthasar's presentation of the economic *kenosis* as founded within the intra-divine relations of reciprocal surrender.[47] "The archetype is the *circumincessio* of the divine Hypostases and their total 'being for one another,' but this is always mediated by what, on earth, was the sacrament of *communio*, the surrender of the Son's Body by the Father in the Holy Spirit [...]. This surrender, too, remains an eternal archetype, the economic side of the inner-trinitarian relationships."[48] In the Eucharist is thus united, as Adrienne would have it, the grace of the Father, who gives the Son to the believer, and the grace of the Son, who gives the believer within himself to the Father. Hence the unity of the objective and subjective graces of redemption: the grace "of the giver" and the grace "of being able to give."[49]

43. Ibid., q. 4, a. 3, ad. 4. Cf. Balthasar, *Theo-Drama* III, 222; and *The Theology of Karl Barth*, 197.
44. See Balthasar, *Theo-Logic* II, 186; *Theo-Drama* II, 288; and "Creation and the Trinity," 291.
45. Thomas Aquinas, *ST* I, q. 32, a. 1, ad. 3.
46. Emery, "Contemporary Questions about God," 801. Cf. Thomas Aquinas, cf. *ST* I, q. 37, a. 2; ad. 2 and 3.
47. See for example Balthasar, *Theo-Drama* V, 98; *Explorations in Theology* IV, 138; and *Mysterium Paschale*, 28. Cf. Speyr, *John* II, 188; and *Das Wort und die Mystik* II, 52.
48. Balthasar, *Theo-Drama* V, 483.
49. Speyr, *Das Wort und die Mystik* II, 524.

It is thus also by way of the Eucharist that the believer might gratefully acknowledge his or her being as a gift from the Father and lovingly receive the Eucharist as nourishment from the Son through, in both cases, the Spirit's mediation. As the recipient of both, he or she is a gift of God to God,[50] of each of the divine persons to the others: a gift which so much bears the image of God that the believer, unlike all other earthly beings, is analogically related to divine freedom.

Faith and love, with which hope is conjoined, are to be understood primarily as the expression of the eternal life communicated to man [...]. Love itself is the surrender of one's entire will and being through faith, in the conviction that God merits to be placed first in every respect and is deserving of total surrender; in a trust, too, that in its knowledge surpasses all knowledge. And it is precisely in this infinite surrender and self-renunciation, in this absolute preference of the Thou to the I, that the life of the Trinity consists; for it is a life in which the Persons can be conceived only 'relatively'; that is, through one another.[51]

Thus is mediated within the economy of salvation—from Creator to creature—what is eternally "realized" within the immanent Trinity: "the most profound intimacy in the most absolute distinction."[52]

An Analogy of Reciprocal Surrender: Divine "Enrichment" or Human Fulfillment?

This mediation within the economy of what is eternally realized within the immanent Trinity is the basis of Balthasar's analogy of reciprocal surrender between the triune God and the human creature, such that we might speak of circumincession in the case of the divine persons and of integration in the case of human freedom with respect to divine freedom. Hence, Balthasar reasons, "just as God can be one with the other Divine Persons *in* himself, he is just as capable in his freedom of becoming one with the others outside himself."[53]

"God's will, embracing the entire, infinitely diversified heaven is so generous that it draws into itself all the fullness of redeemed human freedoms, pride of place being given to that of the incarnate Son." It does so, Balthasar specifies, as both the *Alpha*—"the originating will, providing the (analytic) norm for all freedom"—and the *Omega*: "the (synthetic) will": not, to be

---

50. See, for example, Balthasar, *Theo-Drama* II, 262; and *Theo-Drama* V, 507 and 521. Cf. Speyr, *World of Prayer*, 74; *Mary in the Redemption*, 41; and *Light and Images*, 18–19.
51. Balthasar, *Explorations in Theology* I, 168–69.
52. Ouellet, "Adrienne von Speyr et le samedi saint de la théologie," 43.
53. Balthasar, *Epilogue*, 86; see also *Theo-Drama* II, 119; and *The Glory of the Lord* VI, 87.

sure, one "that is the resultant of all the others," as Balthasar's translator would (incorrectly) have it, but rather: one who wills to incorporate all other (created) wills into itself.[54] Indeed, "created freedom can only be perfected within the context of absolute freedom," Balthasar claims in terms that resonate with Thomistic doctrine.[55] As for absolute freedom, it "is identical with love":[56] with, that is to say, the reciprocal surrender of the divine hypostases.

From this perspective, the divine likeness within the human person is anything but static, for the Christian does not image God in the manner that "a finished, discrete copy reflects its prototype." Rather, because the prototype itself exists only within a relationship of dynamic communion, "the 'copy' must continue to be open to the 'prototype'"; there must be a real "sharing between them."[57] This sharing, Angelo Cardinal Scola has good reason to argue, is on the level of freedom.[58] Without granting that divine freedom infringes or otherwise overrides human freedom[59] and thus also "creaturely spontaneity," Balthasar argues that created freedom is in fact oriented "to the Prototype and Origin of all freedom" so as to be assimilated both actively and passively to God's will.[60] Hence—to take it still one step further—it is by way of self-giving surrender, which is the archetypal "law of life" of the Trinity, on the one hand, and the highest act of the spiritual creature, on the other hand, that the latter is willingly integrated into the divine communion, so as also to be analogically related to divine freedom.[61]

It is precisely in this sense, in fact, that Balthasar follows Adrienne in pre-

---

54. Balthasar, *Theo-Drama* V, 486. I thus propose the following translation of the above passage: "it [the divine will] nonetheless also wills to be simultaneously synthetic with respect to all that is given." Cf. *Theodramatik* IV: *Das Endspiel* (Einsiedeln: Johannes Verlag, 1983), 446: "*so will er doch gleichzeitig auch der aus allen sich ergebende synthetische sein.*"

55. Cf. Thomas Aquinas, *ST* I-II, q. 5, a. 5, ad. 1; q. 62, a. 1; and *Comp* 106.

56. Balthasar, *Theo-Logic* III, 240. Similarly, "we should not forget," Balthasar insists, "that, while God can posit the creature as "the other," he himself never becomes "the Other"; he remains *Non Aliud*" (ibid., 235).

57. Balthasar, *Theo-Drama* V, 99; cf. *Theo-Drama* III, 527; *Theo-Logic* I, 237; Schrijver, *Le merveilleux accord*, 55; and Palakeel, *The Use of Analogy in Theological Discourse*, 123.

58. Scola, *The Nuptial Mystery*, 235–36. Cf. Balthasar, *Theo-Drama* II, 123; *Theo-Drama* III, 223; *The Threefold Garland*, 31; *The God Question and Modern Man*, 114; and *Theo-Logic* III, 239–40. In a similar manner, it might be argued from a Thomistic perspective that human freedom acts as a sort of bridge, and thus a continuity, between the so-called natural happiness of the human being and his or her supernatural happiness. See Jean Porter, "Desire for God: Ground of the Moral Life in Aquinas," *Theological Studies* 47 (1986): 48–68.

59. See Balthasar, *Epilogue*, 121; *A Theology of History*, 61; and *Theo-Drama* II, 123.

60. Balthasar, *Theo-Drama* V, 485; see also *Epilogue*, 122; and *My Work*, 114.

61. Speyr, *Korinther* I, 89; cf. Balthasar, *Theo-Drama* V, 89; *Theo-Drama* II, 259; and *Explorations in Theology* I, 168–69. On the integration of the spiritual creature into divine communion by way of surrender, see *Gaudium et Spes*, no. 24 (*DZ* 4324); Balthasar, *Explorations in Theology* IV, 203 and 341; *Theo-Logic* I, 9; *Theo-Drama* II, 259; *Mysterium Paschale*, 28; Speyr, *John* II, 188; and *Das Wort und die Mystik* II, 52.

senting, as we saw already in chapter one, the idea of a "divine 'conversation,'" which from all eternity "envisages the possibility of involving a non-divine world in the Trinity's love."[62]

The whole point of this distinction between the created and the uncreated is that, in it, the glory of God shall fulfill itself "superabundantly" in the freedom of the creature. It follows, then, that the self-fulfilling Word of God, that is his perfect self-giving, must elicit a perfect answer from and in the free creature; absolute freedom must not force or overpower the creature's freedom. In affirming this, we must maintain the whole span of tension: for, on the one hand, the full Word [*Wort*] both presupposes and effects the full answer [*Antwort*]—otherwise it does not really reach man, does not really become "flesh"; and, on the other hand, the presence of perfect self-giving, which is now the definite model of ethical human action, faces man with a far more acute decision than all previous forms of ethics. Only after God has uttered his absolute Yes to man can man utter his absolute No to God: genuine atheism is a post-Christian phenomenon.[63]

Despite his famous call to hope "that all men be saved,"[64] Balthasar's theo-dramatic vision of redemption thus leaves open the door to "tragedy": to an outcome that Balthasar acknowledges as "tragic, not only for man, who can throw away life's meaning and his own salvation, but also"—and this, of course, is where his eschatological account rubs hard against the Thomistic account of the same—"for God himself, who is compelled to judge where he wished to heal; in the extreme case he is compelled to judge precisely because he only wished to bring love to man."[65]

It would thus seem—ironically enough, given my criticism of Balthasar's redemption by substitution in chapter five, which seems to constrict human freedom—that the latter is capable, within Balthasar's *Theo-Drama*, of put-

---

62. Balthasar, *Theo-Drama* V, 509. Cf. Speyr, *World of Prayer*, 76.
63. Balthasar, *Theo-Drama* II, 123; see also *The Threefold Garland*, 30–31.
64. See Balthasar, *Dare We Hope*; see also *Epilogue*, 122–23.
65. Balthasar, *Theo-Drama* V, 193; see also *Love Alone Is Credible*, 91. St. Thomas adds an important clarification to this quandary in his presentation of divine mercy: "Mercy is especially to be attributed to God, as seen in its effect, but not as an affection of passion. In proof of which it must be considered that a person is said to be merciful [*misericors*], as being, so to speak, sorrowful at heart [*miserum cor*]; being affected with sorrow at the misery of another as though it were his own. Hence it follows that he endeavors to dispel the misery of this other, as if it were his; and this is the effect of mercy. To sorrow, therefore, over the misery of others belongs not to God; but it does most properly belong to Him to dispel that misery, whatever be the defect we call by that name. Now defects are not removed, except by the perfection of some kind of goodness: and the primary source of goodness is God" (*ST* I, q. 21, a. 3). Gilles Emery thus has good reason to hold that "God in his merciful activity knows neither pain nor suffering—certainly not because of a lack or a defect, but because of his eminent perfection—and then it is his *Love* that we are naming, Divine Love working to heal human beings and their misery. Scripture gives us a name, a word to signify this perfection: God is *Agape* (1 John 4:8). Is the perfection and the nobility of compassion a *suffering* or a *quasi-suffering*? Is it not rather the *unchanging love of God*?" ("The Question of Evil and the Mystery of God in Charles Journet," 261).

ting real constraints upon divine freedom: to, that is to say, alter the "script" within the midst of the dramatic action itself. This, indeed, is the question that for Balthasar is at the heart of the sacred mysteries: how can divine freedom create another freedom that is really free, all in remaining itself supremely free? Or to put it another way, how can finite freedom "fulfill itself in infinite freedom [...] without making infinite freedom somehow finite, without relegating it to one existent entity among others[?]"[66]

Balthasar's theodramatic approach refuses to resolve the question in an easy answer. He admits: "The possibility of distinguishing between God—who 'is all' (Sir 43:27) and thus needs nothing—and a world of finite beings who need God remains the fundamental mystery."[67] The theologian of Lucerne thus insists upon retaining the mystery within his analogy of freedoms, which "reciprocally enrich each other in self-lessness."[68] This does not mean, however, that finite freedom can "enrich" the Trinity. "We cannot say that God only attains his ultimate fullness by involving himself with the world, that he needs the world," Balthasar insists. Nor can we legitimately hold "that God's goodness radiates forth of its very essence, so that it *has to* communicate itself."[69] God can, however, Balthasar clearly proposes, "enrich" himself.

By this idea of God enriching himself is "not" meant, Balthasar clarifies, that the reason for creation is "God's will to procure his own ('accidental') glorification (primary goal) by leading rational creatures to share his blessedness (secondary goal)." Rather, the theologian of Lucerne proposes, "the creature is drawn into the reciprocal acts of love within the Godhead, so that the collaboration of each Divine Person in the work of creation is intended to magnify the 'glory' of the Others." And, because the "inner participation of creatures in the life of the Trinity becomes an internal gift from each Divine Person to the Other," this Trinitarian conception of the mystery—the only one which can properly account for "the final goal of creation, the *gloria Dei (formalis)*"—"overcomes every appearance of a merely external 'glorification.'"[70]

Of course, "the whole event of salvation is not an affair interior to God,"

---

66. Balthasar, *Theo-Drama* II, 228; see also *My Work*, 117. For, as St. Thomas would have it, "God loses no dignity no matter how closely a creature draws near to Him [or, by the same logic, away from Him], although this makes the creature grow in dignity. For He communicates His goodness to creatures in such wise that He Himself suffers no loss" (*SCG* IV, c. 55, 3).

67. Balthasar, *Theo-Drama* II, 119.

68. Ibid., 228; see also 262.

69. Balthasar, *Theo-Drama* V, 507; see also *Theo-Drama* II, 261.

70. Balthasar, *Theo-Drama* V, 507. God, Adrienne explains, "gives himself to man, but he also gives man to himself [to God], so that man stands in the midst of a flowing exchange" (Speyr, *Light and Images*, 19).

Balthasar admits. In fact, when the eternal Word is spoken by the Father "into the world of men," it "must [...] resound from the world": not only from the Word, who is "always" already "an answer to him," but also from other human beings. Such, in fact, is a necessary consequence of the Incarnation, as Balthasar sees it; for Christ is human "only *with* others; the only humanity is cohumanity."[71] If, however, God desires "to hear" his word echoed from "outside" of himself, his purpose is finally to incorporate all of humanity into his one Word: the Word who dwells, by grace, in the hearts of those who know and love him.[72] Like the eternal Son, who "receives his being from the Father as the Word uttered by him (Jn 3:32; 8:26; 8:40; 15:15)," we, to whom it has been given to hear him "are meant to receive him as the Father's Word (Jn 6:45; 8:43, 47)—which, in turn, presupposes that we are 'of God' (8:47), that we are 'of truth' (18:37), that is, that the Holy Spirit is present in us as 'hearers.'"[73] Or, to put it in Speyrian terms, he thus allows us to enter into "the eternal conversation between Father, Son and Spirit": "to dialogue with God the Invisible, [...] to enter his holiest of holies," to participate not only in "God's action [by way of Christian missions] but [also] in God himself [by loving contemplation]."[74]

If, in fact, already in this life we are given a share in the divine life by grace, then eternal happiness "cannot" consist, Balthasar reasons, in simply "beholding" God. Ultimately we are meant to live "not over against God, but in him." Arguing in terms borrowed directly from Catholic doctrine, Balthasar presents our fate as that of being "'intimately associated (*proxime adsistere*) with the processions of the Divine Persons,' so as to "share in the bliss of the Most Holy and Undivided Trinity' ([Pius XII,] *Mystici Corporis*, DS [DZ] 3815)."[75]

This is what it means, as Aquinas would have it, "to possess [*habere*]"[76] a divine person: "to be 'conformed' to the Son and to the Holy Spirit who are sent to us," Gilles Emery explains, "and to be united to the divine Persons as 'object' [sic] of knowledge and of love, that is, to be caught up in the divine Persons known and loved by faith (and then by the vision) and by charity (fruition)."[77] The beatific vision should thus not be thought of as "a grasp, or enclos-

---

71. Balthasar, *The Threefold Garland*, 30–31.   72. Cf. Thomas Aquinas, *ST* I, q. 38, a. 1.
73. Balthasar, *Theo-Logic* III, 370–71.   74. Speyr, *World of Prayer*, 76–77.
75. Balthasar, *Theo-Drama* V, 425; see also *Theo-Drama* II, 230–42, 272, and 284; *Theo-Drama* III, 341–42; *Theo-Logic* I, 227–72; and *Theo-Logic* III, 448. The reference to Pope Pius XII is also valid for the more recent (English-Latin) edition of *DZ*.
76. Thomas Aquinas, *ST* I, q. 38, a. 1; cf. q. 45, a. 7.
77. Emery, *Trinity, Church, and the Human Person*, 150. Emery defines "fruition" as "the union of love with the divine Persons who are the ultimate end of the human being and in whom the human being finds his happiness" (ibid.).

ing" within finite minds of God. On the contrary, it is, as Fergus Kerr reads Aquinas, "an enjoyment in which one is enraptured—captured—by, rather than capturing, the One by whom one is enraptured."[78] It follows—as proper to the teaching of Aquinas, but also that of Balthasar[79]—that "God is not an object like others that we possess and can deal with as we please. It is we who are possessed by him, even in the noetic order." If, therefore, he is considered as an "object" of our knowledge, this means more properly that "he draws our intelligence to himself as an intelligible pole, from which it is suspended."[80]

As if to resonate with Balthasar's analogy of surrender, Mark McIntosh recognizes in the doctrine of St. Thomas that "at the highest level of [human] knowing and loving, the intellect and the will are progressively *available* to God. All is grace and therefore nothing is happening in the intellect or the will except what God is doing; and in God, knowing and loving are aspects of the one Trinitarian act of existence."[81] This is why, Balthasar admits, "we are bound to agree with Thomas Aquinas" when the latter teaches that the creature who has the greatest charity will also have the fullest "participation of the light of glory [...], because where there is the greater charity, there is the more desire; and desire in a certain degree makes the one desiring apt and prepared to receive the object desired. Hence he who possesses the more charity, will see God the more perfectly, and will be the more beatified."[82] As for Balthasar, he is convinced: "Infinite love will not be caught and held, but the more love there is, the more it can penetrate what exceeds its grasp."[83] "There is therefore a simple conclusion to the controversy over whether eternal beatitude consists in vision or in love," Balthasar explains. "It can consist only in the loving 'vision' of love, for what else but love is there to see in God, and how else can it be seen except from within love?"[84]

A Challenge for Balthasarian Scholars: Situating His Appropriation of Adrienne's Doctrine within the Tradition

Given their complementary approaches to human perfection, it is not surprising that St. Thomas and Balthasar are further united in the common

---

78. Kerr, *After Aquinas*, 160.
79. See Balthasar, *Theo-Drama* V, 425. For an excellent treatment of the differences between St. Thomas and Balthasar regarding the nature of faith in this life and the beatific vision in the next, see Donneaud, "Hans Urs von Balthasar contre saint Thomas d'Aquin sur la foi du Christ."
80. Nicolas, *Dieu connu comme inconnu*, 112.   81. McIntosh, *Mystical Theology*, 71.
82. Thomas Aquinas, *ST* I, q. 12, a. 6.   83. Balthasar, *Theo-Logic* III, 448.
84. Balthasar, *Love Alone Is Credible*, 146.

conviction that theological knowledge is "a form of reflection deriving from a kind of active participation in God's self-knowledge, which is no less than God's own self."[85] Indeed, these words by which Anna Williams describes St. Thomas's perspective resonate with Balthasar's own insistence that the theologian should constantly seek to study the divine mysteries from within the consciousness of Christ. This occurs, more specifically, by way of the Spirit's inspiration and the humility that allows the Christian to be appropriated for God's purposes.[86]

To be sure, humility and theological rigor need not—indeed ought not—be opposed, but any theological "analysis" of the creature's relation to God will, Balthasar maintains, more accurately be described and practiced as a synthesis, whence his method of infolding (*Einfaltung*),[87] as comparable—thus goes the thesis of Gilbert Narcisse—to the Thomistic approach of integration or the properly Thomistic argument of fittingness, which Jean-Pierre Torrell qualifies as "the only properly theological argument."[88] The latter should not be mistaken for a process of "deductive claims," Torrell explains, for the angelic doctor seeks "neither to prove the truths of the faith, nor to demonstrate other truths from those that we hold by faith, but simply to highlight the connections between the truths that we believe and, finally, to show how all of these might be explained from God." The French Dominican thus points to the "visualizing"[89] function of Aquinas's theology.

As for Balthasar, far from dissecting the various mysteries of the Christian faith in such a way as to disengage them from their life-giving center, he

---

85. Williams, "Mystical Theology Redux," 58.

86. Such is also what Mark McIntosh presents (in his exposition of Balthasar) as "mystical consciousness." See McIntosh, *Mystical Theology*, 102.

87. See, for example, Balthasar, *Our Task*, 44n22; *Convergences*, 12; *My Work*, 10; *Theo-Logic* II, 210, 213, and 314; (with Albus) "Spirit and Fire," 593; and *Theo-Logic* I, 8. Cf. Martinelli, *La Morte di Cristo come Rivelazione dell'amore Trinitario*, 108; John R. Sachs, "Hans Urs von Balthasar," in Donald W. Musser and John L. Price (eds.), *A New Handbook to Christian Theologians* (Nashville, Tenn.: Abingdon, 1996), 498; Peter Casarella, "Hans Urs von Balthasar, Erich Przywara's *Analogia Entis*, and the Problem of a Catholic *Denkform*," in White, *The Analogy of Being*, 205–6; Henri de Lubac, "A Witness of Christ in the Church: Hans Urs von Balthasar," in Schindler, *Hans Urs von Balthasar: His Life and Work*, 272; Lochbrunner, *Analogia Caritatis*, 55–56; and (from a critical standpoint) Kilby, *Balthasar: A (Very) Critical Introduction*, 72–93.

88. Jean-Pierre Torrell, "Préface" to Gilbert Narcisse, *Les raisons de Dieu: Argument de convenance et esthétique théologique selon saint Thomas d'Aquin et Hans Urs von Balthasar* (Fribourg: Éditions Universitaire, 1997), xiii. Narcisse further explains that the argument of fittingness simultaneously holds to a truth of faith (a realized fact) "*and* [to] God's sovereign freedom and wisdom to effectively realize this fact" (ibid., 107). The Thomistic argument of integration is well summarized by Jean-Hervé Nicolas: "Adapted to the human mode of knowing, the revelation of the unique, simple and universal divine Truth multiplies it into a plurality of particular truths, which—by their internal order—reproduce, in their manner, the original unity from which they arise and to which they return the spirit" (*Dieu connu comme inconnu*, 266).

89. Torrell, *La Somme de Saint Thomas* (Paris: Cerf, 1998), 75.

too seeks their "integration"[90] within the whole of Christian (and thus Trinitarian) revelation, as is evident in his constant insistence upon the unity of spirituality and the science of God, as we saw in chapter two. This insistence by Balthasar upon the integration of theo-logy and theo-praxis was certainly not isolated by what Claudia Lee presents as his "passionate preoccupation"[91] with Christian mysticism and its role within the Church. This preoccupation, in turn, can hardly be isolated from what he perceived as Adrienne's mission of bringing mysticism back from the "clandestine existence" that has been its sorry fate within official theology in modern times, to what he esteemed its rightful place within the "center of salvation history": the history, that is to say, of "the exchange between the word of God in Christ and the hearing and responding to this word by the Bride-Church."[92]

Sadly, Balthasar's engagement with Adrienne's mission—which implied his own mission (as he understood it) of introducing and training her (precisely as her confessor) "in the central christological mystery of the Son's obedience to the Father"[93] and of "fitting" (precisely as a well-trained theologian) her extraordinary experiences "into the tradition of the Church,"[94] and even of winning for her "a reputation as one of Christianity's truly great mystics"[95]—will not necessarily speak in Balthasar's favor among many academically-minded theologians.

There furthermore remains the question of the authenticity of Adrienne's mysticism. This question is hardly facilitated by the fact that Balthasar is apparently the only eyewitness to the mystical phenomena in Adrienne's life, including the mystical manner in which her works were written. Balthasar explains, in fact, that he and Adrienne once invited a young Jesuit friend to

---

90. See Balthasar, *My Work*, 105. "Truth is the *whole*" (*Does Jesus Know Us?*, 67). Gilbert Narcisse thus refers to Balthasar's "vigorous logic of unity," according to his conviction, no doubt, that the whole of revelation exists in the single form of Christ, together with his Church, which in turn points to the unity-in-difference of the three divine persons in the Trinity. See Narcisse, *Les Raisons de Dieu*, 60. See also Balthasar and Albus, "Spirit and Fire," 593; Balthasar, *Convergences*; and *Theo-Logic* I, 8 (cf. Kilby, *Balthasar: A (Very) Critical Introduction*, 87).

91. Lee, "The Role of Mysticism within the Church as Conceived by Hans Urs von Balthasar," 106. See also McIntosh, *Mystical Theology*, 101.

92. Balthasar, *First Glance at Adrienne von Speyr*, 89; cf. *Explorations in Theology* I, 201.

93. Balthasar, *Our Task*, 19. In another context, Balthasar explains the manner in which this was carried out: "Adrienne was able to 'transmit' instructions from heaven in total disinterestedness and without any personal authority, and could forget them under obedience just as completely. She transmitted to me—as the representative of authority—a complete and often very varied and complicated 'program,' which was mainly concerned with penitential exercises. 'Under obedience,' she would forget it completely, and I was obliged to impose the program 'with authority'" (Balthasar, *First Glance at Adrienne von Speyr*, 69–70).

94. Balthasar, *Our Task*, 58. It bears repeating that it was to this end that he understood the significance of his vast theological training. See ibid., 39–45.

95. Lee, "The Role of Mysticism within the Church as Conceived by Hans Urs von Balthasar," 118.

assist at one of Adrienne's dictations, but she apparently stopped after a few words. "It was no good. She could only dictate to her confessor. It was up to him to pass on the result to the Church."[96]

Even her works (other than some of the posthumous volumes) reveal little if anything of Adrienne's subjective experience: a fact which corresponds to her own insistence that the mystic must be transparent before the divine object, even to the point of anonymity; hence the constant emphasis upon the objective word of God revealed by Christ rather than upon her own subjective state or experience. If not for certain of the posthumous volumes, which remain difficult to access, even in the original German, there is in fact little or nothing to be found in Adrienne's vast opus that would necessarily reveal or otherwise bespeak the mystical nature of their transmission. We are thus left to judge the authenticity of her mysticism with nothing more than Balthasar's word and the objective content of her work.

If, furthermore, Balthasar did not go to greater pains to exposit the extraordinary phenomena of her life—indeed, he even insisted that one refrain from reading the more obviously mystical works until only after studying the "major works [*ihre Hauptwerke*],"[97] among which he points out the biblical commentaries (especially those of the Gospel of St. John, the Pauline letters, and the Catholic epistles), *Handmaid of the Lord, Confession,* and *World of Prayer*—this is because he accords far greater importance to the objective value of her work as evidence of its inspired origin.[98] "All the various aspects of her charism are," he argued, "directed concentrically at a deeper interpretation of revelation."[99]

It has been among the primary aims of this book to present her theology in a manner that might facilitate this judgment (that of the objective value and inspired origin of Adrienne's works) by providing a general exposition of her theological anthropology without diverging from the "whole" that Balthasar judged necessary for an adequate appreciation of her work.[100] Admittedly, I have done so from the perspective of one already convinced of their authenticity, of one who recognizes in her insights not merely the spark

---

96. Balthasar, *Our Task*, 18n11; see also 60n23.

97. See Balthasar, introduction to Balthasar, Chantraine, and Scola, *Adrienne von Speyr und ihre kirchliche Sendung*, 12–13.

98. "The criterion of her mysticism's authenticity lies primarily, if not exclusively, in the *quality* of what she did and what she had and has to say" (Balthasar, *Our Task*, 72). In this same book, he explains: "The posthumous works are not yet generally available. Their circulation has been restricted up to now [1984], so that Adrienne's objective message, which is so important for the Church, might first be heard and pondered" (ibid., 15). See also Balthasar and Albus, "Spirit and Fire," 574.

99. Balthasar, *Our Task*, 9–10.

100. Ibid., 15.

of genius that I had once thought to originate in Balthasar's work, but also the call to holiness and the challenge to live holiness in the form of an "ecclesial existence": that of a life lived in service of the Church and the world for love of Christ. I have likewise written from the perspective of one recognizing in the combined figures of Adrienne and Balthasar a single "Gestalt,"[101] possessing what they themselves believed to be a common mission. While one might argue that I am—in virtue of these convictions—less than objective in my presentation, I am perhaps also better suited to attest to the truth of Balthasar's observation that the "more one attends [in Adrienne's theology] to the whole, the clearer the inner coherence of the parts become."[102]

Indeed, it has been my purpose to serve others in perceiving the whole which I have exposited as Trinitarian love in the form of the reciprocal surrender of the divine Persons. Each of the previous chapters might thus be considered an exposition, from still another angle, of this same fundamental intuition: that creaturely (especially human) being, precisely in its natural (and thus also willed) directedness beyond itself, is a particularly fitting image of divine life. I nonetheless admit that my exposition of Adrienne's theological anthropology—as facilitated by Balthasar's insights and as complemented by the same—represents a very meager beginning, especially if one considers the almost countless number of themes that one might touch upon in Adrienne's vast corpus; and let us not forgot the complementary and perhaps still vaster opus of Balthasar.

Within this context of admitting my own limitations, it behooves me to express a sincere hope that the work I have merely begun here might provide a springboard for other scholarly studies. I urge those who would do so—no matter how convinced they are of the prophetic nature of the common work of Balthasar and Adrienne—to seriously entertain the often very challenging questions and concerns of their critics. It would be terribly negligent with respect not only to Balthasar's personal example of constantly seeking the synthesis that marks his understanding of Catholicism, but also (and as might be considered part of the same) to his tremendous and overarching effort to theologically support and frame Adrienne's rich spiritual insights, to simply dismiss these criticisms. Hence, for example, rather than ignoring the apparent contradiction between Balthasar's opposition to a "bottom-up" theology—as is evident in his refutation of Rahner's transcendental Christology[103]—and his own attempt to explain the Trinity by way of analogies

---

101. Cf. Lochbrunner, *Analogia Caritatis*, 321.
102. Balthasar, *Our Task*, 15.
103. The debate between Balthasar and Rahner is evident in the former's *Love Alone Is Credible*,

drawn from human beings, we must show that it is resolved in his characteristically katalogical perspective.

Still more significant than these concerns, it seems to me, is one that I wish to address not so much to Balthasar as to his disciples. This concern, more specifically, is one that I might frame as the question of whether it is possible to have it both ways: to attempt to surpass the constraints of a negative theology by employing images, metaphors, and analogies borrowed from Adrienne's (presumably) mystically-inspired theology and to simultaneously take refuge in the idea of "mystery" when those images are criticized as being in (at least) apparent contradiction with Christian doctrine. Hence Balthasar addresses, for example, a "negative incomprehensibility" which, in virtue of Christian revelation, becomes "a positive one. For it is far more incomprehensible that the Eternal God, in his freedom, should set forth to come to us, caring for us by means of his Incarnation, Cross and Eucharist."[104]

Beyond our attempt to reconcile Balthasar's doctrine with certain non-negotiable aspects of Christian doctrine—such as the immutable nature of the Godhead, the single divine nature of the Trinity (as implying a single divine intellect and a single divine will), and the real distinction of the divine and human natures of Christ, doctrines which we examined in chapter seven—we might also address the validity of Balthasar's extensive use of metaphors borrowed largely from Adrienne. In so doing, we do well to heed the counsel of Jean-Hervé Nicolas, who argues for the "irreplaceable" role of metaphors in theological discourse—"not only as examples that illustrate the intelligible truth, but also as symbols which contain it." He nonetheless maintains that certain rules for their use must be respected, the first of which is that they must contain "no error."[105] From this perspective, the question that concerns us is whether Balthasar's particular use of metaphors does in fact, as his critics argue, risk the introduction of error in our conception of God.

---

and to some extent, *Engagement with God*. See also Balthasar, *My Work*, 51–60; (with Albus), "Spirit and Fire"; *Theo-Drama* IV, 273–84; "Current Trends in Catholic Theology"; Henri-Jérôme Gagey and Vincent Holzer (eds.), *Balthasar, Rahner: Deux pensées en contraste* (Paris: Bayard, 2005); Louis Roberts, "The Collision of Rahner and Balthasar," *Continuum* 5 (1968): 753–57; Kilby, "Balthasar and Karl Rahner," in Oakes and Moss, *The Cambridge Companion to Hans Urs von Balthasar*, 256–68; Rowan Williams, "Balthasar and Rahner," in Riches, *The Analogy of Beauty*, 11–34; Mansini, "Rahner and Balthasar on the Efficacy of the Cross"; Schenk, "Ist die Rede vom leidenden Gott theologisch zu vermeiden?"; Dalzell, *The Dramatic Encounter of Divine and Human Freedom in the Theology of Hans Urs von Balthasar*, 183–86; and the symposium on "Balthasar and Rahner on Nature and Grace" published in the English edition of *Communio* 18 (1991): 207–80.

104. Balthasar, *Theo-Drama* II, 260. See also the criticism in Kilby, *Balthasar: A (Very) Critical Introduction*, 93.

105. Nicolas, *Dieu connu comme inconnu*, 247–49.

In my own confrontation with this important question, I cannot help but raise still another: should the disciple of Balthasar be any less vigilant in attempting to situate the master's doctrine within the tradition than was the master himself (Balthasar) in his own attempt to situate Adrienne's mysticism within the same tradition? Assuredly, the growing number of important criticisms of Balthasar's theology—most of which point to difficulties arising directly out of Adrienne's mystical language and insights—might be perceived as evidence that his attempt was not always immediately or obviously successful. This, of course, is not sufficient reason to condemn his theology (nor hers) as unorthodox, especially given the undeniable phenomenon of its universal appeal and mounting popularity, particularly among so-called traditional theologians,[106] a fact which might also (but not necessarily) be understood as bespeaking something of its Catholicity. In that regard, it is worth mentioning a short excerpt from the homily of Joseph Cardinal Ratzinger at the funeral liturgy for Balthasar: "What the Pope [John Paul II] intended to express by this mark of distinction, and of honor [that of naming Balthasar to the cardinalate], remains valid: no longer only private individuals but the Church itself, in its official responsibility, tells us that he is right in what he teaches of the Faith, that he points the way to the sources of living water—a witness to the word which teaches us Christ and which teaches us how to live."[107]

On the other hand, no service is rendered to Balthasar's enormous undertaking—including, most especially, all that he did to encourage, preserve, foster, and theologically situate the profound and presumably mystical insights of Adrienne—if we simply refuse to enter into conversation with other theologians who, no less than we, are sincerely seeking to serve the living Word of God as it is expressed throughout the rich and very broad tradition of Catholic teaching. We do well, for example, to heed the important concern of Richard Schenk (echoed, as it were, by Karen Kilby) when he writes: "The claim by Balthasar to present a 'seamless theology,' without seeming to allow room for debate on individual tracts or arguments, a theology of that 'truth which is so true, that it can even maintain and sustain itself beyond the

---

106. Hence John D. O'Connor asks "how such an audacious theology has come to be so influential among many 'traditional' theologians, including the present pope [Benedict XVI]" (book review of Pitstick, *Light in Darkness*, in *New Blackfriars* 88 [November 2007]: 747).

107. Joseph Ratzinger, "Homily at the Funeral Liturgy of Hans Urs von Balthasar (Lucerne, July 1, 1988)," reprinted in Schindler, *Hans Urs von Balthasar: His Life and Work*, 295. See also the telegram from Pope John Paul II to Joseph Cardinal Ratzinger: "Your participation at the solemn funeral services [of Hans Urs von Balthasar] will be an expression of the high esteem in which the person and the life work of this great priest and theologian are held by the Holy See" (in ibid., 289).

bounds of the principle of non-contradiction,' might seem to evoke a sense of 'take it or leave it': an impression which not all the followers of Balthasar are quick to discourage."[108] Schenk objects, more specifically, that Balthasar's equating of the Christ event with "the economic *id quo majus cogitari nequit*" [that which nothing greater can be thought] implies a "sapiential claim [which he compares to that of Leibniz] to 'know' what is the most fitting course of action for God to take."[109] "Since [however] no finite good is unsurpassable," Schenk rightfully reasons, "no sapiential definition of what God must do is convincing."[110]

It is terribly unfortunate—even ironic—however, that Schenk would accuse Balthasar of the very thing that the latter most seeks to avoid: reducing the Godhead—and thus also God's "plans" as it were—to a dimension graspable by human reason. Like Adrienne, whom Balthasar presents as "overwhelmed and as though possessed by the thought that God is the 'ever greater,'"[111] Balthasar grants but one limit to the "act" of revelation: that of our understanding.[112] Only "in order to be capable of being understood as God's conclusive self-expression and accepted in faith" must the Word of God—which in Christ "sum[s] up all words [...] into one single word which contains all others within it"—"fulfill the condition which Anselm set for the idea of God." This condition, more specifically, is to be that "beyond which something greater cannot be thought," a condition that Balthasar recognizes as "self-evidently" fulfilled in "God's self-expression as absolute love in himself," which in turn is revealed "in Jesus Christ's Incarnation, Passion and Resurrection." Hence, "every cognitive formulation of this self-demonstration of God" must "refer beyond itself to absolute love, which not only factually but essentially 'passes all understanding' (Eph 3:19)."[113]

Hence, as Balthasar sees it, dogmas—but also every metaphor and anal-

---

108. Richard Schenk, "The Epoché of Factical Damnation? On the Cost of Bracketing Out the Likelihood of Final Loss," *Logos* 1, no. 3 (1997): 143. Cf. Kilby, *A (Very) Critical Introduction*, 55 and 104.

109. Richard Schenk, "The Epoché of Factical Damnation," 143–44. Balthasar explicitly refutes this charge in his *Theo-Drama* II, 268–69. Schenk's reference is to Henrici, "A Sketch of Von Balthasar's Life," 33: "An aesthetic of God's glory blazing forth in the world became really possible only when von Balthasar came to see the descent of Christ, the economic *id quo majus cogitari nequit*, as the form in which God reveals himself in the world."

110. Schenk, "The Epoché of Factical Damnation," 145; cf. Balthasar, *Theo-Drama* II, 259.

111. See Balthasar, *First Glance at Adrienne von Speyr*, 62; Speyr, *John* II, 79; and *Mary in the Redemption*, 100. Cf. *The Catechism of the Catholic Church*, no. 230, with reference to St. Augustine of Hippo.

112. See, for example, Balthasar, *Love Alone Is Credible*, 87n1; *The Glory of the Lord* I, 37; and *Theo-Drama* II, 119. Cf. Thomas Aquinas, *ST* I, q. 12, a. 1. Concerning the "act" character of God's revelation, see Balthasar, *Convergences*, 39.

113. Balthasar, *Convergences*, 80–81; see also "God is His Own Exegete," 282; *Explorations in Theology* III, 363–87; and Palakeel, *The Use of Analogy in Theological Discourse*, 106.

ogy that he and Adrienne employ to describe the inner-Trinitarian life and the work of redemption—are "nothing other than aspects of the love which manifests itself and yet remains mystery within revelation." To see it otherwise would be, he argues, to let knowledge triumph over love and to allow human reason to "conquer" God such that "at this instant—first in theology, then in the Church, then in the world—God is 'dead.'"[114] Indeed, "a God who could be expressed to the end in finite words (and deeds!) would no longer be God but an idol. But a God who did not wish to give himself away to this extreme end [namely, death on the Cross], but withheld a piece of himself from us and for himself, would also no longer be our God; here too, he would be an idol."[115]

From this perspective it seems that Schenk and Balthasar would certainly agree that we can never do away with the mystery at the heart of the theological enterprise and thus also with the important challenge of Christian faith: that we seek "to understand the love of Christ which is beyond all understanding" (cf. Eph 3:19). "The mystery does not allow itself to be won by logic and concepts," Balthasar maintains. "And this is finally the danger of all theology."[116] My hope, then, is this: that the mystery beyond understanding might provide a common ground for dialogue among those convinced of Ratzinger's claim that Balthasar "points the way to the sources of living water" and those who fear that his theology would drown us instead.[117]

Any such dialogue will however, it seems to me, require of those of us in the first group that we be willing—without necessarily abandoning the rich mystical (and in this case largely metaphorical) language that Balthasar valued as efficaciously serving to express the mystery of the triune God—to situate these same insights in metaphysical terms, borrowed from philosophy, which share Balthasar's goal of passing beyond the constraints of negative theology so as to say something positive (albeit non-limiting) of the unfathomable mystery of the triune God. It is nonetheless important to add, with Mark McIntosh, that "it would be a hermeneutical fault to read mystical language in a positivistic fashion, reducing it to a direct report of 'things' that 'happened'—whether in external events or interior sensations—or as enjoining would-be mystics to cultivate particular feelings, attitudes, or spiritual

---

114. Balthasar, *Convergences*, 13–14; see also *My Work*, 105, where he explains that "the multiplicity of dogmas is only the mediation of the unique 'dogma,' Jesus Christ, by all the parts." Such is also his argument in (with Albus), "Spirit and Fire," 593.

115. Balthasar, *Theo-Logic* II, 279–80.

116. Balthasar and Albus, "Spirit and Fire," 578. Cf. Balthasar, *Convergences*, 94–95.

117. For a first attempt, see Gilbert Narcisse, "Le réalisme thomiste," in Serge-Bonino, et al., *Thomistes ou de l'actualité de saint Thomas d'Aquin* (Toulouse: Parole et Silence, 2003), 49–65.

stances. Mystical language is, rather, more like lenses for viewing what cannot be seen; it is describing in a simple or direct sense neither God nor the mystic's experiences but evoking an *interpretive framework* within which the readers of the text may come to recognize and participate in their own encounters with God."[118] On the other hand, within the specific context of an attempt to resolve certain recent "problems" of "understanding […] God's *kenosis*," Pope John Paul II acknowledges that "a coherent solution […] will not be found without philosophy's contribution."[119]

To be sure, one might—with Jean-Hervé Nicolas—accord to mystical theology "a pure and simple superiority over notional theology,"[120] while simultaneously admitting that it is dependent upon notional theology to express the 'inexpressible' mystery of its experience and to judge its authenticity.[121] From this point of view, a notional theology serves mystical theology[122] just as the latter serves the former by pointing out "the inadequacy of [its] concepts, the poverty of [its] formulations, [and] the heaviness of [its] reasoning."[123] In short, "the two theologies mutually complete and sustain one another."[124]

As for judging Adrienne's dependency upon metaphors in her particular form of mysticism, we might again follow Nicolas's twofold acknowledgement of the "irreplaceable role" of metaphor in *all* theological discourse. Not only is metaphor "an instrument of revelation,"[125] Nicolas explains, but it also serves an important "pedagogical" function, precisely because it is natural to human beings "to attain the intelligible from the experience of what is sensed."[126] And because God, precisely as incorporeal, cannot be sensed, we can never think of him without the use of some metaphor.[127] It follows that the theologian "naturally" employs them "not only as examples illustrating intelligible truth, but also as symbols containing it."[128] Adrienne's own reasoning might be applied here:

---

118. McIntosh, *Mystical Theology*, 124. This should be kept in mind when Karen Kilby faults Balthasar's theology for "transgress[ing] the usual bounds of theology […] to know more than can be known" (*Balthasar: A (Very) Critical Introduction*, 114).

119. Pope John Paul II, *Fides et Ratio*, no. 93.   120. Nicolas, *Dieu connu comme inconnu*, 399.
121. See ibid., 405–6.   122. See ibid., 408.
123. Ibid., 411.   124. Ibid., 412.

125. Ibid., 247. In revealed knowledge, the proper concept is "wrapped in the metaphor itself." For example, "the image of an upward spatial movement evoked by the term *ascension* conceals the concept of *the return to the Father*, [who is] the term of the temporal mission of the Incarnation" (ibid.); see also 245.

126. Ibid., 247. Cf. Thomas Aquinas, *ST* I, q. 1, a. 9.

127. Nicolas, *Dieu connu comme inconnu*, 166. "The highest and purest intellectual speculations" presuppose "more or less precise imaginative representations, which are often vague and imprecise, but which cannot be avoided" (ibid.).

128. Ibid., 248.

In initiating us into his inner-divine world of love, showing us ways to his Trinitarian nature and guiding us into the 'greater-than' of his being, God lets us keep our human concept with all its inadequacy because it can be transformed through grace. [...] We must use what experience we as Christians have of God as access to his nature, as a means of interpreting his being. To renounce this would be to shut ourselves in our earthly world and reject the most precious gifts which give access to God.[129]

What is more, Nicolas argues—as if to defend Adrienne's own particular use of metaphors—that a second, derived, but nonetheless significant role of metaphors is that of saving us from the "permanent" temptation of imagining that we possess knowledge of God as we do of other objects. "Metaphorical designation, by its very crudeness [*grossièreté*], awakens the spirit from this illusion" and reminds us that God far surpasses every concept we use to designate him.[130] From this point of view, moreover, it is not the higher, more abstract metaphors that might be considered preferable, but those that are the most material. There is much less risk of confusing God with a citadel, Nicolas explains, than with the concept of light.[131] Or in the words of the angelic doctor, "similitudes drawn from things farthest away from God form within us a truer estimate that God is above whatsoever we may say or think of Him."[132]

On the other hand, in arguing for the validity, or even necessity, of employing metaphors both in the transmission and reception of the faith, Nicolas nonetheless insists that they ought not to be used—and this point is of no small significance to the discussion at hand—as explanations of the faith, whence our return to the challenge of expressing the content of Adrienne's mystical teaching in metaphysical terms, or in what Nicolas refers to as notional theology.[133] Of course, it might be granted that metaphysical language is not always accessible to recent theologians, given what I consider to be a certain philosophical poverty in various theological faculties and seminaries, and it might be thought to lack something of the appeal that mystical (including much patristic) and scriptural language offers to the human spirit, which is universally moved by beauty and yearning for love. Hence, Nicolas addresses the power of metaphor "to awaken affectivity" and "to provoke emotions within us" as well as "outbursts of love."[134] One might, moreover, fear a return to the neo-scholasticism of Balthasar's day, as we briefly de-

---

129. Speyr, *World of Prayer*, 35.
130. Nicolas, *Dieu connu comme inconnu*, 166. See also the application of this principle to the notion of God's anger by Jean-Pierre Torrell in *Pour nous les hommes et pour notre salut*, 234–40.
131. See Nicolas, *Dieu connu comme inconnu*, 167.
132. Thomas Aquinas, *ST* I, q. 1, a. 9, ad. 3.
133. Nicolas, *Dieu connu comme inconnu*, 249.
134. Nicolas, *Dieu connu comme inconnu*, 166.

scribed it in chapter one, which was perhaps motivated more by intellectual curiosity than by a reverent love of God and the obedience that it entails. It is likely with good reason that Balthasar feared the narrowing of the Catholic fullness of faith to "fit" what he judged a "rigid" rationalistic tendency of his time, sometimes "politically, rather than spiritually minded" and "often with immensely destructive consequences."[135]

Despite his preference for mystical images and the language of Scripture, Balthasar clearly recognized the need for metaphysics, and he was never explicitly opposed to the spirit of high (as opposed to modern or neo-) scholasticism. "In order to be a serious theologian," he maintained, "one must also, indeed, first, be a philosopher; one must—precisely also in the light of revelation—have immersed oneself in the mysterious structures of creaturely being."[136] It would, for example, be "a mistake to strip the revealed world of the inchoate philosophical understanding it contains [...] on the pretext that it is simply based on ultimate intramundane categories (for example, the immutability of numbers and natural laws)."[137]

We thus have good reason to believe that Balthasar would actually encourage the precisions that metaphysical language offers in formulating the truths of our faith. Indeed, he explicitly holds that "the increase of the conceptual materials and other 'thought forms'" available thanks to scholasticism "permit a more exact description of the core content of revelation."[138] Furthermore, we need only consider the fact that the Church has chosen precisely this language—the language of metaphysics—for expressing and preserving the doctrinal truths of her faith. Emmanuel Perrier has in fact good reason to argue that we ought not to think of dogmatic formulations as imposing particular philosophical categories upon the faith, but rather of marking, by means of these very concepts, "the intrinsic limits of human intelligence in its comprehension of," for example, "the unity of the two natures of Christ"[139] or of the three divine persons in the one divine nature. Still more positively, Jean-Pierre Torrell argues that dogmatic formulations "are not an obstacle to understanding the faith, but a beacon which enlightens the path and precisely delimits [*balise*] it."[140] At the very minimum, the serious scholar of Balthasar ought therefore—or, again, so it seems to me—to demonstrate a certain willingness to employ this same metaphysical language in an attempt

---

135. Balthasar, *The Theology of Henri de Lubac*, 29 and 31.
136. Balthasar, *Theo-Logic* I, 8; see also *Theo-Logic* II, 173.
137. Balthasar, *Theo-Drama* II, 278.
138. Balthasar, "The Fathers, the Scholastics, and Ourselves," 385.
139. Perrier, "L'enjeu christologique de la satisfaction (I)," 130.
140. Torrell, *Pour nous les hommes et pour notre salut*, 203.

to situate apparent "novelties" of the theology of Balthasar and Adrienne within the context of these metaphysically expressed dogmatic truths. To refuse to do so would arguably amount to abandoning "the centrality of Christ in favor of a concept."[141]

Again, this need not imply that we superimpose a systematic frame or a theological "system" upon a mystery that both Balthasar and Adrienne insisted could not be systematized.[142] It does, however, mean taking seriously the questions of their critics. Hence, we might join Gilbert Narcisse, for example, in asking whether Balthasar's frequent recourse to Adrienne's insights—often cited *verbatim*—is not "abusive"[143] or misleading, especially when he refers to her as an authority at the very junctions of his arguments that might be considered philosophically weak or theologically questionable. Despite what Narcisse positively esteems as Balthasar's attempt "to enter more directly into the mystery of the personal Trinitarian relations precisely as personal," the French Dominican nonetheless shuns various "inacceptable propositions," not unlike those that we visited in our refutation of Blankenhorn and Pitstick in chapter seven of this volume.

The following question thus emerges: "Is this [Balthasar's] systematic Trinitarian foundation based *primarily* upon theological argumentation? Or *especially* upon a speculation involving diverse theses? Or again, and most probably—it seems—upon profound theological, 'mystical,' realities which still require that they be purged of their excessive formulations and [that they be] better argued so as to demonstrate not only their profundity, but also in what [sense] they are true?"[144]

The Question of Interpreting Adrienne von Speyr's Presumably Mystical Experiences

In responding to this important question—and I admit from the outset that I agree with Narcisse on the latter of the three possibilities[145]—I

---

141. Ibid., 132.

142. See for example Balthasar, *First Glance at Adrienne von Speyr*, 50; *My Work*, 105; *Explorations in Theology* IV, 333; *Explorations in Theology* I, 54; and *The Grain of Wheat*, 21–22.

143. Narcisse, "Participer à la vie trinitaire," 120.

144. Ibid., 128. This important question is not far from that posed by Bernhard Blankenhorn with regard to Balthasar's theology of Holy Saturday: "Does the theology [of Balthasar] follow the visions [of Adrienne], or at least seek its justification in their concreteness? Or does the theology shape the interpretation of the visions, which surely cannot be direct windows into [for example] Christ's consciousness in hell that are easily translatable into human language? What is the determining factor behind Balthasar's conclusions?" (Blankenhorn, book review of Pitstick's *Light in Darkness*, 953). See also Schenk, "The Epoché of Factical Damnation," esp. 127–28.

145. Such is also the interpretation of Roten; see his "Two Halves of the Moon," 85. Roten exam-

think it important to acknowledge that, contrary to the claim of Johann Roten, Balthasar did not understand himself to be Adrienne's interpreter. Although Roten admits that the "initiative is all Adrienne's where the contents and the formulation of her message are concerned,"[146] he nonetheless concludes: "They are kneeling and sitting theology united; the overflowing abundance carried in the womb of the woman and the representative function of *the man, called upon to interpret and formulate*—all these aspects of a complementary thematic can be found in the different facets of the double mission."[147] In fact, Balthasar explicitly proclaims his conviction that Adrienne's mission was "not only one of experience, of the dark night and other christological states, but also quite expressly one of interpretation."[148] Therefore, he appears to have perceived a twofold mystical charism operative in her dictations: that of vision and that of the interpretation of these visions by way of divine inspiration, which is likewise a grace.[149] "A[drienne] said it was 'very variable,'" Balthasar explains. "It could be given 'partly in words, partly in gestures and intimations,' or simply by the showing of 'great connections.'"

When she dictates, A[drienne] translates what she has seen—the *species impressa*, as it were. What was shown could then remain, so to speak, in store in order to be brought out again later at the time of dictation. At that moment everything is once more in place, as fresh as ever, even though months have passed. The ideas are absolutely clear; they do not need to be looked for. The only matter that requires occasional consideration is the language to be used to express the ideas.[150]

In this regard, Jacques Maritain offers some helpful insights:

We know that in Heaven the blessed do not use words and speech to converse among themselves. On the other hand, we also know that God uses instrumentally what is in the mind of the prophet. [...] Let us suppose that a person of heaven who appears and speaks, does not utter audible words, but rather *reads* [...] in the soul of the messenger [...]. Then one can think that utterances coming from Heaven, and really heard, and authentically transmitted, have passed through the instrumentality of typical or 'archetypal' mental perspectives present in the unconscious of the spirit of the messenger, without, for all this, the meaning or the letter of the message being changed, such as it was intended from on high to reach us. When someone from

---

ines twelve themes (not including the specifically Marian themes) which he believes to reflect Adrienne's "direct influence on von Balthasar's opus." See also 76–78.

146. Ibid., 72.

147. Ibid., 85; emphasis added.

148. Balthasar, *Our Task*, 18–19; see also *First Glance at Adrienne von Speyr*, 97; and "General Introduction to the Posthumous Works" in Speyr, *Book of All Saints* I, 13.

149. On the grace of interpretation, see Balthasar, *Our Task*, 89.

150. Ibid., 62.

Heaven speaks [...] it is necessary to understand them (to understand their 'literal sense') according to the spirit of him who causes these words to be heard.[151]

When it comes to understanding the visions entrusted by heaven, as it were, to Adrienne, Balthasar explains how this occurred:

> A[drienne] asks me not to write for a moment but just to listen. She explains the thing to me, perhaps with some images and analogies, and then I write down a continuous paragraph, as faithful as possible to these illustrations. This is another reason why it may be possible in a number of dictations to detect my "style." [...] She was well aware of the limits of theological language, but the precision of her statements distinguishes her clearly from so many mystics who think that one can only stammer about God. There may have been an interplay here between her own intelligence and love of clarity and the concepts she learned from me when she was being instructed [in preparation for her reception into the Catholic Church].[152]

We might argue, of course, that despite the specific "interpretations" that Adrienne herself has offered to her mystical visions, Balthasar has undoubtedly taken these (the interpretations) at least one step further. On the one hand, he provided her with a certain conceptual assistance during the dictations, as he explains in the above citation—including, no doubt, his willing offer of an already very rich literary, philosophical, and theological (including scriptural and patristic) vocabulary.[153] To be sure, this does not mean that he is responsible for the content of the dictations, nor that she merely described an experience that he then put into his own words. Instead, Balthasar explains that he was led by Adrienne, who spoke "in the Spirit" until he understood what she had been given to transmit:

> H[ans] U[rs] does not influence her. She just dissects, dismembers, the unified things she sees. A[drienne] does not think that there is any great connection between these two facts—that I am theologically trained, and she is not. But it is true that contemporary theology is not (or not yet) in a position to understand what is shown. If someone reads A. and says, 'That's pure H. U.,' sometimes they may be right. When A. sees yellow and H. U. sees blue, she may occasionally have to put herself into the position where he sees blue, so that she can lead him from there to where she sees yellow. There may be points in the speaking in the Spirit when H. U. outlines certain things. But this does not affect the final outcome, only the way to it. H. U. is her public. There is no other way.[154]

---

151. Jacques Maritain, *Notebooks*, trans. Joseph W. Evans (Albany, N.Y.: Magi Books, 1984), 91–92.
152. Balthasar, *Our Task*, 62–63, with extensive reference to Speyr, *Erde und Himmel* II.
153. See Balthasar, *Our Task*, 38 and 44–45.
154. Ibid., 18; cf. Speyr, *Erde und Himmel* II, 458.

On the other hand, Balthasar's role as Adrienne's "public" nonetheless implied far more than being a simple stenographer. Besides helping her to express what she experienced—an act that necessarily implied that he was also somehow involved in the interpretation of her experiences—he also clarified certain questions or unknown details for her. There were times, for example, when he was able to figure out who or what she was seeing: "One night she saw the prayer of 'a St. Gregory,' but she did not know his name," Balthasar explains. "However, once she had described his prayer, it became clear to me beyond doubt that it could only be St. Gregory Nazianzen."[155]

Beyond these already significant aspects of his mission beside Adrienne, one might note the manner in which he took up her insights into his own work, developing and contextualizing them within Church tradition, as he believed them to be rightfully understood. The substance of her theology, Balthasar attests, "derives from her."

> All I attempted to do was gather it up and embed it in a space, such as the theology of the Fathers, that of the Middle Ages and the modern age, with which I was fairly familiar. My contribution consisted in providing a comprehensive theological horizon, so that all that was new and valid in her thought would not be watered down or falsified, but be given space to unfold. With a mere textbook-theology one could not have captured Adrienne's work; it required a knowledge of the great tradition to realize that her original propositions in no way contradicted it. The Holy Spirit may suddenly illuminate parts of revelation that have always been there, but have not been sufficiently reflected upon.[156]

To be sure, Balthasar admits that his "own ideas and way of thinking were not extinguished but rather enriched" by what he received from Adrienne.[157] It would, however, be worth pursuing the question of their shared mission, which Johann Roten presents as "essentially theological, in the comprehensive meaning of this word."[158] If, in fact, Adrienne's work "corresponds in themes and tone to those of my own books," Balthasar argues, this follows as a consequence of the fact that their missions "interpenetrate."[159] It is precisely in this sense that one might best understand Joseph Ratzinger's presentation of their relationship in terms of prophet and theologian.

Hans Urs von Balthasar is unthinkable without Adrienne von Speyr. I think that one could show in the case of all great theological figures that new theological

---

155. Balthasar, *Our Task*, 45.
156. Balthasar and Scola, *Test Everything*, 88.
157. Balthasar, *Our Task*, 72–73.
158. Roten, "The Two Halves of the Moon," 71. Theirs, Roten argues, is the mission "to receive and to transmit, to ponder, 'interpret,' and to implant the word of God in human history" (ibid.).
159. Balthasar, *My Work*, 21.

emergences [*Aufbrüche*] only become possible when there is first a prophetic breakthrough [*Durchbrüche*]. As long as one proceeds only rationally, there is essentially nothing new that emerges. It might be increasingly more precise in its systematization; ever more subtle questions will be raised, but the original breakthroughs giving rise to great theology simply do not emerge from the rational enterprise of theology, but [rather] from the charismatic, prophetic impulse. In this respect, I believe that prophecy and theology belong tightly bonded together. Theology, understood as scientific theology in the strictest sense is not prophetic, but it will be truly living theology, only when it is energized from and illuminated by a prophetic impulse.[160]

Perhaps still more helpful than this explanation of their shared mission in terms of prophet and theologian is Balthasar's own presentation of his relationship with Adrienne in terms of the unity between "spirit [Adrienne] and institution [Balthasar],"[161] as exemplified in the unity of Mary and Peter: a unity requiring what he perceived as the strictest obedience on the part of both (Adrienne and Balthasar).[162] In that regard, Balthasar's presentation of the objective and subjective aspects of the Spirit's role in building up the body of Christ in terms of office and charism is also pertinent, as is Adrienne's treatment of the relation between authority and love in the Church; and, of course, these other intuitions might be further developed within the context of my exposition in chapter six of what Adrienne and Balthasar present as typically "male" and "female" missions.[163]

It would thus seem—to respond to Narcisse's question above—that Balthasar's "systematic Trinitarian foundation" is indeed based "upon profound theological, 'mystical,' realities." This is even the case, I might add, if we join Peter Henrici in the observation that "the earliest works came into

---

160. Joseph Cardinal Ratzinger, "Das Problem der christlichen Prophetie. Neils Christian Hvidt im Gespräch mit Joseph Kardinal Ratzinger," *Internationale katholische Zeitschrift "Communio"* 28 (March–April 1999): 183. Similar is Rino Fisichella's presentation of their shared mission in terms of the complementarity of prophet and doctor in "Hans Urs von Balthasar et Adrienne von Speyr: l'inseparabilità delle due opere," *Communio* (Italian edition) 156 (1997): 61–74. See also Servais, "Per una valutazione dell'influsso di Adrienne von Speyr su Hans Urs von Balthasar," 80–83.

161. See Balthasar, *My Work*, 107; see also the essay "Spirit and Institution" in *Explorations in Theology* IV, 209–43; and (with Albus), "Fire and Spirit," 583–84. Cf. Speyr, *Die Wort und die Mystik* I, 25; and *Hohelied*, 50–51.

162. On the obedience required of Balthasar and Adrienne, see for example Balthasar, *Our Task*, 19–20 and 69–71. On the unity of Mary and Peter, see Balthasar, *Theo-Drama* III, 358–60; *The Office of Peter and the Structure of the Church*, 208; *Mary for Today*, 67; *Explorations in Theology* II, 157–66; Antonio Sicari, "Mary, Peter and John: Figures of the Church," *Communio* 19 (1992): 189–207; and John Saward, "Mary and Peter in the Christological Constellation: Balthasar's Ecclesiology," in Riches, *The Analogy of Beauty*, 105–32.

163. On the relation between office and charism, see for example Balthasar and Scola, *Test Everything*, 64–65; and Balthasar, *Theo-Logic* III, 308. On the relation between authority and love in the Church, see Balthasar, *First Glance*, 52–53; and Speyr, *John* IV, 159–443. On male and female missions, see Balthasar, *Our Task*, 16–17.

being independently [of Adrienne's influence]."¹⁶⁴ Balthasar, after all, considered all of these earlier works as a sort of preparation for the mission of handing on Adrienne's mystical doctrine to the Church.¹⁶⁵ He was, moreover, convinced that what one "makes of his natural gifts depends entirely on the mission that God has designed for him,"¹⁶⁶ and he unquestionably understood his mission as entailing the transmission of Adrienne's mystical experiences and dictations to the Church.¹⁶⁷

Without denying the authenticity of this mission or his faithfulness and competency in accomplishing it and without, furthermore, attempting to circumvent the question—still worth pursuing—of whether Balthasar might validly claim the "right" to draw upon Adrienne's presumably mystical experiences "as a direct source for theological construction,"¹⁶⁸ I would, furthermore, respond affirmatively to what is also implied in Narcisse's question. Balthasar's theology—no less than that of Adrienne, although the former preferred to speak of their "common theological work"¹⁶⁹ and referred to Adrienne's books as "'my' greatest life's work"¹⁷⁰—might well be served by a thorough questioning of all that is in (at least apparent) contradiction with certain aspects of Christian doctrine. This theology might, in other words, be rendered more credible by being "purged" (to borrow from Narcisse) or "purified" (to borrow from the *Catechism*)¹⁷¹ of certain images or concepts that might lead to misunderstanding, especially in what may be thought in opposition to Christian doctrine.

To be sure, this would entail not so much a "purging" of language, as

---

164. Henrici, "A Sketch of Von Balthasar's Life," 31.

165. This is particularly apparent in Balthasar, *Our Task*, 35–45, wherein he explains how his formation served him in this mission. He also explains how Adrienne "quite independently" (42) took up certain themes that he had already been studying or found interesting at the time preceding his encounter with her in 1940. See also Balthasar, *My Work*, 105.

166. Balthasar, *The Christian State of Life*, 75. See chapters one and two of the present volume for more detail.

167. See Balthasar, *Our Task*, 18n11. "Today [1968], after her death, her work appears far more important to me than mine, and the publication of her still unpublished writings takes precedence over all personal work of my own" (*First Glance at Adrienne von Speyr*, 13).

168. McIntosh, *A Christology from Within*, 26. See also Moss, "The Saints," 81–82. Not surprisingly, Balthasar is often criticized on precisely this point. See, for example, see Schenk, "Ist die Rede von leidenden Gott zu vermeiden?", 235–37; "The Epoché of Factical Damnation," 127–28; Kerr, "Adrienne von Speyr and Hans Urs von Balthasar," 32; Blankenhorn, book review of *Light in Darkness*, 953; Narcisse, "Participer à la vie trinitaire," 120; and O'Connor, book review of *Light in Darkness*, 747.

169. Such is the estimation of Balthasar, as evident in the chapter heading ("Our Common Theological Work") given in *Our Task*, 47.

170. Balthasar and Albus, "Spirit and Fire," 574.

171. Because God transcends all creatures, "we must," *The Catechism of the Catholic Church* teaches, "continually purify our language of everything in it that is limited, imagebound or imperfect, if we are not to confuse our image of God—'the inexpressible, the incomprehensible, the invisible, the ungraspable'—with our human representations. Our human words always fall short of the mystery of God" (no. 42).

(more importantly) a vigorous theological interpretation of Adrienne's mystical formulations which Balthasar perhaps too quickly takes up into his own work without first calming, as it were, the metaphorical language, or without attempting to explain it.[172] He has, no doubt, good reason for doing so: perhaps out of respect for her mission,[173] which—as we saw above—he believed to include the interpretation of her visions; perhaps for esteem of her person, whom he judged as possessing the "confessional attitude" that she proclaimed throughout her work as typically Christian, namely, "the permanent and fundamental openness of the whole soul to God and to the appropriate confessor or superior."[174] This attitude permitted her (and this constitutes the third possible reason) to exercise what he esteemed to be a certain objectivity with regard to the heavenly message that she received.

One might, on the other hand, rightfully ask whether objectivity in this sense of transmission—from God to the mystic—suffices to assure an objectivity in the other sense: from the mystic to the community of faith. Again, Maritain's insights are of help: "When someone from Heaven speaks […] it is necessary to understand them (to understand their 'literal sense') according to the spirit of him who causes these words to be heard." This means, for example, that "when realized" God's purposes "will doubtless appear very different from the image which we could form of them—all of this designated in terms essentially mysterious which, even reported exactly as they were heard, are true 'literally' as to the general practical sense which is intended to be communicated to us, but not as to the particular mental perspectives, nor to the particular imagery, nor to the words taken according to the human measure through whose instrumentality a transcendent thought is signified to us."[175]

Balthasar might also—and I think this to be highly probable—have simply incorporated Adrienne's images into his theology because he thought that the mystery of faith is best served by such a language. Perhaps, finally, he was convinced that Adrienne's mystical language is properly ecclesial (and thus theological). Finding echoes in other mystical writers recognized as such by the Church, in the Fathers and in Scripture, this language is (as Balthasar would have it) not unknown to the tradition.[176] With real respect not only for these (probable) "reasons" as to why Balthasar simply appropri-

---

172. See, for example, Emery's critique in "The Immutability of the God of Love and the Problem of Language Concerning the 'Suffering of God,'" 51, as well as my treatment of the problematic he points to here in chapter five of the present volume.

173. See Balthasar, *First Glance at Adrienne von Speyr*, 13.

174. Balthasar, *Our Task*, 27. See also ibid., 19. 175. Maritain, *Notebooks*, 93.

176. This is implied, for example, in his interview with Scola (*Test Everything*, 88). See also Lee, "The Role of Mysticism within the Church as Conceived by Hans Urs von Balthasar," 121.

ated Adrienne's mystical language and imagery without practicing a certain "purifying" distance—and the liturgical reference here is purposeful insofar as it implies the return of the object (in this case, the language) from the holy realm to the profane world—I insist that any such interpretative effort on our part must not impose a theological "system" upon their work.

What I have in mind is, rather, drawing out certain questionable phrases, images, and doctrines—whether from his opus, hers, or both—in an attempt to understand their meaning within the whole of their common theological work, on the one hand, and within the whole of the rich and vast Catholic tradition (including most especially the Thomistic tradition), on the other. This tradition is the source of the fourfold criteria that Balthasar proposes for judging the authenticity of Adrienne's mysticism: that her teaching be subject to magisterial scrutiny, that it originate within the Church, that it contribute to the Church's edification, and that it be in consonance with canonical revelation.[177]

Hence, for example, we might ask the meaning of one of her apparently contradictory statements dictated from within, Balthasar explains, an experiences of "God-forsakenness": the experience of being "in the hole [*Loch*],"[178] as she put it. In this particular passage, cited by Gilles Emery from part of the posthumous works[179] as an example of how Adrienne's complex doctrine of Christ's dereliction might have misled Balthasar, she claims that "not only Christ's humanity suffers, but [that] the whole Trinity is engaged [*beteiligt*]" in the Son's experience of estrangement on the Cross: even—she further explains—to the extent that the Trinity might be conceived of as "destroyed [*zerstört*]" in itself. Adrienne admits that this is merely a human expression of an unfathomable mystery, and "yet [it] is truer than if one were to say that the divinity cannot suffer, and [that] the Father as God is not engaged in the Son's suffering."[180]

Given the (presumable) intensity of her suffering at the moment of this dictation, one might ask whether this theologically unacceptable statement does not betray a valid theological concern: that of maintaining a common divine will within the Godhead despite the experience—"from within" Christ's human consciousness[181]—of being severed (as it were) from the Fa-

---

177. See Lee, "The Role of Mysticism within the Church as Conceived by Hans Urs von Balthasar," 112.

178. For an explanation, see Balthasar's introduction to Speyr, *Kreuz und Hölle* I, 13.

179. See Emery, "The Immutability of the God of Love and the Problem of Language Concerning the 'Suffering of God,'" 51.

180. See Speyr, *Erde und Himmel* II, no. 1471 (157).

181. In his foreword to Speyr, *The Passion from Within*, Balthasar explains that her meditations

ther through terrible psychological suffering which cannot be expressed otherwise than as (the feeling of) abandonment, as typifies what the tradition presents as the dark night of faith.[182]

Here, then, there can be no question, as Richard Schenk seems to suggest, of trying to explain human suffering by way of theodicy.[183] Adrienne can in no way be accused of putting God on trial in an attempt to prove his innocence vis-à-vis the atrocities of world events (including most especially that of her own suffering) which God certainly might have prevented. Rather, in the suffering of this woman, like that of all authentic mystics (let us give her—at least for the sake of argumentation—the benefit of the doubt), we are confronted (as were presumably she and Balthasar) with the very real question of interpreting the sufferings of a God who reveals himself thus: in the human sufferings of his incarnate Son as they are transmitted by Scripture, of course, but also (albeit privately) in the experiences of those whom he has admitted therein.

Granted, one might question the validity not only of Adrienne's mystical experiences, but also (it bears repeating) of Balthasar's almost unwavering decision to draw upon them as a source for his theology, even to the point that it often reads like a novel, as Karen Kilby maintains and Francesca Murphy indirectly refutes.[184] If, however, we might presume—even for the sake of argumentation—the validity of those experiences, then might we not also, and almost inevitably, ask: what are we to make of them theologically?

This question of interpretation is, of course, complicated by the fact that Adrienne not only experienced certain mystical states but was also charged, as I explained above, with what Balthasar believed to be the specific task of interpreting them. This conviction—in light of which Balthasar claims to have "in no way enlarged, rounded off, [or] set off" what he witnessed and heard of Adrienne's experiences entrusted to him in the form of dictations—

---

there (and the same is certainly true of the content of *Kreuz und Hölle* I-II and of much of *Erde und Himmel* I-III) "are always concerned with the interior aspect of the Passion event, mostly with the interior states and experiences of Christ [...]. Such experiences of the interior states of persons and events were a very special charism given to Adrienne von Speyr, here as in her other works. It is evidently not a question of 'empathy' or of psychologizing, but rather a 'being admitted,' which becomes particularly clear because these in-sights [*Ein-Sichten*] always prove to be important in relation to salvation history (or 'theologically')" (Balthasar in Speyr, *The Passion from Within*, 7).

182. See my treatment of this theme in the postcript of chapter five.
183. See his "Ist die Rede von leidenden Gott zu vermeiden?"
184. See Kilby, *Balthasar: A (Very) Critical Introduction*, 114 and 151. As for Francesca Aran Murphy, she argues that Balthasar's theodramatic vision provides an alternative to narrative theologies, such as those of, for example, George Lindbeck (to whom Kilby dedicates her book); Robert Jenson; and Herbert McCabe. See Francesca Aran Murphy, *God Is Not a Story: Realism Revisited* (Oxford: Oxford University Press, 2007).

ought not to prevent us, however, from effectively interpreting (that is to say, situating) Adrienne's texts within the whole of the Christian (especially Catholic) tradition, which—it bears repeating—is what Balthasar himself attempted to do.[185]

Indeed, Balthasar does well to point Adrienne's readers in the direction of threefold and constantly "pending [*schwebendes*] balance" to be maintained while examining her obviously more mystical works and doctrines: the balance (1) "between the lived experience and the theological truths contained therein"; (2) between the personal experience of suffering (by Adrienne) and its objective expression in the form of the dictations recorded by Balthasar (who acted simultaneously as stenographer, "official representative of the Church" and "an accompanying friend"); and (3) "between the sensual and the spiritual aspects of the experience."[186] And we might add, as does Balthasar elsewhere,[187] (4) between the mysterious participated experience of Adrienne—that is, her mystical suffering, which is simultaneously physical, psychological, and spiritual, and which presupposes her mystical consciousness—and the actual experience of the God-man (in his twofold consciousness as man and as God) who has invited her to participate therein.

If, therefore, we might be willing to give her the benefit of the doubt, then rather than shying away from the specific theological task of interpreting both her experiences and her doctrine, we might instead allow her experiences to interpret her doctrine (as I proposed in the example above) and her doctrine to interpret her experiences (as I proposed in my postscript to chapter five of this volume). "What is at issue," as Balthasar sees it, "is the presentation of the mystery, how it is that obedience enabled the Son of God to bear the whole of the world's sin, what this bearing of sin meant for him experientially, what inconceivable landscapes of suffering emerged here—constantly new views, perspectives, unexpected changes, in which the suffering is deepened and intensified—how the experience of time is thus eliminated, what the anxiety, the abandonment by God, the separation from men and from the Mother [Mary] mean for the Son, and so forth."[188]

From this perspective, one might question whether, in interpreting her (presumably) mystical share in the consciousness of Christ, Adrienne—theologically uneducated as she was—did not often pass too quickly from this experience (that of Christ's *human* consciousness, regardless of the su-

---

185. See Balthasar and Scola, *Test Everything*, 88.
186. Balthasar, "Einleitung," in Speyr, *Kreuz und Hölle* I, 11–12.
187. See Balthasar, "General Introduction to the Posthumous Works," in Speyr, *Book of All Saints* I, 13.
188. Ibid.

pernatural means of her participation therein) to her doctrine of his *divine consciousness* and thus also to the divine nature. From within what Balthasar presents as her experience of mystically partaking of Christ's "interior state," Adrienne explains, for example: "As God, he knows about the panic he suffers as man; the consciousness of his mission is overlaid at times so that the human panic may, so to speak, directly touch his divinity. As God he robs himself of clear vision; as God, he closes the door against any hope and consolation, against everything that binds the Son to the Father."[189]

Assuredly there is no surer way to enter into the mystery of Christ's divinity (and thus the mystery of the whole Godhead) than by way of his humanity,[190] but the two ought never to be confused or combined, even when both belong to the one divine Person of God's Son.[191] In fact, I am convinced that Adrienne's intention in the passage cited above and other similar passages is precisely that of clarifying the Son's unity with the Father (their common divine will, which she—mistakenly, I would argue—presents as a commonality in suffering) and the adherence of Christ's human will to the divine will despite the terrible experience of "estrangement" from God.

Balthasar explains, for example, that Adrienne's presentation of what the bearing of sin meant for the Son of God experientially "constantly takes place in the dialectic between distance and proximity, the complete separation and then once again the reconciliation of the suffering sinner, as something Adrienne feels with the suffering Lord: though experiential, her participation is indirect; to describe this in a proper way belongs to the most difficult and important aspects of her mission to undergo the passion."[192] At any rate, while Balthasar esteems that "the implications of Adrienne's Holy Saturday and other 'hellish' experiences—for theology, mysticism, and ordinary Christian life—are incalculable," he also suggests that we "not forget that, for Adrienne, despite all attempts at clarification, this experience remained an absolute mystery, resisting resolution into the formulas of any 'dialectic.'"[193]

To summarize, problematic passages such as the one mentioned above cannot be simply dismissed; nor, however, ought they to be detached from the context wherein they originate: namely, the attempt to bring to expres-

---

189. Speyr, *The Passion from Within*, 61–62; see also Balthasar's foreword in ibid., 7.
190. See Gilles Emery, "*Theologia* and *Dispensatio*: The Centrality of the Divine Missions in St. Thomas's Trinitarian Theology," *The Thomist* 74, no. 4 (2010): 515–61, esp. 546. See also chapter seven of this volume, wherein is addressed the complexities of this question with regard to the two natures of Christ.
191. Cf. *DZ* 302.
192. Balthasar, "General Introduction to the Posthumous Works," in Speyr, *Book of All Saints* I, 13; see also Balthasar, *Theo-Logic* II, 357–58.
193. Balthasar, *Our Task*, 65–66.

sion a profound (presumably) mystical experience. Neither, still, should they be detached—and Balthasar insists upon this point—from the rest of Adrienne's profound and extensive works, most of which are dedicated to biblical commentary and spiritual themes. Indeed, these works seen as a whole provide, Balthasar explains, the base or pedestal (*Sockel*) upon which the theme of the paschal mysteries in Adrienne's work ought to be set.[194] It is for this reason that Balthasar cautions Adrienne's reader against too quickly engaging her posthumous works, which are of an apparently more mystical nature, and whose contents are not always easy to reconcile with authentic Catholic teaching (at least not obviously so).

On the other hand, such audacious, even "dangerous," language is—it bears repeating—no reason to deny the authenticity of Adrienne's mystical experiences, nor of her mission (as Balthasar saw it) to contribute to a more profound understanding of the faith. Helpful in understanding what I mean by this statement are the reflections of Jacques Maritain concerning his own appropriation of the message of Mélanie Calvat, the visionary of La Salette:

> I would prefer to say: "I believe in the full authenticity of the reported words": without implying, for all that, that everything said must be taken "literally," according to the usual sense of this expression, that is to say, as to the essentially human measure or to the essentially human modality which our words entail in common earthly usage. [...] The people of Heaven employ human language, which cannot precisely signify purely and simply "literally" what they themselves mean to say; the literal sense of what they tell us surpasses our words and remains therefore essentially charged with mystery, whereas a kind of immoderation—in "too much" (*overstatement*) or in "not enough" (*understatement*)—introduces itself into our words such as they employ them. The voices of Joan of Arc in her prison told her that she was going to be delivered:—that is to say, not! This meant to climb the funeral-pile, and to be delivered in this manner from the English and from their prelates, and also delivered from this perishable flesh, and *delivered from evil,* and free to see her God.[195]

Beyond, therefore, the challenge to disciples of Balthasar to reconsider the often very pointed and well-placed questions of his critics—most of which address (at least indirectly) his appropriation of Adrienne's experiences or teaching—is the challenge to these same critics to reconsider Balthasar's teaching in light of these same experiences and teaching. By this I obviously do not mean that these critics should be willing to compromise their vocation to teach (and thus implicitly defend) the faith. Far more important to those unconvinced of the doctrine of Balthasar and Adrienne than the will-

---

194. See Balthasar, "Einleitung," in Speyr, *Kreuz und Hölle* I, 14.
195. Maritain, *Notebooks,* 91; cf. McIntosh, *Mystical Theology,* 124.

ingness to "kindly" bend in their direction is, indeed, the courageous attempt to bring to light certain errors or possible misunderstandings in this doctrine. Nor would I suggest that metaphysically-minded theologians should be willing to "adapt" the formulas of faith in terms borrowed from a mystical or metaphorical language such as Adrienne and Balthasar (or even Scripture or the Fathers) have to offer. However, these same theologians ought not, it seems to me—at least not if they wish to retain an authentically "Catholic" spirit—simply condemn all that is not immediately graspable by human reason in the theological formulations of Adrienne and Balthasar.[196]

Of particular pertinence in this context are the wise words of Etienne Gilson in a private letter to Henri de Lubac, whom he considers therein as both a "theologian of great stature" and "a humanist in the great tradition of humanist theologians."

> Humanist theologians usually do not love the scholastics, and they are almost always hated by the scholastics. Why? In part, it seems to me, because the latter understand only univocal propositions and those that seem to be univocal. The former, by contrast, are more interested in the truth that the proposition attempts to formulate and that always partly escapes it. Then the latter no longer understand; they become restless, and, because they cannot be certain that what escapes them is not false, they condemn it as a matter of principle, because that is more *secure*.[197]

To be sure, security is hardly to be found in the theological perspective of Adrienne and Balthasar: one which challenges us to jump into deep waters (cf. Lk 5:5). Because God's revelation in Scripture "is not primarily a doctrine but the occurrence of a deed," it must in fact be answered, as Balthasar would have it, "not with (faith-) knowledge, but with a life (in the Holy Spirit)."[198] It is not enough to "unite ourselves outwardly"—to rally in favor of a dogmatic doctrine, for example—for "the question is whether the grace will be given us to collect ourselves inwardly as well."[199] This means, more specifically, that the "innermost disposition" of the theologian—like that of all Christians—which was previously thought of as "the most private thing" that he or she could possess, is henceforth "conceivable to him only in light of the dogma of God's Incarnation."[200]

---

196. It is with good reason that Blankenhorn argues, for example, in his review of *Light in Darkness*, 954: "In the end, her [Pitstick's] polemics set up an obstacle to a just evaluation of Balthasar's thought. She does not show how some of his insights might at least highlight the ways in which Christology still needs to develop, even if Balthasar's original proposal for such a development is not altogether successful. Does Balthasar really have nothing to teach us about Christ's suffering and death?" See also Schmitt, *The Sacrament of Confession as a "Sequela Christi" in the Writings of A. von Speyr*, 246.

197. Cited by Balthasar in *The Theology of Henri de Lubac*, 14.

198. Balthasar, *Convergences*, 39. Cf. Speyr, *John* III, 101; and *John* I, 21.

199. Balthasar, *Convergences*, 13.

200. Balthasar, *The Glory of the Lord* I, 254.

Balthasar reminds the theologian that whatever knowledge he or she might think to possess ought only to convict him or her of ignorance (cf. 1 Cor 8:2). Dogmatic knowledge is no exception to this rule, he insists, which is to say that it too is "subject to the paradox which applies to all Christian truth, that the content of what is given always overflows to an infinite degree the vessel into which it is poured." Hence the task of the theologian is not that of simply arguing from certain established premises (defined dogmatic truths) in order to draw from them "automatic conclusions." Rather, it is that of proceeding with every step of one's thinking "as a direct hearing and obeying of the living Spirit of Jesus."[201] Similarly Adrienne cautions those who would attempt to formulate truths of faith. When, in fact, our understanding is not constantly nourished by God's meaning, we tend to set boundaries to what is absolutely unbounded. Adrienne thus argues that our dogmatic formulations must be so inspired by the Spirit that no limitations are thereby set to the infinite word spoken by the Lord.[202] The only way to adequately transmit the truths of faith is, as they would both conclude, to be so enraptured by the person of Christ that one is willingly employed as his instrument.

As Christ is the Father's exegete in virtue of his receptivity, we too are called not merely to speak God's word, but to bear it (him) in our very persons, or more accurately said, to become living members of his body in service of his truth (and thus of his person). "This is the fundamental law for all Christian ethics, and even for all Christian knowledge: to carry out one's action in conjunction with what has already been done in its fullness, and therefore to bring about and perfect that which has already been brought about and perfected, since it is only in this way that what is revealed in itself becomes revealed also to us: 'Beloved, if God so loved us, we ought also to love one another. No man has ever seen God; [but] if we love one another, then God abides in us and his love is perfected in us' (1 Jn 4:11–12)."[203]

Such is the attitude that dominates the theology of Balthasar.[204] This is an attitude to which he was perhaps already inclined in virtue of his Ignatian education with its emphasis upon *soli Deo gloria*, but one that was also largely cultivated by his close and long collaboration with Adrienne von Speyr. For Adrienne, the entire mystery of the human person might be summarized

---

201. Balthasar, *A Theology of History*, 108; see also *Explorations in Theology* I, 186.
202. See Speyr, *Das Wort und die Mystik* I, 43 and II, 26.
203. Balthasar, *Love Alone Is Credible*, 116–17.
204. "I consider my own theology to be like the finger of John pointing to the fullness of revelation in Jesus Christ, which is unfolded in the immense fullness of its reception in the history of the Church, above all in the mediation of the saints" (Balthasar and Albus, "Spirit and Fire," 574).

in terms of loving surrender, because quite simply—as she "saw" it—this attitude is divine before it is human. It nonetheless remains for the Christian to be stretched, as it were, to the infinite measure of God's own surrender.

"God is a consuming fire," Balthasar explained in the first book that he wrote under Adrienne's influence.[205] "He begins with a small flame, and before you realize it he has gotten total hold of you and you are caught. If you let yourself be caught you are lost, for heavenwards there are no limits. He is God—accustomed to infinity. He sucks you upwards like a cyclone, whirls you up and away like a waterspout. Look out: man is made for measure and for limits, and only in the finite does he find rest and happiness. But this God knows nothing of measure. He is a seducer of hearts."[206] We thus end where we began: in a circular movement leading from God to the human being and from the human being to God. At the center of this movement stands the divine person of Christ in whom the "exhaustive taking possession of man on the part of God [...] is already as such an adaptation of man to the measure of God,"[207] and all of this within the overriding mystery of Trinitarian surrender.

The movement that circulates from God and back to God in faith, love and hope, in the mission and the sacraments, is not a movement from unity to plurality and back to unity but contains the original, unity itself, and as such contains the Word. [...] The glory of the Father in his unity is so great that he cannot do otherwise than give his glory to God himself, that is, to the Son. The Father therefore demonstrates his glory and his unity by giving his Son to the world and communicates himself to us in the Son, for in no other way can he communicate the uniqueness of his unity.[208]

There could hardly be a better word with which to conclude this volume than "unity." I have learned from undertaking this study that true unity presupposes differences which are in no way suppressed but are only heightened within the positive or fruitful "tension" realized by reciprocal surrender, as is archetypically the case in the holy Trinity. Such are the differences-in-unity of the common theology of Adrienne von Speyr and Hans Urs von Balthasar. Such also is the difference-in-unity, or unity-in-difference, of this theology in comparison and contrast with that of St. Thomas Aquinas. And such, ultimately, is the richness of Catholicism, as founded ultimately within the mystery of the triune God. For, as Adrienne puts it, "in God unity and distance are not opposites but full and eternally fruitful unity."[209]

---

205. See Henrici, "A Sketch of Balthasar's Life," 31.
206. Balthasar, *Heart of the World*, 117–18.
207. Balthasar, *The Glory of the Lord* I, 475.
208. Speyr, *John* I, 122. In the official translation, "Word" appears in lower case, but it is clear within the context that Adrienne refers thereby to the second person of the Trinity.
209. Speyr, *World of Prayer*, 48.

BIBLIOGRAPHY

Works of Adrienne von Speyr
(edited by Hans Urs von Balthasar)

Translated Works

Book of All Saints, Part One. With a general introduction to the posthumous works by Hans Urs von Balthasar, ed., 1–19; and with a particular introduction to the present volume by Balthasar, 20–24. Translated by David C. Schindler. San Francisco: Ignatius Press, 2008. [*Das Allerheiligen Buch* I. Volume 1.1 of *Die Nachlasswerke*. Einsiedeln: Johannes Verlag, 1966].

The Boundless God. Translated by Helena M. Tomko. San Francisco: Ignatius Press, 2004. [*Der grenzenlose Gott*. Einsiedeln: Johannes Verlag, 1955, 1981²].

The Christian State of Life. Translated by Mary Frances McCarthy. San Francisco: Ignatius Press, 1986. [*Christlicher Stand*. Einsiedeln: Johannes Verlag, 1956].

Confession. With foreword by Hans Urs von Balthasar, ed., 9–10. Translated by Douglas W. Stott. San Francisco: Ignatius Press, 1985. [*Die Beichte*. Einsiedeln: Johannes Verlag, 1960, 1982²].

The Countenance of the Father. Translated by David Kipp. San Francisco: Ignatius Press, 1997. [*Das Angesicht des Vaters*. Einsiedeln: Johannes Verlag, 1955, 1981²].

The Cross: Word and Sacrament. Translated by Graham Harrison. San Francisco: Ignatius Press, 1983. [*Kreuzeswort und Sakrament*. Einsiedeln: Johannes Verlag, 1957].

Elijah. Translated by Brian McNeil. San Francisco: Ignatius Press, 1990. [*Elija*. Einsiedeln: Johannes Verlag, 1972].

The Gates of Eternal Life. Translated by Corona Sharp. San Francisco: Ignatius Press, 1983. [*Die Pforten des ewigen Lebens*. Einsiedeln: Johannes Verlag, 1953].

Handmaid of the Lord. Translated by E. A. Nelson. San Francisco: Ignatius Press, 1985. [*Magd des Herrn*. Trier: Johannes Verlag Einsiedeln, 1969, 1988³].

The Holy Mass. With foreword by Hans Urs von Balthasar, ed., 7–9. Translated by Helena M. Saward. San Francisco: Ignatius Press, 1999. [*Die heilige Messe*. Einsiedeln: Johannes Verlag, 1980].

John I: *The Word Becomes Flesh. Meditations on John 1–5*. Translated by Lucia Wiedenhöver and Alexander Dru. San Francisco: Ignatius Press, 1994. [*Das Wort wird Fleisch*. Volume 1 of *Betrachtungen über das Johannesevangelium Kapitel 1–5*. Einsiedeln: Johannes Verlag, 1949].

John II: *Discourses of Controversy. Meditations on John 6–12*. With foreword by Hans Urs von Balthasar, ed., 7–8. Translated by Brian McNeil. San Francisco: Ignatius Press, 1993.

[*Die Streitreden. Betrachtungen über das Johannesevangelium Kapitel 6–12*. Einsiedeln: Johannes Verlag, 1949].

John III: The Farewell Discourses. Meditations on John 13–17. With foreword by Hans Urs von Balthasar, ed., 7–8. Translated by E. A. Nelson. San Francisco: Ignatius Press, 1987. [*Die Abschiedsreden. Betrachtungen über Johannes 13–17*. Einsiedeln: Johannes Verlag, 1948].

John IV: The Birth of the Church. Meditations on John 18–21. Translated by David Kipp. San Francisco: Ignatius Press, 1991. [*Geburt der Kirche. Betrachtungen über Kapitel 18–21 des Johannesevangeliums*. Einsiedeln: Johannes Verlag, 1949, 1998²].

The Letter to the Colossians. Translated by Michael J. Miller. San Francisco: Ignatius Press, 1998. [*Der Kolosserbrief*. Einsiedeln: Johannes Verlag, 1957, 1993²].

The Letter to the Ephesians. With preface by Hans Urs von Balthasar, ed., 9–11. Translated by Adrian Walker. San Francisco: Ignatius Press, 1996. [*Der Epheserbrief*. Einsiedeln: Johannes Verlag, 1949. Also published under the title *Kinder des Lichtes*, 1983²].

Light and Images: Elements of Contemplation. With introduction by Hans Urs von Balthasar, ed., 11–15. Translated by David Schindler, Jr. San Francisco: Ignatius Press, 2004. [*Das Licht und die Bilder: Elemente der Kontemplation*. Einsiedeln: Johannes Verlag, 1955, 1986²].

Lumina and New Lumina. With prefatory note by Hans Urs von Balthasar, ed., 7–10. Translated by Adrian Walker. San Francisco: Ignatius Press, 2008. [*Lumina und Neue Lumina*. Einsiedeln: Johannes Verlag, 1968, 1974²].

Mary in the Redemption. With introduction by Hans Urs von Balthasar, ed., 7–9. Translated by Helena M. Tomko. San Francisco: Ignatius Press, 2003. [*Maria in der Erlösung*. Einsiedeln: Johannes Verlag, 1979, 1999³].

The Mission of the Prophets. With foreword by Hans Urs von Balthasar, ed., 7–9. Translated by David Kipp. San Francisco: Ignatius Press, 1996. [*Die Sendung der Propheten*. Einsiedeln: Johannes Verlag, 1953].

My Early Years. With foreword by Hans Urs von Balthasar, ed., 9–14. Translated by Mary Emily Hamilton and Dennis D. Martin. San Francisco: Ignatius Press, 1995. [*Aus meinem Leben: Fragment einer Selbstbiographie*. Einsiedeln: Johannes Verlag, 1968, 1984²].

The Mystery of Death. Translated by Graham Harrison. San Francisco: Ignatius Press, 1988. [*Das Geheimnis des Todes*. Einsiedeln: Johannes Verlag, 1953].

The Passion from Within. With foreword by Hans Urs von Balthasar, ed., 7–9. Translated by Lucia Wiedenhöver. San Francisco: Ignatius Press, 1998. [*Die Passion von Innen*. Einsiedeln: Johannes Verlag, 1981].

They Followed His Call: Vocation and Asceticism. With foreword by Hans Urs von Balthasar, ed., 7–8. Translated by Erasmo Leiva-Merikakis. San Francisco: Ignatius Press, 1986. [*Sie folgten seinem Ruf: Berufung und Askese*. Einsiedeln: Johannes Verlag, 1955, 1976²].

Three Women and the Lord. Translated by Graham Harrison. San Francisco: Ignatius Press, 1986. [*Drei Frauen und der Herr*. Einsiedeln: Johannes Verlag, 1978].

The Victory of Love: A Meditation on Romans 8. With foreword by Hans Urs von Balthasar, ed., 7–9. Translated by Lucia Wiedenhöver. San Francisco: Ignatius Press, 1990. [*Der Sieg der Liebe: Betrachtungen über Römer 8*. Einsiedeln: Johannes Verlag, 1953].

With God and with Men: Prayers. Translated by Adrian Walker. San Francisco: Ignatius Press, 1995. [*Bei Gott und bei den Menschen: Gebete*. Einsiedeln: Johannes Verlag, 1992].

The World of Prayer. With foreword by Hans Urs von Balthasar, ed., 9–11. Translated by Graham Harrison. San Francisco: Ignatius Press, 1985. [*Die Welt des Gebetes*. Einsiedeln: Johannes Verlag, 1951, 1992²].

Untranslated Works

Achtzehn Psalmen. Einsiedeln: Johannes Verlag, 1957.
Apokalypse: Betrachtungen über die geheime Offenbarung. With introduction (Zur Einführung) by Hans Urs von Balthasar, ed., 7–13. Einsiedeln: Johannes Verlag, 1950, 1999³.
Arzt und Patient. With foreword (Vorwort des Herausgebers) by Hans Urs von Balthasar, ed., 7–8. Einsiedeln: Johannes Verlag, 1983.
Bereitschaft: Dimensionen christlichen Gehorsams. With introduction (Einleitung) by Hans Urs von Balthasar, ed., 3–4. Einsiedeln: Johannes Verlag, 1975.
Das Allerheiligen Buch II. Volume 1.2 of *Die Nachlasswerke.* With foreword (Vorwort) by Hans Urs von Balthasar, ed., 11–12. Published privately (Privatdruck). Einsiedeln: Johannes Verlag, 1977.
Das Buch vom Gehorsam. With foreword (Vorwort) by Hans Urs von Balthasar, ed., 7–8. Einsiedeln: Johannes Verlag, 1966.
Das Fischernetz. Volume 2 of *Die Nachlasswerke.* With introduction (Einleitung) by Hans Urs von Balthasar, 7–12. Published privately (Privatdruck). Einsiedeln: Johannes Verlag, 1969.
Das Hohelied. With foreword (Vorwort) by Hans Urs von Balthasar, ed., 5–6. Einsiedeln: Johannes Verlag, 1972.
Das Themenheft. With foreword (Vorwort) by Hans Urs von Balthasar, ed., 5–6. Einsiedeln: Johannes Verlag, 1977.
Das Wort und die Mystik I: *Subjektive Mystik.* Volume 6 of *Die Nachlasswerke.* With foreword (Vorwort des Herausgebers) by Hans Urs von Balthasar, ed., 10–14. Published privately (Privatdruck). Einsiedeln: Johannes Verlag, 1970.
Das Wort und die Mystik II: *Objektive Mystik.* Volume 5 of *Die Nachlasswerke.* With foreword (Vorwort des Herausgebers) by Hans Urs von Balthasar, ed., 15–17. Published privately (Privatdruck). Einsiedeln: Johannes Verlag, 1970.
Der Mensch vor Gott. Einsiedeln: Johannes Verlag, 1966.
Die Bergpredigt: Betrachtungen über Matthäus 5–7. Einsiedeln: Johannes Verlag, 1948.
Die katholischen Briefe I: *Der Jakobusbrief und die Petrusbriefe.* With introduction (Einleitung) by Hans Urs von Balthasar, ed., 5–26. Einsiedeln: Johannes Verlag, 1961.
Die katholischen Briefe II: *Die Johannesbriefe.* Einsiedeln: Johannes Verlag, 1961.
Die Schöpfung. With prefatory note (Vorbemerkung) by Hans Urs von Balthasar, ed., 7–9. Einsiedeln: Johannes Verlag, 1972.
Dienst der Freude: Betrachtungen über den Philipperbrief. With foreword (Vorwort) by Hans Urs von Balthasar, ed., 5–6. Einsiedeln: Johannes Verlag, 1951.
Erde und Himmel I: *Einübungen.* Volume 8 of *Die Nachlasswerke.* With foreword (Vorwort) by Hans Urs von Balthasar, ed., 5–9. Published privately (Privatdruck). Einsiedeln: Johannes Verlag, 1975.
Erde und Himmel II: *Die Zeit der großen Diktate.* Volume 9 of *Die Nachlasswerke.* With foreword (Vorwort) by Hans Urs von Balthasar, ed., 5–7. Published privately (Privatdruck). Einsiedeln: Johannes Verlag, 1975.
Erde und Himmel III: *Die späten Jahre.* Volume 10 of *Die Nachlasswerke.* With foreword (Vorwort) by Hans Urs von Balthasar, ed., 5–7. Published privately (Privatedruck). Einsiedeln: Johannes Verlag, 1976.
Gebetserfahrung. Einsiedeln: Johannes Verlag, 1965, 1978².
Geheimnis der Jugend. Volume 7 of *Die Nachlasswerke.* With introduction (Einleitung) by Hans Urs von Balthasar, ed., 7–11. Published privately (Privatdruck). Einsiedeln: Johannes Verlag, 1966.

Gleichnisse des Herrn. Einsiedeln: Johannes Verlag, 1966.
Ignatiana. Volume 11 of *Die Nachlasswerke*. With foreword (Vorwort) by Hans Urs von Balthasar, ed., 9–14. Published privately (Privatdruck). Einsiedeln: Johannes Verlag, 1974.
Isaias: Erklärung ausgewählter Texte mit einem Anhang zu den Visionen Daniels. With foreword (Vorwort) by Hans Urs von Balthasar, ed., 7–8. Einsiedeln: Johannes Verlag, 1958.
Job. With foreword (Vorwort) by Hans Urs von Balthasar, ed., 7–8. Einsiedeln: Johannes Verlag, 1972.
Korinther I. With foreword (Vorwort) by Hans Urs von Balthasar, ed., 5–8. Einsiedeln: Johannes Verlag, 1956.
Kostet und Seht: Ein theologisches Lesebuch. With foreword (Vorwort) by Hans Urs von Balthasar, ed., 13–14. Trier: Johannes Verlag Einsiedeln, 1988.
Kreuz und Hölle I: *Die Passionen*. Volume 3 of *Die Nachlasswerke*. With introduction (Einleitung) by Hans Urs von Balthasar, ed., 7–14. Published privately (Privatdruck). Einsiedeln: Johannes Verlag, 1966.
Kreuz und Hölle II: *Auftragshöllen*. Volume 4 of *Die Nachlasswerke*. With introduction (Einleitung) by Hans Urs von Balthasar, ed., 9–12. Published privately (Privatdruck). Einsiedeln: Johannes Verlag, 1972.
Markus: Betrachtungspunkte für eine Gemeinschaft. With foreword (Vorwort des Herausgebers) by Hans Urs von Balthasar, ed., 9–10. Einsiedeln: Johannes Verlag, 1971.
Passion nach Matthäus. Einsiedeln: Johannes Verlag, 1957.
Theologie der Geschlechter. Volume 12 of *Die Nachlasswerke*. With foreword (Vorwort des Herausgebers) by Hans Urs von Balthasar, ed., 7–9. Published privately (Privatdruck). Einsiedeln: Johannes Verlag, 1969.
Über die Liebe. With afterword (Nachwort) by Hans Urs von Balthasar, ed., 137–38. Einsiedeln: Johannes Verlag, 1976.

Works by Hans Urs von Balthasar

For a complete bibliography, see Cornelia Capol and Claudia Müller. *Hans Urs von Balthasar. Bibliography 1925–2005*. Einsiedeln: Johannes Verlag, 2005.

Translated Works

The Balthasar Reader. Edited by Medard Kehl and Werner Löser. Translated by Robert J. Daly and Fred Lawrence. New York: Crossroad, 1982.
The Christian and Anxiety. Translated by Dennis D. Martin and Michael J. Miller. With a foreword by Yves Tourenne, translated by Adrian Walker. San Francisco: Ignatius Press, 1994. [*Der Christ und die Angst*. Trier: Johannes Verlag Einsiedeln, 1951, 1989²].
Christian Meditation. Translated by Mary Theresilde Skerry. San Francisco: Ignatius Press, 1989. [*Christlich meditieren*. Freiburg im Breisgau: Herder, 1984].
The Christian State of Life. Translated by Mary Frances McCarthy. San Francisco: Ignatius Press, 1983. [*Christlicher Stand*. Einsiedeln: Johannes Verlag, 1977, 1981²].
Convergences: To the Source of Christian Mystery. Translated by E. A. Nelson. San Francisco: Ignatius Press, 1983. [*Einfaltungen. Auf Wegen christlicher Einigung*. Munich: Kösel, 1969].
Cosmic Liturgy: The Universe According to Maximus the Confessor. Translated by Brain E. Daley. San Francisco: Igantius Press and Communio Books, 2003. [*Kosmische Liturgie. Das Weltbild Maximus' des Bekenners*. Einsiedeln: Johannes Verlag, 1961].

Credo: Meditations on the Apostles' Creed. Translated by David Kipp. San Francisco: Ignatius Press, 2002, 2005². [*Credo. Meditationen zum Apostolischen Glaubenbekenntnis*. Freiburg im Breisgau: Herder, 1989].

Dare We Hope "That All Men Be Saved"? With a Short Discourse on Hell. Translated by David Kipp and Lothar Krauth. San Francisco: Ignatius Press, 1988. [*Was dürfen wir hoffen?* Einsiedeln: Johannes Verlag, 1986; and *Kleiner Diskurs über die Hölle*. Ostfildern: Schwabenverlag, 1987].

Does Jesus Know Us? Do We Know Him? Translated by Graham Harrison. San Francisco: Ignatius Press, 1983. [*Kennt uns Jesus—Kennen wir ihn?* Freiburg in Breisgau, Basel, Wien: Herder, 1980, 1980²].

Elucidations. Translated by John Riches. San Francisco: Ignatius Press, 1998. [*Klarstellungen. Zur Prüfung der Geister*. Freiburg im Breisgau: Herder, 1971].

Engagement with God. The Drama of Christian Discipleship. Translated by John Halliburton. San Francisco: Ignatius Press, 2008. [*In Gottes Einsatz leben*. Einsiedeln: Johannes Verlag, 1971, 1972²].

Epilogue. Translated by Edward T. Oakes. San Francisco: Ignatius Press, 2004. [*Epilog*. Trier: Johannes Verlag Einsiedeln, 1987].

Explorations in Theology I: *The Word Made Flesh*. Translated by A. V. Littledale and Alexander Dru. San Francisco: Ignatius Press, 1989. [*Skizzen zur Theologie* I: *Verbum Caro*. Einsiedeln: Johannes Verlag, 1960].

Explorations in Theology II: *Spouse of the Word*. Translated by A. V. Littledale, Alexander Dru, Brian McNeil, John Saward, and Edward T. Oakes. San Francisco: Ignatius Press, 1991. [*Skizzen zur Theologie* II: *Sponsa Verbi*. Einsiedeln: Johannes Verlasg, 1961].

Explorations in Theology III: *Creator Spirit*. Translated by Brian McNeil. San Francisco: Ignatius Press, 1993. [*Skizzen zur Theologie* III: *Spiritus Creator*. Einsiedeln: Johannes Verlag, 1967].

Explorations in Theology IV: *Spirit and Institution*. Translated by Edward T. Oakes. San Francisco: Ignatius Press, 1995. [*Skizzen zur Theologie* IV: *Pneuma und Institution*. Einsiedeln: Johannes Verlag, 1974].

First Glance at Adrienne von Speyr. Translated by Antje Lawry and Sergia Englund. San Francisco: Ignatius Press, 1981. [*Erster Blick auf Adrienne von Speyr*. Einsiedeln: Johannes Verlag, 1968].

The Glory of the Lord: A Theological Aesthetics I: *Seeing the Form*. Translated by Erasmo Leiva-Merikakis. Edited by Joseph Fessio and John Riches. San Francisco: Ignatius Press, 1982, 1989. [*Herrlichkeit. Eine theologische Ästhetik*. Band I. *Schau der Gestalt*. Einsiedeln: Johannes Verlag, 1961, 1967²].

The Glory of the Lord: A Theological Aesthetics II: *Studies in Theological Style: Clerical Styles*. Translated by Andrew Louth, Francis McDonagh, and Brian McNeil. Edited by John Riches. San Francisco / New York: Ignatius Press / Crossroads, 1984. [*Herrlichkeit. Eine theologische Ästhetik*. Band II. *Fächer der Stile*. Teil 1: *Klerikale Stile*. Einsiedeln: Johannes Verlag, 1962, 1969²].

The Glory of the Lord: A Theological Aesthetics III: *Studies in Theological Styles: Lay Styles*. Translated by Andrew Louth, John Saward, Martin Simon, and Rowan Williams. Edited by John Riches. Edinburgh / San Francisco: T. & T. Clark / Ignatius Press, 1986. [*Herrlichkeit. Eine theologische Ästhetik*. Band II: *Fächer der Stile*. Teil 2: *Laikale Stile*. Einsiedeln: Johannes Verlag, 1962, 1969²].

The Glory of the Lord: A Theological Aesthetics IV: *The Realm of Metaphysics in Antiquity*.

Translated by Brian McNeil, Andrew Louth, John Saward, Rowan Williams, and Oliver Davies. Edited by John Riches. Edinburgh / San Francisco: T. & T. Clark / Ignatius Press, 1989. [*Herrlichkeit. Eine theologische Ästhetik*. Band III, 1: *Im Raum der Metaphysik*. Teil 1: *Altertum*. Einsiedeln: Johannes Verlag, 1965, 1975²].

The Glory of the Lord: A Theological Aesthetics V: *The Realm of Metaphysics in the Modern Age*. Translated by Oliver Davies, Andrew Louth, Brian McNeil, John Saward, and Rowan Williams. Edited by Rian McNeil and John Riches. San Francisco: Ignatius Press, 1991. [*Herrlichkeit. Eine theologische Ästhetik*. Band III, 1: *Im Raum der Metaphysik*. Teil 2: *Neuzeit*. Einsiedeln: Johannes Verlag, 1965, 1975²].

The Glory of the Lord: A Theological Aesthetics VI: *Theology. The Old Covenant*. Translated by Brian McNeil and Erasmo Leiva-Merikakis. Edited by John Riches. San Francisco: Ignatius Press, 1991. [*Herrlichkeit. Eine theologische Ästhetik*. Band III, 2: *Theologie*. Teil 1: *Alter Bund*. Einsiedeln: Johannes Verlag, 1967].

The Glory of the Lord: A Theological Aesthetics VII: *Theology. The New Covenant*. Translated by Brian McNeil. Edited by John Riches. San Francisco: Ignatius Press, 1989. [*Herrlichkeit. Eine theologische Ästhetik*. Band III. 2: *Theologie*. Teil 2: *Neuer Bund*. Einsiedeln: Johannes Verlag, 1969].

The God Question and Modern Man. With foreword by John Macquarrie. Translated by Hilda Graef. New York: Seabury Press, 1967. [*Die Gottesfrage des heutigen Menschen*. Wien: Herold, 1956. Newly edited by Alois M. Haas. Einsiedeln: Johannes Verlag, 2009].

The Grain of Wheat: Aphorisms. Translated by Erasmo Leiva-Merikakis. San Francisco: Ignatius Press, 1995. [*Das Weizenkorn*. Einsiedeln: Johannes Verlag, 1953].

Heart of the World. Translated by Erasmo S. Leiva. San Francisco: Ignatius Press, 1979. [*Das Herz der Welt*. Zurich: Arche, 1945, 1953³].

In the Fullness of Faith: On the Centrality of the Distinctively Catholic. Translated by Graham Harrison. San Francisco: Ignatius Press, 1988. [*Katholisch. Aspekte des Mysteriums*. Einsiedeln: Johannes Verlag, 1975].

The Laity and the Life of the Counsels: The Church's Mission in the World. Translated by Brian McNeil and David C. Schindler. San Francisco: Ignatius Press, 2003. [*Gottbereites Leben: Der Laie und der Rätestand. Nachfolge Christi in der heutigen Welt*. Einsiedeln: Johannes Verlag, 1993].

Life Out of Death: Mediations on the Easter Mystery. Translated by Davis Perkins. Philadelphia: Fortress Press, 1985. [*Leben aus dem Tod: Betrachtungen zum Ostermysterium*. Freiburg im Breisgau: Verlag Herder, 1984].

Light of the Word. Brief Reflections on the Sunday Readings. Translated by Dennis D. Martin. San Francisco: Ignatius Press, 1993. [*Licht des Wortes: Skizzen zu allen Sonntagslesungen*. Einsiedeln: Freiburg im Breisgau, 1987, 1992²].

Love Alone Is Credible. Translated by David C. Schindler. San Francisco: Ignatius Press, 2004. [*Glaubhaft ist nur Liebe*. Einsiedeln: Johannes Verlag, 1963, 1985⁵].

Mary for Today. Translated by Robert Nowell. San Francisco: Ignatius Press, 1988. [*Maria für heute*. Wien: Herder, 1987, 1988²].

The Moment of Christian Witness. Translated by Richard Beckley. San Francisco: Ignatius Press, 1994. [*Cordula oder der Ernstfall*. Trier: Johannes Verlag Einsiedeln, 1966, 1987⁴].

My Work: In Retrospect. Translated by Brian McNeil, Kenneth Batinovich, John Saward and Kelly Hamilton. San Francisco: Ignatius Press, 1993. [*Mein Werk. Durchblicke*. Einsiedeln and Freiburg im Breisgau: Johannes Verlag, 1990].

Mysterium Paschale, The Mystery of Easter. Translated by Aidan Nichols. Edinburgh: T. & T. Clark, 1990. [*Theologie der drei Tage*. Einsiedeln: Benziger, 1969].

New Elucidations. Translated by Mary Theresilde Skerry. San Francisco: Ignatius Press, 1986. [*Neue Klarstellungen*. Einsiedeln: Johannes Verlag, 1979].

The Office of Peter and the Structure of the Church. Translated by André Emery. San Francisco: Ignatius Press, 1986. [*Der antirömische Affekt. Wie lässt sich das Papsttum in der Gesamtkirche integrieren*. Freiburg im Breisgau: Herder, 1974].

Our Task: A Report and a Plan. Translated by John Saward. San Francisco: Ignatius Press and Communio Books, 1994. [*Unser Auftrag: Bericht und Entwurf*. Einsiedeln: Johannes Verlag, 1984].

Paul Struggles with His Congregation. The Pastoral Message of the Letters to the Corinthians. Translated by Brigitte L. Bojarska. San Francisco: Ignatius Press, 1992. [*Paulus ringt mit seiner Gemeinde*. Trier: Johannes Verlag Einsiedeln, 1988].

Prayer. Translated by Graham Harrison. San Francisco: Ignatius Press, 1986. [*Das betrachtende Gebet*. Einsiedeln: Johannes Verlag, 1955].

Presence and Thought: An Essay on the Religious Philosophy of Gregory of Nyssa. Translated by Mark Sebanc. San Francisco: Ignatius Press and Communio Books, 1995. [*Présence et pensée. Essai sur la philosophie religieuses de Grégoire de Nysse*. Paris: Beauchesne, 1988].

Razing the Bastions: On the Church in this Age. With a foreword by Bishop Christoph Schönborn. Translated by Brian McNeil. San Francisco: Ignatius Press, 1993. [*Schleifung der Bastionen: Von der Kirche in dieser Zeit*. Einsiedeln: Johannes Verlag, 1952, 1954[4]].

A Short Primer for Unsettled Laymen. Translated by Michael Waldstein. San Francisco: Ignatius Press, 1985, 1987[2]. [*Kleine Fibel für verunsicherte Laien*. Einsiedeln: Johannes Verlag, 1980].

Theo-Drama: Theological Dramatic Theory I: *Prolegomena*. Translated by Graham Harrison. San Francisco: Ignatius Press, 1988. [*Theodramatik* I: *Prolegomena*. Einsiedeln: Johannes Verlag, 1983].

Theo-Drama: Theological Dramatic Theory II: *The Dramatis Personae: Man in God*. Translated by Graham Harrison. San Francisco: Ignatius Press, 1990. [*Theodramatik* II: *Die Personen des Spiels*. Teil 1: *Der Mensch in Gott*. Einsiedeln: Johannes Verlag, 1976].

Theo-Drama: Theological Dramatic Theory III: *The Dramatis Personae: Persons in Christ*. Translated by Graham Harrison. San Francisco: Ignatius Press, 1992. [*Theodramatik* II: *Die Personen des Spiels*. Teil 2: *Die Personen in Christus*. Einsiedeln: Johannes Verlag, 1978].

Theo-Drama: Theological Dramatic Theory IV: *The Action*. Translated by Graham Harrison. San Francisco: Ignatius Press, 1994. [*Theodramatik* III: *Die Handlung*. Einsiedeln: Johannes Verlag, 1980].

Theo-Drama: Theological Dramatic Theory V: *The Last Act*. Translated by Graham Harrison. San Francisco: Ignatius Press, 1998. [*Theodramatik* IV: *Das Endspiel*. Einsiedeln: Johnannes Verlag, 1983].

Theo-Logic. Theological Logical Theory I: *Truth of the World*. Translated by Adrian J. Walker. San Francisco: Ignatius Press, 2000. [*Theologik* I: *Wahrheit der Welt*. Einsiedeln: Johannes Verlag, 1985].

Theo-Logic. Theological Logical Theory II: *Truth of God*. Translated by Adrian J. Walker. San Francisco: Ignatius Press, 2004. [*Theologik* II: *Wahrheit Gottes*. Einsiedeln: Johannes Verlag, 1985].

Theo-Logic. Theological Logical Theory III: *The Spirit of Truth*. Translated by Graham Harrison. San Francisco: Ignatius Press, 2005. [*Theologik* III: *Der Geist der Wahrheit*. Einsiedeln: Johannes Verlag, 1987].

A Theological Anthropology. No translator noted. New York: Sheed and Ward, 1967. [*Das Ganze im Fragment. Aspekte der Geschichtstheologie*. Einsiedeln: Benziger, 1963].

The Theology of Henri de Lubac: An Overview. Translated by Joseph Fessio, Michael Waldstein, and Susan Clements. San Francsico: Ignatius Press, 1991. [*Henri de Lubac: Sein organisches Lebenswerk*. Freiburg im Breisgau: Johannes Verlag Einsiedeln, 1976].

A Theology of History. No translator noted. San Francisco: Ignatius Press, 1994. [*Theologie der Geschichte*. Einsiedeln: Johannes Verlag, 1950].

The Theology of Karl Barth: Exposition and Interpretation. Translated by Edward T. Oakes. San Francisco: Ignatius Press, 1992. [*Karl Barth. Darstellung und Deutung seiner Theologie*. Olten / Köln: Summa Verlag / Jakob Hegner, 1951; and Einsiedeln: Johannes Verlag, 1976⁴].

The Threefold Garland: The World's Salvation in Mary's Prayer. Translated by Erasmo Leiva-Merikakis. San Francisco: Ignatius Press, 1982. [*Der dreifache Kranz. Das Heil der Welt im Mariengebet*. Einsiedeln: Johannes Verlag, 1977].

Truth is Symphonic: Aspects of Christian Pluralism. Translated by Graham Harrison. San Francisco: Ignatius Press, 1987. [*Die Wahrheit ist symphonisch. Aspekte des christlichen Pluralismus*. Einsiedeln: Johannes Verlag, 1972].

Two Sisters in the Spirit: Thérèse of Lisieux and Elizabeth of the Trinity. Translated by Donald Nichols, Anne Elizabeth Englund, and Dennis Martin. San Francisco: Ignatius Press, 1992. [*Schwestern im Geist: Therese von Lisieux und Elisabeth von Dijon*. Einsiedeln: Johannes Verlag, 1970].

Unless You Become Like This Child. Translated by Erasmo Leiva-Merikakis. San Francisco: Ignatius Press, 1991. [*Wenn ihr nicht werdet wie dieses Kind*. Ostfildern: Schwabenverlag, 1988].

Who is Christian? Translated by John Cumming. New York: Newman Press, 1967. [*Wer ist ein Christ?* Einsiedeln: Benziger, 1965, 1966³].

You Crown the Year with Your Goodness. Radio Sermons. Translated by Graham Harrison. San Francisco: Ignatius Press, 1989. [*"Du krönst das Jahr mit deiner Huld". Psalm 65, 12. Radiopredigten*. Einsiedeln: Johannes Verlag, 1982].

You Have Words of Eternal Life. Scripture Meditations. Translated by Dennis Martin. San Francisco: Ignatius Press, 1991. [*Du hast Worte ewigen Lebens. Schriftbetrachtungen*. Trier: Johannes Verlag Einsiedeln, 1989].

Untranslated Works

Apokalypse der deutschen Seele. Studien zu einer Lehre von letzten Haltungen. Bd. I: *Der deutsche Idealismus*. Salzburg: A. Pustet, 1937. Bd. II: *Im Zeichen Nietzsches*. Salzburg: A. Pustet, 1939. Bd. III: *Die Vergöttlichung des Todes*. Salzburg: A. Pustet, 1939.

Besondere Gnadengaben und die zwei Wege menchlichen Lebens. Summa Theologica II-II, qq. 171–182. Kommentiert von Hans Urs von Balthasar. Volume 23 of Thomas Aquinas, *Die deutsche Thomas-Ausgabe*. Edited by Heinrich M. Christmann. Munich and Salzburg: Gemeinschaftsverlag, 1954.

Homo Creatus Est. Volume 5 of *Skizzen zur Theologie* [*Explorations in Theology*]. Einsiedeln: Johannes Verlag, 1986.

Co-Authored

Balthasar, Hans Urs von, and Joseph Ratzinger. *Mary: The Church at the Source*. Translated by Adrian Walker. San Francisco: Ignatius Press and Communio Books, 2005. [*Maria. Kirche im Ursprung*. Freiburg im Breisgau, Basel, Wien: Herder, 1980].

———, Joseph Ratzinger, and Heinz Schürmann. *Principles of Christian Morality*. Translated by Graham Harrison. San Francisco: Ignatius Press, 1986. [*Prinzipien Christlicher Moral*. Einsiedeln: Johannes Verlag, 1975].

——— and Angelo Scola. *Test Everything, Hold Fast to What Is Good. An Interview with Hans Urs von Balthasar by Angelo Scola*. Translated by Maria Shrady. San Francisco: Ignatius Press, 1989. [*Prüfet alles—das Gute behalten*. Ostfildern Stuttgart: Schwabenverlag, 1986].

——— and Adrienne von Speyr. *Au cœur du mystère rédempteur*. Paris: CLD, 1980.

Works Co-Edited

In addition to editing all of the works by Adrienne von Speyr listed above, Balthasar has co-edited the following:

Balthasar, Hans Urs von, Georges Chantraine, and Angelo Scola, eds. *Adrienne von Speyr und ihre kirchliche Sendung. Akten des römischen Symposiums (27.–29. September 1985)*. With an introduction by Hans Urs von Balthasar, 12–16. Einsiedeln: Johannes Verlag, 1986.

———, eds. *La mission ecclésiale d'Adrienne von Speyr. Actes du colloque romain (27–29 septembre 1985)*. With an introduction by Hans Urs von Balthasar, ed., 11–16. Paris and Namur: Éditions Lethielleux and Culture et Vérité, 1986.

Articles and Contributions

"Action and Contemplation." In Hans Urs von Balthasar, *Explorations in Theology* I: *The Word Made Flesh*, 227–40. Translated by A. V. Littledale and Alexander Dru. San Francisco: Ignatius Press, 1989. ["Aktion und Kontemplation." In Hans Urs von Balthasar, *Skizzen zur Theologie* I: *Verbum Caro*, 245–59. Einsiedeln: Johannes Verlag, 1960].

"Adrienne von Speyr (1902–1967). Die Miterfahrung der Passion und Gottverlassenheit." *Geist und Leben* 58 (1985): 61–66.

"Adrienne von Speyr et le sacrement de pénitence." *Nouvelle Revue Théologique* 107, no. 3 (1985): 394–403. ["Adrienne von Speyr e il Sacramento della Confessione." *Il Nuovo Areopago, rivista trimestrale di cultura* (Roma) 2, no. 3 (1983): 218–24].

"Adriennes Charisma." In *Adrienne von Speyr und ihre kirchliche Sendung. Akten des römischen Symposiums, 27.–29. September 1985*, 173–78. Edited by Hans Urs von Balthasar, Georges Chantraine, and Angelo Scola. Einsiedeln: Johannes Verlag, 1986. [More complete is the French translation: "Le charisme d'Adrienne." In *La mission ecclésiale d'Adrienne von Speyr. Actes du colloque romain*, edited by Hans Urs von Balthasar, Georges Chantraine, and Angelo Scola, 187–93. Paris and Namur: Éditions Lethielleux and Culture et Vérité, 1986].

"Characteristics of Christianity." In Hans Urs von Balthasar, *Explorations in Theology* I: *The Word Made Flesh*, 161–80. Translated by A. V. Littledale with Alexander Dru. San Francisco: Ignatius Press, 1989. ["Merkmale des Christlichen." In Hans Urs von Balthasar, *Skizzen zur Theologie* I: *Verbum Caro*, 172–94. Einsiedeln: Johannes Verlag, 1960].

"Charis and Charisma." Translated by Brian McNeil. In Hans Urs von Balthasar, *Explorations in Theology* II: *Spouse of the Word*, 301–14. San Francisco: Ignatius Press, 1991. ["Charis und Charisma." In Hans Urs von Balthasar, *Skizzen zur Theologie*, II: *Sponsa Verbi*, 319–31. Einsiedeln: Johannes Verlag, 1961].

"Christian Prayer." Translated by André Emery. *Communio* 5, no. 1 (1978): 15–22 [Presentation at the Catholic University of America, October 1, 1977].

"Christian Universalism." In Hans Urs von Balthasar, *Explorations in Theology* I: *The Word Made Flesh*, 253–54. Translated by A. V. Littledale with Alexander Dru. San Francisco:

Ignatius Press, 1989. ["Christlicher Universalismus." In Hans Urs von Balthasar, *Skizzen zur Theologie* I: *Verbum Caro*, 260–75. Einsiedeln: Johannes Verlag, 1960].

"Christological and Ecclesial Obedience." In Hans Urs von Balthasar, *Explorations in Theology* IV: *Spirit and Institution*, 139–67. Translated by Edward T. Oakes. San Francisco: Ignatius Press, 1995. ["Christologie und kirchlicher Gehorsam." In Hans Urs von Balthasar, *Skizzen zur Theologie* IV: *Pneuma und Institution*, 133–61. Einsiedeln: Johannes Verlag, 1974].

"The Contemporary Experience of the Church." Translated by A. V. Littledale with Alexander Dru. In Hans Urs von Balthasar, *Explorations in Theology* II: *Spouse of the Word*, 11–41. San Francisco: Ignatius Press, 1991. ["Kirchenerfahrung dieser Zeit." In Hans Urs von Balthasar, *Skizzen zur Theologie* II: *Sponsa Verbi*, 1–44. Einsiedeln: Johannes Verlag, 1961].

"The Council of the Holy Spirit." In Hans Urs von Balthasar, *Explorations in Theology* III: *Creator Spirit*, 245–67. Translated by Brian McNeil. San Francisco: Ignatius Press, 1993. ["Das Konzil des Heiligen Geistes." In Hans Urs von Balthasar. *Skizzen zur Theologie* III: *Spiritus Creator*, 218–36. Einsiedeln: Johannes Verlag, 1967].

"Creation and the Trinity." Translated by Stephen Wentworth Arndt. *Communio* 15, no. 4 (1988): 285–93. ["Schöpfung und Trinität." In *Internationale katholische Zeitschrift Communio* 17 (1988): 205–12].

"Current Trends in Catholic Theology and the Responsibility of the Christian." No translator named. *Communio* 5, no. 1 (1978): 77–85 [Presentation at the Catholic University of America, October 2, 1977].

"Das literarische Werk Adriennes von Speyr." In *Adrienne von Speyr und ihre spirituelle Theologie. Symposium zu ihrem 100. Geburtstag*, edited by Hans Urs von Balthasar Stiftung, 125–31. Einsiedeln: Johannes Verlag, 2002.

"The Descent into Hell." In Hans Urs von Balthasar, *Explorations in Theology* IV: *Spirit and Institution*, translated by Edward T. Oakes, 401–14. San Francisco: Ignatius Press, 1995. ["Abstieg zur Hölle." In Hans Urs von Balthasar, *Skizzen zur Theologie*, IV: *Pneuma und Institution*, 387–400. Einsiedeln: Johannes Verlag, 1974].

"Die Würde der Frau." *Internationale katholische Zeitschrift: Communio* 11, no. 4 (1982): 346–52. Also in Hans Urs von Balthasar, *Skizzen zur Theologie* V: *Homo Creatus Est*, 134–41. Einsiedeln: Johannes Verlag, 1986.

"Exerzitien und Theologie." *Orientierung: Katholische Blätter für weltanschauliche Information* 12 (1948): 229–32.

"The Fathers, the Scholastics, and Ourselves." *Communio* 24, no. 2 (1997): 345–96. ["Patristik, Scholastik und wir." *Theologie der Zeit* (Wien) 3 (1939): 65–104].

"*Fides Christi*: An Essay on the Consciousness of Christ." Translated by Edward T. Oakes. In Hans Urs von Balthasar, *Explorations in Theology* II: *Spouse of the Word*, 43–79. San Francisco: Ignatius Press, 1991. ["Fides Christi." In Hans Urs von Balthasar, *Skizzen zur Theologie* II: *Sponsa Verbi*, 45–79. Einsiedeln: Johannes Verlag, 1961].

"God is His Own Exegete." Translated by Stephen Wentworth Arndt. *Communio* 13, no. 4 (1986): 280–87. ["Gott ist sein eigener Exeget." *Internationale katholische Zeitschrift: Communio* 15, no. 1 (1986): 8–13].

"Immediacy to God." In Hans Urs von Balthasar, *Explorations in Theology* III: *Creator Spirit*, translated by Brian McNeil, 335–51. San Francisco: Ignatius Press, 1993. ["Unmittelbarkeit zu Gott." In Hans Urs von Balthasar, *Skizzen zur Theologie* III: *Spiritus Creator*, 296–311. Einsiedeln: Johannes Verlag, 1967].

"The Implications of the Word." In Hans Urs von Balthasar, *Explorations in Theology* I:

The Word Made Flesh, translated by A. V. Littledale and Alexander Dru, 47–68. San Francisco: Ignatius Press, 1989. ["Implikationen des Wortes." In Hans Urs von Balthasar, *Skizzen zur Theologie* I: *Verbum Caro*, 48–72. Einsiedeln: Johannes Verlag, 1960].

"Jesus and Forgiveness." Translated by Josephine Koeppel. *Communio* 11, no. 4 (1984): 222–34. ["Jesus und das Verzeihen." *Internationale katholische Zeitschrift: Communio* 13 (1984), 406–17].

"Kenosis of the Church?" In Hans Urs von Balthasar, *Explorations in Theology* IV: *Spirit and Institution*, translated by Edward T. Oakes, 125–38. San Francisco: Ignatius Press, 1995. ["Kenose der Kirche?" In Hans Urs von Balthasar, *Skizzen zur Theologie* IV: *Pneuma und Institution*, 119–32. Einsiedeln: Johannes Verlag, 1974].

"The Marian Principle." In Hans Urs von Balthasar, *Elucidations*, translated by John Riches, 101–13. San Francisco: Ignatius Press, 1998. ["Das Marianische Prinzip." *Klarstellungen. Zur Prüfung der Geister*, 65–72. Freiburg im Breisgau: Herder, 1971].

"Maria und der Geist." *Geist und Leben* 56 (1983): 173–77.

"Movement Toward God." In Hans Urs von Balthasar, *Explorations in Theology* III: *Creator Spirit*, translated by Brian McNeil, 15–55. San Francisco: Ignatius Press, 1993. ["Bewegung zu Gott." In Hans Urs von Balthasar, *Skizzen zur Theologie* III: *Spiritus Creator*, 13–50. Einsiedeln: Johannes Verlag, 1967].

"Nine Propositions on Christian Ethics." In Joseph Ratzinger, Heinz Schürmann, and Hans Urs von Balthasar, *Principles of Christian Morality*, translated by Graham Harrison, 77–104. San Francisco: Ignatius Press, 1986.

"On the Concept of Person." Translated by Peter Verhalen. *Communio* 13, no. 1 (1986): 18–26. ["Zum Begriff der Person." In Hans Urs von Balthasar, *Skizzen zur Theologie* V: *Homo Creatus Est*, 93–102. Einsieden: Johannes Verlag, 1986].

"On the Task of Catholic Philosophy in Our Time." Translated by Brian McNeil. *Communio* 20, no. 1 (1993): 147–87. ["Von der Aufgaben der katholischen Philosophie in der Zeit." *Annalen der Philosophischen Gesellschaft der Innerschweiz* 3, nos. 2/3 (1946/1947): 1–38].

"On Vicarious Representation." In Hans Urs von Balthasar, *Explorations in Theology* IV: *Spirit and Institution*, translated by Edward T. Oakes, 415–22. San Francisco: Ignatius Press, 1995. ["Über Stellvertretung." In Hans Urs von Balthasar, *Skizzen zur Theologie*, IV: *Pneuma und Institution*, 401–9. Einsiedeln: Johannes Verlag, 1974].

"The Place of Theology." In Hans Urs von Balthasar, *Explorations in Theology* I: *The Word Made Flesh*, translated by A. V. Littledale and Alexander Dru, 149–60. San Francisco: Ignatius Press, 1989. ["Der Ort der Theologie." In Hans Urs von Balthasar, *Skizzen zur Theologie* I: *Verbum Caro*, 159–71. Einsiedeln: Johannes Verlag, 1960].

"Pourquoi je suis devenu prêtre?" In *Pourquoi je me suis fait prêtre: témoignages recueillis*, edited by Jorge Sans Villa, 19–22. Tournai: Centre diocésain de documentation, 1961. ["Por qué me hice Sacerdote." In *Por qué me hic Sacerdote*, edited by Jorge Sans Villa, 29–32. Salamanca: Ed. Sigueme, 1959].

"Preliminary Remarks on the Discernment of Spirits." In Hans Urs von Balthasar, *Explorations in Theology* IV: *Spirit and Institution*, translated by Edward T. Oakes, 337–51. San Francisco: Ignatius Press, 1995. ["Vorerwägungen zur Unterscheidung des Geistes." In Hans Urs von Balthasar, *Skizzen zur Theologie* IV: *Pneuma und Institution*, 325–39. Einsiedeln: Johannes Verlag, 1974].

"Revelation and the Beautiful." In Hans Urs von Balthasar. *Explorations in Theology* I: *The Word Made Flesh*, translated by A. V. Littledale and Alexander Dru, 95–126. San Francisco: Ignatius Press, 1989. ["Offenbarung und Schönheit." In Hans Urs von Balthasar,

Skizzen zur Theologie I: *Verbum Caro*, 100–134. Einsiedeln: Johannes Verlag, 1960].
"Spirit and Fire: An Interview with Hans Urs von Balthasar," by Michael Albus. *Communio* 32, no. 3 (2005): 573–93. ["Geist und Feuer. Ein Gespräch mit Hans Urs von Balthasar." *Herder Korrespondenz* 30, no. 2 (1976): 72–82].
"Spirituality." In Hans Urs von Balthasar, *Explorations in Theology* I: *The Word Made Flesh*, translated by A. V. Littledale and Alexander Dru, 211–26. San Francisco: Ignatius Press, 1989. ["Spiritualität." In Hans Urs von Balthasar, *Skizzen zur Theologie* I: *Verbum Caro*, 226–44. Einsiedeln: Johannes Verlag, 1960].
"Summa Summarum." In Hans Urs von Balthasar, *Explorations in Theology* III: *Creator Spirit*, translated by Brian McNeil, 363–87. San Francisco: Ignatius Press, 1993. ["Summa Summarum." In Hans Urs von Balthasar, *Skizzen zur Theologie* III: *Spiritus Creator*, 322–44. Einsiedeln: Johannes Verlag, 1967].
"Theologie des Abstiegs zur Hölle." In *Adrienne von Speyr und ihre kirliche Sendung. Akten des römischen* Symposiums, edited by Hans Urs von Balthasar, George Chantraine, and Angelo Scola, 138–46. Einsiedeln: Johannes Verlag, 2002.
"Theology and Sanctity." In Hans Urs von Balthasar, *Explorations in Theology* I: *The Word Made Flesh*, translated by A. V. Littledale and Alexander Dru, 181–209. San Francisco: Ignatius Press, 1989. ["Theologie und Heiligkeit." In Hans Urs von Balthasar, *Skizzen zur Theologie* I: *Verbum Caro*, 195–225. Einsiedeln: Johannes Verlag, 1960].
"The Threefold Presence of Christ." In Hans Urs von Balthasar, *You Crown the Year with Your Goodness. Radio Sermons*, translated by Graham Harrison, 128–34. San Francisco: Ignatius Press, 1989. ["Dreifache Gegenwart Christi." In Hans Urs von Balthasar. "*Du krönst das Jahr mit deiner Huld*". *Psalm 65, 12. Radiopredigten*, 114–19. Einsiedeln: Johannes Verlag, 1982].
"Two Modes of Faith." In Hans Urs von Balthasar, *Explorations in Theology* III: *Creator Spirit*, translated by Brian McNeil, 85–102. San Francisco: Ignatius Press, 1993. ["Zwei Glaubensweisen." In Hans Urs von Balthasar, *Skizzen zur Theologie* III: *Spiritus Creator*, 76–91. Einsiedeln: Johannes Verlag, 1967].
"Understanding Christian Mysticism." In Hans Urs von Balthasar, *Explorations in Theology* IV: *Spirit and Institution*, translated by Edward T. Oakes, 309–35. San Francisco: Ignatius Press, 1995. ["Zur Ortsbestimmung christlicher Mystik." In Hans Urs von Balthasar, *Skizzen zur Theologie*, IV: *Pneuma und Institution*, 298–324. Einsiedeln: Johannes Verlag, 1974].
"What Is Distinctively Christian in the Experience of God?" In Hans Urs von Balthasar, *Explorations in Theology* IV: *Spirit and Institution*, translated by Edward T. Oakes, 29–40. San Francisco: Ignatius Press, 1995. ["Das unterscheidend Christliche der Gotteserfahrung." In Hans Urs von Balthasar, *Skizzen zur Theologie*, IV: *Pneuma und Institution*, 26–37. Einsiedeln: Johannes Verlag, 1974].
"Who Is Man?" In Hans Urs von Balthasar, *Explorations in Theology* IV: *Spirit and Institution*, translated by Edward T. Oakes, 15–28. San Francisco: Ignatius Press, 1995. ["Wer ist der Mensch?" In Hans Urs von Balthasar, *Skizzen zur Theologie*, IV: *Pneuma und Institution*, 13–25. Einsiedeln: Johannes Verlag, 1974].
"Who Is the Church?" In Hans Urs von Balthasar, *Explorations in Theology* II: *Spouse of the Word*, translated by A. V. Littledale and Alexander Dru, 143–91. San Francisco: Ignatius Press, 1991. ["Wer ist die Kirche?" In Hans Urs von Balthasar, *Skizzen zur Theologie* II: *Sponsa Verbi*, 148–202. Einsiedeln: Johannes Verlag, 1961].
"Women Priests?" In Hans Urs von Balthasar, *New Elucidations*, translated by Mary Theresil-

de Skerry, 187–98. San Francisco: Ignatius Press, 1986. ["Frauenpriestertum?" In Hans Urs von Balthasar, *Neue Klarstellungen*, 109–15. Einsiedeln: Johannes Verlag, 1979].

"A Word on *Humanae Vitae.*" *Communio* 20, no. 3 (1993): 437–50. Also printed in Hans Urs von Balthasar, *New Elucidations*, translated by Sr. Mary Theresilda Skerry, 204–28. San Francisco: Ignatius Press, 1986. ["Ein Wort zu 'Humanae Vitae.'" *Neue Klarstellungen*, 119–28. Einsiedeln: Johannes Verlag, 1979].

"Zur Ortsbestimmung christlicher Mystik." In Werner Beierwaltes, Hans Urs von Balthasar, and Alois M. Haas, *Grundfragen der Mystik*, 37–71. Einsiedeln: Johannes Verlag, 1974.

Works by St. Thomas Aquinas

Compendium theologiae seu brevis compilatio theologiae ad fratrem Raynaldum. Volume 42 of the Leonine edition. Rome: Editori di San Tommaso, 1979. [*Compendium of Theology*. Translated by Cyril Vollert. London: Herder, 1952].

De potentia. In *Quaestiones disputatae*. Volume 2. Edited by Pio Bazzi. Turin and Rome: Marietti, 1965. [*On the Power of God*. Literally translated by the English Dominican Fathers. Eugene, Ore.: Wipf & Stock Publishers, 2004. Previous edition: Westminster, Md.: The Newman Press, 1932].

Expositio libri Boetii De Hebdomadibus. Leonine edition, volume 50. Rome / Paris: Commissio leonina / Editions du Cerf, 1992.

Expositio Salutationis Angelicae. In *The Three Greatest Prayers*. Translated by Laurence Shapcote. London: Burns Oates & Washbourne LTD, 1937.

Quaestiones Disputatae De Veritate. Leonine edition, volume 22 (3 vols.). Rome: Editori di San Tommaso, 1975–76. [*On Truth*. Translated by James V. McGlynn and Robert W. Schmidt. Edited by Robert W. Mulligan. Chicago: H. Regnery, 1952–54; Indianapolis: Hackett, 1994].

Scriptum super libros Sententiarum. Volumes 1–2. Edited by Pierre Mandonnet. Paris: Lethiellieux, 1929.

Scriptum super libros Sententiarum. Volumes 3–4. Edited by Maria F. Moos. Paris: Lethiellieux, 1933 and 1947.

Summa contra Gentiles. Leonine edition. Volumes 13–15. Rome: Editori di San Tommaso, 1918, 1926, 1930. [*Summa contra Gentiles*. Translated into English by Anton C. Pegis, James F. Anderson, Vernon J. Bourke, and Charles J. O'Neil. Notre Dame, Ind.: University of Notre Dame Press, 1997].

Summa theologiae. Translated by Fr. Laurence Shapcote, OP. Edited by John Mortensen and Enrique Alarcón. Volumes 13–20 of the Latin/English Edition of the *Works of St. Thomas Aquinas*. Lander, Wyo.: The Aquinas Institute for the Study of Sacred Doctrine, 2012. The Latin text is based on the Leonine Edition, transcribed by Roberto Busa and revised by Enrique Alarcón.

Super Evangelium S. Ioannis lectura. In *Commentary on the Gospel of John*. Translated by Fr. Fabian R. Larcher, OP. Edited by the Aquinas Institute. Volumes 35–36 of the Latin/English Edition of the *Works of St. Thomas Aquinas, Biblical Commentaries*. Lander, Wyo.: The Aquinas Institute for the Study of Sacred Doctrine, 2013. The Latin text is based on the 1972 Marietti edition.

Super Epistolam B. Pauli ad Colossenses. In *Commentary on the Letters of Saint Paul to the Philippians, Colossians, Thessalonians, Timothy, Titus, and Philemon*. Translated by Fabien R. Larcher. Edited by John Mortensen and Enrique Alarcón. Volume 40 of the

Latin/English edition of the *Works of St. Thomas Aquinas, Biblical Commentaries*. Lander, Wyo.: The Aquinas Institute for the Study of Sacred Doctrine, 2012. The Latin text is based on the Marietti 1953 edition, prepared by Raffaele Cai, transcribed by Roberto Busa and revised by Enrique Alarcón.

Super I Epistolam B. Pauli ad Corinthios lectura. In *Commentary on the Letters of Saint Paul to the Corinthians*. Translated by Fabien R. Larcher, Elisabeth Mortensen, and Daniel Keating. Edited by John Mortensen and Enrique Alarcón. Volume 38 of the Latin/English Edition of the *Works of St. Thomas Aquinas, Biblical Commentaries*. Lander, Wyo.: The Aquinas Institute for the Study of Sacred Doctrine, 2012. The Latin text is based on the Marietti 1953 edition, prepared by Raffaele Cai, transcribed by Roberto Busa and revised by Enrique Alarcón.

Super II Epistolam B. Pauli ad Corinthios lectura. In *Commentary on the Letters of Saint Paul to the Corinthians*. Translated by Fabien R. Larcher, Elisabeth Mortensen, and Daniel Keating. Edited by John Mortensen and Enrique Alarcón. Volume 38 of the Latin/English Edition of the *Works of St. Thomas Aquinas, Biblical Commentaries*. Lander, Wyo.: The Aquinas Institute for the Study of Sacred Doctrine, 2012. The Latin text is based on the Marietti 1953 edition, prepared by Raffaele Cai, transcribed by Roberto Busa and revised by Enrique Alarcón.

Super Epistolam B. Pauli ad Ephesios lectura. In *Commentary on the Letters of Saint Paul to the Galatians and Ephesians*. Translated by Fabien R. Larcher and Matthew L. Lamb. Edited by John Mortensen and Enrique Alarcón. Volume 39 of the Latin/English Edition of the *Works of St. Thomas Aquinas, Biblical Commentaries*. Lander, Wyo.: The Aquinas Institute for the Study of Sacred Doctrine, 2012. The Latin text is based on the Marietti 1953 edition, prepared by Raffaele Cai, transcribed by Roberto Busa and revised by Enrique Alarcón.

Super Epistolam B. Pauli ad Galatas lectura. In *Commentary on the Letters of Saint Paul to the Galatians and Ephesians*. Translated by Fabien R. Larcher and Matthew L. Lamb. Edited by John Mortensen and Enrique Alarcón. Volume 39 of the Latin/English Edition of the *Works of St. Thomas Aquinas, Biblical Commentaries*. Lander, Wyo.: The Aquinas Institute for the Study of Sacred Doctrine, 2012. The Latin text is based on the Marietti 1953 edition, prepared by Raffaele Cai, transcribed by Roberto Busa and revised by Enrique Alarcón.

Super Epistolam B. Pauli ad Philipenses lectura. In *Commentary on the Letters of Saint Paul to the Philippians, Colossians, Thessalonians, Timothy, Titus, and Philemon*. Translated by Fabien R. Larcher. Edited by John Mortensen and Enrique Alarcón. Volume 40 of the Latin/English Edition of the *Works of St. Thomas Aquinas, Biblical Commentaries*. Lander, Wyo.: The Aquinas Institute for the Study of Sacred Doctrine, 2012. The Latin text is based on the Marietti 1953 edition, prepared by Raffaele Cai, transcribed by Roberto Busa and revised by Enrique Alarcón.

Super Epistolam B. Pauli ad Romanus lectura. In *Commentary on the Letter of Saint Paul to the Romans*. Translated by Fabien R. Larcher. Edited by John Mortensen and Enrique Alarcón. Volume 37 of the Latin/English Edition of the *Works of St. Thomas Aquinas, Biblical Commentaries*. Lander, Wyo.: The Aquinas Institute for the Study of Sacred Doctrine, 2012. The Latin text is based on the 1953 Marietti edition, prepared by Raffaele Cai, transcribed by Roberto Busa and revised by Enrique Alarcón.

Secondary Sources

(For an up-to-date list of the secondary literature on Hans Urs von Balthasar, see: *http://home page.bluewin.ch/huvbslit.*)

Aertsen, Jan A. *Medieval Philosophy and the Transcendentals: The Case of Thomas Aquinas.* Leiden: Brill, 1996.

———. *Nature and Creature: Thomas Aquinas's Way of Thought.* Leiden: Brill, 1988.

Agacinski, Sylviane. *Femmes entre sexe et genre.* Paris: Seuil, 2012.

Albrecht, Barbara. *Eine Theologie des Katholischen: Einführung in das Werk Adriennes von Speyr.* Volume 1: *Durchblick in Texten.* Einsiedeln: Johannes Verlag, 1972.

———. *Eine Theologie des Katholischen: Einführung in das Werk Adriennes von Speyr.* Volume 2: *Darstellung.* Einsiedeln: Johannes Verlag, 1973.

———. "Speyr (Adrienne von)." *Dictionnaire de spiritualité ascétique et mystique, doctrine et histoire,* XIV (Paris: Beauchesne, 1990).

Albus, Michael and Hans Urs von Balthasar. "Spirit and Fire: An Interview with Hans Urs von Balthasar." *Communio* 32, no. 3 (2005): 573–93. ["Geist und Feuer. Ein Gespräch mit Hans Urs von Balthasar." *Herder Korrespondenz* 30, no. 2 (1976): 72–82].

Alszeghy, Zoltán and Maurizio Flick. *Fondamenti di una antropologia teologica.* Florence: Libreria Ed. Fiorentina, 1970.

Althaus, Paul. *Die christliche Wahrheit: Lehrbuch der Dogmatik.* Gütersloh: C. Bertelsmann, 1952³.

Anonymous Jesuit. "Arm um zu bereichern." In *Adrienne von Speyr und ihre kirchliche Sendung. Akten des römischen Symposiums (27.–29. September 1985),* edited by Hans Urs von Balthasar, Georges Chantraine, and Angelo Scola, 36–39. Einsiedeln: Johannes Verlag, 1986. ["Pauvre pour enrichir." In *La mission ecclésiale d'Adrienne von Speyr. Actes du colloque romain (27–29 septembre 1985),* edited by Hans Urs von Balthasar, Georges Chantraine, and Angelo Scola, 38–42. Paris / Namur: Éditions Lethielleux / Culture et Vérité, 1986].

Anonymous member of The Community St. John. "Kurze Darstellung der Johannesgemeinschaft." In *Adrienne von Speyr une ihre kirchliche Sendung. Akten des römischen Symposiums (27.–29. September 1985),* edited by Hans Urs von Balthasar, Georges Chantraine, and Angelo Scola, 49–57. Einsiedeln: Johannes Verlag, 1986. ["Brève présentation de l'Institut Saint-Jean." In *La mission ecclésiale d'Adrienne von Speyr. Actes du colloque romain (27–29 septembre 1985),* edited by Hans Urs von Balthasar, Georges Chantraine, and Angelo Scola, 55–63. Paris / Namur: Éditions Lethielleux / Culture et Vérité, 1986].

Augustine of Hippo. *Confessionum / Confessions.* Œuvres *de Saint Augustin* (Bibliothèque Augustinienne), volume 13. Translated by Eugène Tréhorel and Guilhem Bouissou. Edited by M. Skutella. Paris: Desclée de Brouwer, 1992. English translation by R. S. Pine-Coffin (Harmondsworth, Middlesex, England: Penguin Books, 1961, 1975¹¹).

———. *De Doctrina Christiana.* Œuvres *de Saint Augustin* (Bibliothèque Augustinienne), volume 11/2. Translated by Madeleine Moreau. Edited by Isabelle Bochet and Goulven Madec. Paris: Etudes Augustiniennes, 1997. English translation: *Teaching Christianity. The Works of Saint Augustine. A Translation for the 21st Century* I/11. Translated by Edmund Hill. Edited by John E. Rotelle. New Haven, N.Y.: New City Press, 1996, 1997.

———. *De Trinitate.* Bibliothèque Augustinienne, volume 16. *La Trinité,* Livres VIII-XV. Translated by Paul Agaësse. Paris: Institute d'Études Augustiniennes, 1997. [English translation: *A Select Library of the Nicene and Post-Nicene Fathers of the Christian Church,* volume III. St. Augustine on The Holy Trinity, Doctrinal Treatises, Moral Treatises. Edited by Philip Schaff. Grand Rapids, Mich.: Eerdmans, 1978].

———. *In Johannis Evangelium. Homélies sur l'Évangile de Saint Jean*. Bibliothèque Augustinienne, volume 71. Translated by Marie-François Berrouard. Paris: Desclée de Brouwer, 1969. PL 35:1977–2062. [*Patrologiae Latina*, volume 35: *Sancti Aurelii Augustini Hipponesis Episcopi*. Edited by Jacques-Paul Migne. Opera Omnia 3. pars 2. Paris, 1842]. English translation of selected passages: "Homilies on the Gospel of John." In William A. Jurgens, *The Faith of the Early Fathers*, volume III, 115–24. Collegeville, Minn.: Liturgical Press, 1979].

———. *Sermo* 25. "*De verbis Evangelii Matth*. XII, vers 41–50." PL 46:932–40. [*Patrologiae Latina*, volume 46: *Sancti Aurelii Augustini Hipponesis Episcopi*. Edited by Jacques-Paul Migne. *Opera Omnia* 11, pars 1. Paris, 1864].

———. *Sermo* 169. "*De verbis apostoli. Ephes, cap. VI, 23.*" PL 38:911–26. [*Patrologiae Latina*, volume 38: *Sancti Aurelii Augustini Hipponesis Episcopi*. Edited by Jacques-Paul Migne. *Opera Omnia* 5, pars 1. Paris, 1841].

———. *Sermo* 196. "*In Natali Domini*, XIII." PL 38:1019–21. [*Patrologiae Latina*, volume 38: *Sancti Aurelii Augustini Hipponesis Episcopi*. Edited by Jacques-Paul Migne. *Opera Omnia* 5, pars 1. Paris, 1841].

———. *Sermo* 215. "In redditione symboli." PL 38:1072–76. [*Patrologiae Latina*, volume 38: *Sancti Aurelii Augustini Hipponesis Episcopi*. Edited by Jacques-Paul Migne. *Opera Omnia* 5, pars 1. Paris, 1841].

Auricchio, John. *The Future of Theology*. New York: Alba House, 1970.

Babini, Ellero, "Jesus Christ: Form and Norm of Man according to Hans Urs von Balthasar." In *Hans Urs von Balthasar: His Life and Work*, edited by David L. Schindler, 221–30. San Francisco: Ignatius Press and Communio Books, 1991.

Barrett, Melanie Susan. *Love's Beauty at the Heart of the Christian Moral Life. The Ethics of Catholic Theologian Hans Urs von Balthasar*. Lewiston, Penn.: Edwin Mellen Press, 2009.

Barth, Karl. *Church Dogmatics*. Volume IV. Translated by G. W. Bromiley. Edinburgh: T. & T. Clark, 1956. [*Die kirchliche Dogmatik*. Volume IV, 1. *Die Lehre von der Versöhnung*. Zürich: Evangelischer Varlag, 1953].

Bätzing, Georg. "Homesickness for God: Adrienne von Speyr's *Confession*." *Communio* 31, no. 4 (2004): 548–56.

Beattie, Tina. "A Man and Three Women—Hans, Adrienne, Mary and Luce." *New Blackfriars* 79, no. 927 (1998): 97–105.

———. *New Catholic Feminism: Theology and Theory*. London: Routledge, 2006.

Beaudin, Michel. *Obéissance et solidarité: Essai sur la christologie de Hans Urs von Balthasar*. Montréal: Editions Fides, 1989.

Beauvoir, Simone. *The Second Sex*. Translated by H. M. Parshley. New York: Vintage Books, 1989. [*Le Deuxième Sexe*. I: *Les faits et les mythes*. II: *L'expérience vécue*. Paris, Gallimard, 1949, 1976].

Benedict XVI, Pope. Encyclical Letter, *Deus caritas est / God is Love*. December 25, 2005. San Francisco: Ignatius Press, 2006.

———. "Meditation of His Holiness Benedict XVI during the First General Congregation." Special Assembly for the Middle East of the Synod of Bishops. Synod Hall. Monday, 11 October 2010. http://www.vatican.va/holy_father/benedict_xvi/speeches/2010/october/documents/hf_ben-xvi_spe_20101011_meditazione_en.html

Berg, Blaise R. *Christian Marriage according to Adrienne von Speyr*. PhD diss., Pontifical Lateran University, Pontifical John Paul II Institute of Studies on Marriage and Family, 2003.

Birot, Antoine. "The Divine Drama, From the Father's Perspective: How the Father Lives Love in the Trinity." *Communio* 30, no. 3 (2003): 406–29.

———. *La dramatique trinitaire de l'amour: Pour une introduction à la théologie trinitaire de Hans Urs von Balthasar et Adrienne von Speyr.* Paris: Parole et Silence, 2009.

———. "Le fondement christologique et trinitaire de la différence sexuelle chez Adrienne von Speyr." *Revue Catholique Internationale: Communio* 31, nos. 5–6 (2006): 123–35.

———. "'God in Christ, Reconciled the World to Himself': Redemption in Balthasar." *Communio* 24, no. 3 (1997): 259–85.

———. "Le Mystère Pascal expression suprême de l'Amour trinitaire selon Adrienne von Speyr et Hans Urs von Balthasar." *Communio* 24, nos. 5–6 (1999): 127–38.

Blanchette, Oliva. "The Logic of Perfection in Aquinas." In *Thomas Aquinas and His Legacy*, edited by David M. Gallagher, 107–30. Washington, D.C.: The Catholic University of America Press, 1994.

Blankenhorn, Bernhard-Thomas. "Balthasar's Method of Divine Naming." *Nova et Vetera* (English edition) 1, no. 2 (2003): 245–67.

———. "Book review of Alyssa Pitstick, *Light in Darkness: Hans Urs von Balthasar and the Catholic Doctrine of Christ's Descent into Hell* (Grand Rapids, Mich: Eerdmans, 2007)." *Nova et Vetera* (English edition) 6, no. 4 (2008): 951–84.

———. "The Good as Self-Diffusive in Thomas Aquinas." *Angelicum* 79, no. 4 (2002): 803–37.

Boersma, Hans. *Nouvelle Théologie and Sacramental Ontology: A Return to Mystery.* Oxford: Oxford University Press, 2009.

Boethius. *Contra Eutychen et Nestorium.* In *Traités théologiques*, 62–121. Translated and presented by Axel Tisserand. Paris: Flammarion, 2000.

———. *Liber de Persona et Duabus Naturis.* PL 64:1247–1412. [*Patrologia Latina*, volume 64: *Manlii Severini Boetii Opera Omnia.* Edited by Jacques-Paul Migne. Paris, 1847].

Bonino, Serge-Thomas. "La simplicité de Dieu." In *Instituto San Tommaso, Studi 1996*, edited by Dietrich Lorenz, 117–52. Studia Pontificiae Universitatis a S. Thomas Aquinate in Urbe, Nuova serie 3. Rome: Pontificia Università San Tommaso d'Aquino in Roma Angelicum, 1997.

———, ed. *Surnaturel: A Controversy at the Heart of Twentieth-Century Thomistic Thought.* Translated by Robert Williams. Translation revised by Matthew Levering. Naples, Fla.: Sapientia Press, 2009. [*Surnaturel. Une controverse au cœur du thomisme au XXe siècle.* Actes du colloque organisé par l'Institut Saint-Thomas-d'Aquin les 26–27 mai 2000 à Toulouse. Publié par la *Revue thomiste*, 102, no. 1 (2001)].

Borella, Jean. *Penser l'analogie.* Paris: Ad Solem, 2000.

———. *The Sense of the Supernatural.* Translated by G. John Champoux. Edinburgh: T. & T. Clark, 1998. [*Le sens du surnaturel.* Geneva: Ad Solem, 1996].

Bouyer, Louis. *The Christian Mystery: From Pagan Myth to Christian Mysticism.* Translated by Illtyd Trethowan. Edinburgh: T. & T. Clark, 1990. [*Mysterion, du mystère à la mystique.* Paris: O. E. I. L., 1986, 1999].

Boyle, John F. "St. Thomas and the Analogy of *Potentia Generandi*." *The Thomist* 64 (2000): 581-592.

Bremond, Henri. *Histoire littéraire du sentiment religieux en France depuis la fin des guerres de religion jusqu'à nos jours*, volumes VII and VIII: *La métaphysique des saints*. Paris: Bloud et Gay, 1928.

Brock, Stephen L. "Harmonizing Plato and Aristotle on *Esse*: Thomas Aquinas and the *De hebdomadibus*." *Nova et Vetera* (English edition) 5, no. 3 (2007): 465–94.

Buckley, James J. "Balthasar's Use of the Theology of Aquinas." *The Thomist* 59, no. 4, (1995): 517–45.

Bulgakov, Sergei Nikolaevich. *Le verbe incarné: Agnus Dei*. Translated by Constantin Andronikof. Lausanne: Editions l'Age d'Homme, 1982; Paris: Aubier, 1943.

Campodonico, Angelo. "Hans Urs von Balthasar's Interpretation of the Philosophy of Thomas Aquinas." Translated by Joseph G. Trabbic. In *Nova et Vetera* (English edition) 8, no. 1 (2010): 33–53.

Capol, Cornelia and Claudia Müller. *Hans Urs von Balthasar. Bibliography 1925–2005*. Einsiedeln: Johannes Verlag, 2005.

Casarella, Peter. "Hans Urs von Balthasar, Erich Przywara's *Analogia Entis*, and the Problem of a Catholic *Denkform*." In Thomas Joseph White, ed., *The Analogy of Being: Invention of the Antichrist or the Wisdom of God?* Grand Rapids, Mich.: Eerdmans, 2011: 192–206.

The Catechism of the Catholic Church. New York: Doubleday, 1995.

Catry, Patrick. "Spuren Gottes." In *Adrienne von Speyr und ihre kirchliche Sendung. Akten des römischen Symposiums (27.–29. September 1985)*, edited by Hans Urs von Balthasar, Georges Chantraine, and Angelo Scola, 19–35. Einsiedeln: Johannes Verlag, 1986. ["Des traces de Dieu." In *La mission ecclésiale d'Adrienne von Speyr. Actes du colloque romain (27–29 septembre 1985)*, edited by Hans Urs von Balthasar, Georges Chantraine, and Angelo Scola, 19–37. Paris and Namur: Éditions Lethielleux and Culture et Vérité, 1986].

Cessario, Romanus. *The Moral Virtues and Theological Ethics*. Notre Dame, Ind.: University of Notre Dame Press, 1991.

Chantraine, Georges, Hans Urs von Balthasar, and Angelo Scola, eds. *Adrienne von Speyr und ihre kirchliche Sendung. Akten des römischen Symposiums (27.–29. September 1985)*. Einsiedeln: Johannes Verlag, 1986. [*La mission ecclésiale d'Adrienne von Speyr. Actes du colloque romain (27–29 septembre 1985)*. Paris and Namur: Éditions Lethielleux and Culture et Vérité, 1986].

Chapp, Larry. "Revelation." In *The Cambridge Companion to Hans Urs von Balthasar*, edited by Edward Oakes and David Moss, 11–23. Cambridge: Cambridge University Press, 2004, 2006.

Chapp, Larry S. and Rodney A. Howsare, eds. *How Balthasar Changed My Mind*. New York: Crossroad, 2008.

Chenu, Marie-Dominique. *Introduction à l'étude de Saint Thomas d'Aquin*. Montréal / Paris: Institute d'études médievales / Vrin, 1950.

Clarke, Norris. "Response to Long." *The Thomist* 61, no. 4 (1997): 617–24.

———. "Response to Long's Comments." *Communio* 21, no. 1 (1994): 165–69.

Congregation for the Doctrine of the Faith. *Instruction on Christian Freedom and Liberation* (March 22, 1986). Washington, D.C.: United States Catholic Conference, 1986. [In *Compendium of Creeds, Definitions, and Declarations on Matters of Faith and Morals*, 43rd edition. Originally edited by Heinrici Denzinger. Revised, enlarged, and in collaborations with Helmut Hoping, edited by Peter Hünnermann in German (2010) and in English by Robert Fastiggi and Anne Englund Nash, nos. 4750–76. San Francisco: Ignatius Press, 2012.]

———. *Letter to the Bishops of the Catholic Church on the Collaboration of Men and Women in the Church and in the World*, signed by Joseph Ratzinger, Prefect and Angelo Amato, Secretary (May 31, 2004). Boston: Pauline Books & Media, 2004.

Council, Constantinople (Third). Session 18, September 16, 681. In *Compendium of Creeds, Definitions, and Declarations on Matters of Faith and Morals*, 43rd edition. Originally edited by Heinrich Denzinger. Revised, enlarged, and in collaborations with Helmut Hoping, edited by Peter Hünnermann in German (2010) and in English by Robert Fastiggi and Anne Englund Nash, nos. 553–59. San Francisco: Ignatius Press, 2012.

Council, Fourth Lateran. November 11–30, 1215. Chapter 2. *The False Doctrine of Joachim of Fiore*. In *Compendium of Creeds, Definitions, and Declarations on Matters of Faith and Morals*, 43rd edition. Originally edited by Heinrich Denzinger. Revised, enlarged, and in collaborations with Helmut Hoping, edited by Peter Hünnermann in German (2010) and in English by Robert Fastiggi and Anne Englund Nash, nos. 803–9. San Francisco: Ignatius Press, 2012.

Council, Nicaea (First Ecumenical). Nicene Creed, June 19, 325. In *Compendium of Creeds, Definitions, and Declarations on Matters of Faith and Morals*, 43rd edition. Originally edited by Heinrich Denzinger. Revised, enlarged, and in collaborations with Helmut Hoping, edited by Peter Hünnermann in German (2010) and in English by Robert Fastiggi and Anne Englund Nash, nos. 125–26. San Francisco: Ignatius Press, 2012.

Council, Vatican II. October 11, 1962 to December 8, 1965. In *Compendium of Creeds, Definitions, and Declarations on Matters of Faith and Morals*, 43rd edition. Originally edited by Heinrich Denzinger. Revised, enlarged, and in collaborations with Helmut Hoping, edited by Peter Hünnermann in German (2010) and in English by Robert Fastiggi and Anne Englund Nash, nos. 4001–5. San Francisco: Ignatius Press, 2012. [In *Vatican Council II. The Conciliar and Post Conciliar Documents*. Edited by Austin Flannery. Collegeville, Minn.: The Liturgical Press, 1975, 1979[4]]

———. *Ad Gentes Divinitus*. Decree on the Church's Missionary Activity. December 7, 1965. In *Vatican Council II. The Conciliar and Post Conciliar Documents*. Edited by Austin Flannery, 813–62. Collegeville, Minn.: The Liturgical Press, 1975, 1979[4]. This decree does not appear in Denzinger.

———. *Dei Verbum*. Dogmatic Constitution on Divine Revelation. November 18, 1965. In *Compendium of Creeds, Definitions, and Declarations on Matters of Faith and Morals*, 43rd edition. Originally edited by Heinrich Denzinger. Revised, enlarged, and in collaborations with Helmut Hoping, edited by Peter Hünnermann in German (2010) and in English by Robert Fastiggi and Anne Englund Nash, nos. 4201–35. San Francisco: Ignatius Press, 2012. [In *Vatican Council II. The Conciliar and Post Conciliar Documents*. Edited by Austin Flannery, 750–65. Collegeville, Minn.: The Ligurgical Press, 1975, 1979[4]].

———. *Gaudium et Spes*. Pastoral Constitution on the Church in the Modern World. December 7, 1965. In *Compendium of Creeds, Definitions, and Declarations on Matters of Faith and Morals*, 43rd edition. Originally edited by Heinrich Denzinger. Revised, enlarged, and in collaborations with Helmut Hoping, edited by Peter Hünnermann in German (2010) and in English by Robert Fastiggi and Anne Englund Nash, nos. 4301–45. San Francisco: Ignatius Press, 2012. [In *Vatican Council II. The Conciliar and Post Conciliar Documents*. Edited by Austin Flannery, 930–1001. Collegeville, Minn.: The Liturgical Press, 1975, 1979[4]].

———. *Lumen Gentium. Dogmatic Constitution on the Church*. November 5, 1964. In *Compendium of Creeds, Definitions, and Declarations on Matters of Faith and Morals*, 43rd edition. Originally edited by Heinrich Denzinger. Revised, enlarged, and in collaborations with Helmut Hoping, edited by Peter Hünnermann in German (2010) and in English by Robert Fastiggi and Anne Englund Nash, nos. 4101–79. San Francisco: Ignatius Press, 2012. [In *Vatican Council II. The Conciliar and Post Conciliar Documents*. Edited by Austin Flannery, 350–426. Collegeville, Minn.: The Liturgical Press, 1975, 1979⁴.]

Cottier, Georges. *Le désir de Dieu. Sur les traces de saint Thomas*. Paris: Parole et Silence, 2002.

———. "Metaphysics and Mysticism." *Nova et Vetera* (English edition) 1, no. 2 (2003): 269–82.

Crammer, Corinne. "One Sex or Two? Balthasar's Theology of the Sexes." In *Cambridge Companion to Hans Urs von Balthasar*, edited by Edward T. Oakes and David Moss, 93–112. Cambridge: Cambridge University Press, 2004, 2006.

Crawford, David S. "Christian Community and the States of Life: A Reflection on the Anthropological Significance of Virginity and Marriage." *Communio* 29, no. 2 (2002): 337–65.

———. "Of Spouses, the Real World, and the 'Where' of Christian Marriage." *Communio* 33, no. 1 (Spring 2006): 100–116.

Crowley, Paul G. "*Instrumentum Divinitatis* in Thomas Aquinas: Recovering the Divinity of Christ." *Theological Studies* 52, no. 3 (1991): 451–75.

Dalzell, Thomas G. *The Dramatic Encounter of Divine and Human Freedom in the Theology of Hans Urs von Balthasar*. Bern: Peter Lang, 1997.

———. "The Enrichment of God in Balthasar's Trinitarian Eschatology." *Irish Theological Quarterly* 66, no. 1 (2001): 3–18.

Daniélou, Jean. "Les orientations présentes de la pensée religieuse." *Études* 249, no. 4 (April 1946): 5–21.

Dauphinais, Michael and Matthew Levering, eds. *Reading John with St. Thomas: Theological Exegesis and Speculative Theology*. Washington, D.C.: The Catholic University of America Press, 2005.

Davies, Oliver. "The Theological Aesthetics." In *Cambridge Companion to Hans Urs von Balthasar*, edited by Edward T. Oakes and David Moss, 131–42. Cambridge: Cambridge University Press, 2004, 2006.

D'Costa, Gavin. *Sexing the Trinity: Gender, Culture and the Divine*. London: SCM Press, 2000.

De Lubac, Henri. *At the Service of the Church: Henri de Lubac Reflects on the Circumstances that Occasioned His Writings*. Translated by Anne Elizabeth Englund. San Francisco: Communio Books / Ignatius Press, 1993. [*Mémoire sur l'occasion de mes écrits*. Namur, Belgium: Culture et Verité, 1989].

———. *La révélation divine*. Paris: Cerf, 1983.

———. *The Mystery of the Supernatural*. Translated by Rosemary Sheed. New York: Crossroad, 1998. [*Le mystère du surnaturel*. Paris: Aubier, 1965].

———. *Surnatural. Études historiques*. Paris: Aubier-Montaigne, 1946; Desclée de Brouwer, 1991.

———. *Théologie dans l'histoire*, II: *Questions disputées et résistance au nazisme*. Paris: Desclée de Brouwer, 1990.

———. "A Witness of Christ in the Church: Hans Urs von Balthasar." In *Hans Urs von Balthasar: His Life and Work*, edited by David L. Schindler, 271–88. San Francisco: Ignatius Press and Communio Books, 1991. [*Un Témoin du Christ Hans Urs von Balthasar*. Paris: Desclée de Brouwer, 1965].

Denzinger, Heinrich. *Compendium of Creeds, Definitions, and Declarations on Matters of Faith and Morals*, 43rd edition. Revised, enlarged and, in collaboration with Helmut Hoping, edited by Peter Hünnermann in German. Edited in English by Robert Fastiggi and Anne Englund Nash. San Francisco: Ignatius Press, 2012. [*Kompendium der Glaubensbekenntnisse und kirchlichen Lehrentscheidungen*. Freiburg im Breisgau: Verlag Herder, 2010].

DiNoia, Augustine J. "American Catholic Theology at Century's End: Postconciliar, Postmodern, Post-Thomistic." *The Thomist* 54, no. 3 (1990): 499–518.

———. "Karl Rahner." In *The Modern Theologians*. Volume I. Edited by David F. Ford, 183–204. Oxford: Basil Blackwell, 1989.

———. "Philosophical Theology in the Perspective of Religious Diversity." *Theological Studies* 49, no. 3 (1988): 401–16.

Dinechin, Olivier de. "*Kathos*: La similitude dans l'évangile selon Saint Jean." *Recherches de Science et Religion* 58, no. 2 (1970): 195–236.

Dol, Jean-Noël. "L'inversion trinitaire chez Hans Urs von Balthasar." *Revue thomiste* 100, no. 2 (2000): 201–38.

Donneaud, Henri. "Hans Urs von Balthasar contre saint Thomas d'Aquin sur la foi du Christ." *Revue thomiste* 97, no. 2 (1997): 335–54.

Dupré, Louis. *The Enlightenment and the Intellectual Foundations of Modern Culture*. New Haven, Conn.: Yale University Press, 2004.

———. "The Glory of the Lord: Hans Urs von Balthasar's Theological Aesthetic." In *Hans Urs von Balthasar: His Life and Work*, edited by David L. Schindler, 183–206. San Francisco: Ignatius Press and Communio Books, 1991.

Dupuis, Jacques and Josef Neuner, eds. *The Christian Faith: The Doctrinal Documents of the Catholic Church*. New York: Alba House, 1982.

Durand, Emmanuel. "L'image créée et sa destination trinitaire. Discernement sur les fondements de l'eschatologie chez Balthasar." *Transversalités* no. 104 (2007): 231–46.

Elshtain, Jean Bethke. *Sovereignty: God, State, and Self*. New York: Basic Books, 2008.

Emery, Gilles. "Contemporary Questions about God." *Nova et Vetera* (English edition) 8, no. 4 (2010): 799–811. ["Questions d'aujourd'hui sur Dieu." In Serge-Thomas Bonino (ed.), *Thomistes ou de l'actualité de saint Thomas d'Aquin*, 87–98. Paris: Parole et Silence, 2003.]

———. "The Dignity of Being a Substance: Person, Subsistence, and Nature." *Nova et Vetera* (English edition) 9, no. 4 (2011): 991–1001.

———. "The Ecclesial Fruit of the Eucharist in St. Thomas Aquinas." Translated by Therese C. Scarpelli. In Gilles Emery, *Trinity, Church, and the Human Person*, 155–72. Ave Maria, Fla.: Sapientia Press, 2007. ["Le fruit ecclesial de l'Eucharistie chez saint Thomas d'Aquin." *Nova et Vetera* (French) 72 (1997): 25–40].

———. "Essentialism or Personalism in the Treatise on God in St. Thomas Aquinas?" In Gilles Emery. *Trinity in Aquinas*, translated by Matthew Levering, 165–208. Naples, Fla.: Sapientia Press, 2003, 2006². ["Essentialisme ou personnalisme dans le traité de Dieu chez saint Thomas d'Aquin?" *Revue thomiste* 98 (1998): 5–38].

———. "The Immutability of the God of Love and the Problem of Language Concerning the 'Suffering of God.'" In *Divine Impassibility and the Mystery of Human Suffering*, edited by James F. Keating and Thomas J. White, 27–76. Grand Rapids, Mich.: Eerdmans, 2009. [This is an amplified version of the French original: "L'immutabilité du Dieu d'amour et les problèmes du discours sur la 'souffrance de Dieu." *Nova et Vetera* 74, no. 1 (1999): 5–37].

———. "La relation création." *Nova et Vetera* 88, no. 1 (2013): 9–43.

———. "Mission invisibles et missions visibles: Le Christ et son Esprit." *Revue thomiste* 106, nos. 1–2 (2006), 51–99.

———. "A Note on St. Thomas and the Greek Fathers." Translated by Jennifer Harms and John Baptist Ku. In Emery, *Trinity, Church and the Human Person: Thomistic Essays*, 193–207. Ave Maria, Fla.: Sapientia Press, 2007. [A former version of this essay was published in French: "Saint Thomas d'Aquin et l'Orient chrétien." *Nova et Vetera* (French) 74, no. 4 (1999): 19–36].

———. "Personne humaine et relation: la personne se définit-elle par la relation?" *Nova et Vetera* 87, no. 1 (2014): 7–29.

———. "The Personal Mode of Trinitarian Action in St. Thomas Aquinas." Translated by Matthew Levering. In Emery, *Trinity, Church, and the Human Person: Thomistic Essays*, 115–53. Naples, Fla.: Sapientia Press, 2007. ["Le mode personnel de l'agir trinitaire suivant Thomas d'Aquin." *Freiburger Zeitschrift für Philosophie und Theologie* 50 (2003): 334–53].

———. "The Question of Evil and the Mystery of God in Charles Journet." Translated by Robert E. Williams and Paul Gondreau. In Emery, *Trinity, Church, and the Human Person: Thomistic Essays*, 237–62. Naples, Fla.: Sapientia Press, 2007. ["La question du mal et le mystère du Dieu chez Charles Journet." In *Charles Journet: Un témoin du XXe siècle*, 301–25. Actes de la Semaine théologique de l'Université de Fribourg, Faculté de théologie, 8–12 avril 2002. Paris: Parole et Silence, 2003.]

———. "La Relation de creation." *Nova et Vetera* 88, no. 1 (2013): 9–43.

———. "*Theologia* and *Dispensatio*: The Centrality of the Divine Missions in St. Thomas's Trinitarian Theology." *The Thomist* 74, no. 4 (2010): 515–61.

———. *La Trinité créatrice: Trinité et création dans les commentaires aux Sentences de Thomas d'Aquin et de ses précurseurs Albert le Grand et Bonaventure*. Paris: Vrin, 1995.

———. "La Trinité, le Christ et l'homme: Théologie et métaphysique de la personne." In *L'humain et la personne*, edited by François-Xavier Putallaz and Bernard N. Schumacher, 175–93. Paris: Cerf, 2008.

———. *The Trinitarian Theology of St. Thomas Aquinas*. Translated by Francesca Aran Murphy. Oxford: Oxford University Press, 2007, 2010². [*La théologie trinitaire de saint Thomas d'Aquin*. Paris: Cerf, 2004, 2005].

———. *The Trinity: An Introduction to Catholic Doctrine on the Triune God*. Translated by Matthew Levering. Washington, D.C.: The Catholic University of America Press, 2011. [*La Trinité: Introduction théologique à la doctrine catholique sur Dieu Trinité*. Paris: Les Éditions du Cerf, 2009].

———. *Trinity, Church, and the Human Person: Thomistic Essays*. Naples, Fla.: Sapientia Press, 2007. [This is a collection of essays previously published in French in various journals.]

———. *Trinity in Aquinas*. Naples, Fla.: Sapientia Press, 2003, 2006.

———. "The Unity of Man, Body and Soul, in St. Thomas Aquinas." Translated by Therese C. Scarpelli. In Emery, *Trinity, Church and the Human Person: Thomistic Essays*, 209–35. Naples, Fla.: Sapientia Press, 2007. ["L'unité de l'homme, âme et corps, chez saint Thomas d'Aquin." *Nova et Vetera* (French) 75, no. 2 (2000): 53–76].

Escobar, Pedro. "Hans Urs von Balthasar: Christologian." *Communio* 2, no. 3 (1975): 300–316.

Esperienza mistica e teologia. Ricerca epistemologica sulle proposte di Hans Urs von Balthasar (25–26 May 2000). 14th colloquium of theology in Lugano. *Revista Teologica di Lugano* 6, no. 1 (2001).

Espezel, Alberto. "Quelques aspects de la sotériologie de Hans Urs von Balthasar." *Nouvelle*

revue théologique 112, no. 1 (1990): 80–92.
Faggioli, Massimo. *Vatican II: The Battle for Meaning*. New York: Paulist Press, 2012.
Farley, Margaret, A. "New Patterns of Relationship: Beginnings of a Moral Revolution." *Theological Studies* 36, no. 4 (1975): 627–46.
Feingold, Lawrence. *The Natural Desire to See God according to St. Thomas Aquinas and His Interpreters*. Naples, Fla.: Sapientia Press, 2010.
Fessio, Joseph. "Comment lire Adrienne?" In *La mission ecclésiale d'Adrienne von Speyr. Actes du colloque romain (27–29 septembre 1985)*, edited by Hans Urs von Balthasar, Georges Chantraine, and Angelo Scola, 172–83. Paris and Namur: Éditions Lethielleux and Culture et Vérité, 1986. ["Wie liest man Adrienne von Speyr?" In *Adrienne von Speyr und ihre kirchliche Sendung. Akten des römischen Symposiums (27.–29. September 1985)*, edited by Hans Urs von Balthasar, Georges Chantraine, and Angelo Scola, 158–72. Einsiedeln: Johannes Verlag, 1986].
Fields, Stephen. "Balthasar and Rahner on the Spiritual Senses." *Theological Studies* 57, no. 2 (1996): 224–41.
Fiorenza, Elisabeth Schüssler. *In Memory of Her: Feminist Theological Reconstruction of Christian Origins*. New York: Crossroad, 1984.
Fiorenza, Francis Schüssler. *Foundational Theology: Jesus and the Church*. New York: Crossroad, 1985.
Fisichella, Rino. "Hans Urs von Balthasar e Adrienne von Speyr: l'inseparabilità delle due opere." *Communio*, Italian edition, 156, no. 4 (1997): 61–74.
Ford, David F. "Introduction to Modern Christian Theology." In David F. Ford, ed., *The Modern Theologians*, 1–19. Volume I. Oxford: Basil Blackwell, 1989.
———, ed. *The Modern Theologians*. Volume I. Oxford: Basil Blackwell, 1989.
Fort, Gertrud von le. *The Eternal Woman*. Translated by Placid Jordan. San Francisco: Ignatius Press, 2010. [*Die ewige Frau*. München: Josef Kösel and Friedrich Pustet, 1934].
Franks, Angela Franz. "Trinitarian *Analogia Entis* in Hans Urs von Balthasar." *The Thomist* 62, no. 4 (1998): 533–59.
Gagey, Henri-Jérôme and Vincent Holzer, eds. *Balthasar, Rahner: Deux pensées en contraste*. Paris: Bayard, 2005.
Gallagher, David. "Goodness and Moral Goodness." In *Thomas Aquinas and His Legacy*, edited by David M. Gallagher, 37–60. Washington, D.C.: The Catholic University of America Press, 1994.
———, ed. *Thomas Aquinas and His Legacy*. Washington, D.C.: The Catholic University of America Press, 1994.
Gallagher, John A. *Time Past, Time Future: An Historical Study of Catholic Moral Theology*. New York: Paulist Press, 1990.
Gardiner, Anne Barbeau. "Anne Barbeau Gardiner answers Jacques Servais." *New Oxford Review* 69, no. 8 (September 2002): 42–45.
Gardner, Lucy and David Moss. "Difference—the Immaculate Concept? The Laws of Sexual Difference in the Theology of Hans Urs von Balthasar." *Modern Theology* 14, no. 3 (July 1998): 377–401.
———. "Something Like Time; Something Like the Sexes: An Essay in Reception." In *Balthasar at the End of Modernity*, edited by Lucy Gardner, David Moss, Benjamin Quash, and Graham Ward, 69–137. Edinburgh: T. & T. Clark, 1999.
Gardner, Lucy, David Moss, Ben Quash, and Graham Ward, eds. *Balthasar at the End of Modernity*. Edinburgh: T. & T. Clark, 1999.
———. "Correcting the Deposit of Faith? The Dubious Adrienne von Speyr." *New Oxford*

Review 69, no. 8 (September 2002): 31–36.

Garrigou-Lagrange, Reginald. "La nouvelle théologie, où va-t-elle ?" *Angelicum* 23, nos. 3–4 (1946): 126–45.

———. "Vérité et immutabilité du dogme." *Angelicum* 24, nos. 2–3 (1947): 124–39.

Garrigues, Jean-Miguel. "La doctrine de la grâce habituelle dans ses sources scripturaires et patristiques." *Revue thomistie* 103, no. 2 (2003): 179–202.

Gawronski, Raymond. *Word and Silence: Hans Urs von Balthasar and the Spiritual Encounter between East and West*. Edinburgh: T. & T. Clark, 1995.

Geiger, Louis-Bertrand. "L'homme image de Dieu, à propos de *Summa Theologiae* I, 93, 4." In Geiger, *Penser avec Thomas d'Aquin*. Etudes thomistes présentées par Ruedi Imbach, 111–38. Paris / Fribourg: Cerf / Editions universitaires Fribourg Suisse, 2000.

———. *Le problème de l'amour chez Saint Thomas d'Aquin*. Paris / Montréal: Vrin / Institue d'Études Médiévales, 1952.

Gillespie, Michael Allen. *The Theological Origins of Modernity*. Chicago: University of Chicago Press, 2008.

Gillette, Gertrude. "Augustine and the Significance of Perpetua's Words: 'And I was a man.'" *Augustinian Studies* 32, no. 1 (2001): 115–25.

Gilson, Etienne. *Thomism: The Philosophy of Thomas Aquinas*. Translated by Armand Augustine Maurer and Laurence K. Shook. Toronto: Pontifical Institute of Mediaeval Studies, 2002[6]. [*Le thomisme. Introduction à la philosophie de saint Thomas d'Aquin*. Paris: Vrin, 1989[6]].

Gonzalez, Michelle A. "Hans Urs von Balthasar and Contemporary Feminist Theology." *Theological Studies* 65, no. 3 (2004): 566–95.

Greiner, Maximilian. "The Community of St. John: A Conversation with Cornelia Capol and Martha Gisi." In *Hans Urs von Balthasar: His Life and Work*, edited by David L. Schindler, 87–101. San Francisco: Ignatius Press and Communio Books, 1991.

Greiner, Susanne. "Die Würde der Frau. Ihre Bedeutung in der Theologie Hans Urs von Balthasar." In *Hans Urs von Balthasar. Gestalt und Werk*, edited by Karl Lehmann and Walter Kaspers, 285–97. Köln: Communio, 1989.

Gregory of Nazianzus. *Episola* 101: *Ad Cledonium presbyterum*. PG 37:175–91. [*Patrologiae Graeca*, volume 37: *Sancti Patris Nostri Gegorii theologi vulgo Nazianzeni Archiepiscopi Constantinopolitani*. Edited by Jacques-Paul Migne. Paris, 1857].

Grillmeier, Aloys. *Christ in Christian Tradition: From the Apostolic Age to Chalcedon (451)*. Translated by John S. Bowden. New York: Sheed and Ward, 1965.

Guerriero, Elio. *Hans Urs von Balthasar*. Translated by Frances Georges-Catroux. Paris: Desclée, 1993 [French edition]. *Hans Urs von Balthasar. Eine Monographie*. Johannes, Einsiedeln: Johannes Verlag, 1993 [German edition]. *Hans Urs von Balthasar*. Cinisello Balsamo (Milano): Edizioni Paoline, 1991 [original Italian edition].

Hans Urs von Balthasar Stiftung, ed. *Adrienne von Speyr und ihre spirituelle Theologie : die Referate am Symposium zu ihrem 100 Geburtstag* (September 2002) im Freiburg im Breisgau (Einsiedeln: Johannes Verlag, 2002).

Harris, Harriet A. "Should We Say that Personhood is Relational?" *Scottish Journal of Theology* 51, no. 2 (1998): 214–34.

Harrison, Victoria S. "*Homo Orans*: Von Balthasar's Christo-Centric Philosophical Anthropology." *Heythrop Journal* 40, no. 3 (1999): 280–300.

Healy, Nicholas J. *The Eschatology of Hans Urs von Balthasar*. Oxford: Oxford University Press, 2005.

——— and David L. Schindler. "For the Life of the World: Hans Urs von Balthasar on the Church as Eucharist." In *The Cambridge Companion to Hans Urs von Balthasar*, edited by Edward T. Oakes and David Moss, 51–63. Cambridge: Cambridge University Press, 2004.

———. "Henri de Lubac on Nature and Grace: A Note on Some Recent Contributions to the Debate," *Communio* 35, no. 4 (2008): 535–64.

Hemmerle, Klaus. *Thesen zu einer trinitarischen Ontologie*. Einsiedeln: Johannes Verlag, 1976.

Henrici, Peter. *Hans Urs von Balthasar: Aspekte seiner Sendung*. Einsiedeln: Johannes Verlag, 2008.

———. "The Philosophy of Hans Urs von Balthasar." In *Hans Urs von Balthasar: His Life and Work*, edited by David L. Schindler, 149–67. San Francisco: Ignatius Press and Communio Books, 1991.

———. "Response to Louis Dupré." In *Catholicism and Secularization in America: Essays on Nature, Grace, and Culture*, edited by David L. Schindler, 74–79. Huntington, Ind.: Our Sunday Visitor and Communio Books, 1990.

———. "A Sketch of Von Balthasar's Life." In *Hans Urs von Balthasar: His Life and Work*, edited by David L. Schindler, 7–43. San Francisco: Ignatius Press and Communio Books, 1991.

Hofer, Andrew. "Balthasar's Eschatology on the Intermediate State." *Logos* 12, no. 3 (2009): 148–72.

Hoffmann, Norbert. *Kreuz und Trinität. Zur Theologie der Sühne*. Einsiedeln: Johannes Verlag, 1982.

Holzer, Vincent and Henri-Jérôme Gagey, eds. *Balthasar, Rahner: Deux pensées en contraste*. Paris: Bayard, 2005.

Howsare, Rodney A. *Balthasar: A Guide for the Perplexed*. London: T. & T. Clark, 2009.

——— and Larry S. Chapp, eds. *How Balthasar Changed My Mind*. New York: Crossroad, 2008.

Hütter, Reinhard. "Aquinas on the Natural Desire for the Vision of God: A Reflection on *Summa Contra Gentiles* III, c. 25 *après* Henri de Lubac." *The Thomist* 73, no. 4 (2009): 523–91.

———. "Attending to the Wisdom of God—from Effect to Cause, from Creation to God: A *Relecture* of the Analogy of Being according to Thomas Aquinas." In *The Analogy of Being: Invention of the Antichrist or the Wisdom of God?*, edited by Thomas Joseph White, 209–45. Grand Rapids, Mich.: Eerdmans, 2011.

———. "*Desiderium Naturale Visionis Dei—Est autem duplex hominis beatitudo sive felicitas*: Some Observations about Lawrence Feingold's and John Milbank's Recent Interventions in the Debate over the Natural Desire to See God." *Nova et Vetera* (English edition) 5, no. 1 (2007): 81–132.

Ide, Pascal. *Être et mystère. La philosophie de Hans Urs von Balthasar*. Bruxelles: Culture et Vérité, 1995.

———. *Une théologie de l'amour: L'amour, centre de la Trilogie de Hans Urs von Balthasar*. Bruxelles: Lessius, 2012.

———. "Une théologie du don. Les occurrences de *Gaudium et spes*, nr. 24, § 3 chez Jean-Paul II." *Anthropotes* 17, no. 1 (2001): 149–78; 17, no. 2 (2001): 313–44.

Ignatius of Loyola. *Spiritual Exercises*. Translated by Anthony Mottola with an introduction by Robert W. Gleason. New York: Image Books, 1964.

International Theological Commission. "Theology, Christology, Anthropology" [1981]. In *International Theological Commission. Texts and Documents*, Volume I: *1969–1985*, 207–23.

San Francisco: Ignatius Press, 1989.

———. "Communion and Stewardship: Human Persons Created in the Image of God" (2004). In *International Theological Commission. Texts and Documents*. Volume II: *1986–2007*, 319–51. San Francisco: Ignatius Press, 2009.

Irenaeus of Lyons. *Adversus Haereses*. In *Contre les hérésies: édition critique d'après les versions arménienne et latine*. Translated and edited by Adelin Roussea, Louis Doutreleau, et al. Volume I, 1: Sources chrétiennes 263. Paris: Cerf, 1979. Volume I, 2: Sources chrétiennes 264. Paris: Cerf, 1979. Volume II, 1: Sources chrétiennes 293. Paris: Cerf, 1982. Volume II, 2: Sources chrétiennes 294. Paris: Cerf, 1982. Volume III, 1: Sources chrétiennes 211. Paris: Cerf, 1974. Volume IV. Sources chrétiennes 100. Paris: Cerf, 1974. Volume V, 1: Sources chrétiennes 152. Paris: Cerf, 1969. Volume V, 2: Sources chrétiennes 153. Paris: Cerf, 1969.

———. *Demonstratio. Démonstrations de la prédicatation apostolique*. Translated by L. M. Froideveaux. *Sources chrétiennes* 62. Paris: Cerf, 1959, 1971, 1995.

———. *The Scandal of the Incarnation: Irenaeus Against the Heresies*. Selected and introduced by Hans Urs von Balthasar. Translated by John Saward. San Francisco: Ignatius Press, 1990. [*Irenäus: Gott im Fleisch und Blut*. Einsiedeln: Johannes Verlag, 1981].

John of the Cross. *Dark Night of the Soul*. Translated and edited by E. Allison Peers. New York: Image Books, 1959³. [*La nocha oscrua del alma*. In *Obras de San Juan de la Cruz, Doctor de la Iglesia*, II: *Subida y Noche oscrua*. Edited by Silverio de Santa Teresa. Burgos: Monte Carmelo, 1929–31].

John Paul II, Pope. *Centesimus Annus*. Encyclical Letter. *On the Hundredth Anniversary of Rerum Novarum* (May 1, 1991). Boston: Pauline Books and Media, 1991.

———. *Dives in Misericordia*. Encyclical Letter. *On the Mercy of God* (November 13, 1980). Boston: St. Paul Editions, 1980.

———. *Dominum et Vivificantem*. Encyclical Letter. *On the Holy Spirit in the Life of the Church and the World* (May 18, 1986). Boston: Pauline Books and Media, 1986.

———. *Ecclesia de Eucharistia*. Encyclical Letter. *On the Eucharist in its Relationship to the Church* (April 17, 2003). Washington, D.C.: United States Conference of Catholic Bishops, 2003.

———. *Evangelium Vitae*. Encyclical Letter. On *the Gospel of Life* (1995). Boston: Pauline Books and Media, 1995.

———. *Familiaris Consortio*. Apostolic Exhortation. *On the Role of the Christian Family in the Modern World* (November 22, 1981). Boston: St. Paul Editions, 1981.

———. *Fides et Ratio*. Encyclical Letter. *On Faith and Reason* (September 14, 1998). Washington, D.C.: United States Catholic Conference, 1998.

———. *Gratissimam Sane. Letter to Families* (February 2, 1994). Boston: St. Paul Books and Media, 1994.

———. *Laborem Exercens*. Enyclcial Letter. *On Human Work* (1981). Washington, D.C.: Office for Publishing and Promotion Services, United States Catholic Conference, 1981.

———. *Letter to Women*. Written on the occasion of the Fourth World Conference on Women in Beijing. June 29, 1995. In *Origins: CNS Documentary Service* 25, no. 9 (July 27, 1995): 137 and 139–143.

———. *Man and Woman He Created Them: A Theology of the Body*. Edited by Michael Waldstein. New York: Paulist Press, 2006.

———. *Mulieris Dignitatem*. Apostolic Letter. On *the Dignity and Vocation of Women* (August 15, 1988). Boston: Pauline Books and Media, 1988.

———. *Redemptor Hominis*. Enyclical letter. *On the Redeemer of Man* (1979). Boston:

St. Paul Editions, 1979.

———. *Redemptoris Mater*. Encyclical Letter. *On the Mother of the Redeemer* (March 25, 1987). Boston: St. Paul Books and Media, 1987.

———. *Rosarium Virginis Mariae*. Encyclical Letter. *On the Rosary of the Virgin Mary* (October 16, 2002). Boston: Daughters of St. Paul, 2002.

———. *Sollicitudo Rei Socialis*. Encyclical Letter. *On Social Concern* (1987). Boston: Pauline Books and Media, 1987.

———. *Veritatis Splendor*. Encyclical Letter. *On the Splendor of Truth* (1993). Washington, D.C.: United States Catholic Conference, 2003.

Journet, Charles. *The Church of the Incarnate Word*. Translated by A. H. C. Downes. London and New York: Sheed and Ward, 1955. [*L'Église du Verbe incarné: essai de théologie spéculative*, I-III. Paris: Desclée de Brouwer, 1941, 1951, 1969].

———. "La place de l'homme dans l'univers." *Nova et Vetera* 83, no. 4 (2008): 371–98.

Kasper, Walter, and Karl Lehmann, eds. *Hans Urs von Balthasar. Gestalt und Werk*. Köln: Communio, 1989.

Keating, Daniel A. *Deification and Grace*. Naples, Fla.: Sapientia Press, 2007.

Kehl, Medard. "Hans Urs von Balthasar: A Portrait." In *The Von Balthasar Reader*, edited by Medard Kehl and Werner Löser, 3–54. New York: Crossroad, 1982.

Kerr, Fergus. "Adrienne von Speyr and Hans Urs von Balthasar." *New Blackfriars* 79, no. 923 (January 1998): 26–32.

———. *After Aquinas: Versions of Thomism*. Oxford: Blackwell, 2002.

———. "Discipleship of Equals or Nuptial Mystery?" *New Blackfriars* 75, no. 884 (July/August 1994): 344–54.

———. "Foreword: Assessing this 'Giddy Synthesis.'" In *Balthasar at the End of Modernity*, edited by Lucy Gardner, David Moss, Ben Quash, and Graham Ward, 1–13. Edinburgh: T. & T. Clark, 1999.

———. *Immortal Longings: Versions of Transcending Humanity*. Notre Dame, Ind.: University of Notre Dame Press, 1997.

———. *Twentieth-Century Theologians: From Neoscholasticism to Nuptial Mysticism*. Oxford: Blackwell, 2007.

Kilby, Karen. *Balthasar: A (Very) Critical Introduction*. Grand Rapids, Mich.: Eerdmans, 2012.

———. "Balthasar and Karl Rahner." In *The Cambridge Companion to Hans Urs von Balthasar*, edited by Edward T. Oakes and David Moss, 256–68. Cambridge: Cambridge University Press, 2004, 2006.

Krempel, Anton. *La Doctrine de la relation chez Saint Thomas. Exposé historique et systématique*. Paris: Vrin, 1952.

Krenski, Thomas Rudolf. *Passio Caritatis. Trinitarische Passiologie im Werk Hans Urs von Balthasar*. Einsiedeln: Johannes Verlag, 1990.

Kupczak, Jaroslaw. *Destined for Liberty: The Human Person in the Philosophy of Karol Wojtyla / John Paul II*. Washington, D.C.: The Catholic University of America Press, 2000.

Kwasniewski, Peter A. "St. Thomas, *Extasis*, and Union with the Beloved." *The Thomist* 61, no. 4 (1997): 587–603.

———. "Solitude, Communion, and Ecstasy." *Communio* 26, no. 2 (Summer 1999): 371–92.

Labourdette, Michel. "Chronique de théologie morale." *Revue thomiste*, 74, no. 1 (1966): 277–97.

———. *Cours de théologie morale. Petit cours I: Morale fondamentale*. Préface du cardinal Georges Cottier et avant-propos du fr. Thierry-Dominique Humbrecht. Paris: Paroles et Silence, 2010.

Langevin, Gilles. "*Capax Dei.*" *La Créature intellectuelle et l'intimité de Dieu.* Paris: Desclée de Brouwer, 1966.
Lee, Claudia. "The Role of Mysticism within the Church as Conceived by Hans Urs von Balthasar." *Communio* 16, no. 1 (1989): 105–26.
Lehmann, Karl and Walter Kasper, eds. *Hans Urs von Balthasar. Gestalt und Werk.* Köln: Communio, 1989.
Leo XIII, Pope. Aeterni Patris. Encyclical letter on the restoration of Christian Philosophie. August 4, 1879. [In *Compendium of Creeds, Definitions, and Declarations on Matters of Faith and Morals,* 43rd edition. Originally edited by Heinrici Denzinger. Revised, enlarged, and in collaborations with Helmut Hoping, edited by Peter Hünnermann in German (2010) and in English by Robert Fastiggi and Anne Englund Nash, nos. 3135–3146. San Francisco: Ignatius Press, 2012.]
Léonard, Jean. "Geschmeidigkeit und Humor." In *Adrienne von Speyr und ihre kirchliche Sendung. Akten des römischen Symposiums (27.–29. September 1985)*, edited by Hans Urs von Balthasar, Georges Chantraine, and Angelo Scola, 40–48. Einsiedeln: Johannes Verlag, 1986. ["L'élasticité de l'esprit et humour." In *La mission ecclésiale d'Adrienne von Speyr. Actes du colloque romain (27–29 septembre 1985)*, edited by Hans Urs von Balthasar, Georges Chantraine, and Angelo Scola, 45–52. Paris and Namur: Éditions Lethielleux and Culture et Vérité, 1986].
Léthel, François-Marie. *Théologie de l'agonie du Christ: la liberté humaine du Fils de Dieu et son importance sotériologique mises en lumière par Saint Maxime le confesseur.* Paris: Beauchesne, 1979.
Levering, Matthew. "Hans Urs von Balthasar on the Cross as Analog for the Trinity." In Matthew Levering, *Scripture and Metaphysics: Aquinas and the Renewal of Trinitarian Theology,* 120–32. Oxford: Blackwell Publishing, 2004, 2006.
———. *Predestination: Biblical and Theological Paths.* Oxford University Press, 2011.
——— and Michael Dauphinais, eds. *Reading John with St. Thomas: Theological Exegesis and Speculative Theology.* Washington, D.C.: The Catholic University of America Press, 2005.
———. *Scripture and Metaphysics: Aquinas and the Renewal of Trinitarian Theology.* Oxford: Blackwell Publishing, 2004, 2006.
Livi, Antonio. "The Philosophical Category of 'Faith' at the Origins of Modern Scepticism." *Nova et Vetera* (English edition) 1, no. 2 (2003): 321–40.
Lochbrunner, Manfred. *Analogia Caritatis. Darstellung und Deutung der Theologie Hans Urs von Balthasars.* Wien: Herder, 1981.
Lombardo, Nicholas. *The Logic of Desire: Aquinas on Emotion.* Washington, D.C.: The Catholic University of America Press, 2011.
Long, Steven A. *Analogia Entis: On the Analogy of Being, Metaphysics, and the Act of Faith.* Notre Dame, Ind.: University of Notre Dame Press, 2011.
———. *Natura Pura: On the Recovery of Nature in the Doctrine of Grace.* New York: Fordham Press, 2010.
———. "Obediential Potency, Human Knowledge, and the Natural Desire for God." *International Philosophical Quarterly* 37, no. 1 (1997): 45–63.
———. "On the Loss, and the Recovery, of Nature as a Theonomic Principle: Reflections on the Nature/Grace Controversy." *Nova et Vetera* (English edition) 5, no. 1 (2007): 133–84.
———. "On the Possibility of a Purely Natural End for Man." *The Thomist* 64, no. 2 (2000): 211–37.
———. *The Teleological Grammar of the Moral Act.* Naples, Fla.: Sapientia Press, 2007.
López, Antonio. "Eternal Happening: God as an Event of Love." *Communio* 32, no. 2 (2005):

214-45.

Loughlin, Gerard. "Sexing the Trinity." *New Blackfriars* 79 (1998): 18-25.

Louth, Andrew. "The Place of Heart of the World in the Theology of Hans Urs von Balthasar." In *The Analogy of Beauty: The Theology of Hans Urs von Balthasar*, edited by John Riches, 147-63. Edinburgh: T. & T. Clark, 1986.

Maas, Wilhelm. "Das Geheimnis des Karsamstags." In *Adrienne von Speyr und ihre kirchliche Sendung. Akten des römischen Symposiums (27.-29. September 1985)*, edited by Hans Urs von Balthasar, Georges Chantraine, and Angelo Scola, 128-37. Einsiedeln: Johannes Verlag, 1986.

———. *Gott und die Hölle. Studien zum Decensus Christi*. Einsiedeln: Johannes Verlag, 1979.

Malloy, Christopher J. "Participation and Theology: A Response to Schindler's "What's the Difference?" *Nova et Vetera* (English edition) 5, no. 3 (2007): 619-46.

Mansini, Guy. "The Abiding Significance of de Lubac's *Surnaturel*." *The Thomist* 73, no. 4 (2009): 593-619.

———. "Balthasar and the Theodramatic Enrichment of the Trinity." *The Thomist* 64, no. 4 (2000): 499-519.

———. "Rahner and Balthasar on the Efficacy of the Cross." *Irish Theological Quarterly* 63, no. 3 (1998): 232-49.

Margerie, Bertrand de. "Note on Balthasar's Trinitarian Theology." *The Thomist* 64, no. 1 (2000): 127-30.

Maritain, Jacques. *Approaches to God*. Translated by Peter O'Reilly. New York: Macmillian, 1967³. [*Approches de Dieu*. Paris: Alsatia, 1953].

———. *De Bergson à Thomas d'Aquin. Oeuvres complètes*, VIII. Fribourg / Paris: Éditions Universitaires Fribourg / Éditions Saint-Paul, 1989.

———. *Notebooks*. Translated by Joseph W. Evans. Albany, N.Y.: Magi Books, 1984. [*Carnet de notes*. Paris: Desclée de Brouwer, 1965 and in *Oeuvres complètes*, volume XII, 125-427. Fribourg / Paris: Editions Universitaires Fribourg Suisse / Editions Saint-Paul, 1992].

Martinelli, Paolo. *La morte di Cristo come rivelazione dell'amore trinitario nella teologia di Hans Urs von Balthasar*. Milano: Jaca Book, 1995.

Matro, Justin. *Christian Suffering in the Spiritual Writings of Adrienne von Speyr*. PhD diss., Pontifical Gregorian University, 1999.

Mayer, Rupert Johannes. "Zum *desiderium naturale visionis Dei* nach Johannes Duns Scotus und Thomas de Vio Cajetan. Eine Anmerkung zum Denken Henri de Lubacs." *Angelicum* 85 (2008): 737-63.

McCool, Gerald A. "Why St. Thomas Stays Alive." *International Philosophical Quarterly* 30, no. 3 (September 1990): 257-87.

McIntosh, Mark. *A Christology from Within: Spirituality and the Incarnation in Hans Urs von Balthasar*. Notre Dame, Ind.: University of Notre Dame Press, 2000.

———. *Mystical Theology*. Oxford: Basil Blackwell, 1998.

Menke, Karl-Heinz. *Stellvertetung. Schlüsselbegriff christlichen Lebens und theologische Grundkategorie*. Einsiedeln: Johannes Verlag, 1991.

Mettepenningen, Jürgen. *Nouvelle Théologie—New Theology. Inheritor of Modernism, Precursor of Vatican II*. London: T. & T. Clark, 2010.

Milbank, John. *The Suspended Middle: Henri de Lubac and the Debate Concerning the Supernatural*. Grand Rapids, Mich.: Eerdmans, 2005.

Mongrain, Kevin. *The Systematic Thought of Hans Urs von Balthasar: An Irenaean Retrieval*. New York: Herder & Herder, 2002.

Montagne, Bernard. *La Doctrine de l'analogie de l'être d'après Saint Thomas d'Aquin*. Paris:

Cerf, 2008.

Moss, David. "The Saints." In *Cambridge Companion to Hans Urs von Balthasar*, edited by Edward T. Oakes and David Moss, 79–92. Cambridge: Cambridge University Press, 2004, 2006.

——— and Edward T. Oakes, eds. *The Cambridge Companion to Hans Urs von Balthasar*. Cambridge: Cambridge University Press, 2004, 2006.

———. "Introduction." In *The Cambridge Companion to Hans Urs von Balthasar*, edited by Edward T. Oakes and David Moss, 1–8. Cambridge: Cambridge University Press, 2004, 2006.

——— and Lucy Gardner. "Difference—the Immaculate Concept? The Laws of Sexual Difference in the Theology of Hans Urs von Balthasar." *Modern Theology* 14, no. 3 (July 1998): 377–401.

———. "Something Like Time; Something Like the Sexes: An Essay in Reception." In *Balthasar at the End of Modernity*, edited by Lucy Gardner, David Moss, Benjamin Quash, and Graham Ward, 69–137. Edinburgh: T. & T. Clark, 1999.

———, Lucy Gardner, Ben Quash, and Ward Graham, eds. *Balthasar at the End of Modernity*. Edinburgh: T. & T. Clark, 1999.

Mouroux, Jean. *The Christian Experience: An Introduction to a Theology*. Translated by George Lamb. New York: Sheed and Ward, 1954. [*L'expérience chrétienne. Introduction à la théologie*. Paris: Aubier, 1952].

Müller, Claudia and Cornelia Capol. *Hans Urs von Balthasar. Bibliographie 1925–2005*. Einsiedeln: Johannes Verlag, 2005.

Muers, Rachel. "The Mute Cannot Keep Silent: Barth, von Balthasar, and Irigaray, on the Construction of Women's Silence." In *Challenging Women's Orthodoxies in the Context of Faith*, edited by Susan Frank Parsons, 109–20. Sydney: Ashgate, 2000.

———. "A Question of Two Answers: Difference and Determination in Barth and Von Balthasar," *Hethrop Journal* 60 (1999): 265–79.

Murphy, Francesca Aran. *God Is Not a Story: Realism Revisited*. Oxford: Oxford University Press, 2007.

Nandkisore, Robert. *Hoffnung auf Erlösung. Die Eschatologie im Werk Hans Urs von Balthasars*. Rome: Editrice Pontificia Università Gregoriana, 1997.

Narcisse, Gilbert. *Le Christ en sa beauté. Hans Urs von Balthasar et saint Thomas d'Aquin* I: *Christologie*. Magny-les-Hameaux, France: Socéval Éditions, 2005.

———. *Le Christ en sa beauté. Hans Urs von Balthasar. Saint Thomas d'Aquin* II: *Textes annotés*. Magny-les-Hameaux, France: Socéval Éditions, 2005.

———. "Le Christ selon Saint Thomas." In Serge-Thomas Bonino et al., *Thomistis ou de l'actualité de saint Thomas d'Aquin*, 115–29. Paris: Parole et Silence, 2003.

———. *Les raisons de Dieu. Argument de convenance et esthétique théologique selon saint Thomas d'Aquin et Hans Urs von Balthasar*. Fribourg: Éditions Universitaire, 1997.

———. "Le réalisme thomiste." In Serge-Thomas Bonino, et al., *Thomistes ou de l'actualité de saint Thomas d'Aquin*, 49–65. Paris: Parole et Silence, 2003.

———. "Participer à la vie trinitaire." *Revue thomiste* 96, no. 1 (1996): 107–28.

———. "The Supernatural in Contemporary Theology." In *Surnaturel: A Controversy at the Heart of Twentieth-Century Thomistic Thought*, edited by Serge-Thomas Bonino, translated by Robert Williams and revised by Matthew Levering, 295–309. Naples, Fla.: Sapientia Press, 2009. ["Le surnaturel dans la théologie contemporaine," *Revue thomiste* 101, no. 1 (2001): 312–28].

Neuner, Josef and Jacques Dupuis, eds. *The Christian Faith: The Doctrinal Documents of the Catholic Church*. New York: Alba House, 1982.
Nichols, Aidan. "Adrienne von Speyr and the Mystery of Atonement." *New Blackfriars* 73, no. 856 (1992): 542–53.
———. *No Bloodless Myth: A Guide through Balthasar's Dramatis*. Washington, D.C.: The Catholic University of America Press, 2000.
———. "Thomism and the Nouvelle Théologie." *The Thomist* 64, no. 1 (2000): 1–19.
Nicolas, Jean-Hervé. *Dieu connu comme inconnu. Essai d'une critique de la connaissance théologique*. Paris: Desclée de Brouwer, 1966.
———. *Les profondeurs de la grâce*. Paris: Beauchesne, 1969.
———. "Les rapports entre la nature et le surnaturel dans les débats contemporains." *Revue Thomiste*, 95, no. 1 (1995): 339–416.
———. *Synthèse dogmatique. Complément*. Paris / Fribourg, Switzerland : Beauchesne / Editions Universitaires Fribourg, 1993.
Nicolas, Marie-Joseph. "Introduction à la *Somme théologique*." In Thomas Aquinas, *Somme théologique* I, 17–66. Paris: Cerf, 1984.
———. "Le corps humain." *Revue thomiste* 79, no. 3 (1979): 357–87.
———. "Le corps humain et sa résurrection." *Revue thomiste* 79, no. 4 (1979): 533–45.
———. "L'idée de nature dans la pensée de saint Thomas d'Aquin." In *Revue thomiste* 74, no. 4 (1974): 533–90.
Nygren, Anders. *Agape and Eros*. Translated by Philip S. Watson. Chicago: University of Chicago Press, 1982.
Oakes, Edward T. "Balthasar, Early and Late." *Modern Theology* 23, no. 4 (October 2007): 617–23.
———. "*Descensus* and Development: A Response to Recent Rejoinders." *International Journal of Systematic Theology* 13, no. 1 (2011): 3–24.
———. "The Internal Logic of Holy Saturday in the Theology of Hans Urs von Balthasar. *International Journal of Systematic Theology* 9 (2007): 184–99.
———. "Introduction." In *The Cambridge Companion to Hans Urs von Balthasar*, edited by David Moss and Edward T. Oakes, 1–8. Cambridge: Cambridge University Press, 2004, 2006.
———. *Pattern of Redemption: The Theology of Hans Urs von Balthasar*. London: Continuum, 1994.
———. "The Surnaturel Controversy: A Survey and a Response." *Nova et Vetera* (English edition) 9, no. 3 (2011): 625–56.
——— and David Moss, eds. *The Cambridge Companion to Hans Urs von Balthasar*. Cambridge: Cambridge University Press, 2004, 2006.
——— and Alyssa Lyra Pitstick. "Balthasar, Hell and Heresy: An Exchange." *First Things* (December 2006): 25–29.
———. "More on Balthasar, Hell, and Heresy." *First Things* (January 2007): 16–18.
O'Connor, John D. "Review of Alyssa Pitstick's book, *Light in Darkness: Hans Urs von Balthasar and the Catholic Doctrine of Christ's Descent into Hell* [Grand Rapids, Mich.: Eerdmans, 2007]." In *New Blackfriars* 88 (November 2007): 745–47.
O'Donnell, John. *Hans Urs von Balthasar*. Collegeville, Minn.: Liturgical Press, 1992.
———. "Hans Urs von Balthasar: The Form of his Theology." In *Hans Urs von Balthasar: His Life and Work*, edited by David L. Schindler, 207–20. San Francisco: Ignatius Press and Communio Books, 1991.

———. "Man and Woman as *Imago Dei* in the Theology of Hans Urs von Balthasar." *Clergy Review* 68, no. 4 (1983): 117–28.
O'Hanlon, Gerard. *The Immutability of God in the Theology of Hans Urs von Balthasar*. Cambridge: Cambridge University Press, 1990.
Olsen, Glenn. "The Return of Purpose." *Communio* 33, no. 4 (Winter 2006): 666–81.
O'Meara, Thomas. *Thomas Aquinas Theologian*. Notre Dame, Ind.: University of Notre Dame Press, 1997.
O'Neil, Colman Eugene. "L'homme ouvert à Dieu (Capax Dei)." In *L'Anthropologie de saint Thomas* (Conférences organisées par la Faculté de théologie et la Société philosophique de Fribourg à l'occasion du 7ème centenaire de la mort de saint Thomas d'Aquin), ed. N[orbert] A. Luyten, 54–74. Fribourg, Switzerland: Editions universitaires, 1974.
O'Rourke, Fran. *Pseudo-Dionysius and the Metaphysics of Aquinas*. Leiden: Brill, 1992.
Ouellet, Marc. "Adrienne von Speyr et le Samedi Saint de la théologie." In *Adrienne von Speyr und ihre spirituelle Theologie. Symposium zu ihrem 100. Geburtsta*g, edited by Hans Urs von Balthasar Stiftung, George Chantraine, and Angelo Scola, 31–56. Einsiedeln: Johannes Verlag, 2002.
———. *Divine Likeness: Toward a Trinitarian Anthropology of the Family*. Translated by Philip Milligan and Linda M. Cicone. Grand Rapids, Mich.: Eerdmanns, 2006. [*Divine resemblance: Le mariage et la famille dans la mission de l'Eglise*. Montréal: Éditions Anne Sigier, 2006].
———. "The Foundations of Christian Ethics according to Hans Urs von Balthasar." In *Hans Urs von Balthasar: His Life and Work*, edited by David L. Schindler, 231–49. San Francisco: Ignatius Press and Communio Books, 1991. Also appeared in *Communio* 17, no. 3 (Fall 1990): 375–401.
———. *L'existence comme mission. L'anthropologie théologique de Hans Urs von Balthasar*. Rome: Pontifical Gregorian University, 1983.
———. "The Message of Balthasar's Theology to Modern Theology." *Communio* 23, no. 2 (1996): 270–99. ["Le Message de la théologie de Balthasar à la théologie moderne." In *Hans Urs von Balthasar. Mission et Médiation*, edited by Peter Henrici, Aloïs Haas, Walter Gut, Herbert Meier, Jacques Servais, and Marc Ouellet, 141–72. Saint Maurice, Switzerland: Éditions Saint Augustin, 1998].
———. "Theological Perspectives on Marriage." *Communio* 31, no. 3 (Fall 2004): 419–34.
Palakeel, Joseph. *The Use of Analogy in Theological Discourse: An Investigation in Ecumenical Perspective*. Rome: Editrice Pontificia Università Gregoriana, 1995.
Papanikolaou, Aristotle. "Person, *Kenosis* and Abuse: Hans Urs von Balthasar and Feminist Theologies in Conversation." *Modern Theology* 19, no. 1 (January 2003): 41–65.
Paradiso, Marcello. *Il blue e il giallo. Hans Urs von Balthasar e Adrienne von Speyr: Un'avventura spirituale*. Torino: Effatà, 2009.
Perrier, Emmanuel. "L'enjeu christologique de la satisfaction (I)." *Revue thomiste* 103, no. 1, 2 (2003): 105–36.
———. "L'enjeu christologique de la satisfaction (II)." *Revue thomiste* 103, no. 2 (2003): 203–47.
Pesarchick, Robert A. *The Trinitarian Foundation of Human Sexuality as Revealed by Christ according to Hans Urs von Balthasar. The Revelatory Significance of the Male Christ and the Male Ministerial Priesthood*. Rome: Editrice Pontificia Università Gregoriana, 2000.
Pieper, Josef. *Faith, Hope, Love*. Translated by Richard Winston, Clara Winston, and Mary Frances McCarthy. San Francisco: Ignatius Press, 1997. [*Über den Glauben. Ein philoso-*

phischer Traktat (1962). In *Werke in acht Bänden*, volume 4, edited by Berthold Wald. 11 volumes. Hamburg: Felix Meiner, 1995–2008].

———. *The Four Cardinal Virtues*. Translated by Richard and Clara Winston, Lawrence E. Lynch, and Daniel F. Coogan. Notre Dame, Ind.: University of Notre Dame Press, 1966. [*Traktat über die Klugheit* (1937). In *Werke in acht Bänden*, volume 4, edited by Berthold Wald. 11 volumes. Hamburg: Felix Meiner, 1995–2008].

Pinckaers, Servais. *Morality: The Catholic View*. Prefaced by Alasdair MacIntyre and translated by Michael Sherwin. South Bend, Ind.: St. Augustine's Press, 2001. [*La morale catholique*. Paris: Cerf / Fides, 1991].

———. "The Natural Desire to See God." *Nova et Vetera* (English edition) 8, no. 3 (2010): 627–46. ["Le désir natural de voir Dieu." *Nova et Vetera* (French edition) 60, no. 4 (1976): 255–73].

———. *The Pursuit of Happiness—God's Way: Living the Beatitudes*, translated by Sr. Mary Thomas Noble. Staten Island, N.Y.: St. Paul's, 1998. [*La Quête du bonheur*. Paris: Téqui, 1979].

———. *The Sources of Christian Ethics*. Translated by Mary Thomas Noble from the third edition. Washington, D.C.: The Catholic University of America Press, 1995. [*Les sources de la morale chrétienne: sa méthode, son contenu, son histoire*. Fribourg / Paris: Editions Universitaires / Cerf, 1985, 2007^4].

Pitstick, Alyssa Lyra. "Development of Doctrine, or Denial? Balthasar's Holy Saturday and Newman's *Essay*." *International Journal of Systematic Theology*, 11, no. 2 (2009): 129–45.

———. *Light in Darkness: Hans Urs von Balthasar and the Catholic Doctrine of Christ's Descent into Hell*. Grand Rapids, Mich.: Eerdmans, 2007.

——— and Edward T. Oakes. "Balthasar, Hell and Heresy: An Exchange." *First Things* (December 2006): 25–29.

———. "More on Balthasar, Hell, and Heresy." *First Things* (January 2007): 16–18.

Pius IX, Pope. *Ineffabilis Deus*. Apostolic Constitution Defining the Immaculate Conception. December 8, 1854. In *Compendium of Creeds, Definitions, and Declarations on Matters of Faith and Morals*, 43rd edition, originally edited by Heinrici Denzinger; revised, enlarged, and in collaboration with Helmut Hoping, edited by Peter Hünnermann in German (2010) and in English by Robert Fastiggi and Anne Englund Nash from the German edition edited by Peter Hünnermann, nos. 2800–2804. San Francisco: Ignatius Press, 2012].

Pius XII, Pope. *Mediator Dei*, Encyclical Letter. "On the Sacred Litury." November 20, 1947. In *Compendium of Creeds, Definitions, and Declarations on Matters of Faith and Morals*, 43rd edition, originally edited by Heinrici Denzinger; revised, enlarged, and in collaboration with Helmut Hoping, edited by Peter Hünnermann in German (2010) and in English by Robert Fastiggi and Anne Englund Nash from the German edition edited by Peter Hünnermann, nos. 3840–55. San Francisco: Ignatius Press, 2012.

———. *Mystici corporis*. Encyclical letter "On the Mystical Body of Christ." June 29, 1943. In *Compendium of Creeds, Definitions, and Declarations on Matters of Faith and Morals*, 43rd edition, originally edited by Heinrici Denzinger; revised, enlarged, and in collaboration with Helmut Hoping, edited by Peter Hünnermann in German (2010) and in English by Robert Fastiggi and Anne Englund Nash from the German edition edited by Peter Hünnermann, nos. 3800–3822. San Francisco: Ignatius Press, 2012.

Plé, Albert. *Par devoir ou par plaisir*. Paris: Cerf, 1980.

Pontifical Biblical Commission. "The Interpretation of the Bible in the Church." In *Origins:*

CNS Documentary Service 23 (January 6, 1994): 497–524.
Porter, Jean. "Desire for God: Ground of the Moral Life in Aquinas." *Theological Studies* 47, no. 1 (1986): 48–68.
Pouliquen, Tanguy Marie. *Libres en Christ. La liberté chrétienne selon l'anthropologie de Hans Urs von Balthasar*. Nouan-le-Fuzelier, France: Éditions des Béatitudes, 2008.
Potterie, Ignace de la. *La vérité dans Saint Jean*. Volume II: *Le croyant et la vérité*. Analecta Biblica Investigationes Scientificae in Res Biblicas 74. Rome: Biblical Institute Press, 1977.
Potworowski, Christophe. "Christian Experience in Hans Urs von Balthasar." *Communio* 20, no. 1 (Spring 1993): 107–17.
Przywara, Erich. *Analogia Entis*. Einsiedeln: Johannes Verlag, 1962^2.
Quash, Ben. "Drama and the Ends of Modernity." In *Balthasar at the End of Modernity*, edited by Ben Quash, Lucy Gardner, David Moss, and Graham Ward, 139–71. Edinburgh: T. & T. Clark, 1999.
———, Lucy Gardner, David Moss, and Graham Ward, eds. *Balthasar at the End of Modernity*. Edinburgh: T. & T. Clark, 1999.
Rahner, Karl. *Im Gespräch I*. Edited by Paul Imhof and Herbert Biallowons. Munich: Kösel Verlag, 1982.
———. "The Present Situation of Catholic Theology." In Karl Rahner. *Theological Investigations* XXI. London: Darton, Longman and Todd, 1988, 70–77. ["Zur momentanen Situation der katholischen Theologie," in Karl Rahner, *Schriften zur Theologie*, XV: *Wissenschaft und Christlicher Glaube*, Bearbeitet von Paul Imhof, 76–83. Einsiedeln: Benziger Verlag, 1983].
———. "Remarks on the Dogmatic Treatise 'De Trinitate.'" In Karl Rahner, *Theological Investigations* IV, translated by Joseph Donceel, 79–102. New York: Crossroad, 1998. ["Bemerkungen zum dogmatischen Traktat 'De Trinitate.'" In Karl Rahner, *Schriften zur Theologie*, IV: *Neuere Schriften*, 103–33. Einsiedeln: Benziger Verlag, 1964].
Ratzinger, Joseph. "Das Problem der christlichen Prophetie, Neils Christian Hvidt im Gespräch mit Joseph Kardinal Ratzinger." *Internationale katholische Zeitschrift Communio* 28, no. 2 (March–April 1999): 177–88.
———. "Homily at the Funeral Liturgy of Hans Urs von Balthasar." (Lucerne, July 1, 1988). Reprinted in David L. Schindler, ed., *Hans Urs von Balthasar: His Life and Work*, 291–95. San Francisco: Ignatius Press and Communio Books, 1991.
——— and Hans Urs von Balthasar. *Mary: The Church at the Source*. Translated by Adrian Walker. San Francisco: Ignatius Press and Communio Books, 2005. [*Maria. Kirche im Ursprung*. Freiburg im Breisgau: Herder, 1980].
Remy, Gérard. "La déréliction du Christ." *Revue Thomiste* 98, no. 1 (1998): 39–94.
———. "Le merveilleux et la nuit divine: Un aspect de l'expérience mystique d'Adrienne von Speyr." In Patrick Dondelinger, ed., *Faut-il croire au merveilleux? Actes du colloque de Metz*, 103–34. Paris: Les Editions du Cerf, 2003.
Reno, Russell R. "Was Balthasar A Heretic?" *First Things*, October 15, 2008. http://www.firstthings.com/web-exclusives/2008/10/was-balthasar-a-heretic.
Riches, John, ed. *The Analogy of Beauty: The Theology of Hans Urs von Balthasar*. Edinburgh: T. & T. Clark, 1986.
———. "Hans Urs von Balthasar." In David F. Ford, ed., *The Modern Theologians: An Introduction to Christian Theology in the Twentieth Century*, 1:237–54. Oxford: Blackwell, 1989.
Roberts, Louis. "The Collision of Rahner and Balthasar." *Continuum* 5, (1968): 753–57.
Rocca, Gregory P. *Speaking the Incomprehensible God: Thomas Aquinas on the Interplay of*

Positive and Negative Theology. Washington, D.C.: The Catholic University of America Press, 2004.

Rondet, Henri. *The Grace of Christ: A Brief History of the Theology of Grace*. Translated by Tad W. Guzie. New York: Newman Press, 1966. [*Gracia Christi*, Paris: Beauchesne, 1948].

Roten, Johann G. "Hans Urs von Balthasar's Anthropology in Light of His Marian Thinking." *Communio* 20, no. 2 (1993): 306–33.

———. "The Two Halves of the Moon: Marian Anthropological Dimensions in the Common Mission of Adrienne von Speyr and Hans Urs von Balthasar." *Communio* 16, no. 3 (Fall 1989): 419–45. [Reprinted in David L. Schindler, ed., *Hans Urs von Balthasar: His Life and Work*, 65–86. San Francisco: Ignatius Press and Communio Books, 1991].

Sachs, Randall J. "Current Eschatology: Universal Salvation and the Problem of Hell." *Theological Studies* 52, no. 2 (1991): 227–54.

———. "Hans Urs von Balthasar." In Donald W. Musser and John L. Price, eds., *A New Handbook to Christian Theologians*, 496–504. Nashville, Tenn.: Abingdon, 1996.

———. *The Pneumatology and Christian Spirituality of Hans Urs von Balthasar*. PhD diss., University of Tübingen, 1984.

Sara, Juan M. "*Descensus ad Inferos*, Dawn of Hope. Aspects of the Theology of Holy Saturday in the Trilogy of Hans Urs von Balthasar." *Communio* 32, no. 3 (Fall 2005): 541–72.

Saward, John. "Mary and Peter in the Christological Constellation: Balthasar's Ecclesiology." In John Riches, ed., *The Analogy of Beauty: The Theology of Hans Urs von Balthasar*, 105–32. Edinburgh: T. & T. Clark, 1986.

Scheeben, Matthias Joseph. *Nature and Grace*. Translated by Cyril Vollert. Eugene, Ore.: Wipf & Stock, 2009.

Schenk, Richard. "The Epoché of Factical Damnation? On the Cost of Bracketing Out the Likelihood of Final Loss." *Logos* 1, no. 3 (1997): 122–54.

———. "Ist die Rede vom leidenden Gott theologisch zu vermeiden? Reflexionen über den Streit von K. Rahner und H. U. von Balthasar." In Peter Koslowski and Friedrich Hermanni, eds., *Der leidende Gott. Eine philosophische und theologische Kritik*, 225–39. Munich: Wilhelm Fink Verlag, 2001.

Schiettecatte, Johannes. *Disponiblité aimante. L'attitude d'amour johannique chez Adrienne von Speyr à la lumière de l'exégèse contemporaine*. PhD diss., Pontifical Theology Faculty "Teresianum," 1998.

Schindler, David C. *Hans Urs von Balthasar and the Dramatic Structure of Truth: A Philosophical Investigation*. New York: Fordham University Press, 2004.

———. "Truth and the Christian Imagination: The Reformation of Causality and the Iconoclasm of the Spirit." *Communio* 33, no. 4 (Winter 2006): 521–39.

Schindler, David L. "Catholic Theology, Gender, and the Future of Western Civilization." In David L. Schindler, *Heart of the World, Center of the Church: "Communio" Ecclesiology, Liberalism, and Liberation*, 237–74. Grand Rapids, Mich.: Eerdmans, 1996.

———, ed. *Catholicism and Secularization in America: Essays on Nature, Grace, and Culture*. Huntington, Ind.: Our Sunday Visitor and Communio Books, 1990.

———, ed. *Hans Urs von Balthasar: His Life and Work*. San Francisco: Ignatius Press and Communio Books, 1991.

———. Postscript to his article "Modernity and the Nature of a Distinction." In Rodney A. Howsare and Larry S. Chapp, eds., *How Balthasar Changed my Mind*, 255–58. New York: Crossroad, 2008.

———. "Preface." In David L. Schindler, ed., *Hans Urs von Balthasar: His Life and His Work*, xi–xiii. San Francisco: Ignatius Press and Communio Books, 1991.

———. "The Significance of World and Culture for Moral Theology: *Veritatis Splendor* and the 'Nuptial-Sacramental' Nature of the Body." *Communio* 31, no. 1 (Spring 2004): 111–42.

Schindler, David L. and Nicholas Healy. "For the Life of the World: Hans Urs von Balthasar on the Church as Eucharist." In Edward T. Oakes and David Moss, eds., *The Cambridge Companion to Hans Urs von Balthasar*, 51–63. Cambridge: Cambridge University Press, 2004.

Schmitt, William. *The Sacrament of Confession as a "Sequela Christi" in the Writings of A. von Speyr*. PhD diss., Pontifical Lateran University, Pontifical John Paul II Institute of Studies on Marriage and Family, 1999.

Schmitz, Kenneth L. *At the Center of the Human Drama: The Philosophical Anthropology of Karol Wojtyla / Pope John Paul II*. Washington, D.C.: The Catholic University of America Press, 1993.

———. "Created Receptivity and the Philosophy of the Concrete." *The Thomist* 61, no. 3 (1997): 339–71.

———. "The First Principle of Personal Becoming." In Kenneth Schmitz, *The Texture of Being: Essays in First Philosophy*, edited by Paul O'Herron, 183–97. Washington, D.C.: The Catholic University of America Press, 2007.

———. *The Gift: Creation*. Milwaukee, Wis.: Marquette University Press, 1982.

———. "Modernity Meets Tradition: The Philosophical Originality of Karol Wojtyla." *Crisis* (April 1994): 30–36.

———. "The Solidarity of Personalism and the Metaphysics of Existential Act." In Kenneth Schmitz. *Texture of Being Essays in First Philosophy*, edited by Paul O'Herron, 132–45. Washington, D.C.: The Catholic University of America Press, 2007.

———. "Taking the Measure of the Philosophical Project: Modernity Meets Tradition." In Kenneth Schmitz, *At the Center of the Human Drama: The Philosophical Anthropology of Karol Wojtyla / John Paul II*, 121–46. Washington, D.C.: The Catholic University of America Press, 1993.

Schrijver, Georges de. *Le merveilleux accord de l'homme et de Dieu. Étude de l'analogie de l'être chez Hans Urs von Balthasar*. Leuven: Leuven University Press, 1983.

Schumacher, Bernard. "La personne comme conscience de soi performante au cœur du débat bioéthique. Analyse critique de la position de John Locke." *Laval théologique et philosophique* 64, no. 3 (2008): 709–43.

———. *A Philosophy of Hope: Josef Pieper and the Contemporary Debate on Hope*. New York: Fordham University Press, 2003.

Schumacher, Michele M. "The Concept of Redemption in the Theology of Hans Urs von Balthasar." *Theological Studies* 60, no. 1 (1999): 53–71.

———. "Feminine Experience and Christian Experience." In Michele M. Schumacher, ed., *Women in Christ: Towards a New Feminism*, 169–200. Grand Rapids, Mich.: Eerdmans, 2004.

———. "Feminism, Nature and *Humanae Vitae*: What's Love Got to do with It?" *Nova et Vetera* (English edition) 6, no. 4 (2008): 879–99.

———. "John Paul II's Theology of the Body on Trial: Responding to the Accusation of the Biological Reduction of Women." *Nova et Vetera* (English Edition) 10, no. 2 (Spring 2012): 463–84.

———. "An Inseparable Connection: The Fruitfulness of Conjugal Love and the Divine Norm." *Nova et Vetera* (English edition) 1, no. 2 (Fall 2003): 137–58.

―――. "The Nature of Nature in Feminism, Old and New: From Dualism to Complementary Unity." In Michele M. Schumacher, ed., *Women in Christ: Towards a New Feminism*, 17–51. Grand Rapids, Mich.: Eerdmans, 2004.

―――. "The Prophetic Vocation of Women and the Order of Love." *Logos: A Journal of Catholic Thought and Culture* 2, no. 2 (1999): 147–92.

―――. "Therese, Woman in the Church." *Logos: A Journal of Catholic Thought and Culture* 3, no. 3 (2000): 122–51.

―――. "Towards a New Feminist Theology of the Body." In Michele M. Schumacher, ed., *Women in Christ: Towards a New Feminism*, 201–31. Grand Rapids, Mich.: Eerdmans, 2004.

―――. "Towards a Spirituality of Poverty." *Nova et Vetera* (English edition) 3, no. 3 (Spring 2005): 217–30.

―――. "A Woman in Stone or in the Heart of Man? Navigating between Naturalism and Idealism in the Spirit of *Veritatis Splendor*." *Nova et Vetera* (English edition) 11, no. 4 (2013): 1249–86.

―――, ed. *Women in Christ: Toward a New Feminism*. Grand Rapids, Mich.: Eerdmans, 2004.

Scola, Angelo. *Hans Urs von Balthasar: A Theological Style*. No translator named. Grand Rapids, Mich.: Eerdmans, 1995. [*Hans Urs von Balthasar: Un stile teologico*. Milan: Jaca Book, 1991].

―――. *The Nuptial Mystery*. Translated by Michelle K. Borras. Grand Rapids, Mich.: Eerdmanns, 2005. [*Il mistero nuziale. 1. Uomo-donna 2. Matimonio-Famiglia*. Rome: PulMursia, 1998–2000].

―――. "The Nuptial Mystery: A Perspective for Systematic Theology?" *Communio* 30, no. 2 (Summer 2003): 208–33.

―――. *Test Everything: Hold Fast to What is Good. An Interview with Hans Urs Von Balthasar*. Translated by Maria Shrady. San Francisco: Ignatius Press, 1989. [*Prüfet alles— das Gute behaltet*. Ostfildern Stuttgart: Schwabenverlag, 1986].

―――, Hans Urs von Balthasar, and Georges Chantraine, eds. *La mission ecclésiale d'Adrienne von Speyr. Actes du colloque romain (27–29 septembre 1985)*. Paris / Namur: Éditions Lethielleux / Culture et Vérité, 1986. [*Adrienne von Speyr und ihre kirchliche Sendung. Akten des römischen Symposiums (27.–29. September 1985)*. Einsiedeln: Johannes Verlag, 1986].

Servais, Jacques. "The Community of St. John." Translated by Michael M. Waldstein. *Communio* 19, no. 2 (1992): 208–19.

―――. "Confession as a Sacrament of the Father of Mercy According to Adrienne von Speyr." *Communio* 26, no. 2 (1999): 343–57.

―――. "Finding God in All Things." *Communio* 30, no. 2 (2003): 260–81.

―――. "Freedom as Christ's Gift to Man in the Thought of Hans Urs von Balthasar." Translated by Dino Gerard D'Agata. *Communio* 29, no. 4 (2002): 556–78.

―――. "The Lay Vocation in the World According to Balthasar." No translator noted. *Communio* 23, no. 4 (1996): 656–76.

―――. "Per una valutazione dell'influsso di Adrienne von Speyr su Hans Urs von Balthasar." *Rivista Teologica di Lugano* 6, no. 1 (2001): 67–89.

―――. "Préface." In Tanguy Marie Pouliquen. *Libres en Christ. La liberté chrétienne selon l'anthropologie de Hans Urs von Balthasar*, 15–18. Nouan-le-Fuzelier, France: Éditions des Béatitudes, 2008.

―――. "A Response from Jacques Servais." *New Oxford Review* 69, no. 8 (September 2002):

36–42.

———. "The *Ressourcement* of Contemporary Spirituality under the Guidance of Adrienne von Speyr and Hans Urs von Balthasar." Translated by David Louis Schindler, Jr. *Communio* 23, no. 2 (1996): 300–321. ["Ressourcement de la vie spirituelle, sous la conduit d'Adrienne von Speyr et de Hans Urs von Balthasar." In Peter Henrici, Aloïs Haas, Walter Gut, Herbert Meier, Jacques Servais, Marc Ouellet (eds.), *Hans Urs von Balthasar. Mission et Médiation*. Saint Maurice, Switzerland: Éditions Saint Augustin, 1998, 119–40].

———. *Théologie des exercises spirituels: Hans Urs von Balthasar interprète saint Ignace*. Bruxelles: Culture et Vérité, 1996.

Sherwin, Michael. *By Knowledge and by Love: Charity and Knowledge in the Moral Theology of St. Thomas Aquinas*. Washington, D.C.: The Catholic University of America Press, 2005.

———. "Happiness and Its Discontents." *Logos: A Journal of Catholic Thought and Culture* 13, no. 4 (2010): 35–59.

Shivanandan, Mary. *Crossing the Threshold of Love: A New Vision of Marriage in the Light of John Paul II's Anthropology*. Edinburgh: T. & T. Clark, 1999.

Sicari, Antonio. "Hans Urs von Balthasar: Theology and Holiness." In David L. Schindler, ed., *Hans Urs von Balthasar: His Life and Work*, 121–32. San Francisco: Ignatius Press and Communio Books, 1991.

———. "Mary, Peter and John: Figures of the Church." Translated by Michael M. Waldstein. *Communio* 19, no. 2 (1992): 189–207.

Sinoni, Paola Ricci. *Adrienne von Speyr: Storia di una esistenza teologica*. Torino: Società Editrice Internazionale, 1996.

Smulders, Peter. "L'Église sacrement du salut." In Guilherme Baraúna, ed., *L'église de Vatican II. Études autour de la Constitution conciliaire sur l'Église* II, 313–38. Collection *Unam Sanctum*, 51b. Paris: Cerf, 1966.

Sokolowski, Robert. *Eucharistic Presence: A Study in the Theology of Disclosure*. Washington, D.C.: The Catholic University of America Press, 1993.

Somme, Luc-Thomas. *La divinisation dans le Christ*. Texts of St. Thomas Aquinas translated and commented upon by Luc-Thomas Somme. Geneva: Ad Solem, 1998.

———. *Fils adoptifs de Dieu par Jésus Christ*. Paris: Vrin, 1997.

Spencer, Archie. "Causality, the Analogia Entis, and Karl Barth." *Nova et Vetera* (English Edition) 6, no. 2 (2008): 329–76.

Steck, Christopher. *The Ethical Thought of Hans Urs von Balthasar*. New York: Crossroad, 2001.

Stein, Edith. *Der Aufbau der menschlichen Person. Vorlesung zur philosophischen Anthropologie*. Gesamtausgabe 14. Wein: Herder, 2004.

———. "The Ethos of Women's Professions." In *The Collected Works of Edith Stein*. Volume 2: *Essays on Women*, edited by Lucy Gelber and Romaeus Leuven, 43–57. Washington, D.C.: ICS Publications, 1987, 1996². ["Das Ethos der Frauenberufe." (1930). In Edith Stein, *Die Frau. Ihre Aufgabe nach Natur und Gnade*, from *Edith Stein Gesamtausgabe*, 13:16–29. Wien: Herder, 2000, 2005³].

———. "The Separate Vocations of Man and Woman according to Nature and Grace." In *The Collected Works of Edith Stein*. Volume 2: *Essays on Women*, edited by Lucy Gelber and Romaeus Leuven, 59–85. Washington, D.C.: ICS Publications, 1987, 1996². ["Beruf des Mannes und der Frau nach Natur- und Gnadenordnung" (1931). In Edith Stein, *Die Frau. Ihre Aufgabe nach Natur und Gnade*, from *Edith Stein Gesamtausgabe*, 13:56–78. Wien: Herder, 2000, 2005³].

———. "Spirituality of the Christian Woman." In *The Collected Works of Edith Stein*.

Volume 2: *Essays on Women*, edited by Lucy Gelber and Romaeus Leuven, 87–128. Washington, D.C.: ICS Publications, 1987, 1996². ["Christliches Frauenleben" (1942). In Edith Stein, *Die Frau. Ihre Aufgabe nach Natur und Gnade*, from *Edith Stein Gesamtausgabe*, 13:79–114. Wien: Herder, 2000, 2005³].

Streng, Sibylle von. "Woman's Threefold Vocation according to Edith Stein." In Michele M. Schumacher, ed., *Women in Christ: Toward a New Feminism*, 105–38. Grand Rapids, Mich.: Eerdmans, 1994.

Strukelj, Anton. "Man and Woman under God: The Dignity of the Human Being according to Hans Urs von Balthasar." *Communio* 20, no. 2 (Summer 1993): 377–88.

Sutton, Agneta. "The Complementarity and Symbolism of the Two Sexes: Karl Barth, Hans Urs von Balthasar, and John Paul II." *New Balckfriars* 87, no. 1010 (July 2006): 418–33.

Sutton, Matthew Lewis. *The Gate of Heaven Opens to the Trinity: The Trinitarian Mysticism of Adrienne von Speyr*. PhD diss., Marquette University, 2007.

———. *Heaven Opens: The Trinitiarian Mysticism of Adrienne von Speyr*. Minneapolis: Fortress Press, 2014.

Taylor, Charles. *Sources of the Self: The Making of Modern Identity*. Cambridge, Mass.: Harvard University Press, 1989.

Teresa of Avila. *Interior Castle*. Translated and edited by Edgar Allison Peers. New York: Image Books, 1989. [*Moradas, conceptos, exclamaciones*. Volume IV, *Obras de Sta. Teresa de Jesus*. Biblioteca Mistica Carmelitana. Edited by P. Silverio de Santa Teresa. Burgos: Tipografía de 'El Monte Carmelo', 1917].

Tillich, Paul. *Systematic Theology*. Volume I. Chicago: University of Chicago Press, 1951.

Torrell, Jean-Pierre. *Christ and Spirituality in St. Thomas Aquinas*. Translated by Bernhard Blankenhorn. Washington, D.C.: The Catholic University of America Press, 2011. [This is a compilation of various articles orignally published in French.]

———. *Encyclopédie, Jésus le Christ chez Saint Thomas d'Aquin*. Texte de la Tertia Pars (ST III^a) traduit et commenté, accompagné de données historiques et doctrinales et de cinquante Textes. Paris: Cerf, 2008.

———. *Le Christ en ses mystères. La vie et l'œuvre de Jésus selon saint Thomas d'Aquin*. Volume I. Paris: Desclée de Brower, 1999.

———. *Pour nous les hommes et pour notre salut. Jésus notre Rédemption*. Paris: Cerf, 2014.

———. "Préface." In Gilbert Narcisse. *Les Raisons de Dieu. Argument de convenance et esthétique théologique selon saint Thomas d'Aquin et Hans Urs von Balthasar*. Fribourg, Switzerland: Éditions Universitaires Fribourg, 1997.

———. *Saint Thomas Aquinas*. Volume 2: *Spiritual Master*. Translated by Robert Royal. Washington, D.C.: The Catholic University of America Press, 2003. [*Saint Thomas d'Aquin, Maître Spirituel*. Fribourg / Paris: Editions Universitaires Fribourg / Cerf, 1996].

———. "Saint Thomas d'Aquin et la science du Christ. Une relecture des questions 9–12 de la 'Tertia Pars' de la 'Somme théologique.'" In Jean-Pierre Torrell, *Recherches thomasiennes*, 198–213. Paris: Vrin, 2000.

———. *La Somme de Saint Thomas*. Paris: Cerf, 1998.

Treitler, Wolfgang. "Foundations of Authentic Theology." In David L. Schindler, ed., *Hans Urs von Balthasar: His Life and Work*, 169–82. San Francisco: Ignatius Press and Communio Books, 1991.

Tromp, Sabastian. "De nativitate ecclesiae ex Corde Jesus in Cruce." *Gregorianum* 13, no. 4 (1932): 489–527.

Tschipke, Theophil. *Die Menschheit Christi als Heilsorgan der Gottheit: Unter Besonderer Berücksichtigung der Lehre des heiligen Thomas von Aquin*. Freiburg im Breisgau: Herder,

1940. Translated into French by Philibert Secrétan, *L'humanité du Christ comme instrument de salut de la divinité*. Fribourg, Switzerland: Academic Press / St. Paul, 2003.

Turek, Margaret M. *Towards a Theology of God the Father: Hans Urs von Balthasar's Theodramatic Approach*. New York: Peter Lang, 2001.

Ulrich, Ferdinand. *Homo Abyssus. Das Wagnis der Seinsfrage*. Einsiedeln: Johannes Verlag, 1961.

Vollmer de Marcellus, Beatriz. "New Feminism: A Sex-Gender Reunion." In Michele M. Schumacher, ed., *Women in Christ: Towards a New Feminism*, 52–66. Grand Rapids, Mich.: Eerdmans, 2004.

———. *The Ontological Differentiation of Human Gender: A Critique of the Philosophical Literature between 1965 and 1995*. Philadelphia: Xlibris, 2004.

Waldstein, Michael. "The Analogy of Mission and Obedience: A Central Point in the Relation between *Theologia* and *Oikonomia* in St. Thomas Aquinas's *Commentary on John*." In Michael Dauphinais and Matthew Levering, eds., *Reading John with St. Thomas Aquinas: Theological Exegesis and Speculative Theology*, 92–112. Washington, D.C.: The Catholic University of America Press, 2005.

———. "Introduction by Michael Waldstein." In John Paul II, *Man and Woman He Created Them: A Theology of the Body*, 1–128. Translated by Michael Waldstein. Boston: Pauline Books & Media, 2006.

Walker, Adrian J. "The Gift of Simplicity: Reflections on Obedience in the Work of Adrienne von Speyr." *Communio* 34, no. 4 (2007): 573–84.

Wallner, Karl Josef. *Gott als Eschaton. Trinitarische Dramatik als Voraussetzung göttlicher Universalität bei Hans Urs von Balthasar*. Heiligenkreuz bei Baden, Austria: Verein der Heiligenkreuzer Hochschulfreunde, 1992.

———. "Love Alone: Hans Urs von Balthasar as a Master of Theological Renewal," *Communio* 32, no. 3 (Fall 2005): 517–40.

Ward, Graham, Ben Quash, Lucy Gardner, and David Moss, eds. *Balthasar at the End of Modernity*. Edinburgh: T. & T. Clark, 1999.

White, Thomas Joseph, ed. *The Analogy of Being: Invention of the Antichrist or the Wisdom of God?* Grand Rapids, Mich.: Eerdmans, 2011.

———. "Intra-Trinitarian Obedience and Nicene-Chalcedonian Christology." *Nova et Vetera* (English edition) 6, no. 2 (2008): 377–402.

———. "Jesus' Cry on the Cross." *Nova et Vetera* (English edition) 5, no. 3 (2007): 555–81.

———. "Kenoticism and the Divinity of Christ Crucified." *The Thomist* 75, no. 1 (2011): 1–41.

———. "The 'Pure Nature' of Christology: Human Nature and *Gaudium et Spes* 22." *Nova et Vetera* (English edition) 8, no. 2 (2010): 283–322.

———. "The Voluntary Action of the Earthly Christ and the Necessity of the Beatific Vision." *The Thomist* 69, no. 4 (2005): 497–534.

———. "Von Balthasar and Journet on the Universal Possibility of Salvation and the Twofold Will of God." *Nova et Vetera* (English edition) 4, no. 3 (2006): 633–66.

———. *Wisdom in the Face of Modernity: A Study in Thomistic Natural Theology*. Naples, Fla.: Sapientia Press, 2009.

Williams, Anna N. "Deification in the *Summa Theologiae*: A Structural Interpretation of the *Prima Pars*," *The Thomist* 61 (1997): 219–55.

———. *The Ground of Union: Deification in Aquinas and Palamas*. Oxford: Oxford University Press, 1999.

———. "Mystical Theology Redux: The Pattern of Aquinas' *Summa Theologiae*." *Modern*

Theology 13, no. 1 (1997): 53–74.

Williams, Rowan. "Balthasar and Rahner." In John Riches, ed., *The Analogy of Beauty: The Theology of Hans Urs von Balthasar*, 11–34. Edinburgh: T. & T. Clark, 1986.

Wojtyla, Karol. *The Acting Person. A Contribution to Phenomenological Anthropology*. Translated by Andrzej Potocki. Volume X of *Analecta Husserliana*. Dordrecht: D. Reidel Publishing Company, 1979.

———. "Human Nature as the Basis of Ethical Formation." In John Paul II (Karol Wojtyla). *Person and Community, Selected Essays*, translated by Theresa Sandok, 95–99. New York: Peter Lang, 1993.

———. *Love and Responsibility*. Translated by H. T. Willetts. San Francisco: Ignatius Press, 1993.

———. *Sources of Renewal: The Implementation of Vatican II*. Translated by P. S. Falla. San Francisco: Harper & Row, 1979.

———. "The Person: Subject and Community." In John Paul II (Karol Wojtyla). *Person and Community, Selected Essays*, translated by Theresa Sandok, 219–61. New York: Peter Lang, 1993.

———. "The Personal Structure of Self-Determination." In John Paul II (Karol Wojtyla). *Person and Community, Selected Essays*, translated by Theresa Sandok, 187–95. New York: Peter Lang, 1993.

Zeitz, James V. "Przywara and von Balthasar on Analogy." *The Thomist* 52, no. 3 (1988): 473–98.

INDEX OF NAMES

Aertsen, Jan, 38n69, 360n15, 362, 413
Agacinski, Sylviane, 273n158, 413
Albrecht, Barbara, 4n11, 74n29, 75n30, 298n325, 413
Albus, Michael, 1n1, 2n3, 6n23, 29n17, 57n205, 76n34, 127n175, 347n246, 372n87, 373n90, 374n98, 376n103, 379n114, 379n116, 387n161, 388n170, 396n204, 410, 413
Althaus, Paul, 207n55, 413
Anselm of Canterbury, 2n3, 80n60
Ambrosius Autpertus, 193
Athanasius of Alexandria, 144n285, 170n50
Augustine of Hippo, 29, 112n78, 128, 135n228, 160, 170, 194, 211, 285n236, 315, 319, 378n100, 413
Auricchio, John, 29n16, 414

Babini, Ellero, 11n44, 102n17, 127n175, 414
Baius, Michael, 340
Barrett, Melanie, 119n125, 414
Barth, Karl, 8, 13, 56n199, 201n19, 242, 335–36, 339–40, 305n358, 414
Basil the Great, 123
Bätzing, Georg, 86n102, 414
Beattie, Tina, 8n35, 72n19, 251–52, 256, 296, 303-304, 414
Beaudin, Michel, 202n29, 209, 259n75, 310n13, 414
Beauvoir, Simone de, 253, 414
Benedict XV, Pope, 2n4
Benedict XVI, Pope, 12n48, 25, 39, 233n238, 237n264, n268, 268n134, 269n139, 270n146, 377n106, 414. See also Ratzinger, Joseph Cardinal
Berg, Blaise R., 4n12, 75n30, 414
Birot, Antoine, xi, 6n22, 201n18, 310n13, 311n21, 415
Blanchette, Oliva, 415
Blankenhorn, Bernhard, OP, xi, 206n51, 315n47, 320–24, 329, 331, 337, 341, 348n251, 383, 388n168, 395n196, 415
Boersma, Hans, 29n16, 415
Boethius, Anicius M. S., 119, 120n128, 319n79, 415
Bonino, Serge-Thomas, 33n38, 415
Borella, Jean, 170n54, 415
Bouyer, Louis, 78n46, 415
Boyle, John, 48
Braus, Allison, OCD, xii
Bremond, Henri, 77, 415
Brock, Stephen L., 361n20, 416
Buckley, James, J., 319n78, 416
Bulgakov, Sergei, 341, 416

Cajetan, Thomas de Vio, 110n59
Calvat, Mélanie, 394
Campodonico, Angelo, 416
Capol, Cornelia, 9n37, 74n29, 100n3, 121n139, 298n325, 416
Casarella, Peter, 30n23, 372n87, 416
Catry, Patrick, 75n30, 416
Cessario, Romanus, 139n253, 416
Chantraine, George, 3n9, 6n22, 416
Chapp, Larry, 72n17, 416
Chenu, Marie-Dominique, 11n42, 34n42, 105n30, 416
Clarke, Norris, 313, 355n289, 416
Congregation for the Doctrine of the Faith 157n388, 268n133, 416-417
Cottier, Georges, 106n36, 107n41, 129n186, 315n47, 361, 418
Crammer, Corinne, 251, 252n34, 253–54, 256, 262n90, 283n218, 418
Crawford, David, 15n66, 264n110, 418
Crowley, Paul G., 324n109, 418
Cullmann, Oscar, 242
Cyril of Alexandria, 170n50, 332n149

Daniélou, Jean, 28, 418
Dalzell, Thomas G., 60n232, 113n85, 311n22,

312n25, 331n143, 334n163, 376n103, 418
Dauphinais, Michael, 84n93, 418
Davies, Oliver, 75n32, 418
D'Costa, Gavin, 249n15, 255, 418
De Lubac, Henri, 7, 15n64, 71n14, 108n52, 110n59, 114n88, 117n111, 372n87, 395, 406, 418
Denzinger, Heinrich, xiii, 61, 416, 417, 418-19
Dinechin, Olivier de, 234n243, 419
DiNoia, J. Augustine, 30n20, 419
Dionysius the Areopagite, 216n197
Dol, Jean-Noël, 204n39, 331, 333n151, 419
Donneaud, Henri, 68n1, 84n92, 117n111, 121n141, 371n79, 419
Dupré, Louis, 29n17, 112n77, 419
Dupuis, Jacques, 419
Dürr, Emil, 91n133, 273n161
Durand, Emmanuel, 352–54, 419

Elizabeth of the Trinity, 73
Elshtain, Jean Bethke, 104n20, 419
Emery, Gilles, OP, xi, 11n46, 36–37, 39n80, 40-41, 48n136, 52, 106n33, 107n43, 109n53, 112n74, 120n130, 160, 161n74, 165n25, 171n54, 187n176, 200n17, 205n47, 309n9, 316n58, 324n109, 335n167, 335n170, 338n194, 342n215, 343n218, 344n225, 353–54, 359, 360n15, 360n16, 362–63, 365n46, 368n65, 370, 389n172, 390, 393n190, 419-20
Escobar, Pedro, 420
Espezel, Alberto, 202n24, 420-21
Faggioli, Massimo, 29n16, 421
Farley, Margaret, 283n218, 421
Feingold, 108n52, 117n111, 421
Fessio, Joseph, 6n22, 97n163, 421
Fields, Stephen, 30n20, 421
Fiorenza, Elisabeth Schüssler, 296n312, 421
Fiorenza, Francis Schüssler, 30n20, 421
Fisichella, Rino, 387n160, 421
Ford, David F., 30n20, 421
Fort, Gertrud von le, 272, 421
Franks, Angela Franz, 347n244, 421

Gagey, Henri-Jérôme, 376n103, 421
Gallagher, David, 114n90, 421
Gallagher, John A., 29n16, 114n88, 421
Gardiner, Anne Barbeau, 10n39, 22, 188n189, 421
Gardner, Lucy, 8n35, 15n54, 31, 33n37, 252–55, 257n66, 258–61, 421-22
Garrigou-Lagrange, Reginald, 422
Garrigues, Jean-Miguel, 101n10, 422
Gawronski, Raymond, 75n30, 256n58, 422
Geiger, Louis-Bertrand, 106n35, 109n54, 361n21, 422
Gillespie, Michael Allen, 112n77, 117n77, 422
Gillette, Gertrude, OSB, 277n189, 422
Gilson, Etienne, 395, 422
Gisi, Martha, 100n3
Goethe, Johann Wolfgang, 29n17
Gonzalez, Michelle, 8n35, 76n34, 253n38, 254n45, 255n53, 296, 347n244, 422
Gray, Alison, xii
Gregory of Nazianzus, 169, 386, 422
Greiner, Maximilian, 100n3, 121n139, 422
Greiner, Susanne, 254n45, 422
Gregory of Nyssa, 43n109, 116, 405, 422
Grillmeier, Aloys, 170n50, 422
Guerriero, Elio, 74n30, 422

Harris, Harriet A., 354n285, 422
Harrison, Victoria S., 11n46, 113n85, 422
Healy, Nicholas J., 5n16, 31n27, 42, 56n195, 108n52, 231n215, 257n63, 309, 310n10, 310n11, 310n11, 313–14, 315n44, 316n67, 317–18, 323n101, 325, 326n119, 329-31, 335n169, 336n178, 338, 349n253, 422-23
Hegel, G. W. F., 50, 340
Hemmerle, Klaus, 58n210, 60n227, 342n217, 423
Henrici, Peter, 8n35, 28n14, 71n14, 99n1, 108n47, 114n88, 296n314, 304n354, 378n109, 387, 388n164, 397n205, 423, 430, 436
Hofer, Andrew, 423
Hoffman, Norbert, 201n23, 204n44, 423
Holzer, Vincent, 376n103, 423
Hütter, Reinhard, xii, 30n21, 117n111, 423

Ide, Pascal, xii, 14n63, 347n244, 423
Ignatius of Loyola, 18, 80, 95-98, 112–13, 114n92, 115, 117-118, 119n124, 121n139, 179, 261, 238n274, 298n324, 333n156, 396, 423
International Theological Commission, 14n59, 349n254, 355n290, 423-24
Irenaeus of Lyons, 7–8, 6364n251, 123, 133n210, 138, 144n285, 151n345, 167n32, 169-70n50, 185n160, 263n100, 289n261, 333n156, 423
Irigaray, Luce, 8n35, 249n15

Joan of Arc, 394
John of the Cross, 243n298, 424
John Damascene, 45, 160
John the Evangelist, 80n60, 133–34, 144, 155, 184, 222, 238–39, 291–95, 291n273, 292n278, 295n303, 300, 326–28, 370
John Paul II, Pope, 2n4, 12n53, 14-15, 88n117, 115, 122n143, 137n239, 139n253, 145n295, 147n304,

151n335, 155n372, 157n388, 162, 163n15, 171n54, 180n128, 184n152, 187n182, 193n219, n225, 194n230, 200n17, 210n70, 212–14, 215n102, 216, 229–30, 237n273, 241n291, 234n302, 243n302, 248, 253n35, 264n110, 268, 270n140, 271n148, 273n159, 274n165, 276n178, 278n190, 278n192, 279, 280n203, 281n207, n211, 287n242, 293n289, 304n357, 305n357, n358, 353, 377, 380, 424-25. See also Wojtyla, Karol.

Kaegi, Werner, 91n133, 273n161
Kaliba, Clemens, 58n210
Kasper, Walter, 254n45, 425
Keating, Daniel, 101n10, 425
Kehl, Medard, 101n7, 245
Kerr, Fergus, 5, 8, 14–15, 22n83, 28n13, 30n20, 71n13, 90n130, 107n31, 256n58-59, 268, 312, 322n94, 364, 371, 245
Kilby, Karen, 15n66, 72n17, 74n28, 78n49, 104n20, 205, 256n58, 256n60, 311, 331, 377, 372n87, 373n90, 376n103, 376n104, 378n108, 380n118, 388n168, 391, 245
Kötting, Bernarda, OSB, xii
Krempel, Anton, 425
Krenski, Thomas Rudolf, 31n24, 202n24, 425
Kupczak, Jaroslaw, 425
Kwasniewski, Peter, 105n28, 270n142, 425

Labourdette, Michel, 425
Langevin, Gilles, 107n38, 426
Laven, Gloria Therese, OCD, xii
Lee, Claudia, 70n11, 72n19, 373, 389n176, 390n177, 426
Lehmann, Karl, 254n45, 426
Leibniz, Gottfried Wilhelm, 378
Leo I, Pope, 169
Leo XIII, Pope 2n4, 426
Léonard, Jean, 75n30, 426
Léthel, F.-M., 334n162, 426
Levering, Matthew, xii, 47, 84n93, 319, 349n244, 426
Livi, Antonio, 426
Lochbrunner, Manfred, 6n21, 349n244, 372n87, 375n101, 426
Lombardo, Nicholas E., 114n90, 315n48, 426
Long, Steven A., 106n36, 108n52, 124n172, 320, 322n94, 338, 426
López, Antonio, 60n232, 312n25, 426-427.
Loughlin, Gerard, 249n15, 250–51, 253n40, 303n350, 427
Louth, Andrew, 304n354, 427
Lubac, Henri de: see De Lubac, Henri

Maas, Wilhelm, 344, 348n247, n249, 427
Malloy, Christopher J., 427
Margerie, Bertrand de, 310n12, 311n21, 313n33, 314, 427
Mansini, Guy, OSB, 7n30, 119, 202n24, 203n35, 205–6, 313n33, 320, 376n103, 427
Maritain, Jacques, 106, 384, 385n151, 389, 394, 427
Martinelli, Paolo, 6n22, 55n193, 372n87, 427
Mary Magdalene, 94n150, 96, 235–36, 264, 290n264
Matro, Justin, 74n12, 24n90, 75n30, 427
Maximus the Confessor, 116, 123, 324n106, 334
Mayer, Rupert Johannes, OP, 110, 427
McIntosh, Mark, 49-50n150, 71-72n17, 81n72, 116, 242, 347n244, 371, 372n86, 373n91, 379, 380n118, 388n168, 394n195, 427
Menke, Karl-Heinz, 141, 201n22, 209n68, 427
Mettepenningen, Jürgen, 29n16, 427
Milbank, John, 7n30, 333n156, 427
Moingt, Joseph, 2n3
Mongrain, Keven, 5n15, 7, 22n83, 427
Moock, Wilhelm, 58n210
Moss, David, 5n21, 8n35, 13n54, 31, 33n37, 72, 76, 82n74, 252–55, 258–61, 427-28
Müller, Claudia, 9n37, 402, 416, 428
Muers, Rachel, 8n35, 257-258n66, 296n312, 428
Murphy, Francesca, 391, 428

Nandkisore, Robert, 6n22, 428
Narcisse, Gilbert, 7n30, 53-54n183, 71n13, 106n33, 205n47, 313n33, 331, 345, 354n285m 372, 373n90, 379n117, 383, 387–88, 428
Nestorius, 329n137, 332n149
Neuner, Josef, 429
Newman, John Henry, 29
Nichols, Aidan, 28n11, 57-58n207, 74-75n30, 347n244, 348n247, 429
Nicolas, Jean-Hervé, 94n149, 101n10, 108n52, 376, 371n80, 372, 380–81, 376n105, 380-381, 429
Nicolas, Marie-Joseph, 34n43, 44n110, 60n232, 106n35, 108n51, 124n153, 127n179, 132n203, 165n25, 312, 315 n47, 429
Nygren, Anders, 114n91, 429

Oakes, Edward T., SJ, xii, 5, 6n21, 29n17, 31n27, 75n32, 104n20, 318, 429
O'Connor, John D., 377n106, 388n168, 429
O'Donnell, John, 117n114, 119n124, 215n104, 255n54, 261n86, 347n244, 429-30
O'Hanlon, Gerard, 60n232, 79n57, 204n45, 312n25, 313, 341n207, 430
Olsen, Glenn, 430

O'Meara, Thomas, 28n13, 29, 430
O'Neil, Colman E., 10, 30n21, 107n38, 109n54, 430
Origen, 38, 116, 123
O'Rourke, Fran, 34n43, n44, 108n49, 315n47, 316n58, 361, 430
Ouellet, Marc, 6n22, 15n66, 69n7, 102n17, 113n85, 121n136, 202n29, 344, 348n247, n249, 363, 366n52, 430

Palakeel, Joseph, 13n55, 54n183, 56n195, 58, 312n26, 358n5, 367n57, 378n113, 430
Pannenburg, Wolfhart, 2n3
Papanikolaou, Aristotle, 252n34, 430
Paradiso, Marcello, 6n22, 430
Paschasius Radbertus, 193
Perrier, Emmanuel, 2n3, 56n197, 171n59, 182n142, 211n82, 214n98, 382, 430
Pesarchick, Robert A., 255n54, 261n86, 430
Pieper, Josef, 114, 139n253, 430
Pinckaers, Servais, 11n42, 78n44, 114n91, 115–16, 431
Pitstick, Alyssa Lyra, 5, 205n47, 311n21, 322n95, 324n109, 331, 332n150, 342–44, 346–47, 349, 383, 395n196, 431
Pius IX, Pope, 151n334, 431
Pius XII, Pope, 134n220, 185n162, 189n191, n194, 212, 370, 431
Plé, Albert, 114n90, 431
Pontifical Biblical Commission, 68n3, 431
Porter, Jean, 367n58, 432
Potterie, Ignace de la, 84n93, 432
Pouliquen, Tanguy Marie, 209n68, 210n71, 432
Potworowski, Christophe, 70n11, 82n77, 345, 432
Przywara, Erich, 7n31, 16, 30n23, 57, 58n208, 358n5, 372n87, 432

Quash, Ben, 8n35, 432

Rahner, Karl, 2n3, 28n13, 29, 30n20, 71n13, 104n20, 202n24, 314n42, 360, 375, 432
Ratzinger, Joseph Cardinal, 6, 14n64, 70, 339, 121n137, 122n144, 155n367, 159n397, 238n247, 257n64, 258n67, 260n79, 262n93, 263n100, 287n245, 294n302, 339, 360n16, 377, 379, 386, 387n160, 432. See also Benedict XVI, Pope
Rémy, Gérard, 348n247, 432
Reno, Russell R., 5n19, 432
Richard of St. Victor, 319
Roberts, Louis, 376n103, 432
Rocca, Gregory P., 110n60, 315, 361, 432-33.
Roten, Johann, 57n202, 69n7, 76, 106n36, 118n119, 150n327, 296n314, 297, 383n145, 384, 386, 433

Sachs, John Randall, 326n119, 347n244, 348n247, 372n87, 433
Sara, Juan M., 348n247, 433
Saward, John, 387n162, 433
Scheeben, Matthias Joseph, 123n151, 433
Schelling, Friedrich, 314
Schenk, Richard, 71n13, 205n47, 314n42, 376n103, 377–79, 383n144, 388n168, 391, 433
Schiettecatte, Johannes 4n12, 434
Schillebeeckx, Edward, 2n3
Schindler, David C., 315n44, 359, 433
Schindler, David L., 4-5n15, 15n66, 31n27, 75n33, 108n47, 231n215, 255n54, 347n244, 349n244, 433-34
Schmitt, William, 4n122, 75n30, 86n102, 201n23, 203n31, n37, 241, 395n196, 434
Schmitz, Kenneth, 42, 273-274n163, 434
Schrijver, Georges de, 13n55, n57, 56n195, n199, 58n208, 72n22, 73, 82n75, 113n79, 329n137, 324n110, 329n137, 347n244, 367n57, 434
Schumacher, Bernard, xii, 42-43n103, 47n128, 120n129, 354n285, 434
Schumacher, Michele M., 15n65, 78n46, 89n119, 205n47, 210n75, 229n200, 247n9, 263n99, 272n157-158, 278n193, 279n196, 281n207, 296n315, 314n42, 434-35
Scola, Angelo Cardinal, 2n5, 3n7, n9, 6n22, 15n66, 28n14, 35, 57n205, 61n236, 65n259, n260, n261, 69n6, 118, 141, 165n28, 181n139, 192n218, 209, 210n69, 248n14, 256n58, 269n314, 302n342, 308n1, 322n94, 337, 363n30, 367, 386n156, 387n162, n163, 389n176, 392n185, 407, 410, 413, 416, 421, 426, 430, 435
Servais, Jacques, SJ, xi, 6, 10n39, 6n22, 61n235, 69n7, 72n19, 86n102, 99n1, 100n3, 113n85, 120n139, 210n71, 298n326, 387n160, 435-36
Sherwin, Michael, OP, xi, 113n86, 114n91, 208n61, 436
Shivanandan, Mary, 15n66, 436
Sicari, Antonio, 4n15, 69–70, 94n147, 387n162, 436
Siewerth, Gustav, 7n31
Sinoni, Paola Ricci, 74n30, 436
Smulders, Peter, 171n60, 436
Somme, Luc-Thomas, 101n10, 436
Spencer, Archie, 13n55, 436
Steck, Christopher, 111n73, 119, 145n161, 436
Stein, Edith, 43-44n110, 270n141, 275, 276n175, 436-37

Streng, Sibylle von, 276n175, 437
Strukelj, Anton, 254n45, 256n58, 437
Sutton, Agneta, 254n45, 305n358, 437
Sutton, Matthew Lewis, 4n12, 75n30, 76n38, 437

Taylor, Charles, 104n20, 437
Teresa of Avila, 243n298
Therese of Lisieux, 73
Tillich, Paul, 437
Torrell, Jean-Pierre, OP, xi, 28n13, 78n50, 101n10, 104, 106n33-34, 109n54, 114n88, 133n210, 139n253, 161n4, 165n27, 174n81, 200n15-16, 203n38, 205n47, 206, 207n54, n57, 208n62, 211n78, 216-217n115, 219n125, 227n188, 229n204, 243n298-299, 316n58, 332n149, 348n251, 362n27, 363-64, 372, 381n130, 382, 437
Trietler, Wolfgang, 31n24, 437
Tromp, Sabastian, 135n228, 437
Tschipke, Theophil, 161n4, 170n50, 324n109, 437-38
Turek, Margaret M., 54n183, 325n118, 341n211, 438

Ulrich, Ferdinand 7n31, 438
Vetö, Étienne, xiin2
Vollmer de Marcellus, Beatriz, 272-73n158, 279n195, 438
Von le Fort, Gertrud, see Fort, Gertrud von le

Waldstein, Michael, xii, 14, 84n93, 132n205, 144n291, 318b74, 438
Walker, Adrian J., 69n7, 438
Wallner, Karl Josef, 438
White, Thomas Joseph, OP, xii, 30n21, 39n80, 126n172, 205n47, 322n93, 329, 334-35, 336n178, 338n190, 438
Williams, Anna, 33n38, 37, 38n73, 38n75 47, 49n141, 77-78n44, 107n46, 109-112, 360n18, 364, 372, 438-39
Williams, Rowan, 376n103, 439
Wojtyla, Karol, 330n139, 434, 439. See also John Paul II, Pope
Zeitz, James V., 30n23, 58n208, 439

SUBJECT INDEX

abandonment: attitude of, 93, 97, 360; Adrienne's experience of, 240, 390–91; of Christ and the Christian to God, 245, 352; as the experience of the dark night, 391–92; of God by the sinner, 215, 241; and hell, 344; of the sinner by God, 245; of the Son by the Father, 143–44, 203, 206, 209, 215, 221–22, 224, 226, 240–45, 341, 347, 392. *See also* hell; faith; redemption; sin; surrender

admirabile commercium. *See* exchange

analogy: of Adam-Eve reciprocity to describe the Trinity, 303; of anthropological "tensions" to describe the Trinity, 9, 16, 42, 55, 360; awakening of self-consciousness by another's love as a description of the eternal generation of the Word, 46; Barth's understanding of, 13n55; of being, 11, 32–36, 57n207, 58, 338–40, 346, 363; caution in the application of worldly terms to divine revelation, 327n125; to Christ and his revelation, 327n125; of Christ-Church union to describe the Trinity, 189, 262–63, 265, 284, 291; Christology as Word-made-flesh, 11, 19, 31, 55–56, 134, 167, 309, 319, 323–25, 331, 336–39, 357–58; as complemented by katalogy, 10, 61–63, 163, 249, 264–65, 303, 346, 353, 362–63; of creation, 338, 346; between Creator and creatures as strictly one-directional, 38–39, 315–18, 338, 361, 364–65; of the dual-unity of man and woman to describe the Trinity, 21, 262, 282–83, 307; of the Eucharist to describe the Trinity, 302; the Eucharistic fruitfulness of the Trinity to describe the fruitfulness of Mary's maternity, 152; of freedom to describe the Trinity, 15, 35, 41–57, 111–12, 214, 259, 308–11, 366–69; of giving and receiving to describe the Trinity, 46–47, 53, 58, 70, 136, 147, 262, 278, 309, 343; of human person to describe God, 10; of human love to describe the Trinity, 46–53, 60, 214–18, 222–23, 234, 279–80, 354, 366; of intersubjectivity, 319; of man-woman-child unity to describe the Trinity, 267, 270–71, 283, 301; as marked by the "greater dissimilitude" between Creator and creature, 16–17, 24, 26, 30–31, 33, 48, 62, 78–79, 121, 132, 167, 250–51, 256, 261, 303–4, 331, 339, 344, 354, 357; of marriage to describe the Creator-creature relation, 254–63, 273, 276–77; as religious, 13; of the processions of speech and love to describe the Trinity, 32–41, 110–11, 319, 340; of *proportionalitas*, 13, 55, 317, 339; as reasoning from creature to Creator, 15, 28, 30; of sexual relations to describe the Christian's reception of grace, 130–31, 136–37; of sexual relations to describe the Eucharist and the Trinity, 265n112, 302–3, 351–52; of surrender to describe the Trinity, 9, 16, 27, 57–63, 209, 271–72, 358–59, 366, 371, 375; of "tension" between the sexes to describe nature-grace relation, 303; in theology, 357; of the unity of transcendence and immanence in all being to describe the Trinity, 35; of the transcendentals to describe the Trinity, 258–360. *See also* anthropomorphism; archetype; Church; image of God; *katalogy*

Annunciation, 151, 193

anonymity, 76, 85, 197n4, 287

anthropology: as theological, 9–11, 14, 24, 54, 57, 126–27, 134, 213n92, 258, 273, 304, 337–38

anthropomorphism, 1, 10, 26, 61, 206, 314, 325, 341. *See also* metaphor

archetype: Christ and the Church of marriage, 21, 181, 267; Christ as "concrete universal," 127; Christ of confession, 202; Christ of creation, 11, 56, 337; Christ of faith, 17, 67–68, 84, 93n142, 121n141; Christ of human fulfillment, 355; Christ of the human person, 134, 173, 271, 309, 324; Christ and Mary of the human couple, 264, 267, 288, 291–92, 300, 302;

447

archetype *(cont.)*
  Christ of masculine and feminine, 21, 255n51, 261, 283–87, 290–91; Christ of obedience, 81; Christ of the "right *proportio*" between Creator and creature or the "concrete *analogia entis*," 11, 55–56, 122, 134, 167, 321–24, 331, 335, 337–38, 349; Christ of surrender, 9, 68, 81, 84; the circumincession of the divine persons with respect to the economic kenosis, 58, 164–65, 341, 344, 346–47, 349–50, 365; Creator of the human person, 10, 24, 126; definition of, 360; the "distance" between the divine persons of the "distance" between Creator and creature, 45; divine freedom of created freedom, 358, 366–67; the divine processions of the economic acts, 50–51, 352; the divine processions of human love, 16; the divine will of human will, 366; the eternal generation of the Son of his kenosis in time, 160; the Eucharist of sexual relations, 302; Father-Son relation of the Christ-Church relation, 189; God of all perfection, 364; God's word as the "measure" of the human being, 81; the *Logos* of creation, 38–40, 54, 55, 81, 361; Mary of the Church, 21, 163, 165, 197, 238, 254, 287, 294, 296, 291n269; Mary of the disciple, 238; Mary of the human being, 264; Mary of a "theological person," 150–56, 192–93, 290, 355n293; Mary and John of the Marian-Petrine union of the Church, 291–95; Mary of woman, 253, 263–64, 287, 294, 295; the sacraments of corporal life, 179–80; the Son's eternal consent to the Incarnation of his obedience in time, 352; Trinity of change and possibility, 318; Trinity of the Christ-Church relation, 262; Trinity of difference, 27, 31–32, 59, 318, 346–47, 359–60, 397; Trinity of the Eucharist, 58, 164–65, 302, 350; Trinity of fecundity, 265; Trinity of human experience and relations, 141n164, 249; Trinity of relation between the sexes, 21, 271, 299, 302, 304, 353, 358–60; Trinity of spirit–body tension, 167; Trinity of surrender, 367, 397; Trinity of transcendental properties of being, 52, 358–59. *See also* analogy; Christ; Church; confession; *katalogy*; Mary; person; predestination; Trinity

Arianism, 47, 49, 50, 322, 328, 341, 343n221
Aristotelianism, 25, 32, 35, 63, 105n30, 132, 161–62, 165–66, 315, 361–62. *See also* metaphysics; teleology; theology
Ascension of Christ, 168, 188, 291, 306
Assumption of Mary, 176

beatific vision: of Christ, 203n31, 222n153, 348n251, 393; of the Christian, 109–11, 370–71; conditions of, 364
beatitude. *See* fulfillment of the human person
baptism, 212, 231

Catholicism, 1, 2, 9, 15, 22, 58, 72, 96, 103, 156, 178, 188, 199, 210, 213–14, 217n115, 241, 252, 308, 336, 357, 370, 373, 375, 377, 382, 385, 390, 392, 394–95, 397
Catalogy. *See Katalogy*
charisma: of Adrienne, 68–70, 89–97, 176n102, 190, 221, 240–41, 297–98, 374, 384–85, 389, 390n181; and *charis* (grace), 68, 93–94, 388; of the prophet, 89, 92, 386–87; of the saints, 93. *See also* grace; mission; mysticism
Christ: in communion with other human beings, 370; as "concrete *analogia entis*," 11, 134, 323–24, 331, 336–39, 346; consciousness of, 119–22, 223–25, 242, 324–27, 332, 345, 392–93; dual-orientation of, 13, 184, 201, 227, 283, 291, 309, 331, 340, 346; as Head of the Church, 105, 106n34, 141n267, 145, 167, 169n45, 170, 182, 188–89, 200, 207–8, 211, 235, 304–6, 355; as New Adam, 21, 58, 63, 152n345, 162, 173, 175, 184, 200, 218, 247, 256–57, 264, 267, 271, 282, 286, 292, 295n306, 305, 337n181; person-mission identity of, 144, 220, 325; two natures of, 40, 56, 167, 169–70, 182, 205–6, 223–24, 226–27, 320–36, 338, 341, 357, 376, 382. *See also* archetype; Church; Incarnation; mediation; mission; obedience; person; revelation; sacraments; Trinity
Church: born on Calvary, 135n228, 156, 285, 295; as bride of Christ, 21, 78, 170, 185, 189–90, 192–93, 197, 235, 238, 260, 262, 284, 287–91, 301n341, 303, 305–6; of the apostles, 155–56, 294–96; as communion, 237, 291–92, 304n357; as continuing Christ's mission, 138n248, 158, 168, 185, 396; corporal dimension of, 178; as infallible, 295–96; as Marian and Petrine (Spirit and institution), 262, 291–96, 300, 387; as ministerial, 294–96, 300–301; as mystical body of Christ, 106, 138, 164, 168–71, 178, 183, 185–92, 200, 211, 216n115, 228, 235, 286, 291; as new Eve, 21, 156, 285, 291; as originating in Mary, 21, 156–57, 163, 165, 195, 197, 237–38, 287, 291n269, 294–96; and the sacraments, 139, 182; from the wounds of Christ, 168. *See also* archetype; Catholicism; Christ; Church; Mary; mediation; sacraments
Church Fathers. *See* Fathers of the Church

circumincession. *See* Trinity
Community of St. John, 100, 266, 287, 298n324
Communion. *See* Eucharist; exchange; image; human fulfillment; mediation; saints; surrender; Trinity
conscience, 213, 229
confession: attitude of, 136, 292, 389; Christ as archetype of, 202; effect of, 226; Mary as archetype of, 292; sacrament of, 294. *See also* sacraments
consecrated life. *See* States of Life
conversion. *See* grace; human freedom; redemption
Council: of Chalcedon, 127n173, 200, 309–10, 322, 341; of Constantinople II, 101; of Constantinople III, 205–6; Fourth Lateran, 30n23, 78, 132n208, 250n19, 331, 342, 344, 354; of Nicaea, 172, 334n164; Vatican II, 1, 14, 68n3, 111n73, 126, 162n11, 169n49, 171, 182n141, 185n159, 189n191, 190n199, 193n224, 199n13, 249–50, 254n43, 289n261, 290n265, 291n269, 294n302, 337, 353
creation: as an act of love of the divine persons for one another, 64, 174–75; in Christ, 174–76; not by divine emanation, 44; divine processions as cause of, 31, 40, 45, 174, 359; as free gift of God, 32, 365; for purpose of assimilating things to himself, 108; by the Word and in the Word, 38–39, 45, 340. *See also* archetype; divine freedom

dark night of faith. *See faith*
descent. *See* hell; kenosis; surrender
desire. *See* natural desire
distance in the Trinity. *See* metaphor
divine freedom: as absolute, 50, 105n30; 338–39, 349, 368–69, 372n88; as "challenged" by human freedom, 26, 112, 222, 229, 368–69; as eliciting a response from created freedom, 12, 230, 363, 368; as eternally surrendered, 45; as groundless, 25; as identical with divine being, 54; as identical with love, 50–51, 367; as responsible for creation, 16, 25, 32, 45, 112, 365, 367; and revelation, 346, 349, 351; as surpassing the created order, 38–39, 49; as surpassing human understanding, 112, 344, 349; as united to finite freedom, 366; as willing to enter into relation with us, 25. *See also* human freedom; immutability of God; Incarnation; metaphor; predestination; redemption; surrender; Trinity
divine Incarnation. *See* Incarnation

Enlightenment, 104
eschatology. *See* beatific vision; divine freedom; fulfillment; hell; hope for universal salvation; human freedom; predestination; teleology
ethics, 21, 24, 115–17, 119n125, 368, 396
Eucharist: Christ as personification of, 230; and Christ's return to the Father, 227; as a continuation of the Incarnation, 125, 134–37, 160, 163, 169n47, 182–92; as gift of the Father and of the Son, 123; as incorporating us into Christ, 135, 146, 163, 168, 175, 178, 186–87, 227, 236; as fruit of Christ's passion, 216, 284; Mary's role in, 194–96, 293, 295; as originating in Trinitarian "surrender," 58, 123, 152, 164–65, 220, 236, 239, 302; as the sacramental body of Christ, 170, 178, 186–87; as sacrificial, 168; as a salvific exchange, 146; Spirit's role in, 136, 168–69; 365; as Trinitarian, 345, 347, 365–66. *See also* analogy; archetype
exemplar. *See* archetype
exchange: between Christ and Church or Christ and members, 24, 132, 146, 169–71, 188, 192, 231, 239, 373; between Christ and Mary, 152–54; of love, 231, 272, 278; between man and woman, 266, 279, 283–84; as salvific (*admirabile commercium*), 24, 132, 143–44, 166–67, 169–70, 204, 217n115. *See also* grace; mediation; recapitulation; redemption; saints; surrender; Trinity
experience: of Adrienne as married, 91, 273; of Adrienne as physician, 91, 190, 266, 273n161; as religious, 81, 128, 381; as source for theology, 21, 62, 71, 381. *See also* mysticism; suffering; theology

faith: as adherence or reception, 88, 155; of Adrienne, 68, 88, 94–98, 298n326; as assent, 77, 88, 93n142, 101, 121, 128, 135, 146–49, 155, 157; as availability, 84–86; content of, 17–18, 84–85, 151, 155; corporal dimension of, 177–78; dark night of, 203n37, 221, 223, 235n248, 240n288, 242–45, 384, 391; as disposition or virtue, 84, 121–22, 132n106, 151; as expropriation, 82, 130; Ignatius's understanding of, 117; and justification, 211; and knowledge, 208n61, 366; Luther's understanding of, 117; of Mary as origin of the Church's faith, 86, 135, 151–52, 155–56, 159, 186, 194–95, 237–38, 284n110, 289, 293–95, 298n326; as meritorious, 135, 192; and mysticism, 87, 95; as response, 18, 88, 157; as a revelatory disposition, 68, 81–86; as "stretching" to God's "measure," 137, 142–43, 147–49, 156;

faith (*cont.*)
as surrender of the will, 366; and theology, 76; two dimensions (subjective and objective) of, 17–18, 68, 75, 84–87, 89, 94, 155–56. *See also* archetype; experience; grace; knowledge; obedience; sacraments; surrender; virtue
Fathers of the Church, 123, 135, 143–44, 167, 169–70, 204, 230, 277n189, 289n261, 315, 324n109, 348n251, 381, 386, 389, 395
fiat of Mary. *See* faith
finite freedom. *See* human freedom
forsakenness of Christ on the Cross. *See* abandonment
freedom. *See* divine freedom; human freedom; mission; person

gender, 256n60, 272, 279, 296
grace: the beatific vision as, 371; as capital, 182, 211, 216n107; of contemplation, 98; of conversion, 20, 207, 209–14, 216, 223; as enriching the creature, not the Creator, 317–18; as given and received (correspondence), 12, 87–88, 131, 135–36, 142–43, 212, 231, 303, 365, 368; as indwelling, 103; and nature, 36–38, 61–63, 93, 104–23, 130–31, 141, 174, 247, 269n139, 276–78, 303, 337, 361–62; as participation in Christ's consciousness, 372n86; as participation in Christ's filiation, 101, 121, 127, 187, 198, 228, 239; as participation in Christ's mission, 93, 102, 121, 150, 198, 239; as participation in divine nature, 98, 103, 127, 129, 132–34, 166, 183n146, 219n125; as participation in Trinitarian love and surrender, 355; as prevenient, 121, 140, 146, 365, 368; as receptivity, 231; as redemptive, 271; as reserved to the intelligent creature, 36; and surrender, 11, 128, 143n178, 228; as sacramental, 236. *See also* mediation

hell: Adrienne's experience of, 213n90, 344n228, 347–48, 393; Christ's experience of, 205–6, 223; Christ's descent into, 97, 347. *See also* abandonment; experience; kenosis; mysticism
hierarchy: of being, 34–35, 361–62; of Creator over creature, 261–62; in the Church, 295–96, 301, 386–87; of Christ over the Church, 253–55, 305–6; between love and knowledge, 113n86, 371; in marriage (between man and woman), 190, 253–54, 305–7; in the Trinity, 16, 46–47, 49, 51–52, 261–62, 305–7, 335, 345, 352. *See also* archetype; Christ; Trinity
Holy Saturday. *See* hell; kenosis; mysticism
Holy Spirit: in the life of the Christian, 36, 85–86, 122, 145–49, 169, 186, 188, 195, 213–14, 217, 228, 267, 269, 302, 332, 356, 370, 372; in the life of the Church, 168–69, 386, 389; in the life of Jesus, 168–71, 202, 204, 218, 227n192, 231n21; as inspiring the theologian, 396; in the Trinity, 47, 64–65, 80, 219–20, 225, 313, 333; as uniting creation and redemption, 145; as unity of Father and Son, 333; and the unity of love, 40, 47, 267. *See also* mediation; mission; Trinity
homo ecclesiasticus. *See* Person
hope for universal salvation, 63, 245, 368. *See also* divine freedom; human freedom; human fulfillment; predestination
human freedom: as capable of rejecting the grace of salvation, 368; of Christ, 116, 324, 334; as involved in the "theodrama," 26, 168, 222, 229, 262–63, 363, 368–70; as liberated by redemption, 209–10; meaning of, 116–18, 121–22, 358; as oriented to the good, 115–17; as oriented to and fulfilled in divine freedom, 20, 55, 104–22, 167, 209, 212, 214, 216–17, 255, 257, 332, 355, 358, 364, 366–69; as oriented to self-gift, surrender, 42, 146, 157, 353, 355, 358–59; as respected by divine freedom, 45, 107–9, 121, 146–47, 168, 170, 208–9, 213, 216–17, 229, 255, 259–60, 262, 304n357, 363, 367; as responsible for Christ's death, 206–7, 221n145; two poles of, 42; of woman with respect to man, 251n22, 253n36, 255. *See also* analogy; Christ; divine freedom; faith; human fulfillment; merit; mission; obedience; predestination
human fulfillment: as assimilation to God, 24, 108, 242–43, 361–62, 370; as availability for God, 87; as beatitude, 106, 111, 370–71; by charity, 36, 371; as communion with God, 105–6, 110, 123, 126–29, 157–58; as integration of human freedom into divine freedom, 18, 23, 110–12, 121, 353, 355–56, 366–71; as participation in God's nature (knowledge and love), 38; potency as, 313–14; through gift of self, 14, 42–43, 142, 157, 280, 304n357, 353; by mission, 145; two ends of, 108–9, 117n111, 362, 367n58; two ways of conceiving of, 361–62. *See also* beatific vision; grace; human freedom; image; mission; person; predestination; surrender
hylomorphism, 165n25
hypostatic union. *See* Christ

Immaculate Conception, 151, 155–56, 176, 193n224, 261, 263, 285, 355n293
image: Adam of Christ, 174; human person of God, 10, 35–36, 104–5, 107, 110–11, 119,

SUBJECT INDEX   451

123–24, 126, 239, 268–71, 306, 309, 355, 360, 367; Christ of the Father, 230; Christ of God, 54, 174; human communion of Trinity, 268, 354; finite freedom of infinite freedom, 358; God's image of us, 123–24; love of God, 345; as restored on the Cross, 173; Son of Father, 54, 122, 230

immanence: between Christ and the Christian, 82–83, 103, 133, 187, 240

immutability of God, 25, 38–39, 44–45, 175n96, 199, 205n47, 222n153, 313, 315–17, 320, 361, 369, 376. *See also* divine freedom; metaphor

Incarnation: as an act of love of the divine persons for one another, 174–76, 219–20, 331, 345, 348; as an act of obedience, 136, 331; as continuing in Christian and Church, 82, 138–40, 143–44, 158, 163, 166–67, 170, 182–92, 200, 228, 256–57; as Father's gift, 122, 183–84, 236; the fittingness of, 105n30, 108n46, 318n75; the fittingness of human nature for, 330; as God's surrender, 12, 16, 44–45, 61n235, 160, 164, 166, 207, 221, 284n225, 331, 376; as implying human fellowship, 370; Mary's role in, 151–52, 154, 163, 170, 172, 194–95, 284, 293, 295; as mediation, 31, 105, 133, 136, 166–67, 171, 179, 182, 238–39, 397; by the power of the Holy Spirit, 233n234; reality of, 168, 177–78, 324n108; as revelation of God's triune love, 16, 164, 172–76, 204, 219, 221, 349–50; as a salvific event, 163, 171–73, 175, 211, 247, 348; of the Son in reason of his place in the Trinity, 331; of the Son as willed, 345. *See also* Church; divine freedom; Eucharist; kenosis; predestination; redemption

indifference (Ignatian), 92, 97, 113

influence: of Adrienne on Balthasar, 2–3, 5–10, 19, 22–23, 31, 41, 51, 57–58, 70–71, 75–76, 78, 121n141, 167, 199, 212–13, 267, 281, 297, 299, 302n347, 304, 309–11, 323, 333, 335–37, 347, 352, 358, 374–76, 383–84, 396; of Balthasar on Adrienne, 385–86

Kantianism, 114

katalogy: Adrienne and Balthasar's preference for, 60–61; 337; definition of, 10, 15–16, 30–31, 65–66, 138, 346, 362; examples in Adrienne's theology, 10, 61–62, 98, 126, 127, 138, 163–64, 176, 179–82, 247, 299, 302–3, 305; 346, 350; examples in Balthasar's theology, 13, 16, 21, 24, 31, 46, 48, 55, 115, 122, 165–67, 201, 292, 346–48; 357–58; examples elsewhere in the tradition, 14; examples in St. Thomas's theology, 40,

48, 247–48, 292, 362–65. *See also* archetype; divine freedom; human freedom

kenosis: in Adrienne's theology, 347; in Balthasar's theology, 344–50; as the "depositing" of the divinity, 223, 311n21, 321; of God eliciting that of man, 12, 44–45; interpretation of with philosophy's contribution, 380; as love, 345; as revelation of Trinitarian love, 343, 345, 347; as selflessness, 347; and transcendence, 167; in the Trinity (Ur-Kenosis), 22, 46, 167–68, 207, 341–44, 349–50, 352, 365. *See also* archetype; descent; hell; Incarnation; surrender

knowledge: as dogmatic, 396; by faith, 87; God's, 39, 41, 49, 365, 379; human persons' of God, 37, 78–80, 142, 216, 365, 370–71, 381, 388n171, 396; of human persons as limited, 142, 364; of human persons as participating in God's, 34, 36–38, 109–11, 370–71; human persons' of themselves and of being, 43; and love, 109, 113n86, 371; Mary's of the Old Testament prophecies, 155; as philosophical and theological, 363–64, 372; as surpassed by love, 371. *See also* divine freedom; faith; mysticism; theology

love: as commanded, 199, 217–20, 230–31, 234, 238–39; as diffusive, 215–16, 230; as dynamic, 273, 275; as eliciting a response, 42, 46, 85, 136, 216, 226, 229–31, 234, 239–40, 280–81; as foundation of the divine processions, 46–53; for God and neighbor as united, 218, 236–38; of God as responsible for the events of salvation, 50–51; of human beings as participating in the divine, 32, 218–19, 228–32, 234, 238–40, 307, 355; between man and woman, 136, 271–83, 306; as the meaning of freedom, 42, 114, 366; as presupposing difference, 59, 267, 357; as presupposing distance, 253; reciprocity of, 146, 212, 228–31, 236, 276, 302, 307; as total surrender, 366; of the Trinity as central dogma, 345; of the Trinity as center of Balthasar's theology, 347. *See also* freedom, divine; freedom, human; surrender; Trinity

marriage: of Adrienne, 91n133, 273n161; as analogy, 158, 170, 180–81, 185–88, 192, 235; of Mary and Joseph, 195; as sacrament (spiritual signification of), 21, 147, 179–81, 265, 292, 303, 307. *See also* analogy; Church

Mary: as co-redeemer, 263, 289; and the Eucharist, 193–94, 294–95; as mother of Christ; 151–54, 163, 170, 172, 176, 181, 194–95, 261, 293;

Mary (cont.)
  as mother of Christians, 103, 152, 155, 194, 238; as new Eve and Bride of Christ, 152, 156, 158, 176, 192–95, 238, 260–61, 263–64, 287, 289, 293, 301n341, 305. *See also* archetype; Assumption; Church; faith; Immaculate Conception; mediation; merit; mission; saints; surrender

Mass, 135, 155, 175, 235. *See also* Eucharist

mediation: of the apostles, 294; of Christ, 11, 14, 31–32, 34, 67, 89, 105–6, 122, 135, 167, 174, 182, 184, 230, 283–86, 290–91, 303, 305, 339–40, 346, 393, 397; of Christ's humanity, 161, 169–73, 323–24, 329n137; of the Christian, 239; of the Church, 291, 294; of the Holy Spirit, 55, 86, 122, 136, 218, 267, 302, 366; of man for woman and woman for man, 269; of Mary, 98, 153, 155, 159, 238, 261, 291–94; of priesthood, 294, 296n314; of the sacraments, 136–37, 140, 146, 169, 236. *See also* Eucharist; exchange; sacrament; surrender

mercy, 212, 215–17, 229, 344n225, 368n65

merit: of Christ, 211, 217n115; of Christians, 20, 134–35, 138, 140, 208n63, 212; of Mary, 153n347

metaphor: of being "challenged" by human freedom, 26, 222, 229, 368–69; of "distance" in the Trinity, 31, 45, 59, 79, 204–5, 309, 312, 342, 346, 352–53; of divine "conversation," 26, 174, 333, 368, 370; of divine "enrichment," 366–71; of divine "happening" or "event," 204, 206, 311–12, 320, 333; of divine "obedience," 209, 286, 310, 323, 329–34; of divine "suffering," 200–201, 204, 321, 329–30, 341, 344, 368n65, 390; of divine "vulnerability," 216; of "faith" in the Trinity, 85n96; of gift-giving in the Trinity, 26, 47, 58, 174–76, 313, 321, 365–66, 369; of God "experiencing" human love, 240; of God "as greater" than himself, 79–80, 307, 311–12; of God's "heart," 107–8; of God as "seducer," 397; of God as "sexual," 20–21, 251, 254–59, 265, 273, 284–86, 301; of God's "womb," 45, 251, 341; of God's "wrath," 203, 205–6, 225, 381n130; interpretation of, 240–41, 388–89; of "loss" in the Trinity, 341–44; of "pleasure" in the Trinity, 175; of "prayer" in the Trinity, 141n264, 147, 174, 333; of "realms of freedom" in the Trinity, 41, 46, 51–52, 309–11, 333–36, 351–52; of the "renunciation" of the divine persons, 227; of "separation" between the divine persons, 312; of "surprise" in the Trinity, 320–21, 329, 341; of "tensions" in the Trinity, 9, 59, 163, 199, 249; validity of in theological argumentation, 10n39, 22, 342–43, 376, 381–83, 388n171; of woman as "answer" and "answering gaze," 253. *See also* kenosis

metaphysics: Balthasar's appreciation of, 382; and doctrinal formulation, 45, 343, 382; and meta-anthropology, 28, 205–6; as oriented to theology, 22, 27, 109–11, 225, 343, 337–40; and the rooting of consciousness in being, 43; and the saints, 77–78. *See also* philosophy

method. *See* theology

mission: of Adrienne, 3n9, 73–74, 94, 213n90, 297, 373, 384, 393–94; of Balthasar, 76, 100, 383; of Balthasar and Adrienne as shared, 2–3, 6–9, 22–23, 69, 71, 74–75, 88, 100, 297–99, 373–75, 383–87, 392, 397; body in service of, 181; of Christ, 31n25, 40, 164, 220, 225–26, 231, 283, 285–86, 300, 309, 318, 326, 332, 346; of the Christian in Christ, 81–82, 84, 122, 137, 140–41, 154, 169, 181, 196–97, 209, 239; of the Church, 164, 168, 305–6; of divine persons, 34, 37, 40, 326–27, 345; and ecclesial existence, 375; and expropriation, 82; of John the Apostle, 291–95, 300; of Mary, 77, 148, 151, 153–56, 192–95, 237–38, 288–89, 300; of man and woman, 291–301, 387; and obedience, 131–32, 136, 331; as oscillating, 260–61, 281–86, 291; over psychology, 78; of the theologian, 76, 394, 396. *See also* charism; grace; person; Trinity

monophysitism. *See* Christ

mysticism: Adrienne's experiences of, 63, 91n134, 97, 190, 191n209, 199, 201–3, 212–13, 240, 242, 297–98, 347, 373–74, 384–85, 390–91; Adrienne's theory of, 8, 86–92, 374; Balthasar's preoccupation with, 373; characteristics of, 87, 164; criteria for judging authenticity of, 390; and faith, 87, 95; interpretation of, 19, 22, 71–73, 240–45, 383–94; language of, 79, 381–82; as nuptial, 15; and obedience, 13n57; as source for theology, 21, 71–73, 94–98, 388. *See also* charisma; experience; mission; sin

natural desire: 106–8, 112, 114n88, 122, 210, 340n202

nature. *See* Christ; human freedom; human fulfillment; grace; image; Trinity

neo-scholasticism, 77, 338, 381–82, 395

Nestorian heresy, 329n137

night of faith. *See* faith

nouvelle théologie. *See* theology

obedience: of Adrienne, 92, 95, 373n93, 387, 389; as availability, 87; as "blind," 113; body

SUBJECT INDEX 453

as instrument of, 19, 161–62, 164, 179, 191, 300, 323; of Christ, 12n53, 67, 83–84, 86, 144–45, 161–62, 167–68, 195, 197–98, 203, 219–23, 223n162, 226–28, 284–86, 290, 300, 318, 326–28, 331n145, 345, 347, 373n93, 392; of the Christian (as a participation in Christ's), 12–13, 18, 24, 67, 122, 126, 140, 145, 148–49, 195, 199, 217–18; of creation as participating in Christ's, 61; as determining our growth in holiness, 147–48; as grace, 87–88; the Incarnation as an act of, 136, 331; as kenosis, 340; of Mary, 88, 195, 290, 300; as revelatory, 67, 83, 162, 168, 330, 345; teleological aspect of, 13; of the theologian, 80–81; in the Trinity, 331–34; as vowed, 195n234, 299–300. *See also* metaphor; states of life; surrender; virtue

pantheism, 61, 165
patristics. *See* Fathers of the Church
penance, 97, 181, 212, 290n264, 294. *See also* confession
perfection of the human person. *See* fulfillment of human person
person: Balthasar's theological understanding of, 18, 73, 94, 97, 101–5, 119–22, 134, 144–45, 149–56, 196–97, 198, 226, 238, 242, 257; distinction between divine and human, 353–54. *See also* Christ; human freedom; human fulfillment; Mary; mission; Trinity
phenomenology, 43n110, 95, 164, 252–53, 275
philosophy. *See* Kantianism; metaphysics; phenomenology; neo-platonism
predestination: of Christ, 105n30, 172–76, 181, 331, 333; of the Cross, 345; by the eternal law, 340; of the human person in Christ, 63, 173–76, 302; of human persons to participate in the intra-Trinitarian love, 370; of Mary, 263–64. *See also* archetype; divine freedom; Immaculate Conception
priesthood: as accompanied by the prayer of the religious woman, 300; of Christ, 225; as combining passive and active functions, 225–26; and confession, 266, 294; mission of as linked to Mary's mission, 292–96. *See also* mediation
processions of divine persons. *See* Trinity
prototype. *See* archetype

recapitulation: of Adam in Christ, 63–64, 173; of creation in Christ, 173, 185, 358; of the human person in Christ, 18; of the sinner in the "distance" between Father and Son, 204. *See also* Christ; exchange; redemption

receptivity in the Trinity: 23, 46, 54, 56, 309–18, 320–21, 326–27, 331–32, 335–37, 343, 352–53, 355n289. *See also* surrender; Trinity
redemption: as contrition and certainty of God's mercy, 229–30; corporal dimension of, 177; five motifs of, 201n18; as a gift of the divine persons to one another, 365; as incorporation into the Trinity, 20, 128, 214, 217, 228, 231, 286; mystical doctrine of, 169, 172–73, 176; by obedience, 392; as renewal of human nature, 184, 285; as satisfaction, 2n3, 207n59, 211n78, 348n251; by substitution, 19, 55, 200–214, 216–17, 282; as union with Christ, 164, 186–87, 236. *See also* exchange; grace; Incarnation; kenosis; mediation; recapitulation; sacrament; suffering
resurrection of Christ, 168, 184–85, 328n129
revelation: as act, 68, 395; Christ of creation, 338–40; Christ of his divine sonship, 223, 227, 327; Christ of the Father, 12, 14n61, 19–20, 50, 58, 83–84, 88, 130n195, 198, 239, 284, 286, 309, 319–20, 323–30, 334–37, 340, 346, 397; Christ as fullness of, 1, 29, 88, 167, 171, 189, 378; Christ of God, 11, 29, 324, 340; Christ of the human person, 11, 14n61, 126–27, 263, 309, 340, 349; Christ of his love for the Father, 85, 162, 215, 219–20, 232; Christ of the Trinity, 67, 167, 219, 309, 319–20, 323–24, 333, 340; Christ's humanity of his divinity, 318–19, 324–25, 328–31, 393; Christ of the love of God, 239, 349; Christ's obedience as, 144–45, 167, 220, 227, 345, 347–50; Christ as only source of, 319; Christ's suffering as, 341, 391; the Christian of Christ, 81–83, 396; the Church of Christ, 189; creation in service of, 16, 24, 61–62, 338–40, 346, 381; Cross as, 206, 221–22, 235, 349; Christ's agony in Gethsemane of the Trinity, 333–36; development of, 386; as evoking a response, 395; human person of God, 10, 269; by God's free initiative, 50; human body of the Trinity, 163; of Father in the Son, 83–84, 327–28; kenosis as, 345, 347; Mary's experience as source of, 155, 237–38, 293–94, 298n326; mysticism as form of, 390–91; as necessary to human persons, 365; as only access to the Trinity, 319; Scripture as source of, 318; transmission of, 389. *See also* Christ; experience; Incarnation; knowledge; mysticism; sin; surrender; theology

sacraments: Christ as archetype of, 161, 167n37, 171, 181–83; Christ as personification of, 134n219, 182; Christ at work in, 139; as containing love, 231n217; the human body as, 162;

sacraments (*cont.*)
as incorporating us into Christ, 168, 179, 182; as incorporating us into the Trinity, 397; from the open heart and wounds of Christ, 135n228, 168, 291, 294; as requiring faith for their efficacy, 135; role of the Holy Spirit in, 122; as sharing in Christ's mission, 102, 137. *See also* archetype; baptism; Eucharist; marriage; mediation

sacrifice: of the Cross, 155, 207n54, 229–31; death as the final, 168n43; one of Head and body, 169, 217n115, 233n234, 235, 239–40

saints: and the Church, 92, 188, 192; communion of, 20, 70, 184n154, 198, 237, 240n285; and degrees of holiness, 93; as interpreters of theodrama, 21, 71, 73, 77, 81–82; mission of, 72, 76; as theologians, 77

self-realization. *See* human freedom; fulfillment of the human person; grace; mission; person; surrender

sexual complementarity, 247, 264–67, 272–73, 282, 297, 307. *See also* analogy; Church; marriage; metaphor

similitude. *See* analogy; archetype; metaphor

sin: Christ's mystical incurring of, 177n105, 184, 201n24, 243; as distance for God, 342; as limiting 142, 228, 269–70; as original, 166; as refusal of God, 207, 213–14, 229–30, 243; revelation of, 184, 210, 213–15, 222, 229; as unlikeness to God, 306. *See also* redemption

Spirit. *See* Holy Spirit

states of life: consecrated life, 147, 274, 299–300, 303, 307; lay state, 99; Mary as bridging, 193, 292; secular institutes, 99; the vows of, 86, 99, 299–300; a "third" state denied by Adrienne, 147, 180, 265n117. *See also* Community of St. John; marriage; virginity

substitution. *See* redemption

suffering: of Adrienne, 95, 297–98; of Christ, 172–73, 223–25; 234–35, 229, 282, 287–88, 290; of Christian as participation in Christ's, 12n12, 135, 184–85, 234–35, 286–87; of Church, 287; as characteristically male and female, 282, 290; of Mary, 155, 287–90; as vicarious, 141, 177n105, 201–2, 204, 209, 210n74, 225, 235n253. *See also* metaphor

surrender: as active and passive, 58, 130–31, 227n186, 230, 262, 272, 281, 308–9; as assent, 308; as availability or readiness, 85, 113, 115, 272, 308, 331, 335; of Christ to Christian and Church, 11, 13, 163, 168, 192, 228, 230–31, 257, 290, 305–6; of Christ to the Father, 11, 13, 19, 167, 228, 245, 257, 306, 331, 351; as confession, 292; as descent, 223; as devotion, 121, 157; of divine persons to one another, 9, 11, 16, 20, 23–24, 27, 44, 46, 54, 58, 160, 164–65, 168, 214, 227, 271, 308–9, 340, 359, 365, 397; as eliciting surrender in return, 351; as Eucharistic, 175, 302; as expropriation, 360; as fruitful, 279–80; as gift, 130, 184, 272, 308; of God as primary to man as responsive, 77, 158–59, 163–64, 192, 214–17, 228, 257; as incorporating us into the Trinity, 121, 199, 302, 345, 355, 358; as indifference, 113; as initiating, 137, 257, 272, 276, 306; as kenotic, 345; as letting-be, 335; as love, 16, 168, 223, 237, 240, 276, 331, 348, 375; "masculine" and "feminine" forms of, 181, 262, 266, 271–91, 301, 306; of Mary, 86, 157–58, 194–95, 291, 293–94; as a mediating concept, 11, 14, 54–57, 293–94, 331, 358; as obedience, 121, 157, 331, 358; as participated, 228, 235; as receptive, 12, 85, 98, 158–59, 184, 214, 293, 306, 308, 313, 335; as revelatory, 9, 68, 84, 101, 167, 277, 280, 286, 336, 355; as salvific/perfecting, 24, 111, 209, 214, 216, 229–30, 242, 305–6, 366; as self-giving, 313; as transcending, 166–67, 268; as transparency, 86, 294; as unifying, 17, 137, 273. *See also* analogy; faith; Incarnation; kenosis; mediation; obedience

tension: as anthropological, 9, 16, 64; as "difference-in-unity," 23, 59, 266; love as, 64–65, 196, 267; as a mediating concept, 303; by reciprocal surrender, 397. *See also* analogy; metaphor; Trinity

teleology, 18, 42, 61–62, 105–10, 113–15, 117, 122, 150, 266, 273, 303, 314, 362–64. *See also* divine freedom; eschatology; human freedom; image; metaphysics; predestination

theodrama. *See* divine freedom; human freedom; human fulfillment; mission; person; redemption; surrender

theological person. *See* archetype; mission; person

theology: as aesthetical, 114, 372n88; as apophatic, 78, 80, 311; and the argument of fittingness, 105n30, 108n46, 210–11, 318n75, 330, 372; complementarity of mystical and notional theology, 380–81; as experiential or mystical, 21, 62, 68, 71–72, 80–81, 94, 97, 266, 273, 276–77, 297–99, 372; as prophetic, 386–87; as systematic, 8n36, 18, 24n86, 76n34, 383; by convergence or integration, 1, 76n34, 130, 304, 308n2, 344–45, 372–74; as correlation, 29–30;

SUBJECT INDEX

language of, 78–80, 343, 388–89; and mystery, 376; and mysticism, 296, 311, 373, 379–83, 386–88; *la nouvelle théologie*, 28–29; and philosophy, 37, 53–54, 337, 362–65; and prayer, 75, 111; and revelation, 16; and sanctity, 4n13, 17, 68–69, 75, 77, 338; and spirituality, 77–78, 81, 337–38. *See also* analogy; experience; influence; katalogy; mysticism; revelation; saints

transcendence: and the categories of being, 35; of the couple in the child, 162–63, 301; as descent, 10n41, 66, 167; by surrender, 12, 19, 111, 350

transcendentals, 35, 52, 358–60

Trinity: circumincession, 58–60, 132, 189, 311–12, 318, 346, 350, 352, 365; divine persons, 27, 56, 144, 309, 326–27, 329, 366; the identity of attributes, 39, 41; as immanent and as economic, 37, 40–41, 50–51, 206, 219, 232, 317, 326, 341–42, 347, 365–66, 369–70; inseparability of divine essence and the processions, 36, 51–53, 342–43, 350n265, 366; "inversion" of, 145n297, 204n39, 330–31, 333n151; love as definition of, 46, 48–49, 50, 52–53, 316, 349; one divine essence, 319n79, 328; one divine will, 221, 224, 228, 260, 308, 310, 312, 333–36, 352, 376, 390–91; one nature, three persons 46, 51, 328; personal appropriations, 174, 206, 308, 327, 329, 331, 335; processions, 16, 30, 40, 44, 46–60, 206, 286, 309, 326, 328; unity of action in, 328, 365; unity of love in the Trinity, 27, 47, 52, 100, 215, 217, 219, 221–38, 240, 271, 305–6, 345, 366; unity-in-difference, 9, 16, 27, 59, 65, 80, 222, 254, 304, 342, 346, 359–60, 393, 397. *See also* analogy; archetype; Christ; divine freedom; hierarchy; Holy Spirit; knowledge; generation of Son by Father; love; metaphor; mission; receptivity in the Trinity; revelation

Vatican II. *See* Council

virginity, 168n43, 190, 264–65, 274, 284, 288, 292–95, 307. *See also* states of life

virtue: Christ as exemplary of, 211; Christian's as share in Christ's, 11–12, 84, 138–41, 306; as theological, 36–37. *See also* archetype; faith; grace; knowledge; love

wrath of God. *See* metaphor

A Trinitarian Anthropology: Adrienne von Speyr & Hans Urs von Balthasar in Dialogue with Thomas Aquinas was designed in Garamond and composed by Kachergis Book Design of Pittsboro, North Carolina. It was printed on 60-pound House Natural Smooth and bound by Sheridan Books of Ann Arbor, Michigan.

www.ingramcontent.com/pod-product-compliance
Lightning Source LLC
Chambersburg PA
CBHW020312010526
44107CB00054B/1817